TRANSLATOR AND EDITOR:
Rabbi David Strauss

MANAGING EDITOR:
Baruch Goldberg

ASSOCIATE EDITOR:
Dr. Jeffrey M. Green

COPY EDITOR:
Alec Israel

BOOK DESIGNER:
Ben Gasner

GRAPHIC ARTIST:
Michael Etkin

TECHNICAL STAFF:
Muriel Stein

Random House Staff

PRODUCTION MANAGER:
Richard Elman

ART DIRECTOR:
Bernard Klein

CHIEF COPY EDITOR:
Amy Edelman

THE TALMUD

THE STEINSALTZ EDITION

VOLUME XX

TRACTATE SANHEDRIN

PART VI

Volume XX

Tractate Sanhedrin

Part VI

Random House

New York

THE TALMUD

תלמוד בבלי

THE STEINSALTZ EDITION

Commentary by Rabbi Adin Steinsaltz (Even Yisrael)

 Published in the United States by
Random House, Inc., New York, and simultaneously in Canada by
Random House of Canada Limited, Toronto.

This is an English translation of a work originally published
in Hebrew by The Israel Institute for Talmudic Publications,
Jerusalem, Israel.

Library of Congress Cataloging-in-Publication Data
(Revised for volume XX)
The Talmud
English, Hebrew, Aramaic.
Includes bibliographical references.
Contents: v. 1. Tractate Bava metzia—
v. 20. Tractate Sanhedrin, pt. 6
Accompanied by a reference guide.
I. Title.
BM499.5.E4 1989 89-842911
ISBN 0-394-57665-9 (guide)
ISBN 0-394-57666-7 (v. 1)
ISBN 0-375-50247-5 (v. 20)

Random House website address: www.atrandom.com
Printed in the United States of America on acid-free paper

2 4 6 8 9 7 5 3

First Edition

"And you shall teach them diligently to your children..."

This volume is lovingly dedicated in honor of

Our Parents

Harriett and Mende Lerner
Judy and Warren Michelson
Sylvia and Jerome Rose

And Our Children

Stephanie, Coby, Tyler and Sara

In appreciation of the heritage that has been given to us and in the hope that we will do as well with our children as our parents did with us in imbuing a love of and commitment to the traditions of our people.

Traci and Mark Lerner

"ושננתם לבניך"

כרך זה מוקדש באהבה

להורינו

צביה בת מרדכי וחיה שרה
משה מנחם מנדל בן מרדכי הכהן וינטה דבורה
חנה שיינדל בת אברהם בנימין ובפציה רוניא
וולף דוד בן צבי הירש ורחל לאה
שרה רבקה בת מנשה וחייקי
יוסף בן יצחק ושושנה

ולילדינו

ינטה דבורה פייגה בת מרדכי הכהן ותרצה
וולוול בן מרדכי הכהן ותרצה
דניאל מנשה בן מרדכי הכהן ותרצה
חיה בת מרדכי הכהן ותרצה

בהוקרה על המורשת שזכינו בה ובתקווה שנצליח להנחיל לילדינו כשם שהורינו הנחילו לנו אהבה ומחוייבות למסורת עמנו.

תרצה בת וולוול ושרה רבקה
מרדכי בן משה מנחם מנדל הכהן וחנה שיינדל

The Steinsaltz Talmud in English

The English edition of the Steinsaltz Talmud is a translation and adaptation of the Hebrew edition. It includes most of the additions and improvements that characterize the Hebrew version, but it has been adapted and expanded especially for the English reader. This edition has been designed to meet the needs of advanced students capable of studying from standard Talmud editions, as well as of beginners, who know little or no Hebrew and have had no prior training in studying the Talmud.

The overall structure of the page is similar to that of the traditional pages in the standard printed editions. The text is placed in the center of the page, and alongside it are the main auxiliary commentaries. At the bottom of the page and in the margins are additions and supplements.

The original Hebrew-Aramaic text, which is framed in the center of each page, is exactly the same as that in the traditional Talmud (although material that was removed by non-Jewish censors has been restored on the basis of manuscripts and old printed editions). The main innovation is that this Hebrew-Aramaic text has been completely vocalized and punctuated, and all the terms usually abbreviated have been fully spelled out. In order to retain the connection with the page numbers of the standard editions, these are indicated at the head of every page.

We have placed a *Literal Translation* on the right-hand side of the page, and its punctuation has been introduced into the Talmud text, further helping the student to orientate himself. The *Literal Translation* is intended to help the student to learn the meaning of specific Hebrew and Aramaic words. By comparing the original text with this translation, the reader develops an understanding of the Talmudic text and can follow the words and sentences in the original. Occasionally, however, it has not been possible to present an exact literal translation of the original text, because it is so different in structure from English. Therefore we have added certain auxiliary words, which are indicated in square brackets. In other cases it would make no sense to offer a literal translation of a Talmudic idiom, so we have provided a close English equivalent of the original meaning, while a note, marked "lit.," explaining the literal meaning of the words, appears in parentheses. Our purpose in presenting this literal translation was to give the student an appreciation of the terse and enigmatic nature of the Talmud itself, before the arguments are opened up by interpretation.

Nevertheless, no one can study the Talmud without the assistance of commentaries. The main aid to understanding the Talmud provided by this edition is the *Translation and Commentary,* appearing on the left side of the page. This is Rabbi Adin Steinsaltz's highly regarded Hebrew interpretation of the Talmud, translated into English, adapted and expanded.

This commentary is not merely an explanation of difficult passages. It is an integrated exposition of the entire text. It includes a full translation of the Talmud text, combined with explanatory remarks. Where the translation in the commentary reflects the literal translation, it has been set off in bold type. It has also been given the same reference numbers that are found both in the original text and in the literal translation. Moreover, each section of the commentary begins with a few words of the Hebrew-Aramaic text. These reference numbers and paragraph headings allow the reader to move from one part of the page to another with ease.

There are some slight variations between the literal translation and the words in bold face appearing in the *Translation and Commentary.* These variations are meant to enhance understanding, for a juxtaposition of the literal translation and the sometimes freer translation in the commentary will give the reader a firmer grasp of the meaning.

The expanded *Translation and Commentary* in the left-hand column is intended to provide a conceptual understanding of the arguments of the Talmud, their form, content, context, and significance. The commentary also brings out the logic of the questions asked by the Sages and the assumptions they made.

Rashi's traditional commentary has been included in the right-hand column, under the *Literal Translation.* We have left this commentary in the traditional "Rashi script," but all quotations of the Talmud text appear in standard square type, the abbreviated expressions have all been printed in full, and Rashi's commentary is fully punctuated.

Since the *Translation and Commentary* cannot remain cogent and still encompass all the complex issues that arise in the Talmudic discussion, we have included a number of other features, which are also found in Rabbi Steinsaltz's Hebrew edition.

At the bottom of the page, under the *Translation and Commentary*, is the *Notes* section, containing additional material on issues raised in the text. These notes deepen understanding of the Talmud in various ways. Some provide a deeper and more profound analysis of the issues discussed in the text, with regard to individual points and to the development of the entire discussion. Others explain Halakhic concepts and the terms of Talmudic discourse.

The *Notes* contain brief summaries of the opinions of many of the major commentators on the Talmud, from the period after the completion of the Talmud to the present. Frequently the *Notes* offer interpretations different from that presented in the commentary, illustrating the richness and depth of Rabbinic thought.

The *Halakhah* section appears below the *Notes.* This provides references to the authoritative legal decisions reached over the centuries by the Rabbis in their discussions of the matters dealt with in the Talmud. It explains what reasons led to these Halakhic decisions and the close connection between the Halakhah today and the Talmud and its various interpreters. It should be noted that the summary of the Halakhah presented here is not meant to serve as a reference source for actual religious practice but to introduce the reader to Halakhic conclusions drawn from the Talmudic text.

English commentary and expanded translation of the text, making it readable and comprehensible

Hebrew/Aramaic text of the Talmud, fully vocalized, and punctuated

Literal translation of the Talmud text into English

Marginal notes provide essential background information

Hebrew commentary of Rashi, the classic explanation that accompanies all editions of the Talmud

Numbers link the three main sections of the page and allow readers to refer rapidly from one to the other

Notes highlight points of interest in the text and expand the discussion by quoting other classical commentaries

REALIA

קַלְתָּה Her basket. The source of this word is the Greek κάλαθος, kalathos, and it means a basket with a narrow base.

Illustration from a Greek drawing depicting such a basket of fruit.

CONCEPTS

פֵּאָה *Pe'ah*. One of the presents left for the poor (מַתְּנוֹת עֲנִיִּים). The Torah forbids harvesting "the corners of your field," so that the produce left standing may be harvested and kept by the poor (Leviticus 19:9).

The Torah did not specify a minimum amount of produce to be left as *pe'ah*. But the Sages stipulated that it must be at least one-sixtieth of the crop.

Pe'ah is set aside only from crops that ripen at one time and are harvested at one time. The poor are allowed to use their own initiative to reap the *pe'ah* left in the fields. But the owner of an orchard must see to it that each of the poor gets a fixed share of the *pe'ah* from places that are difficult to reach. The poor come to collect *pe'ah* three times a day. The laws of *pe'ah* are discussed in detail in tractate *Pe'ah*.

TRANSLATION AND COMMENTARY

[1] **and her husband threw her a bill of divorce into her lap or into her basket**, which she was carrying on her head, [2] would you say **here, too**, that **she would not be divorced**? Surely we know that the law is that she *is* divorced in such a case, as the Mishnah (*Gittin* 77a) states explicitly!

אֲמַר לֵיהּ [3] **Rav Ashi said** in reply **to** Ravina: The woman's **basket is** considered to be **at rest, and it is she who walks beneath it.** Thus the basket is considered to be a "stationary courtyard," and the woman acquires whatever is thrown into it.

MISHNAH הָיָה רוֹכֵב [4] **If a person was riding on an animal and he saw an ownerless object** lying on the ground, **and he said to another person** standing nearby, **"Give** that object **to me,"** [5] if **the other person took** the ownerless object **and said, "I have acquired it for myself,"** [6] he has **acquired it** by lifting it up, even though he was not the first to see it, and the rider has no claim to it. [7] But **if, after he gave** the object **to** the rider, the person who picked it up **said, "I acquired** the object **first,"** [8] **he** in fact **said nothing**. His words are of no effect, and the rider may keep it. Since the person walking showed no intention of acquiring the object when he originally picked it up, he is not now believed when he claims that he acquired it first. Indeed, even if we maintain that when a person picks up an ownerless object on behalf of someone else, the latter does *not* acquire it automatically, here, by *giving* the object to the rider, he makes a gift of it to the rider.

GEMARA תְּנַן הָתָם [9] **We have learned elsewhere** in a Mishnah in tractate *Pe'ah* (4:9): **"Someone who gathered *pe'ah*** — produce which by Torah law [Leviticus 23:22] is left unharvested in the corner of a field by the owner of the field, to be gleaned by the poor — **and said, 'Behold, this** *pe'ah* which I have gleaned **is** intended **for so-and-so the poor man,'** [10] **Rabbi Eliezer says:** The person who gathered the *pe'ah* **has acquired it**

בִּרְשׁוּת הָרַבִּים [1] וְזָרַק לָהּ גֵּט לְתוֹךְ חֵיקָהּ אוֹ לְתוֹךְ קַלְתָּהּ — [2] הָכָא נַמִּי דְּלָא מְגָרְשָׁה? [3] אֲמַר לֵיהּ: קַלְתָּהּ מֵינָח נַיְיחָא, וְאִיהִי דְּקָא מְסַגְּיָא מִתּוּתָהּ.

מִשְׁנָה [4] הָיָה רוֹכֵב עַל גַּבֵּי בְהֵמָה וְרָאָה אֶת הַמְּצִיאָה, וְאָמַר לַחֲבֵירוֹ "תְּנָה לִי", [5] נְטָלָהּ וְאָמַר, "אֲנִי זָכִיתִי בָּהּ", [6] זָכָה בָּהּ. [7] אִם, מִשֶּׁנְּתָנָהּ לוֹ, אָמַר, "אֲנִי זָכִיתִי בָּהּ תְּחִלָּה", [8] לֹא אָמַר כְּלוּם.

גְּמָרָא [9] תְּנַן הָתָם: "מִי שֶׁלִּיקֵּט אֶת הַפֵּאָה וְאָמַר, 'הֲרֵי זוֹ לִפְלוֹנִי עָנִי', [10] רַבִּי אֱלִיעֶזֶר

LITERAL TRANSLATION

in a public thoroughfare [1] and [her husband] threw her a bill of divorce into her lap or into her basket, [2] here, too, would she not be divorced?

[3] He said to him: Her basket is at rest, and it is she who walks beneath it.

MISHNAH [4] [If a person] was riding on an animal and he saw a found object, and he said to another person, "Give it to me," [5] [and the other person] took it and said, "I have acquired it," [6] he has acquired it. [7] If, after he gave it to him, he said, "I acquired it first," [8] he said nothing.

GEMARA [9] We have learned there: "Someone who gathered *pe'ah* and said, 'Behold this is for so-and-so the poor man,' [10] Rabbi Eliezer says:

RASHI

קלתה – סל שעל ראשה, שנותנת בה כלי מלאכתה וטווי שלה. **הכי נמי דלא הוי גיטא** – והאנן תנן במסכת גיטין (עז,א): זרק לה גיטה לתוך חיקה או לתוך קלתה – הרי זו מגורשת!

משנה לא אמר כלום – דאפילו אמרינן המגביה מציאה לחבירו לא קנה חבירו, כיון דיהבה ליה – קנייה ממה נפשך. אי קנייה קמא דלא מתכוין להקנות לחבירו – הא יהבה ניהליה במתנה. ואי לא קנייה קמא משום דלא היה מתכוין לקנות – הויא ליה הפקר עד דמטא לידיה דהאי, וקנייה האי במאי דעקרה מידיה דקמא לשם קנייה.

גמרא מי שליקט את הפאה – אדם בעלמא שאינו בעל שדה. דאי בבעל שדה – לא אמר רבי אליעזר זכה. דליכא למימר "מגו דזכי לנפשיה", דאפילו הוא עני מוזהר הוא שלא ללקט פאה משדה שלו, כדאמר בשחיטת חולין (קלא,ב): "לא תלקט לעני" – להזהיר עני על שלו.

NOTES

מִי שֶׁלִּיקֵּט אֶת הַפֵּאָה If a person gathered *pe'ah*. According to *Rashi*, the Mishnah must be referring to someone other than the owner of the field. By Torah law the owner of a field is required to separate part of his field as *pe'ah*, even if he himself is poor, and he may not take the *pe'ah* for himself. Therefore the "since" (מגו) argument

HALAKHAH

קַלְתָּה A woman's basket. "If a man throws a bill of divorce into a container that his wife is holding, she thereby acquires the bill of divorce and the divorce takes effect." (*Shulḥan Arukh, Even HaEzer* 139:10.)

הַמְלַקֵּט פֵּאָה עֲבוּר אַחֵר A person who gathered *pe'ah* for someone else. "If a poor person, who is himself entitled to collect *pe'ah*, gathered *pe'ah* for another poor person, and said, 'This *pe'ah* is for X, the poor person,' he acquires the *pe'ah* on behalf of that other poor person. But if the person who collected the *peah* was wealthy, he does not acquire the *pe'ah* on behalf of the poor person. He must give it instead to the first poor person who appears in the field," following the opinion of the Sages, as explained by Rabbi Yehoshua ben Levi. (*Rambam, Sefer Zeraim, Hilkhot Mattenot Aniyyim* 2:19.)

On the outer margin of the page, factual information clarifying the meaning of the Talmudic discussion is presented. Entries under the heading *Language* explain unusual terms, often borrowed from Greek, Latin, or Persian. *Sages* gives brief biographies of the major figures whose opinions are presented in the Talmud. *Terminology* explains the terms used in the Talmudic discussion. *Concepts* gives information about fundamental Halakhic principles. *Background* provides historical, geographical, and other information needed to understand the text. *Realia* explains the artifacts mentioned in the text. These notes are sometimes accompanied by illustrations.

The best way of studying the Talmud is the way in which the Talmud itself evolved – a combination of frontal teaching and continuous interaction between teacher and pupil, and between pupils themselves.

This edition is meant for a broad spectrum of users, from those who have considerable prior background and who know how to study the Talmud from any standard edition to those who have never studied the Talmud and do not even know Hebrew.

The division of the page into various sections is designed to enable students of every kind to derive the greatest possible benefit from it.

For those who know how to study the Talmud, the book is intended to be a written Gemara lesson, so that, either alone, with partners, or in groups, they can have the sense of studying with a teacher who explains the difficult passages and deepens their understanding both of the development of the dialectic and also of the various approaches that have been taken by the Rabbis over the centuries in interpreting the material. A student of this kind can start with the Hebrew-Aramaic text, examine Rashi's commentary, and pass on from there to the expanded commentary. Afterwards the student can turn to the Notes section. Study of the *Halakhah* section will clarify the conclusions reached in the course of establishing the Halakhah, and the other items in the margins will be helpful whenever the need arises to clarify a concept or a word or to understand the background of the discussion.

For those who do not possess sufficient knowledge to be able to use a standard edition of the Talmud, but who know how to read Hebrew, a different method is proposed. Such students can begin by reading the Hebrew-Aramaic text and comparing it immediately to the *Literal Translation*. They can then move over to the *Translation and Commentary*, which refers both to the original text and to the *Literal Translation*. Such students would also do well to read through the *Notes* and choose those that explain matters at greater length. They will benefit, too, from the terms explained in the side margins.

The beginner who does not know Hebrew well enough to grapple with the original can start with the *Translation and Commentary*. The inclusion of a translation within the commentary permits the student to ignore the *Literal Translation*, since the commentary includes both the Talmudic text and an interpretation of it. The beginner can also benefit from the *Notes*, and it is important for him to go over the marginal notes on the concepts to improve his awareness of the juridical background and the methods of study characteristic of this text.

Apart from its use as study material, this book can also be useful to those well versed in the Talmud, as a source of additional knowledge in various areas, both for understanding the historical and archeological background and also for an explanation of words and concepts. The general reader, too, who might not plan to study the book from beginning to end, can find a great deal of interesting material in it regarding both the spiritual world of Judaism, practical Jewish law, and the life and customs of the Jewish people during the thousand years (500 B.C.E.–500 C.E.) of the Talmudic period.

Contents

THE TALMUD
THE STEINSALTZ EDITION

VOLUME XX
TRACTATE SANHEDRIN
PART VI

Introduction to Chapter Ten

אֵלּוּ הֵן הַנֶּחֱנָקִין

"And he that smite his father, or his mother, shall surely be put to death. And he that steal a man, and sell him, or if he be found in his hand, he shall surely be put to death." (Exodus 21:15-16.)

"If a man be found stealing any of his breathen of the Children of Israel, and makes a slave of him, or sell him; then that thief shall die: and you shall put evil away from among you." (Deuteronomy 24:7.)

"And the man that will do presumptuously, and will not hearken to the priest that stands to minister there before the Lord your God, or to the judge, even that man shall die: and you shall put away the evil from Israel. And all the people shall hear, and fear, and do no more presumptuously." (Deuteronomy 17:12-13.)

"But the Prophet, which shall presume to speak a word in My name, which I have not commanded him to speak, or that shall speak in the name of other gods, even that Prophet shall die." (Deuteronomy 18:20.)

"And the man that commits adultery with another man's wife, even he that commits adultery with his neighbor's wife, the adulterer and the adulteress shall surely be put to death." (Leviticus 20:10.)

The laws of execution by strangulation that are clarified in this chapter have no inner connection to each other, because the transgressions punishable by strangulation are different from each other in nature and gravity. Two of these are mentioned in the Ten Commandments, two are connected with laws of forbidden sexual relations, and two for other types of transgression. Most of the transgressions punishable by strangulation are approached in this chapter through Halakhic Midrash in order to determine their precise boundaries, testimony regarding them, and the like. However, two other subjects are clarified in this chapter, whose importance transcends the issue of the laws of capital punishment: The rebellious elder and the false Prophet. The similarity between these two transgressors lies not only in that their crimes are between themselves and God, or between themselves and society, but because they constitute a challenge to the authority of Torah law, although to a great degree their actions are based on principles that are found in the Halakhah.

The rebellious elder is a Rabbi who refuses to accept the authority of the majority of his colleagues and issues a Halakhic ruling contrary to their opinion. A false Prophet (and also an idolatrous Prophet) undermines the authority of the Torah through the power of his ostensible prophecy. In both cases the precise limits of the definition of the transgression are very important. For in principle every Rabbi has permission to study and examine matters according to his intellectual abilities and knowledge of Torah, and he also has the right to disagree and to innovate within the Halakhah. Consequently, it is very important to set the boundaries of this freedom of inquiry and opinion and to determine when a Rabbi is allowed to oppose the opinion of other Rabbis and when he oversteps the bounds and rebels against the accepted norms of the Halakhah. This also applies to a Prophet. On the one hand, the Torah requires every person, and all the apparatus of government among the Jews, to obey the words of a Prophet, even to the extent, in certain cases, of overthrowing and changing that apparatus. Therefore, precise distinctions are necessary to determine when a Prophet acts within the area of his authority and when he becomes a false Prophet whose words are not to be obeyed, and who is subject to execution.

TRANSLATION AND COMMENTARY

MISHNAH [1]**These are** the transgressors **who are liable to** the penalty of death by **strangulation:** [2]**Someone who strikes his father or his mother,** as the verse states (Exodus 21:15): "And he that strikes his father, or his mother, shall be surely put to death"; [3]**someone who kidnaps a Jew** and sells him to another person, as the verse states (Exodus 21:16): "And he that steals a man, and sells him, if he be found in his hand, he shall surely be put to death"; [4]**an elder who rebels against the court,** as the verse states (Deuteronomy 17:12): "And the man who will act presumptuously, and will not hearken to the priest...that man shall die"; [5]someone who claims to be a divinely inspired Prophet, but proves to be a **false Prophet, as well as someone who prophesies in the name of an idol,** as the verse states (Deuteronomy 18:20): "But the prophet, who shall presume to speak a word in My name, which I have not commanded him to speak, or who shall speak in the name of other gods, that prophet shall die"; [6]**someone who has intercourse with a married woman,** as the verse states (Leviticus 20:10): "And the man who commits adultery with another man's wife...the adulterer and the adulteress shall surely be put to death"; [7]**witnesses who conspire against the** married **daughter of a priest,** falsely testifying that she committed adultery, for they are not subject to the penalty that they sought to inflict upon her, but rather to the penalty that they sought to inflict upon her lover, as the verse states (Deuteronomy 19:19): "Then you shall do to him, as he had thought to have done to his brother" — to his brother, and not to his sister; **and the lover** of the married daughter of a priest, as the verse states (Leviticus 21:9): "She shall be burnt with fire" — the daughter of a priest who commits adultery is liable to death by burning, but her lover is not.

LITERAL TRANSLATION

MISHNAH [1]These are those who are strangled: [2]Someone who strikes his father or his mother; [3]and someone who kidnaps a Jew (lit., "who steals a soul of Israel"); [4]and an elder who rebels against the court; [5]and a false Prophet; and someone who prophesies in the name of an idol; [6]and someone who has intercourse with another man's wife; [7]and witnesses who conspire against the daughter of a priest, and her lover.

אֵלּוּ

[1]הֵן הַנֶּחֱנָקִין: [2]הַמַּכֶּה אָבִיו וְאִמּוֹ; [3]וְגוֹנֵב נֶפֶשׁ מִיִּשְׂרָאֵל; [4]וְזָקֵן מַמְרֵא עַל פִּי בֵּית דִּין; [5]וּנְבִיא הַשֶּׁקֶר; וְהַמִּתְנַבֵּא בְּשֵׁם עֲבוֹדָה זָרָה; [6]וְהַבָּא עַל אֵשֶׁת אִישׁ; [7]וְזוֹמְמֵי בַּת כֹּהֵן, וּבוֹעֲלָהּ.

RASHI

משנה אלו הן הנחנקין, ממרא על פי בית דין – כמו "ממרים הייתם עם ה'" (דברים ט), שמסרב על פי בית דין הגדול שבלשכת הגזית. וזוממי בת כהן – אף על פי שהם היו מחייבין אותה שריפה, אין נדונין אלא במיתה שהיו מחייבין לבועל – והיינו חנק כשאר בא על אשת איש, כדמפרש קרא היא תשרף – ולא בועלה, וזוממיה ילפינן מ"כאשר זמם לעשות לאחיו", "לאחיו" – ולא לאחותו. ובועלה – בנשואה בת כהן קמיירי אבל ארוסה בועלה בסקילה.

NOTES

אֵלּוּ הֵן הַנֶּחֱנָקִין **These are those who are strangled.** In the standard editions of the Babylonian Talmud, "These are those who are strangled," is the tenth chapter of tractate *Sanhedrin,* and "All of Israel has a portion in the World to Come" is the eleventh chapter. But according to many Rishonim, the order of these two chapters is reversed, "These are those who are strangled," is the eleventh chapter, and "All of Israel has a portion in the World to Come," the tenth chapter. This is also the order of the chapters in the Mishnah and in the Jerusalem Talmud. Two explanations are offered for this ordering of the chapters. The second half of tractate *Sanhedrin* deals with the various modes of judicial execution. Thus, it first completes its discussion of those liable to death by decapitation (which began in chapter nine, and which ends in "All of Israel has a portion" with the laws governing a condemned city), and then it proceeds to discuss those liable to death by strangulation. Moreover, the Gemara in tractate *Makkot* implies that tractate *Makkot* is a continuation of tractate *Sanhedrin* (according to some, it was originally part of *Sanhedrin*), and the beginning of tractate *Makkot* is in fact connected to the end of "These are those who are strangled" (see *Rabbi David Bonfil, Ran, Rashi* in *Makkot,* and others). As for the order found in the standard editions of the Talmud, the Rishonim explain that "All of Israel has a portion" is rightfully the last chapter in the tractate, for it deals with principles of faith, resurrection, and those who have a portion in the World to Come (see *Meiri,* and others).

מִתְנַבֵּא בְּשֵׁם עֲבוֹדָה זָרָה **Someone who prophesies in the name of an idol.** *Ramban* (in his commentary on the Torah) explains that we are not dealing here with a person who prophesied that people should worship an idol, for

HALAKHAH

אֵלּוּ הֵן הַנֶּחֱנָקִין **These are those who are strangled.** "Six types of offender are liable to death by strangulation: Someone who has intercourse with a married woman (this includes someone who has intercourse with the married daughter of a priest, and witnesses who conspired against the daughter of a priest (*Radbaz, Lehem Mishneh*); someone who wounds his father or his mother; someone who kidnaps a Jew; a rebellious elder; a false Prophet; and someone who prophesies in the name of an idol." (*Rambam, Sefer Shofetim, Hilkhot Sanhedrin* 15:13.)

גמרא [1]״מַכֶּה אָבִיו וְאִמּוֹ״. [2]מְנָלַן? [3]דִּכְתִיב: ״וּמַכֵּה אָבִיו וְאִמּוֹ מוֹת יוּמָת״. [4]וְכָל מִיתָה הָאֲמוּרָה בַּתּוֹרָה סְתָם אֵינָהּ אֶלָּא חֶנֶק.
[5]אֵימָא עַד דְּקָטֵיל לֵיהּ מִיקְטַל! [6]סָלְקָא דַּעְתָּךְ? קָטַל חַד — בְּסַיִיף, [7]וְאָבִיו בְּחֶנֶק? [8]הָנִיחָא לְמַאן דַּאֲמַר חֶנֶק קַל. [9]אֶלָּא לְמַאן דַּאֲמַר חֶנֶק חָמוּר, מַאי אִיכָּא לְמֵימַר?
[10]אֶלָּא, [11]מִדִּכְתִיב: ״מַכֵּה אִישׁ וָמֵת מוֹת יוּמָת״, [12]וּכְתִיב: ״אוֹ בְאֵיבָה הִכָּהוּ בְיָדוֹ וַיָּמֹת״ — [13]שְׁמַע מִינָּהּ: כָּל הֵיכָא דְּאִיכָּא

LITERAL TRANSLATION

GEMARA [1]"Someone who strikes his father or his mother." [2]From where do we [know this]? [3]For it is written: "And he that strikes his father, or his mother, shall be surely put to death." [4]And every death stated in the Torah without specification is strangulation.
[5]Say: Unless he kills him!
[6]Does it enter your mind [that if] he killed someone — by the sword; [7]and his father — by strangulation?
[8]It is well according to the one who says strangulation is lenient. [9]But according to the one who says strangulation is severe, what is there to say?
[10]Rather, [11]since it is written: "He who strikes a man, so that he dies, shall be surely put to death," [12]and it is written: "Or in enmity strikes him with his hand, that he dies" — [13]infer from this: Wherever there is

TRANSLATION AND COMMENTARY

GEMARA מַכֶּה [1]We learned in the Mishnah: **"Someone who strikes his father or his mother** is liable to death by strangulation." [2]The Gemara asks: **From where do we know this** law? [3]The Gemara explains: This is derived from **the verse** that **states** (Exodus 21:15): **"And he that strikes his father, or his mother, shall be surely put to death."** [4]**And** there is a rule that **wherever the Torah speaks of execution without specifying** the mode of execution, it **is** referring to **strangulation** (see *Sanhedrin* 52b).

אֵימָא [5]The Gemara asks: How do we know that a person is liable to the death penalty for merely striking his parent? Why not **say** that someone who strikes his father is not liable to the penalty of strangulation **unless he kills him?**

סָלְקָא דַּעְתָּךְ [6]The Gemara answers: **Could you** possibly **think that if** someone **killed an** ordinary **person,** he is liable to death **by the sword** (decapitation) as we learned in the previous chapter (76b), that a murderer is subject to decapitation, [7]**but** if he killed **his father,** he is liable only to death **by strangulation?**

הָנִיחָא [8]The Gemara rejects this argument: **This is acceptable according to the** Tanna **who says** that **strangulation is** a more **lenient** method of execution than decapitation, for it stands to reason that the punishment for killing one's father should be no less severe than the punishment for killing a stranger. [9]**But according to the** Tanna **who says** that **strangulation is** a more **severe** method of execution than decapitation, **what is there to say?** Someone who kills his father might indeed be liable to the more severe punishment of death by strangulation.

אֶלָּא [10]The Gemara answers: **Rather,** the wording of the verse itself proves that a person is liable to be punished for striking his father or his mother, even if he did not kill them. [11]**Since the verse** regarding a murderer **states** (Exodus 21:12): **"He that strikes a man, so that he dies, shall be surely put to death,"** [12]**and** another **verse** regarding a murderer **states** (Numbers 35:21): **"Or in enmity strikes him with his hand, that he dies;** he that struck him shall surely be put to death, for he is a murderer," both verses specifying that the offender struck his victim and killed him — [13]it is legitimate to **infer from this** that **wherever** the Torah

RASHI

גמרא סלקא דעתך — בתמיה. **קטן חד בסייף** — כדתנן בפרקין לעיל (סנהדרין עו,ב) אלו הן הנהרגים הרוצח, ועיר הנדחת. **מאי איכא למימר** — הכא דאיכא למדרש דאביו בחנק. **אלא מדכתיב מכה איש ומת** — היכא דבעי מיתה מפרש מיתה בהדיא.

NOTES

such a person is liable to stoning for inciting others to idol worship, even if he prophesied in the name of God. Nor are we dealing here with a person who claims that an idol came to him in a dream and told him to admonish others to fulfill the Torah's commandments, for such a person is exempt from all punishment. Rather, we are dealing with someone who claims that a certain idol is God, and he issues a commandment in its name, or foretells the future in its name.

כָּל הֵיכָא דְּאִיכָּא הַכָּאָה סְתָם, לָאו מִיתָה הוּא Wherever there is smiting without specification, it is not death. The Rishonim note that the verse (Leviticus 24:17), "And he that smites [יַכֶּה] the life of any man [נֶפֶשׁ אָדָם] shall surely die," mentions smiting without specifying that the assailant killed

HALAKHAH

כָּל מִיתָה הָאֲמוּרָה בַּתּוֹרָה סְתָם אֵינָהּ אֶלָּא חֶנֶק Every death stated in the Torah without specification is strangulation. "Wherever the Torah speaks of execution without specifying the mode of execution, it refers to strangulation." (*Rambam, Sefer Kedushah, Hilkhot Issurei Biah* 1:6.)

הַכָּאָה סְתָם, [1]לָאו מִיתָה הוּא. [2]וְאִיצְטְרִיךְ לְמִיכְתַּב ״מַכֵּה אִישׁ״ וְאִיצְטְרִיךְ לְמִכְתַּב ״כָּל מַכֵּה נֶפֶשׁ״. [3]דְּאִי כָּתַב רַחֲמָנָא: [4]״מַכֵּה אִישׁ וָמֵת״, [5]הֲוָה אָמִינָא: ״אִישׁ״, דְּבַר מִצְוָה — אִין, [6]קָטָן — לָא. [7]כָּתַב רַחֲמָנָא: ״כָּל מַכֵּה נֶפֶשׁ״. [8]וְאִי כָּתַב רַחֲמָנָא: ״כָּל מַכֵּה נֶפֶשׁ״, [9]הֲוָה אָמִינָא: אֲפִילּוּ נְפָלִים, [10]אֲפִילּוּ בֶּן שְׁמוֹנָה. [11]צְרִיכִי. [12]וְאֵימָא: אַף עַל גַּב דְּלָא עָבֵיד בֵּיהּ חַבּוּרָה. [13]אַלְּמָה תְּנַן: ״הַמַּכֶּה אָבִיו וְאִמּוֹ״ אֵינוֹ חַיָּיב עַד שֶׁיַּעֲשֶׂה בָּהֶן חַבּוּרָה?

LITERAL TRANSLATION

smiting without specification, [1]it is not death. [2]And it was necessary to write: "He who strikes a man," [3]and it was necessary to write: "Whoever kills any person." [4]For had the Torah (lit., "the Merciful") written: "He who strikes a man, so that he dies," [5]I might have said: "A man," who is obligated by the commandments — yes; [6]a minor — no. [7][Therefore] the Torah wrote: "Whoever kills any person." [8]And had the Torah written: "Whoever kills any person," [9]I might have said: Even nonviable infants, [10]even [an infant] born after the eight [months]. [11]It was necessary.

[12]But say: Even if he did not inflict a wound upon him. [13]Why did we learn: "Someone who strikes his father or his mother is not liable unless he inflicted a wound upon them"?

RASHI

אפילו נפלים – כגון בן תשעה וראשו אטום, או שיש לו שני גבין דלא חיי.

TRANSLATION AND COMMENTARY

mentions **striking without specifying** that the assailant killed his victim, [1]**it is not** referring to a blow that caused **death.** Since the verse regarding a person who struck his father or his mother does not specify that he killed them, the son must be liable to the death penalty even if he did not kill his parent.

וְאִיצְטְרִיךְ [2]The Gemara continues: **It was necessary** for the Torah **to write** (Exodus 21:12): **"He who strikes a man,** so that he dies, shall be surely put to death," [3]**and it was necessary** for it **to write** (Numbers 35:30): **"Whoever kills any person,** the murderer shall be put to death by the mouth of witnesses." Neither verse is extraneous. [4]**For had the Torah** only **written: "He who strikes a man, so that he dies,** he shall surely be put to death," [5]**I might have said** that if someone kills an adult **"man" who is obligated by the** Torah's **commandments,** the killer is **indeed** liable to the death penalty. [6]But if he only kills **a minor,** who is not bound by the Torah, he would **not** be liable to receive that punishment. [7]**Therefore, the Torah wrote: "Whoever kills** any person, the murderer shall be put to death," teaching that a killer is liable to the death penalty for killing any person, even a minor. [8]**And had the Torah** only **written: "Whoever kills any man,** the murderer shall be put to death," [9]**I might have said** that a killer is liable **even** if he killed **a** full-term but **nonviable infant,** [10]and **even** if he **killed a** premature **infant born after** only **eight months** of gestation, which is also assumed to be nonviable. Therefore, the Torah wrote: "He who strikes a man, so that he dies, he shall surely be put to death," teaching that a killer is only liable to the death penalty for killing a viable human being. [11]Thus, **it was necessary** for the Torah to write both verses.

וְאֵימָא [12]The Gemara asks: **But** if this is the source for the son's liability for striking his father, then we should **say** that a person is liable for striking his father, **even if he did not inflict a wound upon him.** [13]**Why,** then, **did we learn** in the next Mishnah (85b): **"Someone who strikes his father or his mother is not liable** to the death penalty **unless he inflicted a wound upon** him or her"?

NOTES

his victim, but it is nevertheless clear that the verse refers to someone who killed another person. They distinguish between "smiting" — which refers to smiting without killing — and "smiting a life" — which refers to killing (see *Rabbi David Bonfil, Ran*).

אִישׁ — קָטָן A man, and a minor. *Tosafot* and others cite an alternative reading, "A man — yes, a woman — no." The Rishonim comment: Surely we have a principle that the Torah equates men and woman with respect to all of its punishments. How, then, could we have thought of saying that, if someone killed a woman, he is not liable to punishment? They answer that this principle applies only in cases where the Torah uses a masculine grammatical form. But in cases where the Torah states explicitly, "man," women are indeed excluded unless there is some other term in the verse that comes to include women in that law (see *Tosafot, Rabbi David Bonfil, Ran*).

HALAKHAH

כָּל מַכֵּה נֶפֶשׁ Whoever kills any person. "A person is liable to the death penalty for killing another person, whether his victim was an adult or a minor, whether a male or a female." (*Rambam, Sefer Nezikin, Hilkhot Rotzeaḥ* 2:6.)

TRANSLATION AND COMMENTARY

אָמַר קְרָא [1]The Gemara answers: This is derived from **the verse** that **states** (Leviticus 24:21): "And **he who strikes a man,** he shall restore it; **and he who strikes a beast,** he shall be put to death." According to traditional hermeneutic principles, when the Torah juxtaposes two different laws in this way, it means that they are subject to the same rules. Hence, we apply the same rule to someone who strikes an animal as we do to someone who strikes another man, and we say: [2]**Just as he who strikes a beast** is not liable for the damage that he causes **unless he inflicts a wound upon it,** [3]**for** another **verse states** (Leviticus 24:18): "And he that strikes the **soul** of a beast shall make it good," and the word soul (*nefesh*) implies the spilling of blood, **so, too,** is **he that strikes a man** (a parent) [4]not liable to the death penalty **unless he inflicts a wound** upon him.

מַתְקִיף לָהּ [5]**Rabbi Yirmeyah strongly objected** to this proof: **But according to this, if someone weakened** an animal **by** loading it with **stones** without causing a wound, **so, too, would he not be liable** for the damage that he caused? [6]Surely a person is liable for all the damage that he causes to another person's property! **Rather,** if the word "soul" **does not refer to the soul of a beast** — [7]**for surely** a person **is liable** for the damage that he causes to an animal, **even if he weakens** it **by** loading it with **stones,** without causing a wound — [8]**it refers to the soul of a man** (a parent). Thus, the verse teaches that someone who strikes his father or his mother is not liable to the death penalty unless he inflicted a wound upon him or her.

אֶלָּא [9]The Gemara asks: If this law is derived from the verse "And he who strikes the soul of a beast," and by the hermeneutic principle, "If it does not refer to A, then it refers to B," **why do I need the analogy** of the verse: "And he who strikes a man...and he who strikes a beast"? What new law is derived by way of the juxtaposition of those two prohibitions? [10]The Gemara explains: The verse is needed **for that which was taught by a Sage of the School of Ḥizkiyah.** According to that Sage, the juxtaposition of these two verses teaches that, just as we make no distinction between damage caused inadvertently and damage caused deliberately when someone strikes an animal, but rather we oblige the tortfeasor to pay in all cases, similarly if someone kills another person, we make no distinction between an inadvertent act and deliberate homicide, and we exempt the killer from paying damages in all cases, because he is liable to forfeit his life.

הָנִיחָא [11]The Gemara comments: **This is acceptable according to those who accept** the position of **the Sage of the School of Ḥizkiyah.** [12]**But according to those who do not accept** the position of **the Sage of the School of Ḥizkiyah,** [13]**why do I need the analogy** of the verse: "And he that strikes a beast...he that strikes a man"? What new law does the juxtaposition of those two prohibitions teach us?

מַה [14]The Gemara explains: The juxtaposition of these two prohibitions teaches us that, **just as someone who inflicts a wound upon a beast in order to remedy** it by letting its blood, for example, **is exempt** from

[1]אָמַר קְרָא: ״מַכֵּה אָדָם וּמַכֵּה בְהֵמָה״. [2]מַה מַּכֵּה בְהֵמָה — עַד דְּעָבֵיד בָּהּ חַבּוּרָה, [3]דִּכְתִיב בָּהּ: נֶפֶשׁ, אַף מַכֵּה אָדָם — [4]עַד דְּעָבֵיד חַבּוּרָה.

[5]מַתְקִיף לָהּ רַב יִרְמְיָה: אֶלָּא מֵעַתָּה, הִכְחִישָׁהּ בַּאֲבָנִים הָכִי נַמִי דְּלָא מִיחַיַּיב? [6]אֶלָּא: אִם אֵינוֹ עִנְיָן לְנֶפֶשׁ בְּהֵמָה, [7]דְּהָא אִי נַמִי הִכְחִישָׁהּ בַּאֲבָנִים חַיָּיב, [8]תְּנֵיהוּ עִנְיָן לְנֶפֶשׁ אָדָם.

[9]אֶלָּא הֶקֵּישָׁא לָמָּה לִי? [10]לְכִדְתַנְיָא דְּבֵי חִזְקִיָּה.

[11]הָנִיחָא לְמַאן דְּאִית לֵיהּ תַּנָּא דְּבֵי חִזְקִיָּה. [12]אֶלָּא לְמַאן דְּלֵית לֵיהּ תַּנָּא דְּבֵי חִזְקִיָּה, [13]הֶיקֵּישָׁא לָמָּה לִי?

[14]מַה מַּכֵּה בְּהֵמָה לִרְפוּאָה

LITERAL TRANSLATION

[1]The verse says: "He who strikes a man...and he who strikes a beast." [2]Just as he who strikes a beast — unless he inflicts a wound upon it, [3]for it is written: *Nefesh*; so, too, he who strikes a man — [4]unless he inflicts a wound.

[5]Rabbi Yirmeyah strongly objected: But now, if he weakened it with stones, so also he would not be liable? [6]Rather, if it does not refer to the soul of a beast, [7]for surely even if he weakened it with stones, he is liable, [8]it refers to the soul of a man.

[9]Then why do I need the analogy? [10]For that which was taught [by a Sage] of the School of Ḥizkiyah.

[11]It is acceptable according to the one who has the Sage of the School of Ḥizkiyah. [12]But according to the one who does not have the Sage of the School of Ḥizkiyah, [13]why do I need the analogy?

[14]Just as someone who strikes a beast for a cure

RASHI

דכתיב ביה נפש — ונפש משמע דם, דהוה חבורה. הכחישה — לבהמה. באבנים — דלא עשה בה חבורה. לנפש אדם — דהיינו אביו, דאף על גב דלא בעינן מיתה — חבורה מיהא בעינן. אלא הקישא למה לי — דאתקש מכה אדם למכה בהמה בחד קרא, הואיל וילפת ליה מ״אם אינו ענין״. לכדתניא דבי חזקיה — בבבא קמא [״בהמניח״] (לה,א) לפטור חייבי מיתות שוגגין מן התשלומין: מה מכה בהמה לא חלקת בו וכו׳. הניחא וכו׳ — פלוגתא דרבי יוחנן ורבי שמעון בן לקיש בכתובות באלו נערות (לד,ב). מה מכה בהמה לרפואה — כגון מקיז דם פטור מן

TRANSLATION AND COMMENTARY

paying compensation, for he did not cause the animal any damage, [1]**so, too, is someone who** inflicts a wound on his father's body in order to cure him **exempt** from the death penalty. [2]**For the** following **question was** raised in discussion among the Sages: What **is the law about a son letting his father's blood?** [3]**Rav Matenah said:** Letting one's father's blood is permitted, for the verse states (Leviticus 19:18): **"And you shall love your neighbor as yourself,"** teaching that you are only forbidden to do unto others what you would not want others to do unto you. Since a person wants others to let his blood, he is permitted to let his father's blood when medically necessary, even though he causes him an injury. [4]**Rav Dimi bar Hinana said:** Letting one's father's blood is permitted, for the verse states: **"He who strikes a man...and he who strikes a beast."** [5]The juxtaposition of these two laws teaches us that, **just as someone who inflicts a wound upon a beast in order to cure it is exempt** from paying compensation, [6]**so, too, is someone who inflicts a wound upon** his father **in order to** cure him **exempt** from the death penalty.

רַב [7]It was related that **Rav did not allow his son to remove a thorn,** lest he cause him a wound and violate the prohibition against inflicting a wound upon one's father. [8]It was further related that **Mar the son of Ravina did not allow his son to lance an abscess** to let the pus flow out, **lest he cause him a wound,** [9]**and** he **be** liable for **an unintentional violation of a prohibition.**

אִי הָכִי [10]The Gemara asks: **If it is so,** that Mar the son of Ravina was concerned about this issue, then he should have barred not only his son, but **everyone else as well** from lancing his abscess.

אַחֵר [11]The Gemara answers: Mar the son of Ravina would allow **another person** to lance his abscess, for even if he would inadvertently cause him an injury, it would only be **an unintentional violation of an** ordinary **negative commandment** derived from the verse (Deuteronomy 25:3): "And he may not exceed; lest, if he should exceed." [12]But Mar the son of Ravina would not allow **his son** to lance his abscess, for if a son inadvertently

פָּטוּר, [1]אַף מַכֵּה אָדָם לִרְפוּאָה
פָּטוּר. [2]דְּאִיבַּעְיָא לְהוּ: בֵּן מַהוּ
שֶׁיָּקִיז דָּם לְאָבִיו? [3]רַב מַתָּנָא
אָמַר: ״וְאָהַבְתָּ לְרֵעֲךָ כָּמוֹךָ״.
[4]רַב דִּימִי בַּר חִינָּנָא אָמַר:
״מַכֵּה אָדָם...וּמַכֵּה בְּהֵמָה״.
[5]מַה מַכֵּה בְּהֵמָה לִרְפוּאָה
פָּטוּר, [6]אַף מַכֵּה אָדָם לִרְפוּאָה
פָּטוּר.
[7]רַב לָא שָׁבֵיק לִבְרֵיהּ לְמִישְׁקַל
לֵיהּ סִילְוָא. [8]מָר בְּרֵיהּ דְּרָבִינָא
לָא שָׁבֵיק לִבְרֵיהּ לְמִיפְתַּח לֵיהּ
כַּוְותָא, [9]דִּילְמָא חָבֵיל, וַהֲוָה
לֵיהּ שִׁגְגַת אִיסּוּר.
[10]אִי הָכִי אַחֵר נַמִי!
[11]אַחֵר, שִׁיגְגַת לָאו. [12]בְּנוֹ,

LITERAL TRANSLATION

is exempt, [1]so, too, is someone who strikes a man for a cure exempt. [2]For it was asked of them: What [is the law about] a son letting the blood of his father? [3]Rav Matenah said: "And you shall love your neighbor as yourself." [4]Rav Dimi bar Hinana said: "He who strikes a man...and he who strikes a beast." [5]Just as someone who strikes a beast for a cure is exempt, [6]so, too, is someone who strikes a man for a cure exempt.

[7]Rav did not allow his son to remove a thorn from him. [8]Mar the son of Ravina did not allow his son to lance an abscess, lest he injure him, [9]and it be an unintentional [violation of a] prohibition.

[10]If so, someone else also!

[11]Someone else, an unintentional [violation of a] negative commandment. [12]His son,

RASHI

התשלומין, שהרי לא הזיקה. אף מכה אדם — דהיינו אביו. לרפואה פטור — ממיתה, ואף על גב דחבורה היא. ואהבת לרעך כמוך — לא הוזהרו ישראל מלעשות לחבריהם אלא דבר שאינו חפץ לעשות לעצמו. סילוא — קוץ ישב לו בבשרו. למפתח ליה כוותא — כויה, להוציא ליחה ממנה. אי הכי אחר נמי — לא ליפתח, שהרי כל ישראל הוזהרו על חבלת חבירו דכתיב (דברים כה) ״לא יוסיף פן יוסיף״. שגגת לאו — כשאין מתכוין הוי שגגה באיסור שזדונו לאו בעלמא, דקיל.

NOTES

מַכֵּה אָדָם לִרְפוּאָה **Someone who smites a man for a cure.** The Rishonim deal at length with the responsibility of a physician whose treatment caused his patient injury or death. Some distinguish between a physician who treated the patient's ailments with medications, and one who performed surgery. Some Rishonim argue that, since the Torah permits a physician to practice medicine (and even commands him to do so), if he made an error that caused his patient injury or death he is not regarded as having acted unwittingly (*shogeg*) — so that he still bears a certain responsibility, but rather he is considered as having acted under force (*ones*) — so that he bears no liability (see *Rabbi David Bonfil, Ran* in the name of *Ramban, Margoliyot HaYam*).

HALAKHAH

בֵּן מַהוּ שֶׁיָּקִיז דָּם לְאָבִיו? **What is the law about a son letting the blood of his father?** "A son should not remove a thorn that is stuck in his father's flesh, lest he inflict a wound upon him. Similarly, if the son is a bloodletter or a doctor, he should not draw his father's blood, or perform any surgery upon him, even though the wound that he

TRANSLATION AND COMMENTARY

causes his father an injury, he **unintentionally violates a prohibition** that is **subject to the punishment of strangulation.**

וְהָדִתְנַן [1]The Gemara asks: Regarding **that which we have learned** in the Mishnah (*Shabbat* 17:20): "One is permitted to handle **a** small **sewing needle** on Shabbat **in order to** use it to **remove a thorn**" — one may ask: Why is a person permitted to remove a thorn on Shabbat? [2]**Let us be concerned that,** while removing the thorn, **he may inflict a wound, and** he **will have unintentionally violated a Torah prohibition** that is **subject to the punishment of stoning.**

הָתָם [3]The Gemara answers: **There,** we say that a person is permitted to remove a thorn on Shabbat, for even if he inflicts a wound, **that would be** regarded as an act of **damage,** and an action is forbidden on Shabbat only if it has a constructive purpose.

הָנִיחָא [4]The Gemara objects: **This is acceptable according to the** authority **who says that someone who commits** an act of **damage** on Shabbat **is exempt** from liability. [5]**But according to the** authority **who says that** even **someone who commits** an act of **damage** on Shabbat **is liable** for violating Shabbat, **what is there to say?**

מַאן [6]The Gemara answers: **Which** Tanna **said that someone who commits** an act of **damage** on Shabbat **is liable?** [7]**It is Rabbi Shimon.** [85A] [8]**And surely Rabbi Shimon** himself **said:** [9]If a person performed **work** on Shabbat **that is not necessary for its own sake,** meaning that it was not done for the same purpose for which that work was performed in the Sanctuary in the wilderness, but for some other purpose, **he is exempt** from liability. For example, extinguishing a fire to save fuel, rather than to produce coals (the purpose for which extinguishing was performed in the Sanctuary), is considered work that is not necessary for its own sake. Thus, a person is permitted to remove a thorn on Shabbat, even according to Rabbi Shimon who says that someone who commits an act of damage on Shabbat is liable. If he causes a wound while removing the thorn, it is not for the same purpose for which that work was performed in the Sanctuary in the wilderness.

שִׁגְגַת חֶנֶק.
[1]וְהָדִתְנַן: ״מַחַט שֶׁל יָד לִיטּוֹל בָּהּ אֶת הַקּוֹץ״ — [2]לֵיחוּשׁ דִּילְמָא חֲבֵיל, וְהָוְיָא לָהּ שִׁגְגַת סְקִילָה!
[3]הָתָם מְקַלְקֵל הוּא.
[4]הָנִיחָא לְמַאן דַּאֲמַר מְקַלְקֵל פָּטוּר. [5]אֶלָּא לְמַאן דַּאֲמַר חַיָּיב, מַאי אִיכָּא לְמֵימַר?
[6]מַאן שָׁמַעְתְּ לֵיהּ דַּאֲמַר מְקַלְקֵל בְּחַבּוּרָה חַיָּיב? [7]רַבִּי שִׁמְעוֹן הִיא, [85A] [8]וְרַבִּי שִׁמְעוֹן, הָאָמַר: [9]כָּל מְלָאכָה שֶׁאֵינָהּ צְרִיכָה לְגוּפָהּ, פָּטוּר עָלֶיהָ.

LITERAL TRANSLATION

an unintentional [violation of a prohibition subject to the punishment of] strangulation.

[1]And that which we have learned: "A sewing needle to remove a thorn with it" — [2]let us be concerned that he might cause an injury, and it will be an unintentional [violation of a prohibition subject to the punishment of] stoning!

[3]There, he does damage.

[4]This is acceptable according to the one who says [that] someone who causes damage is exempt. [5]But according to the one who says [that] someone who causes damage is liable, what is there to say?

[6]About whom did you hear that he said [that] someone who causes damage is liable? [7]It is Rabbi Shimon. [85A] [8]And Rabbi Shimon, surely he says: [9]Any work that is not necessary for its own sake, he is exempt for it.

RASHI

מחט של יד – היא מחט קטנה שתופרין בה בגדים – ניטלת בשבת ליטול בה את הקוץ, ומשום דקתני לה להלן במסכת שבת בפרק ״כל הכלים״ (קכב,ב) גבי ושל שקאין לפתוח בו את הדלת, קרי ליה להא קטנה מחט של יד. **דילמא חביל** – ועביד חבורה בשבת. **מקלקל הוא** – וכל המקלקלין פטורין בחלול שבת, דמלאכת מחשבת כתיב, ואין מחייב אמקלקל אלא ר׳ שמעון, ומקלקל בחבורה ר׳ שמעון נמי לא מחייב אלא במתכוון לכך דהוי צריך לחבלה, אבל הנוטל קוץ אין צריך לחבלה וברצונו לא יחבל. **ורבי שמעון אית ליה מלאכה שאינה צריכה לגופה פטור עליה** – בפרק ״המצניע״ (שבת צג,ב) גבי המוציא את המת במטה.

BACKGROUND

מְלָאכָה שֶׁאֵינָהּ צְרִיכָה לְגוּפָהּ Any work that is not necessary for its own sake. Work on Shabbat is only prohibited by Torah law if it is מְלָאכָה מַחֲשֶׁבֶת — creative, purposeful work intentionally performed. Rabbi Shimon adds another element — that the work must be "necessary for its own sake." In his view, a person is only liable if he did the work for the same purpose for which it was done in the Sanctuary in the wilderness. But if he did the work for some other purpose, he is exempt. For example, if a person dug a hole in the ground, not because he wanted the hole, but because he needed the earth, he is not liable to be punished for digging a hole on Shabbat. Similarly, if a person inflicted a wound while removing a thorn on Shabbat, he is exempt, because he did not do the work for the same purpose for which that work had been performed in the Sanctuary.

HALAKHAH

would inflict is for medical purposes. *Rema* adds that this only applies when another person is available to do the same task. But if there is nobody else to do it, and the father is in distress, the son may draw his father's blood or perform surgery on him as is necessary."

מַחַט שֶׁל יָד A sewing needle. "A person is permitted to handle a needle on Shabbat in order to remove a thorn from his flesh, for removing a thorn is permitted on Shabbat (provided that he takes cares not to inflict a wound; *Shulḥan Arukh HaRav*)." (*Shulḥan Arukh, Oraḥ Ḥayyim* 308:11.)

מְקַלְקֵל פָּטוּר Someone who causes damage is exempt. "If someone performs an action that is destructive in nature, with no constructive purpose, he is not liable for violating Shabbat (though the action itself is forbidden by Rabbinic decree)." (*Rambam, Sefer Zemanim, Hilkhot Shabbat* 1:17.)

[1] בָּעוּ מִינֵּיהּ מֵרַב שֵׁשֶׁת: בֵּן מַהוּ שֶׁיֵּעָשֶׂה שָׁלִיחַ לְאָבִיו לְהַכּוֹתוֹ וּלְקַלְּלוֹ?
[2] אָמַר לְהוּ: וְאַחֵר מִי הִתִּירוּ?
[3] אֶלָּא כְּבוֹד שָׁמַיִם עָדִיף, [4] הָכָא נַמִי כְּבוֹד שָׁמַיִם עָדִיף.
[5] מֵיתִיבִי: "וּמַה מִּי שֶׁמְּצֻוֶּה לְהַכּוֹתוֹ, מִצְוָה שֶׁלֹּא לְהַכּוֹתוֹ, [6] מִי שֶׁאֵינוֹ מְצֻוֶּה לְהַכּוֹתוֹ, אֵינוֹ דִּין שֶׁמִּצְוָה שֶׁלֹּא לְהַכּוֹתוֹ"?
[7] מַאי לָאו: אִידִי וְאִידִי בִּמְקוֹם מִצְוָה, [8] הָא — בִּבְנוֹ, הָא — בְּאַחֵר!

LITERAL TRANSLATION

[1] They asked Rav Sheshet: What [is the law] about a son becoming an agent [of a court against] his father to flog him or to curse him?
[2] He said to them: And who allowed someone else?
[3] Rather, the honor of Heaven takes precedence. [4] Here, too, the honor of Heaven takes precedence.
[5] They raised an objection: "If [regarding] someone whom one is commanded to strike, there is a commandment not to strike him, [6] [regarding] someone whom one is commanded not to strike, all the more so is there a commandment not to strike him." [7] Is it not that this and that are where there is a commandment, [8] and this — regarding his son; and that — regarding someone else?

TRANSLATION AND COMMENTARY

בָּעוּ מִינֵּיהּ [1] **Rav Sheshet was asked** the following question: **What is the law about a son acting as a agent** of the court **to flog his father,** if he became liable to the punishment of lashes, **or to curse** him, if he became liable to the punishment of excommunication?

אָמַר לְהוּ [2] Rav Sheshet **said to them: Who allowed someone else** to act as an officer of the court and administer the punishments of flogging and excommunication? Surely every Jew is bound by the general prohibitions against striking or cursing a fellow Jew! Nevertheless, officers of the court are permitted to administer the penalty of flogging, as the verse states (Deuteronomy 25:3): "Forty stripes he may give him," and to pronounce a curse, as the verse states (Numbers 5:21): "And the priest shall say to the woman, The Lord shall make you a curse and an oath among your people"! [3] **Rather,** it must be that **the honor of Heaven takes precedence** over the honor of man. For the sake of God's honor, which was violated when the offender committed his transgression, an officer of the court is permitted to violate the offender's honor. [4] **Here, too, the honor of Heaven takes precedence** over the honor due to one's father, and so a son may serve as an officer of the court and administer the punishments of flogging and excommunication against his father.

מֵיתִיבִי [5] **An objection was raised** against Rav Sheshet from a Baraita, which states: **"If regarding someone whom one is commanded to flog, there is** nevertheless a **commandment not to strike him** with even a single blow that is not administered as part of the punishment that is due him, [6] then **regarding someone whom one is commanded not to flog, all the more so should there be a commandment not to strike him."** The Gemara proposes an explanation for this obscure Baraita: [7] **Is it not that,** regarding both **this** one **and that** one — someone whom one is commanded to flog and someone whom one is commanded not to flog — **there is a commandment** to administer lashes to an offender? [8] **And** when the Baraita speaks of **this** one, whom one is commanded not to flog, it refers to an officer of the court who is the offender's **son** and is therefore forbidden to flog his father, **and** when the Baraita speaks of **that** one, whom one is commanded to flog, it refers to an officer of the court who is **someone else,** not the offender's son, and who may therefore administer the punishment of lashes. The Baraita is based on the following *kal vaḥomer* argument: Regarding someone whom an officer of the court who is not the offender's son is commanded to flog, as the verse states (Deuteronomy 25:3): "Forty stripes he may give him," there is a commandment not to strike the offender with even a single extra blow, as that same verse continues: "And not exceed"; therefore, regarding someone whom an officer of the court is commanded not to flog, because that officer of the court is the offender's son, all the more so should there be a commandment upon the son not to strike his father with even a single blow that is not administered as part of the punishment due him. In any case, the Baraita assumes that a son may not administer the punishment of lashes to his father, and this against the position of Rav Sheshet!

RASHI

מהו שיעשה שליח — בית דין לאביו אם נתחייב אביו נדוי או מלקות. **ואחר מי התירו** — לקללו ולהכות את חבירו והלא כל ישראל הוזהרו על הכאת חביריהם ועל קללתם כדילפינן ב"ארבע מיתות" (סנהדרין נח,ב) אפילו הכי נעשה שליח בית דין לכך, דכתיב (דברים כה) "ארבעים יכנו" וכתיב (במדבר ה) "יתן ה' אותך". **ומה מי שמצוה להכותו** — ברייתא תניא הכי במכילתא. **מאי לאו אידי ואידי** — מצוה ואינה מצוה תרוייהו במקום מצוה והא בבנו והא באחר והכי קאמר ויליף אזהרה למכה אביו.

NOTES

בֵּן מַהוּ שֶׁיֵּעָשֶׂה שָׁלִיחַ לְאָבִיו לְקַלְּלוֹ? What is the law about a son becoming a deputy to his father to curse him? The Geonim ask whether a son may impose an oath upon his father with whom he has a monetary dispute, if a curse is

[1]לָא, אִידִי וְאִידִי לָא שְׁנָא בְּנוֹ וְלָא שְׁנָא אַחֵר. [2]וְלָא קַשְׁיָא: כָּאן בִּמְקוֹם מִצְוָה, [3]כָּאן שֶׁלֹּא בִּמְקוֹם מִצְוָה. [4]וְהָכִי קָתָנֵי: וּמַה בִּמְקוֹם מִצְוָה, שֶׁמִּצְוֶה לְהַכּוֹתוֹ, [5]מִצְוָה שֶׁלֹּא לְהַכּוֹתוֹ, [6]שֶׁלֹּא בִּמְקוֹם מִצְוָה, שֶׁאֵינוֹ מְצֻוֶּה לְהַכּוֹתוֹ, [7]אֵינוֹ דִּין שֶׁמִּצְוָה שֶׁלֹּא לְהַכּוֹתוֹ? [8]תָּא שְׁמַע: ״הַיּוֹצֵא לֵיהָרֵג, וּבָא בְּנוֹ וְהִכָּהוּ וְקִילְּלוֹ, חַיָּיב. [9]בָּא אַחֵר וְהִכָּהוּ וְקִילְּלוֹ, פָּטוּר״. [10]וְהָוֵינַן בָּהּ: מַאי שְׁנָא בְּנוֹ וּמַאי שְׁנָא אַחֵר? [11]וְאָמַר

LITERAL TRANSLATION

[1]No, [regarding] this and that there is no distinction between his son and someone else. [2]And there is no difficulty: Here, in the place of a commandment, [3][and] here not in the place of a commandment. [4]And it teaches as follows: Since in the place of a commandment, that one is commanded to strike him, [5]there is a commandment not to strike him, [6]not in the place of a commandment, that one is not commanded to strike him, [7]all the more so is there a commandment not to strike him. [8]Come [and] hear: "[If] someone was going out to be executed, and his son came and struck him or cursed him, he is liable. [9][If] someone else came and struck him or cursed him, he is exempt." [10]And we discussed it: How is his son different, and how is someone else different? [11]And

RASHI

ומה אחר שמצוה להכותו במקום מצוה — דכתיב יכנו. **מצוה שלא להכותו** — יותר מארבעים, דכתיב (דברים כה) "ולא יוסיף פן יוסיף", בנו שאינו מצוה להכותו — אפילו במקום מצוה, אלמא אינו נעשה שליח לכך — אינו דין שמוזהר שלא להכותו שלא במקום מצוה. **ומה במקום מצוה שמצוה להכותו מצוה שלא להכותו** — יותר מארבעים, שלא במקום מצוה לא כל שכן ויליף אזהרה למכה אביו או חבירו מהכא. **בא אחר והכהו וקיללו פטור** — קסלקא דעתך פטור ממלקות.

TRANSLATION AND COMMENTARY

לָא [1]The Gemara rejects this proof: **No, regarding this** one **and that** one — someone whom one is commanded to flog and someone whom one is commanded not to flog — **there is no distinction between** an officer of the court who is the offender's **son and** an officer of the court who is **someone else.** [2]**And there is no difficulty** in understanding the Baraita: **Here, there is a commandment** to administer lashes, [3]**and here, there is no commandment** to administer lashes. [4]The Baraita means to **teach as follows:** The warning against striking one's father or any other person is derived by the following *kal vahomer* argument: **If** when **there is a commandment** to administer lashes, **and** the officer of the court **is commanded to strike** the offender, [5]**there is** nevertheless **a commandment not to strike him** with even a single extra blow — [6]then, when **there is no commandment** to administer lashes, **and nobody is commanded to strike** another person, [7]**all the more so** should **there be a commandment not to strike him** with any blow whatsoever. Thus, it may not be inferred from here that a son may not administer the punishment of lashes to his father.

תָּא שְׁמַע [8]**Come and hear** another proof against Rav Sheshet from the following Baraita: "**If** a capital offender **was being taken out for execution, and his son came and struck him or cursed him,** the son **is liable** to the death penalty. [9]But **if someone else came and struck or cursed** the man as he was being taken out for execution, **he is exempt.**" [10]**And we raised a difficulty** concerning this Baraita: **Why is** the law that applies to the man's **son different from** the law that applies to **another person?** If the son is liable to the death penalty for cursing or striking his father as he is being taken out for execution, why should another person who strikes or curses the condemned criminal be exempt from punishment? Surely every Jew is bound by the general prohibitions against striking or cursing a fellow Jew, prohibitions punishable by lashes! [11]**And Rav Ḥisda**

NOTES

attached to the oath. Some suggest that in such a case the son should transfer his rights to another person, and thus allow that other person to impose the oath upon his father.

HALAKHAH

הַיּוֹצֵא לֵיהָרֵג, וּבָא בְּנוֹ וְהִכָּהוּ **If someone was going out to be executed, and his son came and struck him.** "Even if someone's father or mother was a sinner convicted of a capital offense, and is now being taken out for execution, the son may not strike or curse him or her; but if he struck or cursed him or her, the son is exempt. If the parent has repented, then the son is liable to be punished for striking or cursing him or her, and subject to the death penalty for his offense," following the Gemara. (*Rambam, Sefer Shofetim, Hilkhot Mamrim* 5:12; *Shulḥan Arukh, Yoreh De'ah* 241:4.)

בָּא אַחֵר וְהִכָּהוּ **If someone else came and struck him.** "If someone other than his or her son struck a person who was being taken out for execution, the assailant is exempt, even if the convicted criminal has repented. But if the person who slapped him caused the condemned person shame, he is liable to pay monetary compensation to the dead man's heirs." (*Rambam, Sefer Shofetim, Hilkhot Mamrim* 5:12.)

TRANSLATION AND COMMENTARY

said: This applies **when they were** urging and **pressing** the condemned criminal **to go out** for execution, **but he would not go out** on his own and had to be taken out by force. If in such a case the criminal's son strikes or curses his father, he is liable to be punished, but if another person does the same thing, he is not liable. According to this Baraita, even if the son is acting for the court, he is forbidden to strike or curse his father, and if he does strike or curse him, he is liable to the death penalty, against the opinion of Rav Sheshet!

רַב שֵׁשֶׁת [1]The Gemara rejects this proof: **Rav Sheshet** can **explain** the Baraita as referring to **when they were not pressing** the condemned criminal **to go out** for execution. Rather, the criminal was going out on his own, and the son or some other person came and struck or cursed him on his own initiative.

אִי הָכִי [2]The Gemara comments: **If so,** then not only the criminal's son, but **also** any **other person** who struck or cursed the criminal should be liable to punishment.

אַחֵר [3]The Gemara answers: If **another person** struck or cursed the condemned criminal, he is exempt, for a condemned criminal who is being taken out for execution **is** regarded as **a dead man,** and someone who strikes or curses a dead man is not subject to punishment.

וְהָאָמַר רַב שֵׁשֶׁת [4]The Gemara asks: **But surely Rav Sheshet** himself **said: If** someone **put** another person **to shame while he was asleep, and** that other person **died** in his sleep, so that he never knew he had been humiliated, the offender **is** nevertheless **liable** to pay monetary compensation to the dead man's heirs, for they suffered shame when their father was humiliated. Similarly the person who struck or cursed the condemned criminal as he was being taken out for execution should be liable to pay monetary compensation to the criminal's heirs. Why, then, does the Baraita say that he is exempt, implying that he is not even liable for monetary compensation?

הָכָא [5]The Gemara answers: **We are dealing here** in the Baraita **with a blow** that caused such slight injury that it **was not worth** even **a perutah** in damages.

רַב חִסְדָּא: בִּמְסָרְבִין בּוֹ לָצֵאת וְאֵינוֹ יוֹצֵא.
[1]רַב שֵׁשֶׁת מוֹקֵי לָהּ בְּשֶׁאֵין מְסָרְבִין בּוֹ לָצֵאת.
[2]אִי הָכִי, אַחֵר נַמִּי!
[3]אַחֵר — גַּבְרָא קְטִילָא הוּא.
[4]וְהָאָמַר רַב שֵׁשֶׁת: בִּיְּישׁוֹ יָשֵׁן וָמֵת, חַיָּיב!
[5]הָכָא בְּמַאי עָסְקִינַן — בְּשֶׁהִכָּהוּ הַכָּאָה שֶׁאֵין בָּהּ שָׁוֶה פְּרוּטָה.

LITERAL TRANSLATION

Rav Ḥisda said: When they are pressing him to go out, but he does not go out.

[1]Rav Sheshet explains it when they are not pressing him to go out.

[2]If so, someone else also!

[3]Someone else — he is a dead man.

[4]But surely Rav Sheshet said: [If] he put him to shame while he was asleep, and he died, he is liable!

[5]What we are dealing with here is if he struck him with a blow that does not have the value of a perutah.

RASHI

ואינו יוצא — ואשמעינן דבנו אינו נעשה שליח בית דין לכופו לצאת וקשיא לרב ששת. הכי גרסינן: **והאמר רב ששת ביישו ישן ומת חייב** — ביישו ישן ומת מתוך שינתו. **חייב** — דהא מתביישין בניו והאי נמי לא שנא.

BACKGROUND

פְּרוּטָה Perutah. The perutah was the smallest coin in circulation among Jews in antiquity. For Halakhic purposes the Sages decreed that the perutah had a certain absolute value, which was that of approximately half a gram of silver. But the term was sometimes used broadly to designate any copper coin of low value. Thus coins known as "perutot" may have been worth more or less than the Halakhically determined value of a perutah.

NOTES

הַכָּאָה שֶׁאֵין בָּהּ שָׁוֶה פְּרוּטָה A blow that does not have the value of a perutah. There is a general rule that a person cannot become liable to different penalties for the same offense. Thus, if a person committed an offense that is subject to a financial penalty and to flogging, he can only be subjected to one of the two penalties. In general, when the financial penalty is mentioned explicitly in the Torah, the offender becomes liable to that penalty, and is therefore exempt from lashes. This is the law that applies to someone who causes another person bodily injury. If the injury is subject to monetary compensation, he becomes liable to the financial penalty, and is exempt from lashes. But if the injury was so slight that it was not subject to monetary compensation, since it was not worth even a perutah in damages, the offender becomes liable to the punishment of lashes for violating a negative commandment of the Torah.

HALAKHAH

בִּיְּישׁוֹ יָשֵׁן וָמֵת If he put him to shame while he was asleep, and he died. "If someone put another person to shame while he was asleep, he is liable to pay him compensation. If the victim died in his sleep, so that he never knew he had been humiliated, the offender cannot be forced to pay compensation to the victim's heirs, but if those heirs seize money from the offender, we do not require them to return it to him." (*Shulḥan Arukh, Ḥoshen Mishpat* 420:35.)

הַכָּאָה שֶׁאֵין בָּהּ שָׁוֶה פְּרוּטָה A blow that does not have the value of a perutah. "If someone struck another person with a blow that causes an injury that was worth at least a perutah in damages, he is liable to pay monetary compensation, and is exempt from lashes. But if he inflicted an injury that was worth less than a perutah in damages, he is subject to lashes by Torah law." (*Shulḥan Arukh, Ḥoshen Mishpat* 420:2.)

LITERAL TRANSLATION

[1]But surely Rabbi Ammi said in the name of Rabbi Yoḥanan: [If] he struck him with a blow that does not have the value of a perutah, he is flogged! [2]What is [the meaning of] "exempt," which he said? He is exempt from monetary compensation. [3]This implies that his son is liable to pay monetary compensation. [4]Rather, with his law; [5]here, too, with his law. [6]Rather, [regarding] someone else, the reason that he is exempt — because the verse states: [7]"And a prince among your people you shall not curse" — when he does the deeds of your people. [8]Granted, cursing, [but] from where do we [know about] striking? [9]We compare striking to cursing. [10]If so, his son also!

[1]וְהָאָמַר רַבִּי אַמִי אָמַר רַבִּי יוֹחָנָן: הִכָּהוּ הַכָּאָה שֶׁאֵין בָּהּ שָׁוֶה פְּרוּטָה, לוֹקֶה!
[2]מַאי "פָּטוּר" דְּקָאָמַר? פָּטוּר מִמָּמוֹן.
[3]מִכְּלָל דִּבְנוֹ חַיָּיב בְּמָמוֹן
[4]אֶלָּא, בְּדִינוֹ: [5]הָכָא נַמִי — בְּדִינוֹ!
[6]אֶלָּא: אַחֵר הַיְינוּ טַעְמָא דְּפָטוּר — דְּאָמַר קְרָא: [7]"וְנָשִׂיא בְעַמְּךָ לֹא תָאֹר" — בְּעוֹשֶׂה מַעֲשֵׂה עַמְּךָ.
[8]הָתֵינָח קְלָלָה, הַכָּאָה מְנָלַן?
[9]דְּמַקְשִׁינַן הַכָּאָה לִקְלָלָה.
[10]אִי הָכִי, בְּנוֹ נַמִי!

TRANSLATION AND COMMENTARY

וְהָאָמַר רַבִּי אַמִי [1]The Gemara objects: **But surely Rabbi Ammi said in the name of Rabbi Yoḥanan: If** the assailant **struck** another person **with a blow that** caused such slight injury that it **was not worth** even **a perutah** in damages, **he is flogged!** Why, then, does the Baraita say that someone who struck or cursed a condemned criminal as he was being taken out for execution is exempt, implying that he is totally exempt from all penalties?

מַאי "פָּטוּר" [2]The Gemara answers: **What** does the Baraita mean when it says that a person who struck or cursed the condemned criminal **is "exempt"**? It means that **he is exempt from monetary compensation,** but he is indeed liable to the punishment of flogging.

מִכְּלָל [3]This solution is problematic, because it **implies that** when the Baraita says that **the son** is liable, it means that he **is liable to pay monetary compensation.** But we just said that the Baraita is dealing with a blow that caused such slight injury that it was not worth even a perutah in damages. [4]**Rather,** when the Baraita says that the son is liable, it means that he is liable to **his penalty,** the death sentence. [5]**Here, too,** then, when the Baraita says that the other person is exempt, it means that he is exempt from **his penalty,** from lashes. Thus, the question returns: Why is the law that applies to the offender's son different from the law that applies to someone else? If the son is liable to the death penalty for striking or cursing his father as he was taken out for execution, why should another person who struck or cursed the condemned criminal be exempt from lashes?

אֶלָּא [6]The Gemara explains: **Rather, the reason that the other person is exempt is that the verse** from which we learn that it is forbidden to curse a Jew **states** (Exodus 22:27): [7]**"And a prince among your people you shall not curse,"** and the words "among your people" serve as a qualification teaching that you are only forbidden to curse Jews **who act in the manner of "your people,"** Jews who keep the Torah. A condemned criminal who is being taken out for execution does not fall under this category, so there is no prohibition against cursing him.

הָתֵינָח קְלָלָה [8]The Gemara asks: **Granted,** that a person is exempt from liability for **cursing** a condemned criminal, **but from where do we know** that he is also exempt from liability for **striking** him? The verse from which we learn that it is forbidden to strike a Jew does not qualify that prohibition, limiting it to Jews who act in the manner of "your people"!

דְּמַקְשִׁינַן [9]The Gemara answers: **We learn** the law regarding **striking** a fellow Jew **by analogy from** the law regarding **cursing** a fellow Jew.

אִי הָכִי [10]The Gemara objects: **If so,** then **his son** should **also** be exempt from liability for striking or cursing his wicked father!

RASHI

מכלל — דחייב דקתני גבי בנו ממון קאמר בתמיה והא באין בה שוה פרוטה מוקמת לה. אלא — על כרחך חייב בדינו קאמר מיתה. הכא נמי — דתני גבי אחר פטור — בדינו קאמר, וממלקות פטר ליה ואכתי מאי שנא. בעושה מעשה עמך — וזה שעובר עבירה שחייב מיתה לאו עושה מעשה עמך הוא. התינח קללה — דכתיב ביה בעמך. מקשינן — כלומר גמרינן במה מצינו ואיכא דאמרי היקשא דכתיב "מכה אביו" ו"מקלל אביו" גבי הדדי ב"אלה המשפטים" אלא שמקרא אחד מפסיק ביניהם. אי הכי בנו נמי — דהא לא כתיב אזהרה במקלל אביו אלא במקלל חברו שאביו בכלל עמך בפרק "ארבע מיתות" (סנהדרין סו,א).

HALAKHAH

עוֹשֶׂה מַעֲשֵׂה עַמְּךָ **When he does the deeds of your people.** "A Jew who embarrasses a fit member of the people of Israel has no share in the World to Come. A Jew who curses such a person is subject to lashes. A Jew who strikes

[1]כִּדְאָמַר רַב פִּינְחָס: בְּשֶׁעָשָׂה תְּשׁוּבָה. [2]הָכִי נַמִי — בְּשֶׁעָשָׂה תְּשׁוּבָה.
[3]אִי הָכִי, אַחֵר נַמִי!
[4]אָמַר רַב מָרִי: "בְעַמְּךָ" — [5]בַּמְקוּיָּם שֶׁבְּעַמְּךָ.
[6]אִי הָכִי בְּנוֹ נַמִי!
[85B] [7]מִידֵי דַּהֲוָה לְאַחַר מִיתָה.
[8]מַאי הֲוָה עֲלָהּ? [9]אָמַר רַבָּה בַּר רַב הוּנָא, וְכֵן תָּנָא דְּבֵי רַבִּי יִשְׁמָעֵאל: [10]"לַכֹּל אֵין הַבֵּן נַעֲשֶׂה שָׁלִיחַ לְאָבִיו לְהַכּוֹתוֹ וּלְקַלְּלוֹ, חוּץ מִמֵּסִית, [11]שֶׁהֲרֵי אָמְרָה תּוֹרָה: 'וְלֹא תַחְמֹל וְלֹא תְכַסֶּה עָלָיו'".

LITERAL TRANSLATION

[1]As Rav Pineḥas said: When he repented. [2]Here, too, when he repented.
[3]If so, someone else also!
[4]Rav Mari said: "Among your people" — [5]among the enduring of your people.
[6]If so, his son also!
[85B] [7]As it is regarding after death.
[8]What was there about it? [9]Rabbah bar Rav Huna said, and so it was taught by [a Sage] of the School of Rabbi Yishmael: [10]"For all [offenses] a son does not become an agent to [punish] his father to flog him or to curse him, except for [the crime of] incitement, [11]for the Torah said: 'You shall not spare or conceal [the inciter].'"

RASHI

דרב פנחס — משמיה דרבא במסכת חגיגה בסוף חומר בקודש. במקוים — הראוי להתקיים ולא זה שנגמר דינו. מידי דהוה לאחר מיתה — דילפינן לקמן מקלל לאחר מיתה חייב. ואם תאמר: והתנן מכה לאחר מיתה פטור — והכא מחייב ליה אהכאה דקתני הכהו וקללו — היינו טעמא דפטור מכה לאחר מיתה משום דבעינן חבורה ולאחר מיתה ליכא חבורה, דליכא "נפש" דנפקא ליה לעיל מ"נפש" ויוצא ליהרג איכא חבורה דחי הוא אלא דסופו למות.

TRANSLATION AND COMMENTARY

כִּדְאָמַר רַב פִּינְחָס [1]The Gemara replies by applying a suggestion made by Rav Pineḥas in connection with a similar problem (*Ḥagigah* 26a). The Mishnah, there, states that a thief who stole a utensil and claims that he did not render it ritually impure is believed. **Rav Pineḥas said** that the Mishnah's ruling applies only **if** the thief **repented.** [2]Accordingly, **here, too,** we can explain our Baraita as applying only if the father who was being taken out for execution **repented.** Thus, his son who struck or cursed him is liable to the death penalty.

אִי הָכִי [3]The Gemara objects: **If so,** then **some other person** who struck or cursed the condemned criminal as he was being taken out for execution should **also** be liable, for once the criminal has repented, he is once again included "among your people"!

אָמַר רַב מָרִי [4]**Rav Mari said:** The words, **"among your people,"** qualify the prohibition in another way as well, [5]teaching that you are only forbidden to curse Jews who are **among the enduring of your people,** meaning that they are fit to live an ordinary life in the future, unlike someone who was sentenced to death.

אִי הָכִי [6]The Gemara objects: **If it is so,** that there is no liability for striking or cursing a person who is not fit to live an ordinary life in the future, then the condemned criminal's **son** should **also** be exempt from liability for striking or cursing his father!

מִידֵי דַּהֲוָה [85B] [7]The Gemara answers: A son is liable to the death penalty if he curses his father while he is being taken out for execution, **just as** he is liable to that punishment if he curses him **after his death,** as we will learn in the next Mishnah. And so, too, is he liable if he strikes his father while he is being taken out for execution, though he is exempt if he strikes him after his death.

מַאי [8]The Gemara raised numerous objections against Rav Sheshet, but it was unable to bring conclusive proof against his position, and so it asks: **What conclusion was** reached about the matter? May a son act as an officer of the court and administer the punishments of flogging and excommunication, or not? [9]**Rabbah bar Rav Huna said, and so it was taught** in a Baraita **by a Sage of the School of Rabbi Yishmael:** [10]**"For** practically **all** offenses **a son may not act as an agent** of the court **to flog his father,** if he became liable for lashes, **or to curse him,** if he became liable for excommunication, **except if** his father was found guilty of **inciting** others to worship idols, [11]**for** regarding that offender **the Torah said** (Deuteronomy 13:9): **'You shall not spare or conceal him.'"**

NOTES

שֶׁהֲרֵי אָמְרָה תּוֹרָה: וְלֹא תַחְמֹל **For the Torah said: You shall not spare.** The passage regarding a person who incites others to worship idols begins (Deuteronomy 13:7): "If your brother, the son of your mother, or your son, or

HALAKHAH

such a person violates a negative commandment." (*Rambam, Sefer Nezikin, Hilkhot Ḥovel U'Mazik* 3:7, 5:1; *Sefer Mishpatim, Hilkhot Sanhedrin* 26:2.)

אֵין הַבֵּן נַעֲשֶׂה שָׁלִיחַ לְאָבִיו **A son does not become an agent against his father.** "A son may not act as an officer of the court to flog his father who has become liable to the punishment of lashes, nor may he act as an officer of the court to pronounce a ban against his father who has become liable to the punishment of excommunication, except if the father was found guilty of inciting others to worship idols." (*Rambam, Sefer Shofetim, Hilkhot Mamrim* 5:13; *Shulḥan Arukh, Yoreh De'ah* 241:5.)

משנה [1]הַמַּכֶּה אָבִיו וְאִמּוֹ אֵינוֹ חַיָּיב עַד שֶׁיַּעֲשֶׂה בָּהֶן חַבּוּרָה. [2]זֶה חוֹמֶר בִּמְקַלֵּל מִבְּמַכֶּה, [3]שֶׁהַמְקַלֵּל לְאַחַר מִיתָה חַיָּיב, [4]וְהַמַּכֶּה לְאַחַר מִיתָה — פָּטוּר.

גמרא [5]תָּנוּ רַבָּנַן: ״׳אָבִיו וְאִמּוֹ קִלֵּל׳, [6]לְאַחַר מִיתָה. [7]שֶׁיָּכוֹל, הוֹאִיל וְחַיָּיב בְּמַכֶּה וְחַיָּיב בִּמְקַלֵּל — [8]מַה מַּכֶּה אֵינוֹ חַיָּיב אֶלָּא מֵחַיִּים, [9]אַף הַמְקַלֵּל אֵינוֹ חַיָּיב אֶלָּא מֵחַיִּים. [10]וְעוֹד, קַל וָחוֹמֶר: [11]וּמַה מַּכֶּה — שֶׁעָשָׂה בּוֹ שֶׁלֹּא ׳בְּעַמְּךָ׳

LITERAL TRANSLATION

MISHNAH [1]Someone who smites his father or his mother is not liable unless he inflicts a wound upon them. [2]This is a stringency regarding someone who curses over someone who smites, [3]for someone who curses after death is liable, [4]and someone who smites after death is exempt.

GEMARA [5]Our Rabbis taught: "'His father or his mother he has cursed' — [6]after death. [7]For I might [have thought] that since he is liable [to be punished] for smiting, and he is liable [to be punished] for cursing — [8]just as someone who smites is only liable during his lifetime, [9]so, too, is someone who curses only liable during his lifetime. [10]And furthermore, [there is] a *kal vaḥomer:* [11]If someone who smites — regarding whom it made [someone who is] 'not among your people'

TRANSLATION AND COMMENTARY

MISHNAH הַמַּכֶּה [1]**Someone who smites his father or his mother is not liable** to the death penalty **unless he inflicted a wound upon him or her.** [2]On **this** matter, the law **regarding someone who curses** his father or his mother **is more stringent than** the law **regarding someone who smites** them: [3]**Someone who curses** his father or his mother **after** his or her **death is liable** to death by stoning, [4]**whereas someone who smites** either of them **after** his or her **death is exempt** from punishment.

GEMARA תָּנוּ רַבָּנַן [5]**Our Rabbis taught** the following Baraita: "The seemingly extraneous words (Leviticus 20:9): **'His father or his mother he has cursed,'** [6]come to teach that even someone who curses a parent **after** his or her **death** is liable to the death penalty. [7]For had the Torah not written those words, **I might have thought that** someone who curses a dead parent is exempt, based on the following arguments: **Since** a son **is liable to be punished for smiting** a parent, **and he is** also **liable to be punished for cursing** a parent, it is legitimate to draw an analogy between them: [8]**Just as someone who smites** his parent **is only liable** if he committed the offense **during** the parent's **lifetime,** [9]**so, too, should someone who curses** his parent **be liable** to be punished **only** if he committed the offense **during** the parent's **lifetime.** [10]**And furthermore, there is a *kal vaḥomer*** argument which suggests that a person should be exempt for cursing a dead parent: [11]For **smiting** a parent is a prohibition **regarding which** the Torah **made someone who does not act in the manner of 'your people'** and does observe the Torah **like someone who acts in the manner of 'your**

RASHI

משנה שהמקלל לאחר מיתה חייב — כדיליף בגמרא. והמכה לאחר מיתה פטור — דחבורה ליכא.

גמרא אביו ואמו קלל — קרא יתירא הוא דהא כתיב רישיה דקרא "אשר יקלל את אביו ואת אמו". מכה שעשה שלא בעמך כבעמך — דגבי הכאה לא כתיב "בעמך" למעוטי שאינו עושה מעשה עמך והאי תנא סבר לא מקשינן הכאה לקללה, מפני המקרא, המפסיק בינתים.

NOTES

your daughter, or the wife of your bosom, or your friend who is as your own soul, entice you secretly." Some suggest that the words, "or your friend who is as your own soul," refer to one's father. According to this, the Torah states explicitly that one may not spare a person who incites others to idolatry, even if he is one's own father.

הַמַּכֶּה וְהַמְקַלֵּל **Someone who smites and someone who curses.** Our commentary follows *Rashi, Rabbi David Bonfil,* and others, who explain that someone who strikes his father or his mother after his or her death is exempt from punishment, for a son who strikes his parent is only liable to the death penalty if he inflicts a wound, and after death a wound can no longer be inflicted. *Rabbenu Yehonatan* explains this exemption differently. A son is only liable to be punished for cursing or striking his parent if he cursed or struck the parent in his presence. If a son struck his father or his mother after his or her death, he cannot be said to have struck him or her in his or her presence. But if he cursed him or her after his or her death, he is considered to have cursed him or her in his or her presence, for the parent's soul continues to exist even after death. Others suggest that since a physical blow relates only to a person's body, and after death the

HALAKHAH

עַד שֶׁיַּעֲשֶׂה בָּהֶן חַבּוּרָה **Unless he inflicted upon him or her a wound.** "Someone who strikes his father or his mother is liable to death by strangulation, only if he inflicted a wound upon his parent. If he did not inflict a wound, he has violated a negative commandment, as if he had struck any other Jew." (*Rambam, Sefer Shofetim, Hilkhot Mamrim* 5:5; *Shulḥan Arukh, Yoreh De'ah* 241:1, *Rema.*)

הַמְקַלֵּל לְאַחַר מִיתָה **Someone who curses after death.** "Someone who curses his father or his mother, even after the parent's death, is liable to death by stoning." (*Rambam, Sefer Shofetim, Hilkhot Mamrim* 5:1; *Shulḥan Arukh, Yoreh De'ah* 241:1.)

הַמַּכֶּה לְאַחַר מִיתָה **Someone who smites after death.** "Someone who strikes his father or his mother after the parent's death is exempt." (*Rambam, Sefer Shofetim, Hilkhot Mamrim* 5:5.)

TRANSLATION AND COMMENTARY

people' and observes the Torah, for the Torah forbids a person to strike his parent, even if he is a wicked sinner. [1]However, a person **is not liable** if he committed this offense **after** his parent's **death.** [2]Therefore, one would think that **all the more so** for **cursing** a parent, a prohibition **regarding which** the Torah **did not make someone who does not act in the manner of your people like someone who acts in the manner of 'your people'** (for one is only forbidden to curse a parent who keeps the Torah) a person **should not be liable** if he committed his offense **after** his parent's **death.** [3]To forestall that erroneous conclusion, **the Torah states: 'His father or his mother he has cursed,'** teaching that someone who curses his father or his mother even **after** his or her **death** is liable to the death penalty."

הָנִיחָא [4]The Gemara comments: **This is acceptable according to Rabbi Yonatan, according to whom the verse, "His father or his mother** he has cursed," **is extraneous,** and so it can be understood as teaching that someone who curses a parent even after his or her death is liable to the death penalty. [5]**But according to Rabbi Yoshiyah,** who says that those words are needed to teach us something else, **what is there to say?** [6]**For it was taught** in a Baraita: "The verse states (Leviticus 20:9): 'For everyone [*ish ish*] who curses his father or his mother shall surely be put to death; his father and his mother he has cursed; his blood shall be upon him.' It would have sufficed for the word *'ish* [man]' to have been written once. [7]**What did** the Torah mean to **teach by** writing it twice, ***'ish ish'***? [8]The word is doubled in order **to include a daughter, a person whose genitals are undeveloped** so that it is impossible to determine his or her sex, **and a hermaphrodite** who has both male and female reproductive organs. Even though these people do not fall under the category of *ish,* the doubling of that word includes them in the prohibition against cursing one's parents. The wording of the verse allows for the interpretation: [9]'For everyone **who curses his father *and*** [וְאֶת] **his mother.'** If only the first part of the verse had been stated, [10]**I would know only** that the son is liable if he curses both **his father *and* his mother.** Since there is no disjunctive expression in the verse, the phrase 'his father and his mother' is treated as a single unit, implying that there is no liability for cursing only one parent. [11]**From where** do I know that he is also punished if he curses **his father without his mother, or his mother without his father?** [12]**The** latter part of the **verse states: 'His father and his mother he has cursed.'** Since in the first half of the verse the word 'curses' appears next to the word 'father,' whereas in the second half of the

[1]כְּ׳בְעַמְּךָ׳ — לֹא חִיֵּיב בּוֹ לְאַחַר מִיתָה, [2]מְקַלֵּל שֶׁלֹּא עָשָׂה בּוֹ שֶׁלֹּא ׳בְעַמְּךָ׳ כְּ׳בְעַמְּךָ׳ — אֵינוֹ דִּין שֶׁלֹּא חִיֵּיב בּוֹ לְאַחַר מִיתָה. [3]תַּלְמוּד לוֹמַר: ׳אָבִיו וְאִמּוֹ קִלֵּל׳ — לְאַחַר מִיתָה״.

[4]הָנִיחָא לְרַבִּי יוֹנָתָן דְּמִיַּיתַּר לֵיהּ קְרָא, ״אָבִיו וְאִמּוֹ״, [5]אֶלָּא לְרַבִּי יֹאשִׁיָּה, מַאי אִיכָּא לְמֵימַר? [6]דְּתַנְיָא: ״׳אִישׁ אִישׁ׳, [7]מָה תַּלְמוּד לוֹמַר ׳אִישׁ אִישׁ׳? [8]לְרַבּוֹת בַּת, טוּמְטוּם, וְאַנְדְּרוֹגִינוֹס. [9]׳אֲשֶׁר יְקַלֵּל אֶת אָבִיו וְאֶת אִמּוֹ׳, [10]אֵין לִי אֶלָּא אָבִיו וְאִמּוֹ, [11]אָבִיו שֶׁלֹּא אִמּוֹ, אִמּוֹ שֶׁלֹּא אָבִיו מִנַּיִין? [12]תַּלְמוּד לוֹמַר: ׳אָבִיו וְאִמּוֹ

LITERAL TRANSLATION

like [someone who is] 'among your people' — [1]it did not make liable after death, [2]all the more so someone who curses — regarding whom it did not make [someone who is] 'not among your people' like [someone who is] 'among your people' — it did not make liable after death. [3]The Torah states: 'He cursed his father or his mother' — after death."

[4]This is acceptable according to Rabbi Yonatan, according to whom the verse, "His father or his mother," is extraneous. [5]But according to Rabbi Yoshiyah, what is there to say? [6]For it was taught: "'*Ish ish.*' [7]What is taught by *'Ish ish'*? [8]To include a daughter, a person whose genitals are hidden [or undeveloped], and a hermaphrodite. [9]'Who curses his father and his mother.' [10]I have only his father *and* his mother. [11]From where [do I know] his father without his mother, [or] his mother without his father? [12]The verse teaches: 'His father and his mother he has

RASHI

לא חייב בו לאחר מיתה — דהא חבורה כתיב. **לרבות בת** — טומטום ואנדרוגינוס. **אין לי אלא אביו ואמו** — שניהם יחד.

NOTES

body no longer suffers any pain, a son who strikes his dead parent is exempt. But a curse relates to a person's soul which lives on after his or her death, and so a son bears liability even if he cursed his or her parent after his death.

HALAKHAH

בַּת, טוּמְטוּם, וְאַנְדְּרוֹגִינוֹס A daughter, a person whose genitals are undeveloped, and a hermaphrodite. "Regarding the prohibitions against striking or cursing a parent, there is no difference between a son and a daughter. Even a person with hidden or undeveloped genitals, or a hermaphrodite who has both male and female reproductive organs, is included in the prohibition." (*Rambam, Sefer Shofetim, Hilkhot Mamrim* 5:1.)

קִלֵּל׳, ¹אָבִיו קִלֵּל, אִמּוֹ קִלֵּל. ²דִּבְרֵי רַבִּי יֹאשִׁיָּה. ³רַבִּי יוֹנָתָן אוֹמֵר: מַשְׁמַע שְׁנֵיהֶן כְּאֶחָד, וּמַשְׁמַע אֶחָד וְאֶחָד בִּפְנֵי עַצְמוֹ, ⁴עַד שֶׁיְּפָרֵט לְךָ הַכָּתוּב ׳יַחְדָּיו׳״. ⁵מְנָא לֵיהּ? ⁶נָפְקָא לֵיהּ מִ״וּמְקַלֵּל אָבִיו וְאִמּוֹ מוֹת יוּמָת״. ⁷וְאִידָךְ? ⁸הַהוּא מִיבָּעֵי לֵיהּ לְרַבּוֹת בַּת, טוּמְטוּם וְאַנְדְּרוֹגִינוֹס. ⁹וְתֵיפּוֹק לֵיהּ מֵ״אִישׁ אִישׁ״! ¹⁰דִּבְּרָה תּוֹרָה כִּלְשׁוֹן בְּנֵי אָדָם. ¹¹וְלִיתְנֵי: חוֹמֶר בַּמַּכֶּה מִבַּמְקַלֵּל, ¹²שֶׁהַמַּכֶּה עָשָׂה בּוֹ שֶׁ׳לֹּא בְּעַמְּךָ׳ כִּ׳בְעַמְּךָ׳,

LITERAL TRANSLATION

cursed,' [1][implying that] he has cursed his father, he has cursed his mother. [2][These are] the words of Rabbi Yoshiyah. [3]Rabbi Yonatan says: It means the two of them together, and it means [each] one separately, [4]unless the verse specifies to you 'together.'" [5]From where does he [know]? [6]He derives it from: "And he who curses his father, or his mother, shall surely be put to death." [7]And the other one? [8]That he needs to include a daughter, a person whose genitals are hidden [or undeveloped], and a hermaphrodite. [9]But derive it from: *"Ish ish"*! [10]The Torah spoke in the language of people. [11]But let it teach: This is a stringency regarding someone who smites more than someone who curses, [12]for regarding someone who smites it made [someone who is] 'not among your people' like [someone who is] 'among your people,'

TRANSLATION AND COMMENTARY

verse the word 'cursed' appears next to the word 'mother,' [1]**it may be inferred that** a person is liable whether **he cursed his father** or **cursed his mother.** [2]**This is the viewpoint of Rabbi Yoshiyah.** [3]But **Rabbi Yonatan** disagrees and **says:** The second half of the verse is not needed to teach us that someone is liable even if he cursed only one of his parents, because that ruling can be derived from the wording of the first half of the verse. A formulation such as his father and his mother **means the two of them together and it means each one separately,** [4]**unless the verse** in the Torah **specifically uses** the expression **'together.'** According to Rabbi Yonatan, a copulative *vav* may indicate conjunction, meaning 'and,' but it may also indicate disjunction, meaning 'or,' unless there is explicit proof from the rest of the verse that it must be understood in the conjunctive sense." According to Rabbi Yonatan, since the first half of the verse teaches us that someone is liable to be punished even if he cursed only one parent, the second half of the verse is there to teach us that someone is liable to be punished for cursing a deceased parent. But according to Rabbi Yoshiyah, the second half of the verse is needed to teach us that a person is liable to be punished if he cursed only one of his parents. [5]**From where,** then, **does he know** that a person is liable to be punished if he cursed a deceased parent?

נָפְקָא לֵיהּ [6]The Gemara explains: Rabbi Yoshiyah **derives this from** another verse dealing with the same matter (Exodus 21:17): **"And he who curses his father, or his mother, shall surely be put to death."** Since that verse is not needed to teach that someone who curses a parent is liable to the death penalty, for that law is already learned from the verse in Leviticus, it may teach that he is liable to that punishment for cursing a deceased parent.

וְאִידָךְ [7]The Gemara asks: What does **the other** Sage — Rabbi Yonatan — derive from the verse in Exodus? [8]The Gemara explains: According to Rabbi Yonatan, **that** verse **is needed to include** in the prohibition **a daughter, a person whose genitals are undeveloped, and a hermaphrodite.**

וְתֵיפּוֹק לֵיהּ [9]The Gemara comments: **But** let Rabbi Yonatan **derive** that law **from** the words ***"ish ish,"*** as that law was derived in the Baraita cited above!

דִּבְּרָה תּוֹרָה [10]The Gemara continues: According to Rabbi Yonatan, **the Torah spoke** here **in the language of men.** The doubling of the word *"ish"* is purely stylistic, with no special Halakhic significance. Therefore, the verse in Exodus was needed to teach us that a woman or a person whose gender is in doubt is also included in the prohibition.

וְלִיתְנֵי [11]The Gemara now makes a point concerning the Mishnah: The Mishnah **should** also **have taught** as follows: On **this** matter, **the law regarding someone who smites** his father or his mother **is more stringent than** the law **regarding someone who curses** them: [12]Regarding the prohibition against **smiting** a parent, the Torah **made someone who does not act in the manner of "your people"** and does not keep the Torah, **like someone who acts in the manner of "your people,"** and keeps the Torah, for the Torah forbids a person to

RASHI

אביו קילל ואמו קילל — בראש המקרא סמך קללה לאביו ובסוף סמך לאמו. **עד שיפרט לך הכתוב יחדיו** — וכמו שפרט בחורש בשור ובחמור מדפרט לך שמע מינה דאי לא הוי יחדו הוה משמע שור לבדו וחמור לבדו, והא אביו ואמו דרישא דרשינן נמי או אביו או אמו וסיפא לאתויי לאחר מיתה. **מ״ומקלל אביו״** — ד״ואלה המשפטים״. **ואידך** — דמפיק לאחר מיתה מ״אביו ואמו קילל״. **וליתני נמי וכו׳** — אמתניתין קאי דקתני: זה חומר במקלל מבמכה.

LITERAL TRANSLATION

[1] which is not so regarding someone who curses. [2] He maintains: We compare striking to cursing. [3] Is this to say that these Tannaim are like these Tannaim? [4] For it was taught in one [Baraita]: "[Regarding] a Cuthean you are commanded about striking him, but you are not commanded about cursing him." [5] And it was taught in another [Baraita]: "You are not commanded about cursing him, nor about striking him." [6] They thought: All (lit., "the whole world") agree [that] Cutheans are genuine converts. [7] Is it not that they disagree about this, [8] that the one Sage maintains: We compare striking to cursing, [9] and the other Sage maintains: We do not compare striking to cursing?

[1] מה שֶׁאֵין כֵּן בִּמְקַלֵּל! [2] קָסָבַר: מַקְשִׁינַן הַכָּאָה לִקְלָלָה. [3] לֵימָא הָנֵי תַּנָּאֵי כְּהָנֵי תַּנָּאֵי? [4] דְּתָנֵי חֲדָא: ״כּוּתִי אַתָּה מְצוּוֶּה עַל הַכָּאָתוֹ, וְאִי אַתָּה מְצוּוֶּה עַל קִלְלָתוֹ״. [5] וְתַנְיָא אִידָךְ: ״אִי אַתָּה מְצוּוֶּה לֹא עַל קִלְלָתוֹ, וְלֹא עַל הַכָּאָתוֹ״. [6] סַבְרוּהָ: דְּכוּלֵּי עָלְמָא כּוּתִים גֵּירֵי אֱמֶת הֵן. [7] מַאי לָאו בְּהָא קָמִיפַּלְגִי, [8] דְּמָר סָבַר: מַקְשִׁינַן הַכָּאָה לִקְלָלָה, [9] וּמָר סָבַר: לָא מַקְשִׁינַן הַכָּאָה לִקְלָלָה?

TRANSLATION AND COMMENTARY

strike his parent, even if he is a wicked sinner, [1] **but this is not so regarding** the prohibition against **cursing** a parent, for one is only forbidden to curse a parent who keeps the Torah.

קָסָבַר [2] The Gemara answers: The author of our Mishnah **maintains** that **we learn** the law regarding **striking** another person **by analogy from** the law regarding **cursing** him. Just as the prohibition against cursing another Jew applies only to a Jew who keeps the Torah, so, too, does the prohibition against striking another Jew apply only to a Jew who keeps the Torah. Similarly, the prohibitions against cursing and striking a parent apply only to a parent who keeps the Torah.

לֵימָא [3] The Gemara now suggests that the Tannaitic controversy in our passage, as to whether we learn the law about striking another Jew by analogy from the law regarding cursing him, parallels another Tannaitic controversy: **Is this to say that** the views of **these Tannaim** — the Tanna of our Mishnah and the Tanna of the Baraita cited above — **parallel** the views of **these Tannaim** — the Tannaim of the following two Baraitot? [4] **For in one Baraita it was taught: "A Cuthean** — a term used to describe the Samaritans, a non-Jewish people who settled in Samaria and the surrounding territory after the exile of the ten tribes, and who converted to Judaism, but were not scrupulous in the observance of the commandments — **you are forbidden to strike, but you are not forbidden to curse,** for the Cutheans do not keep the Torah properly, and are therefore not included among 'your people.'" [5] **And in another Baraita it was taught:** "A Cuthean **you are neither forbidden to curse, nor** are you forbidden **to strike.**" [6] The Gemara, which wished to equate the two Tannaitic controversies, initially **assumed** that **both** the Tanna who says that striking a Cuthean is forbidden and the Tanna who says that striking a Cuthean is not forbidden **agree that the Cutheans were genuine converts,** but since they later abandoned Jewish practices, they are no longer governed by those laws that apply only to Jews who observe the Torah. [7] **Is it not,** then, **that they disagree about** the following matter? [8] **One Sage** — the Tanna who says that just as one is not forbidden to curse a Cuthean, so, too, one is not forbidden to strike him — **maintains** that **we learn** the law about **striking** another person **by analogy from** the law about **cursing** him. Just as the prohibition against cursing another Jew applies only to a Jew who keeps the Torah, so, too, the prohibition against striking another Jew applies only to a Jew who keeps the Torah. [9] **And the other Sage** — the Tanna who says that even though one is not forbidden to curse a Cuthean, striking him is forbidden — **maintains** that **we do not learn** the law about **striking** another person **by analogy from** the law regarding **cursing** him. The prohibition against cursing another Jew applies only to a Jew who keeps the Torah, but no similar qualification applies to the prohibition against striking him. Thus, the Tannaitic controversy regarding whether or not one is forbidden to strike a Cuthean parallels the controversy between the Tanna of our Mishnah and the Tanna of the Baraita cited above about whether it is forbidden to strike a parent who does not observe the Torah.

RASHI

לימא הני תנאי – תנא דמתניתין דלא תנא חומר במכה שעשה בו שלא בעמך כבעמך ותנא דברייתא דלעיל דתנא ומה מכה שעשה בו. **גירי אמת הן** – מתחילתן גרים גמורים היו ועכשיו הרשיעו וישראל שאינו עושה מעשה עמך הוא וכי היכי דעל קללתו פטור על הכאתו נמי פטור.

NOTES

כּוּתִי אַתָּה מְצוּוֶּה עַל הַכָּאָתוֹ Regarding a Cuthean you are commanded about striking him. *Meiri* notes that while by Torah law a convert to Judaism is not liable to be punished for striking or cursing his father or mother, by Rabbinic decree he may not strike or curse or even insult them, lest people say that, with his conversion, he went from a level of higher sanctity to a level of lower sanctity and his obligations decreased.

¹לָא, דְּכוּלֵּי עָלְמָא לָא מַקְשִׁינַן הַכָּאָה לִקְלָלָה. ²וְהָכָא בְּהָא קָמִיפַּלְגִי: ³מָר סָבַר: כּוּתִים גֵּירֵי אֱמֶת הֵן, ⁴וּמָר סָבַר: כּוּתִים גֵּירֵי אֲרָיוֹת הֵן. ⁵אִי הָכִי, הַיְינוּ דְּקָתָנֵי עֲלָהּ: ⁶״וְשׁוֹרוֹ כְּיִשְׂרָאֵל״? ⁷אֶלָּא, שְׁמַע מִינָּהּ: בְּהֶיקֵּישָׁא פְּלִיגִי. ⁸שְׁמַע מִינָּהּ.

מִשְׁנָה ⁹הַגּוֹנֵב נֶפֶשׁ מִיִּשְׂרָאֵל אֵינוֹ חַיָּיב עַד שֶׁיַּכְנִיסֶנּוּ לִרְשׁוּתוֹ, ¹⁰רַבִּי יְהוּדָה

LITERAL TRANSLATION

[1]No, all agree [that] we do not compare striking to cursing. [2]And here they disagree about this: [3]One Sage maintains: Cutheans are genuine converts, [4]and the other Sage maintains: Cutheans are lion-converts. [5]If so, [how may we understand] that which was taught on it: [6]"And his ox is like [that of] a Jew"? [7]Rather, infer from this: They disagree about the comparison. [8]Infer from this.

MISHNAH [9]Someone who kidnaps a soul of Israel is not liable unless he brings him into his possession. [10]Rabbi Yehuda

RASHI

גירי אריות הן — והרי הם כנכרים גמורים. **אי הכי** — דטעמא דפטור משום דגירי אריות הן. **היינו דתנא עלה** — בתמיה, בהך מתניתין דקתני אינו מצווה לא על הכאתו ולא על קללתו קתני ושורו כישראל שור שלנו שנגח את שורו ושורו שנגח שלנו תם משלם חצי נזק ומועד משלם נזק שלם, ואילו דנכרים תנן שור של ישראל שנגח שור של נכרי פטור ושל נכרי שנגח שור של ישראל בין תם בין מועד משלם נזק שלם.

משנה שיכניסנו לרשותו — דכתיב (שמות כא) "ונמצא בידו" ותניא במכילתא: "ונמצא" — אין מציאה בכל מקום אלא בעדים, "בידו" — אין בידו אלא ברשותו וכן הוא אומר (במדבר כא) "ויקח את כל ארצו מידו".

TRANSLATION AND COMMENTARY

לָא [1]The Gemara rejects the equation of these two Tannaitic disputes: **No, both** the Tanna who says that striking a Cuthean is forbidden and the Tanna who says that it is not forbidden agree **that we do not learn** the law regarding **striking** another Jew **by analogy from** the law regarding **cursing** him. [2]**And here,** on the matter of Cutheans, the Tannaim **disagree about** the following issue: [3]**One Sage maintains** that the **Cutheans were genuine converts,** but since they later abandoned Jewish practices, they are no longer governed by those laws that apply only to Jews who observe the Torah. Thus, one is not forbidden to curse a Cuthean, for the prohibition against cursing applies only to Jews who observe the Torah, but one is forbidden to strike him, for no similar qualification was applied to the prohibition against striking another Jew. [4]**And the other Sage maintains** that the **Cutheans were "lion-converts"** (a reference to II Kings 17:25-26), people who converted under fear and duress, so their conversion to Judaism was not valid. Since a Cuthean is not a Jew, one is neither forbidden to curse him nor forbidden to strike him.

אִי הָכִי [5]The Gemara raises an objection against this interpretation of the Tannaitic dispute: **If it is so,** that the Tanna of the Baraita which taught that one is neither forbidden to curse nor forbidden to strike a Cuthean, maintains that the Cutheans were "lion-converts," so that they remained non-Jews, how, then, may we understand **that which was taught** later in that Baraita: [6]**"But his ox is** treated **like that of a Jew"**? This implies that if an ox belonging to a Jew gored an ox belonging to a Cuthean, or if an ox belonging to a Cuthean gored an ox belonging to a Jew — the first three times, its owner is required to pay only half-damages, and afterwards, he is required to pay for all the damage that his ox caused. If a Cuthean were a non-Jew, then the law should be different, for if an ox belonging to a Jew gored an ox belonging to a non-Jew, its owner is exempt, and if an ox belonging to a non-Jew gored an ox belonging to a Jew, its owner is liable for full damages even the first time that his animal caused damage!

אֶלָּא [7]The Gemara concludes: **Rather, infer from this** that the Tannaim **disagree about** whether we learn the law regarding striking another Jew by analogy from the law regarding cursing him, as was argued above. The Gemara confirms that this is the only possible way to understand the Tannaitic dispute: [8]Indeed, **infer from this** that the Tannaim disagree about that matter.

MISHNAH הַגּוֹנֵב [9]We learned in the first Mishnah in the chapter that someone who kidnaps another Jew is liable to death by strangulation. The following Mishnah comes to clarify some of the laws relating to that offense: **Someone who kidnaps** another **Jew is not liable** to the death penalty, **unless he brought** his victim **into his possession,** as the verse states (Exodus 21:16): "And he that steals a man, and sells him, if he be found *in his hand,* he shall surely be put to death," the words "in his hand" implying that there is no liability until the kidnapper brings his victim into his possession. [10]**Rabbi Yehudah says:** A kidnapper is

HALAKHAH

הַגּוֹנֵב נֶפֶשׁ מִיִּשְׂרָאֵל **Someone who kidnaps a member of Israel.** "If someone kidnaped another Jew, he is not liable to death by strangulation, unless he brought his victim into his possession, used him as one would use a slave, even if the benefit that he derived from him was worth less than a perutah, and then sold him to another person," following the Sages in the Mishnah. (*Rambam, Sefer Nezikin, Hilkhot Genevah* 9:2.)

TRANSLATION AND COMMENTARY

not liable to the death penalty, **unless he brought** his victim **into his possession, and used him** as one would use a slave, [1]**as the verse states** (Deuteronomy 24:7): "If a man is found stealing any of his brethren of the children of Israel **and deals with him as a slave, or sells him;** then that thief shall die."

הַגּוֹנֵב [2]If **someone kidnapped his** own **son,** the Tannaim disagree: **Rabbi Yishmael the son of Rabbi Yoḥanan ben Berokah says** that the father **is liable** to the death penalty, like any other kidnapper. [3]But **the Sages exempt him**.

גָּנַב [4]If **someone kidnapped a person who is half slave and half free man** (a non-Jewish slave who had been owned jointly by two or more Jewish masters, and who was set free by one of them), the Tannaim disagree: [5]**Rabbi Yehudah says** that the kidnapper **is liable,** like any other kidnapper. [6]But **the Sages exempt him.**

GEMARA וְתַנָּא קַמָּא [7]The Gemara asks: Can it be that **the** anonymous **first Tanna** of the Mishnah **does not require** the kidnapper to have subjected his victim to **slave-like service,** to make him liable to the death penalty? Surely the Torah states explicitly (Deuteronomy 24:7): "And deals with him as a slave"!

אָמַר [8]**Rabbi Aḥa the son of Rava said:** Indeed, even the anonymous first Tanna of the Mishnah agrees with Rabbi Yehudah that a kidnapper is not liable to the death penalty unless he used his victim as one would use a slave. [9]The practical difference **between** their two positions relates to **slave-like service** rendered by the victim to the kidnapper that is worth **less than the value of a perutah.** According to the anonymous first Tanna of the Mishnah, the kidnapper is liable to the death penalty, even if he had subjected his victim to service that is worth less than the value of a perutah, and according to Rabbi Yehudah, he is only liable for that punishment if he had made use of him to the value of a perutah, the smallest coin of legal significance.

בָּעֵי רַבִּי יִרְמְיָה [10]**Rabbi Yirmeyah asked** about the following two cases: **If someone kidnapped** another person **and sold him** for temporary use **while he was asleep, what is the law?** [11]Or **if someone** kidnapped **a** pregnant **woman,** and **sold** her for temporary use **with respect to the fetus** in her womb, **what is the**

אוֹמֵר: עַד שֶׁיַּכְנִיסֶנּוּ לִרְשׁוּתוֹ וְיִשְׁתַּמֵּשׁ בּוֹ, [1]שֶׁנֶּאֱמַר: "וְהִתְעַמֶּר בּוֹ וּמְכָרוֹ".

[2]הַגּוֹנֵב אֶת בְּנוֹ — רַבִּי יִשְׁמָעֵאל בְּנוֹ שֶׁל רַבִּי יוֹחָנָן בֶּן בְּרוֹקָה מְחַיֵּיב, [3]וַחֲכָמִים פּוֹטְרִין.

[4]גָּנַב מִי שֶׁחֶצְיוֹ עֶבֶד וְחֶצְיוֹ בֶּן חוֹרִין — [5]רַבִּי יְהוּדָה מְחַיֵּיב, [6]וַחֲכָמִים פּוֹטְרִין.

גמרא [7]וְתַנָּא קַמָּא לָא בָּעֵי עִימּוּר?

[8]אָמַר רַבִּי אַחָא בְּרֵיהּ דְּרָבָא: [9]עִימּוּר פָּחוֹת מִשָּׁוֶה פְּרוּטָה אִיכָּא בֵּינַיְיהוּ.

[10]בָּעֵי רַבִּי יִרְמְיָה: גְּנָבוֹ וּמְכָרוֹ יָשֵׁן, מַהוּ? [11]מָכַר אִשָּׁה

LITERAL TRANSLATION

says: Unless he brings him into his possession and uses him, [1]as it is stated: "And deals with him as a slave, or sells him."

[2]Someone who kidnaps his son — Rabbi Yishmael the son of Rabbi Yoḥanan ben Berokah says he is liable, [3]and the Sages exempt [him].

[4][If] someone kidnapped someone who is half slave and half free man — [5]Rabbi Yehudah says he is liable, [6]but the Sages exempt [him].

GEMARA [7]And the first Tanna does not require enslavement?

[8]Rabbi Aḥa the son of Rava said: [9]Enslavement of less than the value of a perutah is between them.

[10]Rabbi Yirmeyah asked: [If] he kidnapped him and sold him while he was asleep, what [is the law]? [11][If] he sold a woman

RASHI

גמרא עמור — שמוש. גנבו ומכרו כשהוא ישן מהו — לקמן מפרש לה הבעיא. מכר אשה לעוברה — גנב אשה מעוברת ומכרה לעוברה שלא מכר הגוף שלה אלא שיהא עובר מכור.

HALAKHAH

הַגּוֹנֵב אֶת בְּנוֹ **Someone who kidnaps his son.** "If someone kidnapped his own son or brother who was still a minor, he is not liable to the death penalty," following the Sages of the Mishnah against Rabbi Yehudah. (*Rambam, Sefer Nezikin, Hilkhot Genevah* 9:5.)

גָּנַב מִי שֶׁחֶצְיוֹ עֶבֶד וְחֶצְיוֹ בֶּן חוֹרִין **If someone kidnapped someone who is half slave and half free.** "If someone kidnapped a person who is half slave and half free, he is not liable to the death penalty," following the Sages of the Mishnah against Rabbi Yehudah. (*Rambam, Sefer Nezikin, Hilkhot Genevah* 9:6.)

גְּנָבוֹ וּמְכָרוֹ יָשֵׁן **If he kidnapped him and sold him while he was asleep.** "If someone kidnapped a person in his sleep, then used him while he was sleeping, and then sold him while he was still sleeping, he is exempt from the death penalty, for the matter was not resolved in the Gemara, and wherever the law regarding capital punishment is in doubt, we follow the more lenient position (*Maggid Mishneh*)." (*Rambam, Sefer Nezikin, Hilkhot Genevah* 9:3.)

מָכַר אִשָּׁה לְעוּבָּרָהּ **If he sold a woman for her fetus.** "If someone kidnapped a pregnant woman, and sold her with

TRANSLATION AND COMMENTARY

law? [1]**Is this** regarded as **having used** the kidnap victim as one would have used a slave, **or not?**

וְתֵיפּוֹק לֵיהּ [2]The Gemara comments: **Let** Rabbi Yirmeyah **learn** the answer to his questions from the fact that **there was no slave-like service** here **at all,** for in what possible way could the kidnapper have used the sleeping victim or the fetus as a slave?

לָא צְרִיכָא [3]The Gemara answers: **No,** Rabbi Yirmeyah's questions **were necessary** with respect to the following cases: [4]As for someone who kidnapped another person and sold him **while he was asleep,** a question arises **if** the kidnapper made use of his victim by **leaning on him.** [5]And as for someone who kidnapped a pregnant **woman,** and sold her together with her fetus, a question arises **if** the kidnapper **stood her up in the wind** so that it not blow on him, and the fetus gave him greater protection. In both cases, the kidnapper used his victim, but the question remains: [6]**Is this** regarded as **having used** the kidnap victim as one would have used a slave, **or not?**

תֵּיקוּ [7]The Gemara does not find an answer to Rabbi Yirmeyah's questions, and so it concludes: The questions raised in the previous passage **remain unresolved.**

תָּנוּ רַבָּנַן [8]**Our Rabbis taught** a related Baraita: "The verse regarding a kidnapper states (Deuteronomy 24:7): **'If a man is found stealing any of his brethren** of the children of Israel and deals with him as a slave, or sells him; then that thief shall die.' Had I only had this verse, **I would only know** that **a man who kidnapped** another person is liable to the death penalty. [9]**From where,** then, **do I know** that if the kidnapper was **a woman,** she, too, is liable? [10]That is learned from **the verse** that **states** (Exodus 21:16): **'And he who steals a man,** and sells him, if he is found in his hand, he shall surely be put to death.' Since the verse does not specify who it was who stole the man (in the Hebrew, the subject of the verb 'steals' is missing altogether) it implies that even a female kidnapper is liable. And had I only had the clauses: 'If a man be found stealing any [*nefesh*] of his brethren,' and: 'And he that steals a man,' [11]**I would only know** that **a man who kidnapped either a man or a woman, and a woman who kidnapped a man** are liable, for the verse dealing with a male kidnapper does not specify the gender of his victim (the word *nefesh,* rendered here as 'any,' is gender-neutral), but the verse dealing with a female kidnapper specifies that her victim is a male ('and he that steals a man'). [12]**From where,** then, **do I know** that if **a woman kidnapped** another **woman,** she, too, is liable? [13]That is learned from the continuation of **the verse** that **states: 'Then that thief shall die'** — [14]which implies that the death penalty is imposed **in any case,** whatever the gender of the kidnapper or his victim."

לְעוּבָּרָהּ, מַהוּ? [1]יֵשׁ דֶּרֶךְ עִימּוּר בְּכָךְ, אוֹ אֵין דֶּרֶךְ עִימּוּר בְּכָךְ? [2]וְתֵיפּוֹק לֵיהּ דְּלֵיכָּא עִימּוּר כְּלָל! [3]לָא צְרִיכָא. [4]יָשֵׁן — דִּזְגָא עֲלֵיהּ. [5]אִשָּׁה — דְּאוֹקְמָא בְּאַפֵּי זִיקָא. [6]דֶּרֶךְ עִימּוּר בְּכָךְ אוֹ אֵין דֶּרֶךְ עִימּוּר בְּכָךְ, מַאי? [7]תֵּיקוּ.

[8]תָּנוּ רַבָּנַן: ״׳כִּי יִמָּצֵא אִישׁ גֹּנֵב נֶפֶשׁ מֵאֶחָיו׳, [9]אֵין לִי אֶלָּא אִישׁ שֶׁגָּנַב, אִשָּׁה מִנַּיִין? [10]תַּלְמוּד לוֹמַר: ׳וְגֹנֵב אִישׁ׳. [11]אֵין לִי אֶלָּא אִישׁ שֶׁגָּנַב, בֵּין אִשָּׁה וּבֵין אִישׁ, וְאִשָּׁה שֶׁגָּנְבָה אִישׁ, [12]אִשָּׁה שֶׁגָּנְבָה אִשָּׁה מִנַּיִין? [13]תַּלְמוּד לוֹמַר: ׳וּמֵת הַגַּנָּב הַהוּא׳ — [14]מִכָּל מָקוֹם״.

LITERAL TRANSLATION

for her fetus, what [is the law]? [1]Is there a way of enslavement in it or is there not a way of enslavement in it?

[2]Let him learn it that there is no enslavement at all!

[3]No, it was necessary. [4][While] he was asleep — when he leaned on him. [5]A woman — when he stood her up in the wind. [6]Is there a way of enslavement in it or is there no way of enslavement in it?

[7]Let it stand.

[8]Our Rabbis taught: "'If a man is found stealing a soul of his brethren.' [9]I have only a man who stole. From where [do I know about] a woman? [10]The verse states: 'And he that steals a man.' [11]I have only a man who stole, either a man or a man, and a woman who stole a man. [12]From where [do I know about] a woman who stole a woman? [13]The verse states: 'Then that thief shall die' — [14]in any case."

RASHI

דליבא עימור – לא בישן ולא בעובר. **דזגא עליה** – דסמך עליו. **דאוקמי באפי זיקא** – וכל כמה שהוא עבה מועיל יותר להגין בפני הרוח. **אין לי אלא איש** – כשהגנב איש. **וגונב איש** – שהנגנב איש ולא אשה, וקרא קמא דלא קפיד הנגנב למהוי איש דכתיב ״נפש״ הלכך אין לי אלא איש שגנב בין איש בין אשה, דהיכא דגנב הוי איש, כתוב ״גונב נפש״ ואשה שגנבה איש דכתיב ״וגונב איש״ וגונב אפילו אשה גונבת משמע.

HALAKHAH

respect to the fetus in her womb, he is exempt from the death penalty, for the matter was not resolved in the Gemara, and wherever the law regarding capital punishment is in doubt, we follow the more lenient position." (*Rambam, Sefer Nezikin, Hilkhot Genevah* 9:4.)

דִּזְגָא עֲלֵיהּ **Where he leaned on him.** "If the kidnapper sat or leaned on his victim, he is liable, even though he derived benefit that was worth less than a perutah, and even if the

TRANSLATION AND COMMENTARY

תַּנְיָא אִידָךְ [1]It was also **taught in another Baraita:** "The verse regarding a kidnapper states (Deuteronomy 24:7): **'If a man is found stealing any** [*nefesh*] **of his brethren** of the children of Israel and deals with him as a slave, or sells him; then that thief shall die.' [2]The comprehensive term, *nefesh* (translated here as 'any') implies that the kidnapper **is liable** to be punished **whether he kidnapped a man, or a woman, or a convert, or an emancipated slave, or a minor.** [3]**If someone kidnapped** another Jew, **but did not sell him, or if someone sold** another Jew, **but** the sold person **was still in his** own **possession,** meaning that he was never actually 'stolen,' the kidnapper **is exempt** from liability. [4]**If someone** kidnapped another person, and **sold** the victim **to** the victim's own **father or to his brother, or to one of his** other **relatives,** the kidnapper **is liable.** [5]If **someone kidnapped a slave,** he is **exempt** from punishment." [86A] [6]**A Tanna taught** this Baraita — which states that if someone kidnapped another person, and sold the victim to the victim's own father or to his brother, or to one of his other relatives, the kidnapper is liable — **before Rav Sheshet.** [7]Rav Sheshet **said to him: I teach** a different Baraita, which states: [8]**"Rabbi Shimon says:** The verse that states (Deuteronomy 24:7): 'If a man is found stealing any **of his brethren'** implies that a kidnapper is not liable **unless he removed** his victim **from the possession of his brothers."** [9]How, then, can **you say** that if someone kidnapped another person, and sold the victim to the victim's own father or brother, he **is liable?** Surely, in such a case the victim was not "removed from the possession of his brothers"! [10]Rather, you must emend your Baraita and **teach:** "If someone kidnapped another person, and sold the victim to the victim's own father or to his brother, or to one of his other relatives, the kidnapper **is exempt."**

מַאי קוּשְׁיָא [11]The Gemara asks: **What was** Rav Pappa's **difficulty?** [12]**Perhaps this** Baraita, which states that a kidnapper is not liable unless he removed his victim from the possession of his brothers, follows the position of **Rabbi Shimon,** [13]and **that** Baraita, which states that a kidnapper is liable even if he sold his victim to the victim's own father or brother, follows the position of **the Sages** who disagree with Rabbi Shimon!

[1]תַּנְיָא אִידָךְ: ״׳כִּי יִמָּצֵא אִישׁ גֹּנֵב נֶפֶשׁ מֵאֶחָיו׳ — [2]אֶחָד הַגּוֹנֵב אֶת הָאִישׁ, וְאֶחָד הַגּוֹנֵב אֶת הָאִשָּׁה, וְאֶחָד גֵּר וְאֶחָד עֶבֶד מְשׁוּחְרָר וְקָטָן — חַיָּיב. [3]גְּנָבוֹ וְלֹא מְכָרוֹ, מְכָרוֹ וַעֲדַיִין יֶשְׁנוֹ בִּרְשׁוּתוֹ פָּטוּר. [4]מְכָרוֹ לְאָבִיו אוֹ לְאָחִיו, אוֹ לְאֶחָד מִן הַקְּרוֹבִים, חַיָּיב. [5]הַגּוֹנֵב אֶת הָעֲבָדִים פָּטוּר״. [86A] [6]תָּנֵי תַּנָּא קַמֵּיהּ דְּרַב שֵׁשֶׁת. [7]אֲמַר לֵיהּ: אֲנִי שׁוֹנֶה: [8]״רַבִּי שִׁמְעוֹן אוֹמֵר: ׳מֵאֶחָיו׳ — עַד שֶׁיּוֹצִיאֶנּוּ מֵרְשׁוּת אֶחָיו״. [9]וְאַתְּ אָמְרַתְּ חַיָּיב? [10]תְּנֵי: פָּטוּר.
[11]מַאי קוּשְׁיָא? [12]דִּילְמָא, הָא רַבִּי שִׁמְעוֹן, [13]הָא רַבָּנַן!

LITERAL TRANSLATION

[1]It was taught in another [Baraita]: "'If a man is found stealing a soul of his brethren.' [2]Whether he stole a man, or he stole a woman, or a convert, or an emancipated slave or a minor — he is liable. [3][If] he kidnapped him, but did not sell him, [or] if he sold him, but he is still in his possession, he is exempt. [4][If] he sold him to his father or to his brother, or to one of his relatives, he is liable. [5]Someone who steals slaves is exempt." [86A] [6]A Tanna taught before Rav Sheshet. [7]He said to him: I teach: [8]"Rabbi Shimon says: Of his brethren — until he removes him from the possession of his brethren." [9]And you say he is liable? [10]Teach: He is exempt. [11]What is the difficulty? [12]Perhaps, this is Rabbi Shimon, [13]this is the Sages!

RASHI

הגונב — מכל מקום, והכלו דרשינן לה בספרי למעוטי גונב עבד. **ועדיין ישנו ברשותו** — ברשות הנגנב עצמו, שעדיין לא הכניסו גנב ברשותו. **פטור** — שהרי לא גנבו. **לאביו** — אביו של נגנב. **תני תנא** — להך מתניתין דקתני: מכר לאביו חייב.

HALAKHAH

victim was sleeping," following the Gemara. (*Rambam, Sefer Nezikin, Hilkhot Genevah* 9:2.)

אֶחָד הַגּוֹנֵב אֶת הָאִישׁ, וְאֶחָד הַגּוֹנֵב אֶת הָאִשָּׁה **Whether he stole a man, or he stole a woman.** "A kidnapper is liable, whether his victim was an adult or a minor, a man or a woman, a Jew from birth or a convert, or an emancipated slave." (*Rambam, Sefer Nezikin, Hilkhot Genevah* 9:6.)

גְּנָבוֹ וְלֹא מְכָרוֹ **If he kidnapped him, but did not sell him.** "If someone kidnapped another person, used him, and sold him, but never brought him into his own possession, or if he kidnapped him, brought him into his own possession, and used him, but never sold him, or if he sold him before he used him, or if he used him, and sold him to one of the victim's own relatives, he is exempt from liability" (following *Rambam*'s reading of the Gemara; *Maggid Mishneh*). (*Rambam, Sefer Nezikin, Hilkhot Genevah* 9:3.)

הַגּוֹנֵב אֶת הָעֲבָדִים **Someone who steals slaves.** "If someone kidnapped a slave (even if he is half free), he is exempt," following the Baraita, and as is implied by the Mishnah. (*Rambam, Sefer Nezikin, Hilkhot Genevah* 9:1.)

TERMINOLOGY

סְתָם מַתְנִיתִין רַבִּי מֵאִיר An anonymous Mishnah is Rabbi Meir. The final redaction of the Tannaitic works mentioned in our passage was not done by the Sages mentioned here, but rather by other Sages. The Mishnah was put in its final form by Rabbi Yehudah HaNasi, the *Tosefta* was edited by Rabbi Ḥiyya and Rabbi Oshaya, and *Sifra* and *Sifrei* were redacted by one of the Sages of the School of Rav, or some even later authority. Different versions of each of these collections of Tannaitic teachings existed, from which the editors chose one. For example, Rabbi Yehudah HaNasi formulated the Mishnah based on the earlier version of Rabbi Meir, and not on the slightly different versions of Rabbi Yehudah or Rabbi Shimon. The same thing applies to the other Tannaitic works mentioned in our passage.

TRANSLATION AND COMMENTARY

לָא סָלְקָא [1] The Gemara rejects this argument: **You cannot** possibly **say this, for** the Baraita cited by the Tanna was taken from the Halakhic Midrash to the Books of Numbers and Deuteronomy known as *Sifrei*, [2] and **Rabbi Yoḥanan said: An anonymous Mishnah** follows the view of **Rabbi Meir.** [3] **An anonymous *Tosefta*** follows the view of **Rabbi Neḥemyah.** [4] **An anonymous passage in** the Halakhic Midrash to the Book of Leviticus known as ***Sifra*** follows the view of **Rabbi Yehudah.** [5] **An anonymous passage in** the Halakhic Midrash to the Books of Numbers and Deuteronomy known as ***Sifrei*** follows the view of **Rabbi Shimon.** [6] **And all of them are in accordance with** the views of **Rabbi Akiva,** for Rabbi Meir, Rabbi Neḥemyah, Rabbi Yehudah, and Rabbi Shimon were all disciples of Rabbi Akiva. Thus, an anonymous passage found in *Sifrei* cannot be in disagreement with the view of Rabbi Shimon.

הַגּוֹנֵב בְּנוֹ [7] We learned in our Mishnah: "If **someone kidnapped his** own **son,** the Tannaim disagree: Rabbi Yishmael the son of Rabbi Yoḥanan ben Berokah says that the father is liable to the death penalty, like any other kidnapper. But the Sages exempt him." [8] For **what reason** do **the Sages** exempt a person who kidnapped his own son? [9] **Abaye said: The verse states** (Deuteronomy 24:7): **"If a man is found** stealing any of his brethren of the children of Israel"— [10] thus **excluding** someone who steals **another person who is** already **found** in his hands. Thus, a father is exempt if he kidnaps his own son, for a son is regarded as being "found" in his father's hands.

אֲמַר לֵיהּ [11] **Rav Pappa said to Abaye: But now,** if we follow this method of interpretation, then regarding the verse (Deuteronomy 22:22): **"If a man is found lying with a woman married to a husband,** they shall both of them die," [12] we should also say that the words **"if a man is found"** [13] **exclude someone who had** already previously **been** often **found** together with married women. [14] This implies that, with **the house of So-and-so** (a distinguished family which the Gemara did not want to shame by mentioning it by name), **where** married women **were** often **found** in the company of men who were not their husbands, [15] those men and women who committed adultery **should** also **be exempt** from the death penalty.

[1] לָא סָלְקָא דַּעְתָּךְ, [2] דְּאָמַר רַבִּי יוֹחָנָן: סְתָם מַתְנִיתִין רַבִּי מֵאִיר. [3] סְתָם תּוֹסֶפְתָּא רַבִּי נְחֶמְיָה. [4] סְתָם סִפְרָא רַבִּי יְהוּדָה. [5] סְתָם סִפְרֵי רַבִּי שִׁמְעוֹן. [6] וְכוּלְּהוּ אַלִּיבָּא דְּרַבִּי עֲקִיבָא.

[7] "הַגּוֹנֵב בְּנוֹ". [8] מַאי טַעְמָא דְּרַבָּנַן? [9] אֲמַר אַבַּיֵי: דְּאָמַר קְרָא: "כִּי יִמָּצֵא" — [10] פְּרָט לְמָצוּי.

[11] אֲמַר לֵיהּ רַב פַּפָּא לְאַבַּיֵי: אֶלָּא מֵעַתָּה, "כִּי יִמָּצֵא אִישׁ שֹׁכֵב עִם אִשָּׁה בְּעֻלַת בַּעַל", [12] הָכִי נַמִי, "כִּי יִמָּצֵא" — [13] פְּרָט לְמָצוּי! [14] כְּגוֹן שֶׁל בֵּית פְּלוֹנִי דִּשְׁכִיחָן גַּבַּיְיהוּ, [15] הָכִי נַמִי דְּפְטִירִי?

LITERAL TRANSLATION

[1] This cannot enter your mind, [2] for Rabbi Yoḥanan said: An anonymous Mishnah is Rabbi Meir. [3] An anonymous *Tosefta* is Rabbi Neḥemyah. [4] An anonymous [passage] in *Sifra* is Rabbi Yehudah. [5] An anonymous [passage in] *Sifrei* is Rabbi Shimon. [6] And all of them are in accordance with Rabbi Akiva.

[7] "Someone who kidnaps his son." [8] What is the reason of the Sages? [9] Abaye said: For the verse states: "If [a man] be found" — [10] to the exclusion of someone who is found.

[11] Rav Pappa said to Abaye: But now, "If a man be found lying with a woman married to a husband," [12] so, too, "If [a man] be found" — [13] to the exclusion of someone who is found! [14] Like the house of So-and-so where they are found by them, [15] so, too, they are exempt?

RASHI

סתם ספרא — תורת כהנים. **סתם ספרי** — ספר וידבר ומשנה תורה, והאי סתמא ד"כי ימצא איש" במשנה תורה הוא. **אליבא דרבי עקיבא** — ממה שלמדו מרבי עקיבא אמרום. **של בית פלוני** — לא רצה להזכיר שמם שחשובין היו, ובזה לא היו נוהגין כדת שהיו הרבה דרין בבית אחד אנשים ונשים, והיו מצויין תמיד עם נשי חביריהן, ולא שמתייחדין.

NOTES

כִּי יִמָּצֵא — פְּרָט לְמָצוּי "If a man is found" — to the exclusion of someone who is found. *Ran* explains that, even according to the Gemara's conclusion, the formulation, "if a man is found [כִּי יִמָּצֵא]," does indeed exclude "someone who is found." But as applied in the case of kidnapping, the formulation, "if a man is found," would exclude a kidnapper who was already "found" before the kidnapping. Such an exclusion would have no practical significance, for here we are interested in excluding a victim who was already found in his kidnapper's hands before the kidnapping, as when someone kidnaps his own son or student. This can only be derived from the verse, "if he is found in his hand," which teaches that a kidnapper is only liable if his victim is *now* "found" in his hands, but not if his victim had previously been in his hands.

שֶׁל בֵּית פְּלוֹנִי Like the house of So-and-so. We find in several places that, when the Gemara speaks of some blemish in a certain family, it does not mention that family by name, whether out of respect for that family (see *Rashi*), or out of fear of that family. *Rambam* explains that in such cases the family's name is not mentioned in order to teach us the severity of the prohibition against speaking ill of other people.

TRANSLATION AND COMMENTARY

אֲמַר לֵיהּ [1]Abaye **said to** Rav Pappa: When I adduced Biblical support for the position of the Rabbis, [2]**I** meant to **say** that they derive their view **from** the verse, (Exodus 21:16): "And he who steals a man, and sells him, **if he is found in his hand,** he shall surely be put to death." The extraneous words, "if he is found in his hand," teach that the kidnapper is only liable if his victim is now found in his hands, to the exclusion of someone who steals someone who was previously in his hands, as in the case of a father who kidnaps his son.

אֲמַר רָבָא [3]**Rava said:** Since a father is exempt from the death penalty if he kidnaps his own son, because his son was in his father's hands prior to the kidnapping, it **therefore** follows that a similar exemption applies to **those who teach the Bible to** young **children and those who teach the Mishnah to** more advanced **Rabbinic students.** [4]These students **are considered as if they have been in their** master's **hands, and** so those teachers **are exempt** from the death penalty if they kidnap one of their disciples.

גָּנַב [5]Our Mishnah continues: "If **someone kidnapped a person who is half slave** and half free [a non-Jewish slave who was owned jointly by two or more Jewish masters, and who was set free by one of them], the Tannaim disagree: Rabbi Yehudah says that the kidnapper is liable, like any other kidnapper. But the Sages exempt him." Before analyzing the dispute in our Mishnah, [6]the Gemara first cites another dispute between Rabbi Yehudah and the Sages which **we learned elsewhere** in the Mishnah (*Bava Kama* 87a): "If someone caused an injury to another person's non-Jewish slave, he is liable to be penalized for all five categories of damages for which a person who injures someone must reimburse him: Injury, pain, medical costs, loss of livelihood, and humiliation. [7]**Rabbi Yehudah** disagrees and **says:** Non-Jewish **slaves are not entitled to compensation for humiliation."** [8]The Gemara asks: **What is the reasoning of Rabbi Yehudah?** [9]The Gemara explains: **The verse** from which we learn the obligation to compensate for humiliation **states** (Deuteronomy 25:11): **"When men strive together one with his brother,** and the wife of the one draws near to deliver her husband out of the hand of he who smites him." The words, "one with his brother" imply that the obligation to compensate for humiliation only applies to **someone who has consanguinity** — family ties recognized by the Halakhah. [10]This **excludes a** non-Jewish **slave, who has no consanguinity,** for there is no legal relationship between a non-Jewish slave and even his closest family. [11]**And** how do **the Rabbis** who disagree with Rabbi Yehudah counter this argument? According to the Rabbis, even a non-Jewish slave is entitled to compensation for humiliation, for he, too, is included under the heading of "his brother." [12]A non-Jewish slave **is** regarded as a Jew's **brother in commandments,** for he is obligated to fulfill all the commandments that are not bound by time.

[1]אֲמַר לֵיהּ: [2]אֲנָא מִ״וְּנִמְצָא בְיָדוֹ״ קָאָמִינָא.

[3]אֲמַר רָבָא: הִלְכָּךְ, הָנֵי מִיקְרֵי דַרְדְּקֵי וּמַתְנוּ רַבָּנַן — [4]כִּמְצוּיִּין בִּיָדָן דָּמוּ, וּפְטִירִי.

[5]״גָּנַב מִי שֶׁחֶצְיוֹ וכו׳״. [6]תְּנַן הָתָם: [7]״רַבִּי יְהוּדָה אוֹמֵר: אֵין לַעֲבָדִים בּוֹשֶׁת״. [8]מַאי טַעְמָא דְּרַבִּי יְהוּדָה? [9]אָמַר קְרָא: ״כִּי יִנָּצוּ אֲנָשִׁים יַחְדָו אִישׁ וְאָחִיו״ — מִי שֶׁיֵּשׁ לוֹ אַחֲוָה, [10]יָצָא עֶבֶד שֶׁאֵין לוֹ אַחֲוָה. [11]וְרַבָּנַן? [12]אָחִיו הוּא בַּמִּצְוֹת.

LITERAL TRANSLATION

[1]He said to him: [2]I said from [the verse:] "If he is found in his hand."

[3]Rava said: Therefore, [regarding] those who teach the Bible to children and the Mishnah to the Rabbis — [4]they are considered as if they were found in their hands, and they are exempt.

[5]"[If] someone kidnapped someone who is half [slave], etc." [6]We have learned elsewhere: [7]"Rabbi Yehudah says: Slaves are not entitled to [compensation for] humiliation." [8]What is the reason of Rabbi Yehudah? [9]The verse states: "When men strive together one with his brother" — someone who has consanguinity, [10]to the exclusion of a slave who has no consanguinity. [11]And the Rabbis? [12]He is his brother in the commandments.

RASHI

ונמצא — קרא יתירא הוא, דאי ללמד שימצא בעדים — מ״כי ימצא״ נפקא. **כמצויין בידו דמו** — התלמידים מצויין תמיד בבית הרב, ואם גנב הרב אחד מתלמידיו ומכרו — אינו נהרג. **אין לעבדים בושת** — המבייש את העבד לא חייבתו תורה לתת דמי בשתו. **וכי ינצו אנשים יחדיו והכה איש וגו׳** — מהתם נפקא לן חיוב בשת, דכתיב ״וקצותה את כפה״ — ממון, אתה אומר ממון, או אינו אלא ממש נאמר כאן לא תחוס עינך ונאמר להלן בעדים זוממין (דברים יט) ״לא תחוס עינך״, מה להלן ממון — אף כאן ממון. **עבד שאין לו אחוה** — ואפילו עם אחיו בני אביו דכתיב (בראשית כב) ״עם החמור״ עם הדומה לחמור, אינו אלא כבהמה. **אחיו הוא במצות** — בכל מצות שהאשה חייבת בהן עבד חייב בהן, דגמר ״לה״ ״לה״ מאשה.

HALAKHAH

מִיקְרֵי דַרְדְּקֵי **Those who teach the Bible to children.** "If a teacher kidnapped one of the children whom he was teaching, even if he used him and sold him to another person, he is exempt from the death penalty." (*Rambam, Sefer Nezikin, Hilkhot Genevah* 9:5.)

בּוֹשֶׁת עֲבָדִים **The humiliation of slaves.** "If someone caused an injury to another person's non-Jewish slave, he is liable (to the slave's master) for all five categories of damages,

TRANSLATION AND COMMENTARY

וְהָכָא [1]The Gemara now asks: **And here,** regarding kidnapping, **how does Rabbi Yehudah interpret the verse,** "If a man is found stealing any of his brethren of the Children of Israel"? [2]The Gemara explains: Rabbi Yehudah **maintains** that the words, **"of his brethren" exclude** non-Jewish **slaves,** for, according to Rabbi Yehudah, non-Jewish slaves are not included under the heading of "brothers," as non-Jewish slaves have no consanguinity. [3]The words, **"the Children of Israel," exclude someone who is half slave and half free.** [4]However, the letter *mem* ("of") in the expression, **"of the Children of Israel** [מִבְּנֵי יִשְׂרָאֵל]," restricts this regulation even further, for it implies that the law applies only to some of the Children of Israel. It, too, **excludes someone who is half slave and half free.** [5]**This is,** therefore, a case of **one restrictive expression following another restrictive expression,** [6]**and** the rule is that when **one restrictive expression follows another restrictive expression,** it **amplifies.** That is to say, when one restrictive expression appears after another, the two expressions together are treated as an amplificatory expression. Thus, argues Rabbi Yehudah, someone who kidnaps a person who is half slave and half free is liable, like any other kidnapper.

וְרַבָּנַן [7]The Gemara asks: **And** how do **the Rabbis** who disagree with Rabbi Yehudah interpret this verse? [8]The Gemara explains: The interpretation, according to which the words, **"of his brethren," exclude** non-Jewish **slaves, does not seem reasonable to** the Rabbis, [9]**for** a non-Jewish slave is obligated to fulfill all the commandments that are not bound by time. Hence he **is** regarded as a Jew's **brother in the commandments,** and we must look elsewhere for a source that teaches us that there is no liability for the kidnapping of a non-Jewish slave. [10]In the Rabbis' view, the two restrictive expressions, **"the Children of Israel,"** and the letter *mem* in the expression, **"of the Children of Israel,"** are not an instance of one restrictive expression following another restrictive expression. [11]**One excludes** non-Jewish **slaves, and the** other **one excludes someone who is half slave and half free.** Hence, argue the Rabbis, someone who kidnaps a person who is half slave and half free is indeed exempt from the death penalty.

אַזְהָרָה [12]The Gemara asks: **Where** does the Torah issue **a warning** that **one** is forbidden to **kidnap another person?** Punishment cannot be imposed for a crime unless the Torah issued an explicit warning that the act is forbidden. [13]**Rabbi Yoshiyah says:** The prohibition against kidnapping is learned **from** that which is stated in the Ten Commandments (Exodus 20:13): **"You shall not steal."** [14]**Rabbi Yoḥanan says:** The prohibition is derived **from** the verse regarding a Jewish slave (Leviticus 25:42), which states: **"They shall not be sold as slaves."**

[1]וְהָכָא הֵיכִי דָּרֵישׁ רַבִּי יְהוּדָה? [2]סָבַר: "מֵאֶחָיו" — לְאַפּוּקֵי עֲבָדִים. [3]"בְּנֵי יִשְׂרָאֵל" — לְמַעוּטֵי מִי שֶׁחֶצְיוֹ עֶבֶד וְחֶצְיוֹ בֶּן חוֹרִין. [4]"מִבְּנֵי יִשְׂרָאֵל" — לְמַעוּטֵי מִי שֶׁחֶצְיוֹ עֶבֶד וְחֶצְיוֹ בֶּן חוֹרִין. [5]הֲוֵי מִיעוּט אַחַר מִיעוּט, [6]וְאֵין מִיעוּט אַחַר מִיעוּט אֶלָּא לְרַבּוֹת.

[7]וְרַבָּנַן? [8]"מֵאֶחָיו" לְאַפּוּקֵי עֲבָדִים, לָא מַשְׁמַע לְהוּ, [9]דְּהָא אָחִיו הוּא בַּמִּצְוֹת. [10]"בְּנֵי יִשְׂרָאֵל", "מִבְּנֵי יִשְׂרָאֵל" — [11]חַד לְמַעוּטֵי עֶבֶד, וְחַד לְמַעוּטֵי מִי שֶׁחֶצְיוֹ עֶבֶד וְחֶצְיוֹ בֶּן חוֹרִין.

[12]אַזְהָרָה לְגוֹנֵב נֶפֶשׁ מִנַּיִן? [13]רַבִּי יֹאשִׁיָּה אָמַר: מִ"לֹּא תִּגְנֹב". [14]רַבִּי יוֹחָנָן אָמַר: מִ"לֹּא יִמָּכְרוּ מִמְכֶּרֶת עָבֶד".

LITERAL TRANSLATION

[1]And here, how does Rabbi Yehudah interpret [the verse]? [2]He maintains: "Of his brethren" — to the exclusion of slaves. [3]"The Children of Israel" — to the exclusion of someone who is half slave and half free. [4]"Of the Children of Israel" — to the exclusion of someone who is half slave and half free. [5]This is one restrictive expression after another restrictive expression, [6]and there is no restrictive expression after another restrictive expression except to amplify.

[7]And the Rabbis? [8]"Of his brethren" — to the exclusion of slaves, does not seem reasonable to them, [9]for he is your brother in the commandments. [10]"The Children of Israel," "Of the Children of Israel" — [11]one to the exclusion of a slave, and one to the exclusion of someone who is half slave and half free.

[12]From where [do I know] a warning for someone who kidnaps? [13]Rabbi Yoshiyah says: From: "You shall not steal." [14]Rabbi Yoḥanan says: From: "They shall not be sold as slaves."

RASHI

והכא — במתניתין בגונב נפש דכתיב "מאחיו". היכי דריש — רבי יהודה לחייב על מי שחציו עבד. מאחיו למעוטי עבדים — דהא לרבי יהודה אין לו אחוה, מ"בני" יתירא דריש ליה, דהוה ליה למכתב "מאחיו בני ישראל". מלא תגנוב — האמור בעשרת הדברות, דבגונב נפשות מתוקם לקמן בשמעתין.

BACKGROUND

אֵין מִיעוּט אַחַר מִיעוּט אֶלָּא לְרַבּוֹת **One restrictive expression after another restrictive expression amplifies.** Some explain that this rule is based on the principle of logic, according to which a double negative implies a positive. Alternatively, the rule is based on the number of extraneous words in the verse. Since the second restrictive expression is not needed to limit the law taught in the verse, for the law was already limited by the first restrictive expression, that extraneous word must be treated as an amplificatory expression.

HALAKHAH

including humiliation," against the opinion of Rabbi Yehudah. (*Rambam, Sefer Nezikin, Hilkhot Ḥovel U'Mazik* 4:10.)

[1]וְלָא פְּלִיגִי. [2]מָר קָא חָשֵׁיב לָאו דִּגְנֵיבָה, [3]וּמָר קָא חָשֵׁיב לָאו דִּמְכִירָה.

[4]תָּנוּ רַבָּנַן: "'לֹא תִּגְנֹב' [5]בְּגוֹנֵב נְפָשׁוֹת הַכָּתוּב מְדַבֵּר. [6]אַתָּה אוֹמֵר בְּגוֹנֵב נְפָשׁוֹת. [7]אוֹ אֵינוֹ אֶלָּא בְּגוֹנֵב מָמוֹן? [8]אָמַרְתָּ: צֵא וּלְמַד מִשְּׁלֹשׁ עֶשְׂרֵה מִדּוֹת שֶׁהַתּוֹרָה נִדְרֶשֶׁת בָּהֶן. [9]דָּבָר הַלָּמֵד מֵעִנְיָינוֹ. [10]בַּמֶּה הַכָּתוּב מְדַבֵּר — בִּנְפָשׁוֹת. [11]אַף כָּאן, בִּנְפָשׁוֹת".

[12]תַּנְיָא אִידָךְ: "'לֹא תִּגְנֹבוּ' — [13]בְּגוֹנֵב מָמוֹן הַכָּתוּב מְדַבֵּר. [14]אַתָּה אוֹמֵר בְּגוֹנֵב מָמוֹן. [15]אוֹ אֵינוֹ אֶלָּא בְּגוֹנֵב נְפָשׁוֹת? [16]אָמַרְתָּ: צֵא וּלְמַד מִשְּׁלֹשׁ עֶשְׂרֵה מִדּוֹת שֶׁהַתּוֹרָה נִדְרֶשֶׁת בָּהֶן. [17]דָּבָר הַלָּמֵד מֵעִנְיָנוֹ. [18]בַּמֶּה הַכָּתוּב מְדַבֵּר — בְּמָמוֹן. [19]אַף כָּאן, בְּמָמוֹן".

[20]אִיתְּמַר: עֵידֵי גְנֵיבָה וְעֵידֵי מְכִירָה בְּנֶפֶשׁ שֶׁהוּזְמוּ —

LITERAL TRANSLATION

[1]And they do not disagree. [2]The one counts the prohibition of stealing, [3]and the one counts the prohibition of selling.

[4]Our Rabbis taught: "'You shall not steal' — [5]Scripture speaks about someone who kidnaps. [6]You say about someone who kidnaps. [7]But might it not be about someone who steals money? [8]You say: Go out and learn from the thirteen principles by which the Torah is interpreted. [9]Something learned from its context. [10]What is Scripture speaking about? Capital offenses. [11]Here, too, a capital offense."

[12]It was taught in another [Baraita]: "'You shall not steal' — [13]Scripture speaks about someone who steals money. [14]You say about someone who steals money. [15]But might it not be about someone who kidnaps? [16]You say: Go out and learn from the thirteen principles by which the Torah is interpreted. [17]Something learned from its context. [18]What is Scripture speaking about? Money. [19]Here, too, money."

[20]It was stated: Witnesses to the stealing and witnesses to the sale in [a case of] kidnapping who were refuted —

TRANSLATION AND COMMENTARY

וְלָא פְּלִיגִי [1]The Gemara explains that the two Amoraim **do not** actually **disagree,** but rather they complement one another. [2]**One** Amora — Rabbi Yoshiyah — **counts the prohibition against** the initial **stealing** of another person, [3]**and the other** Amora — Rabbi Yoḥanan — **counts the prohibition against selling** the kidnap victim into slavery.

תָּנוּ רַבָּנַן [4]**Our Rabbis taught** the following Baraita: "The verse in the Ten Commandments states (Exodus 20:13): **'You shall not steal.'** [5]**Scripture speaks** here **about someone who kidnaps** another person. [6]**You say** that the verse refers here to **someone who kidnaps** another person. [7]**But might it not be** that the verse refers to **someone who steals money?** [8]**Go and learn** the meaning of these words, 'you shall not steal,' by one of **the thirteen** hermeneutic **principles through which the Torah is interpreted:** [9]An unclear verse may be **interpreted in light of the context** in which it appears. [10]**What** other offenses **does Scripture refer to** here in the Ten Commandments? **Capital offenses** such as murder and adultery. [11]**Here, too,** then, the verse must be referring to **a capital offense** — kidnapping, and not stealing money."

תַּנְיָא אִידָךְ [12]**It was** also **taught in another Baraita:** "The verse states (Leviticus 19:11): **'You shall not steal,** neither deal falsely, neither lie to one another.' [13]**Scripture speaks** here **about someone who steals money.** [14]**You say** that the verse refers here to **someone who steals money.** [15]**But might it not be** that the verse refers to **someone who kidnaps** another person? [16]**Go out and learn** the meaning of these words, 'you shall not steal,' by one of **the thirteen principles through which the Torah is interpreted:** [17]An unclear verse may be **interpreted in light of the context** in which it appears. [18]**What** other offenses **does Scripture refer to** in this passage? Prohibitions involving **money** such as fraud, robbery, and the withholding of wages. [19]**Here, too,** then, the verse must be referring to a prohibition involving **money:** Stealing money, and not kidnapping."

אִיתְּמַר [20]**It was stated** that the Amoraim disagree about the following matter: If there were two sets of witnesses **in a case of kidnapping** — one set of **witnesses** who testified that the defendant **kidnapped** another person, and a second set of **witnesses** who testified that he **sold** his victim — and both set of witnesses **were refuted** and shown to be false, conspiring witnesses, the Amoraim disagree about the law.

RASHI

דבר הלמד מעניינו — אם אי אתה יודע במה הכתוב מדבר צא ולמד מפרשה שכתוב בה, ולפי הפרשה הוא נכתב אצלה, וכאן במה כל הענין מדבר — בנפשות, "לא תרצח" ו"לא תנאף" כל אלה חייבי מיתות בית דין — אף "לא תגנוב" — בגניבה שיש בה מיתת בית דין. **לא תגנובו** — בפרשת "קדושים תהיו". **משלש עשרה מדות** — זו היא אחת מהן שיהא הדבר מעניינו למד. **במה הכתוב מדבר** — הענין של מטה ושל מעלה מזו. **בממון** — "לא תעשוק את רעך" (ויקרא יט). **עידי גניבה ועידי מכירה** — שני כיתי עדים, אחת העידה שגנב את הנפש, ואחת העידה שמכר — אין נהרגין, כדמפרש טעמא ואזיל, וכיון דאינהו לא מקטלי — איהו נמי אם לא הוזמו לא מקטיל, דהויא לה עדות שאי אתה יכול להזימה, ולא משכחת לה דמקטיל אלא בכת אחת שמעידין על הגניבה ועל המכירה.

TRANSLATION AND COMMENTARY

[1]**Ḥizkiyah says:** Even though false, conspiring witnesses ordinarily pay the penalty that they had sought to inflict upon the defendant by their testimony, here the witnesses **are not executed.** [2]**Rabbi Yoḥanan** disagrees and **says:** The witnesses **are** indeed **executed.**

חִזְקִיָּה [3]The Gemara now explains the two sides of this Amoraic dispute: **Ḥizkiyah agrees with Rabbi Akiva, who said:** The verse that states (Deuteronomy 19:15): "At the mouth of two witnesses, or at the mouth of three witnesses, shall the matter be established," [4]teaches that witnesses must testify about an entire **"matter" — and not half a "matter."** Here one set of witnesses testified about the actual kidnapping, and a second set of witnesses testified about the sale of the kidnap victim, so each set of witnesses testified about half a matter. The defendant could not have been executed on the basis of such testimony, and so the refuted witnesses are not subject to the penalty ordinarily imposed upon false, conspiring witnesses. [5]**Rabbi Yoḥanan agrees with the Rabbis, who** disagreed with Rabbi Akiva and **said:** [6]A set of witnesses can testify about an entire **matter** — or **even half a matter,** provided there is another set of witnesses who can complete their testimony by testifying about the other half of the matter.

וּמוֹדֶה [7]On a related issue, **Ḥizkiyah agrees that** if **the second set of witnesses regarding a rebellious son were refuted** and shown to be false, conspiring witnesses, they **are executed.** We learned earlier in this tractate (71a) that a rebellious son had first to be brought before a court of three judges. If they convicted him, on the testimony of a set of witnesses who saw him stealing and eating meat and drinking wine in a ravenous manner, he would be flogged. If the boy sinned again, he would be brought before a court of twenty-three judges. If they convicted him, on the testimony of a second set of witnesses who saw him committing the same offenses, he would be sentenced to death. Ḥizkiyah agrees that if that second set of witnesses were refuted and shown to be false, conspiring witnesses, they are subject to the penalty that they had sought to have imposed on the rebellious son. In such a case we do not say that, since the rebellious son could not have been executed without the testimony of the first set of witnesses, the second set of witnesses testified about only half a matter. [8]The reason: **The first** set of witnesses **can say:** [86B] [9]**"We came to** offer testimony on the basis of which the boy **would be flogged,"** and the boy was indeed flogged on the basis of their testimony. We view that testimony as independent, [10]**and** regard **the second** set of witnesses as those who **offered the entire testimony** on the basis of which the boy would have been executed.

מַתְקִיף לָהּ [11]**Rav Pappa strongly objected to this** version of the dispute between Ḥizkiyah and Rabbi Yoḥanan: [12]**If it is so,** that Ḥizkiyah agrees that the second set of witnesses regarding a rebellious son are

[1]חִזְקִיָּה אָמַר: אֵין נֶהֱרָגִין. [2]רַבִּי יוֹחָנָן אָמַר: נֶהֱרָגִין.
[3]חִזְקִיָּה דַּאֲמַר כְּרַבִּי עֲקִיבָא, דַּאֲמַר: [4]"דָּבָר" — וְלֹא חֲצִי דָבָר. [5]וְרַבִּי יוֹחָנָן אָמַר כְּרַבָּנַן, דַּאֲמַרִי: [6]"דָּבָר" — וַאֲפִילּוּ חֲצִי דָבָר.
[7]וּמוֹדֶה חִזְקִיָּה בָּעֵדִים הָאַחֲרוֹנִים שֶׁל בֵּן סוֹרֵר וּמוֹרֶה שֶׁהוּזְמוּ שֶׁנֶּהֱרָגִין, [8]מִתּוֹךְ שֶׁיְּכוֹלִים לוֹמַר הָרִאשׁוֹנִים: [86B] [9]"לְהַלְקוֹתוֹ בָּאנוּ", [10]וְהָנֵי אַחֲרִינֵי — כּוּלֵּיהּ "דָּבָר" קָא עָבְדִי לֵיהּ.
[11]מַתְקִיף לָהּ רַב פַּפָּא: [12]אִי הָכִי עֵידֵי מְכִירָה נַמִי לִיקְטְלֵיהּ,

LITERAL TRANSLATION

[1]Ḥizkiyah says: They are not executed. [2]Rabbi Yoḥanan says: They are executed.

[3]Ḥizkiyah said like Rabbi Akiva, who said: [4]"Matter" — and not half a matter. [5]And Rabbi Yoḥanan said like the Rabbis, who said: [6]"Matter" — even half a matter.

[7]And Ḥizkiyah agrees that the last [set of] witnesses regarding a rebellious son who were refuted are executed, [8]for the first ones can say: [86B] [9]"We came to flog him," [10]and these last ones did to him the entire "matter."

[11]Rav Pappa strongly objected to this: [12]If so, they should also execute the witnesses to the sale,

RASHI

פלוגתא דרבי עקיבא ורבנן — בבבא בתרא ב"חזקת הבתים", על פי שנים עדים יקום דבר — ולא חצי דבר, והאי חצי דבר הוא אלא כל כת וכת דאי לאו עידי גניבה אינו נהרג משום עידי מכירה, שיכול לומר: עבדי מכרתי, ואי לאו מכירה נמי לא מיחייב אגניבה. **בעדים האחרונים של בן סורר ומורה** — דתנן לעיל (עא,א): מתרין בו בפני שלשה ומלקין אותו, חזר וקלקל — נדון בעשרים ושלשה, מתרין בו אביו ואמו בפני הדיינין, וכשבאין עדים ראשונים ומעידין עליו שאכל תרטימר בשר ושתה חצי לוג יין מגניבה — מלקין אותו, כדכתיב "ויסרו אותו" דהיינו מלקות, חזר וקלקל — נדון בעשרים ושלשה למיתה, ומודה חזקיה בהנך אחרונים העידו שחזר וקלקל, שהוזמו — שנהרגין, ולא אמרינן שחצי דבר הוא, דאי לאו סהדותא דקמאי לא מקטיל בסהדותא דהני — אלא אמרינן הואיל ויש עונש על פי ראשונים שזה לקה על ידה, תו לא שייכא ההוא סהדותא קמייתא בהני בתרייתא, והני בתראי כוליה דבר קא עבדי. **להלקותו באנו** — ולא הועדנו להמיתו שלא ידענו שסופו לחזור ולקלקל.

HALAKHAH

עֵידֵי גְּנֵיבָה וּמְכִירָה **Witnesses to the stealing and the sale.** "If two witnesses testified that they saw the defendant

[1]מִתּוֹךְ שֶׁיְּכוֹלִין עֵידֵי גְנֵיבָה
לוֹמַר: [2]״לְהַלְקוֹתוֹ בָּאנוּ״. [3]וְכִי
תֵּימָא דְּקָסָבַר חִזְקִיָּה דְּלָא לָקֵי
— [4]וְהָא אִיתְּמַר: [5]עֵידֵי גְנֵיבָה
בְּנֶפֶשׁ שֶׁהוּזְמוּ, [6]חִזְקִיָּה וְרַבִּי
יוֹחָנָן. [7]חַד אָמַר: לוֹקִין. [8]וְחַד
אָמַר: אֵין לוֹקִין. [9]וְאָמְרִינַן:
תִּסְתַּיֵּים דְּחִזְקִיָּה דַּאֲמַר לוֹקִין,
[10]מִדַּאֲמַר חִזְקִיָּה: אֵין נֶהֱרָגִין.
[11]דְּאִי רַבִּי יוֹחָנָן, כֵּיוָן דַּאֲמַר:

LITERAL TRANSLATION

[1]since the witnesses to the stealing can say: [2]"We came to flog him." [3]And if you say that Ḥizkiyah maintains that he is not flogged — [4]but surely it was stated: [5][Regarding] witnesses to the stealing who were refuted in [a case of] kidnapping, [6]Ḥizkiyah and Rabbi Yoḥanan [disagree]. [7]One says: They are flogged. [8]And one says: They are not flogged. [9]And we said: It stands to reason that it was Ḥizkiyah who said [that] they are flogged, [10]for Ḥizkiyah said: They are not executed. [11]For if it was Rabbi Yoḥanan, since he said:

TRANSLATION AND COMMENTARY

subject to execution if they were found to be false, conspiring witnesses, then he should **also** agree that in a case of kidnapping, the second set of **witnesses** who testified that the kidnapper had **sold** his victim **are subject to execution,** if they were found to be false, conspiring witnesses, [1]**for the** first set of **witnesses** who testified that the defendant had **kidnapped** the victim **can say:** [2]**"We came to** offer testimony on the basis of which the defendant **would be flogged."** Like the first testimony regarding the rebellious son, our testimony should be viewed as a separate unit. [3]**And if you** should **suggest that Ḥizkiyah** himself **maintains that** a kidnapper who did not sell his victim **is not subject to flogging** (so the first set of witnesses cannot say that they offered testimony on the basis of which the defendant would be flogged), that is problematic, [4]**for surely it was stated** that the Amoraim disagree about that matter. [5]**In a case of kidnapping,** if the set of **witnesses** who testified that the defendant **kidnapped** someone **were refuted** and shown to be false, conspiring witnesses, before the second set of witnesses testified that the defendant sold his victim, [6]**Ḥizkiyah and Rabbi Yoḥanan disagree** about the law. [7]**One** of these Amoraim — Ḥizkiyah or Rabbi Yoḥanan — **says:** Those witnesses are liable to the penalty that they sought to inflict, so **they are flogged.** [8]**And the other** Amora **says: They are not flogged.** [9]**And** when we discussed the matter, **we said: It stands to reason that it was Ḥizkiyah who said that** the refuted witnesses **are subject to flogging,** [10]**for Ḥizkiyah said** that if the set of witnesses who testified that the defendant kidnapped someone were refuted only after the second set of witnesses testified that the defendant sold his victim, **they are not executed.** [11]**For if it was Rabbi Yoḥanan** who said that the refuted witnesses are subject to flogging, there is a difficulty, for it was Rabbi Yoḥanan who **said** that if the set of witnesses who testified that the defendant kidnapped someone were refuted only after the second set of

RASHI

להלקותו באנו — על הגניבה, ולא ידענו שימכרנו. דלא לקי — אגניבה לחודה, משום דהוה ליה לאו שניתן לאזהרת מיתת בית דין, שאם ימכרנו — יהרג. עידי גניבה בנפש — שהעידוהו שגנב נפש. מדאמר חזקיה אין נהרגין — אם הוזמו לאחר שבאו עידי מכירה, משום הכי לוקין, שהרי אין סופן למות על עדות זו ולא הוי לגבייהו לאו שניתן לאזהרת מיתת בית דין. דאי רבי יוחנן כיון דאמר נהרגין — אם באו עידי מכירה אחרי כן קודם הזמה, ונגמר דינו על פי שתי הכתות והוזמו, היכי לקו אם הוזמו קודם שבאו עידי מכירה — הא הוה ליה לאו ״דלא תענה״ לגבייהו בשעה שהעידו לאו שניתן לאזהרה שלא להעיד כן, שאם יעידו ולא

NOTES

עֵידֵי גְנֵיבָה בְּנֶפֶשׁ **Witnesses to the stealing.** The dispute between Ḥizkiyah and Rabbi Yoḥanan regarding witnesses who testified that the defendant kidnapped someone and were later refuted is based on a disagreement about the nature of the prohibition against kidnapping. According to Ḥizkiyah, kidnapping constitutes a separate prohibition, the violation of which is subject to flogging, and selling the victim is a second prohibition, the violation of which is subject to the death penalty. According to Rabbi Yoḥanan, there is a single prohibition, kidnapping and selling. Someone who kidnaps and sells another person is liable to the death penalty, but someone who only kidnaps another person is exempt from lashes, for the crime of kidnapping is punishable by judicial execution (*Rabbi David Bonfil, Ran*).

תִּסְתַּיֵּים דְּחִזְקִיָּה דַּאֲמַר **It stands to reason that it was Ḥizkiyah.** It does not necessarily follow from Ḥizkiyah's ruling — that the witnesses who testified that the defendant kidnapped someone are not executed — that he maintains that those witnesses can be subject to flogging. Perhaps those witnesses are not executed because they only testified about half a "matter." But it follows from Rabbi Yoḥanan's ruling, that those witnesses are executed. Since Rabbi Yoḥanan maintains that they cannot be subject to flogging, Ḥizkiyah must maintain that they can be subject to flogging. Since the Gemara was dealing with the position of Ḥizkiyah, it formulates its argument in terms of Ḥizkiyah.

HALAKHAH

kidnapping the victim, and two other witnesses testified that they saw him selling the victim, and then the witnesses to the sale were refuted, or even if the witnesses to the kidnapping were refuted, the refuted witnesses are subject to execution," following Rabbi Yoḥanan, against Resh Lakish. (*Rambam, Sefer Shofetim, Hilkhot Edut* 21:9.)

[1]נֶהֱרָגִין, [2]הֲוָה לֵיהּ לָאו שֶׁנִּיתַּן לְאַזְהָרַת מִיתַת בֵּית דִּין, [3]וְכָל לָאו שֶׁנִּיתַּן לְאַזְהָרַת מִיתַת בֵּית דִּין, אֵין לוֹקִין עָלָיו. [4]אִיהוּ לָא לָקֵי, אִינְהוּ הֵיכִי לָקוּ?

[5]אֶלָּא אֲמַר רַב פַּפָּא: [6]בְּעֵידֵי מְכִירָה דְּכוּלֵּי עָלְמָא לָא פְּלִיגִי דְּנֶהֱרָגִין, [7]כִּי פְּלִיגִי? — בְּעֵידֵי גְנֵיבָה. [8]חִזְקִיָּה אָמַר: אֵין נֶהֱרָגִין — גְּנֵיבָה לְחוּדָהּ קַיְימָא, וּמְכִירָה לְחוּדָהּ קַיְימָא. [9]רַבִּי יוֹחָנָן אָמַר: נֶהֱרָגִין — גְּנֵיבָה אַתְחַלְתָּא דִּמְכִירָה הִיא.

LITERAL TRANSLATION

[1]They are executed, [2]it is a [violation of a] prohibition which serves as a warning for judicial execution, [3]and [regarding] any prohibition which serves as a warning for judicial execution, they are not flogged for it. [4]If he is not flogged, how can they be flogged?

[5]Rather, Rav Pappa said: [6]Regarding witnesses to the sale, all agree (lit., "the whole world does not disagree") that they are executed. [7]When do they disagree? Regarding witnesses to the stealing. [8]Hizkiyah says: They are not executed — the stealing stands by itself, and the sale stands by itself. [9]Rabbi Yoḥanan says: They are executed — the stealing is the beginning of the sale.

TRANSLATION AND COMMENTARY

witnesses testified that the defendant sold his victim, [1]**they are executed.** [2]Thus, the first set of witnesses violated **a prohibition which,** if all the necessary conditions are fulfilled, **is punishable by judicial execution.** [3]**And regarding a prohibition which is punishable by judicial execution,** a transgressor **is not subject to flogging,** even if certain conditions prevent the court from administering the death penalty. Rabbi Yoḥanan said that if the set of witnesses who testified that the defendant kidnapped someone were refuted after the second set of witnesses testified that the defendant sold his victim, they are executed. Therefore he cannot say that if the first set of witnesses were refuted before the second set of witnesses offered their testimony, they are subject to flogging. Since, as we have demonstrated, Ḥizkiyah said that if the witnesses who testified that the defendant kidnapped someone were refuted before a second set of witnesses testified that the defendant sold his victim, they are subject to flogging, Ḥizkiyah must also maintain that if the witnesses were not refuted, the kidnapper himself is subject to flogging, [4]for **if the kidnapper is not subject to flogging, how can** the refuted witnesses **be subject to flogging?** Surely they can only be liable to the penalty that they sought to inflict upon the defendant!

אֶלָּא [5]**Rather, Rav Pappa said:** If there were two sets of witnesses in a case of kidnapping — one set of witnesses who testified that the defendant kidnapped someone, and a second set of witnesses who testified that the defendant sold his victim — and both sets of witnesses were refuted and shown to be false, conspiring witnesses, [6]**regarding the witnesses** who testified that the defendant **sold** his victim, **both** Ḥizkiyah and Rabbi Yoḥanan agree that the witnesses **are executed.** [7]**About what do they disagree?** They only disagree **about the witnesses** who testified that the defendant **kidnapped** someone. [8]**Ḥizkiyah says** that **they are not executed,** for **the kidnapping stands by itself** as an independent offense that is subject to flogging, **and the sale** of the kidnap victim **stands by itself** as a separate offense that is subject to the death penalty. Therefore the witnesses who testified that the defendant kidnapped someone only offered testimony on the basis of which the defendant would be flogged. [9]**Rabbi Yoḥanan** disagrees and **says** that the witnesses who testified that the defendant kidnapped someone **are** also **executed,** for **kidnapping is the beginning** of an offense which culminates in **the sale** of the victim. The perpetrator is subject to the death penalty, and so the witnesses who testified that the defendant kidnapped someone offered testimony on the basis of which the defendant would be executed.

RASHI

יוזמו עד שיבאו עידי מכירה ויגמר דינו ויוזמו — יומתו. וכל לאו שניתן לאזהרת מיתת בית דין אין לוקין עליו — ואפילו יפטרו מן המיתה, שהרי לא לאזהרת מלקות ניתן. אינהו היכי לקו — הא לאו "כאשר זמם" הוא, ואי משום "לא תענה" (שמות כ) — לאו שאין בו מעשה הוא. בעידי מכירה כולי עלמא לא פליגי דנהרגין — אם נגמר דינו על פי שתי הכתות. לחודה קיימא — ועידי גניבה אינן באין להורגו אלא להלקותו, אבל עידי מכירה שבאין עמהן ואומרין שהתרו בו למיתה — מונעין אותו ממלקות ומחייבין אותו מיתה, והויא לה מכירה דבר שלם. אתחלתא דמכירה — דקסבר רבי יוחנן לא לקי עלה, דלאו שניתן לאזהרת מיתת בית דין, ואינן באין אלא להורגו, ואף על גב דשתיהן צריכות זו לזו והוה ליה

NOTES

לָאו שֶׁנִּיתַּן לְאַזְהָרַת מִיתַת בֵּית דִּין **A prohibition that serves as a warning for judicial execution.** If, when all the necessary conditions are fulfilled, a violated prohibition is punishable by execution, then a person who violates the prohibition is not given the punishment of lashes, even if certain conditions prevent the court from administering the death penalty. This principle is somewhat similar to the view of Ḥizkiyah, that if a violated prohibition can sometimes lead to the death penalty, the violation of that prohibition can never create a monetary liability.

אִינְהוּ הֵיכִי לָקוּ **How can they be flogged.** *Rashi* writes that the witnesses are not liable to lashes for violating the prohibition stated in Exodus 20:13: "You shall not bear false witness against your neighbor," even though false, conspiring witnesses are occasionally flogged for violating that prohibition. It has been argued that lashes are only imposed

TRANSLATION AND COMMENTARY

וּמוֹדֶה [1]The Gemara notes that **Rabbi Yoḥanan agrees that** if **the first set of witnesses regarding a rebellious son were refuted** and shown to be false, conspiring witnesses, they **are not executed,** [2]**for they can say: "We came** merely **to** offer testimony on the basis of which the boy **would be flogged."**

אָמַר אַבַּיֵי Purposely using language that sounds self-contradictory in order to gain our attention, [3]**Abaye said: All agree about** one set of witnesses regarding **a rebellious son and all agree about** a second set of witnesses regarding **a rebellious son,** [4]**and there is a dispute** between those Amoraim **about** one set of witnesses against **a rebellious son** who were found to be false, conspiring witnesses. [5]The Gemara explains: **All** — including Rabbi Yoḥanan — **agree** that if **the first set of witnesses** who testified against **a rebellious son** were later refuted, they **are not executed,** [6]**for they can say: "We came** merely **to** offer testimony on the basis of which the boy **would be flogged."** [7]**And all** — including Ḥizkiyah — **agree** that if **the second set of witnesses regarding a rebellious son** were refuted, they **are executed,** [8]**for the first set of witnesses can say: "We came** merely **to** offer testimony on the basis of which the boy **would be flogged,"** [9]**and** we therefore regard the second set of witnesses as those who **offered the entire testimony** on the basis of which the boy would have been executed. [10]**And there is a dispute** between Ḥizkiyah and Rabbi Yoḥanan **about** witnesses who testified against **a rebellious son when two** witnesses **said: "We saw** the boy **steal** money from his father again, after he was flogged," [11]**and two** other witnesses **said: "We saw** the boy **eat** meat and drink wine purchased with the stolen money." If those witnesses were later refuted and found to be false, conspiring witnesses, Ḥizkiyah says that they are not

[1]וּמוֹדֶה רַבִּי יוֹחָנָן בָּעֵדִים הָרִאשׁוֹנִים שֶׁל בֵּן סוֹרֵר וּמוֹרֶה שֶׁהוּזְמוּ שֶׁאֵין נֶהֱרָגִין, [2]מִתּוֹךְ שֶׁיְּכוֹלִין לוֹמַר: ״לְהַלְקוֹתוֹ בָּאנוּ״.

[3]אֲמַר אַבַּיֵי: הַכֹּל מוֹדִים בְּבֵן סוֹרֵר וּמוֹרֶה, וְהַכֹּל מוֹדִים בְּבֵן סוֹרֵר וּמוֹרֶה, [4]וּמַחֲלוֹקֶת בְּבֵן סוֹרֵר וּמוֹרֶה. [5]הַכֹּל מוֹדִים בְּבֵן סוֹרֵר וּמוֹרֶה — בָּעֵדִים הָרִאשׁוֹנִים שֶׁאֵין נֶהֱרָגִין, [6]מִתּוֹךְ שֶׁיְּכוֹלִין לוֹמַר: ״לְהַלְקוֹתוֹ בָּאנוּ״. [7]וְהַכֹּל מוֹדִים בְּבֵן סוֹרֵר וּמוֹרֶה, בָּעֵדִים אַחֲרוֹנִים שֶׁנֶּהֱרָגִים, [8]מִתּוֹךְ שֶׁעֵדִים הָרִאשׁוֹנִים יְכוֹלִין לוֹמַר: ״לְהַלְקוֹתוֹ בָּאנוּ״, [9]וְהָנֵי כּוּלֵּיהּ ״דָּבָר״ קָא עָבְדִי לֵיהּ. [10]וּמַחֲלוֹקֶת בְּבֵן סוֹרֵר וּמוֹרֶה: ״שְׁנַיִם אוֹמְרִים בְּפָנֵינוּ גָּנַב״, [11]וּשְׁנַיִם אוֹמְרִים: ״בְּפָנֵינוּ אָכַל״.

LITERAL TRANSLATION

[1]And Rabbi Yoḥanan agrees about the first [set of] witnesses regarding a rebellious son who were refuted, that they are not executed, [2]for they can say: "We came to flog him."

[3]Abaye said: All agree about a rebellious son, and all agree about a rebellious son, [4]and there is a dispute about a rebellious son. [5]All agree about a rebellious son that the first [set of] witnesses are not executed, [6]for they can say: "We came to flog him." [7]And all agree about a rebellious son that the last [set of] witnesses are executed, [8]for the first [set of] witnesses can say: "We came to flog him," [9]and these did to him the entire "matter." [10]And there is a dispute about a rebellious son [when] two say: "He stole before us," [11]and two say: "He ate before us."

RASHI

כל חדא וחדא תלי דבר — מיקטל כרבנן. ומודה רבי יוחנן בעדים הראשונים של בן סורר ומורה שהוזמו דאין נהרגין — דאינהו ודאי למלקות אתו, כדכתיב "ויסרו אותו" (דברים כא). הכל מודים כו' — כלומר, יש עדים בבן סורר ומורה שהכל מודים באחת כתותיו לפטור, ויש כת שהכל מודים בו לחיוב, ויש כת בבן סורר ומורה שנחלקו חזקיה ורבי יוחנן לפי מה שמשמעו במחלוקתן. שנים אומרים בפנינו גנב — משל אביו מעות לקנות בשר ויין בפעם שניה אחר שלקה. ושנים אומרים בפנינו אכל — הבשר ברשות אחרים, דאינו חייב שיגנוב משל אביו ויאכל ברשות אחרים, הנך שתי כתות צריכות זו לזו, ואין הראשונים יכולין לומר: להלקותו באנו — והוה ליה תלי דבר לחזקיה דסבר לה כרבי עקיבא דאמר אין נהרגין, ולרבי יוחנן דאמר נהרגין כרבנן.

NOTES

for violating that prohibition when the witnesses' testimony was not only false, but would have caused some penalty to be inflicted upon the defendant (*Talmidei Rabbenu Peretz*).

HALAKHAH

הַכֹּל מוֹדִים בְּבֵן סוֹרֵר וּמוֹרֶה All agree about a rebellious son. "If the first set of witnesses who testified against a rebellious son were later refuted, they are not executed, for they can claim that they had come to offer testimony on the basis of which the boy would be flogged. But if the second set of witnesses who testified against a rebellious son were later refuted, they are executed, for the boy would have been put to death on the basis of their testimony," following the Gemara. (*Rambam, Sefer Shofetim, Hilkhot Edut* 21:9.)

שְׁנַיִם אוֹמְרִים בְּפָנֵינוּ גָּנַב, וּשְׁנַיִם אוֹמְרִים: בְּפָנֵינוּ אָכַל Where two say: He stole before us, and two say: He ate before us. "If two of the latter witnesses against a rebellious son testified that they had seen him steal, and two others of

TRANSLATION AND COMMENTARY

executed, and Rabbi Yoḥanan says that they are executed. In such a case, each set of two witnesses completes the testimony offered by the other, for a rebellious son is not put to death unless witnesses testify that he stole money from his father, and that he ate meat and drank wine purchased with the stolen money. Ḥizkiyah agrees with Rabbi Akiva, who said that witnesses must testify about an entire matter, and not half a matter. Here, one set of witnesses testified about the stealing, and a second set of witnesses testified about the eating, so each set of witnesses testified about half a matter. Since the boy could not have been executed on the basis of testimony by either pair of witnesses by themselves, the refuted witnesses are not subject to the penalty ordinarily imposed on false, conspiring witnesses. Rabbi Yoḥanan agrees with the Rabbis who said that a set of witnesses can testify about either an entire matter or half a matter. Since the boy could have been executed on the basis of such testimony, the refuted witnesses are subject to the penalty ordinarily imposed on false, conspiring witnesses.

[1]אָמַר רַב אַסִי: עֵדֵי מְכִירָה בַּנֶּפֶשׁ שֶׁהוּזְמוּ אֵין נֶהֱרָגִין, [2]מִתּוֹךְ שֶׁיָּכוֹל לוֹמַר עַבְדִּי מָכַרְתִּי.

[3]אָמַר רַב יוֹסֵף: כְּמַאן אָזְלָא הָא שְׁמַעֲתָא דְּרַב אַסִי? — [4]כְּרַבִּי עֲקִיבָא, דְּאָמַר: [5]״דָּבָר״ — וְלֹא חֲצִי דָבָר.

[6]אֲמַר לֵיהּ אַבַּיֵי: דְּאִי כְּרַבָּנַן, נֶהֱרָגִין? [7]הָא ״מִתּוֹךְ״ קָאָמַר! [8]אֶלָּא, אֲפִילּוּ תֵּימָא רַבָּנַן, [9]וּבִדְלָא אָתוּ עֵידֵי גְנֵיבָה.

LITERAL TRANSLATION

[1]Rav Assi said: Witnesses to the sale of the person (lit., "soul") who were refuted are not executed, [2]since he can say: "I sold my slave."

[3]Rav Yosef said: In accordance with whom is this teaching of Rav Assi? [4]In accordance with Rabbi Akiva, who said: [5]"Matter" — and not half a matter.

[6]Abaye said to him: But [does it follow that,] according to the Sages, they are executed? [7]But he said: "Since!" [8]Rather, you can even say [in accordance with] the Sages, [9]and when witnesses to the stealing did not come.

RASHI

עידי מכירה בנפש — ולא באו עידי גניבה על כך לפנינו. **הא מתוך קאמר** — אפילו חצי דבר אין כאן, שהרי היה לו להציל נפשו מבית דין בטענה זו. **ובדלא אתו עידי גניבה** — קאמר רב אסי וכדפרישית שהיה יכול לומר עבדי מכרתי.

אָמַר [1]**Rav Assi said:** If a set of witnesses testified that the defendant sold someone to another person, but there were no witnesses to a kidnapping, and **the witnesses to the sale were refuted,** and shown to be false, conspiring witnesses, **they are not executed,** [2]**for** the defendant **could have said:** "The person whom **I sold** was not a kidnap victim, but rather **my slave."** Since the defendant could not have been convicted on the basis of the witnesses' testimony. The witnesses are not subject to the death penalty for their false testimony.

אָמַר רַב יוֹסֵף [3]**Rav Yosef asked: In accordance with whose** position **was this teaching of Rav Assi** taught? [4]**In accordance with** the position of **Rabbi Akiva, who said** that the verse which states (Deuteronomy 19:15): "At the mouth of two witnesses, or at the mouth of three witnesses, shall the matter be established," [5]teaches that witnesses must testify about an entire **matter — and not half a matter.** Testimony about the sale of the kidnap victim, only regards half a matter. Since the defendant could not have been executed on the basis of such testimony, the refuted witnesses are not subject to the penalty ordinarily imposed upon false, conspiring witnesses.

אֲמַר לֵיהּ [6]**Abaye said to him** in astonishment: **But** does it follow from what you said that, **according to the Sages** who disagree with Rabbi Akiva and say that a set of witnesses can indeed testify about half a matter, the witnesses to the sale **would be executed?** [7]**But** surely Rav Assi **said:** The witnesses to the sale are not executed, **for** the defendant could have said that it was his slave whom he had sold. Even the Rabbis who disagree with Rabbi Akiva only say that a set of witnesses can testify about a half a matter, if there is another set of witnesses who can complete their testimony by testifying about the second half of the matter. But here there are no witnesses to the kidnapping. [8]**Rather, you can say** that Rav Assi's ruling was taught **even according to the Sages** who disagree with Rabbi Akiva, [9]**and** we are dealing with a case **where witnesses to the** actual **kidnapping did not come** forth.

HALAKHAH

the latter witnesses testified that they had seen him eat, and they were all refuted, they are all subject to execution," following Rabbi Yoḥanan. (*Rambam, Sefer Shofetim, Hilkhot Edut* 21:9.)

עֵדֵי מְכִירָה בַּנֶּפֶשׁ שֶׁהוּזְמוּ **Witnesses to the sale who were refuted.** "If two witnesses testified that they saw the defendant selling someone to a third party, but there were no witnesses to the kidnapping itself, and the witnesses to the sale were refuted, they are not subject to execution. The defendant could not have been put to death on the basis of their testimony, for he could have claimed that it was a slave that he had sold. If witnesses to the kidnapping came forward and testified after the witnesses to the sale were refuted, they are not subject to execution, even if we saw them signaling to the witnesses to the sale," following the Gemara. (*Rambam, Sefer Shofetim, Hilkhot Edut* 21:9.)

TRANSLATION AND COMMENTARY

אִי הָכִי 1The Gemara asks: **If so, what** does Rabbi Assi **say?** Surely the defendant could never have been convicted on the basis of the witnesses' testimony, for there was no proof that anyone was kidnapped!

לָא צְרִיכָא 2The Gemara answers: **No, it was necessary** for Rabbi Assi to teach us that if the witnesses to the sale were refuted, and shown to be false, conspiring witnesses, they are not executed, **even** when in **the end,** after the witnesses to the sale gave their testimony, witnesses to the kidnapping **came** and testified. In such a case, we might have thought that the false witnesses to the sale are indeed subject to the death penalty, for the defendant could have been executed on the basis of the testimony offered by the two sets of witnesses together.

וְאַכַּתִּי 3The Gemara asks: **But still, what** does Rabbi Assi come **to say?** Surely the witnesses to the sale cannot be executed, for when they gave their testimony, the defendant could not have been convicted on the basis of what they said, and they can claim that they did not know that the witnesses to the kidnapping would come and testify after them!

לָא צְרִיכָא 4The Gemara answers: **No, it was necessary** for Rabbi Assi to teach us that if the witnesses to the sale were refuted, they are not executed, even **if** we saw the witnesses to the sale and the witnesses to the kidnapping **signaling** each other, indicating that the first pair knew that the second pair would testify after them. 5**You might have said that signaling has** Halakhic **significance,** and so the two sets of witnesses are considered as a single unit. 6**Therefore,** Rabbi Assi comes and **teaches us** that the witnesses' **signaling has no** Halakhic **significance,** and that unless the two sets of witnesses come together to testify against the defendant, they are not regarded as a single unit. Hence the witnesses to the sale who were refuted cannot be executed, for the defendant could not have been convicted on the basis of their testimony.

MISHNAH זָקֵן מַמְרֵא 7Our Mishnah clarifies the laws regarding a rebellious elder, who was included in the first Mishnah in our chapter among those liable to death by strangulation: **A rebellious elder** — a Sage who was duly ordained and fit to serve in the Sanhedrin, but who himself followed a practice that contradicted the opinion of the majority of the Sages of his generation — is liable to death by strangulation, 8**as it is stated** (Deuteronomy 17:8-12): **"If there arise a matter too hard for you in judgment**...then shall you arise, and go up to the place which the Lord your God shall choose. And you shall come to the priests the Levites, and to the judge that shall be in those days, and inquire; and they shall tell you the sentence of judgment. And

1אִי הָכִי מַאי לְמֵימְרָא? 2לָא צְרִיכָא דְּאַף עַל גַּב דְּאָתוּ לְבַסּוֹף. 3וְאַכַּתִּי מַאי לְמֵימְרָא? 4לָא צְרִיכָא דְּקָא מְרַמְּזִי רְמוּזֵי. 5מַהוּ דְּתֵימָא רְמִיזָא מִילְּתָא הִיא. 6קָא מַשְׁמַע לָן: רְמִיזָא לָאו כְּלוּם הוּא.

מִשְׁנָה 7זָקֵן מַמְרֵא עַל פִּי בֵּית דִּין, 8שֶׁנֶּאֱמַר: ״כִּי יִפָּלֵא

LITERAL TRANSLATION

1If so, what is there to say?

2No, it was necessary even when they came at the end.

3But still, what is there to say?

4No, it was necessary when they signaled. 5Lest you say signaling is something. 6[Therefore] it teaches us: Signaling is nothing.

MISHNAH 7An elder who rebels against the court, 8as it is stated: "If there arise

RASHI

לבסוף — אחר שהעידו עידי מכירה באו עידי גניבה ונגמר הדין על פי שניהם. **ואכתי מאי למימרא** — כשהעידו הראשונים לא היה הדין ראוי ליגמר על פיהם, ויכולין לומר: לא היינו יודעין שיבואו עידי גניבה עלינו. **דקא מרמזי רמוזי** — הני להני.

NOTES

זָקֵן מַמְרֵא עַל פִּי בֵּית דִּין An elder who rebels against the court. According to *Meiri,* a rebellious elder was only liable to the death penalty if he issued a ruling that contradicted a unanimous decision of the Great Sanhedrin. But if he contradicted a ruling of the Great Sanhedrin that was merely a majority opinion, he was exempt from the death penalty.

HALAKHAH

זָקֵן מַמְרֵא An elder who rebels. "If a Torah Sage issued a ruling which contradicted the opinion of the judges sitting on a local court, they all went to Jerusalem and appeared before the court sitting at the entrance to the Temple Mount. If the dissenting elder did not accept that court's decision, they all went to the court sitting at the entrance to the Temple Courtyard. If the dissenting elder did not accept that court's decision either, they all went to the Great Sanhedrin sitting in the Chamber of Hewn Stone, whose decision was final. If the dissenting elder went back to his home town and continued teaching in accordance with his own opinion, he was exempt. But if he issued a practical ruling, or if he himself acted in accordance with his own position, he was subject to execution, even if he did not receive a warning." (*Rambam, Sefer Shofetim, Hilkhot Mamrim* 3:8.)

מִמְּךָ דָבָר לַמִּשְׁפָּט״.
[1]שְׁלֹשָׁה בָּתֵּי דִינִין הָיוּ שָׁם,
[2]אֶחָד יוֹשֵׁב עַל פֶּתַח הַר הַבַּיִת,
[3]וְאֶחָד יוֹשֵׁב עַל פֶּתַח הָעֲזָרָה,
[4]וְאֶחָד יוֹשֵׁב בְּלִשְׁכַּת הַגָּזִית.
[5]בָּאִין לְזֶה שֶׁעַל פֶּתַח הַר
הַבַּיִת, וְאוֹמֵר: [6]״כָּךְ דָּרַשְׁתִּי,
וְכָךְ דָּרְשׁוּ חֲבֵירִי. [7]כָּךְ לִימַּדְתִּי,
וְכָךְ לִימְּדוּ חֲבֵירַי״. [8]אִם שָׁמְעוּ
— אָמַר לָהֶם, וְאִם לָאו —
בָּאִין לָהֶן לְאוֹתָן שֶׁעַל פֶּתַח
עֲזָרָה. [9]וְאוֹמֵר: ״כָּךְ דָּרַשְׁתִּי
וְכָךְ דָּרְשׁוּ חֲבֵירַי״. [10]כָּךְ
לִימַּדְתִּי, וְכָךְ לִימְּדוּ חֲבֵירַי.
[11]אִם שָׁמְעוּ, אָמַר לָהֶם. [12]וְאִם
לָאו, אֵלּוּ וְאֵלּוּ בָּאִין לְבֵית דִּין

LITERAL TRANSLATION

a matter too hard for you in judgment."

[1]There were three courts there, [2]one sitting at the entrance to the Temple Mount, [3]and one sitting at the entrance to the Temple Courtyard, [4]and one sitting in the Chamber of Hewn Stone. [5]They come to the one at the entrance to the Temple Mount, and he says: [6]"Thus have I expounded, and thus have my colleagues expounded. [7]Thus have I taught, and thus have my colleagues taught." [8]If they heard, he says to them, and if not, they come to those who are at the entrance to the Temple Courtyard. [9]And he says: "Thus have I expounded, and thus have my colleagues expounded. [10]Thus have I taught, and thus have my colleagues taught." [11]If they heard, he says to them. [12]And if not, these and those come to the great court

TRANSLATION AND COMMENTARY

you shall do according to the sentence, which they of that place which the Lord shall choose shall tell you....And the man who acts with malice, and does not heed the priest...or the judge, that man shall die." Wherever the Torah speaks of execution without specifying the mode of death, it refers to death by strangulation.

שְׁלֹשָׁה [1]**There were three courts** in Jerusalem, to which all Halakhic matters about which there was any doubt were brought for clarification and decision. [2]**One** court of twenty-three judges **sat at the entrance to the Temple Mount,** [3]**another** superior court of twenty-three judges **sat at the entrance to the Temple Courtyard, and** the highest court, [4]the Great Sanhedrin consisting of seventy-one judges, **sat in the Chamber of Hewn Stone.** If a Sage issued a ruling, and his colleagues sitting on the local court disagreed with his decision, they would bring the matter to the Jerusalem courts. [5]**They would** first **appear before** the court sitting **at the entrance to the Temple Mount,** where the Sage with the dissenting opinion would **say:** [6]**"Thus have I expounded** the Torah, **and thus have my colleagues expounded** it. [7]**Thus have I taught** the law to my students, **and thus have my colleagues taught** it to theirs." [8]**If** the members of the court sitting at the entrance to the Temple Mount **heard** the law on the matter from their teachers, **they told** it to **them** as they heard it. **If** those judges did **not** have a tradition on the matter, the Sage with the dissenting opinion and his colleagues moved on and **appeared before** the court sitting **at the entrance to the Temple Courtyard.** [9]The Sage with the dissenting opinion **said to** the members of the court: **"Thus have I expounded** the Torah, **and thus have my colleagues expounded** it. [10]**Thus have I taught** the law to my students, **and thus have my colleagues taught** it to theirs." [11]**If** the members of the court sitting at the entrance to the Temple Courtyard **heard** the law on the matter from their teachers, **they told it to them** as they heard it. [12]**If** those judges did **not** have a tradition on the matter, **these and those** — the Sage with the dissenting opinion and his colleagues, as well as the judges before whom they had already appeared — moved on and **appeared before the court in the Chamber of Hewn Stone,** the Great Sanhedrin which was the

RASHI

משנה שלשה בתי דינין היו שם — בירושלים, דמשמעי בה קרא ״וקמת ועלית״. אחד יושב על פתח הר הבית — הוא שער המזרחי שלפנים מן החיל לפני עזרת נשים. ואחד יושב למעלה הימנו — כשעברו עזרת נשים ובאין לפני עזרת ישראל. ואחד בלשכת הגזית — שהיא בנויה בתוך העזרה, חציה בקודש וחציה בחול, כדאמרינן בסדר יומא (כה,א). באין לזה שעל פתח הר הבית — זקן זה שהורה בעירו ונחלק בית דין שבעירו עליו, והזקיקו הכתוב לעלות לירושלים ולשאול, ובאין הוא ובית דין שבעירו לבית דין זה שעל פתח הר הבית, שהרי בו פוגעין תחילה.

NOTES

שְׁלֹשָׁה בָּתֵּי דִינִין **There were three courts.** Even though twenty-three judges sat on each of the minor Sanhedrins, whether the court was seated in the rebellious elder's home town, or at the entrance to the Temple Mount, or at the entrance to the Temple Courtyard, those special courts in Jerusalem were regarded as higher courts, for they consisted of the wisest and most knowledgeable judges in the country. The Great Sanhedrin sitting in the Chamber of Hewn Stone was greater than the two special courts sitting at the entrance to the Temple Mount and the entrance to the Temple Courtyard, both in the number and the quality of judges, and the scope of judicial authority.

כָּךְ דָּרַשְׁתִּי וְכָךְ לִימַּדְתִּי **Thus have I expounded, and thus have I taught.** It has been suggested that "expounding" refers to the public dissemination of Torah, whereas "teaching" refers to the teaching of Torah to the inner circle of the elder's disciples. Alternatively, "expounding" refers to a ruling derived from the plain meaning of the text, whereas "teaching" refers to a ruling derived by way of one of the hermeneutic principles according to which the Torah is interpreted (*Tosafot Yom Tov*).

הַגָּדוֹל שֶׁבְּלִשְׁכַּת הַגָּזִית, שֶׁמִּמֶּנּוּ יוֹצֵא תּוֹרָה לְכָל יִשְׂרָאֵל, [1]שֶׁנֶּאֱמַר: ״מִן הַמָּקוֹם הַהוּא אֲשֶׁר יִבְחַר ה׳״.
[2]חָזַר לְעִירוֹ, שָׁנָה וְלִמֵּד בְּדֶרֶךְ שֶׁהָיָה לָמֵד, פָּטוּר. [3]וְאִם הוֹרָה לַעֲשׂוֹת, חַיָּיב, [4]שֶׁנֶּאֱמַר: ״וְהָאִישׁ אֲשֶׁר יַעֲשֶׂה בְזָדוֹן״ — [5]אֵינוֹ חַיָּיב עַד שֶׁיּוֹרֶה לַעֲשׂוֹת. [6]תַּלְמִיד שֶׁהוֹרָה לַעֲשׂוֹת פָּטוּר. [7]נִמְצָא חוּמְרוֹ קוּלּוֹ.

גמרא [8]תָּנוּ רַבָּנַן: [9]״׳כִּי יִפָּלֵא מִמְּךָ דָבָר׳ — [87A] בְּמוּפְלָא שֶׁבְּבֵית דִּין הַכָּתוּב מְדַבֵּר. [10]׳מִמְּךָ׳ — זֶה יוֹעֵץ.

LITERAL TRANSLATION

in the Chamber of Hewn Stone, from which Torah issues forth to all of Israel, [1]as it is stated: "From that place which the Lord shall choose."

[2][If] he returned to his city, and taught again in the way that he had taught, he is exempt. [3]But if he ruled to act, he is liable, [4]as it is stated: "And the man that will act presumptuously" — [5]he is not liable unless he rules to act. [6]A student who ruled to act is exempt. [7]Thus his stringency is his leniency.

GEMARA [8]Our Rabbis taught: [9]"'If there arises a matter too hard for you in judgment' — [87A] Scripture speaks of the distinguished [member] of the court. [10]'For you' — that is a counselor.

TRANSLATION AND COMMENTARY

highest court in Israel and the final authority on Halakhah, and the place **from which Torah issues forth to all of Israel,** [1]**as the verse states** (Deuteronomy 17:10): "And you shall do according to the sentence, which they **of that place which the Lord shall choose** shall tell you; and you shall observe and do according to all that they inform you." The Great Sanhedrin considered the matter and decided the law, and that decision was binding.

חָזַר [2]If the Great Sanhedrin decided against the Sage with the dissenting opinion, and **he returned to his city, and** once **again taught** the law **in the** same **manner that he had taught** it earlier, **he was exempt** from the death penalty, even though his teachings contradicted the decision reached by the Great Sanhedrin. [3]**But if he issued a ruling** to others **to act** in accordance with his dissenting view, or if he himself acted in accordance with his ruling, **he was** regarded as a rebellious elder, and therefore **liable** to death by strangulation, [4]**as the verse states** (Deuteronomy 17:12): **"And the man who acts with malice,** and does not heed the priest...or the judge, that man shall die." [5]That verse comes to teach that a rebellious elder is not liable to the death penalty **unless he issued a ruling to act** in accordance with his dissenting view.

תַּלְמִיד [6]If a Rabbinical **student who** was not yet duly ordained and fit to rule for others **issued a ruling** that contradicted a ruling of the Great Sanhedrin, he **is exempt** from the death penalty, for the law regarding a rebellious elder applies only to a Sage who was duly ordained and fit to serve in the Sanhedrin. [7]**Thus the stringency** that is imposed upon such a person, that he is not fit to issue Halakhic rulings, leads to **a leniency** on his behalf, that he is not sentenced to death for instructing others to follow a practice that contradicts a ruling of the Great Sanhedrin.

GEMARA תָּנוּ רַבָּנַן [8]**Our Rabbis taught** the following Baraita: "The Torah states (Deuteronomy 17:8): 'If there arises a matter too hard for you in judgment, between blood and blood, between plea and plea, and between plague and plague, matters of controversy within your gates; then shall you arise, and go up to the place which the Lord your God shall choose.' [9]**'If there arise a matter too hard** [יִפָּלֵא] **for you in judgment'** — [87A] these words intimate that **Scripture speaks** here **of a distinguished member** [מוּפְלָא] **of the court,** meaning a duly ordained Sage and not a Rabbinical student. [10]**'For you** [מִמְּךָ]' — these words allude to **a counselor** who

RASHI

תלמיד שהורה לעשות – תלמיד שלא הגיע להוראה ונחלק על בית דין שבעירו, ובאו לבית דין הגדול ושאלו, וחזר לעירו והורה כבתחילה – פטור, שאין לסמוך על הוראתו, והתורה לא חייבה אלא מופלא ומומחה לבית דין כדאמרינן בגמרא. **נמצא חומרו קולו** – חומר שהחמירו עליו שאינו ראוי להוראה עד שיהא בן ארבעים שנה, נעשה לו קל לפוטרו מן המיתה.

גמרא במופלא שבבית דין – במומחה לבית דין, למעוטי תלמיד. **ממך זה יועץ** – שנחלק בעיבור השנה הקרוי סוד ועצה,

NOTES

נִמְצָא חוּמְרוֹ קוּלּוֹ **Thus his stringency is his leniency.** Not only does the unordained Rabbinical student violate the prohibition against issuing a ruling that contradicts the Great Sanhedrin, but he also violates the prohibition against issuing any ruling at all, even if it is in accordance with the law. The added severity of his transgression leads to the leniency that he is exempt from the death penalty (*Rambam* in his *Commentary to the Mishnah*).

HALAKHAH

תַּלְמִיד שֶׁהוֹרָה לַעֲשׂוֹת **A student who ruled to act.** "A rebellious elder was only subject to execution if he was a duly ordained Sage fit to issue Halakhic rulings. But if he was still only a Rabbinical student who was not yet duly ordained and fit to rule for others, he was exempt." (*Rambam, Sefer Shofetim, Hilkhot Mamrim* 3:5.)

¹וְכֵן הוּא אוֹמֵר: ׳מִמֵּךְ יָצָא חֹשֵׁב עַל ה׳ רָעָה יֹעֵץ בְּלִיָּעַל׳. ²׳דָּבָר׳ — זוֹ הֲלָכָה. ³׳לַמִּשְׁפָּט׳ — זֶה הַדִּין. ⁴׳בֵּין דָּם לְדָם׳ — בֵּין דַּם נִדָּה, ⁵דַּם לֵידָה, דַּם זִיבָה. ⁶׳בֵּין׳ דִּין לְדִין — בֵּין דִּינֵי נְפָשׁוֹת, דִּינֵי מָמוֹנוֹת, דִּינֵי מַכּוֹת. ⁷׳בֵּין נֶגַע לָנֶגַע׳ — בֵּין נִגְעֵי אָדָם, נִגְעֵי בָתִּים, נִגְעֵי בְגָדִים. ⁸׳דִּבְרֵי׳ — אֵלּוּ הַחֲרָמִים וְהָעֲרָכִין וְהַהֶקְדֵּשׁוֹת. ⁹׳רִיבֹת׳ — זוֹ הַשְׁקָאַת סוֹטָה, ¹⁰וַעֲרִיפַת עֶגְלָה, ¹¹וְטָהֳרַת מְצוֹרָע. ¹²׳בִּשְׁעָרֶיךָ׳ — זוֹ לֶקֶט שִׁכְחָה וּפֵאָה. ¹³׳וְקַמְתָּ׳ — מִבֵּית דִּין. ¹⁴׳וְעָלִיתָ׳ — מְלַמֵּד שֶׁבֵּית הַמִּקְדָּשׁ גָּבוֹהַּ מֵאֶרֶץ יִשְׂרָאֵל,

LITERAL TRANSLATION

[1]And similarly it says: 'There is come out of you one who contrives evil against the Lord, a wicked counselor.' [2]'A matter' — this is a [received] law. [3]'In judgment' — this is a [derived] law. [4]'Between blood and blood' — between menstrual blood, [5]childbirth blood, vaginal bleeding. [6]'Between plea and plea' — between capital cases, monetary cases, cases involving lashes. [7]'Between plague and plague' — between plagues of people, plagues of houses, plagues of garments. [8]'Matters' — these are consecrations, valuations, and dedications. [9]'Controversy' — this is making an unfaithful wife drink, [10]breaking the neck of a heifer, [11]and purifying a leper. [12]'Within your gates' — this is gleanings, forgotten sheaves, and [produce growing in the] corner. [13]'Then you shall arise' — from the court. [14]'And go up' — this teaches that the Temple is higher than [the rest of] Eretz Israel,

TRANSLATION AND COMMENTARY

is fit to offer advice on esoteric Halakhic issues, such as questions dealing with the Jewish calendar. [1]**And similarly the verse states** (Nahum 1:11): **'There is come out of you** [מִמֵּךְ] **one who contrives evil against the Lord, a wicked counselor.'** [2]The words, **'a matter,'** allude to **laws received** by Moses at Sinai, and the words, [3]**'in judgment,'** allude to **laws derived** by the hermeneutic principles, for a Sage who contradicts a ruling of the Great Sanhedrin is liable to the death penalty, whether the Sanhedrin's ruling stemmed from a law given to Moses at Sinai or was deduced using one of the hermeneutic principles. [4]**'Between blood and blood'** — the rebellious elder is liable whether he contradicted a ruling involving **menstrual blood,** [5]or a ruling involving **childbirth blood,** or a ruling involving **vaginal bleeding** of another kind. [6]**'Between plea and plea'** — the rebellious elder is liable whether he contradicted a ruling in a **capital case,** or in a **monetary case,** or in a **case involving lashes.** [7]**'Between plague and plague'** — the rebellious elder is liable whether he contradicted a ruling involving **leprosy** found **on people,** or **leprosy** found **on houses,** or **leprosy** found **on garments.** [8]The word, **'matters'** (lit., "words"), alludes to rulings involving **consecrations, valuations, and dedications** of property or sums of money to the Temple or Temple Treasury, for all of these gifts to the Temple are effected by way of speech. [9]The word **'controversy'** alludes to rulings involving the ceremonies of **making a wife** suspected of infidelity **drink** the bitter waters, [10]**breaking the neck of a heifer** when a murdered person's body is found outside a town, and it is not known who committed the murder, [11]**and purifying a leper.** All of these actions are related to controversies — between a man and his wife, between the murderer and his victim, and between the leper and the people about whom he spoke evil (for leprosy is regarded as a divine punishment for slander). [12]The words **'within your gates'** allude to rulings involving **gleanings** that fell during the harvest, **sheaves** that were **forgotten** in the fields, **and produce growing in the corner** of a field, all of which the property-owner is obligated to leave for the poor, and the poor eat 'within your gates.' [13]**'Then you shall arise' — from the court** that sits in its fixed venue, and to which all the town's residents come. [14]**'And go up** to the place which the Lord your God shall choose' — **this teaches that the Temple** in Jerusalem to which they are headed **is higher than the rest of Eretz Israel,**

RASHI

כדמפרש לקמן. **וכן הוא אומר** — דגבי יועץ כתוב ממך. **זו הלכה למשה מסיני** — שאף עליה הוא נהרג. **למשפט זה הדין** — אם נחלק בדבר הלמד בדין גזירה שוה גם הוא נהרג, דאילו דין ממש כתיב להדיא "בין דין לדין". **בין דם נדה דם לידה כו׳** — שנחלקו בדם נדה, או בדם לידה, או בדם זיבה. **ובין נגע לנגע** — שנחלקו בנגעי אדם או בנגעי בגדים. **דברי ריבות** — הוה ליה למכתב דבר ריב וכתיב "דברי ריבות" — לרבות חרמין וערכין והקדשות שהן באין וחלים על ידי דיבור הפה. **זו השקאת סוטה** — שהיא על ידי ריב שבינה ובין בעלה. **ועריפת העגלה** — שהחלל נהרג על ידי מריבה. **וטהרת מצורע** — שאף נגעים על ידי ריב של לשון הרע הם באים. **זה לקט שכחה ופאה** — שהן לעניים שכתוב בהן "ואכלו בשעריך". **וקמת מבית דין** — מדכתיב "וקמת" מכלל דיושבין עסקינן, והיינו בית דין שיושבין במקום הקבוע להם, עד עת האוכל ושם באין כל הצריכין לדין ולהוראה בכל עיר ועיר, ואזהר רחמנא לבית דין של אותה העיר שהמחלוקת ביניהם לילך ולישאל. **מלמד שבית המקדש גבוה מארץ ישראל** — "וקמת ועלית אל המקום" — שמע מינה אין לך עיר בארץ ישראל שאין ירושלים גבוה ממנה.

TRANSLATION AND COMMENTARY

[1]**and that Eretz Israel is higher than all other countries.** [2]**'To the place' — this teaches that the place** itself that was divinely chosen as the seat of the Sanhedrin **determines** the liability of any elder who contradicts a decision issued there. Only if the Sage contradicted a ruling that was issued by the Sanhedrin while it was sitting in its permanent seat in the place chosen by God is he regarded as a rebellious elder and liable to the death penalty. But if the Sanhedrin reached a decision while sitting elsewhere, a Sage who rebels against that decision is exempt from punishment."

בִּשְׁלָמָא [3]The Gemara asks: **Granted that** the verse teaches that **the Temple** in Jerusalem **is higher than the rest of Eretz Israel,** [4]**for the verse states: "And go up** to the place which the Lord your God shall choose." [5]**But from where does** the Tanna of this Baraita **know that Eretz Israel is higher than all other countries?** The verse is referring to a time when the people of Israel are dwelling in their land, and so when it speaks of "going up" to Jerusalem, it does not refer to going up from other countries! The Gemara explains: Indeed, the Tanna learns that Eretz Israel is higher than all other countries [6]**from** other verses which **state** (Jeremiah 23:7-8): **"Therefore, behold, days are coming, says the Lord, when it shall no longer be said: As the Lord lives, who brought up the Children of Israel out of the land of Egypt. But as the Lord lives, who *brought up* and who led the seed of the house of Israel out of the north country, and from all countries into which I have driven them; and they shall dwell in their own land."** Since the term "brought up" is used regarding the return of the Jewish people from exile, Eretz Israel must be the highest country in the world.

תָּנוּ רַבָּנַן [7]**Our Rabbis taught** the following Baraita: **"A rebellious elder is only liable to** the death penalty if he himself followed a practice or instructed others to follow a practice that contradicted the majority of the Sages of the Great Sanhedrin regarding a matter **whose intentional violation makes one liable to** the penalty of

[1]וְאֶרֶץ יִשְׂרָאֵל גָּבוֹהַּ מִכָּל הָאֲרָצוֹת. [2]'אֶל הַמָּקוֹם' — מְלַמֵּד שֶׁהַמָּקוֹם גּוֹרֵם". [3]בִּשְׁלָמָא בֵּית הַמִּקְדָּשׁ גָּבוֹהַּ מֵאֶרֶץ יִשְׂרָאֵל, [4]דִּכְתִיב: "וְעָלִיתָ". [5]אֶלָּא אֶרֶץ יִשְׂרָאֵל גָּבוֹהַּ מִכָּל הָאֲרָצוֹת מְנָא לֵיהּ? [6]דִּכְתִיב: "לָכֵן הִנֵּה יָמִים בָּאִים נְאֻם ה' (לֹא יֵאָמַר) חַי ה' אֲשֶׁר הֶעֱלָה אֶת בְּנֵי יִשְׂרָאֵל מֵאֶרֶץ מִצְרָיִם כִּי אִם חַי ה' אֲשֶׁר הֶעֱלָה וַאֲשֶׁר הֵבִיא אֶת זֶרַע בֵּית יִשְׂרָאֵל מֵאֶרֶץ צָפוֹנָה וּמִכֹּל הָאֲרָצוֹת אֲשֶׁר הִדַּחְתִּים שָׁם וְיָשְׁבוּ עַל אַדְמָתָם". [7]תָּנוּ רַבָּנַן: "זָקֵן מַמְרֵא אֵינוֹ חַיָּיב אֶלָּא עַל דָּבָר שֶׁזְּדוֹנוֹ כָּרֵת

LITERAL TRANSLATION

[1]and Eretz Israel is higher than all [other] countries. [2]'To the place' — this teaches that the place determines."

[3]Granted that the Temple is higher than [the rest of] Eretz Israel, [4]for it is written: "And go up." [5]But from where does he [know] that Eretz Israel is higher than all [other] countries? [6]For it is written: "Therefore, behold, days are coming, says the Lord, when it shall no longer be said: As the Lord lives, who brought up the Children of Israel out of the land of Egypt. But as the Lord lives, who brought up and who led the seed of the house of Israel out of the north country, and from all countries into which I have driven them; and they shall dwell in their own land."

[7]Our Rabbis taught: "A rebellious elder is only liable for something whose intentional violation is [subject to] excision

RASHI

וארץ ישראל גבוה מכל הארצות — תנא דברייתא קא מסיק למלתיה ולאו מהאי קרא יליף ולקמן מפרש מנלן. **אשר העלה וגו' מכל הארצות אשר הדחתים שם וישבו על אדמתם** — שמע מינה דארעא גבוה מכל הארצות דכתיב "העלה".

NOTES

זָקֵן מַמְרֵא אֵינוֹ חַיָּיב A rebellious elder is only liable. According to *Rambam* (and *Meiri*), a rebellious elder is liable if he issued a ruling that contradicted the Great Sanhedrin, whether he permitted that which the Great Sanhedrin forbade, or he forbade that which the Great Sanhedrin permitted. Others, however, disagree, and say that a rebellious elder is only liable if he permitted that which the Great Sanhedrin forbade. This position is supported by the wording of our Mishnah, "But if he ruled to act," which implies that the rebellious elder ruled that one may do that which is forbidden, but not the other way around (*Tosafot, Rabbi David Bonfil*).

HALAKHAH

מְלַמֵּד שֶׁהַמָּקוֹם גּוֹרֵם This teaches that the place determines. "If the elder rebelled against a ruling which was issued by the Sanhedrin while it was sitting outside the Chamber of Hewn Stone, he is exempt, for the Torah decrees that he is only liable for contradicting a ruling issued in the place that was divinely chosen as the seat of the Sanhedrin." (*Rambam, Sefer Shofetim, Hilkhot Mamrim* 3:7.)

זָקֵן מַמְרֵא אֵינוֹ חַיָּיב אֶלָּא עַל דָּבָר שֶׁזְּדוֹנוֹ כָּרֵת וְשִׁגְגָתוֹ חַטָּאת A rebellious elder is only liable for something whose intentional violation is subject to excision and whose unwitting violation is subject to a sin-offering. "A rebellious elder is only liable to the death penalty if he himself followed a practice or instructed others to follow a practice that contradicted the majority opinion of the

TRANSLATION AND COMMENTARY

excision and whose unwitting violation obligates one to bring **a sin-offering.** [1]**This is the position of Rabbi Meir.** [2]**Rabbi Yehudah says:** A rebellious elder is only liable to the death penalty if he issued a ruling that contradicted that of the Great Sanhedrin about a law **whose source is in the Torah** itself, [3]**but whose clarification is in the words of the Sages.** [4]**Rabbi Shimon says:** A rebellious elder is liable to the death penalty, **even** if his ruling contradicted the opinion of the Great Sanhedrin on only **a single detail of the explanations offered by the Sages** to the words of the Torah."

מַאי טַעְמָא [5]The Gemara now inquires into the reasoning of the three Tannaim whose opinions were recorded in the Baraita: **What is the reasoning of Rabbi Meir?** [6]He **learns** the scope of the term **"matter"** mentioned with regard to a rebellious elder by a *gezerah shavah* from the word **"matter"** mentioned with regard to the bull sacrificed because of an unwitting transgression committed by the community as a whole. [7]**Here,** regarding a rebellious elder, **the verse states** (Deuteronomy 17:8): **"If a *matter* arises that is too hard for you in judgment,"** [8]**and there,** regarding an unwitting transgression committed by the entire community, **the verse states** (Leviticus 4:13): **"And the *matter* is hidden from the eyes of the assembly."** [9]**Just as, there,** we are dealing with **a matter whose intentional violation makes one liable to** the penalty of **excision and whose unwitting violation obligates** one to bring **a sin-offering,** [10]**so, too, here** we must be dealing with **a matter whose intentional violation makes one liable to** the penalty of **excision and whose unwitting violation obligates** one to bring **a sin-offering.**

וְשִׁגְגָתוֹ חַטָּאת. [1]דִּבְרֵי רַבִּי מֵאִיר. [2]רַבִּי יְהוּדָה אוֹמֵר: עַל דָּבָר שֶׁעִיקָּרוֹ מִדִּבְרֵי תוֹרָה, [3]וּפֵירוּשׁוֹ מִדִּבְרֵי סוֹפְרִים. [4]רַבִּי שִׁמְעוֹן אוֹמֵר: אֲפִילּוּ דִּקְדּוּק אֶחָד מִדִּקְדּוּקֵי סוֹפְרִים״.
[5]מַאי טַעְמָא דְּרַבִּי מֵאִיר? [6]גָּמַר ״דָּבָר״ ״דָּבָר״. [7]כְּתִיב הָכָא: ״כִּי יִפָּלֵא מִמְּךָ דָבָר לַמִּשְׁפָּט״, [8]וּכְתִיב הָתָם: ״וְנֶעְלַם דָּבָר מֵעֵינֵי הַקָּהָל״. [9]מַה לְּהַלָּן, דָּבָר שֶׁחַיָּיב עַל זְדוֹנוֹ כָּרֵת וְעַל שִׁגְגָתוֹ חַטָּאת, [10]אַף כָּאן, דָּבָר שֶׁחַיָּיב עַל זְדוֹנוֹ כָּרֵת וְעַל שִׁגְגָתוֹ חַטָּאת.

LITERAL TRANSLATION

and whose unwitting violation is [subject to] a sin-offering. [1][These are] the words of Rabbi Meir. [2]Rabbi Yehudah says: For something whose source is in the Torah, [3]but whose clarification is in the words of the Sages. [4]Rabbi Shimon says: Even a single detail of the explanations of the Sages."

[5]What is the reasoning of Rabbi Meir? [6]He learns "matter" "matter." [7]It is written here: "If a matter arises [that is] too hard for you in judgment," [8]and it is written there: "And the matter is hidden from the eyes of the assembly." [9]Just as there, a matter whose intentional violation is [subject to] excision and whose unwitting violation is [subject to] a sin-offering, [10]so, too, here a matter whose intentional violation is [subject to] excision and whose unwitting violation is [subject to] a sin-offering.

RASHI

מה להלן דבר שחייבים כו׳ — כדילפינן בהוריות.

NOTES

רַבִּי מֵאִיר וְרַבִּי יְהוּדָה Rabbi Meir and Rabbi Yehudah. The Rishonim disagree about the dispute between Rabbi Meir and Rabbi Yehudah, whether Rabbi Yehudah rejects what Rabbi Meir said, or merely adds to it. He cannot totally reject what Rabbi Meir said, for a prohibition whose intentional violation makes one liable to the penalty of excision and whose unwitting violation obligates one to bring a sin-offering is surely a prohibition whose source is in the Torah, and many such prohibitions were clarified by the Sages. Some suggest that Rabbi Yehudah adds to what Rabbi Meir said, arguing that a rebellious elder can become liable to the death penalty even if his dissenting ruling did not involve a prohibition whose intentional violation makes one liable to the penalty of excision and whose unwitting violation obligates one to bring a sin-offering. Rabbi Shimon maintains that he is liable even if his ruling contradicted the opinion of the Great Sanhedrin on a single detail of the explanations offered by the Sages, which is not stated explicitly in the Torah but rather derived by one of the hermeneutic principles. According to this view, even Rabbi Shimon agrees that a rebellious elder is not liable if his ruling contradicted a Rabbinical enactment, but only if his ruling contradicted a ruling derived from the Torah itself (*Rabbi David Bonfil*).

HALAKHAH

Sanhedrin regarding a matter whose intentional violation makes one liable to the penalty of excision, and whose unwitting violation obligates one to bring a sin-offering, or if he issued a contradictory ruling regarding tefillin." (According to *Rambam*, Rabbi Yehudah does not disagree with Rabbi Meir, but rather he adds to what he said, and therefore the law is in accordance with them, against the minority opinion of Rabbi Shimon; *Radbaz, Kesef Mishneh,* and *Leḥem Mishneh.* Moreover, the Gemara discusses the opinion of Rabbi Meir, indicating that the law is in accordance with his opinion.) (*Rambam, Sefer Shofetim, Hilkhot Mamrim* 3:5.)

[1]וְרַבִּי יְהוּדָה? [2]״עַל פִּי הַתּוֹרָה אֲשֶׁר יוֹרוּךָ״ — [3]עַד דְּאִיכָּא ״תּוֹרָה״ וְ״יוֹרוּךָ״.
[4]וְרַבִּי שִׁמְעוֹן? [5]״אֲשֶׁר יַגִּידוּ לְךָ מִן הַמָּקוֹם הַהוּא״ — [6]אֲפִילּוּ כָּל דְּהוּ.
[7]אֲמַר לֵיהּ רַב הוּנָא בַּר חִינָּנָא לְרָבָא: תַּרְגְּמָא לִי לְהָא מַתְנִיתָא אַלִּיבָּא דְּרַבִּי מֵאִיר.
[8]אֲמַר לֵיהּ רָבָא לְרַב פַּפָּא: פּוֹק תַּרְגְּמָא לֵיהּ.
[9]״כִּי יִפָּלֵא״ — [10]בְּמוּפְלָא שֶׁבְּבֵית דִּין הַכָּתוּב מְדַבֵּר. [11]״מִמְּךָ״ — זֶה יוֹעֵץ, שֶׁיּוֹדֵעַ לְעַבֵּר שָׁנִים וְלִקְבּוֹעַ חֳדָשִׁים. [12]כְּדִתְנַן: ״הֵן הֵעִידוּ שֶׁמְּעַבְּרִים אֶת הַשָּׁנָה כָּל אֲדָר, [13]שֶׁהָיוּ אוֹמְרִים עַד הַפּוּרִים״. [14]דְּאִי לְהַאי גִּיסָא, קָא שָׁרֵי חָמֵץ

LITERAL TRANSLATION

[1]And Rabbi Yehudah? [2]"According to the sentence of the Torah which they shall teach you," [3]unless there is "Torah" and "they shall teach you."
[4]And Rabbi Shimon? [5]"Which they of that place shall tell you" — [6]even anything.
[7]Rav Huna bar Ḥinana said to Rava: Explain to me this Baraita according to Rabbi Meir.
[8]Rava said to Rav Pappa: Go out and explain it to him.
[9]"If there arise a matter [that is] too hard" — [10]Scripture speaks of the distinguished [member] of the court. [11]"For you" — that is a counselor, who knows how to intercalate the years and fix the months, [12]as we have learned: "They testified that we may intercalate the year all of Adar, [13]for there were those who said until Purim." [14]For if to this side, he allows leavened bread

TRANSLATION AND COMMENTARY

וְרַבִּי יְהוּדָה [1]The Gemara asks: **And** what is the reasoning of **Rabbi Yehudah?** In his view, the verse that states (Deuteronomy 17:11): [2]"And you shall do **according to the sentence of the Torah which they shall teach you,"** [3]implies that the rebellious elder is not liable **unless** he issued a ruling that contradicted the Great Sanhedrin about a law regarding which there is both **"Torah"** — an explicit Torah source — **and** a need for **"they shall teach you"** — a certain ambiguity that requires Rabbinical clarification.

וְרַבִּי שִׁמְעוֹן [4]And what is the reasoning of **Rabbi Shimon?** [5]He maintains that the verse that states (Deuteronomy 17:10): "And you shall do according to the sentence, **which they of that place shall tell you,"** implies that a rebellious elder is liable to the death penalty even if his ruling contradicted the Great Sanhedrin on [6]**even the smallest** detail of an explanation offered by the Sages to the words of the Torah.

אֲמַר לֵיהּ [7]**Rav Huna bar Ḥinana said to Rava: Explain to me the Baraita** cited above, which interprets the verse, "If a matter arises that is too hard for you," as alluding to all the types of rulings for which a rebellious elder can be sentenced to death **according to Rabbi Meir,** that a rebellious elder is only liable if he himself followed a practice that contradicted a ruling of the Great Sanhedrin on a matter whose witting violation makes one liable to excision. Where do we find a penalty of excision in all of the different areas of law mentioned in the Baraita?

אֲמַר לֵיהּ [8]**Rava said to Rav Pappa: Go out and explain** the Baraita **to** Rav Huna bar Ḥinana.

כִּי יִפָּלֵא [9]Rav Pappa explained the Baraita as follows: **"If a matter arises that is too hard"** — [10]these words intimate that **Scripture speaks** here **of a distinguished member of the court,** meaning a duly ordained Sage and not a Rabbinical student. [11]**"For you"** — these words allude to **a counselor** who is fit to offer advice on esoteric Halakhic issues and who **knows how to intercalate the years** (to decide whether or not to add a second month of Adar) — **and fix the months** (to decide whether a month should be defective, with twenty-nine days, or full, with thirty days). Fixing the calendar against the position of the Great Sanhedrin can lead to liability to the penalty of excision, [12]**for we have learned** in a Mishnah (*Eduyot* 7:7): "Rabbi Yehoshua and Rabbi Papyas **testified that** the court **may intercalate the year during the entire** month **of Adar** (until the twenty-ninth day of the month) and declare the next month a second Adar. Rabbi Yehoshua and Rabbi Papyas had to give this testimony, [13]**because there were those** Sages who disagreed and **said** that the year may only be intercalated **until Purim** (the fourteenth day of Adar)." [14]Now, **if** the Great Sanhedrin ruled **to this side** (like Rabbi Yehoshua and Rabbi Papyas) and the rebellious elder ruled in accordance with the Sages, **he allowed leavened bread** to be eaten **on**

RASHI

תרגמא לי — להאי מתניתא דלעיל, דקתני דמיקטיל אכל הני דחשיב בה הלכה, וגזירה שוה, וערכים, והקדשות, וכולהו הנך דתנא בה דתיתוקס כרבי מאיר דאמר אין חייב אלא על דבר שזדונו כרת וכו׳. **כדתנן הם העידו** — כלומר אי אפלוגתא דהנך תנאי פליגי זקן ממרא ורבנן. **הם העידו** — רבי יהושע ורבי פפיים במסכת עדיות. **שמעברין את השנה כל אדר** — ואף על פי שלא נמלכו לעבר קודם הפורים וקראו את המגילה באדר הראשון ואחר כך ראו שהשנה צריכה להתעבר ועברוה. **שהיו אומרים כו׳** — לפיכך הוצרכו להעיד כן, שהיו שאר חכמים אומרים עד הפורים מעברין ושוב אין מעברין, וטעמא מפרש במסכת ראש השנה דמן הפורים התחילו לדרוש בהלכות הפסח, דתניא: שואלים בהלכות הפסח קודם לפסח שלשים יום, וכי מרחק להו לא צייתי לשלוחי בית דין, שכבר שמעו מן

HALAKHAH

מְעַבְּרִים אֶת הַשָּׁנָה כָּל אֲדָר **We may intercalate the year all of Adar.** "The court may intercalate the year during the

TRANSLATION AND COMMENTARY

what the Great Sanhedrin had established to be **Pesah,** which falls in Nisan, the month following Adar. [1]**And if** the Great Sanhedrin **ruled to the** other **side** (like the Sages who disagree with Rabbi Yehoshua and Rabbi Papyas) and the rebellious elder ruled in accordance with Rabbi Yehoshua and Rabbi Papyas that the year can be intercalated during the entire month of Adar, [2]again **he allowed leavened bread** to be eaten **on** what the Great Sanhedrin had established to be **Pesah,** a transgression that is subject to the penalty of excision.

דָּבָר [3]Rav Pappa continues to explain the Baraita in accordance with the opinion of Rabbi Meir: The words, **"a matter,"** allude to **laws received** by Moses at Sinai. [4]**This refers to the law regarding** vaginal bleeding on **the eleventh day** after the onset of menstruation. By Torah law, a woman is ritually impure for seven days after she begins menstruating, whether she experiences bleeding for only one day or for all seven days. On the eve of the eighth day, she immerses herself in a ritual bath and purifies herself. According to a law received by Moses at Sinai, vaginal bleeding during the next eleven days is governed by different laws. The first secretion of blood during that period makes her ritually impure, and she may not engage in sexual relations. She has the status of "a woman who watches a day as against a day," meaning that she must wait until a day has passed without any vaginal bleeding, and then she may immerse herself in a ritual bath and regain ritual purity. If she experiences vaginal bleeding on three consecutive days during that eleven-day period, she has the status of a *zavah.* She must then examine herself and allow seven days to pass without seeing any discharge before she may begin her purification process, which involves immersion and the bringing of a sacrifice. [5]**It was stated** that the Amoraim disagree about a woman who experienced bleeding on **the tenth** day of this eleven-day period. All agree that if the woman experienced vaginal bleeding on the ninth day, she must "watch a day as against a day," for she can still become a *zavah* if she sees blood again on the tenth and the eleventh days. And all agree that if she experienced bleeding on the eleventh day, she does not have to "watch a day as against a day," for even if she sees blood on the twelfth day, that will be menstrual blood, and not blood that can make the woman a *zavah.* But what is the law if she experienced bleeding on the tenth day? [6]**Rabbi Yohanan said** that **the tenth** day **is like the ninth** day. [7]**And Rabbi Shimon ben Lakish said** that **the tenth** day **is like the eleventh** day. [8]The Gemara explains: **Rabbi Yohanan said: The tenth** day **is like the ninth** day — **just as** if she experienced bleeding on **the ninth** day, she is **required to watch**

בְּפֶסַח, [1]וְאִי לְהַאי גִּיסָא, [2]קָא שָׁרֵי חָמֵץ בְּפֶסַח.

[3]"דָּבָר" — זֶה הֲלָכָה. [4]זוֹ הִלְכוֹת אַחַד עָשָׂר, [5]דְּאִיתְּמַר: עֲשִׂירִי — [6]רַבִּי יוֹחָנָן אָמַר: עֲשִׂירִי כִּתְשִׁיעִי. [7]וְרַבִּי שִׁמְעוֹן בֶּן לָקִישׁ אָמַר: עֲשִׂירִי כְּאַחַד עָשָׂר. [8]רַבִּי יוֹחָנָן אָמַר: עֲשִׂירִי כִּתְשִׁיעִי — מַה תְּשִׁיעִי בָּעֵי

LITERAL TRANSLATION

on Pesah, [1]and if to this side, [2]he allows leavened bread on Pesah.

[3]"A matter" — this is a [received] law. [4]These are the laws regarding the eleventh [day], [5]as it was stated: The tenth — [6]Rabbi Yohanan said: The tenth is like the ninth. [7]And Rabbi Shimon ben Lakish said: The tenth is like the eleventh. [8]Rabbi Yohanan said: The tenth is like the ninth — just as the ninth requires

RASHI

הדרשנים לעשות הפסח בסוף שלשים ואתי לזלזולי בחמץ. **דאי להאי גיסא** — אם אמרו בית דין שבלשכת הגזית שמעברים אחר הפורים, מעוברת, כרבי יהושע ורבי פפיים, והוא אמר אינה מעוברת — קא שרי חמץ בפסח. **ואי איפכא** — נמי שרי חמץ בפסח דזדונו כרת. **הלכות אחד עשר** — יום אחרון של אחד עשר שבין נדה לנדה, קיימא לן אחד עשר יום שבין נדה לנדה הלכה למשה מסיני, משעברו שבעת ימי הנדה אינה חוזרת להיות נדה עד שיעברו אחד עשר יום, דכל דמים שרואה בהם דם זיבה הם, ואם ראתה בהם יום או יומים רצופים שומרת יום שלישי, ואם פסקה ולא ראתה בו טובלת בו ביום וטהורה, ואם ראתה שלשה ימים רצופים הויא זיבה לקרבן ולטבילת מים חיים, ואפליגו רבי יוחנן ורבי שמעון בן לקיש בהלכות יום האחרון: רבי יוחנן אמר: הלכה אחת נאמרה בו, ריש לקיש אמר: שתי הלכות נאמרו בו ליחלק משלפניו, והך פלוגתא בשילהי מסכת נדה ואתמר בתרתי לישני, וחד מנייהו נקט הכא. **עשירי רבי יוחנן אמר הרי הוא בתשיעי** — מה הרואה בתשיעי צריכה להיות שומרת עשירי — שהרי ראויה בצירוף שלשה לזיבה ושמא תראה בעשירי, הרי שנים, ותחזור ותראה באחד עשר — הרי שלשה, אף הרואה בעשירי צריכה להיות שומרת אחד עשר, ואף על פי שעשירי אינו ראוי לצירוף שלשה, שאין שנים עשר מצטרף עמהם לזיבה, דהיכא דלא ראתה שלשה רצופין להיות זבה בהנך אחד עשר יום הוי יום שנים עשר תחלת נדה, והיינו דקאמר רבי יוחנן התם הלכתא אחד עשר, הלכה אחת נאמרה בו ליחלק משלפניו, ומאי איהו דלא בעי שימור להיות שומרת שנים עשר נגדו דהא לאו מימי זיבה הוא, אבל שוה לשלפניו להיות שימור לראיית עשירי, כשם שהעשירי שימור לראיית תשיעי.

HALAKHAH

entire month of Adar, except for the thirtieth day of that month." (*Rambam, Sefer Zemanim, Hilkhot Kiddush Ha-Hodesh* 4:13-14.)

עֲשִׂירִי כִּתְשִׁיעִי **The tenth is like the ninth.** "If a woman experienced vaginal bleeding on the tenth day of the eleven-day period during which she can become a *zavah,* she may immerse herself in a ritual bath on the eleventh day, but she must take care not to touch foods that are intended to be eaten in ritual purity, for if she experiences additional bleeding on that day, everything that she touched

TRANSLATION AND COMMENTARY

the tenth day as against the ninth day, [1]so, too, if she experienced bleeding on **the tenth** day, she is **required to watch** the eleventh day as against the tenth day. [2]**Resh Lakish said: The tenth** day **is like the eleventh** day — **just as** if she experienced bleeding on **the eleventh** day, she **is not required to watch** the twelfth day as against the eleventh day, [3]**so, too,** if she experienced bleeding on **the tenth** day, she **is not required to watch** the eleventh day as against the tenth day. Issuing a ruling on this matter in contradiction to that of the Great Sanhedrin can lead to liability to excision, for someone who engages in sexual relations with a woman who is required to watch a day as against a day violates a prohibition that is subject to excision.

מִשְׁפָּט [4]The words **"in judgment"** allude to **laws derived** by way of the hermeneutic principles through which the Torah is interpreted. [87B] [5]**This refers to a law** like that **regarding** sexual intercourse with a man's **daughter from a woman whom he raped** or seduced but never married, so that the woman is his own daughter, but not the daughter of his wife. Intercourse with one's daughter is punishable by excision, and that prohibition is learned by the hermeneutic principle of *gezerah shavah*. [6]**For Rava said: Rabbi Yitzḥak bar Avudimi said to me:** The punishment imposed on a man for having intercourse with his daughter is derived by a double *gezerah shavah*. [7]The prohibition against intercourse with a daughter **is learned** by a *gezerah shavah* drawn between the words **"theirs"** found in connection with a man's relatives and the word **"they"** found in connection with his wife's relatives. Regarding a man's relatives, the verse states (Leviticus 18:10): "The nakedness of your son's daughter, or of your daughter's daughter, their nakedness you shall not uncover; for *theirs* [*henah*] is your own nakedness." And regarding his wife's relatives, the verse states (Leviticus 18:17): "You shall not uncover the nakedness of a woman and her daughter; neither shall you take her son's daughter, or her daughter's daughter, to uncover her nakedness, for *they* [*henah*] are her near kinswomen; it is wickedness." Just as a man is forbidden to his wife's daughter and granddaughter, so, too, is he forbidden to his own daughter and granddaughter. And just as intercourse with his wife's relatives is called wickedness, so, too, is intercourse with his own relatives called wickedness. [8]The significance of the **"wickedness"** relating to a man who has intercourse with his own daughter **is learned from** the word **"wickedness"** found in the verse (Leviticus 20:14): "And if a man takes a woman and her mother, it is wickedness; they shall be burnt with fire, both he and they." Just as, there, the wickedness is punished by burning, so, too, here, the wickedness is punished by burning.

בֵּין דָּם לְדָם [9]The words **"between blood and blood"** teach that a rebellious elder is liable whether he contradicted a ruling involving **menstrual blood,** [10]or a ruling involving **childbirth blood,** or a ruling involving **vaginal bleeding** other than menstruation. [11]Regarding **menstrual blood,** there is **a dispute** between the

שִׁימּוּר, [1]אַף עֲשִׂירִי בָּעֵי שִׁימּוּר. [2]רֵישׁ לָקִישׁ אָמַר: עֲשִׂירִי כְּאַחַד עָשָׂר — מָה אַחַד עָשָׂר לָא בָּעֵי שִׁימּוּר, [3]אַף עֲשִׂירִי לָא בָּעֵי שִׁימּוּר.

[4]״מִשְׁפָּט״ — זֶה הַדִּין. [87B] [5]דִּין בִּתּוֹ מֵאֲנוּסָתוֹ. [6]דְּאָמַר רָבָא: אָמַר לִי רַב יִצְחָק בַּר אֲבוּדִימִי: [7]אָתְיָא ״הֵנָּה״ ״הֵנָּה״; [8]אָתְיָא ״זִמָּה״ ״זִמָּה״.

[9]״בֵּין דָּם לְדָם״ — בֵּין דַּם נִדָּה, [10]דַּם לֵידָה, דַּם זִיבָה. [11]דַּם נִדָּה

LITERAL TRANSLATION

watching, [1]so, too, the tenth requires watching. [2]Resh Lakish said: The tenth is like the eleventh — just as the eleventh does not require watching, [3]so, too, the tenth does not require watching.

[4]"In judgment" — this is a [derived] law. [87B] [5]This is the law regarding his daughter from a woman whom he raped. [6]For Rava said: Rav Yitzḥak bar Avudimi said to me: [7]"They" is learned from "they"; [8]"wickedness" is learned from "wickedness."

[9]"Between blood and blood" — between menstrual blood, [10]childbirth blood, vaginal bleeding. [11]Menstrual blood

RASHI

וריש לקיש אמר עשירי כאחד עשר — מה אחד עשר לא בעי שימור שנים עשר שהרי אין השנים עשר מימי הזיבה, אף עשירי לא בעי שימור להיות שומרת אחד עשר, דלא נאמרה שומרת יום נגד יום אלא בראויה לצירוף שלישי, הלכך לריש לקיש שתי הלכות נאמרו ביום אחד עשר ליחלק משאר ימים שלפניו, אחת שאינו צריך שימור, ואחת שאין נעשה שימור לראיית עשירי, ואי אפלוג זקן ממרא ורבנן בהלכות אחד עשר כדאיפליגו ריש לקיש ורבי יוחנן הוי דבר שזדונו כרת, על שומרת יום כנגד יום חייב כרת כדכתיב (ויקרא טו) כל ימי זוב טומאה וגו׳ ודרשינן ״ימי״ ו״כל ימי״. **דרב יצחק בר אבודימי** — ״באלו הן הנשרפין״ פרישית לה גבי בתו מאנוסתו דמהאי דינא ילפינן, והוא דבר שזדונו כרת.

HALAKHAH

is ritually impure, following Rabbi Yoḥanan. But if she experienced the first bleeding on the eleventh day of the eleven-day period, she need not watch the twelfth day as against the eleventh day. As for relations with her husband, since Jewish women have accepted the stringency of waiting seven clean days after any vaginal bleeding whatsoever, it makes no difference whether the bleeding was experienced on the tenth day or on the eleventh day. (*Rambam, Sefer Taharah, Hilkhot Metam'ei Mishkav* 5:8.)

LANGUAGE

יָרוֹק Green. For many years the Hebrew word *yarok* ("green") referred to many hues, including leaf green, as it is used in modern Hebrew (also called "Cretan green"), but it also included yellow, as in the expression, "as green as the yoke of an egg." In ancient sources it is not always clear what color the word refers to.

TRANSLATION AND COMMENTARY

Tannaim, **Akavyah ben Mahalalel and the Rabbis,** about a matter that is subject to excision, [1]**as we have learned** in the Mishnah (*Niddah* 19a): "If a woman experiences bleeding of **greenish blood, Akavyah ben Mahalalel says** that blood is regarded as menstrual blood, and therefore the woman is **ritually impure.** [2]**The Rabbis** disagree and **say** that the blood is not menstrual blood, and therefore the woman is **ritually pure.**" Issuing a ruling on this matter in contradiction to the Great Sanhedrin can lead to liability to excision, for a man who engages in sexual relations with a woman while she is menstruating violates a prohibition that is subject to excision.

דַּם לֵידָה [3]Regarding **childbirth blood,** there is **a dispute between** the Amoraim, **Rav and Levi,** about a matter that is subject to excision. Vaginal bleeding experienced by a woman the first seven days after giving birth to a boy, and the first fourteen days after giving birth to a girl, renders her ritually impure. But bleeding which she experiences from eight to forty days after giving birth to a boy, and from fifteen to eighty days after giving birth to a girl is regarded as "blood of purity," and does not render her ritually impure. [4]**It was stated** that Rav and Levi disagreed about the relationship between bleeding immediately following childbirth, and later vaginal bleeding. **Rav said:** All of a woman's vaginal bleeding **has one source** — during the first two weeks (following the birth of a girl) **the Torah declared** the blood **ritually impure,** [5]**and** during the next sixty-six days **the Torah declared it ritually pure,** and after eighty days the Torah declared it once again ritually impure. [6]**And Levi said: There are two** separate **sources** of blood — [7]**when the ritually impure** source of blood **closes** after two weeks, **the ritually pure** source of blood **opens,** [8]and **when the ritually pure** source of blood **closes** at the end of eighty days, **the ritually impure** source of blood **opens** once again, and the woman is once again subject to the laws of menstrual blood. Elsewhere, the Gemara explains that there is a practical difference between Rav and Levi if the woman bleeds continuously between the fourteenth and fifteenth days or between the eightieth and eighty-first day. According to Rav, any bleeding experienced on the fifteenth day is automatically pure, and any bleeding experienced on the eighty-first day is automatically impure. According to Levi, if she continues to bleed on

— בִּפְלוּגְתָּא עֲקַבְיָא בֶּן מַהֲלַלְאֵל וְרַבָּנַן, [1]דִּתְנַן: "דָּם הַיָּרוֹק — עֲקַבְיָא בֶּן מַהֲלַלְאֵל מְטַמֵּא, [2]וַחֲכָמִים מְטַהֲרִין". [3]דַּם לֵידָה — בִּפְלוּגְתָּא דְּרַב וְלֵוִי. [4]דְּאִתְּמַר: רַב אָמַר: מַעְיָן אֶחָד הוּא — [5]הַתּוֹרָה טִמְּאַתּוּ, וְהַתּוֹרָה טִיהֲרַתּוּ. [6]וְלֵוִי אָמַר: שְׁנֵי מַעְיָינוֹת הֵן — [7]נִסְתָּם הַטָּמֵא, נִפְתָּח הַטָּהוֹר; [8]נִסְתָּם

LITERAL TRANSLATION

— [like] the dispute between Akavyah ben Mahalalel and the Rabbis, [1]as we have learned: "Green blood — Akavyah ben Mahalalel declares ritually impure, [2]and the Rabbis declare ritually pure." [3]Childbirth blood — [like] the dispute between Rav and Levi, [4]as it was stated: Rav said: It has one source — [5]the Torah declared it ritually impure, and the Torah declared it ritually pure. [6]And Levi said: There are two sources — [7][when] the ritually impure one closes, the ritually pure one opens; [8][when]

RASHI

הירוק עקביא בן מהללאל מטמא — דם הירוק הוי דם הנדה, ואם אמר זקן ממרא כעקביא בן מהללאל — מייתי לה לחיוב כרת, שפעמים שרואה דם הירוק בתחלת נדותה ולבסוף שני ימים רואה דם אדום ופוסקת, והיא מתחלת למנות שבעה ימים מראיית דם ירוק, וטובלת ומשמשת עם בעלה שני ימים בנדותה — לפי שדם הירוק טהור הוא והיה לה להתחיל למנות מראיית דם אדום. **מעין אחד הוא** — דם הבא בשבועיים של נקיבה — שהוא טמא, ודם הבא לאחר שבועיים — שהוא טהור, ממעין אחד הוא. **התורה טימאתו** — כל שבועיים. **והתורה טיהרתו** — לאחר שבועיים, וחזרה וטימאתו לאחר שכלין ימי טוהר. **ולוי אמר שני מעיינות הן** — **נסתם הטמא** לאחר שבועיים ונפתח הטהור, וכשנסתם הטהור בסוף ימי טוהר — נפתח הטמא, ואמרינן במסכת נדה, מאי בינייהו — בשופעת מתוך שבועיים לאחר שבועיים, או מתוך שמונים לאחר שמונים, לרב — אף על פי שלא פסק מעיינה בתוך שבועיים ויוצא דם לאחר שבועיים ממנה — טהור, וללוי — טמא עד שתפסוק שעה דנימא נסתם הטמא, והשופעת מתוך שמונים לאחר שמונים, לרב — טמאה, ואף על פי שזהו מעין עצמו של ימי טוהר, וללוי — טהורה עד שיפסוק מעין הטהור ויפתח מעין הטמא, ואי

NOTES

דָּם הַיָּרוֹק Green blood. By Torah law, a woman who experiences vaginal bleeding is ritually impure. But the Torah does not define precisely which secretions are regarded as blood for this purpose. The Rabbis concluded that a red secretion of any shade is regarded as blood, but they disagree as to secretions of other colors, whether or not they render a woman ritually impure.

HALAKHAH

דָּם הַיָּרוֹק Green blood. "If a woman experiences vaginal secretion of greenish fluid, she is not ritually impure." (*Shulḥan Arukh, Yoreh De'ah* 188:1.)

מַעְיָן אֶחָד הוּא It has one source. "All cases of vaginal bleeding have one source. What distinguishes between them is the time when the bleeding is experienced. Bleeding experienced at one time renders the woman ritually impure, whereas bleeding experienced at a different time leaves her ritually pure." (*Rambam, Sefer Kedushah, Hilkhot Issurei Bi'ah* 6:1.)

TRANSLATION AND COMMENTARY

the fifteenth day without a break from the previous day, we say that the ritually pure source of blood did not close, so the blood is ritually impure. And if she continues to bleed on the eighty-first day without a break from the previous day, we say that the ritually pure source of blood did not close, so the blood is ritually pure. Issuing a ruling on this matter in contradiction to the Great Sanhedrin can lead to liability for excision, for someone who engages in sexual relations with a woman who is ritually impure because of post-natal or menstrual bleeding violates a prohibition that is subject to excision.

דַּם זִיבָה [1]Regarding other **vaginal bleeding,** there is **a dispute between** the Tannaim, **Rabbi Eliezer and Rabbi Yehoshua,** about a matter that is subject to excision, [2]**as we have learned** in the Mishnah (*Niddah* 36b): **"If** a woman **was in labor** and experienced bleeding **for three** consecutive **days during the eleven-day** period when she is susceptable to become a *zavah*, [3]and then **she experienced relief for a full twenty-four-hour period, and then she gave birth, she is** regarded as **a woman who gave birth while suffering from a flux** of extra-menstrual blood. Thus she is governed by the laws of a *zavah* (meaning that she cannot purify herself until she counts seven clean days, and she must bring a sacrifice). But if she did not experience any relief prior to her delivery, all the vaginal bleeding that she experienced is regarded as related to her labor, and such bleeding is not impure. [4]**This is the position of Rabbi Eliezer.** [5]**Rabbi Yehoshua** disagrees and

הַטָּהוֹר, נִפְתָּח הַטָּמֵא.
[1]דַּם זִיבָה בִּפְלוּגְתָּא דְּרַבִּי אֱלִיעֶזֶר וְרַבִּי יְהוֹשֻׁעַ. [2]דִּתְנַן: ״קִישְׁתָה שְׁלֹשָׁה יָמִים בְּתוֹךְ אַחַד עָשָׂר יוֹם — [3]אִם שָׁפְתָה מֵעֵת לְעֵת וְיָלְדָה, הֲרֵי זוֹ יוֹלֶדֶת בְּזוֹב, [4]דִּבְרֵי רַבִּי אֱלִיעֶזֶר. [5]וְרַבִּי יְהוֹשֻׁעַ אוֹמֵר:

LITERAL TRANSLATION

the ritually pure closes, the ritually impure one opens.

[1]Vaginal bleeding — [like] the dispute between Rabbi Eliezer and Rabbi Yehoshua, [2]as we have learned: "[If] she was in labor for three days during the eleven days — [3]if she was relieved for a full day, and [then] she gave birth, this is a woman who gave birth while suffering from flux; [4][these are] the words of Rabbi Eliezer. [5]And Rabbi Yehoshua says:

RASHI

איפלוג זקן ממרא ורבנן בהא קאתי לידי כרת אי רבנן כרב והוא כלוי — איכא כרת לאחר ימי טוהר, ואי רבנן כלוי והוא כרב — איכא כרת בתחלת ימי טוהר, דרב לקולא ולוי לחומרא. קישתה שלשה ימים בתוך אחד עשר יום כו׳ — כתיב בפרשת זבה באחד עשר יום שבין נדה לנדה, שהם הימים המביאין לידי זיבה ״ואשה כי יזוב זוב דמה ימים רבים״, ותניא בפרק בנות כותים (נדה לו,ב): דמה מחמת עצמה ולא מחמת ולד, מגיד שדם הקישוי שיצא קודם הולד מחמת צער הקישוי אינו מביאה לידי זיבה, וכל שכן דם שלאחר הולד, אבל אם ראתה שלשה ימים רצופין בהן מתוך קושי, ושפתה קודם יציאת הולד יום אחד מעת לעת ששקטה ונחה מצערה, ואחר כך ילדה בין מתוך קושי בין מתוך שופי — הרי זו יולדת בזוב, לפי שכיון שלאחר שלשה שפתה איגלאי מילתא דלאו מחמת ולד אתא, ונעשית בהן זבה למנות שבעה נקיים כדין זבה, וכל זמן שלא תספור שבעה נקיים לא יהא דם שלה דם טוהר ואפילו לאחר שבועיים, ואחר מלאת שמונים שלה צריכה שני קרבנות, אחד ללידתה ואחד לזיבתה.

NOTES

קִישְׁתָה שְׁלֹשָׁה יָמִים **If she was in labor for three days.** A woman is ritually impure for seven days after she begins to menstruate, whether she experiences bleeding for only one day or for all seven days. On the eve of the eighth day (by Torah law, but not according to current practice), she immerses herself in a ritual bath and purifies herself. According to a law received by Moses at Sinai, any bleeding which she experiences during the next eleven days is not governed by the laws applying to menstrual bleeding, but rather by a separate body of law. If she experiences vaginal bleeding on three consecutive days during that eleven-day period, she has the status of a *zavah.* Such a woman must examine herself and allow seven days to pass without seeing any discharge before she may begin her purification process, which involves immersion and the bringing of a sacrifice. If, during labor or delivery, a pregnant woman experiences bleeding related to childbirth, she does not become ritually pure. But if she goes into labor during the eleven-day period during which she is susceptible to becoming a *zavah*, the question arises as whether the bleeding is related to her childbirth, or whether she is giving birth while suffering with prolonged vaginal bleeding. The Mishnah establishes that if the woman experienced relief from her labor pains for a significant period of time, the bleeding is regarded as prolonged vaginal bleeding, and if she did not experience such relief, the bleeding is regarded as related to her labor.

HALAKHAH

קִישְׁתָה שְׁלֹשָׁה יָמִים **If she was in labor three days.** "If a woman went into labor and experienced bleeding, and this took place during the eleven-day-period when she is susceptible to becoming a *zavah*, the law is as follows: If the woman did not experience relief from her labor pains, all her bleeding is regarded as related to her labor, and so she is not governed by the laws of a *zavah.* But if she experienced relief for a full twenty-four-hour period, and then she gave birth, she gave birth while suffering impure vaginal bleeding, and so she is governed by the laws of a *zavah*," following Rabbi Eliezer, against Rabbi Yehoshua. (*Rambam, Sefer Kedushah, Hilkhot Issurei Bi'ah* 7:1.)

TRANSLATION AND COMMENTARY

says: Only if she experienced relief for a full **night and** the following **day,** such as all of **Friday night and Shabbat day,** is her vaginal bleeding impure. But if she experienced relief for a twenty-hour period covering part of two different days, all the bleeding is regarded as related to her labor. [1]When we speak of relief, we mean that the woman **experienced relief from her pain,** even if she did **not** experience relief **from the bleeding.** If the bleeding ceased, but her pains persisted, that is not considered relief, and all her bleeding is regarded as related to her labor." Issuing a ruling on this matter in contradiction to the Great Sanhedrin can lead to liability to excision, for someone who engages in sexual relations with a *zavah* violates a prohibition that is subject to excision.

בֵּין דִּין לְדִין [2]Rav Pappa continues to explain the Baraita in accordance with the opinion of Rabbi Meir: The words **"between plea and plea"** teach that a rebellious elder is liable whether he contradicted a ruling in a **capital case** or in a **monetary case,** or in a **case involving lashes.** [3]Regarding **monetary cases,** there is **a dispute between** the Amoraim, **Shmuel and Rabbi Abbahu,** that has ramifications regarding a matter that is subject to excision. [4]**For Shmuel said:** If **two** laymen **judged** a monetary case, **their judgment is binding** on the litigants, [5]**but** the two judges **are called an impudent court,** for the case should have been heard by a court of three. [6]**Rabbi Abbahu** disagreed and **said: All** the Tannaim **agree** that if two judges adjudicated a monetary case, **their judgment is not binding** on the litigants. Issuing a ruling on this matter in contradiction to the Great Sanhedrin can lead to liability for excision, for, according to Shmuel, money awarded to a person by a court of two is legally his. If he then goes out and betroths a woman with the money, the betrothal is valid. But according to Rabbi Abbahu, such money is considered stolen property, and so the betrothal is invalid. Thus, an improper ruling can lead to liability to excision, for a man who engages in sexual intercourse with a married woman (that is, the betrothed girl, thinking that her betrothal was invalid) violates a prohibition that is subject to excision.

דִּינֵי נְפָשׁוֹת [7]Regarding **capital cases,** there is **a dispute between Rabbi** Yehudah HaNasi **and the Rabbis** that has ramifications regarding a matter that is subject to excision, [8]**for it was taught** in a Baraita dealing with someone who intended to kill one person but killed someone else: **"Rabbi** Yehudah HaNasi **says:** The verse that states (Exodus 21:22): **'Then you shall give life for life,'** refers to **monetary compensation** which the killer must pay to the woman's heirs. [9]**You say** that the verse refers to **monetary compensation, but might**

לַיְלָה וָיוֹם, כְּלֵילֵי שַׁבָּת וְיוֹמוֹ, [1]שֶׁשָּׁפְתָה מִן הַצַּעַר וְלֹא מִן הַדָּם.

[2]"בֵּין דִּין לְדִין" — בֵּין דִּינֵי מָמוֹנוֹת, דִּינֵי נְפָשׁוֹת דִּינֵי מַכּוֹת. [3]דִּינֵי מָמוֹנוֹת — בִּפְלוּגְתָּא דִּשְׁמוּאֵל וְרַבִּי אַבָּהוּ, [4]דְּאָמַר שְׁמוּאֵל: שְׁנַיִם שֶׁדָּנוּ — דִּינֵיהֶם דִּין, [5]אֶלָּא שֶׁנִּקְרָאִין בֵּית דִּין חָצוּף. [6]וְרַבִּי אַבָּהוּ אָמַר: לְדִבְרֵי הַכֹּל אֵין דִּינֵיהֶן דִּין.

[7]דִּינֵי נְפָשׁוֹת — בִּפְלוּגְתָּא דְּרַבִּי וְרַבָּנַן, [8]דְּתַנְיָא: "רַבִּי אוֹמֵר: 'וְנָתַתָּה נֶפֶשׁ תַּחַת נֶפֶשׁ' — מָמוֹן, [9]אַתָּה אוֹמֵר מָמוֹן, אוֹ

LITERAL TRANSLATION

A night and a day, like the night of Shabbat and its day, [1][and] when she was relieved of the pain, and not from the blood."

[2]"Between plea and plea" — between capital cases, monetary cases, cases involving lashes. [3]Monetary cases — [like] the dispute between Shmuel and Rabbi Abbahu, [4]for Shmuel said: Two who judged — their judgment is a judgment, [5]but they are called an impudent court. [6]And Rabbi Abbahu said: According to all, their judgment is not a judgment.

[7]Capital cases — like the dispute between Rabbi [Yehudah] and the Rabbis, [8]as it was taught: "Rabbi says: 'And you shall give life for life' — money. [9]You say money, but

RASHI

לילה ויום — אבל מעת לעת לא חשיב שופי אם שפתה משש שעות של שלישי עד שש שעות של רביעי, הואיל והוה ליה מקצת קושי ביום השופי לא הויא יולדת בזוב, ורבי אליעזר לחומרא, ורבי יהושע לקולא, והיינו דבר שזדונו כרת. **ששפתה מן הצער** — ואין אנו חוששין אם לא שפתה מן הדם. **בפלוגתא דשמואל ורבי אבהו** — וכיון דאפיקו הני בי תרי ממונא מהאי ויהבו להאי בדינא דידהו, והלך זה וקידש אשה באותו ממון — לשמואל מקודשת, לרבי אבהו אינה מקודשת — דהוה ליה קידשה בגזל, וקיימא לן בפרק שני דקידושין (נב, א) גבי מעשה דחמש נשים שנתקדשו בכלכלה: קידשה בגזל — אינה מקודשת, דהשתא אתי לידי כרת, אי רבנן כשמואל וזקן ממרא כרבי אבהו, ואי נמי רבנן כרבי אבהו וזקן ממרא כשמואל אתי לידי כרת דקא משוי להו קידושין, ואי אתי איניש אחרינא לבתר הכי וקדשה מפיק לה מבתרא בלא גט, והוה ליה דבר שזדונו כרת בלא עדים ובלא התראה, דאי איכא עדים והתראה הוי מיתת בית דין, ואי ליכא לא זה ולא זה הוי כרת. **ונתתה נפש תחת נפש** — במתכוין להרוג את זה והרג את זה, ומיחייב ליה רבי ממון ורבנן פטרי, וכפלוגתא באלו הן הנשרפין, ואי תפסו יורשין דהרוג ממונא דהורג ופטר ליה זקן ממרא, וקידשו בו את האשה, לרבי — מקודשת, לרבנן — אינה מקודשת, ואי אתי איניש אחרינא וקידשה — מקודשת לשני, הרי חיוב כרת בדבר.

TRANSLATION AND COMMENTARY

it not refer **actually** to the taking of the killer's **life?** [1]The term **'giving' is mentioned below** (verse 23) — 'Then you shall give life for life,' [2]**and** the term **'giving' is mentioned above** (verse 22) — 'And he shall give as the judges determine.' [3]**Just as, there,** the verse refers to **monetary compensation** for the loss of the unborn fetus, [4]**so, too, here,** the verse refers to **monetary compensation** for the loss of the woman." But the Rabbis disagree with Rabbi Yehudah HaNasi, and say that the assailant is not liable to pay monetary compensation. Issuing a ruling on this matter in contradiction to the Great Sanhedrin can lead to liability to excision, for, according to Rabbi Yehudah, if the victim's heir seized compensation from the assailant, it is legally his, and if he then betrothed a woman with the money, the betrothal is valid. But according to the Sages, the money is stolen, and the betrothal is invalid. If someone else then betrothed the woman, the second betrothal is valid. If the first husband then had intercourse with her, thinking they were betrothed, he would be committing a transgression subject to excision.

דִּינֵי מַכּוֹת [5]Regarding **cases involving lashes,** there is **a dispute between Rabbi Yishmael and the Rabbis** that has ramifications regarding a matter that is subject to excision, [6]**as we have learned** in the Mishnah earlier in the tractate (2a): "A case involving the transgression of a negative commandment which is punishable by **lashes** requires a court of **three** judges. [7]**In the name of Rabbi Yishmael it was said:** Such a case requires a court of **twenty-three."** Issuing a ruling on this matter in contradiction to the Great Sanhedrin can lead to liability to excision, for, according to the Rabbi Yishmael, if a court of three flogged the defendant, they must pay him compensation like anyone else who injures another person. The money is legally his, and if he then betroths a woman with it, the betrothal is valid. But according to the Rabbis, the lashes were administered legally. Thus, if the defendant seized money as compensation, and then betrothed a woman with it, the betrothal is invalid. As above, this situation can give rise to sexual relations punishable by excision.

בֵּין נֶגַע לְנֶגַע [8]Rav Pappa continues to explain the Baraita in accordance with the opinion of Rabbi Meir: The words **"between plague and plague"** teach that a rebellious elder is liable whether his ruling related to **leprosy** found **on people,** or **leprosy** found **on houses,** or **leprosy** found **on garments.** [9]Regarding **leprosy** found **on people,** there is **a dispute between Rabbi Yehoshua and the Rabbis** that has ramifications regarding a matter that is subject to excision, [10]**as we have learned** in the Mishnah (*Negaim* 4:11): **"If the** appearance of **a bright spot** on the skin, minimally the size of a bean, **precedes** the appearance on the same spot of at least two **white hairs,** the afflicted one **is** immediately declared by the priest to be **ritually**

אֵינוֹ אֶלָּא נֶפֶשׁ מַמָּשׁ? [1]נֶאֱמַר 'נְתִינָה' לְמַעְלָה [2]וְנֶאֱמַר 'נְתִינָה' לְמַטָּה. [3]מַה לְהַלָּן — מָמוֹן, [4]אַף כָּאן — מָמוֹן". [5]דִּינֵי מַכּוֹת — בִּפְלוּגְתָּא דְּרַבִּי יִשְׁמָעֵאל וְרַבָּנַן. [6]דִּתְנַן: "מַכּוֹת בִּשְׁלֹשָׁה. [7]מִשּׁוּם רַבִּי יִשְׁמָעֵאל אָמְרוּ: בְּעֶשְׂרִים וּשְׁלֹשָׁה". [8]"בֵּין נֶגַע לְנֶגַע" — בֵּין נִגְעֵי אָדָם, נִגְעֵי בָתִּים, נִגְעֵי בְגָדִים. [9]נִגְעֵי אָדָם — בִּפְלוּגְתָּא דְּרַבִּי יְהוֹשֻׁעַ וְרַבָּנַן, [10]דִּתְנַן: "אִם בַּהֶרֶת קָדַם לַשֵּׂעָר הַלָּבָן, טָמֵא,

LITERAL TRANSLATION

might it not be an actual life? [1]'Giving' is mentioned above, [2]and 'giving' is mentioned below. [3]Just as below — money, [4]so, too, here — money."

[5]Cases involving lashes — [like] the dispute between Rabbi Yishmael and the Rabbis, [6]as we have learned: "Lashes by three. [7]In the name of Rabbi Yishmael they said: By twenty-three."

[8]"Between plague and plague" — between plagues on people, plagues on houses, plagues on garments. [9]Plagues on people — [like] the dispute between Rabbi Yehoshua and the Rabbis, [10]as we have learned: "If the bright spot preceded the white hair, he is ritually impure,

RASHI

נתינה למעלה — גבי נוגף אשה הרה ונתן בפלילים (שמות כא) — דמי ולדות.

בעשרים ושלשה — ואם הלקוהו שלשה, לרבי ישמעאל חייבין לו ממון כשאר חובל בחבירו ומקדש בו את האשה, ולרבנן בדין הלקוהו, ואם תפס ממונו וקידש בו אינה מקודשת.

NOTES

מַכּוֹת בִּשְׁלֹשָׁה **Lashes by three.** It has been asked why the judges would be required to compensate the victim of these lashes, since they themselves did not flog him. Rather, an agent of the court administered the punishment, and since the self-styled court had no legal authority, it could not appoint an agent. Hence the man who flogged the defendant should be personally culpable for the injury he caused (see *Netzot HaḤoshen* and *Tzafnat Pa'ane'aḥ*). This Halakhic problem remains an open question.

HALAKHAH

סָפֵק, אִם בַּהֶרֶת קָדַם **If there is a doubt whether the bright spot preceded.** "In case of doubt whether the appearance

[1]אִם שֵׂעָר לָבָן קָדַם לַבַּהֶרֶת, טָהוֹר. [2]סָפֵק, טָמֵא. [3]רַבִּי יְהוֹשֻׁעַ אוֹמֵר: כֵּהָה״. [4]מַאי ״כֵּהָה״? [5]אָמַר רָבָא: ״כֵּהָה״ טָהוֹר.
[6]נִגְעֵי בָתִּים — בִּפְלוּגְתָּא דְּרַבִּי אֶלְעָזָר בְּרַבִּי שִׁמְעוֹן וְרַבָּנַן. [7]דִּתְנַן: ״רַבִּי אֶלְעָזָר בְּרַבִּי שִׁמְעוֹן אוֹמֵר: לְעוֹלָם אֵין הַבַּיִת טָמֵא עַד שֶׁיֵּרָאֶה כִּשְׁנֵי גְּרִיסִין, עַל שְׁתֵּי אֲבָנִים, בִּשְׁתֵּי כְתָלִים, בְּקֶרֶן זָוִית, אָרְכּוֹ כִּשְׁנֵי גְּרִיסִין וְרָחְבּוֹ כִּגְרִיס״. [8]מַאי טַעְמָא דְּרַבִּי אֶלְעָזָר בְּרַבִּי שִׁמְעוֹן? [9]כְּתִיב ״קִיר״, [10]וּכְתִיב ״קִירֹת״. [11]אֵיזֶהוּ קִיר שֶׁהוּא כְּקִירוֹת? [12]הֱוֵי אוֹמֵר זֶה קֶרֶן זָוִית.

LITERAL TRANSLATION

[1][and] if the white hair preceded the bright spot, he is pure. [2][If there is] a doubt, he is ritually impure. [3]Rabbi Yehoshua says: It became dim." [4]What is [meant by] "it became dim"? [5]Rava said: "It became dim" [means] he is ritually pure.

[6]Plagues on houses — [like] the dispute between Rabbi Elazar the son of Rabbi Shimon and the Rabbis, [7]as we have learned: "Rabbi Elazar the son of Rabbi Shimon says: A house does not become defiled unless [a leprous spot] is seen the size of two barleycorns on two stones, on two walls in a corner, its length two barleycorns and its width one barleycorn." [8]What is the reason[ing] of Rabbi Elazar the son of Rabbi Shimon? [9]It is written "wall," [10]and it is written "walls." [11]Which wall is like walls? [12]Say that is a corner.

TRANSLATION AND COMMENTARY

impure. [1]But **if** the appearance of two **white hairs precedes** the appearance in the same place of **a bright spot,** then he **is** still considered to be **ritually pure.** [2]**In a case of doubt,** the individual **is** declared to be **ritually impure.** [3]**And Rabbi Yehoshua says: It became dim."** [4]**What** did Rabbi Yehoshua mean when he said: **"It became dim"?** [5]**Rava said:** The expression **"it became dim"** means that in a case of doubt we treat the spot as if it has receded, and the afflicted individual **is** still considered to be **ritually pure.** Issuing a ruling on this matter in contradiction to that of the Great Sanhedrin can lead to liability to excision, for if in a case of doubt the afflicted person entered the Temple, the Rabbis maintain that he is liable to excision, whereas according to Rabbi Yehoshua he is exempt from that punishment.

נִגְעֵי בָתִּים [6]Regarding **leprosy** found **on houses,** there is **a dispute between Rabbi Elazar the son of Rabbi Shimon and the Rabbis** that has ramifications regarding a matter that is subject to excision, [7]**as we have learned** in the Mishnah (*Negaim* 12:3): **"Rabbi Elazar the son of Rabbi Shimon says: A house does not become defiled unless a leprous spot the size of two barleycorns is seen on two** adjacent **stones, on two** different **walls** that meet **in the corner** of the house, that spot being **two barleycorns long and one barleycorn wide."** But according to the Rabbis, a house can become defiled even if the leprous spot was not found in the corner. Regarding that Mishnah, the Gemara asks: [8]**What is the reasoning of Rabbi Elazar the son of Rabbi Shimon?** [9]**The verse states** (Leviticus 14:37): "Which in sight are lower than the *wall,*" [10]**and that** same **verse states:** "And, behold, if the plague be in the *walls* of the houses." [11]**Which wall** (singular) **is like walls** (plural)? [12]**Say that** the Torah is referring to a leprous spot found in **the corner** of a house, half on one wall and half on the adjacent wall. Issuing a ruling on this matter in contradiction to the Great Sanhedrin can lead to liability to excision, for if a person entered a house where a leprous spot was found, but not in a corner, and then he entered the Temple, according to the Rabbis, he is liable to excision, whereas according to Rabbi Elazar, the son of Rabbi Shimon, he is exempt.

RASHI

ספק — אם זה קדם אם זה קדם. בהה — כאילו כהה הנגע דהוי מסימני טהרה כשמשתנה הלובן לאחר הסגר, ולרבנן אם נכנס למקדש חייב כרת, ולרבי יהושע פטור. עד שיראה בשני גריסין — שיעור הנגע כגריס על גריס, וכתיב "את האבנים אשר בהן הנגע" — שיהא הנגע על שתי אבנים על כל אחד ואחד שיעור נגע, על שתי כתלים ובקרן זוית, כגון מקצוע דרומית מזרחית אורכו כשני גריסין ורחבו כגריס, שיהא בקיר הדרומי גריס וכן בקיר המזרחי, והנגע כולו מחובר כאחד. מאי טעמא דרבי אליעזר — דבעי קרן זוית. כתיב — "ומראיהן שפל מן הקיר" (ויקרא יד) וכתיב "והנה הנגע בקירות הבית". זה קרן זוית — ורבנן לא בעו קרן זוית, והיכא דליתיה בקרן זוית ונכנס בה אדם ואחר כך נכנס למקדש, לרבנן חייב כרת, לרבי אלעזר ברבי שמעון פטור.

LANGUAGE

אַבְטוֹלְמוֹס **Avtolmos.** This word dervives from the Greek εὔτολμος, *evtolmos,* which means "courageous," or "heroic."

HALAKHAH

of a bright spot on the skin preceded the appearance on the same spot of at least two white hairs, or whether the appearance of two white hairs preceded the appearance in the same place of a bright spot, the individual is declared ritually impure," following the Sages. According to *Rambam,* this is doubtful ritual impurity. (*Rambam, Sefer Taharah, Hilkhot Tum'at Tzara'at* 2:9.)

לְעוֹלָם אֵין הַבַּיִת טָמֵא **A house does not become defiled.** "A house does not become defiled unless a leprous spot the size of two barleycorns is seen on two adjacent stones, but not necessarily on two different walls that meet in a corner of the house," following the Sages who disagree with Rabbi Elazar the son of Rabbi Shimon. (*Rambam, Sefer Taharah, Hilkhot Tum'at Tzara'at* 14:1,7.)

[1]נִגְעֵי בְגָדִים — בִּפְלוּגְתָּא דְּרַבִּי יוֹנָתָן בֶּן אַבְטוֹלְמוֹס וְרַבָּנַן, [2]דְּתַנְיָא: ״רַבִּי יוֹנָתָן בֶּן אַבְטוֹלְמוֹס אוֹמֵר: מִנַּיִן [88A] לִפְרִיחָה בִּבְגָדִים שֶׁהִיא טְהוֹרָה — [3]נֶאֶמְרָה קָרַחַת וְגַבַּחַת בָּאָדָם, [4]וְנֶאֶמְרָה קָרַחַת וְגַבַּחַת בִּבְגָדִים. [5]מַה לְּהַלָּן — פָּרַח בְּכוּלּוֹ טָהוֹר, [6]אַף כָּאן — פָּרַח בְּכוּלּוֹ טָהוֹר״.

[7]״דְּבָרֵי״ — אֵלּוּ הָעֲרָכִין וְהַחֲרָמִים וְהֶקְדֵּישׁוֹת. [8]הָעֲרָכִין — בִּפְלוּגְתָּא דְּרַבִּי מֵאִיר וְרַבָּנַן. [9]דִּתְנַן: ״הַמַּעֲרִיךְ פָּחוֹת מִבֶּן חֹדֶשׁ, [10]רַבִּי מֵאִיר אוֹמֵר: נוֹתֵן

LITERAL TRANSLATION

[1]Plagues on garments — like the dispute between Rabbi Yonatan ben Avtolmos and the Rabbis, [2]as it was taught: "Rabbi Yonatan ben Avtolmos says: From where [do we know] [88A] that an outbreak [of leprosy] on garments is ritually pure? [3]*Karahat* and *gabahat* are mentioned with regard to a person, [4]and *karahat* and *gabahat* are mentioned with regard to garments. [5]Just as there — if it erupted on all of him, he is ritually pure, [6]so, too, here, if it erupted on all of it, it is ritually pure."

[7]"Matters" — these are valuations, consecrations, and dedications. [8]Valuations — like the dispute between Rabbi Meir and the Rabbis, [9]as we have learned: "[If] someone vows the value of [an infant] less than a month old, [10]Rabbi Meir says: He pays

TRANSLATION AND COMMENTARY

נִגְעֵי בְגָדִים [1]Regarding **leprosy** found **on garments,** there is **a dispute between Rabbi Yonatan ben Avtolmos and the Rabbis** that has ramifications regarding a matter that is subject to excision, [2]**as it was taught** in a Baraita: **"Rabbi Yonatan ben Avtolmos says: From where do we know** [88A] **that** if leprous spots **erupt across a garment,** so that the entire garment becomes filled with leprosy, the garment **is** declared **ritually pure?** [3]*Karahat* (baldness of the back of the head) **and** *gabahat* (baldness of the front) **are mentioned with regard to** leprosy found on **a person,** for the verse states (Leviticus 13:42): 'And if there is in the bald head [קָרַחַת] or bald forehead [גַבַּחַת], a white reddish sore,' [4]**and** *karahat* **and** *gabahat* **are mentioned with regard to** leprosy found on **garments,** for the verse states (Leviticus 13:55): 'It is decay on the inner [בְּקָרַחְתּוֹ] or outer surface [בְגַבַּחְתּוֹ].' [5]**Just as, there,** regarding leprosy found on a person, **if** leprous spots **erupted over all his** body, **he is** declared **ritually pure,** as the verses state (Leviticus 13:12-13): 'And if the leprosy breaks out abroad in the skin, and the leprosy covers all the skin of him that has the plague from his head to his foot...he is clean,' [6]**so, too, here,** regarding leprosy found on a garment, **if** leprous spots **erupted over all** the garment, **it** should **be** declared **ritually pure."** But the Rabbis disagree and say that the garment is ritually impure. Issuing a ruling on this matter in contradiction to the Great Sanhedrin can lead to liability to excision, for if someone touched a garment covered completely by leprous spots, and then he entered the Temple, according to the Rabbis he is liable to excision, whereas according to Rabbi Yonatan ben Avtolmos he is exempt.

דְּבָרֵי [7]Rav Pappa continues to explain the Baraita in accordance with the opinion of Rabbi Meir: The word **"matters"** teaches that a rebellious elder is liable whether his ruling related to **valuations,** or **consecrations, or dedications** of property or money to the Temple or the Temple Treasury. [8]Regarding **valuations,** there is **a dispute between Rabbi Meir and the Rabbis** that has ramifications regarding a matter that is subject to excision, [9]**as we have learned** in a Baraita: **"If someone makes a vow,** using the expression, 'I promise to pay the **value of an infant less than a month old,'** [10]**Rabbi Meir says: He** must **pay** the Temple Treasury **the** market **value** of the infant. Ordinarily, when someone makes such a vow, the amount is not calculated according to the presumed market value of the particular person whose value he promised to pay. Rather, it is established according to specific values set by the Torah. Since the Torah did not set a value to a person less than one month old, we assume that someone who promised the value of such a person

RASHI

לפריחה בבגדים — ״אם פרוח תפרח״ הצרעת ונתמלא כל הבגד. **אדם שפרחה בכולו טהור** — דכתיב (ויקרא יג) ״אם פרוח תפרח הצרעת וגו׳״ ופליגי רבנן עליה, והיכא דפרחה בבגד כולו והכניסו למקדש, או הנוגע בו נכנס למקדש — לרבנן חייב ולרבי יונתן פטור. **המעריך פחות מבן חדש** — אמר על פחות מבן חדש: ערכו עלי, והתורה לא נתנה לו ערך דגבי ערכין כתיב (ויקרא כז) ״ואם מבן חדש וגו׳״. **רבי מאיר אומר נותן דמיו** — כמה שהוא נמכר בשוק, דקסבר אין אדם מוציא דבריו לבטלה, ויודע שאין ערך לפחות מבן חדש וגמר ואמר לשם דמים, ולרבנן פטור, ואם בא גיזבר ומשכנו — לרבי מאיר הוי הקדש, ואין אשה מתקדשת בו אלא אם כן יודע בו כדתנן (קידושין נג,ב) ובהקדש — במזיד קידש, בשוגג — לא קידש, ולרבנן לא הוי הקדש והרי הוא של בעלים לקדש בו האשה, והאחר שקדש בו אינה מקודשת, אי נמי: לרבי מאיר הוי הקדש והנהנה ממנו מביא אשם מעילות,

CONCEPTS

עֲרָכִין **Valuations.** Regarding vows made to the Temple Treasury, there is a difference between vows in the form of "valuations" — where a person promises to pay the value ("עֵרֶךְ") of a certain person — and ordinary vows — where a person promises to donate to the Temple the sum that a certain person is worth ("דָּמִים"). When a person makes a vow in the form of a "valuation," the sum to be paid is not calculated according to the presumed market value of the particular person whose value he promised to pay, but rather it is established according to specific values set by the Torah. These values depend only on the sex and the age of the person whose value was promised, and apply to all Jews over one month old. In contrast, when a person vows to donate the sum that a certain person is worth, he pays the presumed market value of the particular person if he were sold as a slave. That value depends on his physique, his health, and his abilities.

HALAKHAH

הַמַּעֲרִיךְ פָּחוֹת מִבֶּן חֹדֶשׁ **If someone vows the value of an infant less than a month old.** "If someone made a vow, saying, 'I promise to pay the value of an infant less than a month old,' he did not say anything," following the Sages. (*Rambam, Sefer Hafla'ah, Hilkhot Arakhin* 1:3.)

TRANSLATION AND COMMENTARY

intended to pay his market value. [1]**The Sages** disagree and **say:** If a person formulated his vow in that manner, **he did not say anything,** and he owes nothing to the Temple Treasury." Issuing a ruling on this matter in contradiction to that of the Great Sanhedrin can lead to liability to excision if the person betrothed a woman with the money set aside to fulfill his vow.

הַחֲרָמִים [2]Regarding **consecrations,** there is **a dispute between Rabbi Yehudah ben Beterah and the Rabbis** that has ramifications regarding a matter that is subject to excision, [3]**as we have learned** in the Mishnah (*Arakhin* 8:6): **"Rabbi Yehudah ben Beterah says:** If someone **consecrates property without specifying** whether he is consecrating it for the maintenance of the Temple, or for use by the priests, it is consecrated **for the maintenance of the Temple,** [4]**as the verse states** (Leviticus 27:28): **'Every consecrated thing is most holy to the Lord.'** [5]**The Sages** disagree and **say:** If someone **consecrates property without specifying** the intended use, it is consecrated **for** use by **the priests,** [6]**as the verse states** (Leviticus 27:21): **'As a consecrated field, the possession of it shall be the priest's.'** [7]**If so, why does the verse state: 'It is most holy to the Lord'?** [8]**That** verse teaches that consecration **applies** both **to the holiest sacrifices and to sacrifices of lesser holiness.** Even sacrifices that have been dedicated for the altar can be consecrated again so that the person who consecrated them must pay their value to the Temple Treasury." Whether property that was consecrated without specification is sacred or mundane has ramifications regarding betrothal and the prohibition against unlawful use of consecrated property which can lead to liability to excision.

דָּמָיו, [1]וַחֲכָמִים אוֹמְרִים: לֹא אָמַר כְּלוּם".

[2]הַחֲרָמִים — בִּפְלוּגְתָּא דְּרַבִּי יְהוּדָה בֶּן בְּתֵירָה וְרַבָּנַן, [3]דִּתְנַן: "רַבִּי יְהוּדָה בֶּן בְּתֵירָה אוֹמֵר: סְתָם חֲרָמִים לְבֶדֶק הַבַּיִת, [4]שֶׁנֶּאֱמַר: 'כָּל חֵרֶם קֹדֶשׁ קָדָשִׁים הוּא לַה'. [5]וַחֲכָמִים אוֹמְרִים: סְתָם חֲרָמִים לַכֹּהֵן, [6]שֶׁנֶּאֱמַר: 'כִּשְׂדֵה הַחֵרֶם לַכֹּהֵן תִּהְיֶה אֲחֻזָּתוֹ'. [7]אִם כֵּן, מַה תַּלְמוּד לוֹמַר: 'קֹדֶשׁ קָדָשִׁים הוּא לַה'? [8]שֶׁחָל עַל קָדְשֵׁי קָדָשִׁים וְעַל קָדָשִׁים קַלִּים".

LITERAL TRANSLATION

his value. [1]And the Sages say: He did not say anything."

[2]Consecrations — like the dispute between Rabbi Yehudah ben Beterah and the Rabbis, [3]as we have learned: "Rabbi Yehudah ben Beterah says: Unspecified consecrations to the maintenance of the Temple, [4]as it is stated: 'Every consecrated thing is most holy to the Lord.' [5]And the Sages say: Unspecified consecrations to the priest, [6]as it is stated: 'As a consecrated field, the possession of it shall be the priest's.' [7]If so, what does the verse teach: 'It is most holy to the Lord'? [8]That it applies to the holiest sacrifices and to sacrifices of lesser holiness."

RASHI

והרי אותו אשם קדשי קדשים והאוכלו בטומאת גופו — חייב כרת, ולרבנן לא הוי הקדש והרי של בעלים הוא — והנהנה ממנו לא מעל, ואם הביא אשם מעילות חולין לעזרה הוא ואין חייבין עליו משום טומאה. **לבדק הבית** — ומועלין בהן. **לכהנים** — ואין מועלין בהם. **שחל על קדשי קדשים** — כדתנן (ערכין כח,ב) מחרים אדם את קדשיו, אם נדר — נותן דמיהם, ואם נדבה — נותן את טובתם כפי חלק שיש לו בה, כדמפרש במסכת ערכין בפרק "המקדיש".

NOTES

שֶׁחָל עַל קָדְשֵׁי קָדָשִׁים וְעַל קָדָשִׁים קַלִּים **It applies to the holiest sacrifices and to sacrifices of lesser holiness.** When a person consecrates property that has already been dedicated to the altar, the consecration does not apply to the animal itself, but rather to its residual value remaining in the owner's hands after the animal was consecrated. Therefore, if the consecrated animal was a *neder,* i.e., he had offered to bring a sacrifice, saying that he undertakes to bring an animal, but not obligating himself to bring a particular animal (in which case, if the animal designated as a sacrifice is lost or dies, he must bring another offering in its place), he must give the Temple Treasury the full value of the animal. But if the consecrated animal was a *nedavah,* i.e., he had undertaken to bring that particular animal as a sacrifice, he must give the Temple Treasury the value of the benefit he derives by offering the animal as a free-will offering. We determine that value by assessing how much a person would be willing to pay to offer such an animal as his own voluntary-offering.

HALAKHAH

סְתָם חֲרָמִים **Unspecified consecrations.** "If someone consecrates property without specifying whether he is consecrating it for the maintenance of the Temple, or he is consecrating it for use by the priests, it is consecrated for use by the priests," following the Sages. (*Rambam, Sefer Hafla'ah, Hilkhot Arakhin* 6:1.)

שֶׁחָל עַל קָדְשֵׁי קָדָשִׁים וְעַל קָדָשִׁים קַלִּים **That it applies to the holiest sacrifices and to sacrifices of lesser holiness.** "A person can consecrate sacrifices that have been dedicated for the altar — both the holiest sacrifices and sacrifices of lesser holiness — so that he must pay their value to the Temple Treasury." (*Rambam, Sefer Hafla'ah, Hilkhot Arakhin* 6:11.)

TRANSLATION AND COMMENTARY

הֶקְדֵּשׁוֹת [1]Regarding **dedications,** there is **a dispute between Rabbi Eliezer ben Ya'akov and the Rabbis** that has ramifications regarding a matter that is subject to excision, [2]**as it was taught** in a Baraita: **"Rabbi Eliezer ben Ya'akov says: Even a hook of consecrated property needs ten people** to assess its value if one is to **redeem it."** The Rabbis disagree and say that an assessment made by three people suffices. Thus, whether we rule in accordance with Rabbi Eliezer ben Ya'akov or in accordance with the Rabbis has ramifications regarding unlawful use of consecrated property, which can lead to being subject to excision.

רִיבֹת [3]The Baraita cited above taught that the word **"controversy"** alludes to rulings involving the ceremonies of **making a woman who is** suspected of infidelity **drink** bitter waters; **breaking the neck of a heifer** when a murdered person's body is found outside a town, and it is not known who caused his death; **and purifying a leper.** [4]As for **making a woman who is** suspected of infidelity **drink** bitter waters, there is **a dispute between Rabbi Eliezer and Rabbi Yehoshua** that has ramifications regarding a matter that is subject to excision, [5]**as we have learned** in the Mishnah (*Sotah* 2a): "Regarding **someone who suspects his wife** of infidelity, the Tannaim disagree. [6]**Rabbi Eliezer says:** The husband **must warn** his wife **in the presence of two** witnesses not to seclude herself with a particular man, **and he** may later **give her** the bitter waters **to drink on the basis of** his evidence or that of another witness who saw the woman seclude herself with the man about whom he is suspicious. [7]**Rabbi Yehoshua says:** The husband **must warn** his wife **in the presence of two** witnesses, **and he** can only **give her** the bitter waters **to drink on the basis of two** witnesses who saw her seclude herself with that other man." This dispute can have ramifications regarding a matter that is subject

[1]הֶקְדֵּשׁוֹת — בִּפְלוּגְתָּא דְּרַבִּי אֱלִיעֶזֶר בֶּן יַעֲקֹב וְרַבָּנַן. [2]דְּתַנְיָא: "רַבִּי אֱלִיעֶזֶר בֶּן יַעֲקֹב אוֹמֵר: אֲפִילּוּ צִינּוֹרָא שֶׁל הֶקְדֵּשׁ צְרִיכָה עֲשָׂרָה בְּנֵי אָדָם לִפְדוֹתָהּ".

[3]"רִיבֹת" — זֶה הַשְׁקָאַת סוֹטָה וַעֲרִיפַת הָעֶגְלָה וְטָהֳרַת מְצוֹרָע. [4]הַשְׁקָאַת סוֹטָה — בִּפְלוּגְתָּא דְּרַבִּי אֱלִיעֶזֶר וְרַבִּי יְהוֹשֻׁעַ. [5]דִּתְנַן: "הַמְקַנֵּא לְאִשְׁתּוֹ, [6]רַבִּי אֱלִיעֶזֶר אוֹמֵר: מְקַנֵּא עַל פִּי שְׁנַיִם, וּמַשְׁקָה עַל פִּי עֵד אֶחָד אוֹ עַל פִּי עַצְמוֹ. [7]רַבִּי יְהוֹשֻׁעַ אוֹמֵר: מְקַנֵּא עַל פִּי

LITERAL TRANSLATION

[1]Dedications — like the dispute between Rabbi Eliezer ben Ya'akov and the Rabbis, [2]as it was taught: "Rabbi Eliezer ben Ya'akov says: Even a hook of consecrated property needs ten people to redeem it."

[3]"Controversy" — this is making an allegedly unfaithful wife drink, breaking the neck of a heifer, and purifying a leper. [4]Making an allegedly unfaithful wife drink — like the dispute between Rabbi Eliezer and Rabbi Yehoshua, [5]as we have learned: "Someone who suspects his wife, [6]Rabbi Eliezer says: He must warn her in the presence of two, and he makes her drink on the basis of one or himself. [7]Rabbi Yehoshua says: He must warn her in the presence

RASHI

צינורא — מזלג קטן שטווין בו זהב. עשרה כהנים — כדמפרש בפרק קמא, עשרה כהניס כתובין בפרשה, אם נפדית בפחות מעשרה בני אדם עדיין הקדש היא ומועלין בה, ולרבנן אין מועלין בה. המקנא לאשתו — המתרה באשתו: אל תסתרי עם איש פלוני. ומשקה על פי עד אחד — שבא ואמר: אני ראיתיה שנסתרה, ואם לא השקה נאסרת עליו, ותנן (סוטה כד,א) אלו לא שותות ולא נוטלות כתובתן: האומרת איני שותה, והיכא דליכא עידי סתירה ואמרה איני שותה — לרבי אליעזר אין לה כתובה, לרבי יהושע יש לה כתובה, שאינה נאסרת עליו, ואם מכרה לאחר כתובתה — קנה, ואם תופס ממונו של זה כדי כתובה — הרי הוא שלו לקדש בו את האשה, ולרבי אליעזר הוי גזל ולא קידש.

NOTES

הַשְׁקָאַת סוֹטָה **Making an allegedly unfaithful wife drink.** The dispute regarding the number of witnesses required in order to give an allegedly unfaithful wife the bitter waters to drink has ramifications regarding a matter that is subject to excision in another way as well. If the husband died before giving his wife the bitter waters to drink, and he did not have any children, she may or may not be able to contract a levirate marriage with his brother. If he could not have given her the bitter waters to drink, because two witnesses to her seclusion are required, she was still his fit wife, and she is permitted to enter into levirate marriage with her deceased husband's brother. But if the husband could have given his wife the bitter waters to drink, because only one witness is required, then she was already forbidden to him, and she is forbidden now to her brother-in-law by a prohibition whose violation is punishable by excision (*Meiri*).

HALAKHAH

מְקַנֵּא עַל פִּי שְׁנַיִם **He must warn her in the presence of two.** "Someone who suspects his wife of infidelity must warn her in the presence of two witnesses not to seclude herself with a particular man, and he can only make her drink the bitter waters on the basis of the evidence of two witnesses," following Rabbi Yehoshua. (*Rambam, Sefer Nashim, Hilkhot Sotah* 1:1,2.)

TRANSLATION AND COMMENTARY

to excision, for a woman who was properly warned and then seen secluding herself with another man is forbidden to her husband until she drinks the bitter waters, and if she refuses to drink the waters, she forfeits her ketubah. Now, if there was only one witness to her seclusion, and she refuses to drink the waters, according to Rabbi Eliezer she is still entitled to her ketubah, whereas according to Rabbi Yehoshua, she forfeits it. And if the woman sold her ketubah, and the husband seized property from the buyer to the value of the ketubah, and then betrothed another woman with that property, according to Rabbi Eliezer the betrothal is not valid, for the man had no right to the money, whereas according to Rabbi Yehoshua the betrothal is valid, for the money was his.

עֲרִיפַת עֶגְלָה [1]As for **breaking the neck of a heifer** when a murder victim is found outside a town, and it is not known who caused his death, there is **a dispute between Rabbi Eliezer and Rabbi Akiva** that has ramifications regarding a matter that is subject to excision, [2]**as we have learned** in the Mishnah (*Sotah* 45b): "When the judges from the Great Sanhedrin measured the distance between the corpse and the nearest town, in order to determine which town must perform the rite of breaking the neck of the heifer, **from which** part of the corpse **would they measure?** [3]**Rabbi Eliezer says: From his navel.** [4]**Rabbi Akiva says: From his nose.** [5]**Rabbi Eliezer ben Ya'akov says: From the place where** a person is usually **made into a corpse, from his neck."** Issuing a ruling on this matter in contradiction to that of the Great Sanhedrin can lead to liability to excision, for if the measurements were made in the wrong way, the heifer is not consecrated, and its owner can use its value to effect a betrothal.

טָהֳרַת מְצוֹרָע [6]As for **purifying a leper,** there is **a dispute between Rabbi Shimon and the Rabbis** that has ramifications regarding a matter that is subject to excision, [7]**as we have learned** in the Mishnah (*Nega'im* 14:9): "Regarding the purification process of a leper, the Torah states (Leviticus 14:14): 'And the priest shall take some of the blood of the guilt-offering, and the priest shall put it upon the tip of the right ear of the one who is to be cleansed, and upon the thumb of his right hand, and upon the great toe of his right foot.' [8]Thus, **if** the leper **does not have a right thumb, great toe, or ear, he can never achieve ritual purification.** This is the position of the anonymous Rabbis of the Mishnah. [9]**Rabbi Eliezer** disagrees and **says:** If the leper is missing his right thumb, great toe, or ear, the priest may **place** the blood **on the place** where the missing

שְׁנַיִם, וּמַשְׁקֶה עַל פִּי שְׁנַיִם״.
[1]עֲרִיפַת עֶגְלָה — בִּפְלוּגְתָּא דְּרַבִּי אֱלִיעֶזֶר וְרַבִּי עֲקִיבָא, [2]דִּתְנַן: ״מֵאַיִן הָיוּ מוֹדְדִין? [3]רַבִּי אֱלִיעֶזֶר אוֹמֵר: מִטִּיבּוּרוֹ. [4]רַבִּי עֲקִיבָא אוֹמֵר: מֵחוֹטְמוֹ. [5]רַבִּי אֱלִיעֶזֶר בֶּן יַעֲקֹב אוֹמֵר: מִמָּקוֹם שֶׁנַּעֲשָׂה חָלָל, מִצַּוָּארוֹ״.
[6]טָהֳרַת מְצוֹרָע — בִּפְלוּגְתָּא דְּרַבִּי שִׁמְעוֹן וְרַבָּנַן, [7]דִּתְנַן: [8]״אֵין לוֹ בֹּהֶן יָד, בֹּהֶן רֶגֶל, אוֹזֶן יְמָנִית, אֵין לוֹ טָהֳרָה עוֹלָמִית. [9]רַבִּי אֱלִיעֶזֶר אוֹמֵר:

LITERAL TRANSLATION

of two, and he makes her drink on the basis of two."

[1]Breaking the neck of a heifer — like the dispute between Rabbi Eliezer and Rabbi Akiva, [2]as we have learned: "From where would they measure? [3]Rabbi Eliezer says: From his navel. [4]Rabbi Akiva says: From his nose. [5]Rabbi Eliezer ben Ya'akov says: From the place where he was made a corpse, from his neck."

[6]Purifying a leper — like the dispute between Rabbi Shimon and the Rabbis, [7]as we have learned: [8]"[If] he does not have a right thumb, great toe, or ear, he can never achieve purification. [9]Rabbi Eliezer says:

RASHI

מאין היו מודדין — לידע אי זו עיר קרובה אל החלל. **מטבורו** — ואותה שקרובה לטבורו תביא את העגלה ולא הקרובה לחוטמו. **רבי עקיבא אומר מחוטמו** — ובמסכת סוטה מפרש טעמא, מר סבר עיקר חיותיה באפיה, ומר סבר עיקר חיותיה בטבוריה. **ממקום שנעשה חלל** — דהיינו מצואריה, דסתם חלל מן הצואר כדמפרש התם "לתת אותך על צוארי חלל רשעים", ותנן (קידושין נו,ג) המקדש בעגלה ערופה אינה מקודשת, ואם מדד זקן ממרא מטיבורו ובית דין מחוטמו והביאו אלו עגלה ואלו עגלה, למר זו עגלה אסורה ואין מקדשין בה, וזו אינה עגלה ומקדשין בה, ולמר הוי איפכא. **אין לו טהרה עולמית** — דבעינן קרא כדכתב, כדאמרן ב"נגמר הדין".

HALAKHAH

מֵאַיִן הָיוּ מוֹדְדִין? From where would they measure? "If a murder victim is found outside a town, and it is not known who caused his death, the distance between the corpse and the nearest town is measured, and the elders of that town perform the rite of breaking the neck of a heifer. The distance is measured from the corpse's nose," following Rabbi Akiva. (*Rambam, Sefer Nezikin, Hilkhot Rotze'aḥ* 9:1,9.)

אֵין לוֹ בֹּהֶן יָד If he does not have a right thumb. "If a leper does not have a right thumb, great toe, or ear, he can never achieve ritual purification." (*Rambam, Sefer Korbanot, Hilkhot Meḥusarei Kaparah* 5:1.)

LITERAL TRANSLATION

He places it on its place, and fulfills [the obligation]. [1]Rabbi Shimon says: He places it on the left [one], and fulfills [the obligation]."

[2]"Within your gates" — this is gleanings, forgotten sheaves, and [produce growing in the] corner. [3]Gleanings — [4]as we have learned: "Two ears are gleanings, three are not gleanings. [5]Two sheaves are forgotten sheaves, [6]three are not forgotten sheaves. [7]Regarding all of them, Bet Shammai say: Three are for the pauper, [8]and four are for the owner."

[9][Produce growing in the] corner — like the dispute between Rabbi Yishmael and the Rabbis, [10]as we have learned: "The mitzvah regarding [produce growing in the] corner is to set aside from the standing grain.

נוֹתֵן לוֹ עַל מְקוֹמוֹ וְיוֹצֵא. [1]רַבִּי שִׁמְעוֹן אוֹמֵר: נוֹתֵן עַל שֶׁל שְׂמֹאל וְיוֹצֵא״.

[2]״בִּשְׁעָרֶיךָ״ — זֶה לֶקֶט שִׁכְחָה פֵּאָה. [3]לֶקֶט — [4]דִּתְנַן: ״שְׁנֵי שִׁבֳּלִין לֶקֶט, שְׁלֹשָׁה אֵינָן לֶקֶט. [5]שִׁכְחָה — שְׁנֵי עוֹמָרִין שִׁכְחָה, [6]שְׁלֹשָׁה אֵינָן שִׁכְחָה. [7]וְעַל כּוּלָּן, בֵּית שַׁמַּאי אוֹמְרִים: שָׁלֹשׁ לֶעָנִי, [8]וְאַרְבַּע לְבַעַל הַבַּיִת״.

[9]פֵּיאָה — בִּפְלוּגְתָּא דְּרַבִּי יִשְׁמָעֵאל וְרַבָּנַן, [10]דִּתְנַן: ״מִצְוַת פֵּיאָה לְהַפְרִישׁ מִן הַקָּמָה.

RASHI

נותן על מקומו — על מקום הבוהן נותן דם האשם וטהור ליכנס למקדש ולאכול קודש, דהיינו זדונו כרת. **שלש אינן לקט** — שאין דרך להפקירן. **שלשה אינן שכחה** — בסיפרא יליף מקראי בפרשת שכחה, ואם נחלק זקן ממרא ואמר: אף שלשה שכחה, ובא עני ונטלן ובא בעל הבית ונטלן הימנו, לזקן ממרא הוי גזל ואין מקדשין בו אשה, ולרבנן מקודשת. **מצות פיאה מפריש מן הקמה** — דכתיב ״לא תכלה״ — אלא הנח לפניהם והם יקצרוהו.

TRANSLATION AND COMMENTARY

appendage should be found, and thus the leper **fulfills his obligation,** and achieves ritual purification. [1]**Rabbi Shimon says:** If the leper is missing his right thumb, great toe, or ear, the priest may **place** the blood **on his left** thumb, great toe, or ear, **and** thus the leper **fulfills his obligation** and achieves ritual purification." Issuing a ruling on this matter in contradiction to that of the Great Sanhedrin can lead to being liable to the punishment of excision, for if a leper enters the Temple or eats of holy things before he achieves purification, he is liable to excision.

בִּשְׁעָרֶיךָ [2]Rav Pappa continues to explain the Baraita in accordance with the opinion of Rabbi Meir: The words **"within your gates"** allude to rulings involving **gleanings** that fell during the harvest, **sheaves** that were **forgotten** in the fields, **and** produce growing in the **corner** of a field. [3]Regarding **gleanings** and forgotten sheaves, there is a dispute between Bet Hillel and Bet Shammai that has ramifications regarding a matter that is subject to excision, [4]**as we have learned** in the Mishnah (see *Pe'ah* 6:5): "If **two ears** of grain fell in one place during the harvest, they are considered **gleanings** which must be left for the poor, but if **three** ears fell in one place, they **are not gleanings,** and so they may be taken by the owner of the field. [5]And similarly, if **two sheaves** of grain were forgotten in the field during harvest, they **are** governed by the law of **forgotten sheaves.** The owner of the field may not return to collect them. Rather, they must be left for the poor. [6]But if **three sheaves** were forgotten in the field, they **are not** governed by the law of **forgotten sheaves,** and so the owner of the field may come back and take them. This is the position of Bet Hillel. [7]**Regarding all of** these agricultural gifts to which the poor are entitled, **Bet Shammai** disagree and **say:** If **three** ears of grain fell in one place, or if three sheaves were forgotten in the field, they must be left **for the pauper.** [8]But if **four** ears of grain fell in one place, or if four sheaves of grain were forgotten in the field, they belong **to the owner** of the field." Issuing a ruling on this matter in contradiction to that of the Great Sanhedrin can lead to liability to excision, for if three ears fell in one place, or three sheaves of grain were forgotten in the field, and a pauper took them and betrothed a woman with them, according to Bet Shammai the betrothal is valid, whereas according to Bet Hillel the betrothal is not valid, for the pauper was not entitled to the grain.

פֵּיאָה [9]Regarding **produce growing in the corner** of a person's field which must be left for the poor, there is **a dispute between Rabbi Yishmael and the Rabbis** that has ramifications regarding a matter that is subject to excision, [10]**as we have learned** in a Baraita: "The preferred way of fulfilling **the commandment regarding produce growing in the corner** of a field **is to set aside** for the poor a portion **of the standing grain,** as the

HALAKHAH

לֶקֶט שִׁכְחָה **Gleanings, forgotten sheaves.** "Two ears of grain that fell in one place during the harvest are considered gleanings, but three ears that fell in one place are not gleanings. Two sheaves of grain that were forgotten in the field during harvest are governed by the law of forgotten sheaves, but three sheaves that were forgotten in the field are not governed by the law of forgotten sheaves." (*Rambam, Sefer Zera'im, Hilkhot Matanot Aniyim* 4:1, 5:14.)

מִצְוַת פֵּיאָה **Produce growing in the corner.** "If someone did not set aside the produce growing in the corner of his field from the standing grain, he must set aside a portion of the sheaves, or a portion of the pile of grain that is

TRANSLATION AND COMMENTARY

verse states (Leviticus 19:9): 'You shall not wholly reap the corners of your field' — but rather you shall leave it for the poor to reap. [1]If the owner of the field **did not set aside** a portion **of the standing grain, he should set aside** a portion of **the sheaves.** [2]**If he did not set aside** a portion **of the sheaves, he should set aside** a portion of **the pile** of grain that is heaped up after threshing, **before he evens it out** and it becomes ready to be tithed. [3]**If he** already **evened out** the pile, and it became ready to be tithed, **he must tithe** the produce **and** then **give** a portion to the poor. [4]**In the name of Rabbi Yishmael they said: Even** if he ground the grain into flour and kneaded the flour into dough, **he** must **set aside** for the poor a portion **of the dough."** But according to the anonymous Rabbis, once a person grinds his grain into flour, he is no longer required to set aside a portion in fulfillment of the commandment to leave the corners of a field for the poor. Issuing a ruling on this matter in contradiction to that of the Great Sanhedrin can lead to liability to excision, for if a person ground his grain into flour, and a pauper took a portion and betrothed a woman with it, according to Rabbi Yishmael the betrothal is valid, whereas according to the Rabbis the betrothal is not valid, for the pauper was not entitled to the flour.

[1]לֹא הִפְרִישׁ מִן הַקָּמָה, יַפְרִישׁ מִן הָעוֹמָרִין. [2]לֹא הִפְרִישׁ מִן הָעוֹמָרִין, יַפְרִישׁ מִן הַכְּרִי עַד שֶׁלֹּא מֵירְחוֹ. [3]מֵירְחוֹ, מְעַשֵּׂר וְנוֹתֵן לוֹ. [4]מִשּׁוּם רַבִּי יִשְׁמָעֵאל אָמְרוּ: אַף מַפְרִישׁ מִן הָעִיסָּה". [5]"שְׁלֹשָׁה בָּתֵּי דִינִין וכו'". [6]אָמַר רַב כָּהֲנָא: הוּא אוֹמֵר מִפִּי הַשְּׁמוּעָה, וְהֵן אוֹמְרִין מִפִּי הַשְּׁמוּעָה, אֵינוֹ נֶהֱרָג. [7]הוּא אוֹמֵר: "כָּךְ הוּא בְּעֵינַי", וְהֵן אוֹמְרִין: "כָּךְ הוּא בְּעֵינֵינוּ", אֵינוֹ נֶהֱרָג. [8]וְכָל שֶׁכֵּן הוּא אוֹמֵר מִפִּי הַשְּׁמוּעָה, וְהֵן אוֹמְרִין: "כָּךְ הוּא בְּעֵינֵינוּ" — אֵינוֹ נֶהֱרָג, [9]עַד שֶׁיֹּאמַר: "כָּךְ

LITERAL TRANSLATION

[1][If] he did not set aside from the standing grain, he should set aside from sheaves. [2][If] he did not set aside from sheaves, he should set aside from the pile before he evens it. [3][If] he evened it, he tithes it, and gives him. [4]In the name of Rabbi Yishmael they said: He even sets aside from dough."

[5]"There were three courts, etc.," [6]Rav Kahana said: [If] he said on the basis of a tradition, and they said on the basis of a tradition, he is not put to death. [7][If] he said: "Thus it appears to me," and they said: "Thus it appears to us," he is not put to death. [8]And all the more so [if] he said on the basis of a tradition, and they said: "Thus it appears to us," he is not put to death. [9]Unless he said: "Thus

RASHI

מרחו — בכרי, נתחייב במעשר דנגמרה מלאכתו, הלכך מעשר תחילה את הכרי מכל מעשרותיו ונותן לו את הפאה, שאילו הפרישה לא היו עניים צריכין לעשרה, דלקט שכחה פאה פטורין מן המעשר. אף מפריש מן העיסה — אם טחנה ולשה, ולתנא קמא טחנה פטור, דקנייה בשינוי, ואם בא עני ונטל כדי פאה משטחנה, לרבי ישמעאל לא הוי גזל, לרבנן הוי גזל.

We have now explained the entire Baraita cited above according to the opinion of Rabbi Meir, that a rebellious elder is liable only if he himself followed a practice or instructed others to follow a practice that contradicted the opinion of the majority of the Sages of the Great Sanhedrin regarding a matter whose intentional violation makes one liable to the penalty of excision and whose unwitting violation obligates one to bring a sin-offering.

שְׁלֹשָׁה [5]We learned in our Mishnah that **there were three courts** in Jerusalem, to which all Halakhic matters about which there was any doubt were brought for clarification and decision, but only if the dissenting elder ruled against a decision issued by the Great Sanhedrin would he become liable to execution. [6]**Rav Kahana said: If** the dissenting elder **said** that he issued his ruling **on the basis of a tradition** that he had received from his teachers, **and** the other Sages **said** that they, too, issued their ruling **on the basis of** such **a tradition,** the dissenting elder **is not put to death.** [7]And similarly, **if** the dissenting elder **said: "Thus** the law **appears to me,"** without basing himself on the authority of a tradition, **and** so, too, the other Sages **said: "Thus** the law **appears to us,"** the dissenting elder **is not put to death.** [8]**And all the more so if** the dissenting elder **said** that he issued his ruling **on the basis of a tradition** that he had received from his teachers, **and** the other Sages **said: "Thus** the law **appears to us,"** without invoking the authority of a tradition, the dissenting elder **is not put to death.** [9]The dissenting elder is not executed **unless he said: "Thus** the law

HALAKHAH

heaped up after threshing. Even if he already ground the grain into flour, and kneaded it into dough, and baked it, he must set aside a portion of the bread." (*Rambam, Sefer Zera'im, Hilkhot Matanot Aniyim* 1:2.)

הוּא אוֹמֵר מִפִּי הַשְּׁמוּעָה **If he said on the basis of a tradition.** "A rebellious elder is liable to the death penalty, even if he issued his ruling on the basis of a tradition that he received from his teachers, and the other Sages issued their ruling as the law appeared to them," following Rabbi Elazar. (*Rambam, Sefer Shofetim, Hilkhot Mamrim* 4:1.)

הוּא בְּעֵינַי״, וְהֵן אוֹמְרִים מִפִּי הַשְּׁמוּעָה. [1]תֵּדַע, שֶׁהֲרֵי לֹא הָרְגוּ אֶת עֲקַבְיָא בֶּן מַהֲלַלְאֵל. [2]וְרַבִּי אֶלְעָזָר אוֹמֵר: אֲפִילּוּ הוּא אוֹמֵר מִפִּי הַשְּׁמוּעָה, וְהֵן אוֹמְרִין: ״כָּךְ הוּא בְּעֵינֵינוּ״, נֶהֱרָג, [3]כְּדֵי שֶׁלֹּא יִרְבּוּ מַחֲלוֹקוֹת בְּיִשְׂרָאֵל. [4]וְאִם תֹּאמַר: מִפְּנֵי מַה לֹּא הָרְגוּ אֶת עֲקַבְיָא בֶּן מַהֲלַלְאֵל? [5]מִפְּנֵי שֶׁלֹּא הוֹרָה הֲלָכָה לְמַעֲשֶׂה.

[6]תְּנַן: [7]״׳כָּךְ דָּרַשְׁתִּי, וְכָךְ דָּרְשׁוּ חֲבֵירַי. [8]כָּךְ לִמַּדְתִּי וְכָךְ לִמְּדוּ חֲבֵירַי׳״. [9]מַאי לָאו דְּהוּא אָמַר מִפִּי הַשְּׁמוּעָה, וְהֵם אוֹמְרִין: ״כָּךְ הוּא בְּעֵינֵינוּ״!

[10]לֹא, הוּא אוֹמֵר: ״כָּךְ הוּא בְּעֵינַי״, וְהֵם אוֹמְרִים מִפִּי הַשְּׁמוּעָה.

[11]תָּא שְׁמַע, דְּאָמַר רַבִּי יֹאשִׁיָּה: שְׁלֹשָׁה דְּבָרִים סָח לִי זְעֵירָא מֵאַנְשֵׁי יְרוּשָׁלַיִם: [12]בַּעַל שֶׁמָּחַל

LITERAL TRANSLATION

it appears to me," and they said on the basis of a tradition. [1]Know [that this is true], for they did not put Akavyah ben Mahalalel to death. [2]And Rabbi Elazar says: Even [if] he said on the basis of a tradition, and they said: "Thus it appears to us," he is put to death, [3]so that disputes in Israel not increase. [4]And if you say: Why did they not put Akavyah ben Mahalalel to death? [5]Because he did not issue a practical ruling.

[6]We have learned: [7]"[The Sage says:] 'Thus have I expounded, and thus have my colleagues expounded. [8]Thus have I taught, and thus have my colleagues taught.'" [9]Is it not that he said on the basis of a tradition, and they said: "Thus it appears to us"?

[10]No, he said: "Thus it appears to me," and they said on the basis of a tradition.

[11]Come [and] hear, for Rabbi Yoshiyah said: Ze'eira of the men of Jerusalem told me three things: [12]A husband who waived

TRANSLATION AND COMMENTARY

appears to me," and the other Sages **said** that they issued their ruling **on the basis of a tradition** that they had received from their teachers, for, by refusing to accept their ruling, the dissenting elder undermines the authority of Rabbinical tradition. [1]**Know that this is true, for** the Sages **did not execute Akavyah ben Mahalalel** when he refused to accept the majority ruling on four different issues (see *Eduyot* 5:6), about which he had received traditions that opposed the dominant view. [2]**Rabbi Elazar** disagreed and **said: Even if** the dissenting elder claimed that he issued his ruling **on the basis of a tradition** that he had received from his teachers, **and** the other Sages **said: "Thus** the law **appears to us,"** without invoking the authority of a tradition, the dissenting elder **is put to death,** [3]**so that** Halakhic **disputes in Israel will not increase in number.** [4]**And if you ask: Why,** then, **did they not execute Akavyah ben Mahalalel** when he refused to accept the majority opinion? [5]The answer is that Akavyah ben Mahalalel was not executed **because he did not issue a practical ruling** that contradicted the opinion of the Great Sanhedrin.

תְּנַן [6]The Gemara raises an objection against Rav Kahana from what **we have learned** in our Mishnah: **"The Sage** with the dissenting opinion **says** to the members of the court: [7]**'Thus have I expounded** the Torah, **and thus have my colleagues expounded** it. [8]**Thus have I taught** the law to my students, **and thus have my colleagues taught** it to theirs.'" [9]**Does this not** also include a dissenting elder who **said** that he issued his ruling **on the basis of a tradition** that he had received from his teachers, **and** the other Sages **said: "Thus** the law **appears to us,"** without invoking the authority of a tradition? And the Mishnah teaches that the dissenting elder is put to death for contradicting the opinion of the majority of the Sages, against the opinion of Rav Kahana!

לֹא [10]The Gemara rejects this proof: **No,** the Mishnah is dealing with a dissenting elder who **said: "Thus** the law **appears to me," and** the other Sages **said** that they issued their ruling **on the basis of a tradition** that they had received from their teachers.

תָּא שְׁמַע [11]**Come and hear** a proof against Rav Kahana, **for Rabbi Yoshiyah said: Ze'eira,** who was one **of the** distinguished **men of Jerusalem, reported three rulings to me:** [12]If **a husband waived the warning** that he

RASHI

עקביא בן מהללאל – נחלק על חכמים בלשכת הגזית בארבעה דברים במסכת עדיות (פרק ה משנה ו), שהיה אומר לבנו בשעת מיתתו חזור בך בארבעה דברים שהייתי אומר, אמר לו: אבא, ואתה מפני מה לא חזרתה בהם? אמר לו: אני שמעתי מפי המרובים, והם שמעו מפי המרובים, הם עמדו בשמועתן, ואני עמדתי בשמועתי, אבל אתה שמעת מפי היחיד וכו׳.

HALAKHAH

בַּעַל שֶׁמָּחַל עַל קִינּוּיוֹ A husband who waived his warning. "If a husband warned his wife not to seclude herself with a particular man, and then waived his warning before she secluded herself with that man, his warning is waived," following the Gemara here and in tractate *Sotah*. (*Rambam, Sefer Nashim, Hilkhot Sotah* 1:7.)

עַל קִינּוּיו, קִינּוּיו מָחוּל, [88B] [1]בֵּן סוֹרֵר וּמוֹרֶה שֶׁרָצוּ אָבִיו וְאִמּוֹ לִמְחוֹל לוֹ — מוֹחֲלִין לוֹ, [2]זָקֵן מַמְרֵא שֶׁרָצוּ בֵּית דִּינוֹ לִמְחוֹל לוֹ — מוֹחֲלִין לוֹ. [3]וּכְשֶׁבָּאתִי אֵצֶל חֲבֵירַי שֶׁבַּדָּרוֹם, עַל שְׁנַיִם הוֹדוּ לִי, עַל זָקֵן מַמְרֵא — לֹא הוֹדוּ לִי, [4]כְּדֵי שֶׁלֹּא יִרְבּוּ מַחֲלוֹקֶת בְּיִשְׂרָאֵל! [5]תְּיוּבְתָּא. [6]תַּנְיָא: "אָמַר רַבִּי יוֹסֵי: מִתְּחִילָּה לֹא הָיוּ מַרְבִּין מַחֲלוֹקֶת בְּיִשְׂרָאֵל. [7]אֶלָּא בֵּית דִּין שֶׁל שִׁבְעִים וְאֶחָד יוֹשְׁבִין בְּלִשְׁכַּת הַגָּזִית, וּשְׁנֵי בָּתֵּי דִּינִין

LITERAL TRANSLATION

his warning, his warning is waived. [88B] [1]A stubborn and rebellious son whose father and mother wished to excuse him — they excuse him. [2]A rebellious elder whom the court wished to excuse, they excuse him. [3]And when I came to my colleagues in the South, about two they agreed with me, about a rebellious elder they did not agree with me, [4]so that disputes in Israel will not be numerous. [5]A refutation.

[6]It was taught: "Rabbi Yose said: At first they would not increase the disputes in Israel. [7]Rather, a court of seventy-one would sit in the Chamber of Hewn Stone, and two courts

TRANSLATION AND COMMENTARY

had given his wife not to seclude herself with a certain man, **his warning is waived.** Thus, if she secluded herself with that other man, she is still permitted to her husband, even if he does not make her drink the bitter waters.

[88B] [1]Regarding **a rebellious son,** if his **father and mother wished to excuse** their son, even after he had been warned and flogged and he sinned again, **they** may indeed **excuse him.** [2]And, similarly, regarding **a rebellious elder,** if **the court wished to excuse him** and not try him for contradicting the majority position of the Great Sanhedrin, **they** may indeed **excuse him.** [3]**And when I came before my colleagues in the South,** and reported these rulings to them, **they agreed with me about** the first **two** rulings, but **they did not agree with me about** the third ruling regarding **a rebellious elder.** [4]They maintained that the court could not excuse the rebellious elder, **so that** Halakhic **disputes in Israel would not increase in number.** Now, since the Rabbis of the South invoked the argument that we are concerned about Halakhic disputes growing in number, it follows that they maintain that the rebellious elder is liable to execution, even if he issued his ruling on the basis of a tradition that he received from his teachers, and the other Sages issued their ruling on the basis of their own judgment. [5]The Gemara concludes: Indeed, this is **a refutation** of the position of Rav Kahana.

תַּנְיָא [6]**It was taught** in a related Baraita: **"Rabbi Yose said: At first,** in the early generations, **there were not many** unresolved Halakhic **disputes in Israel.** [7]**Rather,** doubts about matters of law would be resolved as follows: A High **Court** composed **of seventy-one** judges **would sit in the Chamber of Hewn Stone, and two**

RASHI

על קינויו – שקינא לאשתו: אל תסתרי עם פלוני. קינויו מחול – ואם נסתרה אינה נאסרת עליו. בן סורר ומורה – אף לאחר שהתרו בו וקלקל, והלקוהו וחזר וקלקל, אם רצו למחול ולא הביאוהו לבית דין – מוחלין לו, שהכתוב תלה בהם "ותפשו בו". תיובתא – מדתלי טעמא בשלא ירבו מחלוקת – שמע מינה אפילו הוא אומר מפי השמועה, והן אומרין: כך הוא בעינינו.

NOTES

לֹא הָיוּ מַרְבִּין מַחֲלוֹקֶת בְּיִשְׂרָאֵל **At first they would not increase the disputes in Israel.** Even in earlier times a small number of disputes were never resolved — for example, the unresolved dispute regarding placing hands on the head of a sacrifice offered on a Festival. Therefore, the Baraita uses the expression לֹא הָיוּ מַרְבִּין — "they would not increase, they would not have many."

HALAKHAH

בֵּן סוֹרֵר וּמוֹרֶה שֶׁרָצוּ אָבִיו וְאִמּוֹ לִמְחוֹל לוֹ **A stubborn and rebellious son whose father and mother wished to excuse him.** "If a father and mother excused their rebellious son before he was convicted, he is exempt from the death penalty," following the Gemara. Regarding the point up to which the parents may excuse their rebellious son, *Rambam* follows the Jerusalem Talmud (*Mishneh Lemelekh*). (*Rambam, Sefer Shofetim, Hilkhot Mamrim* 7:8.)

זָקֵן מַמְרֵא שֶׁרָצוּ בֵּית דִּינוֹ לִמְחוֹל לוֹ **A rebellious elder whom the court wished to excuse.** "Even if a court is willing to waive its honor and excuse the rebellious elder and exempt him, it may not do so, lest disputes in Israel increase in number." (*Rambam, Sefer Shofetim, Hilkhot Mamrim* 3:4.)

מִתְּחִילָּה לֹא הָיוּ מַרְבִּין מַחֲלוֹקֶת בְּיִשְׂרָאֵל **At first they would not increase the disputes in Israel.** "When there was a Great Sanhedrin, there were no unresolved Halakhic disputes in Israel. Whenever someone was in doubt about a certain law, he would present his question before the local court. If they knew the answer, they would tell him, and if not, he and the local judges or the court's emissaries would go to Jerusalem and present the issue before the court sitting at the entrance of the Temple Mount. If they did not know the answer, the issue would be brought to the court sitting at the entrance to the Temple Courtyard. If they, too, did not know the answer, the issue would be brought to the Great Sanhedrin sitting in the Chamber of Hewn Stone. And if they did not have a tradition on the matter, they would settle the issue by majority vote." (*Rambam, Sefer Shofetim, Hilkhot Mamrim* 1:4.)

TRANSLATION AND COMMENTARY

lower **courts of twenty-three** judges each **would sit** in Jerusalem, [1]**one at the entrance to the Temple Mount, and one at the entrance to the Temple Courtyard.** [2]**The rest of the courts of twenty-three** judges **would sit in all the towns of Israel.** [3]If a point of law was unclear and **a question had to be asked** because a dispute regarding the matter had arisen among the Sages, **they would pose the question before a local court.** [4]If the members of that court had **heard** the law on the matter from their teachers, **they would tell** it to **them** as they had heard it. [5]If those judges did **not** have a tradition on the matter, the Sages with the conflicting views **would appear before a court in a neighboring town.** [6]If the members of that court had **heard** the law on the matter from their teachers, **they would tell** it to **them** as they had heard it. [7]**If not,** the Sages with the conflicting views **would** go to Jerusalem and **appear before the court** sitting **at the entrance to the Temple Mount.** [8]If those judges had **heard** the law on the matter from their teachers, **they would tell them,** [9]**and if not,** the Sages with the conflicting views **would appear before the court** sitting **at the entrance to the Temple Courtyard.** [10]The Sage with the dissenting opinion **would say: 'Thus have I expounded** the Torah, **and thus have my colleagues expounded** it. [11]**Thus have I taught** the law to my students, **and thus have my colleagues taught** it to theirs.' [12]If the members of that court had **heard** the law on the matter from their teachers, **they would tell** it **to them** as they had heard it. [13]If those judges did **not** have a tradition on the matter, **these and those** — the Sage with the dissenting opinion and his colleagues, as well as the judges before whom they had already appeared — **would come to the Chamber of Hewn Stone,** [14]**where** the Great Sanhedrin **sat** all day **from** the time of the offering of **the daily sacrifice of the morning until** the time of the offering of **the daily sacrifice of the afternoon.** [15]**On the Sabbath and on Festivals,** when the court was not in session, the members of that court would **sit in that area** of the Temple Mount **surrounded by a** low **wall** which was holier than the area of the Temple Mount outside it. [16]**The question would be asked before** the Great Sanhedrin. [17]**If the**

שֶׁל עֶשְׂרִים וּשְׁלשָׁה, [1]אֶחָד יוֹשֵׁב עַל פֶּתַח הַר הַבַּיִת וְאֶחָד יוֹשֵׁב עַל פֶּתַח הָעֲזָרָה, [2]וּשְׁאָר בָּתֵּי דִינִין שֶׁל עֶשְׂרִים וּשְׁלֹשָׁה יוֹשְׁבִין בְּכָל עֲיָירוֹת יִשְׂרָאֵל. [3]הוּצְרַךְ הַדָּבָר לִשְׁאוֹל, שׁוֹאֲלִין מִבֵּית דִּין שֶׁבְּעִירָן. [4]אִם שָׁמְעוּ, אָמְרוּ לָהֶן, [5]וְאִם לָאו — בָּאִין לָזֶה שֶׁסָּמוּךְ לְעִירָן. [6]אִם שָׁמְעוּ, אָמְרוּ לָהֶם, [7]וְאִם לָאו, בָּאִין לָזֶה שֶׁעַל פֶּתַח הַר הַבַּיִת. [8]אִם שָׁמְעוּ, אָמְרוּ לָהֶם, [9]וְאִם לָאו, בָּאִין לָזֶה שֶׁעַל פֶּתַח הָעֲזָרָה. [10]וְאוֹמֵר: ״כָּךְ דָּרַשְׁתִּי וְכָךְ דָּרְשׁוּ חֲבֵירַי, [11]כָּךְ לִמַּדְתִּי וְכָךְ לִמְּדוּ חֲבֵירַי. [12]אִם שָׁמְעוּ, אָמְרוּ לָהֶם, [13]וְאִם לָאו, אֵלּוּ וָאֵלּוּ בָּאִין לְלִשְׁכַּת הַגָּזִית, [14]שֶׁשָּׁם יוֹשְׁבִין מִתָּמִיד שֶׁל שַׁחַר עַד תָּמִיד שֶׁל בֵּין הָעַרְבַּיִם. [15]וּבְשַׁבָּתוֹת וּבְיָמִים טוֹבִים יוֹשְׁבִין בַּחֵיל. [16]נִשְׁאֲלָה שְׁאֵלָה בִּפְנֵיהֶם. [17]אִם שָׁמְעוּ,

LITERAL TRANSLATION

of twenty-three, [1]one would sit at the entrance to the Temple Mount, and one would sit at the entrance to the Temple Courtyard. [2]And the rest of the courts of twenty-three would sit in all the towns of Israel. [3][If] something had to be asked, they would ask the court in their town. [4]If they heard, they would say to them, [5]and if not, they would come to [the court] that was near their town. [6]If they heard, they would say to them, [7]and if not, they would come to [the court] that was at the entrance to the Temple Mount. [8]If they heard, they would say to them, [9]and if not, they would come to [the court] that was at the entrance to the Temple Courtyard. [10]And he would say: 'Thus have I expounded, and thus have my colleagues expounded. [11]Thus have I taught, and thus have my colleagues taught.' [12]If they heard, they would say to them. [13]And if not, these and those would come to the Chamber of Hewn Stone, [14]where they sat from the daily sacrifice of the morning until the daily sacrifice of the afternoon. [15]And on the Sabbath and Festivals, they sat in the area surrounded by a wall. [16]The question would be asked before them. [17]If they heard,

RASHI

יושבין בחיל – מפני שהעם רב ומקום צר להם בלשכה, אי נמי: שלא יהו נראים כיושבין בדין, שבלשכת הגזית היו דנים, וזה עיקר.

BACKGROUND

הַקְרָבַת הַתָּמִיד The daily morning sacrifice. The daily morning sacrifice is offered a half hour before sunrise, when there is light in the eastern sky, at five-thirty in the morning during the spring and autumn. The regular evening sacrifice is offered at nine-thirty (according to the ritual clock), which is three-thirty p.m. during the spring and autumn.

HALAKHAH

שֶׁשָּׁם יוֹשְׁבִין מִתָּמִיד שֶׁל שַׁחַר Where they sat from the daily sacrifice of the morning. "The courts of twenty-three judges and the courts of three judges would convene after the morning service and sit until noon. The Great Sanhedrin would sit from the time of the daily sacrifice of the morning until the time of the daily sacrifice in the afternoon." (*Rambam, Sefer Shofetim, Hilkhot Sanhedrin* 3:1.)

וּבְשַׁבָּתוֹת וּבְיָמִים טוֹבִים And on the Sabbath and Festivals. "On the Sabbath and on Festivals, the Great Sanhedrin would not sit in the Chamber of Hewn Stone, but rather in the Academy on the Temple Mount." (According to *Radbaz*, this Academy was situated in the area of the Temple Mount surrounded by a low wall [the *hail*]; according to *Leḥem Mishnah, Rambam*'s ruling follows the Jerusalem Talmud

TRANSLATION AND COMMENTARY

members of that court had **heard** the law on the matter from their teachers, **they would tell** it to **them, and if** they did **not** have a tradition on the matter, **they would decide** the issue **by vote.** [1]If the matter in dispute involved ritual impurity, and **those who** thought of **declaring** the object or the person **ritually impure were in the majority, they would** establish the law in that manner and **declare** the object or person **ritually impure.** [2]**If those who** thought of **declaring** the object or person **ritually pure were in the majority, they would** establish the law in that manner and **declare** the object or person **ritually pure.** By following this procedure, the Sages decided and settled every Halakhic dispute that arose. [3]**But when the disciples of Shammai and of Hillel who did not wait upon their masters** and study **grew sufficiently in number,** [4]**the disputes in Israel** also **grew in number, and the Torah became like two Torahs.** [5]The Baraita adds: It was **from** the Great Sanhedrin that sat **there** in the Chamber of Hewn Stone that **they would write** missives **and send** them **out to all places,** saying: [6]**Whoever is wise and humble, and people are favorably disposed toward him — let him be a judge in his town.** [7]If the judge succeeded in his local position, **they would raise him up to** sit on the court that convened at the entrance of **the Temple Mount.** [8]If the judge enjoyed continued success, they would elevate him **from there to** sit on the court that convened at the entrance of **the Temple Courtyard.** [9]**And** if the judge also succeeded on the higher court, they would elevate him **from there to** sit on the Great Sanhedrin that convened in **the Chamber of Hewn Stone."**

שָׁלְחוּ מִתָּם [10]Having mentioned the virtue of humility, the Gemara adds: **They sent emissaries from** Eretz Israel: **Who is fit** to enter **the World to Come?** [11]**A man who is modest and humble, who bows when he comes in,**

אָמְרוּ לָהֶם, וְאִם לָאו — עוֹמְדִין לַמִּנְיָן. [1]רַבּוּ הַמְטַמְּאִים, טִמְּאוּ. [2]רַבּוּ הַמְטַהֲרִין, טִהֲרוּ. [3]מִשֶּׁרַבּוּ תַּלְמִידֵי שַׁמַּאי וְהִלֵּל שֶׁלֹּא שִׁמְּשׁוּ כָּל צָרְכָּן — [4]רַבּוּ מַחֲלוֹקֶת בְּיִשְׂרָאֵל, וְנַעֲשֵׂית תּוֹרָה כִּשְׁתֵּי תוֹרוֹת. [5]מִשָּׁם כּוֹתְבִין וְשׁוֹלְחִין בְּכָל מְקוֹמוֹת: [6]כָּל מִי שֶׁהוּא חָכָם וּשְׁפַל בֶּרֶךְ וְדַעַת הַבְּרִיּוֹת נוֹחָה הֵימֶנּוּ — יְהֵא דַּיָּין בְּעִירוֹ. [7]מִשָּׁם מַעֲלִין אוֹתוֹ לְהַר הַבַּיִת, [8]מִשָּׁם לָעֲזָרָה, [9]מִשָּׁם לְלִשְׁכַּת הַגָּזִית". [10]שָׁלְחוּ מִתָּם: אֵיזֶהוּ בֶּן הָעוֹלָם הַבָּא? [11]עַנְוְתָן וּשְׁפַל בֶּרֶךְ,

LITERAL TRANSLATION

they would say to them, and if not, they would decide by vote [lit., 'stand for a count']. [1][If] those who declared it ritually impure were in the majority, they declared it ritually impure. [2][If] those who declared it ritually pure were in the majority, they declared it ritually pure. [3]But when the disciples of Shammai and Hillel who did not wait upon [their masters] grew sufficiently in number, [4]the disputes in Israel grew in number, and the Torah became like two Torahs. [5]From there they would write and send to all places: [6]Whoever is wise, and low of knee, and the opinion of people is favorable toward him — let him be a judge in his town. [7]From there they would raise him up to the Temple Mount, [8][and] from there to the Temple Courtyard, [9][and] from there to the Chamber of Hewn Stone."

[10]They sent from there: Who is fit for the World to Come? [11]A man who is modest and low of knee,

RASHI

משם מעלין אותו — להיות דיין בהר הבית כשמת אחד מהם, ויושב שם עד שמת אחד משל עזרה ומעלין את זה שם, וכולן יש בהם מעלה זה מזה.

NOTES

רַבּוּ הַמְטַהֲרִין, טִהֲרוּ If those who declared it ritually pure were in the majority. Some Rishonim argue that even though the law is decided in accordance with the majority opinion, a rebellious elder is only executed if he contradicted a unanimous decision of the Great Sanhedrin. But if even a single member of the Great Sanhedrin agreed with the rebellious elder, he is not put to death for continuing to promulgate his dissident opinion (*Rabbenu Yehonatan, Meiri*).

חָכָם וּשְׁפַל בֶּרֶךְ Whoever is wise, and low of knee. The qualities mentioned here are derived from the passage dealing with the judges appointed by Moses (Deuteronomy 1:13): "Take wise men, and understanding, and known among your tribes." "Wise men" — judges must be wise; "and known among your tribes" — people must be favorably disposed to them. Judges must also be modest, like Moses, the most modest of men, for it is through Moses that they derive their authority.

HALAKHAH

and the Tosefta, which disagree with our Gemara.) (*Rambam, Sefer Shofetim, Hilkhot Sanhedrin* 3:1.)

מִשָּׁם כּוֹתְבִין וְשׁוֹלְחִין בְּכָל מְקוֹמוֹת From there they would write and send emissaries to all places. "The judges of the Great Sanhedrin would search for suitable judges throughout Eretz Israel. Whomever they found wise, and God-fearing, and humble, and well accepted by the people, they would appoint to sit on a court in his town. From there they would promote him to sit on the court that convened at the entrance of the Temple Mount, and from there to the

[1] שָׁיֵיף עָיֵיל שָׁיֵיף וְנָפֵיק, [1] וְגָרֵיס בְּאוֹרַיְיתָא תְּדִירָא, וְלָא מַחֲזִיק טִיבוּתָא לְנַפְשֵׁיהּ. [2] יָהֲבוּ בֵּיהּ רַבָּנַן עֵינַיְיהוּן בְּרַב עוּלָּא בַּר אַבָּא.

[3] ״חָזַר לְעִירוֹ וְשָׁנָה״. [4] תָּנוּ רַבָּנַן: ״אֵינוֹ חַיָּיב עַד שֶׁיַּעֲשֶׂה כְּהוֹרָאָתוֹ, [5] אוֹ שֶׁיּוֹרֶה לַאֲחֵרִים וְיַעֲשׂוּ כְּהוֹרָאָתוֹ״. [6] בִּשְׁלָמָא ״יוֹרֶה לַאֲחֵרִים וְיַעֲשׂוּ כְּהוֹרָאָתוֹ״ — [7] מֵעִיקָּרָא לָאו בַּר קְטָלָא הוּא, [8] וְהָשְׁתָּא בַּר קְטָלָא הוּא. [9] אֶלָּא ״שֶׁיַּעֲשֶׂה כְּהוֹרָאָתוֹ״, [10] מֵעִיקָּרָא נַמִי בַּר קְטָלָא הוּא! [11] הָתִינַח הֵיכָא דְּאוֹרֵי בְּחֵלֶב וְדָם, [12] דִּמֵעִיקָּרָא לָאו בַּר קְטָלָא הוּא, [13] וְהָשְׁתָּא

LITERAL TRANSLATION

who bows and comes in, bows and goes out, [1] and studies Torah regularly, and does not give himself credit. [2] The Rabbis set their eyes on Ulla bar Abba.

[3] "[If] he returned to his city, and taught again." [4] Our Rabbis taught: "He is not liable unless he acted in accordance with his ruling, [5] or he ruled for others, and they acted in accordance with his ruling." [6] Granted, "unless he ruled for others, and they acted in accordance with his ruling" — [7] initially he was not liable to execution, [8] but now he is liable to execution. [9] But "unless he acted in accordance with his ruling" — [10] even initially he was liable to execution! [11] This is understandable where he ruled about forbidden fat and blood, [12] for initially he was not liable to execution, [13] and now

RASHI

שייף — שוחה נכנס ושוחה יוצא, והכי אמרינן בבבא בתרא (ז,א) גבי תקרת הבית שנחבטה: שוף עול, שוף פוק.

מעיקרא — קודם שבא לבית דין שבלשכת הגזית לישאל לא הוה מיחייב קטלא כל כמה דלא עביד איהו גופיה. מעיקרא נמי בר קטלא הוא — אם עושה עבירה שיש בה מיתת בית דין הוה מיקטיל.

TRANSLATION AND COMMENTARY

and **bows** once again **when he goes out,** [1] **who studies Torah regularly, and does not give himself credit** and think of himself as a distinguished person. [2] When **the** Babylonian **Rabbis** received these guidelines, they immediately **set their eyes upon Ulla bar Abba,** who in their eyes had all of these virtues.

חָזַר [3] **We learned in our Mishnah: "If** the Great Sanhedrin decided against the Sage with the dissenting opinion, and **he returned to his city, and** once **again taught** the law in the same manner, he is exempt from the death penalty, even though his teachings contradict the decision reached by the Great Sanhedrin." [4] **Our Rabbis taught** a related Baraita: "A rebellious elder **is not liable to** execution **unless he** himself **acted in accordance with his** dissenting **ruling,** [5] **or he ruled for others and they acted in accordance with his** dissenting **ruling."** [6] The Gemara comments: **Granted** that we understand why the Baraita said that the rebellious elder is not liable to execution **"unless he ruled for others and they acted in accordance with his** dissenting **ruling,"** [7] for **before** he came to the Great Sanhedrin and asked them to rule on the matter, **he would not have been liable to execution** for the ruling he had issued to others, [8] **but now** that he appeared before the Great Sanhedrin, and they ruled against him, **he is liable to execution** if he ruled for others and they acted in accordance with his ruling. [9] **But** concerning what the Baraita said, that the rebellious elder is not liable to execution **"unless he** himself **acted in accordance with his** dissenting **ruling,"** there is a problem, [10] for **even before** the Great Sanhedrin ruled against him, **he would have been liable to execution** if he himself committed a capital offense! [11] The Gemara adds: We can **well** understand the Baraita if it is referring to a case **where** the rebellious elder **issued a** dissenting **ruling about forbidden fat and blood,** the eating of which is subject to excision, but not capital punishment. [12] **Before** he came to the Great Sanhedrin and asked them to rule on the matter, **he would not have been liable to execution** for acting in accordance with his dissenting ruling, [13] **but now** that he appeared before the Great Sanhedrin, and they ruled against him, **he is liable to**

NOTES

שָׁיֵיף עָיֵיל שָׁיֵיף וְנָפֵיק **Who bows and comes in, bows and goes out.** *Maharsha* understands that this alludes to a modest place of residence. A person who is fit to enter the World to Come lives in a modest dwelling with a low entrance that requires him to bend down in order to enter and exit.

HALAKHAH

court that convened at the entrance of the Temple Courtyard, and from there to the Great Sanhedrin." (*Rambam, Sefer Shofetim, Hilkhot Sanhedrin* 2:8.)

אֵינוֹ חַיָּיב עַד שֶׁיַּעֲשֶׂה כְּהוֹרָאָתוֹ **He is not liable unless he acted in accordance with his ruling.** "If a rebellious elder heard the decision of the Great Sanhedrin, and then returned to his city and continued to teach as he had taught earlier, but did not issue a practical ruling to act in accordance with his view, he is not liable to the death penalty. But if he issued a ruling to others, and they acted in accordance with his ruling, or if he himself acted in accordance with his ruling, he is liable to the death penalty," following the Mishnah and the Gemara. (*Rambam, Sefer Shofetim, Hilkhot Mamrim* 3:5.)

בַּר קְטָלָא הוּא. [1]אֶלָּא הֵיכָא דְּאוֹרֵי בְּחַיָּיבֵי מִיתוֹת בֵּית דִּין, [2]מֵעִיקָּרָא נַמִי בַּר קְטָלָא הוּא! [3]מֵעִיקָּרָא בָּעֵי הַתְרָאָה, [4]הָשְׁתָּא לָא בָּעֵי הַתְרָאָה. [5]מֵסִית דְּלָא בָּעֵי הַתְרָאָה, מַאי אִיכָּא לְמֵימַר? [6]מֵעִיקָּרָא אִי אֲמַר טַעְמָא, מְקַבְּלִינַן מִינֵּיהּ. [7]הָשְׁתָּא אִי אֲמַר טַעְמָא, לָא מְקַבְּלִינַן מִינֵּיהּ.

מִשְׁנָה [8]חוֹמֶר בְּדִבְרֵי סוֹפְרִים מִבְּדִבְרֵי תוֹרָה. [9]הָאוֹמֵר ״אֵין תְּפִילִין״, [10]כְּדֵי

LITERAL TRANSLATION

he is liable to execution. [1]But where he ruled about [offenses] that are punishable by judicial execution, [2]even initially he was liable to execution! [3]Initially he needed a warning, [4]now he does not need a warning. [5][Regarding] an inciter who does not need a warning, what is there to say? [6]Initially, if he gave an explanation, we would accept it from him. [7]Now, if he gives an explanation, we do not accept it from him.

MISHNAH [8]There is a stringency regarding the words of the Sages over the words of the Torah. [9]Someone who says, "There is no tefillin," [10]in order to

TRANSLATION AND COMMENTARY

execution if he acted in accordance with his ruling. [1]**But** regarding the case **where** the rebellious elder **issued a** dissenting **ruling about an offense that is punishable by judicial execution,** there is a difficulty, [2]for **even before** the Great Sanhedrin ruled against him, **he would have been liable to execution** if he himself committed a capital offense!

מֵעִיקָּרָא [3]The Gemara comments: There is nevertheless a difference, for **before** the Great Sanhedrin ruled against him, the rebellious elder **needed a warning** prior to the commission of his offense in order to become subject to execution, just like any other sinner. [4]But **now** that he has appeared before the Great Sanhedrin and they have ruled against him, **he does not need a warning** in order to become subject to execution, for a rebellious elder may be executed for his refusal to accept the rulings of the Great Sanhedrin, even without a warning.

מֵסִית [5]The Gemara comments: This is acceptable if the rebellious elder issued his dissenting ruling about an offense regarding which the transgressor is only liable to execution if he received a warning prior to the commission of his offense. But **what is there to say** if a rebellious elder issued a dissenting ruling about **someone who incites** others to commit idolatry — a sinner **who does not need a warning** in order to become subject to execution? Even before the Great Sanhedrin had ruled against him, the rebellious elder would have been subject to execution if he had incited others to idolatry, even without having received a warning!

מֵעִיקָּרָא [6]The Gemara concludes: There is nevertheless a difference, for **before** the Great Sanhedrin ruled against him, **if** the rebellious elder had **offered** some **explanation** for his behavior, **we would have accepted it from him,** and spared him execution. [7]But **now** that he has appeared before the Great Sanhedrin, and they have ruled against him, **we do not accept** any explanations **from him,** for he heard from the Great Sanhedrin that the incitement in question was forbidden, and yet he acted in accordance with his own dissenting opinion.

MISHNAH חוֹמֶר [8]With respect to a dissenting ruling given by a rebellious elder, **there is a stringency regarding the words of the Sages** — the clarifications offered by the Sages to the words of the Torah — **over the words of the Torah** — that which is stated explicitly in the Torah. If the rebellious elder issued a dissenting ruling regarding a matter known through Rabbinic interpretation or tradition, he is liable to execution. But if he issued a dissenting ruling regarding a matter stated explicitly in the Torah, he is exempt, for a ruling on a matter that is spelled out by the Torah itself has no significance as a ruling. How so? [9]If the rebellious elder **said, "There is no** commandment to put on **tefillin,"** [10]thus instructing

RASHI

מסית דלא בעי התראה — אם היה מסית ומורה טעם היתר ולומר אין בלשון הזה הסתה, מעיקרא נמי מקטיל בלא התראה. **אי אמר טעמא לזכותא** — לאצוליה, אבל השתא אי אמר טעמא לא **מקבלינן** — שהרי שמע מפי בית דין שלא לעשות — והמרה.

משנה האומר אין תפילין פטור — דאין זו הוראה, דזיל קרי בי רב הוא.

NOTES

לָא בָּעֵי הַתְרָאָה **He does not need a warning.** According to *Rosh,* the rebellious elder does not need a warning

HALAKHAH

לָא בָּעֵי הַתְרָאָה **He does not need a warning.** "If the rebellious elder issued a ruling in accordance with his dissenting view, or if he himself acted in accordance with that view, he is liable to the death penalty. He does not need a warning in order to become liable to be executed. Even if he offered an explanation for his ruling, we do not listen to him." (*Rambam, Sefer Shofetim, Hilkhot Mamrim* 3:8.)

לַעֲבוֹר עַל דִּבְרֵי תוֹרָה — פָּטוּר. [1]״חָמֵשׁ טוֹטָפוֹת״, לְהוֹסִיף עַל דִּבְרֵי סוֹפְרִים — חַיָּיב.

גמרא [2]אָמַר רַבִּי אֶלְעָזָר אָמַר רַבִּי אוֹשַׁעְיָא: אֵינוֹ חַיָּיב אֶלָּא עַל דָּבָר שֶׁעִיקָּרוֹ מִדִּבְרֵי תוֹרָה וּפֵירוּשׁוֹ מִדִּבְרֵי סוֹפְרִים. [3]וְיֵשׁ בּוֹ לְהוֹסִיף, וְאִם הוֹסִיף גּוֹרֵעַ. [4]וְאֵין לָנוּ אֶלָּא תְּפִילִּין [5]אַלִּיבָּא דְּרַבִּי יְהוּדָה.

LITERAL TRANSLATION

violate the words of the Torah is exempt. [1]"Five compartments," in order to add to the words of the Sages — he is liable.

GEMARA [2]Rabbi Elazar said in the name of Rabbi Oshaya: He is only liable for something whose source is in the Torah, but whose clarification is in the words of the Sages. [3]And there is in it to add, and if he added, he disqualifies. [4]And we only have tefillin, [5]according to Rabbi Yehudah.

TRANSLATION AND COMMENTARY

others **to violate the** explicit **words of the Torah,** he **is exempt** from execution. But if he disputed the Rabbinic interpretation of the commandment, and said, [1]"There must be **five compartments** in the tefillin worn on the head," thus instructing others **to add to the words of the Sages** (for, according to the Rabbinic interpretation, there are only four such compartments), **he is liable** to execution.

GEMARA אָמַר רַבִּי אֶלְעָזָר [2]**Rabbi Elazar said in the name of Rabbi Oshaya:** A rebellious elder **is only liable** to the death penalty if he issued a ruling that contradicted a ruling of the Great Sanhedrin about a law **whose source is in the Torah** itself, **but whose clarification is in the words of the Sages,** [3]**and** his ruling **adds** an element that goes beyond the Rabbinic interpretation of the law, **and if someone added** that element in accordance with the elder's ruling, **he detracted** from the proper fulfillment of the commandment. [4]**And there is only** one law that fulfills all of these conditions, the law of **tefillin.** The obligation to wear tefillin is derived from the Torah, but it is only through Rabbinic interpretation and tradition that we know that the tefillin worn on the head must have four compartments. However, it is possible to go beyond the Rabbinic interpretation of the law by requiring five such compartments, and that addition disqualifies one's fulfillment of the commandment. By putting on tefillin with five compartments, one violates the prohibition against adding to what is stated in the Torah. [5]And all this was stated **according to Rabbi Yehudah,** who said — above (87a) — that the verse (Deuteronomy 17:11), "And you shall do according to the sentence of the Torah which they shall teach you," implies that the rebellious elder is liable only if he issued a ruling that contradicted a ruling of the Great Sanhedrin about a law regarding which there is both "Torah," an explicit Torah source, and a need for "they shall teach you," a certain ambiguity that requires Rabbinic clarification.

RASHI

חמש טוטפות יש — שאף על פי שאין דבר זה אלא להוסיף על דברי סופרים — חייב, דמדרש דסופרים הוא ״לטטפת״ ״לטטפת״ ״לטוטפות״ הרי כאן ארבע.

גמרא ויש בו להוסיף — על מה שפירשו חכמים. **ואם הוסיף גורע** — ופוסל הראשון בתוספתו. **ואין לנו אלא תפילין** — שעיקרן בתורה, ופירושן מדברי סופרים שהם ארבעה בתים, ויש להוסיף חמשה או יותר, ואם הוסיף — גורע, דקא עבר בבל תוסיף ולא עבד מצוה. **ואליבא דרבי יהודה** — אמר רבי אושעיא למילתיה דאמר לעיל עד דאיכא תורה ויורוך, ואית דאמרי אין לנו אלא תפילין ואליבא דרבי יהודה דאמר צריך להדביק, במנחות בהקומץ רבה (לד,ב), ולא נהירא לי — דההיא בתפילין של יד קאי, ומתניתין טוטפות תאני — והיינו דראש ועוד, מדקא מקשי בסיפא: אי דעבד ארבעה בתים כו׳ — שמע מינה בשל ראש קיימין, דאי בשל יד בית אחד הוא דקא הוי.

NOTES

regarding the offense itself. He must, however, be warned that one is forbidden to issue a ruling or act in a manner that contradicts a ruling of the Great Sanhedrin.

חָמֵשׁ טוֹטָפוֹת Five compartments. The Jerusalem Talmud adds that, regarding this matter, the commandment concerning the mezuzah is like the commandment concerning tefillin.

פֵּירוּשׁוֹ מִדִּבְרֵי סוֹפְרִים Whose clarification is in the words of the Sages. As for the Rabbinic clarification of the details of the commandment concerning lulav, some understand that we are dealing here with the precise identification of the four species, which is not fully clarified in the Torah itself. Others argue that this refers to the number of each species that must be taken. Today, it is customary in certain communities to take more than the minimum number required, particularly myrtle branches. The additional myrtle branches do not invalidate the commandment for we follow the position that a lulav does not need tying.

HALAKHAH

וְאֵין לָנוּ אֶלָּא תְּפִילִּין And we only have tefillin. "If a rebellious elder issued a ruling to add a fifth compartment to the tefillin, he is liable. This ruling applies only in a case where he ruled that one should first fashion tefillin with four compartments, and then add a fifth compartment on the outside (see *Raavad,* who disagrees with this ruling, *Kesef Mishneh, Radbaz,* and *Leḥem Mishneh*)." (*Rambam, Sefer Shofetim, Hilkhot Mamrim* 4:3.)

TRANSLATION AND COMMENTARY

וְהָאִיכָּא [1]The Gemara suggests that there are other laws that fulfill all these conditions: **But surely the** commandment of taking the **lulav** (a palm branch, together with the myrtle, the willow, and the citron, fulfills all the conditions laid down by Rabbi Oshaya) [2]**for the source** of the obligation to take these four species **is** found **in the Torah** itself (Leviticus 23:40), [3]**and the clarification** of the details of the commandment — the precise identification of the four species and the number of each kind that must be taken — **is** found **in the words of the Sages,** [4]**and** a ruling may be given which **adds** an element that goes beyond the Rabbinic interpretation of the law, by adding a fifth species, [5]**and if someone added** that element in accordance with the elder's ruling, **he disqualified** his fulfillment of the commandment!

בְּלוּלָב [6]The Gemara rejects this suggestion: **What do we maintain about a lulav?** [7]**If we maintain that a lulav does not need tying,** and there is no obligation to bind the four species together and take them as a single unit, then taking them together with a fifth species should not invalidate what he did, [8]for **the** four required species **stand by themselves, and** the fifth species which he added **stands by itself.** [9]**But if we maintain that** a lulav **needs tying** meaning that the four species must be bound together as a single unit, [10]then the lulav **was already disqualified** from use when it was first bound together with the fifth species. If someone later took the five species together, he did nothing at that time to invalidate the fulfillment of his obligation. Thus the rebellious elder should not be liable to the ruling that he had issued, according to the conditions set by Rabbi Oshaya.

וְהָאִיכָּא [11]The Gemara asks: **But surely** the commandment of placing **fringes** on the four corners of one's garments fulfills all the conditions laid down by Rabbi Oshaya, [12]**for the source** of the obligation **is** found **in the Torah** itself (Leviticus 15:37-41), **and the clarification** of the details of the commandment — the number of threads that must be placed on each corner — **is** found **in the words of the Sages,** [13]**and** a ruling may be given which **adds** an element that goes beyond the Rabbinic interpretation of the law, such as a fifth thread. [14]**If someone added** that element in accordance with the elder's ruling, **he disqualified** his fulfillment of the commandment!

בְּצִיצִית [15]The Gemara rebuts this argument: **What do we maintain about** the commandment of **fringes?** [16]**If**

[1]וְהָאִיכָּא לוּלָב, [2]דְּעִיקָּרוֹ מִדִּבְרֵי תוֹרָה, [3]וּפֵירוּשׁוֹ מִדִּבְרֵי סוֹפְרִים, [4]וְיֵשׁ בּוֹ לְהוֹסִיף, [5]וְאִם הוֹסִיף גּוֹרֵעַ!

[6]בְּלוּלָב, מַאי סְבִירָא לָן? [7]אִי סְבִירָא לָן דְּלוּלָב אֵין צָרִיךְ אֶגֶד, [8]הַאי לְחוּדֵיהּ קָאֵי [9]וְהַאי לְחוּדֵיהּ קָאֵי, וְאִי סְבִירָא לָן דְּצָרִיךְ אֶגֶד — [10]גָּרוּעַ וְעוֹמֵד הוּא.

[11]וְהָאִיכָּא צִיצִית, [12]דְּעִיקָּרוֹ מִדִּבְרֵי תוֹרָה וּפֵירוּשׁוֹ מִדִּבְרֵי סוֹפְרִים, [13]וְיֵשׁ בּוֹ לְהוֹסִיף, [14]וְאִם הוֹסִיף גּוֹרֵעַ!

[15]בְּצִיצִית מַאי סְבִירָא לָן? [16]אִי

LITERAL TRANSLATION

[1]But surely there is the lulav, [2]for its source is in the Torah, [3]and its clarification is in the words of the Sages, [4]and there is in it to add, [5]and if he added, he disqualifies!

[6]Regarding a lulav, what do we maintain? [7]If we maintain that a lulav does not need tying, [8]this stands by itself and that stands by itself. [9]And if we maintain that it needs tying, [10]it was already disqualified.

[11]But surely there are fringes, [12]for its source is in the Torah, and its clarification is in the words of the Sages, [13]and there is in it to add, [14]and if he added, he disqualifies!

[15]Regarding fringes, what do we maintain? [16]If

RASHI

האי לחודיה קאי — ואין זה גורע. **גרוע ועומד** — דמתחילתו לא עשה כהוגן, שאגד שם תוספת מצוה, ואנן בעינן גורע דהשתא שהיה מתחילתו כשר ופוסלו בתוספתו. **ופירושו מדברי סופרים** — ארבעה חוטין, דילפינן גדיל — שנים, "גדילים" — ארבעה.

NOTES

גָּרוּעַ וְעוֹמֵד הוּא It was already disqualified. According to *Raavad,* the Gemara does not mean to suggest that because the lulav was already disqualified from use when it was first bound with the fifth species, the rebellious elder should not be liable for the ruling that he had issued. But rather the Gemara means to say that the criterion for the elders liability should not be that "if he added, he disqualifies," for here in the case of lulav, the elder is liable even though the lulav was already disqualified from use.

HALAKHAH

לוּלָב אֵין צָרִיךְ אֶגֶד A lulav does not need tying. "By Torah law, one is not required to tie together the palm branch, myrtles, and willows, and so if one took the various species one after the other, he fulfilled the commandment. But the best way to fulfill the commandment involves tying the palm branch, myrtles, and willows together," following the Sages in tractate *Sukkah* (*Maggid Mishneh*). (*Rambam, Sefer Zemanim, Hilkhot Lulav* 7:6.)

TRANSLATION AND COMMENTARY

we maintain that the first knot with which the threads of the fringes must be tied **is not** required **by Torah law,** for by Torah law the threads may be placed on the corners even if they are not tied with a knot then adding a fifth thread should not invalidate a person's fulfillment of the commandment, [1]for **the** four required threads **stand by themselves, and** the added fifth thread **stands by itself.** [2]**And if we maintain** [89A] **that the upper knot** with which the threads of the fringes must be tied **is** required **by Torah law,** then the fringe **was already disqualified** when the five threads were tied together with a knot. If someone later wore the garment with the five-threaded fringes, he did nothing to invalidate the fulfillment of his obligation, and so the rebellious elder should not be liable for the ruling that he had issued, according to the conditions set by Rabbi Oshaya.

אִי הָכִי [3]The Gemara continues: **If so,** we should **also** say the same thing about **tefillin! If someone made** tefillin with **four compartments and** then **brought another** compartment **and placed it** on his head **alongside** the four compartments, the addition of the fifth compartment should not invalidate his fulfillment of the commandment, [4]for the four compartments **stand by themselves, and** the added fifth compartment **stands by itself.** [5]**And if** from the outset **he made** tefillin with **five compartments,** then the tefillin **were already disqualified** from use before he put them on. So when he did put them on, he did nothing new to invalidate the fulfillment of his obligation. Thus, a rebellious elder should not be liable to be punished for the ruling that he issued regarding tefillin, according to the conditions set by Rabbi Oshaya!

הָאָמַר [6]The Gemara answers: There is no comparison between tefillin on the one hand and lulav and fringes on the other, for **surely Rabbi Zera said:** If **the outer compartment** of the tefillin is covered by anything so that it **does not see the air,** it **is disqualified** for use. Thus, if someone made tefillin with four compartments, and then brought another compartment and placed it on his head alongside the four compartments, covering the outer compartment of his tefillin, that act invalidated the fulfillment of the commandment. Thus, a rebellious elder is liable to the death penalty if he issued a ruling adding a fifth compartment to the commandment of tefillin.

MISHNAH אֵין מְמִיתִין [7]A rebellious elder **may not be put to death by the** twenty-three-member **court**

סְבִירָא לָן דְּקֶשֶׁר הָעֶלְיוֹן לָאו דְּאוֹרַיְיתָא, [1]הַאי לְחוּדֵיהּ קָאֵי וְהַאי לְחוּדֵיהּ קָאֵי. [2]וְאִי סְבִירָא לָן [89A] דְּקֶשֶׁר הָעֶלְיוֹן דְּאוֹרַיְיתָא — גָּרוּעַ וְעוֹמֵד. [3]אִי הָכִי, תְּפִילִּין נַמִי! [4]אִי עָבֵיד אַרְבָּעָה בָּתֵּי וְאַיְיתִי אַחֲרִינָא וְאַנַּח גַּבַּיְיהוּ, הַאי לְחוּדֵיהּ קָאֵי וְהַאי לְחוּדֵיהּ קָאֵי, [5]וְאִי עָבֵיד חֲמִשָּׁה בָּתֵּי, גָּרוּעַ וְעוֹמֵד הוּא! [6]הָאָמַר רַבִּי זֵירָא: בַּיִת חִיצוֹן שֶׁאֵינוֹ רוֹאֶה אֶת הָאֲוִיר פָּסוּל.

מִשְׁנָה [7]אֵין מְמִיתִין אוֹתוֹ

LITERAL TRANSLATION

we maintain that the upper knot is not by Torah law, [1]this stands by itself and that stands by itself. [2]And if we maintain [89A] that the upper knot is by Torah law, it was already disqualified.

[3]If so, tefillin also! If he made four compartments and brought another one and placed it on them, [4]this stands by itself and that stands by itself. [5]And if he made five compartments, it was already disqualified.

[6]Surely Rabbi Zera said: An outer compartment that does not see the air is unfit.

MISHNAH [7]They do not put him to death

RASHI

קשר עליון — שעושין סמוך לכנף כשנתלו החוטין ועל ידיהן נעשין חיבור לטלית — לאו דאורייתא (אלא) [כלומר] הלכה למשה מסיני, דפלוגתא היא במנחות (לט,א). האי לחודיה קאי — דכיון דלא נקשר אינו חיבור עם השאר, והראוי למצוה היא המצוה, והעודף כמי שאינו. שאינו רואה את האויר — כגון שהוסיף בית חמישי עליהם בלדו או דבר אחר.

BACKGROUND

קֶשֶׁר עֶלְיוֹן **Upper knot.**

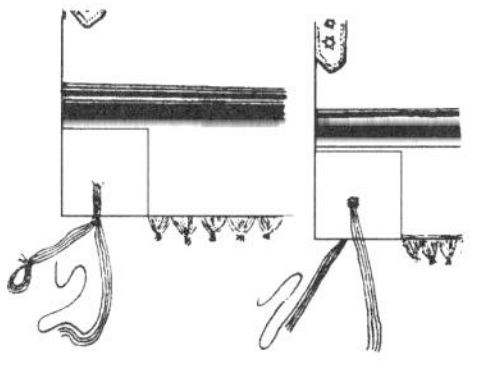

On the right, a fringe passsed through a hole in the garment without any knot. On the left, a fringe tied only with an upper knot. Most commentators maintain that the upper knot is the first one tied when fastening a fringe to a garment, before measuring the length of the fringe.

תְּפִילִּין **Tefillin.**

Photograph of a head phylactery from the Mishnaic period, found in a cave in the Judean Desert.

This photograph clearly shows the four separate chambers of the head phylactery. As noted, if a fifth chamber were added, the outer surface of the phylactery would not be exposed to the air.

NOTES

קֶשֶׁר הָעֶלְיוֹן **The upper knot.** According to *Rashi,* the "upper knot" of the fringes is the knot that is closest to the garment. According to other Rishonim, that knot is the "lower knot," and the "upper knot" is the last knot with which the fringes are tied (*Eshkol, Tosafot* in tractate *Menaḥot, Rabbi David Bonfil*).

HALAKHAH

בַּיִת חִיצוֹן שֶׁאֵינוֹ רוֹאֶה אֶת הָאֲוִיר פָּסוּל **An outer compartment that does not see the air is unfit.** "If the rebellious elder issued a ruling to add a fifth compartment to tefillin, in such a manner that the outer compartments are no longer exposed to the air, the tefillin are disqualified, and the elder is liable to the death penalty." (*Rambam, Sefer Shofetim, Hilkhot Mamrim* 4:3.)

אֵין מְמִיתִין אוֹתוֹ לֹא בְּבֵית דִּין שֶׁבְּעִירוֹ **They do not put him to death in the court in his town.** "A rebellious elder may not be put to death by the court sitting in his home town, nor by the Great Sanhedrin if it was sitting outside of Jerusalem, but only by the Great Sanhedrin sitting in

לֹא בְּבֵית דִּין שֶׁבְּעִירוֹ, [1]וְלֹא בְּבֵית דִּין שֶׁבְּיַבְנֶה. [2]אֶלָּא, מַעֲלִין אוֹתוֹ לְבֵית דִּין הַגָּדוֹל שֶׁבִּירוּשָׁלַיִם. [3]וּמְשַׁמְּרִין אוֹתוֹ עַד הָרֶגֶל, [4]וּמְמִיתִין אוֹתוֹ בָּרֶגֶל, [5]שֶׁנֶּאֱמַר: "וְכָל הָעָם יִשְׁמְעוּ וְיִרָאוּ וְלֹא יְזִידוּן עוֹד". [6]דִּבְרֵי רַבִּי עֲקִיבָא. [7]רַבִּי יְהוּדָה אוֹמֵר: אֵין מְעַנִּין אֶת דִּינוֹ שֶׁל זֶה. [8]אֶלָּא מְמִיתִין אוֹתוֹ מִיָּד, [9]וְכוֹתְבִין וְשׁוֹלְחִין שְׁלוּחִין בְּכָל הַמְּקוֹמוֹת: "אִישׁ פְּלוֹנִי מִתְחַיֵּיב מִיתָה בְּבֵית דִּין".

גמרא [10]תָּנוּ רַבָּנַן: "אֵין מְמִיתִין אוֹתוֹ לֹא בְּבֵית דִּין שֶׁבְּעִירוֹ, [11]וְלֹא בְּבֵית דִּין שֶׁבְּיַבְנֶה. [12]אֶלָּא, מַעֲלִין אוֹתוֹ לְבֵית דִּין הַגָּדוֹל שֶׁבִּירוּשָׁלַיִם, [13]וּמְשַׁמְּרִין אוֹתוֹ עַד הָרֶגֶל, וּמְמִיתִין אוֹתוֹ בָּרֶגֶל. [14]שֶׁנֶּאֱמַר: 'וְכָל הָעָם יִשְׁמְעוּ וְיִרָאוּ'.

LITERAL TRANSLATION

in the court in his town, [1]nor in the court in Yavneh. [2]Rather, they bring him up to the Great Sanhedrin in Jerusalem, [3]and guard him until the Pilgrim Festival, [4]and put him to death on the Pilgrim Festival, [5]as it is stated: "And all the people shall hear, and fear, and no longer act presumptuously." [6][These are] the words of Rabbi Akiva. [7]Rabbi Yehudah says: They do not put off that one's punishment. [8]Rather, they put him to death immediately, [9]and they write, and send messengers to all the places: "So-and-so became liable to judicial execution."

GEMARA [10]Our Rabbis taught: "They do not put him to death in the court in his town, [11]nor in the court in Yavneh. [12]Rather, they bring him up to the Great Sanhedrin in Jerusalem, [13]and guard him until the Pilgrim Festival, and put him to death on the Pilgrim Festival, [14]as it is stated: 'And all the people shall hear, and fear.'

TRANSLATION AND COMMENTARY

sitting **in his** home **town,** even if it was there that he issued his ruling that contradicted the decision of the Great Sanhedrin. [1]**Nor** may he be put to death **by the court** of seventy-one judges sitting **in Yavneh.** After the destruction of the Temple, Rabbi Yoḥanan ben Zakkai reestablished the Great Sanhedrin in the town of Yavneh. Even if the rebellious elder issued a ruling that contradicted a decision of the Great Sanhedrin that had been reached while it was still sitting in Jerusalem, he may not be put to death by the Great Sanhedrin after it has moved elsewhere. [2]**Rather,** if the Great Sanhedrin is still sitting in the Chamber of Hewn Stone, the rebellious elder is **brought to the Great Sanhedrin in Jerusalem,** [3]**he is incarcerated until the** next **Pilgrim Festival** (Pesaḥ, Shavuot or Sukkot), [4]**and he is put to death during** the intermediate days of **the Pilgrim Festival,** when many people are assembled in Jerusalem, and his execution can be most effective as a deterrent, [5]**as the verse states** (Deuteronomy 17:13): **"And all the people shall hear, and fear, and no longer act presumptuously."** [6]**This is the position of Rabbi Akiva.** [7]**Rabbi Yehudah** disagrees and **says:** The rebellious elder's **punishment is not put off** until the next Pilgrim Festival. [8]**Rather, he is put to death immediately** following his appearance before the Great Sanhedrin in Jerusalem, to spare him undue suffering while he is waiting to be executed. [9]But the Sanhedrin **writes** missives **and sends out messengers to all places,** saying: **"So-and-so became liable to judicial execution** for issuing a ruling that contradicts the decision of the majority of the Sages of his generation." Publicizing the rebellious elder's crime and punishment in this manner serves to fulfill the verse, "And all the people shall hear, and fear."

GEMARA תָּנוּ רַבָּנַן [10]**Our Rabbis taught** a Baraita which elaborates on our Mishnah: "A rebellious elder **may not be put to death by the** twenty-three-member **court** sitting **in his home town.** [11]**Nor** may he be put to death **by the court** of seventy-one judges sitting **in Yavneh.** [12]**Rather,** the rebellious elder is **brought to the Great Sanhedrin in Jerusalem,** [13]**he is incarcerated until the** next **Pilgrim Festival** (Pesaḥ, Shavuot or Sukkot), **and he is put to death during** the intermediate days of **the Pilgrim Festival,** when many people are assembled in Jerusalem and his execution can be most effective as a deterrent, [14]**as the verse states** (Deuteronomy 17:13): **'And all the people shall hear, and fear, and no longer act presumptuously.'**

RASHI

משנה כל ישראל ישמעו — צריך להשמיע מיתתו לרבים, שלא יעשה אדם עוד כן. **לא בבית דין שביבנה** — אם נשאלו לבית דין שבלשכת הגזית ואמרו להם, וחזר לעירו ושהה ימים עד שגלתה סנהדרי גדולה ליבנה ועדיין הבית קיים, ואחרי כן הורה כבתחילה — אין ממיתין אותו ביבנה, ואף על פי שהם סנהדרי גדולה — שסוף סוף אין נקבלים שם.

גמרא וכי נאמר וכל העם יראו וייראו — דבעינן שיהו רואין במיתתו.

HALAKHAH

Jerusalem. He is incarcerated in Jerusalem until the next Pilgrim Festival, and put to death by strangulation during the intermediate days of that Festival," following Rabbi Akiva, against the opinion of his disciple, Rabbi Yehudah. (*Rambam, Sefer Shofetim, Hilkhot Mamrim* 3:8.)

LITERAL TRANSLATION

[1][These are] the words of Rabbi Akiva. [2]Rabbi Yehudah said to him: Is it stated: 'They shall see, and fear'? [3]Surely it is only stated: 'They shall hear, and fear.' [4]Why should they put off that one's punishment? [5]Rather, they put him to death immediately, and write, and send [messengers] to all places: [6]'So-and-so became liable to judicial execution.'" [7]Our Rabbis taught: "Four require an announcement: [8]An inciter, a stubborn and rebellious son, a rebellious elder, and false, conspiring witnesses." [9]Regarding all of them it is written: "And all the people," "and all Israel." [10]Regarding false, conspiring witnesses it is written: "And those who remain," [11]because not everybody is fit for testimony.

[1]דִּבְרֵי רַבִּי עֲקִיבָא. [2]אָמַר לוֹ רַבִּי יְהוּדָה: וְכִי נֶאֱמַר: ׳יִרְאוּ וְיִירָאוּ׳? [3]וַהֲלֹא לֹא נֶאֱמַר אֶלָּא: ׳יִשְׁמְעוּ וְיִירָאוּ׳? [4]לָמָּה מְעַנִּין דִּינוֹ שֶׁל זֶה? [5]אֶלָּא, מְמִיתִין אוֹתוֹ מִיָּד, וְכוֹתְבִין וְשׁוֹלְחִין בְּכָל מָקוֹם: [6]״אִישׁ פְּלוֹנִי נִתְחַיֵּיב מִיתָה בְּבֵית דִּין״.

[7]תָּנוּ רַבָּנַן: ״אַרְבָּעָה צְרִיכִין הַכְרָזָה: [8]הַמֵּסִית, וּבֵן סוֹרֵר וּמוֹרֶה, וְזָקֵן מַמְרֵא, וְעֵדִים זוֹמְמִין״. [9]בְּכוּלְּהוּ כְּתִיב בְּהוּ: ״וְכָל הָעָם״ ״וְכָל יִשְׂרָאֵל״. [10]בְּעֵדִים זוֹמְמִין, כְּתִיב: ״וְהַנִּשְׁאָרִים״, [11]דְּלָא כּוּלֵּי עָלְמָא חֲזוּ לְסָהֲדוּתָא.

TRANSLATION AND COMMENTARY

[1]**This is the position of Rabbi Akiva.** [2]**Rabbi Yehudah** disagrees and **says: Does the verse state: 'They shall *see*, and fear'?** This would imply that the rebellious elder must be executed in the presence of all of Israel. [3]**Surely the verse states: 'They shall *hear*, and fear.'** [4]**Why,** then, **should they put off** the rebellious elder's **punishment?** [5]**Rather, he is put to death immediately** following his appearance before the Great Sanhedrin in Jerusalem, and the Sanhedrin **writes** missives **and sends out** messengers **to all places,** saying: [6]**'So-and-so became liable to judicial execution** for issuing a ruling that contradicts the decision of the majority of the Sages of his generation.' In that way all of Israel will hear about the rebellious elder's crime and punishment, their hearts will be filled with fear of God, and they will not act presumptuously anymore."

תָּנוּ רַבָּנַן [7]**Our Rabbis taught** the following Baraita: "Regarding the following **four** capital offenders, **an announcement must be made** as to the nature of the offense for which they are being executed, so that their execution will serve as a deterrent against other people repeating their crimes: [8]**Someone who incites** others to commit idolatry, **a rebellious son, a rebellious elder, and false, conspiring witnesses."** [9]**Regarding all of them** except false, conspiring witnesses, **the verse states: "And all the people,"** or **"and all Israel."** Regarding someone who incites others to commit idolatry, the verse states (Deuteronomy 13:12): "And all Israel shall hear, and fear"; regarding a rebellious son, the verse states (Deuteronomy 21:21): "And all Israel shall hear, and fear"; and regarding a rebellious elder, the verse states (Deuteronomy 17:13): "And all the people shall hear, and fear." [10]But **regarding false, conspiring witnesses, the verse states** (Deuteronomy 19:20): **"And those who remain** shall hear, and fear," [11]**because not everybody is fit** to offer **testimony.** Some Jews, such as women, minors or those guilty of certain transgressions, are disqualified from offering testimony. Hence they can never become false, conspiring witnesses, and only "those who remain" must hear, and fear, and not commit that crime.

RASHI

הכרזה – פלוני מת בבית דין על שעבר עבירה זו, כדי לרדות את האחרים. וכל ישראל – ישמעו וייראו. ובעדים זוממים כתיב והנשארים – ישמעו וייראו, משום דלא שייך למיכתב וכל העם – דלאו כולי עלמא חזו לסהדותא, שיש גזלנין ומלוי ברבית ומועלים בשביעית שהן פסולים לעדות.

NOTES

וְכִי נֶאֱמַר: ׳יִרְאוּ וְיִירָאוּ׳ **Is it stated: They shall see, and fear?** According to Rabbi Akiva, the verse, "and all the people shall hear, and fear," can only be fulfilled when all the people hear of the elder's execution at the same time, and that can only happen on a Pilgrim Festival, when all of Israel is gathered in Jerusalem (*Melo HeRoim*).

לָא כּוּלֵּי עָלְמָא חֲזוּ לְסָהֲדוּתָא **Not everybody is fit for testimony.** Our commentary follows *Rashi*, who explains that the execution of false, conspiring witnesses need not serve as a deterrent against "all Israel," because some people are disqualified from offering testimony and can never become false, conspiring witnesses. Other Rishonim point out several difficulties with *Rashi*'s explanation. *Tosafot* suggests that the Gemara means to say that not everybody is fit for testimony, because a person cannot decide to be a witness, but rather a person who happens to witness a crime is obligated to come forth and offer testimony. Others argue that, regarding someone who incites others to commit idolatry, a rebellious son, and a rebellious elder, an announcement must be made as to the

HALAKHAH

אַרְבָּעָה צְרִיכִין הַכְרָזָה **Four require an announcement.** "Regarding four capital offenders, an announcement must be made informing the entire nation why the offender in each case was sentenced to execution: a rebellious elder, false, conspiring witnesses, someone who incited others to commit idolatry, and a rebellious son, for regarding all of them the Torah states: 'And all of Israel shall hear, and fear.'" (*Rambam, Sefer Shofetim, Hilkhot Mamrim* 3:8; 7:13; *Hilkhot Edut* 18:7.)

TRANSLATION AND COMMENTARY

MISHNAH נְבִיא הַשֶּׁקֶר [1]Our Mishnah comes to clarify the laws regarding the other sinners included in the first Mishnah of our chapter among those liable to death by strangulation: **A false Prophet** — meaning **someone who prophesies what** he himself **did not hear** from God, and what no one else heard from God, **or** someone who prophesies **what was not told to him,** but was told to some true Prophet, and then the false Prophet heard it from him, and declared that the prophecy had been told to him by God — [2]**his death is at the hand of man** by strangulation. [3]**But someone who suppresses a prophecy** told to him by God and does not declare it to the people, [4]**and someone who makes light of the words of a Prophet** and disobeys him, [5]**and a Prophet who transgresses his own words** and fails to fulfill what he has been told to do by God — in each of these cases, [6]the sinner's **death is at the hand of Heaven,** [7]**as the verse states** (Deuteronomy 18:19): "And it shall come to pass, that the man who will not hearken to My words which he shall speak in My name, **I will require it of him**" — meaning death at the hand of Heaven. This verse alludes to each of these three offenses, as will be explained in the Gemara.

הַמִּתְנַבֵּא [8]**Someone who prophesies in the name of an idol, and says: "Thus the idol said** to me," [9]**even if he was precise about the law** that he reported in the name of the idol, and he **declared** what is **ritually impure** according to the Halakhah as being **ritually impure, and** what is **ritually pure** according to the Halakhah as being **ritually pure** — such a person is liable to death by strangulation.

הַבָּא [10]As for **someone who has** sexual **intercourse with a married woman, once** a betrothed woman

LITERAL TRANSLATION

MISHNAH [1]A false Prophet — someone who prophesies what he did not hear, or what was not told to him — [2]his death is at the hand of man. [3]But someone who suppresses his prophecy, [4]and someone who makes light of the words of a Prophet, [5]and a Prophet who transgressed his own words — [6]his death is at the hand of Heaven, [7]as it is stated: "I will require it of him." [8]Someone who prophesies in the name of an idol, and says: "Thus said the idol," [9]even if he was precise about the law to declare the ritually impure ritually impure, and the ritually pure ritually pure. [10]Someone who has intercourse with another man's wife — once

מִשְׁנָה [1]נְבִיא הַשֶּׁקֶר, הַמִּתְנַבֵּא מַה שֶׁלֹּא שָׁמַע, וּמַה שֶׁלֹּא נֶאֱמַר לוֹ — [2]מִיתָתוֹ בִּידֵי אָדָם. [3]אֲבָל הַכּוֹבֵשׁ אֶת נְבוּאָתוֹ, [4]וְהַמְוַותֵּר עַל דִּבְרֵי נָבִיא, [5]וְנָבִיא שֶׁעָבַר עַל דִּבְרֵי עַצְמוֹ — [6]מִיתָתוֹ בִּידֵי שָׁמַיִם, [7]שֶׁנֶּאֱמַר: "אָנֹכִי אֶדְרֹשׁ מֵעִמּוֹ". [8]הַמִּתְנַבֵּא בְּשֵׁם עֲבוֹדָה זָרָה, וְאוֹמֵר: "כָּךְ אָמְרָה עֲבוֹדָה זָרָה", [9]אֲפִילוּ כִּוֵּון אֶת הַהֲלָכָה לְטַמֵּא אֶת הַטָּמֵא וּלְטַהֵר אֶת הַטָּהוֹר. [10]הַבָּא עַל אֵשֶׁת אִישׁ, כֵּיוָן

RASHI

מִשְׁנָה ומה שלא נאמר לו — אף על פי שנאמר לחבירו ונגמרא יליף לה. הכובש נבואתו — שלא אמרה, כגון יונה בן אמיתי. והמוותר על דברי נביא — המפקירם, שלא חשש למה שאמר לו הנביא.

NOTES

nature of the offense, not so that their execution will serve as a deterrent against other people repeating their offense, but as a rebuke aimed at members of the public at large to distance themselves from idol worship, to educate and reprimand their children, and to accept the chain of

Rabbinic tradition and authority. But regarding false, conspiring witnesses, there is no similar general lesson to be derived from their execution, and the announcement is only made so that their execution serves as a deterrent against others repeating their offense (*Rabbi David Bonfil, Ran*).

HALAKHAH

הַמִּתְנַבֵּא מַה שֶׁלֹּא שָׁמַע, וּמַה שֶׁלֹּא נֶאֱמַר לוֹ **Someone who prophesies what he did not hear, or what was not told to him.** "Someone who prophesies what he himself did not hear from God, or who prophesies what was not told to him, but was told to some true Prophet, is a false Prophet, and liable to death by strangulation." (*Rambam, Sefer Mada, Hilkhot Avodah Zarah* 5:8.)

הַמְוַותֵּר עַל דִּבְרֵי נָבִיא **Someone who makes light of the words of a Prophet.** "One is obligated to obey a true Prophet. Whoever disobeys a true Prophet is liable to death at the hand of Heaven." (*Rambam, Sefer Mada, Hilkhot Yesodei HaTorah* 9:2.)

נָבִיא שֶׁעָבַר עַל דִּבְרֵי עַצְמוֹ **A Prophet who transgressed his own words.** "A Prophet who violates his own prophecy, and a Prophet who suppresses his prophecy, is liable to death at the hand of Heaven," following the Mishnah.

(*Rambam, Sefer Mada, Hilkhot Yesodei HaTorah* 9:3.)

הַמִּתְנַבֵּא בְּשֵׁם עֲבוֹדָה זָרָה **Someone who prophesies in the name of an idol.** "If someone prophesies in the name of an idol, saying that the idol told him that there is an obligation to perform or abstain from a certain action — even if that command follows the Halakhah — is liable to death by strangulation," following the Mishnah. (*Rambam, Sefer Mada, Hilkhot Avodah Zarah* 5:6.)

הַבָּא עַל אֵשֶׁת אִישׁ **Someone who has intercourse with another man's wife.** "If someone has sexual intercourse with a married woman — even if she has not yet had intercourse with her husband, but she has already been brought into the marriage chamber, or delivered by her father to her husband's agents — is liable to death by strangulation." (*Rambam, Sefer Kedushah, Hilkhot Issurei Biah* 3:4.)

TRANSLATION AND COMMENTARY

has entered into **the domain of her husband for marriage,** as when she has been delivered by her father to her husband's agents, even though she is still on the road to her husband's house, [1]then **even if she has not** yet **had** sexual **intercourse** with her husband [and is still a virgin], if **someone** else **has intercourse with her,** he **is liable to** death by **strangulation.**

וְזוֹמְמֵי [2]**Witnesses who conspired against the** married **daughter of a priest,** falsely testifying that she committed adultery, **and the lover** of the married daughter of a priest, are liable to death by strangulation, as was explained in the first Mishnah of the chapter. [3]**All false, conspiring witnesses become liable to the same mode of execution** that they had sought to inflict on the defendant by their testimony (see Deuteronomy 19:16-19), [4]**except for witnesses who conspired against the daughter of a priest and her lover.** Even though the witnesses had sought to inflict the penalty of burning, they are liable to death by strangulation — the penalty that would have been administered to her lover.

GEMARA תָּנוּ רַבָּנַן [5]**Our Rabbis taught** a Baraita which discusses the punishments that are administered for the various offenses related to prophecy: **"Three** such offenders — **their death is at the hand of man** by way of strangulation. **And three** such offenders — **their death is at the hand of Heaven.** [6]**Someone who prophesies what he** himself **did not hear** from God, and what no one else heard from God, [7]**and** someone who prophesies **what was not told to him,** but was told to some other Prophet, **and someone who prophesies**

שֶׁנִּכְנְסָה לִרְשׁוּת הַבַּעַל לְנִשּׂוּאִין, [1]אַף עַל פִּי שֶׁלֹּא נִבְעֲלָה — הַבָּא עָלֶיהָ הֲרֵי זֶה בְּחֶנֶק.

[2]וְזוֹמְמֵי בַת כֹּהֵן וּבוֹעֲלָהּ. [3]שֶׁכׇּל הַמּוּזָּמִין מַקְדִּימִין לְאוֹתָהּ מִיתָה, [4]חוּץ מִזּוֹמְמֵי בַת כֹּהֵן וּבוֹעֲלָהּ.

גמרא [5]תָּנוּ רַבָּנַן: "שְׁלֹשָׁה — מִיתָתָן בִּידֵי אָדָם, וּשְׁלֹשָׁה — מִיתָתָן בִּידֵי שָׁמַיִם. [6]הַמִּתְנַבֵּא מַה שֶּׁלֹּא שָׁמַע, וּמַה שֶּׁלֹּא נֶאֱמַר לוֹ. [7]וְהַמִּתְנַבֵּא בְּשֵׁם עֲבוֹדָה זָרָה

LITERAL TRANSLATION

she entered the domain of her husband for marriage, [1]even if she did not have intercourse, someone who has intercourse with her is liable to strangulation.

[2]And witnesses who conspired against the daughter of a priest, and her lover — [3]for all false, conspiring witnesses become liable to the same [mode of] execution, [4]except for witnesses who conspired against the daughter of a priest, and her lover.

GEMARA [5]Our Rabbis taught: "Three [of them] — their death is at the hand of man, and three [of them] — their death is at the hand of Heaven. [6]Someone who prophesies what he did not hear, or what was not told to him, [7]and someone who prophesies in the name of an idol

NOTES

מַקְדִּימִין לְאוֹתָהּ מִיתָה **They become liable to the same mode of execution.** The Rishonim disagree about the significance of the term *makdimim* — "they advance, they do first." *Rashi* (in *Makkot* 2a) explains that they take him out quickly for that same mode of execution, for he has no way of altering his mode of execution. According to *Tosafot*, the Mishnah means to say that the court must first make an attempt to put the false, conspiring witnesses to death by the same mode of execution that they had sought to inflict on the defendant by their testimony, but if that is not possible, they may put them to death by any means at their disposal.

בַּת כֹּהֵן וּבוֹעֲלָהּ **The daughter of a priest, and her lover.** Some understand that the Mishnah's formulation is precise, meaning that only if the witnesses conspired against the daughter of a priest *and* her lover do we say that they are not liable to death by burning, but rather to death by strangulation, the penalty that would have been administered to the lover. But if the witnesses only conspired against the priest's daughter (if her lover was a minor between the ages of nine and thirteen, or if they did not recognize the lover, or he ran away), they are indeed liable to death by burning, the penalty that would have been administered to the priest's daughter (see *Tosafot Yom Tov, Tiferet Yisrael*). But according to *Tosafot* (in *Makkot* 2a), the Mishnah's formulation is imprecise, for the false, conspiring witnesses are liable to strangulation, even if they had only testified against the priest's daughter.

HALAKHAH

מַקְדִּימִין לְאוֹתָהּ מִיתָה **They become liable to the same mode of execution.** "False, conspiring witnesses are liable to the same penalty that they had sought to inflict by their testimony on the defendant. For example, if they had testified about an offense that is subject to death by stoning, and they were refuted, they are liable to death by stoning; and if they had testified about an offense that is subject to death by burning, and they were refuted, they are liable to death by burning." (*Rambam, Sefer Shofetim, Hilkhot Edut* 18:1.)

זוֹמְמֵי בַת כֹּהֵן וּבוֹעֲלָהּ **Witnesses who conspired against the daughter of a priest and her lover.** "If witnesses testified that the daughter of a priest committed idolatry, and she was sentenced to death by burning, and her lover was sentenced to death by strangulation, and then the witnesses were refuted and found to be false, conspiring witnesses, they are liable to death by strangulation." (*Rambam, Sefer Shofetim, Hilkhot Edut* 20:10.)

TRANSLATION AND COMMENTARY

in the name of an idol — the death of each of these offenders **is at the hand of man** by way of strangulation. [1]But **someone who suppresses a prophecy** told to him by God, **and someone who makes light of the words of a Prophet** and disobeys him, [2]**and a Prophet who transgresses his own words,** and fails to fulfill what he has been told to do by God — **the death** of each of these offenders **is at the hand of Heaven."**

מְנָהָנֵי מִילֵּי [3]The Gemara asks: **From where are these regulations derived?** What is their Biblical source? [4]**Rav Yehudah said in the name of Rav: The verse states** (Deuteronomy 18:20): "But the Prophet, who shall presume to speak a word in My name, which I have not commanded him to speak, or that shall speak in the name of other gods, that Prophet shall die." [5]**"But the Prophet, who shall presume to speak a word in My name"** — these words refer to **someone who prophesies what he** himself **did not hear** from God, nor did anyone else hear that prophecy from God. [6]**"Which I have not commanded him to speak"** — implying that there is **someone else** whom I did indeed **command** to speak. [7]So **these** words refer to **someone who prophesies what was not told to him,** but was told to some other Prophet. [8]**"Or that shall speak in the name of other gods"** — **these** words refer to **someone who prophesies in the name of an idol.** [9]And regarding all three offenders, **the verse states: "That Prophet shall die."** [10]**And,** as has been stated several times in this tractate, **whenever the Torah speaks of execution without specifying** the mode of execution, it **is** referring to **strangulation.**

הַכּוֹבֵשׁ [11]The Gemara now offers a source for the second half of the Baraita cited above: **Someone who suppresses a prophecy** told to him by God, [12]**and someone who makes light of the words of a Prophet** and disobeys him, [13]**and a Prophet who transgresses his own words,** and does not do as he has been told by God — **the death** of each of these offenders **is at the hand of Heaven,** [14]**for the verse states** (Deuteronomy 18:19): "And it shall come to pass, that **the man who will not heed** [*lo yishma*] to my words which he shall speak in my name, I will require it of him." According to the plain sense of the text, the verse refers to someone who makes light of the words of a Prophet and disobeys him. [15]But we may also **interpret** the words *lo yishma* (translated here as "not heed") as if they were vocalized *lo yashmi'a*, so that they mean **"not proclaim,"** thus referring to someone who suppresses his prophecy, and fails to proclaim it to the people. [16]And we may also **interpret** those words as if they were vocalized *lo yishama*, so that they mean, **"not obey my words,"** thus referring to someone who transgresses his own words, and fails to do as he had been told

— מִיתָתָן בִּידֵי אָדָם. [1]הַכּוֹבֵשׁ אֶת נְבוּאָתוֹ, וְהַמְוַותֵּר עַל דִּבְרֵי נָבִיא, [2]וְנָבִיא שֶׁעָבַר עַל דִּבְרֵי עַצְמוֹ — מִיתָתָן בִּידֵי שָׁמַיִם״. [3]מְנָהָנֵי מִילֵּי? [4]אָמַר רַב יְהוּדָה אָמַר רַב: דְּאָמַר קְרָא: [5]״אַךְ הַנָּבִיא אֲשֶׁר יָזִיד לְדַבֵּר דָּבָר בִּשְׁמִי״ — זֶה הַמִּתְנַבֵּא מַה שֶּׁלֹּא שָׁמַע. [6]״וַאֲשֶׁר לֹא צִוִּיתִיו״ — הָא לַחֲבֵירוֹ צִוִּיתִיו, [7]זֶה הַמִּתְנַבֵּא מַה שֶּׁלֹּא נֶאֱמַר לוֹ. [8]״וַאֲשֶׁר יְדַבֵּר בְּשֵׁם אֱלֹהִים אֲחֵרִים״ — זֶה הַמִּתְנַבֵּא בְּשֵׁם עֲבוֹדָה זָרָה. [9]וּכְתִיב: ״וּמֵת הַנָּבִיא הַהוּא״. [10]וְכָל מִיתָה הָאֲמוּרָה בַּתּוֹרָה סְתָם אֵינָהּ אֶלָּא חֶנֶק.

[11]הַכּוֹבֵשׁ אֶת נְבוּאָתוֹ, [12]וְהַמְוַותֵּר עַל דִּבְרֵי נָבִיא, [13]וְנָבִיא שֶׁעָבַר עַל דִּבְרֵי עַצְמוֹ — מִיתָתָן בִּידֵי שָׁמַיִם, [14]דִּכְתִיב: ״וְהָאִישׁ אֲשֶׁר לֹא יִשְׁמַע״, [15]קְרִי בֵּיהּ: ״לֹא יַשְׁמִיעַ״, [16]וּקְרִי בֵּיהּ: ״לֹא

LITERAL TRANSLATION

— their death is at the hand of man. [1]Someone who suppresses his prophecy, and someone who makes light of the words of a Prophet, [2]and a Prophet who transgressed his own words — their death is at the hand of Heaven."

[3]From where are these things [derived]? [4]Rav Yehudah said in the name of Rav: For the verse states: [5]"But the Prophet, who shall presume to speak a word in My name" — this is someone who prophesies what he did not hear. [6]"Which I have not commanded him [to speak]" — but someone else I commanded — [7]this is someone who prophesies what was not told to him. [8]"Or who shall speak in the name of other gods" — this is someone who prophesies in the name of an idol. [9]And it is written: "That Prophet shall die." [10]And every death stated in the Torah without specification is strangulation.

[11]Someone who suppresses his prophecy, [12]and someone who makes light of the words of a Prophet, [13]and a Prophet who transgressed his own words — their death is at the hand of Heaven, [14]for it is written: "And the man who will not heed [*yishma*]" — [15]read in it "not proclaim [*yashmi'a*], [16]and read in it "not

RASHI

גמרא והאיש אשר לא ישמע – היינו מוותר. קרי ביה איש אשר לא ישמיע – היינו כובש, וקרי ביה לא ישמע – שהוא עצמו אינו נשמע, היינו עובר על דברי עצמו.

TRANSLATION AND COMMENTARY

by God. [1]And regarding all three offenders, **the verse states: "I will require it of him"** — alluding to death **at the hand of Heaven.**

הַמִּתְנַבֵּא [2]The Gemara now offers an example of each of the offenses relating to prophecy: **"Someone who prophesies what he did not hear"** — [3]**like Zedekiah ben Kena'anah, as the verse states** (I Kings 22:11): **"And Zedekiah ben Kena'anah had made for himself horns of iron,** and he said, Thus says the Lord, With these you shall push Aram until they are wiped out." [4]The Gemara asks: **What should** Zedekiah ben Kena'anah **have done?** [5]Surely, it was **the spirit of Naboth** that **caused him to err, as the verses state** (II Kings 22:20-22): **"And the Lord said, Who shall entice Ahab, that he may go up and fall at Ramot Gilead?...And there came forth a spirit, and stood before the Lord, and said, I will persuade him....And He said, You shall persuade him, and prevail also; go out and do so."** [6]And **Rav Yehudah said: What is meant by** the words, **"Go out"?** Why did God not say merely: "Do so"? God meant to say: [7]**Go out from My presence,** for any being who proposes to act in deceit is not fit to stand before God. [8]And **what is meant by "a spirit"?** [9]**Rabbi Yoḥanan said: The spirit of Naboth the Jezreelite** came to take vengeance against Ahab, by enticing him to wage war against Aram in order to recapture Ramot Gilead. Now, if this spirit was sent by God to deceive the Prophets and trick Ahab, why should Zedekiah ben Kena'anah be liable for false prophecy? Surely his sin was committed inadvertently!

הֲוָה לֵיהּ [10]The Gemara answers: Zedekiah **should have been careful** about the matter, **in accordance with** what **Rabbi Yitzḥak** said, [11]**for Rabbi Yitzḥak said: The same watchword is passed** by the prophetic spirit **to many** different **Prophets,** [12]**but no two Prophets prophecy under the same watchword,** using the very same expressions. [13]For example, **Obadiah said** (Obadiah 1:3): **"The pride of your heart deceived you,"** [14]whereas **Jeremiah said** the same thing in different words (Jeremiah 49:16): **"Your terribleness has deceived you, and the pride of your heart."** And here 400 of Ahab's Prophets all prophesied using the same formulation (I Kings 22:6): "Go up, for the Lord shall deliver it into the hand of the king," as the verse states (I Kings 22:13): "Behold now, the Prophets declare good to the king with one mouth." [15]**Since those** Prophets **all spoke as one,** Zedekiah should have **inferred that they did not say anything** in God's name.

יִשְׁמַע אֶל דְּבָרַי״, [1]וּכְתִיב: ״אָנֹכִי אֶדְרֹשׁ מֵעִמּוֹ״ — בִּידֵי שָׁמַיִם.

[2]״הַמִּתְנַבֵּא מַה שֶּׁלֹּא שָׁמַע״. [3]כְּגוֹן צִדְקִיָּה בֶּן כְּנַעֲנָה, דִּכְתִיב: ״וַיַּעַשׂ לוֹ צִדְקִיָּהוּ בֶן כְּנַעֲנָה קַרְנֵי בַרְזֶל״. [4]מַאי הֲוָה לֵיהּ לְמֶעֱבַד? [5]רוּחַ נָבוֹת אַטְעִיתֵיהּ, דִּכְתִיב: ״וַיֹּאמֶר ה׳ מִי יְפַתֶּה אֶת אַחְאָב וְיַעַל וְיִפֹּל בְּרָמֹת גִּלְעָד... וַיֵּצֵא הָרוּחַ וַיַּעֲמֹד לִפְנֵי ה׳ וַיֹּאמֶר אֲנִי אֲפַתֶּנּוּ וַיֹּאמֶר... תְּפַתֶּה וְגַם תּוּכָל צֵא וַעֲשֵׂה כֵן״. [6]אָמַר רַב יְהוּדָה: מַאי ״צֵא״? [7]צֵא מִמְּחִיצָתִי. [8]מַאי ״רוּחַ״? [9]אָמַר רַבִּי יוֹחָנָן: רוּחוֹ שֶׁל נָבוֹת הַיִּזְרְעֵאלִי.

[10]הֲוָה לֵיהּ לְמִידַק, כִּדְרַבִּי יִצְחָק. [11]דְּאָמַר רַבִּי יִצְחָק: סִיגְנוֹן אֶחָד עוֹלֶה לְכַמָּה נְבִיאִים, [12]וְאֵין שְׁנֵי נְבִיאִים מִתְנַבְּאִין בְּסִיגְנוֹן אֶחָד. [13]עוֹבַדְיָה אָמַר: ״זְדוֹן לִבְּךָ הִשִּׁיאֶךָ״. [14]יִרְמְיָה אָמַר: ״תִּפְלַצְתְּךָ הִשִּׁיא אֹתָךְ זְדוֹן לִבֶּךָ״. [15]וְהָנֵי, מִדְּקָאָמְרִי כּוּלְּהוּ כַּהֲדָדֵי, שְׁמַע מִינָּהּ לָא כְּלוּם קָאָמְרִי.

LITERAL TRANSLATION

obey [*yishama*] my words." [1]And it is written: "I will require it of him" — at the hand of Heaven.

[2]"Someone who prophesies what he did not hear." [3]Like Zedekiah ben Kena'anah, as it is written: "And Zedekiah ben Kena'anah had made for himself horns of iron." [4]What should he have done? [5]The spirit of Naboth caused him to err, as it is written: "And the Lord said, Who shall entice Ahab, that he may go up and fall at Ramot Gilead?...And there came forth a spirit, and stood before the Lord, and said, I will persuade him....And He said, You shall persuade him, and prevail also; go out and do so." [6]Rav Yehudah said: What is [meant by] "Go out"? [7]Go out from My partition. [8]What is [meant by] "a spirit"? [9]Rabbi Yoḥanan said: The spirit of Naboth the Jezreelite.

[10]He should have been careful, like Rabbi Yitzḥak, [11]for Rabbi Yitzḥak said: The same watchword is passed to many Prophets, [12]but no two Prophets prophecy under the same watchword. [13]Obadiah said: "The pride of your heart deceived you"; [14]Jeremiah said: "Your terribleness has deceived you, and the pride of your heart." [15]And these, since they all spoke as one, infer from this that they did not say anything.

RASHI

ויצא הרוח ויאמר אני אפתנו — ״אלא והייתי רוח שקר בפי כל נביאיו״. **סיגנון** — דבר מליצות של רוח הקודש. **עולה לכמה נביאים** — נכנס בלבם, לזה בלשון זה ולזה בלשון זה, והכל אחד.

LANGUAGE

סִגְנוֹן Watchword. This word derives from the Greek σιγνον, *signon,* which is cognate to the Latin *signum,* the main meaning of which is "sign." It can also mean a password or the like.

TRANSLATION AND COMMENTARY

דִּילְמָא [1]The Gemara asks: But **perhaps** Zedekiah **did not know that** law **of Rabbi Yitzḥak,** and so he had no way of knowing that the Prophets were proclaiming a false prophecy!

יְהוֹשָׁפָט [2]The Gemara answers: **Jehoshafat,** king of Judah, **was there, and warned** those present that Ahab's Prophets were false Prophets, [3]**as the verse states** (I Kings 22:7): **"And Jehoshafat said, Is there not here a Prophet of the Lord besides,** that we might inquire of him?" [4]**Responding to** Jehoshafat, Ahab said: **"Surely there are all these** 400 Prophets of mine!" [5]Jehoshafat **said to him: "I have received the following tradition from the house of my father's father,** the House of David: [6]**The same watchword is passed** by way of the prophetic spirit **to many** different **Prophets, but no two Prophets prophecy under the same watchword,** using the very same expressions. Thus, your 400 Prophets must be false prophets, for they all prophesied using the same formulation."

הַמִּתְנַבֵּא [7]The Gemara takes up the next offense related to prophecy: **"Someone who prophesies what was not told to him,** but was told to some true Prophet" — [8]**like Ḥananiah ben Azur, for** when **Jeremiah stood in the upper market** in Jerusalem **and said** (Jeremiah 49:35): **"Thus, says the Lord of hosts, Behold, I will break the bow of Elam,"** [9]**Ḥananiah put forward a *kal vaḥomer* argument on his own:** [10]**If, regarding Elam, who only came to help Babel, the Holy One, blessed be He, said:** [11]**"Behold, I will break the bow of Elam,"** [12]then **all the more so** will **the Babylonians themselves** face destruction. [13]Ḥananiah then **went to the lower market** of Jerusalem, **and said** (Jeremiah 28:2): **"Thus says the Lord** of hosts, the God of Israel, **I have broken the yoke of the king of Babel."** And it is reported that Ḥananiah died shortly thereafter at the hand of God (I Kings 28:15-17).

אֲמַר לֵיהּ [14]**Rav Pappa said to Abaye:** How is this an example of a Prophet who prophesied that which was not told to him, but was told to some other Prophet? [15]Surely this prophecy **was also not told to any other** Prophet. Rather, Ḥananiah should serve as an example of someone who prophesied what he did not hear!

[1]דִּילְמָא לָא הֲוָה יָדַע לֵיהּ לְהָא דְּרַבִּי יִצְחָק!
[2]יְהוֹשָׁפָט הֲוָה הָתָם, וְקָאָמַר לְהוּ, [3]דִּכְתִיב: ״וַיֹּאמֶר יְהוֹשָׁפָט הַאֵין פֹּה נָבִיא עוֹד לַה׳״. [4]אֲמַר לֵיהּ: ״הָא אִיכָּא כָּל הָנֵי״! [5]אֲמַר לֵיהּ: כָּךְ מְקוּבְּלַנִי מִבֵּית אֲבִי אַבָּא: [6]סִיגְנוֹן אֶחָד עוֹלֶה לְכַמָּה נְבִיאִים, וְאֵין שְׁנֵי נְבִיאִים מִתְנַבְּאִים בְּסִיגְנוֹן אֶחָד.
[7]״הַמִּתְנַבֵּא מַה שֶּׁלֹּא נֶאֱמַר לוֹ״. [8]כְּגוֹן חֲנַנְיָה בֶּן עַזּוּר, דְּקָאֵי יִרְמְיָה בְּשׁוּק הָעֶלְיוֹן וְקָאָמַר: ״כֹּה אָמַר ה׳ [צְבָאוֹת] הִנְנִי שֹׁבֵר אֶת קֶשֶׁת עֵילָם״. [9]נָשָׂא חֲנַנְיָה קַל וָחוֹמֶר בְּעַצְמוֹ: [10]מָה עֵילָם שֶׁלֹּא בָּא אֶלָּא לַעֲזוֹר אֶת בָּבֶל, אָמַר הַקָּדוֹשׁ בָּרוּךְ הוּא: [11]״הִנְנִי שֹׁבֵר אֶת קֶשֶׁת עֵילָם״, [12]כַּשְׂדִּים עַצְמָן עַל אַחַת כַּמָּה וְכַמָּה. [13]אֲתָא אִיהוּ בְּשׁוּק הַתַּחְתּוֹן, אָמַר: ״כֹּה אָמַר ה׳ וגו׳ שָׁבַרְתִּי אֶת עֹל מֶלֶךְ בָּבֶל״. [14]אֲמַר לֵיהּ רַב פַּפָּא לְאַבָּיֵי: [15]הַאי לַחֲבֵירוֹ נַמִי לָא נֶאֱמַר!

LITERAL TRANSLATION

[1]Perhaps he did not know that of Rabbi Yitzḥak! [2]Jehoshafat was there, and told them, [3]as it is written: "And Jehoshafat said, Is there not here another Prophet of the Lord?" [4]He said to him: "Surely there are all these!" [5]He said to him: "Thus have I received a tradition from the house of my father's father: [6]The same watchword is passed to many Prophets, but no two Prophets prophecy under the same watchword."

[7]"Someone who prophesies what was not told to him." [8]Like Ḥananiah ben Azur, for Jeremiah stood in the upper market and said: "Thus, says the Lord of hosts, Behold, I will break the bow of Elam." [9]Ḥananiah put forward a *kal vaḥomer* argument on his own: [10]If [regarding] Elam who only came to help Babel, the Holy One, blessed be He, said: [11]"Behold, I will break the bow of Elam," [12]the Chaldeans themselves all the more so. [13]He came to the lower market, [and] said: "Thus says the Lord...I have broken the yoke of the king of Babel." [14]Rav Pappa said to Abaye: [15]This was also not told to another person!

RASHI

ואין שני נביאים מתנבאין בסיגנון אחד – בלשון אחד, ואלו כולן לשון אחד היו אומרים, דכתיב הנה נא כל הנביאים אומרים פה אחד טוב.

NOTES

וַיֹּאמֶר יְהוֹשָׁפָט And Jehoshafat said. The Rabbis understood Jehoshafat's argument in this manner, because it stands to reason that Jehoshafat did not know that all four hundred of Ahab's Prophets were false Prophets. Rather, he knew that their prophecy was false because of the tradition that he had received from his fathers that no two Prophets prophecy under the same watchword (*Maharsha*).

TRANSLATION AND COMMENTARY

אָמַר לֵיהּ [1]Abaye **said to** Rav Pappa: **Since** it is legitimate **to use a** ***kal vaḥomer*** **argument for exposition,** [2]this prophecy **is** regarded **as if it had** actually **been told to** Jeremiah, **but to** Ḥananiah **it had** nevertheless **not been told.**

הַמִּתְנַבֵּא [3]When the Mishnah speaks of **"someone who prophesies in the name of an idol,"** [4]it refers to someone **like the prophets of Baal.**

הַכּוֹבֵשׁ [5]When the Mishnah speaks of **"someone who suppresses a prophecy** told to him by God and does not declare it to the people," [6]it refers to someone **like Jonah ben Amitai** who tried to suppress the prophecy that he was to proclaim regarding Nineveh.

וְהַמְוַותֵּר [7]When the Mishnah speaks of **"someone who makes light of the words of a Prophet** and disobeys him," [8]it refers to someone **like** [89B] **Michah** ben Yimlah's **fellow Prophet,** [9]**as the verse states** (I Kings 20:35): **"And a certain man of the sons of the Prophets** [Michah ben Yimlah] **said to his neighbor in the word of the Lord, Strike me, I pray you. And the man refused to strike him."** [10]And the next verse **states** (I Kings 20:36): **"Then he said to him, Because you have not obeyed** the voice of the Lord, behold, as soon as you have departed from me, a lion shall slay you. And as soon as he departed from him, a lion found him, and slew him." Thus, we see that someone who disobeys a Prophet is liable to death at the hand of Heaven.

וְנָבִיא [11]When the Mishnah speaks of **"a Prophet who transgresses his own words,"** it refers to someone **like Ido the Prophet** who, according to tradition, was the Prophet sent to Jeroboam, [12]and about whom **the verses state** (I Kings 13:8-9): "And the man of God said to the king, If you will give me half of your house, I will not go in with you, neither will I eat bread nor drink water in this place. **For so was it charged me** by the word of the Lord, saying, Eat no bread, nor drink water, nor return by the way that you came"; [13]**and the verse states** (I Kings 13:18): **"He said to him, I am a Prophet also as you are,** and an angel spoke to me by the word of the Lord, saying, Bring him back with you into your house, that he may eat bread and drink water";

[1]אָמַר לֵיהּ: כֵּיוָן דְּאִיתְיְהִיב קַל וָחוֹמֶר לְמִידְרַשׁ, [2]כְּמַאן דְּאִיתְּמַר לֵיהּ דָּמֵי, הוּא נִיהוּ דְּלָא נֶאֱמַר לוֹ.

[3]״הַמִּתְנַבֵּא בְּשֵׁם עֲבוֹדָה זָרָה״. [4]כְּגוֹן נְבִיאֵי הַבַּעַל.

[5]״הַכּוֹבֵשׁ אֶת נְבוּאָתוֹ״. [6]כְּגוֹן יוֹנָה בֶּן אֲמִיתַּי.

[7]״וְהַמְוַותֵּר עַל דִּבְרֵי נָבִיא״. [8]כְּגוֹן [89B] חַבְרֵיהּ דְּמִיכָה, [9]דִּכְתִיב: ״וְאִישׁ אֶחָד מִבְּנֵי הַנְּבִיאִים אָמַר אֶל רֵעֵהוּ בִּדְבַר ה׳ הַכֵּינִי נָא וַיְמָאֵן הָאִישׁ לְהַכּוֹתוֹ״. [10]וּכְתִיב: ״וַיֹּאמֶר לוֹ יַעַן אֲשֶׁר לֹא שָׁמַעְתָּ [וגו׳]״.

[11]״וְנָבִיא שֶׁעָבַר עַל דִּבְרֵי עַצְמוֹ״ — כְּגוֹן עִדּוֹ הַנָּבִיא, [12]דִּכְתִיב: ״כִּי כֵן צִוָּה אֹתִי״, [13]וּכְתִיב: ״וַיֹּאמֶר לוֹ גַּם אֲנִי נָבִיא כָּמוֹךָ״,

LITERAL TRANSLATION

[1]He said to him: Since a *kal vaḥomer* argument was given to be used for exposition, [2]it is as if it was told to him, but to him it was not told.

[3]"Someone who prophesies in the name of an idol." [4]Like the prophets of Baal.

[5]"Someone who suppresses his prophecy." [6]Like Jonah ben Amitai.

[7]"And someone who makes light of the words of a Prophet." [8]Like [89B] Michah's fellow [Prophet], [9]as it is written: "And a certain man of the sons of the Prophets said to his neighbor in the word of the Lord, Strike me, I pray you. And the man refused to strike him." [10]And it is written: "Then he said to him, Because you have not obeyed, etc."

[11]"And a Prophet who transgressed his own words" — like Ido the Prophet, [12]as it is written: "For so was it charged me"; [13]and it is written: "He said to him, I, too, am a Prophet like you";

RASHI

חבריה דמיכה — דכתיב ״ואיש אחד מבני הנביאים אמר אל רעהו בדבר ה׳ הכני נא״, זה היה מיכיהו בן ימלא שנתנבא אותו היום על אחאב ליפול ביד ארם מפני שנפל בן הדד בידו ושלחו לשלום, והיינו דקאמר אחאב ליהושפט ״לא ידבר עלי טוב כי אם רע״ מפני שנתנבא כבר את זו עליו ולא קיבל חבירו את דבריו, דכתיב ״וימאן האיש להכותו״. עדו הנביא — שנתנבא על מזבח ה׳ בבית אל שהיה ירבעם מקטר עליו, ובדברי הימים גבי יאשיהו כתיב — והוא היה עדו. כי כן צוה אותי — בדבר ה׳ לאמר לא תאכל לחם ולא תשתה מים (במקום הזה), ועבר על דברי עצמו ושמע לדברי הנביא השקר ואכל ושתה.

NOTES

חַבְרֵיהּ דְּמִיכָה...עִדּוֹ הַנָּבִיא **Michah's fellow Prophet...Ido the Prophet.** Nowhere is it stated explicitly that "the man of the sons of the Prophets" who told his neighbor to strike him was Michah ben Yimlah, nor is it stated explicitly that the Prophet sent from Judah to prophesy for Jeroboam was Ido, but the Rabbis apparently had traditions regarding both of these identifications. Furthermore, we find that Michah ben Yimlah prophesied a prophecy for Ahab that did not please him, and we find elsewhere an allusion to Ido's prophecy against Jeroboam (II Chronicles 9:29): "And in the visions of Yedo, the seer, against Jeroboam ben Nebat" (*Radak*).

TRANSLATION AND COMMENTARY

[1] **and the verse states** (I Kings 13:19): **"So he went back with him,** and did eat bread in his house, and drank water"; [2] **and the verse states** (I Kings 13:24): **"And when he was gone, a lion met him by the way,** and slew him." Thus, we see that a Prophet who transgresses his own words and fails to fulfill what he has been told to do by God is liable to death at the hand of God.

תָּנֵי תַּנָּא [3] **A Tanna taught** a Baraita **before Rav Ḥisda** which stated: "A Prophet **who suppresses his prophecy** and fails to declare it before the people **is liable to** the punishment of **flogging."**

אֲמַר לֵיהּ [4] Rav Ḥisda **said to** the Tanna: **Is someone who ate figs out of a sieve liable to** the punishment of **flogging?** [5] **Who** saw him before he ate the worms and **warned him** against doing so? A person can only be flogged if he has been warned, and who could know that he was suppressing that prophecy, and issue a proper warning?

אֲמַר אַבַּיֵי [6] **Abaye said: His fellow Prophets** can warn him.

מְנָא יָדְעִי [7] The Gemara asks: But **from where do** his fellow Prophets **know** what prophecy he has received? [8] **Abaye said: For the verse states** (Amos 3:7): **"Surely the Lord God will do nothing, without revealing His secret to His servants the Prophets."**

וְדִילְמָא [9] The Gemara asks: **But perhaps** God **retracted** the evil decree that He wished the Prophet to proclaim, and his fellow Prophets were not yet aware of the change in plans? Thus, even a warning given by his fellow Prophets is at best a warning given under doubt.

אִם אִיתָא [10] The Gemara answers: **If it is true that** God **retracted** the evil decree that He wished the Prophet to proclaim, [11] **He would have notified all the** other **Prophets** as well.

וְהָא יוֹנָה [12] The Gemara asks: **But surely** God **retracted** the evil decree that was issued against the city of Nineveh, **and** Jonah **himself was not notified?**

יוֹנָה מֵעִיקָּרָא [13] The Gemara explains: The prophecy given to Jonah regarding the city of Nineveh was never retracted, for **from the** very **outset Jonah had been told** by way of the prophetic spirit, [14] **"Nineveh will be overturned,"** a prophetic vision which could be interpreted in two ways. [15] Jonah **did not know whether**

[1] וּכְתִיב: ״וַיָּשָׁב אִתּוֹ״, [2] וּכְתִיב: ״וַיֵּלֶךְ וַיִּמְצָאֵהוּ אַרְיֵה״.
[3] תָּנֵי תַּנָּא קַמֵּיהּ דְּרַב חִסְדָּא: ״הַכּוֹבֵשׁ אֶת נְבוּאָתוֹ לוֹקֶה״.
[4] אֲמַר לֵיהּ: מַאן דְּאָכֵיל תַּמְרֵי בְּאַרְבְּלָא לָקֵי? [5] מַאן מַתְרֵי בֵּיהּ?
[6] אֲמַר אַבַּיֵי: חַבְרֵיהּ נְבִיאֵי.
[7] מְנָא יָדְעִי? [8] אֲמַר אַבַּיֵי: דִּכְתִיב: ״כִּי לֹא יַעֲשֶׂה ה׳ [אֱלֹהִים] דָּבָר כִּי אִם גָּלָה סוֹדוֹ״.
[9] וְדִילְמָא הָדְרִי בֵּיהּ.
[10] אִם אִיתָא דְּהָדְרִי בֵּיהּ, [11] אוֹדוּעֵי הָווּ מוֹדְעִי לְכֻלְּהוּ נְבִיאֵי.
[12] וְהָא יוֹנָה, דְּהָדְרִי בֵּיהּ וְלָא אוֹדְעוּהוּ!
[13] יוֹנָה מֵעִיקָּרָא, [14] ״נִינְוֵה נֶהְפָּכֶת״, [15] אָמְרִי לֵיהּ, אִיהוּ לָא

LITERAL TRANSLATION

[1] and it is written: "So he went back with him"; [2] and it is written: "And when he was gone, a lion found him."

[3] A Tanna taught before Rav Ḥisda: "Someone who suppresses his prophecy is flogged."

[4] He said to him: Someone who ate figs out of a sieve is flogged? [5] Who warned him?

[6] Abaye said: His fellow Prophets.

[7] From where do they know? [8] Abaye said: For it is written: "Surely the Lord God will do nothing, without revealing His secret [to His servants the Prophets]."

[9] But perhaps they retracted.

[10] If it is [true] that they retracted, [11] they would have notified all the Prophets.

[12] But surely Jonah, they retracted, and they did not notify him!

[13] From the outset they said to Jonah, [14] "Nineveh will be overturned," [15] [and] he did not

RASHI

תמרי בארבילא – תמרים הנתונים בכברה. **דילמא הדרו ביה** – פמליא של מעלה וניחם על הרעה והם אינם יודעים, והיאך מתרינן בו התראת ספק. **והא יונה דהדרו ביה** – מהפוך את נינוה. **מעיקרא נינוה נהפכת אמרו ליה** – ברוח הקדש, ומשמע נמי לטובה, שיהפכו מעשיהם מרעה לטובה, וכיון ששבו נתקיימה הנבואה ולא מיהדר הוא. **ואיהו דלא ידע** – הוא היה טועה וסבור שהוא לרעה.

NOTES

הַכּוֹבֵשׁ אֶת נְבוּאָתוֹ לוֹקֶה **Someone who suppresses his prophecy is flogged.** The Baraita that states that a Prophet who suppresses his prophecy is liable to flogging must follow the position that even a negative commandment that does not involve an action is subject to lashes (*Talmidei Rabbenu Peretz*). Alternatively, the Baraita is referring here to lashes administered by Rabbinic decree (see *Margoliyot HaYam*).

תַּמְרֵי בְּאַרְבְּלָא **Figs out of a sieve.** It has been suggested that the word *Arbela* is the name of a distant city, and that Rav Ḥisda meant to say as follows: If someone ate figs in far-off Arbela, do we know about it here, so that he should be liable to flogging?

יָדַע אִי לְטוֹבָה אִי לְרָעָה. [1]הַמְוַותֵּר עַל דִּבְרֵי נָבִיא — [2]מְנָא יָדַע דְּאִיעַנַּשׁ? [3]דִּיהַב לֵיהּ אוֹת. [4]וְהָא מִיכָה, דְּלָא יָהֵיב לֵיהּ אוֹת, [5]וְאִיעֲנַשׁ! [6]הֵיכָא דְּמוּחְזָק שָׁאנֵי, [7]דְּאִי לָא תֵּימָא הָכִי, אַבְרָהָם בְּהַר הַמּוֹרִיָּה, [8]הֵיכִי שָׁמַע לֵיהּ יִצְחָק; [9]אֵלִיָּהוּ בְּהַר הַכַּרְמֶל, הֵיכִי סָמְכִי עֲלֵיהּ וְעָבְדִי שְׁחוּטֵי חוּץ? [10]אֶלָּא, הֵיכָא דְּמוּחֲזַק שָׁאנֵי.

[11]״וַיְהִי אַחַר הַדְּבָרִים הָאֵלֶּה וְהָאֱלֹהִים נִסָּה אֶת אַבְרָהָם״. [12]אַחַר מַאי? [13]אָמַר רַבִּי יוֹחָנָן מִשּׁוּם רַבִּי יוֹסֵי בֶּן זִימְרָא: [14]אַחַר דְּבָרָיו שֶׁל שָׂטָן, דִּכְתִיב: ״וַיִּגְדַּל הַיֶּלֶד וַיִּגָּמַל וגו׳״. [15]אָמַר שָׂטָן לִפְנֵי הַקָּדוֹשׁ בָּרוּךְ הוּא: ״רִבּוֹנוֹ שֶׁל עוֹלָם! [16]זָקֵן זֶה חֲנַנְתּוֹ לְמֵאָה שָׁנָה פְּרִי בֶטֶן,

LITERAL TRANSLATION

know whether for good or for bad.

[1]Someone who makes light of the words of a Prophet — [2]from where does he know that he should be punished?

[3]He gives him a sign.

[4]But surely Michah did not give a sign, [5]and he was punished!

[6]When he is established it is different, [7]for if you do not say this, Abraham at Mount Moriah, [8]how did Isaac listen to him; [9]Elijah at Mount Carmel, how did they rely upon him and slaughter outside? [10]Rather, when he is established it is different.

[11]"And it came to pass after these things, that God tested Abraham." [12]After what? [13]Rabbi Yoḥanan said in the name of Rabbi Yose ben Zimra: [14]After the words of Satan, as it is written: "And the child grew, and was weaned, etc." [15]Satan said before the Holy One, blessed be He: "Master of the Universe! [16]That old man You favored after a hundred years with fruit of the womb.

TRANSLATION AND COMMENTARY

this meant that Nineveh would be turned around **for good,** meaning that its inhabitants would repent and improve their ways, **or** that Nineveh would be turned around **for bad,** meaning that the city would be destroyed. Jonah expected the prophecy to be fulfilled in its negative sense, but after the people of Nineveh repented, it became clear that the prophecy was fulfilled in its positive sense.

הַמְוַותֵּר [1]The Gemara raises a question regarding **someone who makes light of the words of a Prophet** and disobeys him: [2]**How does one know** that a person is a true Prophet sent by God so **that he should be punished** for disobeying him?

דִּיהַב לֵיהּ אוֹת [3]The Gemara explains: Here the Prophet **gave him a sign** proving that he was a true Prophet.

וְהָא מִיכָה [4]The Gemara asks: **But surely Michah** ben Yimlah **did not give** his fellow Prophet **a sign** proving that he was a true Prophet, [5]**and** nevertheless the fellow Prophet **was punished** when Michah ordered him in the name of God to strike him, and he refused to do so (see I Kings 20:35-36)!

הֵיכָא [6]The Gemara explains: The law **is different when** the Prophet **has been established** as a true Prophet. When a person is known to be a true Prophet, whatever he says in the name of God must be obeyed. [7]This must be true, **for if you do not say this,** then when **Abraham** went to offer his son Isaac **at Mount Moriah,** [8]**why did Isaac listen to him** and give himself over to be sacrificed? [9]And when the Prophet **Elijah** went to offer sacrifices **on Mount Carmel, why did** people **rely on him and slaughter** sacrifices outside the Temple in Jerusalem, which is severely prohibited by Torah law? [10]**Rather,** the law **is different when** a Prophet has been **established** as a true Prophet.

וַיְהִי [11]Having mentioned the offering of Isaac in passing, the Gemara now discusses the matter at greater length: The verse states (Genesis 22:1): **"And it came to pass after these things, that God tested Abraham."** The Gemara asks: What does the Torah mean by "after these things"? There does not seem to be any link between the story of the offering of Isaac and the previous chapters. [12]**After what** things, then, did God test Abraham? [13]**Rabbi Yoḥanan said in the name of Rabbi Yose ben Zimra:** The Hebrew term *devarim* should be understood here in the sense of "words," rather than "things." [14]**After** hearing **the words of Satan,** God tested Abraham, and this is the order of the events: When Abraham celebrated the weaning of Isaac, **as the verse states** (Genesis 21:8): **"And the child grew, and was weaned,** and Abraham made a great feast on the same day," [15]**Satan said to the Holy One, blessed be He: "Master of the Universe!** [16]When **that old man,** Abraham, **was a hundred** years

RASHI

מנא ידע — האי גברא שזה נביא אמת שהקדוש ברוך הוא עונשו — והלא שמא סבור שזהו נביא שקר לפיכך מוותר על דבריו. **היכא דהוחזק** — שהוא צדיק ונביא אמת. **שאני** — ולא בעי אות. **היכי שמע ליה יצחק** — שהוא דבר אמת מה שלא נאמר לשום אדם להקריב את בנו. **שחוטי חוץ** — שהרי בית המקדש היה בירושלים.

HALAKHAH

הֵיכָא דְּמוּחְזָק שָׁאנֵי When he is established it is different. "If someone who is known to be a true Prophet instructs us to violate a Torah prohibition or commandment on a temporary basis, we are obligated to listen to him." (*Rambam, Sefer Mada, Hilkhot Yesodei HaTorah* 9:3.)

TRANSLATION AND COMMENTARY

old, **You favored** him **with a child.** [1]**From all the feasts that he made** to celebrate the occasion, **did he not have** even **one dove or one pigeon to sacrifice to you** as a thank-offering?" [2]God **said to** Satan: "Do you doubt Abraham's piety? Did **he** not **make this** entire celebration **only on account of his son?** [3]**If I say to him** now: **'Sacrifice your son to Me,' he will** go out **immediately** and **sacrifice him to Me."** [4]**Immediately** "after these words," **"God tested Abraham.... And He said, Take your son, please."**

אָמַר [5]**Rabbi Shimon bar Abba said:** The verse states (Genesis 22:2): "And He said, Take your son, please [*na*]." The word *'na'* **is a term of request.** Why did God beseech Abraham in this manner? [6]**This** situation **may be compared to** that of **a mortal king who** over time **was faced with many** different **wars.** [7]The king **had one** especially mighty **warrior who emerged victorious** from all the various battles. [8]It **once** happened that the king **was facing a** particularly **fierce war.** [9]**He** called his warrior and **said to him: "Please, fight this war for me,** and emerge victorious, **so that** people will **not say** about you: [10]**The earlier** battles that he won **were nothing,** and he is not really a mighty warrior." [11]**So, too, the Holy One, blessed be He, said to Abraham:** "Until now, **I have tested you with a number of tests and you** have **passed all of them.** [12]**Now, pass this** one final **test for me, so that** people **will not say** about you: **The earlier** tests **were nothing,** and Abraham is not really a God-fearing man."

אֶת בִּנְךָ [13]The Gemara now elaborates upon the verse (Genesis 22:2), "And He said, Please take your son, your only son, whom you love, Isaac," for it reflects only one side of the dialogue between God and Abraham: God said to Abraham: "Please, take **your son,"** to which Abraham responded: **"I have two sons** — Ishmael and Isaac." [14]God then added: **"Your only son,"** to which Abraham answered: "Both my sons fall under this category, for **this one is an only son to his mother** Hagar, **and this one is an only son**

[1]מִכָּל סְעוּדָה שֶׁעָשָׂה לֹא הָיָה לוֹ תּוֹר אֶחָד אוֹ גוֹזָל אֶחָד לְהַקְרִיב לְפָנֶיךָ? [2]אָמַר לוֹ: ״כְּלוּם עָשָׂה אֶלָּא בִּשְׁבִיל בְּנוֹ. [3]אִם אֲנִי אוֹמֵר לוֹ: ׳זְבַח אֶת בִּנְךָ לְפָנַי׳, מִיָּד זוֹבְחוֹ״. [4]מִיָּד, ״וְהָאֱלֹהִים נִסָּה אֶת אַבְרָהָם....וַיֹּאמֶר, קַח נָא אֶת, בִּנְךָ״. [5]אָמַר רַבִּי שִׁמְעוֹן בַּר אַבָּא: אֵין נָא אֶלָּא לְשׁוֹן בַּקָּשָׁה. [6]מָשָׁל לְמֶלֶךְ בָּשָׂר וָדָם שֶׁעָמְדוּ עָלָיו מִלְחָמוֹת הַרְבֵּה. [7]וְהָיָה לוֹ גִּבּוֹר אֶחָד וְנִצְּחָן. [8]לְיָמִים עָמְדָה עָלָיו מִלְחָמָה חֲזָקָה. [9]אָמַר לוֹ: ״בְּבַקָּשָׁה מִמְּךָ, עֲמוֹד לִי בְּמִלְחָמָה זוֹ, שֶׁלֹּא יֹאמְרוּ: [10]רִאשׁוֹנוֹת אֵין בָּהֶם מַמָּשׁ״. [11]אַף הַקָּדוֹשׁ בָּרוּךְ הוּא אָמַר לְאַבְרָהָם: ״נִיסִּיתִיךָ בְּכַמָּה נִסְיוֹנוֹת וְעָמַדְתָּ בְּכֻלָּן. [12]עַכְשָׁיו, עֲמוֹד לִי בְּנִסָּיוֹן זֶה, שֶׁלֹּא יֹאמְרוּ: אֵין מַמָּשׁ בָּרִאשׁוֹנִים״. [13]״אֶת בִּנְךָ״ — ״שְׁנֵי בָנִים יֵשׁ לִי״. [14]״אֶת יְחִידְךָ״ — ״זֶה יָחִיד

LITERAL TRANSLATION

[1]From all the feasts that he made, did he not have one dove or one pigeon to sacrifice to you?" [2]He said to him: "He did this only for his son. [3]If I say to him: Sacrifice your son to Me, he will immediately sacrifice him to Me." [4]Immediately, "And God tested Abraham.... And He said, Take your son, please."

[5]Rabbi Shimon bar Abba said: *Na* is a term of request. [6]This is comparable to a king of flesh and blood who was faced with many wars. [7]And he had one warrior who won them. [8]After some time, a fierce war faced him. [9]He said to him: "Please, stand up for me in this war, so that people will not say: [10]The first ones were nothing." [11]So, too, the Holy One, blessed be He, said to Abraham: "I have tested you with a number of tests and you passed all of them. [12]Now, pass this test for me, so that people will not say: The first ones were nothing."

[13]"Your son" — "I have two sons." [14]"Your only son" — "this one is an only son

NOTES

מִכָּל סְעוּדָה שֶׁעָשָׂה לֹא הָיָה לוֹ תּוֹר **From all the feasts that he made, did he not have one dove.** The question has been raised: Surely, the feast that Abraham made to celebrate Isaac's weaning took place years before God asked him to sacrifice his son to Him (according to the Sages, thirty-four years before). What, then, is the connection between the two events? Some suggest that God's command to sacrifice Isaac is connected to the story of Abraham's covenant with Abimelech (as described in Genesis 21:27), for, according to the Midrash, there, too, the covenant was celebrated with a great feast, allowing Satan to level the charge against Abraham that he celebrated a feast for a mortal king, without even offering a dove or a pigeon to God (see *Maharsha*). As for the dove and the pigeon, it has been suggested that Satan argued that Abraham should have learned from his covenant with God, when he was instructed not to divide up the dove and the pigeon (see Genesis 15:10), that he was supposed to bring those birds as an offering to God.

לְאִמּוֹ וְזֶה יָחִיד לְאִמּוֹ". [1]"אֲשֶׁר אָהַבְתָּ" — [2]"תַּרְוַיְיהוּ רְחִימְנָא לְהוּ". "אֶת יִצְחָק". [3]"וְכָל כָּךְ, לָמָּה? [4]כְּדֵי שֶׁלֹּא תִּטָּרֵף דַּעְתּוֹ עָלָיו.

[5]קְדָמוֹ שָׂטָן לַדֶּרֶךְ, [6]אָמַר לוֹ: "הֲנִסָּה דָבָר אֵלֶיךָ תִּלְאֶה?... [7]הִנֵּה, יִסַּרְתָּ רַבִּים וְיָדַיִם רָפוֹת. [8]תְּחַזֵּק כּוֹשֵׁל יְקִימוּן מִלֶּיךָ...כִּי עַתָּה תָּבוֹא אֵלֶיךָ וַתֵּלֶא". [9]אָמַר לוֹ: "אֲנִי בְּתֻמִּי אֵלֵךְ"? [10]אָמַר לוֹ: "הֲלֹא יִרְאָתְךָ כִּסְלָתֶךָ". [11]אָמַר לוֹ: "זְכָר, נָא מִי הוּא נָקִי אָבָד". [12]כֵּיוָן דַּחֲזָא דְּלָא קָא שָׁמַע לֵיהּ, אָמַר לֵיהּ: "וְאֵלַי דָּבָר יְגֻנָּב. [13]כָּךְ שָׁמַעְתִּי מֵאֲחוֹרֵי הַפַּרְגּוֹד: הַשֶּׂה לְעוֹלָה וְאֵין יִצְחָק לְעוֹלָה". [14]אָמַר לוֹ: "כָּךְ עוֹנְשׁוֹ שֶׁל בַּדַּאי, שֶׁאֲפִילּוּ אָמַר אֱמֶת, אֵין שׁוֹמְעִין לוֹ".

LITERAL TRANSLATION

to his mother, and this one is an only son to his mother." [1]"Whom you love" — "I love them both." [2]"Isaac." [3]And all this, why? [4]So that he would not lose his mind.

[5]Satan met him on the road, [6][and] said to him: "If one ventures a word to you, will you be grieved?... [7]Behold, you have instructed many, and you have strengthened the weak hands. [8]Your words have upheld him that was falling....But now it is come upon you, and you are weary." [9]He said to him: "But as for me, I will walk in my honesty." [10]He said to him: "Is not your fear of God your folly?" [11]He said to him: "Recall, now, who that was innocent ever perished." [12]Since he saw that he was not listening to him, he said to him: "Now a word came stealthily to me. [13]Thus I heard from behind the curtain: The lamb is for a burnt-offering, and Isaac is not for a burnt-offering." [14]He said to him: "This is the punishment of a liar, that even when he tells the truth, nobody listens to him."

TRANSLATION AND COMMENTARY

to his mother Sarah." God continued: [1]**"Whom you love,"** to which Abraham **replied: "I love both** of my sons." [2]Finally God spelled out His command: **"Isaac."** [3]The Gemara asks: **And why** did God use **all these** various designations, rather than mentioning Isaac by name from the very beginning? [4]He formulated His command in this roundabout manner **so that** Abraham **not lose his mind** because of the shock at having been instructed by God to offer Him Isaac as a sacrifice.

קְדָמוֹ [5]The Gemara continues with its Aggadic exposition of the story of the binding of Isaac: As Abraham was on his way to sacrifice Isaac, **Satan met him on the road,** and tried to persuade him to disobey God's command. Borrowing the words of Elifaz the Temanite (Job 2:2-5), [6]Satan **said to** Abraham: **"If one ventures a word to you, will you be grieved?** But who can withhold himself from speaking? [7]**Behold, you have instructed many, and you have strengthened the weak hands.** [8]**Your words have upheld him that was falling,** and you have strengthened the feeble knees. **But now it is come upon you, and you are weary** — have you no regrets now that God has commanded you to sacrifice your only son to Him?" [9]Abraham **said to** Satan in response: **"But as for me, I will walk in my integrity** — and not question the will of my Lord." [10]Satan **said to him** once again in the words of Elifaz the Temanite (Job 4:6): **"Is not your fear of God your folly** — if you actually slaughter your son?" [11]Abraham **responded** with Elifaz's own words (Job 4:7): **"Recall, now, who that was innocent ever perished** — surely God is righteous and upright in His judgment." [12]**When** Satan **saw that** Abraham **was paying him no heed, he said to him** (Job 4:12): **"Now a word came stealthily to me,** and my ear took fright of it. [13]**Thus I heard from behind the curtain** separating God from His ministering angels: **A lamb will be** offered to Me **as a burnt-offering, and Isaac will not be** offered to me **as a burnt-offering."** [14]Abraham **said to him:** "You might be right, but **this is the punishment of a liar, that even when he tells the truth, nobody believes him.** Thus, I will continue on my way, and make all my preparations to sacrifice Isaac, as God has instructed me to do."

LANGUAGE

פַּרְגּוֹד **Curtain.** This word apparently derives from an Iranian word related to the root *gund,* meaning to wear clothing. The compound, *pari gund* is probably related to Middle Persian *pardaγ*, meaning "a screen." The image of "behind the screen" derives from the screen that stood before the royal entrance in Persia.

RASHI

הנסה דבר אליך תלאה — וכי היה לאוהבך לנסותך בדבר שהיא תלאה אותך ומכרית את זרעך. **הנה יסרת רבים** — רגילת והחייתה לו כל באי העולם בדברים, ועתה הנה בא להלאותך ולבהלך.

NOTES

הֲנִסָּה דָבָר אֵלֶיךָ **If one ventures a word to you.** The verses cited here from the Book of Job do not refer to Abraham and the binding of Isaac. But the Gemara cites them in order to relate the conversation between Satan and Abraham using the wording of the Bible (*Iyyun Ya'akov*).

אֲחוֹרֵי הַפַּרְגּוֹד **From behind the curtain.** Some understand that whatever is heard "from behind the curtain" will indeed come true, but without compromising man's freedom of choice. Satan heard from behind the curtain that Isaac would not be offered as a burnt-offering. But Abraham paid no heed to what Satan said, for his words could have come true either through a divine command or through Abraham's disobedience (*Tzofnat Pa'ane'aḥ*).

[1]רַבִּי לֵוִי אָמַר: אַחַר דְּבָרָיו שֶׁל יִשְׁמָעֵאל לְיִצְחָק. [2]אָמַר לוֹ יִשְׁמָעֵאל לְיִצְחָק: ״אֲנִי גָּדוֹל מִמְּךָ בְּמִצְוֹת, שֶׁאַתָּה מַלְתָּ בֶּן שְׁמֹנַת יָמִים, [3]וַאֲנִי בֶּן שְׁלֹשׁ עֶשְׂרֵה שָׁנָה״. [4]אָמַר לוֹ: ״וּבְאֵבֶר אֶחָד אַתָּה מְגָרֶה בִּי? [5]אִם אוֹמֵר לִי הַקָּדוֹשׁ בָּרוּךְ הוּא: ׳זְבַח עַצְמְךָ לְפָנַי׳, [6]אֲנִי זוֹבֵחַ״. [7]מִיָּד, ״וְהָאֱלֹהִים נִסָּה אֶת אַבְרָהָם״.

[8]תָּנוּ רַבָּנַן: ״נָבִיא שֶׁהִדִּיחַ — בִּסְקִילָה״. [9]רַבִּי שִׁמְעוֹן אוֹמֵר: בְּחֶנֶק. [10]מַדִּיחֵי עִיר הַנִּדַּחַת — בִּסְקִילָה. [11]רַבִּי שִׁמְעוֹן אוֹמֵר: בְּחֶנֶק.

[12]״נָבִיא שֶׁהִדִּיחַ — בִּסְקִילָה״. [13]מַאי טַעְמָא דְּרַבָּנַן? [14]אָתְיָא ״הַדָּחָה״ ״הַדָּחָה״ מִמֵּסִית. [15]מַה לְּהַלָּן — בִּסְקִילָה, [16]אַף כָּאן בִּסְקִילָה.

[17]וְרַבִּי שִׁמְעוֹן? [18]״מִיתָה״ כְּתִיבָא בֵּיהּ. [19]וְכָל מִיתָה

LITERAL TRANSLATION

[1]Rabbi Levi said: After the words of Ishmael to Isaac. [2]Ishmael said to Isaac: "I am greater than you in commandments, for you were circumcised when you were eight days old, [3]and I when I was thirteen years old." [4]He said to him: "You tease me over one organ? [5]If the Holy One, blessed be He, says to me: 'Sacrifice yourself to me,' [6]I will sacrifice myself." [7]Immediately, "And God tested Abraham."

[8]Our Rabbis taught: "A Prophet who incited — by stoning. [9]Rabbi Shimon says: By strangulation. [10]The inciters of a condemned city — by stoning. [11]Rabbi Shimon says: By strangulation."

[12]"A Prophet who incited — by stoning." [13]What is the reason of the Rabbis? [14]They learn "incitement" "incitement" from an inciter. [15]Just as, there — by stoning, [16]so, too, here by stoning.

[17]And Rabbi Shimon? [18]"Death" is written by him. [19]And every death

RASHI

נביא שהדיח – שמתנבא בשם הקדוש ברוך הוא לעבוד עבודה זרה. **הדחה** – כתיב הכא "כי דבר סרה להדיחך" וכתיב "במסית כי ביקש להדיחך וגו'". **מיתה כתב ביה** – והך גזירה

TRANSLATION AND COMMENTARY

רַבִּי לֵוִי אָמַר [1]The Gemara now suggests another explanation of the verse, "And it came to pass after these things, that God tested Abraham." **Rabbi Levi said: After** hearing **the words of Ishmael to Isaac.** [2]**Ishmael said to Isaac: "I am greater than you with respect to** my observance of God's **commandments, for you were circumcised** as a newborn **when you were** only **eight days old** without your knowledge, and without your consent. [3]**But I** was circumcised **when I was thirteen years old** of my own free will." [4]Isaac **said to** his brother: **"Are you** trying to **tease me** and demonstrate your superiority **with respect to** circumcision which involves only **a single organ?** [5]**If the Holy One, blessed be He, said to me: 'Sacrifice yourself to me,'** [6]**I would** go out immediately and **sacrifice myself** to Him." [7]**Immediately** "after these words," **"God tested Abraham,"** in order to verify that Isaac was indeed prepared to give up his life for Him. Thus, according to this Midrash, Isaac was tested at least as much as his father.

תָּנוּ רַבָּנַן [8]The Gemara returns once again to discuss offenses related to prophecy. **Our Rabbis taught** the following Baraita: **"A Prophet who incited** people to commit idolatry is subject to death **by stoning,** just like an ordinary person who incited an individual to worship an idol. [9]**Rabbi Shimon says:** A Prophet who incited others to commit idolatry is subject to death **by strangulation.** [10]**The inciters of a condemned city** — a city the majority of whose inhabitants were led astray to commit idolatry — are subject to the penalty of death **by stoning,** just like the inciter of a single individual. [11]**Rabbi Shimon says:** The inciters of a condemned city are subject to death **by strangulation."**

נָבִיא [12]The Gemara begins to explain the Baraita clause by clause: **"A Prophet who incited** people to commit idolatry is subject to death **by stoning."** [13]The Gemara asks: **What is the reasoning of the Rabbis?** [14]The Gemara explains: **They learn** the penalty imposed upon a Prophet who incited others to commit idolatry by a *gezerah shavah* drawn between the term of **"incitement"** mentioned with regard to such a Prophet and the term **"incitement"** mentioned **with regard to an** ordinary **inciter.** Regarding an ordinary person who incited an individual to commit idolatry, the verse states (Deuteronomy 13:11): "Because he has sought to draw you away [לְהַדִּיחֲךָ] from the Lord your God," and regarding a Prophet who incited others to commit idolatry, the verse states (Deuteronomy 13:6): "Because he has spoken to turn you away from the Lord…to draw you [לְהַדִּיחֲךָ] out of the way which the Lord your God commanded you to walk in." [15]**Just as, there,** the ordinary inciter is liable to death **by stoning,** as the verse states (Deuteronomy 13: 11): "And you shall stone him with stones," [16]**so, too, here** a Prophet who incited people to commit idolatry is liable to death **by stoning.**

וְרַבִּי שִׁמְעוֹן [17]The Gemara asks: **And** how does **Rabbi Shimon** counter this argument? The Gemara explains: Regarding a Prophet who incited others to commit idolatry, [18]**the verse speaks of "death,"** without specifying the mode of execution, for the verse states (Deuteronomy 13:6): "And that Prophet, or that dreamer of dreams, shall be put to death." [19]**And,** as was stated already several times in the tractate, **whenever the**

TRANSLATION AND COMMENTARY

Torah speaks of execution without specifying the mode of execution, it **is** referring to **strangulation.**

מְדִיחֵי עִיר הַנִּדַּחַת [1]The Baraita continues: **"The inciters of a condemned city** are subject to the penalty of death **by stoning,** just like the inciter of a single individual." [2]The Gemara asks: **What is the reasoning of the Rabbis?** [3]The Gemara explains: **They learn** the penalty imposed upon the inciters of a condemned city by a *gezerah shavah* drawn between the term of **"incitement"** mentioned with regard to such offenders and the term of **"incitement"** mentioned **either with regard to an** ordinary **inciter,** [4]**or with regard to a Prophet who incited** people to commit idolatry. Regarding the inciters of a condemned city, the verse states (Deuteronomy 13:14): "Certain men, wicked persons, are gone out from among you, and have drawn away [וַיַּדִּיחוּ] the inhabitants of their city." A similar term, "to draw you away [לְהַדִּיחֲךָ]," is used regarding an ordinary inciter and a Prophet who incited others to commit idolatry. Just as, there, the ordinary inciter and the Prophet are liable to death by stoning, so, too, are the inciters of a condemned city liable to death by stoning.

וְרַבִּי שִׁמְעוֹן [5]The Gemara asks: **And** how does **Rabbi Shimon** counter this argument? [6]The Gemara explains: **He learns** the penalty imposed upon the inciters of a condemned city by a *gezerah shavah* drawn between the term of **"incitement"** mentioned with regard to such offenders and the term of **"incitement"** mentioned **with regard to a Prophet** who incited people to commit idolatry — who, according to Rabbi Shimon, is liable to death by strangulation.

וְלִיגְמַר מְמֵסִית [7]The Gemara asks: **But let** Rabbi Shimon **learn** the penalty imposed upon the inciters of a condemned city by a *gezerah shavah* **from** the penalty imposed upon **an** ordinary **inciter** who incited an individual to commit idolatry, for even according to Rabbi Shimon, that offender is liable to death by stoning!

דָּנִין [8]The Gemara answers: It is preferable **to learn** the law applying to **someone who incites the community** to commit idolatry (the inciters of a condemned city) by a *gezerah shavah* **from** another law applying to **someone who incites the community** to commit idolatry (a Prophet who incited others to idolatry), [9]**and not to learn** the law applying to **someone who incites the community** to commit idolatry by a *gezerah shavah* **from** the law applying to **someone who incites an individual** to commit idolatry (an ordinary inciter).

אַדְּרַבָּה [10]The Gemara rebuts this: **On the contrary,** it is preferable to **learn** the law applying to **an ordinary person** (the inciters of a condemned city) by a *gezerah shavah* **from** another law applying to **an ordinary person** (an ordinary inciter) [11]**and not to learn** the law applying to **an ordinary person** by a *gezerah shavah* **from** the law applying to **a Prophet.**

וְרַבִּי שִׁמְעוֹן [12]The Gemara asks: **And** how does **Rabbi Shimon** counter this argument? [13]The Gemara explains: **Once** a Prophet **incites** others to commit idolatry, **there is no person more ordinary than he,** and so there is no problem with learning the law regarding the inciters of a condemned city from the law regarding a Prophet who incited others to idolatry.

הָאֲמוּרָה בַּתּוֹרָה סְתָם אֵינָהּ אֶלָּא חֶנֶק.

[1]״מְדִיחֵי עִיר הַנִּדַּחַת — בִּסְקִילָה״. [2]מַאי טַעְמָא דְּרַבָּנַן? [3]גָּמְרִי ״הַדָּחָה״ ״הַדָּחָה״ אוֹ מִמֵּסִית, [4]אוֹ מִנָּבִיא שֶׁהִדִּיחַ.

[5]וְרַבִּי שִׁמְעוֹן? [6]גָּמַר ״הַדָּחָה״ ״הַדָּחָה״ מִנָּבִיא.

[7]וְלִיגְמַר מִמֵּסִית!

[8]דָּנִין מֵסִית רַבִּים מִמֵּסִית רַבִּים, [9]וְאֵין דָּנִין מֵסִיחַ רַבִּים מִמֵּסִית יָחִיד.

[10]אַדְּרַבָּה, דָּנִין הֶדְיוֹט מֵהֶדְיוֹט, [11]וְאֵין דָּנִין הֶדְיוֹט מִנָּבִיא!

[12]וְרַבִּי שִׁמְעוֹן? [13]כֵּיוָן שֶׁהִדִּיחַ, אֵין לְךָ הֶדְיוֹט גָּדוֹל מִזֶּה.

LITERAL TRANSLATION

stated in the Torah without specification can only be strangulation.

[1]"The inciters of a condemned city — by stoning." [2]What is the reasoning of the Rabbis? [3]They learn "incitement" "incitement" either from an inciter, [4]or from a Prophet who incited.

[5]And Rabbi Shimon? [6]He learns "incitement" "incitement" from a Prophet.

[7]But let him learn from an inciter!

[8]We learn about someone who incites many from someone who incites many, [9]and we do not learn about someone who incites many from someone who incites an individual.

[10]On the contrary, we learn an ordinary person from an ordinary person, [11]and we do not learn an ordinary person from a Prophet.

[12]And Rabbi Shimon? [13]Since he incited, you have no ordinary person greater than he.

RASHI

שוה לא גמר מרביה, דאין אדם דן גזירה שוה מעצמו. ורבי שמעון גמר הדחה הדחה מנביא — דבעיר הנדחת אגמריה רביה גזירה שוה מסיני לדון ״הדחה״ ״הדחה״, ומסתברא דמנביא אגמריה הלכה למשה גזירה שוה זו, כדיהיב טעמא למלתיה.

[1]אָמַר רַב חִסְדָּא: [90A] [2]מַחֲלוֹקֶת בְּעוֹקֵר הַגּוּף דַּעֲבוֹדָה זָרָה, [3]וְקִיּוּם מִקְצָת וּבִיטּוּל מִקְצָת דַּעֲבוֹדָה זָרָה, [4]דְּרַחֲמָנָא אָמַר: "מִן הַדֶּרֶךְ" — [5]אֲפִילּוּ מִקְצָת הַדֶּרֶךְ. [6]אֲבָל עוֹקֵר הַגּוּף דִּשְׁאָר מִצְוֹת, [7]דִּבְרֵי הַכֹּל בְּחֶנֶק. [8]וְקִיּוּם מִקְצָת וּבִיטּוּל מִקְצָת דְּבִשְׁאָר מִצְוֹת, [9]דִּבְרֵי הַכֹּל פָּטוּר.

[10]מְתִיב רַב הַמְנוּנָא: "'לָלֶכֶת' —

LITERAL TRANSLATION

[1]Rav Ḥisda said: [90A] [2]The dispute is where he uproots the essence of idolatry, [3]or fulfills part and abrogates part of idolatry, [4]for the Torah (lit., "the Merciful One") said: "Out of the way" — [5]even part of the way. [6]But when he uproots the essence of other commandments, [7]all agree by strangulation. [8]And [when] he fulfills part and abrogates part of other commandments, [9]all agree that he is exempt.

[10]Rav Hamnuna objected: "'To walk' —

TRANSLATION AND COMMENTARY

אָמַר רַב חִסְדָּא [1]**Rav Ḥisda said:** [90A] [2]**The dispute** between the Rabbis and Rabbi Shimon **is** limited to a Prophet who **uprooted the** entire **essence of idolatry,** claiming that he was divinely commanded to prophesy that the prohibition against idolatry was entirely abolished, [3]**and** to a Prophet who **partly fulfilled and partly abrogated** the prohibition **against idolatry,** permitting idol worship only in certain cases. The Rabbis maintain that the Prophet is liable to death by stoning, and Rabbi Shimon maintains that he is liable to death by strangulation. The Prophet is liable even if he only partly abrogated the prohibition, [4]**for the Torah said** (Deuteronomy 13:6): "And that Prophet, or that dreamer of dreams, shall be put to death, because he has spoken to turn you away from the Lord…to draw you out of the way which the Lord your God commands you to walk in," the words **"out of the way"** [5]implying that he is liable **even** if he came only to abrogate **part of the way.** [6]**But** if the Prophet **uprooted the** entire **essence of other commandments,** claiming that he was commanded to prophesy that some other prohibition was entirely abolished, [7]**all agree** — even the Rabbis who disagree with Rabbi Shimon — that he is liable to death **by strangulation.**

The passage from which the Rabbis learn that a Prophet who incites people to sin is liable to death by stoning deals with a Prophet who uprooted the prohibition against idolatry, as the verse states (Deuteronomy 13:3): "And the sign or the wonder comes to pass, of which he spoke to you, saying, Let us go after other gods, which you have not known, and let us serve them." But the penalty imposed upon a Prophet who uprooted some other commandment is derived from the verse (Deuteronomy 18:20): "But the prophet, who shall presume to speak a word in My name, which I have not commanded him to speak, or who shall speak in the name of other gods, that prophet shall die." As noted earlier, an unspecified death penalty refers to death by strangulation. [8]**And** if the Prophet **partly fulfilled and partly abrogated other commandments,** [9]**all agree** — both the Rabbis and Rabbi Shimon — **that he is exempt** from the death penalty, for the verse refers to a Prophet who "speaks a word in My name" — a whole word, and not part of a word.

מְתִיב רַב הַמְנוּנָא [10]**Rav Hamnuna raised an objection** against Rav Ḥisda from a Baraita which taught: "The verse regarding a false prophet who leads others astray reads (Deuteronomy 13:6): 'To draw you out of the way which the Lord your God commands you to walk in.' The words **'to walk'** refer to **positive commandments,**

RASHI

מחלוקת — דרבנן ורבי שמעון בנביא בעוקר כל הגוף בעבודה זרה ואומר "נלטויתי ברוח הקודש מפי הגבורה להתנבאות לעקור כל מצות עבודה זרה מן התורה" או "לקיים מקצת ולבטל מקצת", בהאי הוא דקאמרי רבנן סקילה משום דבהאי ענינא דכתיבא הדחה בנביא דגמרי סקילה מיניה — בעבודה זרה הוא משתעי, דכתיב "ובא האות והמופת וגו' נלכה ונעבדה" — היינו עקירת הגוף ובטול מקצת, התם נמי כתיב בסיפא "יומת כי דבר סרה וגו' להדיחך מן הדרך", ואפילו במקצת במשמע, ומיהו לא מישתעי קרא אלא בעבודה זרה, דדבר למד מענינו. **אבל עוקר הגוף דשאר מצות דברי הכל בחנק** — דנפקא לן מקרא אחרינא האמור בפרשה אחרינא דלא כתיב בה הדחה "אך הנביא אשר יזיד לדבר דבר בשמי" (דברים יח) והיינו מה שלא שמע, וכתיב "ומת הנביא ההוא", וכל מיתה האמורה סתם חנק הוא. **פטור** — דהתם "דבר" כתיב, דבר שלם ולא חצי דבר. **ללכת זו מצות עשה** — ברייתא היא בספרי גבי

NOTES

עוֹקֵר הַגּוּף **He uproots the essence.** A Prophet who uproots one of the Torah's commandments is regarded as a false prophet, even if his prophecy was never refuted — not by another Prophet who is known to be a true Prophet, nor by the failure of the signs that he gave to authenticate his prophecy. There is a difference between a Prophet who uproots the prohibition against idolatry and an ordinary person who comes to incite others to worship an idol. An ordinary inciter is only liable to execution if he incited others to violate a prohibition that is punishable by judicial execution, whereas a Prophet is liable to execution for uprooting any aspect of the prohibition against idolatry, even something that is only forbidden indirectly by a positive commandment (see *Rabbi David Bonfil*).

בִּיטּוּל מִקְצָת דְּבִשְׁאָר מִצְוֹת **When he abrogates part of other commandments.** *Rosh* suggests that a Prophet is exempt if he partly fulfilled and partly abrogated other commandments, because the verse states (Deuteronomy 18:20): "But the Prophet, who shall presume to speak a word in My name," and here all agree that we say: "A word" — and not half a word.

TRANSLATION AND COMMENTARY

and the word [1]**'in'** refers to **negative commandments."** [2]**Now if you think** that this passage refers only to a Prophet who incites others to commit **idolatry,** [3]**where do you find a positive commandment regarding idolatry?** Surely the commandments regarding idolatry are all prohibitions!

תַּרְגְּמָהּ [4]**Rav Ḥisda explained:** There is indeed a positive commandment regarding idolatry (Deuteronomy 12:3): **"And you shall overthrow** their altars, and break their pillars."

רַב הַמְנוּנָא אָמַר [5]Even though his objection was rebutted, **Rav Hamnuna** still disagreed with Rav Ḥisda and **said:** [6]**The dispute** between the Rabbis and Rabbi Shimon **is** limited to a Prophet who **uprooted the** entire **essence** of a commandment, **whether idolatry or other commandments,** [7]**and** to a Prophet who **partly fulfilled and partly abrogated** the prohibition **against idolatry.** The Rabbis maintain that the Prophet is liable to death by stoning, and Rabbi Shimon maintains that he is liable to death by strangulation. The Prophet is liable if he came to uproot the entire essence of any commandment, for the words "to walk in" teach that the Prophet uprooted the entire essence of positive and negative commandments, not just the commandments regarding idolatry. And the Prophet is liable even if he only partly abrogated the prohibition regarding idolatry, [8]**for the Torah said** (Deuteronomy 13:6): "To draw you out of the way which the Lord your God commands you to walk in," and the words **"out of the way"** imply **even part of the way.** [9]**But** if the Prophet **partly fulfilled and partly abrogated other commandments,** [10]**all** — both the Rabbis and Rabbi Shimon — **agree that he is exempt** from the death penalty.

תָּנוּ רַבָּנַן [11]**Our Rabbis taught** a related Baraita: "If **someone prophesies to uproot a matter from the Torah,** he **is liable** to the death penalty. [12]If he prophesies **to partly fulfill and partly abrogate** a commandment, **Rabbi Shimon** says that he is **exempt.** [13]**And regarding idolatry, even if** the Prophet **says: 'Worship** the idol **today, and destroy it tomorrow,'** [14]**all** — both Rabbi Shimon and the Rabbis — **agree that he is liable** to the death penalty."

זוֹ מִצְוַת עֲשֵׂה, [1]'בָּהּ' — זוֹ מִצְוַת לֹא תַּעֲשֶׂה". [2]וְאִי סָלְקָא דַּעְתָּךְ בַּעֲבוֹדָה זָרָה, [3]עֲשֵׂה בַּעֲבוֹדָה זָרָה הֵיכִי מַשְׁכַּחַתְּ לָהּ? [4]תַּרְגְּמָהּ רַב חִסְדָּא: "וְנִתַּצְתֶּם". [5]רַב הַמְנוּנָא אָמַר: [6]מַחֲלוֹקֶת בְּעוֹקֵר הַגּוּף, בֵּין בַּעֲבוֹדָה זָרָה בֵּין בִּשְׁאָר מִצְוֹת, [7]וְקִיּוּם מִקְצָת וּבִיטּוּל מִקְצָת דַּעֲבוֹדָה זָרָה, [8]דְּרַחֲמָנָא אָמַר: "מִן הַדֶּרֶךְ" — אֲפִילּוּ מִקְצָת הַדֶּרֶךְ. [9]אֲבָל קִיּוּם מִקְצָת וּבִיטּוּל מִקְצָת דְּבִשְׁאָר מִצְוֹת — [10]דִּבְרֵי הַכֹּל פָּטוּר. [11]תָּנוּ רַבָּנַן: "הַמִּתְנַבֵּא לַעֲקוֹר דָּבָר מִן הַתּוֹרָה חַיָּיב. [12]לְקַיֵּים מִקְצָת וּלְבַטֵּל מִקְצָת, רַבִּי שִׁמְעוֹן פּוֹטֵר. [13]וּבַעֲבוֹדָה זָרָה, אֲפִילּוּ אוֹמֵר: 'הַיּוֹם עִיבְדוּהָ וּלְמָחָר בַּטְּלוּהָ', [14]דִּבְרֵי הַכֹּל חַיָּיב".

LITERAL TRANSLATION

this is a positive commandment. [1]'In it' — this is a negative commandment." [2]And if it enters your mind regarding idolatry, [3]where do you find a positive commandment regarding idolatry?

[4]Rav Ḥisda explained it: "And you shall overthrow."

[5]Rav Hamnuna said: [6]The dispute is when he uproots the essence, whether regarding idolatry or regarding other commandments, [7]or [when he] fulfills part and abrogates part of idolatry, [8]for the Torah said: "Out of the way" — even part of the way. [9]But [when] he fulfills part and abrogates part of other commandments, [10]all agree that he is exempt.

[11]Our Rabbis taught: "Someone who prophesies to uproot a matter from the Torah is liable. [12]To fulfill part and abrogate part, Rabbi Shimon exempts [him]. [13]And regarding idolatry, even if he says: 'Worship it today, and destroy it tomorrow,' [14]all agree that he is liable."

RASHI

פרשת נביא המדיח דכתב בה הדחה (שם יג) "להדיחך מן הדרך אשר צוך ה' אלהיך ללכת בה וגו'", ודריש קרא יתירא "ללכת" — זו מצות עשה, דמשמע לעשות ולא משמע אזהרה. **בה לא תעשה** — דגמרינן מאשר חטא בה דבלא תעשה מיירי, אלמא דשאר מצות נמי הכא גבי הדחה כתיבי, דאי לא משתעי קרא אלא בעבודה זרה מאי עשה איכא. **ובין בשאר מצות** — דהאי "ללכת בה" לא משמע ליה לרב המנונא א"ונתצתם", דרחמנא אמר "מן הדרך" ואעבודה זרה קאי, דאכתי לא איתרבו שאר מצות בהאי עניינא, ד"ללכת בה" — כולה משמע. **דברי הכל פטור** — ואפילו מחנק, דהתם דבר שלא כתיב ולאו אעוקר דברי תורה האי כי יזיד לדבר דבר קאי, דהתם סקילה הוא — אלא אדברים בעלמא כגון צדקיה בן כנענה. **היום עובדה** — כלומר היינו קיום מקצת וביטול מקצת.

NOTES

הַמִּתְנַבֵּא לַעֲקוֹר דָּבָר מִן הַתּוֹרָה Someone who prophesies to uproot a matter from the Torah. *Rambam* (*Hilkhot Yesodei HaTorah*, chapter 8) explains at length why we are not to listen to a Prophet who abrogates the Torah. The sign with which a Prophet proves the authenticity of his prophecy does not prove the truth of his prophecy, for there is no inherent connection between the sign and the content of the prophecy. The Torah commanded — like any other of the Torah's commandments — that if someone claims to be a Prophet, and offers a sign to prove the veracity of his

[1]אַבַּיֵי סָבַר לָהּ כְּרַב חִסְדָּא, וּמְתָרֵץ לָהּ כְּרַב חִסְדָּא. [2]רָבָא סָבַר לָהּ כְּרַב הַמְנוּנָא, וּמְתָרֵץ לָהּ כְּרַב הַמְנוּנָא. [3]אַבַּיֵי סָבַר לָהּ כְּרַב חִסְדָּא, וּמְתָרֵץ לָהּ כְּרַב חִסְדָּא: [4]הַמִּתְנַבֵּא לַעֲקוֹר דָּבָר מִן הַתּוֹרָה, דִּבְרֵי הַכֹּל בְּחֶנֶק. [5]לְקַיֵּים מִקְצָת וּלְבַטֵּל מִקְצָת, רַבִּי שִׁמְעוֹן פּוֹטֵר, וְהוּא הַדִּין לְרַבָּנַן. [6]וּבַעֲבוֹדָה זָרָה, אֲפִילּוּ אָמַר: ״הַיּוֹם עִיבְדוּהָ וּלְמָחָר בַּטְּלוּהָ״, [7]חַיָּיב. [8]מָר כִּדְאִית לֵיהּ, [9]וּמָר כִּדְאִית לֵיהּ. [10]רָבָא סָבַר לָהּ כְּרַב הַמְנוּנָא, וּמְתָרֵץ לָהּ כְּרַב הַמְנוּנָא. [11]הַמִּתְנַבֵּא לַעֲקוֹר דָּבָר מִן הַתּוֹרָה, בֵּין בַּעֲבוֹדָה זָרָה בֵּין בִּשְׁאָר מִצְוֹת, חַיָּיב. [12]מָר כִּדְאִית לֵיהּ, וּמָר כִּדְאִית לֵיהּ. [13]לְקַיֵּים מִקְצָת וּלְבַטֵּל מִקְצָת בִּשְׁאָר מִצְוֹת, [14]רַבִּי שִׁמְעוֹן פּוֹטֵר, וְהוּא הַדִּין לְרַבָּנַן. [15]וּבַעֲבוֹדָה זָרָה, אֲפִילּוּ אוֹמֵר: ״הַיּוֹם עִיבְדוּהָ וּלְמָחָר בַּטְּלוּהָ, חַיָּיב, [16]מָר כִּדְאִית לֵיהּ, [17]וּמָר כִּדְאִית לֵיהּ.

LITERAL TRANSLATION

[1]Abaye agrees with Rav Ḥisda, and explains it like Rav Ḥisda. [2]Rava agrees with Rav Hamnuna, and explains it like Rav Hamnuna. [3]Abaye agrees with Rav Ḥisda, and explains it like Rav Ḥisda: [4]Someone who prophesies to uproot a matter from the Torah, all agree by strangulation. [5]To fulfill part and abrogate part, Rabbi Shimon exempts [him], and so do the Rabbis. [6]And regarding idolatry, even if he said: "Worship it today, and destroy it tomorrow," [7]he is liable. [8]The one Sage as he maintains, [9]and the other Sage as he maintains.

[10]Rava agrees with Rav Hamnuna, and explains it like Rav Hamnuna. [11]Someone who prophesies to uproot a matter from the Torah, whether regarding idolatry or regarding other commandments, is liable. [12]The one Sage as he maintains, and the other Sage as he maintains. [13]To fulfill part and abrogate part regarding other commandments, [14]Rabbi Shimon exempts [him], and so, too, according to the Rabbis. [15]And regarding idolatry, even if he said: "Worship it today, and destroy it tomorrow," he is liable. [16]The one Sage as he maintains, [17]and the other Sage as he maintains.

TRANSLATION AND COMMENTARY

אַבַּיֵי סָבַר לָהּ [1]The Gemara now explains the relation between the views of the Amoraim and those of the Tannaim: **Abaye agrees with** the position of **Rav Ḥisda, and explains** this Baraita **in accordance with** the position of **Rav Ḥisda,** [2]and **Rava agrees with** the position of **Rav Hamnuna, and explains** this Baraita **in accordance with** the position of **Rav Hamnuna.** The Gemara now explains: [3]**Abaye agrees with** the position of **Rav Ḥisda, and explains** the Baraita **in accordance with** the position of **Rav Ḥisda,** so that it means as follows: [4]If **someone prophesies to** totally **uproot a matter** other than idolatry **from the Torah, all** — both Rabbi Shimon and the Rabbis — **agree** that he is liable to death **by strangulation.** [5]And if he prophesies to **partly fulfill and partly abrogate** that other commandment, **Rabbi Shimon** says that he is **exempt, and so, too, do the Rabbis.** [6]**And regarding idolatry, even if** the Prophet **said: "Worship** the idol **today, and destroy it tomorrow,"** [7]all agree that **he is liable** to the death penalty. [8]**One Sage** — Rabbi Shimon — **follows his position** that he is liable to death by strangulation, [9]**and the other Sage** — the Rabbis — **follows his position** that he is liable to death by stoning.

רָבָא סָבַר לָהּ [10]**Rava agrees with** the position of **Rav Hamnuna, and explains** the Baraita **in accordance with** the position of **Rav Hamnuna,** so that it means as follows: [11]If **someone prophesies to** totally **uproot a matter from the Torah, whether regarding idolatry or regarding other commandments,** he **is liable** to the death penalty. [12]**One Sage** — Rabbi Shimon — **follows his position** that he is liable to death by strangulation, **and the other Sage** — the Rabbis — **follows his position** that he is liable to death by stoning. [13]And if he prophesies **to partly fulfill and partly abrogate** one of the **other commandments,** [14]**Rabbi Shimon** says that he is **exempt, and so, too, do the Rabbis.** [15]**And regarding idolatry, even if** the Prophet **said: "Worship** the idol **today, and destroy it tomorrow," he is liable** to the death penalty. [16]**One Sage** — Rabbi Shimon — **follows his position** that he is liable for death by strangulation, [17]**and the other Sage** — the Rabbis — **follows his position** that he is liable to death by stoning.

RASHI

כרב חסדא — דאמר בעבודה זרה הוא דפליגי, אבל בשאר מצות עוקר הגוף הוא בחנק, וביטול מקצת פטור. **רבי שמעון פוטר והוא הדין לרבנן** — דגבי חנק דבר שלם כתיב, ולרב חסדא הא דנקט רבי שמעון — הא קא משמע לן דרישא דקתני סתמא חייב ואפילו לרבנן בחנק, דר׳ שמעון הוא דקא מחייב חנק ולא סקילה, דשאר מצות בעניינא הדחה דסקילה לא כתיבי. **מר כדאית ליה כו׳** — לרבנן בסקילה לרבי שמעון בחנק, והוא הדין לרבנן ולרב המנונא האי דנקט רבי שמעון — רבותא הוא, כלומר ואפילו מחנק דרבי שמעון פטור, וכל שכן מסקילה דמחייבי ליה רבנן בעוקר את הכל.

NOTES

words, we must listen to him. However, if his words contradict the words of the Torah, then the same source that says we should listen to a Prophet says we should not obey him.

[1]אָמַר רַבִּי אַבָּהוּ אָמַר רַבִּי יוֹחָנָן: בַּכֹּל, אִם יֹאמַר לְךָ נָבִיא: [2]"עֲבוֹר עַל דִּבְרֵי תוֹרָה", שְׁמַע לוֹ, [3]חוּץ מֵעֲבוֹדָה זָרָה, שֶׁאֲפִילּוּ מַעֲמִיד לְךָ חַמָּה בְּאֶמְצַע הָרָקִיעַ, [4]אַל תִּשְׁמַע לוֹ.

[5]תַּנְיָא: "רַבִּי יוֹסֵי הַגְּלִילִי אוֹמֵר: [6]הִגִּיעַ תּוֹרָה לְסוֹף דַּעְתָּהּ שֶׁל עֲבוֹדָה זָרָה, [7]לְפִיכָךְ נָתְנָה תּוֹרָה מֶמְשָׁלָה בָּהּ, שֶׁאֲפִילּוּ מַעֲמִיד לְךָ חַמָּה בְּאֶמְצַע הָרָקִיעַ, [8]אַל תִּשְׁמַע לוֹ".

[9]תַּנְיָא: "אָמַר רַבִּי עֲקִיבָא: חַס וְשָׁלוֹם שֶׁהַקָּדוֹשׁ בָּרוּךְ הוּא מַעֲמִיד חַמָּה לְעוֹבְרֵי רְצוֹנוֹ. [10]אֶלָּא, כְּגוֹן חֲנַנְיָה בֶּן עַזּוּר שֶׁמִּתְּחִלָּתוֹ נְבִיא אֱמֶת, וּלְבַסּוֹף נְבִיא שֶׁקֶר".

[11]"וְזוֹמְמֵי בַּת כֹּהֵן". [12]מְנָהָנֵי מִילֵּי? [13]אָמַר רַב אַחָא בְּרֵיהּ דְּרַב אִיקָא: דְּתַנְיָא: [14]"רַבִּי יוֹסֵי אוֹמֵר: מַה תַּלְמוּד לוֹמַר:

LITERAL TRANSLATION

[1]Rabbi Abbahu said in the name of Rabbi Yoḥanan: Regarding everything, if a Prophet says to you, [2]"Transgress the words of the Torah," listen to him, [3]except for idolatry, for even if he causes the sun to stand for you in the middle of the sky, [4]do not listen to him.

[5]It was taught: "Rabbi Yose the Galilean says: [6]The Torah fully understood (lit., "reached the end of the mind of") idolatry, [7][and] therefore the Torah gave power over it, so that even if [a false prophet] causes the sun to stand for you in the middle of the sky, [8]do not listen to him."

[9]It was taught: "Rabbi Akiva said: Heaven forbid that the Holy One, blessed be He, might cause the sun to stand for those who violate His will. [10]Rather, like Ḥananiah ben Azur who was first a true Prophet, and in the end became a false prophet."

[11]"And witnesses who conspired against the daughter of a priest." [12]From where are these things [derived]? [13]Rav Aḥa the son of Rav Ika said: As it was taught: [14]"Rabbi Yose says: What does the verse teach:

TRANSLATION AND COMMENTARY

אָמַר רַבִּי אַבָּהוּ [1]**Rabbi Abbahu said in the name of Rabbi Yoḥanan: Regarding all** of the Torah's commandments, **if a Prophet** who is known to be a true Prophet **says to you,** [2]**"Transgress the words of the Torah** as a temporary, emergency measure (as when the Prophet Elijah permitted sacrifices to be offered outside of the Temple on Mount Carmel)," you are obligated to **listen to him.** [3]This rule applies to all of the Torah's commandments, **except for idolatry, for** if a Prophet tells you to violate the prohibition against idolatry, then **even if he causes the sun to stand** still **for you in the middle of the sky,** [4]you are **not to listen to him,** for the Torah has already warned you that he is a false prophet.

תַּנְיָא [5]**It was taught** in a Baraita: **"Rabbi Yose the Galilean says:** [6]**The Torah understood** the danger and the seductive power **of idolatry,** [7]**and therefore the Torah gave** us **power** over it, **so that even if** a false prophet **causes the sun to stand** still **for you in the middle of the sky,** [8]you are **not to listen to him."**

תַּנְיָא [9]An opposing view **was taught** in another Baraita: **"Rabbi Akiva said: Heaven forbid that the Holy One, blessed be He, should cause the sun to stand** still in the middle of the sky **for** sinners **who violate His will.** [10]**Rather,** when the Torah speaks of a false prophet who gave a sign and then prophesied to commit idolatry, it is referring to someone **like Ḥananiah ben Azur who was at first a true Prophet, but in the end became a false prophet."**

וְזוֹמְמֵי בַּת כֹּהֵן [11]We have learned in the Mishnah: **"Witnesses who conspired against the** married **daughter of a priest,** falsely testifying that she committed adultery, **and the lover** of the married daughter of a priest, are liable to death by strangulation, and not death by burning, the penalty that would have been imposed upon the priest's daughter." [12]The Gemara asks: **From where is this law derived?** [13]**Rav Aḥa the son of Rav Ika said: As it was taught** in the following Baraita: [14]**"Rabbi Yose says: What does the verse** regarding false, conspiring witnesses come to **teach**

RASHI

אם יאמר לך נביא — המוחזק "עבור על דברי תורה" — הכל לפי תקנת השעה, כגון אליהו בהר הכרמל בשחוטי חוץ. **נתנה התורה ממשלה בה** — כלומר אפילו תראה אותו נביא מושל ועושה כרצונו דכתיב (דברים יג) "ונתן אליך אות או מופת". **שתחילתו נביא אמת** — כגון חנניה הנביא, והאי "ונתן אליך אות" בעודו נביא אמת יתן לך אות בנבואה אחרת, ולבסוף כשיחזור להרשיע יאמר לעבוד עבודה זרה, וסמוך עלי שהרי מוחזק אני על ידי אות ומופת שנתתי לך כבר. (**לרשות הבעל** — כגון מסרה האב לשלוחי הבעל ועדיין היא בדרך, ולא קרינן בה "בית אביה". **לאותה מיתה** — שהיו מחייבין את הנידון. **ובועלה** — כלומר וכל הבועלים נידונין כמיתת הנבעלת, חוץ מבועל בת כהן). **מה תלמוד לומר לאחיו** — לכתוב "כאשר זמם

HALAKHAH

בַּכֹּל, אִם יֹאמַר לְךָ נָבִיא **Regarding everything, if a Prophet says to you.** "If a Prophet who is known to be a true Prophet says that one should violate a Torah prohibition as a temporary, emergency measure, one is obligated to listen to him. This rule applies to all of the Torah's commandments, except for the prohibition against idolatry." (*Rambam, Sefer Mada, Hilkhot Yesodei HaTorah* 9:3.)

TRANSLATION AND COMMENTARY

(Deuteronomy 19:19): **'And you shall do to him, as he had sought to have done to his brother'?** What do the seemingly extraneous words 'to his brother' add? [1]**Regarding all those** women **accused by false witnesses** of adulterous or incestuous intercourse prohibited **by the Torah** — [2]**the witnesses who falsely** testified against them, **and their lovers, are like them** in that they are subject to the mode of execution to which the woman would have been liable. [3]But regarding the **daughter of a priest** who committed adultery, **she is** liable to death **by burning, but her lover is not** liable to death **by burning.** Rather, he is liable to the same punishment to which he would have been liable had he committed adultery with the daughter of an ordinary Israelite: stoning in the case of a betrothed woman, and strangulation in the case of a married woman. If false, conspiring witnesses testified that the married daughter of a priest committed adultery with another man, [4]**I do not know whether** the penalty inflicted upon the witnesses **is the same as** the penalty that they had sought to inflict upon **the man** (strangulation), **or the same as** the penalty that they had sought to inflict upon **the woman** (burning). [5]**When** the verse **says:** 'And you shall do to him, as he had sought **to have done to his brother,'** it teaches that if two different punishments might have been imposed, [6]the false, conspiring witness is liable to the punishment that he had wished to inflict **upon his brother, and not** to the punishment that he sought to inflict **upon his sister."**

'וַעֲשִׂיתֶם לוֹ כַּאֲשֶׁר זָמַם לַעֲשׂוֹת לְאָחִיו׳? [1]לְפִי שֶׁכָּל הַמְזוּמָּמִין שֶׁבַּתּוֹרָה — [2]זוֹמְמֵיהֶן וּבוֹעֲלֵיהֶן כַּיּוֹצֵא בָּהֶן. [3]בַּת כֹּהֵן — הִיא בִּשְׂרֵיפָה, וְאֵין בּוֹעֲלָהּ בִּשְׂרֵיפָה. [4]זוֹמְמִין, אֵינִי יוֹדֵעַ אִם לוֹ הוּקְשׁוּ אִם לָהּ הוּקְשׁוּ. [5]כְּשֶׁהוּא אוֹמֵר לַעֲשׂוֹת לְאָחִיו — [6]לְאָחִיו וְלֹא לַאֲחוֹתוֹ.

הדרן עלך אלו הן הנחנקין

LITERAL TRANSLATION

'And you shall do to him, as he had sought to have done to his brother'? [1]For regarding all those accused by false witnesses in the Torah — [2]their false witnesses and their lovers are like them. [3]The daughter of a priest — she is by burning, but her lover is not by burning. [4]I do not know whether they are compared to him or they are compared to her. [5]When it says: 'To have done to his brother' — [6]to his brother and not to his sister."

RASHI

זמם לעשות" ולישתוק. אם לו הוקשו — לבועל, שהיו מחייבין אותו חנק. **אם לה** — שמחייבין אותה שריפה. **לאחיו לא לאחותו** — כל היכא דבעדותן מחייבין איש ואשה ודינן חלוק כי הכא — לו הוקשו.

הדרן עלך אלו הן הנחנקין

NOTES

לְאָחִיו וְלֹא לַאֲחוֹתוֹ To his brother and not to his sister. There is a general rule that, while the Torah may formulate a particular law in masculine terms, the law applies equally to women. But here the words "to his brother" are totally extraneous, for the verse could have read: "As he had sought to have done." And so it is legitimate to infer: "To his brother," and not to his sister.

Conclusion to Chapter Ten

The laws of adultery and of false, conspiring witnesses were not discussed in detail in this chapter because they had been clarified in earlier chapters, and what distinguishes these transgressions is that they are punishable by strangulation. The laws concerning a person who strikes his father or his mother (or both) were clarified here in comparison to the transgression of cursing one's father and of one's mother and also in relation to instances where there may be some obligation to violate this prohibition. Regarding the crime of kidnapping, details of the Halakhah were clarified here, especially problems deriving from the fact that this transgression, unlike most others, is not a single act, and one cannot be liable to be punished for it unless one combines three elements: kidnapping someone, enslaving him, and selling him.

Regarding the laws of a rebellious elder, it was concluded that this Halakhah is not intended to limit freedom of thought or discussion, but only to prevent the development within the Jewish people of separate sects which will act in different ways. Only a Rabbi who has been ordained and found worthy to teach the Halakhah can be condemned as a rebellious elder, and even when the opinion of such a man contradicts that of all the other Rabbis, and even after the Great Sanhedrin has ruled against his opinion, he is still permitted to hold it, and even to teach it. The rebellious elder is punished only when he instructs other people *to act* in a manner contrary to the accepted Halakhah. Moreover, it is determined that the rebellious elder is punished only when he disagrees with the Oral Law when it is interpreting the written Torah.

The laws governing a false prophet are more complicated and include several different transgressions. When a person prophesies in the name of an idol, no matter what the content of his prophecy may be, he must be executed for that. This is also true when the Prophet orders people to uproot some Torah law or to worship an idol. For such a declaration is false prophecy in its very essence. The Torah, which ordered us to obey the words of a Prophet, also ordered us to remove idolatry from the world in all its forms, and it is what gives authority to the commandments. False prophecy, in its restricted definition, means that a person pretends to be a Prophet though he is not one, that he issues declarations in the name of God, although he has not received them as prophecy, and also that he speaks words of prophecy that are not the entire truth; in all these cases he is a false Prophet and punishable by death.

There are other instances when a Prophet violates the laws of the Torah and must be executed for that, but these are matters left in the hands of Heaven, and God will punish that Prophet for the sin of his false prophecy.

Introduction to Chapter Eleven

כָּל יִשְׂרָאֵל

"Now Korah, the son of Izhar, the son of Kehat, the son of Levi, and Datan and Abiram, the sons of Eliab, and On, the son of the Pelet, sons of Reuben, took courage." (Numbers 16:1.)

"For as the heavens and the new earth, which I will make, shall remain before me, says the Lord, so shall your seed and your name remain." (Isaiah 66:22.)

"And many of them that sleep in the dust of the earth shall awake, some to everlasting life, and some to shame and everlasting contempt." (Daniel 12:2.)

"But you, go your way till the end; for you shall rest, and stand in your lot at the end of the days." (Daniel 12:13.)

"Yea, I lead men, My people Israel, to you, and they shall possess you, and you shall be the inheritance, and you shall not again casue them to be bereaved." (Ezekiel 36:12.)

"And if you hear it said in one of your cities, which the Lord your God has given you to dwell in, saying, Certain men, wicked fellows, are gone out from your midst, and have withdrawn the inhabitants of their city, saying, Let us go and serve other gods, which you have not known. Then shall you enquire, and make search, and ask diligently: and behold, if it be truth, and the thing certain, that such abomination is wrought in your midst; you shall surely smite the inhabitants of that city within the edge of the sword, destroying ity utterly, and all that is therein, and the cattle thereof, with the edge of the sword. And you shall gather all the spoil of it into the midst of the street thereof, and shall burn with fire the city, and all the spoil thereof entirely, for the Lord your God: and it shall be a heap forever; it shall not be built again. And there shall cleave nought of the cursed thing to you hand: that the Lord may turn from the fierceness of his anger, and shew you mercy, and have compassion upon thee, and multiply thee, as he has sworn to your fathers."(Deuteronomy 13:13-18.)

In clarifying the various Halakhot connected to capital offenses, a broad structure has been erected within tractate *Sanhedrin* regarding important commandments in every area of Judaism. Indeed, in this framework only those aspects of the Torah were discussed which are connected to acts, and which, therefore, are subject to judicial intervention. However, to complete this structure, other aspects of the Torah must be discussed, concerning faith and ways of life, which are also fundamental to Judaism. Hence this chapter clarifies all of these subjects and passes judgment on historical figures who exemplify them.

Underlying this chapter is the basic assumption that every Jew has, intrinsically, a portion of the World to Come. That is to say, the immortality of his soul has been promised, giving him a place in the large structure of reward and punishment, the goal of which is the resurrection of the dead and life in the World to Come. This is true of a Jew who seeks to remain within the framework of the Torah and the fear of God. Even if someone sins occasionally, he is not removed from this framework, though he might incur punishment, at the hands of either man or Heaven. However, certain acts that a person might commit without atoning for them remove him from the Jewish people to such a degree that he no longer merits a portion of the World to Come, and this is the greatest of punishments — absolute death after which there is no resurrection or immortality of the soul, annihilation after which nothing remains.

This chapter discusses these transgressions mainly with respect to faith and ways of life. At the same time it clarifies certain principles of faith, including some which were doubted or belittled.

The laws of an idolatrous city, which were discussed earlier in the tractate, conclude this chapter, for they are an extension of the discussion of matters of faith, in that an idolatrous city is an example of an entire community that removes itself from the Jewish people, and which the Jewish people is commanded to extirpate from itself.

כָּל

[1]יִשְׂרָאֵל יֵשׁ לָהֶם חֵלֶק לָעוֹלָם הַבָּא, [2]שֶׁנֶּאֱמַר: ״וְעַמֵּךְ כֻּלָּם צַדִּיקִים; לְעוֹלָם יִירְשׁוּ אָרֶץ; נֵצֶר מַטָּעַי מַעֲשֵׂה יָדַי לְהִתְפָּאֵר״.
[3]וְאֵלּוּ שֶׁאֵין לָהֶם חֵלֶק לָעוֹלָם הַבָּא: [4]הָאוֹמֵר: ״אֵין תְּחִיַּית הַמֵּתִים מִן הַתּוֹרָה״, [5]״וְאֵין תּוֹרָה מִן הַשָּׁמַיִם״, [6]וְאֶפִּיקוֹרוֹס.

LITERAL TRANSLATION

MISHNAH [1]All of Israel has a portion in the World to Come, [2]as it is stated: "Your people also shall be all righteous; they shall inherit the land forever; they shall be the branch of My planting, the work of My hands to be glorified." [3]And these do not have a portion in the World to Come: [4]Someone who says: "There is no resurrection of the dead from the Torah," [5]and "The Torah is not from Heaven," [6]and an *apikoros*.

TRANSLATION AND COMMENTARY

MISHNAH **כָּל יִשְׂרָאֵל** [1]**All** the people **of Israel** — even those who have sinned, and even those who are liable to judicial execution — **have a portion in the World to Come,** [2]**as the verse states** (Isaiah 60:21): **"Your people also shall be all righteous; they shall inherit the land forever; they shall be the branch of My planting, the work of My hands to be glorified."** "Your people shall also be all righteous" includes sinners; "they shall inherit the land forever" refers to the land of the living, the World to Come.

וְאֵלּוּ [3]There are, however, a few exceptions to this rule. **The following** sinners **do not have a portion in the World to Come,** even if they are meticulous in their observance of the Torah, for they deny the fundamental tenets of Judaism: [4]**Someone who says: "There are no** allusions to the **resurrection of the dead in the Torah"**; [5]someone who says: **"The Torah was not** given **from Heaven,** but rather it was written by Moses"; [6]**and an *apikoros*,** a heretic who denigrates the Rabbis and the Torah.

RASHI

משנה כל ישראל יש להם חלק לעולם הבא — מעיקרא איירי בארבע מיתות ומפרש ואזיל להו לכולהו, והדר מפרש הני דאין להם חלק לעולם הבא. הכי גרסינן **האומר אין תחיית המתים מן התורה** — שכופר במדרשים דדרשינן בגמרא לקמן מניין לתחיית המתים מן התורה, ואפילו יהא מודה ומאמין שיחיו המתים אלא דלא רמיזא באורייתא — כופר הוא, הואיל ועוקר שיש תחיית המתים מן התורה — מה לנו ולאמונתו, וכי מהיכן הוא יודע שכן הוא — הלכך כופר גמור הוא. **אפיקורוס** — מפרש בגמרא.

NOTES

חֵלֶק לָעוֹלָם הַבָּא A portion in the World to Come. Our Mishnah speaks of those who have "a portion in the World to Come." Elsewhere (*Ketubot* 103b), the Gemara speaks of those who "are invited, or designated [מְזוּמָּן] for the World to Come." *Tosafot* explains that someone who is designated for the World to Come will enter that world without prior punishment or suffering, whereas someone who only has a portion in the World to Come might first undergo suffering, and only then enjoy his share in the next world.

לָעוֹלָם הַבָּא The World to Come. There is a fundamental dispute between *Rambam* and most other Rishonim regarding the nature of the World to Come that is under discussion in our Mishnah. According to *Rambam*, the World to Come is a world of disembodied souls: A spiritual state that follows the departure of the soul from the body and entails the soul achieving full understanding of God and enjoying eternal bliss. According to *Ramban*, *Ramah*, and *Rabbi Samson of Sens*, the Mishnah refers to the state that will follow the resurrection of the dead and the reuniting of the soul with the body, but will be entirely different from the present world as we know it.

אֵין תְּחִיַּית הַמֵּתִים מִן הַתּוֹרָה There is no resurrection of the dead from the Torah. The Rishonim (*Ramah* and others) note that there are two different readings of this passage. The standard edition of the Talmud follows the reading of *Rashi* and others, according to which the Mishnah refers to someone who denies the Scriptural proofs brought by the Sages for the resurrection of the dead. According to *Rambam* and most Rishonim, the Mishnah refers to someone who says: "There is no resurrection of the dead," denying not only the Scriptural proofs, but the resurrection of the dead itself.

HALAKHAH

כָּל יִשְׂרָאֵל יֵשׁ לָהֶם חֵלֶק לָעוֹלָם הַבָּא All of Israel has a portion in the World to Come. "All the people of Israel have a portion in the World to Come. Even sinners whose transgressions are more numerous than their good deeds are punished for their sins, and then allotted their portion in the World to Come," following the Mishnah. (*Rambam, Sefer Mada, Hilkhot Teshuvah* 3:5.)

אֵלּוּ שֶׁאֵין לָהֶם חֵלֶק לָעוֹלָם הַבָּא These do not have a portion in the World to Come. "A heretic, an *apikoros*, someone who denies the resurrection of the dead, and someone who denies the divine authorship of the Torah do not have a share in the World to Come," following the anonymous Sages of the Mishnah. (*Rambam, Sefer Mada, Hilkhot Teshuvah* 3:6; *Hilkhot Avodah Zarah* 11:12.)

[1]רַבִּי עֲקִיבָא אוֹמֵר: אַף הַקּוֹרֵא בִּסְפָרִים הַחִיצוֹנִים, [2]וְהַלּוֹחֵשׁ עַל הַמַּכָּה, [3]וְאוֹמֵר: ״כָּל הַמַּחֲלָה אֲשֶׁר שַׂמְתִּי בְמִצְרַיִם לֹא אָשִׂים עָלֶיךָ כִּי אֲנִי ה׳ רֹפְאֶךָ״.

[4]אַבָּא שָׁאוּל אוֹמֵר: אַף הַהוֹגֶה אֶת הַשֵּׁם בְּאוֹתִיּוֹתָיו.

[5]שְׁלֹשָׁה מְלָכִים וְאַרְבָּעָה הֶדְיוֹטוֹת אֵין לָהֶן חֵלֶק לָעוֹלָם הַבָּא. [6]שְׁלֹשָׁה מְלָכִים: יָרָבְעָם, אַחְאָב, וּמְנַשֶּׁה. [7]רַבִּי יְהוּדָה אוֹמֵר: מְנַשֶּׁה יֵשׁ לוֹ חֵלֶק לָעוֹלָם הַבָּא, [8]שֶׁנֶּאֱמַר: ״וַיִּתְפַּלֵּל אֵלָיו וַיִּשְׁמַע תְּחִנָּתוֹ וַיְשִׁיבֵהוּ יְרוּשָׁלַיִם לְמַלְכוּתוֹ״. [9]אָמְרוּ לוֹ: לְמַלְכוּתוֹ הֱשִׁיבוֹ, וְלֹא לְחַיֵּי הָעוֹלָם הַבָּא הֱשִׁיבוֹ. [10]אַרְבָּעָה הֶדְיוֹטוֹת: בִּלְעָם, וְדוֹאֵג, וַאֲחִיתוֹפֶל, וְגֵחֲזִי.

גמרא [11]וְכָל כָּךְ לָמָּה? [12]תָּנָא: ״הוּא כָּפַר בִּתְחִיַּית הַמֵּתִים. לְפִיכָךְ לֹא יִהְיֶה לוֹ חֵלֶק בִּתְחִיַּית הַמֵּתִים, [13]שֶׁכָּל מִדּוֹתָיו שֶׁל הַקָּדוֹשׁ בָּרוּךְ הוּא

LITERAL TRANSLATION

[1]Rabbi Akiva says: Also someone who reads heretical books, [2]and someone who mutters an incantation over a wound, [3]and says: "I will put none of these diseases upon you, which I have brought upon Egypt, for I am the Lord that heals you."

[4]Abba Shaul says: Also someone who pronounces the [Divine] Name according to its letters.

[5]Three kings and four ordinary people do not have a portion in the World to Come. [6]Three kings: Jeroboam, Ahab, and Manasseh. [7]Rabbi Yehudah says: Manasseh has a portion in the World to Come, [8]as it is stated: "And he prayed to Him…and He heard his supplication, and brought him back to Jerusalem into his kingdom." [9]They said to him: He restored him to his kingdom, but He did not restore him to life in the World to Come. [10]Four ordinary people: Bilaam, and Doeg, and Achitofel, and Gehazi.

GEMARA [11]And all this, why? [12][A Tanna] taught: "He denied the resurrection of the dead. Therefore he will not have a portion in the resurrection of the dead, [13]for all the punishments of the Holy One, blessed be He,

TRANSLATION AND COMMENTARY

רַבִּי עֲקִיבָא אוֹמֵר [1]**Rabbi Akiva says: Also someone who reads heretical books** containing interpretations of the Bible that do not follow Rabbinic tradition. [2]**And** also **someone who mutters an incantation over a wound** as a remedy, [3]**and says** (Exodus 15:26): **"I will put none of these diseases upon you, which I have brought upon Egypt, for I am the Lord that heals you,"** treating lightly the sanctity of the name of God.

אַבָּא שָׁאוּל אוֹמֵר [4]**Abba Shaul says: Also someone who pronounces the Divine Name** of four letters **as it is written.**

שְׁלֹשָׁה מְלָכִים [5]**Three kings** mentioned in the Bible **and four ordinary people** who reached distinction **do not have a portion in the World to Come.** [6]The **three kings** are **Jeroboam** ben Nabat and **Ahab,** kings of Israel, **and Manasseh,** king of Judah, who all did that which was evil in the sight of God. [7]**Rabbi Yehudah says: Manasseh has a portion in the World to Come,** for he repented of his evil ways, [8]**as the verse states** (II Chronicles 33:13): **"And he** [Manasseh] **prayed to Him,** and He received his entreaty, **and heard his supplication, and brought him back to Jerusalem into his kingdom,"** implying that God pardoned Manasseh for his sins, and so he regained his portion in the World to Come. [9]The Sages **said to** Rabbi Yehudah: A careful reading of the verse in II Chronicles suggests that God only **restored Manasseh to his kingdom, but did not restore him to life in the World to Come,** for he did not repent with all his heart. [10]The **four ordinary people** who do not have a portion in the World to Come are **Bilaam** ben Beor, who was invited by Balak to curse the people of Israel; **Doeg** the Edomite, who slandered David before Saul and caused the death of the priests of Nob; **Achitofel,** who offered Abshalom evil counsel against his father; **and Gehazi,** Elisha's lad who denigrated Rabbinical scholars.

GEMARA וְכָל כָּךְ לָמָּה [11]The Gemara asks: **Why** is someone who says that there are no allusions to the resurrection of the dead in the Torah punished **so severely?** [12]**A Tanna taught** a Baraita which answers this question: "Since this person **denied the resurrection of the dead, he will therefore not have a portion in the resurrection of the dead.** [13]This follows the rule that **all the punishments** meted out by **the Holy One, blessed**

RASHI

ספרים החיצונים — מפרש בגמרא.

NOTES

וְכָל כָּךְ לָמָּה And all this, why? We understand why the other offenders do not have a share in the World to Come, for they reject all the fundamental tenets of faith, and thus remove themselves from the congregation of Israel. But someone who denies the resurrection of the dead only rejects a single tenet of Judaism. Why is he so severely punished? The Gemara answers that the denial of a portion in the World to Come is a fitting punishment for someone who denies the resurrection of the dead, since the punishment fits the crime (*Beer Sheva*).

מִדָּה כְּנֶגֶד מִדָּה. [1]דְּאָמַר רַבִּי
שְׁמוּאֵל בַּר נַחְמָנִי אָמַר רַבִּי
יוֹנָתָן: [2]מִנַּיִין שֶׁכָּל מִדּוֹתָיו שֶׁל
הַקָּדוֹשׁ בָּרוּךְ הוּא מִדָּה כְּנֶגֶד
מִדָּה? [3]שֶׁנֶּאֱמַר: ״וַיֹּאמֶר
אֱלִישָׁע שִׁמְעוּ דְּבַר ה׳ [וגו׳]
כָּעֵת מָחָר סְאָה סֹלֶת בְּשֶׁקֶל
וְסָאתַיִם שְׂעֹרִים בְּשֶׁקֶל בְּשַׁעַר
שֹׁמְרוֹן״. [4]וּכְתִיב: ״וַיַּעַן הַשָּׁלִישׁ
אֲשֶׁר (הַמֶּלֶךְ) נִשְׁעָן עַל יָדוֹ אֶת
אִישׁ הָאֱלֹהִים וַיֹּאמַר הִנֵּה ה׳
עֹשֶׂה אֲרֻבּוֹת בַּשָּׁמַיִם הֲיִהְיֶה
הַדָּבָר הַזֶּה וַיֹּאמֶר הִנְּךָ רֹאֶה
בְּעֵינֶיךָ וּמִשָּׁם לֹא תֹאכֵל״.
[90B] [5]וּכְתִיב: ״וַיְהִי לוֹ כֵּן
וַיִּרְמְסוּ אֹתוֹ הָעָם בַּשַּׁעַר
וַיָּמֹת״.
[6]וְדִילְמָא קִלְלַת אֱלִישָׁע גָּרְמָה
לֵיהּ, [7]דְּאָמַר רַב יְהוּדָה אָמַר
רַב: קִלְלַת חָכָם, אֲפִילּוּ עַל
חִנָּם הִיא בָּאָה.
[8]אִם כֵּן לִכְתּוֹב קְרָא:
״וַיִּרְמְסוּהוּ וַיָּמֹת״. [9]מַאי
״בַּשַּׁעַר״? [10]עַל עִסְקֵי שַׁעַר.
[11]אָמַר רַבִּי יוֹחָנָן: מִנַּיִין
לִתְחִיַּית הַמֵּתִים מִן הַתּוֹרָה,
[12]שֶׁנֶּאֱמַר: ״וּנְתַתֶּם מִמֶּנּוּ [אֶת]
תְּרוּמַת ה׳ לְאַהֲרֹן הַכֹּהֵן״. [13]וְכִי

LITERAL TRANSLATION

are measure for measure." [1]For Rabbi Shmuel bar Naḥmani said in the name of Rabbi Yonatan: [2]From where [do we know] that all the punishments of the Holy One, blessed be He, are measure for measure? [3]For it is stated: "Then Elisha said, Hear the word of the Lord...tomorrow about this time shall a measure of fine flour be sold for a shekel, and two measures of barley for a shekel, in the gate of Shomron." [4]And it is written: "Then the officer on whose hand the king leaned answered the man of God, and said, Behold, if the Lord would make windows in Heaven, might this thing be? And he said, Behold, you shall see it with your eyes, but you shall not eat of it." [90B] [5]And it is written: "And so it happened to him; for the people trampled upon him in the gate, and he died."

[6]But perhaps the curse of Elisha caused him [to die], [7]for Rav Yehudah said in the name of Rav: The curse of a Sage, even without cause, comes [true].

[8]If so, the verse should be written: "For the people trampled upon him, and he died." [9]What is "in the gate"? [10]About matters of the market price.

[11]Rabbi Yoḥanan said: From where [do we know about] the resurrection of the dead from the Torah? [12]For it is stated: "And you shall give of it the Lord's gift to Aaron the priest." [13]Does

TRANSLATION AND COMMENTARY

be He, are expressed in **measure for measure,** the punishment corresponding to the offense." [1]**For Rabbi Shmuel bar Naḥmani said in the name of Rabbi Yonatan:** [2]**From where do we know that all the punishments** meted out by **the Holy One, blessed be He, are** expressed in **measure for measure?** [3]This is derived from the verse that **states** (II Kings 7:1): **"Then Elisha said, Hear the word of the Lord: Thus says the Lord, tomorrow about this time shall a measure of fine flour be sold for a shekel, and two measures of barley for a shekel, in the gate of Shomron."** [4]And the next **verse states** (II Kings 7:2): **"Then the officer on whose hand the king leaned answered the man of God, and said, Behold, if the Lord would make windows in Heaven, might this thing be? And he said, Behold, you shall see it with your eyes, but you shall not eat of it."** [90B] [5]And a later **verse states** (II Kings 7:20): **"And so it happened to him; for the people trampled upon him in the gate, and he died."** The officer who had doubted Elisha's prophecy that grain prices would suddenly drop was trampled to death when the prices fell, and people stormed the market to buy the cheap grain — a punishment that fitted the offense, measure for measure.

וְדִילְמָא [6]The Gemara comments: **But perhaps** the punishment imposed on the officer was not meant to correspond to his offense, but rather **the curse that Elisha** had placed on the officer ("You shall see it with your eyes, but you shall not eat of it") **caused him** to die in that manner. [7]**For Rav Yehudah said in the name of Rav: The curse of a Sage, even** when proclaimed **without** due **cause,** is effective. And all the more so in this case, where Elisha had good reason to curse the officer!

אִם [8]The Gemara answers: **If so, the verse should have written** simply: **"For the people trampled upon him, and he died."** [9]**What is** the significance of the extra words **"in the gate** [*sha'ar*]"? [10]Those words teach that the officer was trampled to death **because** he had ridiculed Elisha's prophecy that **the market price** [another meaning of the Hebrew term *sha'ar*] of grain would suddenly drop.

אָמַר רַבִּי יוֹחָנָן [11]**Rabbi Yoḥanan said: Where is** there an allusion to **the resurrection of the dead in the Torah?** Regarding tithe terumah, that portion of the tithe which the Levite must give to a priest, [12]**the verse states** (Numbers 18:28): **"And you shall give of it the Lord's gift to Aaron the priest."** [13]Now it may be asked: **Did**

RASHI

גמרא ויהי לו כן וירמסו אותו — דבדבר שכפר בו נדון, שלא אכל מעס ונרמס ברגלי הבאים לקנות.

אַהֲרֹן לְעוֹלָם קַיָּים? [1]וַהֲלֹא לֹא נִכְנַס לְאֶרֶץ יִשְׂרָאֵל, שֶׁנּוֹתְנִין לוֹ תְּרוּמָה. [2]אֶלָּא, מְלַמֵּד שֶׁעָתִיד לְחָיוֹת, וְיִשְׂרָאֵל נוֹתְנִין לוֹ תְּרוּמָה. [3]מִכָּאן לִתְחִיַּית הַמֵּתִים מִן הַתּוֹרָה.

[4]דְּבֵי רַבִּי יִשְׁמָעֵאל תָּנָא: "'לְאַהֲרֹן' — כְּאַהֲרֹן. [5]מָה אַהֲרֹן חָבֵר, אַף בָּנָיו חֲבֵרִים.

[6]אָמַר רַבִּי שְׁמוּאֵל בַּר נַחְמָנִי אָמַר רַבִּי יוֹנָתָן: מִנַּיִין שֶׁאֵין נוֹתְנִין תְּרוּמָה לְכֹהֵן עַם הָאָרֶץ? [7]שֶׁנֶּאֱמַר: "וַיֹּאמֶר לָעָם לְיוֹשְׁבֵי יְרוּשָׁלַיִם לָתֵת מְנָת הַכֹּהֲנִים וְהַלְוִיִּם לְמַעַן יֶחֶזְקוּ בְּתוֹרַת ה׳". [8]כָּל הַמַּחֲזִיק בְּתוֹרַת ה׳ יֵשׁ לוֹ מְנָת, וְשֶׁאֵינוֹ מַחֲזִיק בְּתוֹרַת ה׳ אֵין לוֹ מְנָת.

[9]אָמַר רַב אַחָא בַּר אַדָּא אָמַר רַב יְהוּדָה: כָּל הַנּוֹתֵן תְּרוּמָה לְכֹהֵן עַם הָאָרֶץ כְּאִילּוּ נוֹתְנָהּ לִפְנֵי אֲרִי. [10]מָה אֲרִי, סָפֵק דּוֹרֵס וְאוֹכֵל, סָפֵק אֵינוֹ דּוֹרֵס

TRANSLATION AND COMMENTARY

Aaron himself **live long enough** so that tithe terumah was ever given to him? [1]**But surely he did not** even **enter Eretz Israel, where terumah is given.** Why, then, does the verse state that tithe terumah is to be given to Aaron? [2]**Rather, this** verse **teaches that** Aaron **will** indeed **live in the future, and** the people of **Israel will** then **give him terumah.** [3]Thus, we have **here** an allusion to **the resurrection of the dead in the Torah.**

דְּבֵי רַבִּי יִשְׁמָעֵאל [4]The Gemara now cites a Baraita which offers a different interpretation of the same verse. **A Sage of the School of Rabbi Yishmael taught** the following Baraita: "The words **'to Aaron'** teach that terumah may only be given to someone **like Aaron.** [5]**Just as** terumah may be given to **Aaron, who was a** Torah **scholar** dedicated to the precise observance of the commandments, **so, too,** may terumah be given to **his sons who are** Torah **scholars** dedicated to the precise observance of the commandments."

אָמַר [6]Expanding on this subject, **Rabbi Shmuel bar Naḥmani said in the name of Rabbi Yonatan: From where do we know that terumah may not be given to an uneducated priest** who is not scrupulous in his observance of the commandments? [7]This is derived from **the verse** that **states** (II Chronicles 31:4): **"And he commanded the people who dwelt in Jerusalem to give the portion of the priests and the Levites, that they might adhere firmly to the Torah of the Lord."** [8]**Whoever adheres firmly to the Lord's Torah is entitled to a portion** of the priestly gifts, **and whoever does not adhere firmly to the Lord's Torah is not entitled to a portion** of those gifts.

אָמַר [9]**Rav Aḥa bar Adda said in the name of Rav Yehudah: Whoever gives terumah to an uneducated priest** who is not scrupulous in his observance of the commandments **is considered as if he had placed** an animal **before a lion.** [10]**Just as the lion** might **perhaps tear** the animal **to pieces and eat** it, or **perhaps will not tear** the animal **to pieces and eat**

LITERAL TRANSLATION

Aaron live forever? [1]But surely he did not enter into Eretz Israel, where they give him terumah. [2]Rather, this teaches that he will live in the future, and Israel will give him terumah. [3]From here [we know about] the resurrection of the dead from the Torah.

[4][A Sage] of the School of Rabbi Yishmael taught: "'To Aaron' — like Aaron. [5]Just as Aaron is a colleague, so, too, his sons who are colleagues."

[6]Rabbi Shmuel bar Naḥmani said in the name of Rabbi Yonatan: From where [do we know] that we do not give terumah to a priest who is an uneducated person? [7]For it is stated: "And he commanded the people who dwelt in Jerusalem to give the portion of the priests and the Levites, that they might adhere firmly to the Torah of the Lord." [8]Whoever adheres firmly to the Torah of the Lord has a portion, and whoever does not adhere firmly to the Torah of the Lord does not have a portion.

[9]Rav Aḥa bar Adda said in the name of Rav Yehudah: Whoever gives terumah to a priest who is an uneducated person is [considered] as if he placed it before a lion. [10]Just as a lion, perhaps it tears it to pieces and eats, perhaps it does not tear it to pieces

RASHI

(וכי אהרן קיים לעולם — כלומר וכי אהרן חיה כל כך שתנתן לו תרומה — **והלא** לא נכנס לארץ ישראל ומאי האי דקאמר "ונתתם ממנו תרומת ה׳ לאהרן הכהן"). **לעולם קיים** — לאו דווקא, אלא כלומר הלא לא נגזר עליו שיחיה כל כך. **שעתיד לחיות** — לעולם הבא. **דבי רבי ישמעאל תנא** — הא דכתיב לאהרן לאו להכי הוא דאתא, אלא לומר לך כאהרן וכו׳. **מה ארי ספק דורס ואוכל** — ואין אנו יודעין כשנוטל בהמה מן העדר אם דעתו לדורסה ולאוכלה מיד קודם שתסריח, או לא אלא לטרוף ולמלא (חורו) [תאותו] ולאחר זמן יאכלנה כשתסריח, והכי נמי כהן עם הארץ כשאנו נותנין לו תרומה בידו, אין אנו יודעין אם יאכלנה בטהרה או בטומאה. **[אי נמי] ספק דורס שארי דרכו לדרוס ולרמוס בהמה ברגליו ואוכלה כשהיא דרוסה** — מנוולת, ופעמים שנותנה בחורו ואינה מנוולת.

NOTES

סָפֵק דּוֹרֵס וְאוֹכֵל Perhaps it tears it to pieces and eats. Some understand the analogy as follows: Just as a lion sometimes tears its prey to pieces and eats it immediately, and sometimes does not tear its prey to pieces, but rather

TRANSLATION AND COMMENTARY

it, [1]**so, too,** might **an uneducated priest** who is not scrupulous in his observance of the commandments **perhaps eat the terumah in ritual purity** as required, [2]or **perhaps eat it in ritual impurity** and thus violate a severe prohibition.

רַבִּי יוֹחָנָן אָמַר [3]**Rabbi Yoḥanan said: And furthermore,** someone who gives terumah to an uneducated priest **causes** that priest **to die,** [4]**as the verse** regarding terumah **states** (Leviticus 22:9): **"And die therefore, if they profane it,"** teaching that a priest who profanes terumah by eating it in a state of ritual impurity is subject to death at the hand of Heaven.

דְּבֵי רַבִּי אֱלִיעֶזֶר בֶּן יַעֲקֹב [5]**A Sage of the School of Rabbi Eliezer ben Ya'akov taught** a Baraita which states: **"And furthermore,** someone who gives terumah to an uneducated priest **causes** that priest **to bear the iniquity of trespass,** [6]**as the verse states** (Leviticus 22:16): **'And so cause them to bear the iniquity of trespass, when they eat their holy things.'** They bear the weight of many sins when they eat their holy things in a state of ritual impurity."

תַּנְיָא [7]**It was taught** in a Baraita: **"Rabbi Simai says: Where** is there an allusion to **the resurrection of the dead in the Torah?** Referring to God's promise to the Patriarchs, Abraham, Isaac, and Jacob, [8]**the verse states** (Exodus 6:4): **'And I have also established my covenant with them, to give** *them* **the land of Canaan.'** [9]That verse **does not state 'to** give *you* the land of Canaan,' which would have implied that God's promise to the Patriarchs was fulfilled when the land of Canaan was given to their descendants, the people of Israel. [10]**But rather** the verse states **'to** give *them* [= the Patriarchs] the land of Canaan,' implying that God's promise will only be fulfilled when the land of Canaan is given to the Patriarchs themselves. [11]Thus, we have **here** an allusion to **the resurrection of the dead in the Torah.** The Patriarchs will one day rise from the dead and God will give them Eretz Israel and thus keep the covenant that He made with them."

צד״ק [12]The Gemara offers **a mnemonic device** to help the student memorize the various elements of the upcoming discussion: *Tzedek gam geshem kam* (see Note).

וְאוֹכֵל, [1]אַף כֹּהֵן עַם הָאָרֶץ, סָפֵק אוֹכְלָהּ בְּטָהֳרָה, [2]סָפֵק אוֹכְלָהּ בְּטוּמְאָה.

[3]רַבִּי יוֹחָנָן אָמַר: אַף גּוֹרֵם לוֹ מִיתָה, [4]שֶׁנֶּאֱמַר: ״וּמֵתוּ בוֹ, כִּי יְחַלְּלֻהוּ״.

[5]דְּבֵי רַבִּי אֱלִיעֶזֶר בֶּן יַעֲקֹב תָּנָא: ״אַף מַשִּׂיאוֹ עֲוֹן אַשְׁמָה, [6]שֶׁנֶּאֱמַר: ׳וְהִשִּׂיאוּ אוֹתָם עֲוֹן אַשְׁמָה בְּאָכְלָם אֶת קָדְשֵׁיהֶם׳ ״.

[7]תַּנְיָא: ״רַבִּי סִימָאי אוֹמֵר: ׳מִנַּיִין לִתְחִיַּית הַמֵּתִים מִן הַתּוֹרָה? [8]שֶׁנֶּאֱמַר: ׳וְגַם הֲקִמֹתִי אֶת בְּרִיתִי אִתָּם לָתֵת לָהֶם אֶת אֶרֶץ כְּנָעַן׳. [9]׳לָכֶם׳ לֹא נֶאֱמַר, [10]אֶלָּא ׳לָהֶם׳. [11]מִכָּאן לִתְחִיַּית הַמֵּתִים מִן הַתּוֹרָה״.

[12](צד״ק ג״ם גש״ם ק״ם סִימָן).

LITERAL TRANSLATION

and eat, [1]so, too, a priest who is an uneducated person, perhaps he eats it in ritual purity, [2]perhaps he eats it in ritual impurity.

[3]Rabbi Yoḥanan said: He also causes him death, [4]as it is stated. "And die in it therefore, if they profane it."

[5][A Sage] of the School of Rabbi Eliezer ben Ya'akov taught: "He also makes him bear the iniquity of trespass, [6]as it is stated: 'And so make them bear the iniquity of trespass, when they eat their holy things.'"

[7]It was taught: "Rabbi Simai says: From where [do we know] about the resurrection of the dead from the Torah? [8]For it is stated: 'And I have also established my covenant with them, to give them the land of Canaan.' [9]'To you' is not stated, [10]but rather 'to them.' [11]From here [we know about] the resurrection of the dead from the Torah."

[12](A sign: *Tzedek gam geshem kam.*)

RASHI

עון אשמה – עונות הרבה מטעין עליו. **באכלם את קדשיהם** – ומתרגמינן במיכלהון בסואבא ית קודשיהון. **אלא להם** – דמשמע שהבטיח הקדוש ברוך הוא לאבותינו אברהם יצחק ויעקב שיתן להם ארץ ישראל, וכי להם ניתנה – והלא לבניהם ניתנה אלא מלמד שעתידין לחיות ועתיד הקדוש ברוך הוא ליתן להם את ארץ ישראל.

NOTES

carries the prey back to its den whole, so, too, does an uneducated priest sometimes eat his terumah in ritual purity, and sometimes eat it in ritual impurity (*Ramah*).

צד״ק ג״ם גש״ם ק״ם ***Tzedek gam geshem kam.*** According to another reading, the mnemonic device is צר״ק ג״ם גש״ם ק״ם, *Tzerek gam geshem kam,* which would be an acrostic for those who asked questions and offered answers regarding the resurrection of the dead. Those who asked questions: *Tz*edukim (Sadducees), *R*oma'im (Romans), *K*leopatra (Cleopatra), *K*aisar (Caesar), *M*inim (heretics). Those who offered answers: Rabban *G*amliel, Rabbi Yeho*sh*ua, Rabbi *M*eir, Rabban *G*amliel, Rabbi A*m*mi (*Maharsha*).

LANGUAGE (RASHI)

פרונמיי״ש* should be פרומייר, from the Old French *fromier*, meaning "to move."

TRANSLATION AND COMMENTARY

שָׁאֲלוּ מִינִין [1]It was related that **heretics** once **asked Rabban Gamliel** about the resurrection of the dead: **"From where do we know that the Holy One, blessed be He, will resurrect the dead?"** [2]Rabban Gamliel **offered them** proofs **from the Torah, from the Prophets, and from the Writings, but** the heretics **did not accept** those proofs **from him.** [3]He brought the following proof **from the Torah: "The verse states** (Deuteronomy 31:16): **'And the Lord said to Moses, Behold, you shall sleep with your fathers, and rise up'** when the dead are resurrected." The heretics rejected this proof-text, [4]**saying:** "How do you know that the words 'and rise up [וְקָם]' are connected to the preceding words and refer to Moses? [5]**Perhaps** those words are connected to the words that follow and refer to the people of Israel, and so the verse means to say: **'And this people will rise up, and go astray** after the gods of the strangers of the land.'" [6]Rabban Gamliel then brought them a proof **from** the Books of the **Prophets.** [7]**"The verse states** (Isaiah 26:19): **'The dead men of your people shall live, my dead body shall arise. Awake and sing, you that dwell in dust, for your dew is as the dew on herbs, and the earth shall cast out the shades of the dead.'"** The heretics also rejected this proof-text, saying: "Who says that this verse refers to the dead whom God will resurrect in the future? [8]**Perhaps** it refers to **the dead whom Ezekiel resurrected,** for Isaiah lived before Ezekiel, and might have prophesied about the dry bones which Ezekiel was to restore to life." [9]Rabban Gamliel then brought them a proof **from the Writings: "The verse states** (Song of Songs 7:10): **'And the roof of your mouth like the best wine, that goes down smoothly for my beloved, causing the sleepers' lips to murmur.'"** According to Rabban Gamliel, this verse means that the lips of those who are now sleeping in their graves will once again murmur after God resurrects the dead. The heretics rejected this proof-text as well, arguing: "How do you see from there that the dead will come back to life? [10]**Perhaps** they will remain in their graves, and **only their lips will move, like** what **Rabbi Yoḥanan**

[1]שָׁאֲלוּ מִינִין אֶת רַבָּן גַּמְלִיאֵל: "מִנַּיִין שֶׁהַקָּדוֹשׁ בָּרוּךְ הוּא מְחַיֶּיה מֵתִים"? [2]אָמַר לָהֶם מִן הַתּוֹרָה, וּמִן הַנְּבִיאִים, וּמִן הַכְּתוּבִים, וְלֹא קִיבְּלוּ מִמֶּנּוּ. [3]"מִן הַתּוֹרָה, דִּכְתִיב: 'וַיֹּאמֶר ה' אֶל מֹשֶׁה הִנְּךָ שֹׁכֵב עִם אֲבֹתֶיךָ וְקָם'". [4]אָמְרוּ לוֹ: [5]"וְדִילְמָא, 'וְקָם הָעָם הַזֶּה וְזָנָה'". [6]"מִן הַנְּבִיאִים, [7]דִּכְתִיב: 'יִחְיוּ מֵתֶיךָ נְבֵלָתִי יְקוּמוּן הָקִיצוּ וְרַנְּנוּ שֹׁכְנֵי עָפָר כִּי טַל אוֹרֹת טַלֶּךָ וָאָרֶץ רְפָאִים תַּפִּיל'". [8]"וְדִילְמָא, מֵתִים שֶׁהֶחֱיָה יְחֶזְקֵאל". [9]"מִן הַכְּתוּבִים, דִּכְתִיב: 'וְחִכֵּךְ כְּיֵין הַטּוֹב הוֹלֵךְ לְדוֹדִי לְמֵישָׁרִים דּוֹבֵב שִׂפְתֵי יְשֵׁנִים'". [10]"וְדִילְמָא, רַחוּשֵׁי מְרַחֲשָׁן שִׂפְוָותֵיהּ בְּעָלְמָא, כְּרַבִּי יוֹחָנָן,

LITERAL TRANSLATION

[1]Heretics asked Rabban Gamliel: "From where [do we know] that the Holy One, blessed be He, resurrects the dead?" [2]He said to them from the Torah, and from the Prophets, and from the Writings, but they did not accept [it] from him. [3]"From the Torah, as it is written: 'And the Lord said to Moses, Behold, you shall sleep with your fathers, and rise up.'" [4]They said to him: [5]"Perhaps, 'And this people will rise up, and go astray.'" [6]"From the Prophets, [7]as it is written: 'The dead men of your people shall live, my dead body shall arise. Awake and sing, you that dwell in dust, for your dew is as the dew on herbs, and the earth shall cast out the shades of the dead.'" [8]"Perhaps, the dead whom Ezekiel resurrected." [9]"From the Writings, as it is written: 'And the roof of your mouth like the best wine, that goes smoothly for my beloved, causing the sleepers' lips to murmur.'" [10]"Perhaps, only their lips will move, like Rabbi Yoḥanan,

RASHI

הנך שוכב עם אבותיך וקם — הנה אתה מת שוכב, והנה אתה קם — שתחיה לעתיד לבא, והאי וקם אהנך קאי. דילמא וקם העם וזנה — דלקמיה קאי, ולאו אדלעיל, והיינו אחד (מחמשה) מקראות שאין להם הכרע. יחיו מתיך — דמתים שבארץ ישראל יחיו. נבלתי יקומון — אפילו נפלים יחיו, במסכת כתובות. ודילמא מתים שהחיה יחזקאל — דההיא קרא "יחיו מתיך" ישעיה אמרו, והוא קדם ליחזקאל, שנתנבא בימי חזקיה, והיה מתנבא פסוק זה על שהיה עתיד יחזקאל להחיות מתים, אבל לעולם הבא — לא. דובב — *פרונמיי"ש בלעז, כלומר נעות ומתנודדות שפתי ישיני עפר, מכלל שיחיו. מרחשן שפוותיה בעלמא — שפתותיהן נעות מעט בתוך הקבר אבל אין חיין ויוצאין לאויר העולם, וכרבי יוחנן וכו׳.

NOTES

שֹׁכֵב עִם אֲבֹתֶיךָ וְקָם **You shall sleep with your fathers, and rise up.** It is clear that the word וְקָם, "and rise up," relates to the words that follow: "And this people will rise up, and go astray after the gods of the strangers of the land." But there is good reason to say that the word does not relate exclusively to those words, for the word קם denotes elevation and walking erect, and in that sense it is inappropriate to use the term in connection with idol worship. Thus, the word may be understood as relating to the preceding words, "Behold, you shall sleep with your fathers, and rise up," and alluding to the resurrection of the dead (see *Ri'af, Maharsha*).

TRANSLATION AND COMMENTARY

said, **for Rabbi Yoḥanan said in the name of Rabbi Shimon the son of Yehozadak:** [1]**Anybody in whose name a law was stated in this world, his lips will murmur in the grave,** as if he were repeating what he had said while he was alive, [2]**as the verse states: 'Causing the sleepers' lips to murmur.'"** [3]The heretics did not accept any of Rabban Gamliel's proof-texts **until he mentioned** the following **verse to them** as proof of the resurrection of the dead: "The verse states (Deuteronomy 11:21): 'That your days may be multiplied, and the days of your children, [4]in the land **which the Lord swore to your fathers to give them,** as the days of Heaven upon the earth.' [5]The verse **does not state 'to** give **you,' but rather 'to** give **them'** [= your fathers], implying that the fathers will rise from the dead and inherit the land. [6]Thus, we have **here** an allusion to **the resurrection of the dead in the Torah."**

וְיֵשׁ אוֹמְרִים [7]**And some say** that Rabban Gamliel **mentioned this verse to them** (Deuteronomy 4:4): [8]**"But you who cling to the Lord your God are all alive this day."** What does this verse mean to say? [9]Surely, **it is obvious that "every one of you is alive this day,"** for Moses was addressing living people. [10]**Rather,** Moses meant as follows: **Even on a day that the whole world is dead, you** who cling to the Lord **will be alive.** [11]**Just as this day all of you are alive, so, too, in the World to Come all of you will be alive.** Thus, we have here an allusion to the resurrection of the dead in the Torah.

שָׁאֲלוּ רוֹמִיִּים [12]It was related that **the Romans** once **asked Rabbi Yehoshua ben Ḥananyah: "From where do we know that the Holy One, blessed be He,** will **resurrect the dead, and** from where do we know that He **knows what will happen in the future?"** [13]Rabbi Yehoshua ben Ḥananyah **said to them: "Both of these** things **are learned from the** same **verse,** [14]**for the verse states** (Deuteronomy 31:16): **'And the Lord said to Moses, Behold, you shall sleep with your fathers, and rise up; this people will go astray** after the gods of the strangers of the land.' The words 'you shall sleep with your fathers, and rise up' imply that God will resurrect the dead, and the words 'this people will go astray' imply that God knows what will happen in the future." Like the heretics in their argument with Rabban Gamliel on the same verse, the Romans raised an objection: "How do you know that the words 'and rise up [וְקָם]' are connected to the preceding verse and refer to Moses? [15]**Perhaps** those words are connected to the words that follow and refer to the people of Israel, and so the verse means to say: **'And**

דְּאָמַר רַבִּי יוֹחָנָן מִשּׁוּם רַבִּי שִׁמְעוֹן בֶּן יְהוֹצָדָק: [1] כָּל מִי שֶׁנֶּאֶמְרָה הֲלָכָה בִּשְׁמוֹ בָּעוֹלָם הַזֶּה — שִׂפְתוֹתָיו דּוֹבְבוֹת בַּקֶּבֶר, [2] שֶׁנֶּאֱמַר: ׳דּוֹבֵב שִׂפְתֵי יְשֵׁנִים׳ ״. [3] ״עַד שֶׁאָמַר לָהֶם מִקְרָא זֶה: [4] ״ ׳אֲשֶׁר נִשְׁבַּע ה׳ לַאֲבֹתֵיכֶם לָתֵת לָהֶם׳. [5] ׳לָכֶם׳ לֹא נֶאֱמַר, אֶלָּא ׳לָהֶם׳. [6] מִיכָּן לִתְחִיַּית הַמֵּתִים מִן הַתּוֹרָה״. [7] וְיֵשׁ אוֹמְרִים: מִן הַמִּקְרָא הַזֶּה אָמַר לָהֶם: [8] ״וְאַתֶּם הַדְּבֵקִים בַּה׳ אֱלֹהֵיכֶם חַיִּים כֻּלְּכֶם הַיּוֹם״. [9] פְּשִׁיטָא דְּחַיִּים כֻּלְּכֶם הַיּוֹם. [10] אֶלָּא אֲפִילּוּ בְּיוֹם שֶׁכָּל הָעוֹלָם כּוּלָּם מֵתִים, אַתֶּם חַיִּים. [11] מָה הַיּוֹם כּוּלְּכֶם קַיָּימִין, אַף לָעוֹלָם הַבָּא כּוּלְּכֶם קַיָּימִין.

[12] שָׁאֲלוּ רוֹמִיִּים אֶת רַבִּי יְהוֹשֻׁעַ בֶּן חֲנַנְיָה: ״מִנַּיִין שֶׁהַקָּדוֹשׁ בָּרוּךְ הוּא מְחַיֶּה מֵתִים, וְיוֹדֵעַ מַה שֶּׁעָתִיד לִהְיוֹת״? [13] אָמַר לְהוּ: ״תַּרְוַויְיהוּ מִן הַמִּקְרָא הַזֶּה, [14] שֶׁנֶּאֱמַר: ׳וַיֹּאמֶר ה׳ אֶל מֹשֶׁה הִנְּךָ שֹׁכֵב עִם אֲבֹתֶיךָ וְקָם הָעָם הַזֶּה וְזָנָה׳ ״. [15] ״וְדִילְמָא, ׳וְקָם הָעָם הַזֶּה

LITERAL TRANSLATION

for Rabbi Yoḥanan said in the name of Rabbi Shimon the son of Yehozadak: [1]Anybody in whose name a law was stated in this world — his lips will murmur in the grave, [2]as it is stated: 'Causing the sleepers' lips to murmur.'" [3]Until he said this verse to them: [4]"'Which the Lord swore to your fathers to give them.' [5]'To you' is not stated, but rather 'to them.' [6]From here [we know about] the resurrection of the dead from the Torah."

[7]And some say: He said this verse to them: [8]"But you who cling to the Lord your God are all alive this day." [9]It is obvious that you are all alive this day. [10]Rather, even on a day when the whole world is dead, you are alive. [11]Just as this day all of you are alive, so, too, in the World to Come all of you will be alive.

[12]The Romans asked Rabbi Yehoshua ben Ḥananyah: "From where [do we know] that the Holy One, blessed be He, resurrects the dead, and knows what will happen in the future?" [13]He said to them: "Both of them are [learned] from this verse, [14]for it is stated: 'And the Lord said to Moses, Behold, you shall sleep with your fathers, and rise up; this people will go astray.'" [15]"Perhaps, 'And this people will rise up,

RASHI

ולא קבלו ממנו — עד שאמר להם וכו׳. **חיים כלכם היום** — דהאי יום מיותר הוא, דמלי למכתב ״חיים כלכם״ מה תלמוד לומר היום — כהיום, מה היום וכו׳ כך שמעתי. **הנך שוכב עם אבותיך וקם** — הרי תחיית המתים, ״העם הזה וזנה״ — הרי מה שעתיד להיות.

BACKGROUND

זַיַּיפְתֶּם תּוֹרַתְכֶם **You have falsified your Torah.** The Torah scrolls of the Samaritans are different in some respects from those of the Jewish tradition. In addition to slight differences in certain verses, there is also intentional forgery regarding Mount Grizim. For example, the Samaritan version the Ten Commandments contains an explicit injunction to build the Temple on Mount Grizim.

In the end the Samaritans also received many principles from the Jews which are not found in the Pentateuch. However, at some times the differences were extreme, and it is against these that Rabbi Eliezer bar Yose speaks.

TRANSLATION AND COMMENTARY

this people will rise up, and go astray after the gods of the strangers of the land.'" [1]Rabbi Yehoshua ben Ḥananyah **said to them: "Hold on at least to a part** of what I said, for surely this verse teaches **that** God **knows what will happen in the future."**

אִיתְּמַר נַמִּי [2]The same idea **was also stated** in the name of other scholars: **Rabbi Yoḥanan said in the name of Rabbi Shimon ben Yoḥai: [3]From where do we know that the Holy One, blessed be He,** will **resurrect the dead, and** that He **knows what will happen in the future?** Both of these notions are derived from the same verse, [4]**for the verse states** (Deuteronomy 31:16): "And the Lord said to Moses, **Behold, you shall sleep with your fathers, and rise up;** this people will go astray after the gods of the strangers of the land."

תַּנְיָא [5]**It was taught** in a Baraita: **"Rabbi Eliezer the son of Rabbi Yose said: Regarding this matter I proved the fallacy of the books of the Cutheans** [the Samaritans, whose status as Jews was disputed among the Sages], [6]**who said that there are no** allusions to the **resurrection of the dead in the Torah. [7]I said to them: You have falsified your Torah, but it does not avail you. [8]For you say that there are no** allusions to the **resurrection of the dead in the Torah. [9]**But **surely** the verse **says** (Numbers 15:31): **'That soul shall be utterly cut off; his iniquity shall be upon him.'** [10]The words **'that soul shall be utterly cut off'** refer to the sinner's punishment **in this world,** and teach that he will die a premature or sudden death. [11]**When,** then, will the second half of the verse — **'his iniquity shall be upon him'** — **be fulfilled?** [12]**Is it not in the World to Come?** Thus we have here an allusion to the World to Come and the resurrection of the dead in the Torah."

וְזָנָה׳ ״? [1]אָמַר לְהוּ: ״נְקוֹטוּ מִיהָא פַּלְגָא בִּידַיְיכוּ, דְּיוֹדֵעַ מַה שֶׁעָתִיד לִהְיוֹת״.

[2]אִיתְּמַר נַמִּי: אָמַר רַבִּי יוֹחָנָן מִשּׁוּם רַבִּי שִׁמְעוֹן בֶּן יוֹחַאי: [3]מִנַּיִין שֶׁהַקָּדוֹשׁ בָּרוּךְ הוּא מְחַיֶּה מֵתִים, וְיוֹדֵעַ מַה שֶּׁעָתִיד לִהְיוֹת? [4]שֶׁנֶּאֱמַר: ״הִנְּךָ שֹׁכֵב עִם אֲבֹתֶיךָ וְקָם וגו׳ ״.

[5]תַּנְיָא: ״אָמַר רַבִּי אֱלִיעֶזֶר בְּרַבִּי יוֹסֵי: בְּדָבָר זֶה זַיַּיפְתִּי סִפְרֵי כּוּתִים, [6]שֶׁהָיוּ אוֹמְרִים אֵין תְּחִיַּית הַמֵּתִים מִן הַתּוֹרָה. [7]אָמַרְתִּי לָהֶן: זַיַּיפְתֶּם תּוֹרַתְכֶם, וְלֹא הֶעֱלֵיתֶם בְּיֶדְכֶם כְּלוּם. [8]שֶׁאַתֶּם אוֹמְרִים אֵין תְּחִיַּית הַמֵּתִים מִן הַתּוֹרָה. [9]הֲרֵי הוּא אוֹמֵר: ׳הִכָּרֵת תִּכָּרֵת הַנֶּפֶשׁ הַהִיא; עֲוֹנָהּ בָהּ׳. [10]׳הִכָּרֵת תִּכָּרֵת׳ — בָּעוֹלָם הַזֶּה; [11]׳עֲוֹנָהּ בָהּ׳ — לְאֵימַת? [12]לָאו לָעוֹלָם הַבָּא״?

LITERAL TRANSLATION

and go astray.'" [1]He said to them: "Seize at least a part in your hands, that He knows what will happen in the future."

[2]It was also stated: Rabbi Yoḥanan said in the name of Rabbi Shimon ben Yoḥai: [3]From where [do we know] that the Holy One, blessed be He, resurrects the dead, and knows what will happen in the future? [4]For it is stated: "Behold you shall sleep with your fathers, and rise up, etc."

[5]It was taught: "Rabbi Eliezer the son of Rabbi Yose said: Regarding this matter I proved the fallacy of the books of the Cutheans, [6]who said [that] there is no resurrection of the dead from the Torah. [7]I said to them: You have falsified your Torah, but it is of no use to you. [8]For you say [that] there is no resurrection of the dead from the Torah. [9]Surely it says: 'That soul shall be utterly cut off; its iniquity shall be upon it.' [10]'That soul shall be utterly cut off' — in this world; [11]'its iniquity shall be upon it' — when? [12]Is it not in the World to Come?"

RASHI

פלגא בידך — דמהאי קרא נפקא דיודע מה שעתיד. **זייפתם ולא העליתם** — כזב אתם אומרים ואין ממש בדבריכם. **לאו לעולם הבא** — אלמא יש תחיית המתים.

NOTES

זַיַּיפְתִּי סִפְרֵי כּוּתִים **I proved false the books of the Cutheans.** The commentators raise the question: How did the argument put forward by Rabbi Eliezer the son of Rabbi Yose prove the fallacy of the books of the Cutheans? Some suggest he meant to say that, according to the Cutheans' own understanding of the Torah and denial of the resurrection of the dead, their books are false, for various passages have no meaning (*Ri'af*). Alternatively, the Cutheans might have emended those Biblical texts that allude to the resurrection of the dead. Thus, Rabbi Eliezer the son of Rabbi Yose said to them that they gained nothing by falsifying their books, for it is clear to all that those texts were falsified (*Maharsha*).

HALAKHAH

הִכָּרֵת תִּכָּרֵת **Shall utterly be cut off.** "The expression, 'that soul shall utterly be cut off (*hikaret tikaret*),' teaches that a person who is liable to excision will be cut off in two worlds: *hikaret* (in this world), *tikaret* (in the World to Come)." (*Rambam, Sefer Mada, Hilkhot Teshuvah* 8:1.)

TRANSLATION AND COMMENTARY

אָמַר לֵיהּ [1]**Rav Pappa said to Abaye:** Rabbi Eliezer the son of Rabbi Yose **should have said to** the Cutheans that we learn of **the two** worlds **from** the words **"shall utterly be cut off"!** For when the Torah describes the punishment of the blasphemer, it uses the double verb form (Numbers 15:31): "That soul shall utterly be cut off [*hikaret tikaret* — הִכָּרֵת תִּכָּרֵת]." That apparent superfluity teaches that a person who is liable to the punishment of excision will be cut off in two worlds. "Cut off" (*hikaret*) — in this world he will die a premature or sudden death. "Utterly" (*tikaret*) — in the World to Come he will not enjoy eternal life.

אִינְהוּ [2]Abaye said to Rav Pappa: Had Rabbi Eliezer the son of Rabbi Yose put forward that argument, the Cutheans **could have answered:** Nothing can be learned from the double verb form, "shall utterly be cut off," [3]for **the Torah spoke in the language of men.** The double verb form is purely stylistic, with no special significance.

כְּתַנָּאֵי [4]The Gemara notes: **The Tannaim** did in fact disagree about this matter, for it was taught in a Baraita: "The verse states (Numbers 15:31): 'That soul **shall utterly be cut off** (*hikaret tikaret*).' The double verb form is there to teach that a person who is liable to excision will be cut off in two worlds. [5]**'Cut off'** (*hikaret*) **— in this world.** [6]**'Utterly'** (*tikaret*) **— in the World to Come.** [7]**This is the position of Rabbi Akiva.** [8]**Rabbi Yishmael said to him: But surely the** previous verse **states** (Numbers 15:30): [9]**'That person dishonors the Lord; and that soul shall be cut off** (*venikhretah*) from among its people.' If each reference to 'cutting off' in the expression *hikaret tikaret* refers to a different world, then the word *venikhretah* should also refer to a separate world, which would imply an absurdity, [10]for **are there** in fact **three** different **worlds?** [11]**Rather,** the first instance of 'cutting off' — 'and that soul **shall be cut off** (*venikhretah*)' — teaches that a person who is liable to the punishment of excision will be cut off **in this world.** [12]The second instance, 'that soul shall be **cut off** (*hikaret*),' teaches that he will also be cut off **in the World to Come.** [13]And the third instance, **'utterly** (*tikaret*),' does not add anything, for **the Torah spoke in the language of men,** and the double verb form has no special significance."

בֵּין [14]The Gemara asks: According to **both Rabbi Yishmael and Rabbi Akiva, what do we learn from** the words, **"his iniquity shall be upon him,"** the expression from which Rabbi Eliezer ben Rabbi Yose proved to the Cutheans that there is a World to Come? [15]The Gemara explains: Those words are needed **for what was taught** in a Baraita: "Had I only had the words, 'that soul shall be utterly cut off,' **I might have said** that the punishment of excision both in this world and the World to Come is administered **even if** the sinner **repented.** [16]Therefore, **the verse states: 'His iniquity shall be upon him'** — [17]**I only said** that the sinner will be

[1]אָמַר לֵיהּ רַב פַּפָּא לְאַבַּיֵי: וְלֵימָא לְהוּ תַּרְוַיְיהוּ מֵ״הִכָּרֵת תִּכָּרֵת״!

[2]אִינְהוּ הָווּ אָמְרִי לֵיהּ: [3]דִּבְּרָה תּוֹרָה כִּלְשׁוֹן בְּנֵי אָדָם.

[4]כְּתַנָּאֵי: ״ ׳הִכָּרֵת תִּכָּרֵת׳. [5]׳הִכָּרֵת׳ — בָּעוֹלָם הַזֶּה. [6]׳תִּכָּרֵת׳ — לָעוֹלָם הַבָּא. [7]דִּבְרֵי רַבִּי עֲקִיבָא. [8]אָמַר לוֹ רַבִּי יִשְׁמָעֵאל: וַהֲלֹא כְּבָר נֶאֱמַר: [9]׳אֶת ה׳ הוּא מְגַדֵּף וְנִכְרְתָה׳. [10]וְכִי שְׁלֹשָׁה עוֹלָמִים יֵשׁ? [11]אֶלָּא, ׳וְנִכְרְתָה׳ — בָּעוֹלָם הַזֶּה. [12]׳הִכָּרֵת׳ — לָעוֹלָם הַבָּא. [13]׳הִכָּרֵת תִּכָּרֵת׳ — דִּבְּרָה תּוֹרָה כִּלְשׁוֹן בְּנֵי אָדָם״.

[14]בֵּין רַבִּי יִשְׁמָעֵאל וּבֵין רַבִּי עֲקִיבָא, ״עֲוֹנָהּ בָהּ״ מַאי עָבְדִי בֵּיהּ? [15]לְכִדְתַנְיָא: ״יָכוֹל אֲפִילּוּ עָשָׂה תְּשׁוּבָה. [16]תַּלְמוּד לוֹמַר: ׳עֲוֹנָהּ בָהּ׳ — [17]לֹא אָמַרְתִּי

LITERAL TRANSLATION

[1]Rav Pappa said to Abaye: But let him say to them, both [are learned] from "shall utterly be cut off"!

[2]They would have said to him: [3]The Torah spoke in the language of men.

[4]Like the Tannaim: "'Shall utterly be cut off.' [5]'Cut off' — in this world. [6]'Utterly' — in the World to Come. [7][These are] the words of Rabbi Akiva. [8]Rabbi Yishmael said to him: But surely it was already stated: [9]'That person dishonors the Lord; and [that soul] shall be cut off.' [10]Are there three worlds? [11]Rather, 'Shall be cut off' — in this world. [12]'Cut off' — in the World to Come. [13]'Utterly cut off' — the Torah spoke in the language of men."

[14]Both Rabbi Yishmael and Rabbi Akiva, what do they do with: "His iniquity shall be upon him"? [15]For that which was taught: "[I] might [have said] even if he repented. [16]The verse states: 'His iniquity shall be upon him' — [17]I only said

RASHI

מהכרת תכרת — ״הכרת״ — בעולם הזה, ״תכרת״ — לעולם הבא. **אינהו הוו אמרי ליה דברה תורה כלשון בני אדם** — ולהכי אמר להו הכי, כי היכי דלא להוי להו פתחון פה. **הכרת תכרת** — בעבודה זרה כתיב. **והלא כבר נאמר** — בעבודה זרה ״את ה׳ הוא מגדף ונכרתה״, דסבירא להו: ״מגדף״ — היינו עובד עבודה זרה. **וכי שלשה עולמים יש וכו׳** — ורבי עקיבא סבירא ליה דמגדף היינו מברך השם. **והשתא בין לרבי ישמעאל בין לרבי עקיבא עונה בה מאי עבדי ליה** — מבעי ליה וכו׳.

TRANSLATION AND COMMENTARY

punished in that manner **if** he did not repent during his lifetime, so that **his iniquity is** still **upon him."**

שְׁאֲלָה [1] It was related that **Queen Cleopatra** once **had a question for Rabbi Meir, and said: "I know that the dead will come back to life,** [2] **for the verse states** (Psalms 72:16): **'And may they flourish in the city like the grass of the earth,'** teaching that the righteous will one day rise from their graves just as the grass shoots forth from the earth. [3] **But** I have the following question: **When they rise up** from their graves, **will they rise up naked, or will they rise up** already dressed **in their clothing?"** [4] Rabbi Meir **said to her:** "An answer to your question may be reached by way of **a *kal vaḥomer* argument from wheat.** [5] **If wheat, which is buried naked,** i.e., sown without any of the seed coverings, **comes out** of the ground **with several coats** covering the seeds — [6] then **all the more so** should **the righteous who are buried in their clothing** rise from their graves in full garb."

אָמַר לֵיהּ [7] It was further related that **the** Roman **emperor** once **said to Rabban Gamliel: "You say that the dead will come back to life.** [8] But **surely** the dead **turn into dust** in their graves. **Is it possible for dust to come to life?"** [91A] [9] The emperor's **daughter said to** Rabban Gamliel: **"Leave him** to me, **and I will answer him** with a parable. [10] If **there were two potters in our town, one** who **fashioned utensils out of water, and** the other **one fashioned utensils out of clay,** [11] **who would be the greater** of the two?" [12] The emperor **said to** his daughter: "Surely, the potter **who fashioned the utensils out of water."** [13] His daughter **said to him: "If** that potter **can fashion utensils out of water,** [14] then **all the more so** can he fashion utensils **out of clay.** So, too, the Holy One, blessed be He, fashioned the entire world out of water. Surely, then, He can refashion man out of dust."

דְּבֵי רַבִּי יִשְׁמָעֵאל [15] **A Sage of the School of Rabbi Yishmael taught** a related Baraita: "The emperor's question can be answered by way of **a *kal vaḥomer* argument from glass utensils.** [16] **Glass utensils are blown by the breath of flesh and blood,** and **if** those utensils **break, they have a remedy,** for they can be melted

אֶלָּא בִּזְמַן שֶׁעֲוֹנָהּ בָּהּ״.
[1] שָׁאֲלָה קְלֵיאוֹפַּטְרָא מַלְכְּתָא אֶת רַבִּי מֵאִיר: אָמְרָה: ״יָדַעְנָא דְּחַיֵּי שָׁכְבֵי, [2] דִּכְתִיב: ׳וְיָצִיצוּ מֵעִיר כְּעֵשֶׂב הָאָרֶץ׳. [3] אֶלָּא כְּשֶׁהֵן עוֹמְדִין, עוֹמְדִין עֲרוּמִּין, אוֹ בִּלְבוּשֵׁיהֶן עוֹמְדִין״? [4] אָמַר לָהּ: ״קַל וָחוֹמֶר מֵחִיטָּה. [5] וּמָה חִיטָּה שֶׁנִּקְבְּרָה עֲרוּמָה, יוֹצְאָה בְּכַמָּה לְבוּשִׁין, [6] צַדִּיקִים שֶׁנִּקְבָּרִים בִּלְבוּשֵׁיהֶן, עַל אַחַת כַּמָּה וְכַמָּה״.
[7] אָמַר לֵיהּ קֵיסָר לְרַבָּן גַּמְלִיאֵל: ״אָמְרִיתוּ דְּשָׁכְבֵי חַיֵּי. [8] הָא הָווּ עַפְרָא, וְעַפְרָא מִי קָא חַיֵּי״? [91A] [9] אֲמַרָה לֵיהּ בְּרַתֵּיהּ: ״שְׁבַקֵיהּ, וַאֲנָא מַהְדַרְנָא לֵיהּ. [10] שְׁנֵי יוֹצְרִים יֵשׁ בְּעִירֵנוּ, אֶחָד יוֹצֵר מִן הַמַּיִם וְאֶחָד יוֹצֵר מִן הַטִּיט. [11] אֵיזֶה מֵהֶן מְשׁוּבָּח״? [12] אָמַר לָהּ: ״זֶה שֶׁיּוֹצֵר מִן הַמַּיִם״. [13] אָמְרָה לוֹ: ״מִן הַמַּיִם צָר, [14] מִן הַטִּיט לֹא כָּל שֶׁכֵּן״? [15] דְּבֵי רַבִּי יִשְׁמָעֵאל תָּנָא: ״קַל וָחוֹמֶר מִכְּלֵי זְכוּכִית. [16] מַה כְּלֵי זְכוּכִית, שֶׁעֲמָלָן בְּרוּחַ בָּשָׂר וָדָם, נִשְׁבְּרוּ, יֵשׁ לָהֶן תַּקָּנָה,

LITERAL TRANSLATION

when his iniquity is upon him."

[1] Queen Cleopatra asked Rabbi Meir [question]. She said: "I know that the dead will live, [2] for it is written: 'And may they flourish in the city like the grass of the earth.' [3] But when they rise up, will they rise up naked, or will they rise up in their clothing?" [4] He said to her: "A *kal vaḥomer* argument from wheat. [5] If wheat which is buried naked, comes out with several coats, [6] the righteous who are buried in their clothing, all the more so."

[7] The emperor said to Rabban Gamliel: "You say that the dead will live. [8] Surely they become dust, and can dust live?" [91A] [9] His daughter said to him: "Leave him, and I will answer him. [10] There are two potters in our town, one fashions [utensils] out of water, and one fashions [utensils] out of clay. [11] Who is more excellent?" [12] He said to her: "He who fashions [utensils] out of water." [13] She said to him: "If he can fashion [utensils] out of water, [14] all the more so out of clay."

[15] [A Sage] of the School of Rabbi Yishmael taught: "A *kal vaḥomer* argument from glass utensils. [16] If glass utensils, whose formation is by the breath of flesh and blood, break, [and] they have a remedy,

RASHI

שעונה בה — שלא שב קודם מיתה הוי כרת, אבל שב לא. **דחיי שכבי** — שהמתים חיים. **ויציצו מעיר** — שעתידין ישראל לציץ ולפרוח מעיר ירושלים, וכדאמרינן (כתובות קיא,א) הקדוש ברוך הוא עושה להם מחילות לצדיקים והולכין ועולין לירושלים. **אמרה ליה ברתיה** — דקיסר לרבן גמליאל, שבקיה. **שני יוצרים וכו׳** — משל הוא: אלו היו שני יוצרים בעירנו, אחד יוצר כלים מן המים וכו׳. **אמרה לו** — אם כן הקדוש ברוך הוא אם מן המים הוא מצייר, דמטפה סרוחה שהיא כמים הוא מוליד. **מן העפר לא כל שכן** — שבידו. **דבי רבי ישמעאל תנא קל וחומר מכלי זכוכית** — וזו היא תשובה שהשיבה לאביה. **מה כלי זכוכית שעמלן ברוח של אדם** — שכשהוא עושה אותו יש לו שפופרת ונופח לתוכה, וכן נשמע מפי האומנין. **יש להם תקנה** — להתיך ולחזור ולעשות מהן כלי, והא דאמרינן בחגיגה (טו,א): ונותין

TRANSLATION AND COMMENTARY

down and refashioned into new utensils. [1]**Man is formed by the breath of the Holy One, blessed be He,** for it is God who breathes life into him. [2]**All the more so** then should he have a remedy if he dies, and God should be able to refashion him and bring him back to life."

אָמַר לֵיהּ [3]**A certain heretic** once **said to Rabbi Ammi: "You say that the dead will come back to life.** [4]But **surely** the dead **turn into dust** in their graves. [5]**Is it possible for dust to come to life?"** [6]Rabbi Ammi **said to him: "I will explain** the matter **to you by way of a parable.** [7]**What is this like?** [8]**It is like a mortal king who said to his servants: 'Go, and build me a grand palace in a place where there is no water or dirt** with which to build.' [9]The king's servants **went** out **and built** the palace as commanded. [10]**After some time,** the palace **collapsed.** The king called for his servants, [11]**and said to them: 'Go back again and rebuild** the palace **in a place where there is earth and water.'** [12]The servants **said to** the king: **'We are not able to** do that.' [13]The king **became angry with** his servants **and said to them: 'In a place where there was no water or** earth, **you** were able to **build** me a palace. [14]**Now that there is water and earth, all the more so** should you be able to do so.' If, God can make living things from water and earth, you should be able to build a palace from them. [15]**And if you do not believe** that it is possible to bring life to dust, **go out to the valley and** you will **see a** small animal **which today is** still **half flesh and half earth,** [16]but by **tomorrow, it will** have **turned into a creeping creature and become entirely flesh.** [17]And **should you say** that such creatures do not come into being from one moment to the next, but rather they are formed over **an extended** period **of time, go up the mountain and see that today there is only one snail** there, [18]but by **tomorrow,** should **the rain fall,** the mountain **will be entirely filled with snails."**

[1]בָּשָׂר וָדָם שֶׁבְּרוּחוֹ שֶׁל הַקָּדוֹשׁ בָּרוּךְ הוּא, [2]עַל אַחַת כַּמָּה וְכַמָּה".

[3]אָמַר לֵיהּ הַהוּא מִינָא לְרַבִּי אַמִי: "אָמְרִיתוּ דְּשָׁכְבֵי חַיֵּי, [4]וְהָא הָווּ עַפְרָא, [5]וְעַפְרָא מִי קָא חַיֵּי"? [6]אָמַר לֵיהּ: "אֶמְשׁוֹל לְךָ מָשָׁל. [7]לְמָה הַדָּבָר דּוֹמֶה? [8]לְמֶלֶךְ בָּשָׂר וָדָם שֶׁאָמַר לַעֲבָדָיו: 'לְכוּ וּבְנוּ לִי פַּלְטְרִין גְּדוֹלִים בְּמָקוֹם שֶׁאֵין מַיִם וְעָפָר'. [9]הָלְכוּ וּבָנוּ אוֹתוֹ. [10]לְיָמִים נָפְלוּ. [11]אָמַר לָהֶם: 'חִזְרוּ וּבְנוּ אוֹתוֹ בְּמָקוֹם שֶׁיֵּשׁ עָפָר וּמַיִם'. [12]אָמְרוּ לוֹ: 'אֵין אָנוּ יְכוֹלִין'. [13]כָּעַס עֲלֵיהֶם וְאָמַר לָהֶן: בְּמָקוֹם שֶׁאֵין מַיִם וְעָפָר, בְּנִיתֶם. [14]עַכְשָׁיו שֶׁיֵּשׁ מַיִם וְעָפָר עַל אַחַת כַּמָּה וְכַמָּה'! [15]וְאִם אִי אַתָּה מַאֲמִין, צֵא לְבִקְעָה וּרְאֵה עַכְבָּר שֶׁהַיּוֹם חֶצְיוֹ בָּשָׂר וְחֶצְיוֹ אֲדָמָה. [16]לְמָחָר הִשְׁרִיץ וְנַעֲשָׂה כֻּלּוֹ בָּשָׂר. [17]שֶׁמָּא תֹּאמַר לִזְמַן מְרוּבֶּה — עֲלֵה לָהָר וּרְאֵה שֶׁהַיּוֹם אֵין בּוֹ אֶלָּא חִלָּזוֹן אֶחָד. [18]לְמָחָר יָרְדוּ גְּשָׁמִים וְנִתְמַלֵּא כּוּלּוֹ חֶלְזוֹנוֹת".

LITERAL TRANSLATION

[1]flesh and blood [whose formation] is by the breath of the Holy One, blessed is He, [2]all the more so."

[3]A certain heretic said to Rabbi Ammi: "You say that the dead will live. [4]Surely they become dust, [5]and can dust live?" [6]He said to him: "I will tell you a parable. [7]What is this like? [8][It is like] a king of flesh and blood who said to his servants: 'Go, and build me a grand palace in a place where there is no water or earth.' [9]They went and built it. [10]After some time it collapsed. [11]He said to them: 'Go back again and build it in a place where there is earth and water.' [12]They said to him: 'We are not able.' [13]He became angry with them and said to them: 'In a place where there is no water or earth, you built. [14]Now that there is water and earth all the more so!' [15]And if you do not believe, go out to the valley and see a kind of small animal which today is half flesh and half earth. [16]Tomorrow, it will turn into a creeping creature and become entirely flesh. [17]Lest you say after an extended time — go up the mountain and see that today there is only one snail. [18]Tomorrow the rain will fall and it will be entirely filled with snails."

RASHI

לאבדם ככלי זכוכית — לא שאין להם תקנה, אלא שנפסדין לשעתן ואין מתקיימין. **עכשיו שיש מים** — והכי נמי הקדוש ברוך הוא יוצר את האדם מטפה קטנה שאין בה ממש, וכל שכן שיכול לבראתו מן העפר, אי נמי, כל העולם כולו יצר מתוהו. **ואם אי אתה מאמין** — שהקדוש ברוך הוא יוצר מן העפר. **עכבר** — שקורין אשקרו"ל* ויש במינן שאין נבראין על ידי תולדה. **היום** — מתחיל לברא ולצאת מן העפר, ולמחר מהלך כשהוא נברא, כדאמרינן בשחיטת חולין בהעור והרוטב (קכז,א). **ושמא תאמר לזמן מרובה** — שאותו שרץ אינו נברא לאלתר, אלא לזמן מרובה, שבוע או שבועיים, ותהא סבור שאין הקדוש ברוך הוא מחיה המתים לפי שעה. **לך עלה להר וכו'** — **חלזון** — תולעת שיוצא מן הים אחד לשבעים שנה וצובעין בדמו תכלת, ולכתחלה אינו נראה בכל ההר אלא חלזון אחד. **ולמחר** — שהגשמים יורדין מתמלא כולו חלזונות ונראה למורי שבילי חלזון (ראשון) משריצין כולן, אלמא יש בידו לחיות לפי שעה.

BACKGROUND

עַכְבָּר חִלָּזוֹן A small animal and a snail. The animal called עַכְבָּר (lit., "mouse") here is not the small rodent ordinarily referred to by that word but rather a kind of snail or insect, which is aroused from its sleep and begins moving, the way a butterfly emerges from its cocoon. This seems to apply to the simile of the rebirth of snails as well.

LANGUAGE

דִּימוּסָנָאֵי Contesters. This word apparently derives from the Greek δημοσιῶναι, *dimosionai*, meaning "the officials responsible for collecting property taxes." Those who challenged the right of Israel to its land were like the officials who examine the rights of property owners.

TRANSLATION AND COMMENTARY

אָמַר לֵיהּ [1]It was further related that **a certain heretic said to Geviha ben Pesisa: "Woe to you** sinners **who say that the dead will come back to life.** [2]We see with our very own eyes that even **those who are** now **living** eventually **die.** Is it possible, then, to imagine that **those who are** already **dead will come back to life?"** [3]Geviha ben Pesisa **said to** the heretic: **"Woe to you** sinners **who say that the dead will not come back to life.** [4]We see with our very own eyes that **those were never** yet alive **come to life.** [5]So when it comes to **those who were** once **alive,** [6]**all the more so,** then, will they come back to life." [7]The heretic **said to** Geviha ben Pesisa, who was a hunchback: "Did **you call me a sinner?** [8]**If I stand up, I will kick you and remove that hump from your back."** [9]Geviha sarcastically **retorted: "If you** manage to **do that, you shall** surely **be considered an expert doctor,** [10]**and you will** be able to **collect a great fee** for your services."

תָּנוּ רַבָּנַן [11]Having mentioned Geviha ben Pesisa and his debating skills, the Gemara now tells how Geviha ben Pesisa represented the Jewish people before Alexander the Great. **Our Rabbis taught** in *Megillat Ta'anit* a list of days on which there were significant victories and happy events in the history of the Jews during the Second Temple period, as a result of which the Rabbis forbade fasting on them, and in some cases eulogizing as well: [12]"Fasting and eulogizing are forbidden **on the twenty-fourth** day of the month **of Nisan,** for on that day **those who contested** the Jewish people's claim to the land of Israel **were removed from Judah and Jerusalem."** [13]**When the people of** North **Africa came to present a claim against** the people of **Israel before Alexander of Macedonia, they said to him:** [14]**"The land of Canaan is ours, for the verse**

[1]אָמַר לֵיהּ הַהוּא מִינָא לְגְבִיהָא בֶּן פְּסִיסָא: "וַוי לְכוֹן חַיָּיבַיָּא דְּאָמְרִיתוּן מֵיתֵי חַיִּין, [2]דְּחַיִּין מֵיתֵי, דְּמֵיתֵי חַיִּין"? [3]אֲמַר לֵיהּ: "וַוי לְכוֹן חַיָּיבַיָּא דְּאָמְרִיתוּן מֵיתֵי לָא חַיִּין, [4]דְּלָא הָווּ חַיֵּי, [5]דְּהָוֵי חַיֵּי, [6]לֹא כָּל שֶׁכֵּן"? [7]אֲמַר לֵיהּ: "חַיָּיבַיָּא קָרֵית לִי? [8]אִי קָאֵימְנָא, בָּעִיטְנָא בָּךְ וּפַשִׁיטְנָא לַעֲקְמוּתָךְ מִינָּךְ". [9]אֲמַר לֵיהּ: "אִם אַתָּה עוֹשֶׂה כֵּן, רוֹפֵא אוּמָן תִּקָּרֵא, [10]וְשָׂכָר הַרְבֵּה תִּטּוֹל".

[11]תָּנוּ רַבָּנַן: [12]"בְּעֶשְׂרִים וְאַרְבָּעָה בְּנִיסָן, אִיתְנַטִּילוּ דִּימוּסָנָאֵי מִיהוּדָה וּמִירוּשָׁלַיִם". [13]כְּשֶׁבָּאוּ בְּנֵי אַפְרִיקְיָא לָדוּן עִם יִשְׂרָאֵל לִפְנֵי אֲלֶכְּסַנְדְּרוֹס מוֹקְדוֹן, אָמְרוּ לוֹ: [14]"אֶרֶץ כְּנַעַן שֶׁלָּנוּ הִיא,

LITERAL TRANSLATION

[1]A certain heretic said to Geviha ben Pesisa: "Woe to you sinners who say [that] the dead will live. [2][If] the living die, will the dead live?" [3]He said to him: "Woe to you sinners who say [that] the dead will not live. [4][If] those who never were [yet] live, [5]those who were alive, [6]all the more so!" [7]He said to him: "You call me a sinner? [8]If I stand up, I will kick you and remove your hump from you." [9]He said to him: "If you do that, you shall be called an expert doctor, [10]and you shall collect a great fee."

[11]Our Rabbis taught: [12]"On the twenty-fourth of Nisan, the contestors were removed from Judah and Jerusalem." [13]When the people of Africa came to argue against Israel before Alexander of Macedonia, they said to him: [14]"The land of Canaan is ours,

RASHI

גביהא בן פסיסא — כך שמו והיתה לו עקמומיות בגבו כדמוכח לקמן. **ווי לכון חיביא** — אוי לכם לרשעים. **דחיי מתים** — אותן שהן חיין רואין אנו שמתין, והיאך יעלה על דעתנו שהמתים חוזרין וחיים. **דלא הוו** — אותן שלא היו מעולם נוצרין ונולדין וחיין, אותן שהיו כבר — לא כל שכן שחוזרין וחיין. **אמר לו** — מינא. **חייבא קרית לי וכו'** — בא לקנתרו. **דימוסנאי** — עוררין בעלי חמס, שהיו רוצין ליטול חלק ביהודה ובירושלים. **שבאו בני אפריקא לדון וכו'** — ובמגלת תענית חשיב להו כל אותן ימים שנעשה בהן נסים לישראל וקבעום יום טוב, ולהכי קאמר הכא בעשרים וארבעה בניסן, לומר דיום טוב הוא, ואסור בהספד משום נס זה.

NOTES

בְּנֵי אַפְרִיקְיָא The people of Africa. The commentators note that these "people of Africa" were the descendants of the Canaanites (Phoenicians) who had settled in Africa. According to Rabbinic tradition, one of the Canaanite nations (the Girgashites) did not fight Joshua when he conquered the land, but rather left the country peacefully (*R. David Bonfil*).

אֶרֶץ כְּנַעַן שֶׁלָּנוּ הִיא The land of Canaan is ours. The commentators ask: How could the Canaanites have argued before Alexander that the people of Israel had illegally taken possession of the land of Canaan, when Alexander himself became ruler of the world by virtue of military conquest? Thus the Jews' claim to their land should be equally valid by virtue of their military conquest! Some suggest that the Canaanites argued that when the people of Israel were sent into exile by the kings of Assyria and Babylonia, their rights to the Land of Israel by virtue of their earlier conquest were cancelled, and now the Canaanites could claim prior possession of the land (*Maharsha*). Alternatively, the verse that refers to the land as the land of Canaan proves that the land belongs to the Canaanites, and that Israel's conquest of the land was only temporary (*Iyyun Ya'akov*). Or else, they argued that, while "the law of the land" recognizes the right of conquest, surely the Torah of Israel, which is based on a higher level of morality, does not award possession merely on the basis of military conquest (*Be'er Sheva*).

TRANSLATION AND COMMENTARY

states (Numbers 34:2): 'This is the land that shall fall to you for an inheritance, **the land of Canaan with its borders.'** [1]Thus, the Jews have taken the land illegally, for **Canaan was the forefather of our people,** and we are his rightful heirs." [2]When **Geviha ben Pesisa** heard that the people of North Africa had challenged the Jewish people's claim to the Land of Israel, he **said to the Sages:** [3]**"Give me permission, and I will go, and argue against** the people of Africa **before Alexander of Macedonia.** [4]**If they triumph over me** in the debate, you can still **say** to them: **'You have** only **triumphed over an ordinary layman,** and you must now contend with the Sages of Israel.' [5]**And if I triumph over them** in the debate, you can **say to them: 'The Torah of Moses has triumphed over you,'** and you need not attribute the victory to me." [6]The Sages **gave** Geviha **permission** to represent the Jewish people, **and he went and argued with** the people of North Africa before Alexander the Great. [7]Geviha **said to** the North Africans: **"From where do you prove** that the Land of Israel really belongs to you?" [8]**They said:** "We prove it **from** your own **Torah."** [9]Geviha **said to them:** [10]**"I, too,** then **will bring you a proof from that** same **Torah** that the Land of Israel does in fact belong to the Jewish people, [11]**for the verse states** (Genesis 9:25): **'Cursed be Canaan; a servant of servants shall he be to his brethren.'** [12]If **a servant acquired property, to whom does the servant** belong, **and to whom** does **the property** belong? Surely, both the servant and the property belong to the servant's master. Thus you and the Land of Israel belong to us. [13]**And furthermore, many years** have passed **during which you did not serve us** as was mandated by the Torah, so you owe us compensation and must return to servitude. [14]**King Alexander said to them: "Give** Geviha **a** suitable **answer."** [15]The Africans **said to** Alexander: **"Give us three days' time** to consider the matter." [16]Alexander **gave them time** to think. [17]**They examined** the matter **but were not able to find a** convincing **answer.** [18]**They immediately fled, abandoning their fields as they had been sown, and their vineyards as they had been planted.** [19]The Gemara adds **that** the debate took place during **a Sabbatical Year,** [20]so that the people of Israel greatly benefited from the produce that the Africans left in their fields and vineyards.

דִּכְתִיב: ׳אֶרֶץ כְּנַעַן לִגְבֻלֹתֶיהָ׳. [1]וּכְנַעַן אֲבוּהוֹן דְּהָנְהוּ אֱינָשֵׁי הֲוָה״. [2]אָמַר לְהוּ גְּבִיהָא בֶּן פְּסִיסָא לַחֲכָמִים: [3]״תְּנוּ לִי רְשׁוּת וְאֵלֵךְ וְאָדוּן עִמָּהֶן לִפְנֵי אֲלֶכְּסַנְדְּרוֹס מוֹקְדוֹן. [4]אִם יְנַצְּחוּנִי, אִמְרוּ: ׳הֶדְיוֹט שֶׁבָּנוּ נִצַּחְתֶּם׳. [5]וְאִם אֲנִי אֲנַצֵּחַ אוֹתָם, אִמְרוּ לָהֶם: ׳תּוֹרַת מֹשֶׁה נִצַּחְתֶּכֶם׳״. [6]נָתְנוּ לוֹ רְשׁוּת, וְהָלַךְ וְדָן עִמָּהֶם. [7]אָמַר לָהֶם: ״מֵהֵיכָן אַתֶּם מְבִיאִים רְאָיָה״? [8]אָמְרוּ לוֹ: ״מִן הַתּוֹרָה״. [9]אָמַר לָהֶן: [10]״אַף אֲנִי לֹא אָבִיא לָכֶם רְאָיָה אֶלָּא מִן הַתּוֹרָה, [11]שֶׁנֶּאֱמַר: ׳וַיֹּאמֶר אָרוּר כְּנָעַן; עֶבֶד עֲבָדִים יִהְיֶה לְאֶחָיו׳. [12]עֶבֶד שֶׁקָּנָה נְכָסִים – עֶבֶד לְמִי, וּנְכָסִים לְמִי? [13]וְלֹא עוֹד, אֶלָּא שֶׁהֲרֵי כַּמָּה שָׁנִים שֶׁלֹּא עֲבַדְתּוּנוּ״! [14]אָמַר לָהֶם אֲלֶכְּסַנְדְּרוֹס מַלְכָּא: ״הַחֲזִירוּ לוֹ תְּשׁוּבָה״. [15]אָמְרוּ לוֹ: ״תְּנוּ לָנוּ זְמַן שְׁלֹשָׁה יָמִים״. [16]נָתַן לָהֶם זְמַן. בָּדְקוּ וְלֹא מָצְאוּ תְּשׁוּבָה. [17]מִיָּד בָּרְחוּ, וְהִנִּיחוּ שְׂדוֹתֵיהֶן כְּשֶׁהֵן זְרוּעוֹת, וְכַרְמֵיהֶן כְּשֶׁהֵן נְטוּעוֹת. [18]וְאוֹתָהּ שָׁנָה שְׁבִיעִית הָיְתָה.

LITERAL TRANSLATION

as it is written: 'The land of Canaan with its borders.' [1]And Canaan was the forefather of these people." [2]Geviha ben Pesisa said to the Sages: [3]"Give me permission, and I will go, and argue against them before Alexander of Macedonia. [4]If they triumph over me, say: 'You have triumphed over an ordinary person among us.' [5]And if I triumph over them, say to them: 'The Torah of Moses triumphed over you.'" [6]They gave him permission, and he went and argued with them. [7]He said to them: "From where do you bring a proof?" [8]They said to him: "From the Torah." [9]He said to them: [10]"I, too, will bring you a proof only from the Torah, [11]for it is stated: 'Cursed be Canaan; a servant of servants shall he be to his brethren.' [12]A servant who acquired property — the servant to whom, and the property to whom? [13]And furthermore, there are many years during which you did not serve us!" [14]King Alexander said to them: "Give him an answer." [15]They said to him: "Give us three days' time." [16]He gave them time. They checked and did not find an answer. [17]Immediately they fled, and abandoned their fields which were sown, and their vineyards which were planted. [18]And that year was a Sabbatical Year.

RASHI

ארץ כנען לגבולותיה — דלהך ארעא קרי ארץ כנען, ואתם ירשתם שלא כדין, דשלנו הוא, דכנען אבינו היה.

NOTES

הֶדְיוֹט שֶׁבָּנוּ An ordinary person among us. It has been suggested that since Geviha ben Pesisa was a hunchback, he was never formally ordained to serve as a judge (for it is preferable for judges to be free of physical deformities).

[1] שׁוּב פַּעַם אַחַת בָּאוּ בְּנֵי מִצְרַיִם לָדוּן עִם יִשְׂרָאֵל לִפְנֵי אֲלֶכְּסַנְדְּרוֹס מוֹקְדוֹן. [2] אָמְרוּ לוֹ: ״הֲרֵי הוּא אוֹמֵר: ׳וַה׳ נָתַן אֶת חֵן הָעָם בְּעֵינֵי מִצְרַיִם וַיַּשְׁאִלוּם׳. [3] תְּנוּ לָנוּ כֶּסֶף וְזָהָב שֶׁנְּטַלְתֶּם מִמֶּנּוּ״. [4] אָמַר גְּבִיהָא בֶּן פְּסִיסָא לַחֲכָמִים: ״תְּנוּ לִי רְשׁוּת וְאֵלֵךְ וְאָדוּן עִמָּהֶן לִפְנֵי אֲלֶכְּסַנְדְּרוֹס. [5] אִם יְנַצְּחוּנִי, אִמְרוּ לָהֶם: ׳הֶדְיוֹט שֶׁבָּנוּ נִצַּחְתֶּם׳. [6] וְאִם אֲנִי אֲנַצֵּחַ אוֹתָם, אִמְרוּ לָהֶם: ׳תּוֹרַת מֹשֶׁה רַבֵּינוּ נִצְּחַתְכֶם׳״. [7] נָתְנוּ לוֹ רְשׁוּת וְהָלַךְ וְדָן עִמָּהֶן. [8] אָמַר לָהֶן: ״מֵהֵיכָן אַתֶּם מְבִיאִין רְאָיָה״? [9] אָמְרוּ לוֹ: ״מִן הַתּוֹרָה״. אָמַר לָהֶן: ״אַף אֲנִי לֹא אָבִיא לָכֶם רְאָיָה אֶלָּא מִן הַתּוֹרָה, [10] שֶׁנֶּאֱמַר: ׳וּמוֹשַׁב בְּנֵי יִשְׂרָאֵל אֲשֶׁר יָשְׁבוּ בְּמִצְרָיִם שְׁלֹשִׁים שָׁנָה וְאַרְבַּע מֵאוֹת שָׁנָה. [11] תְּנוּ לָנוּ שְׂכַר עֲבוֹדָה שֶׁל שִׁשִּׁים רִיבּוֹא, שֶׁשִּׁיעְבַּדְתֶּם בְּמִצְרַיִם שְׁלֹשִׁים שָׁנָה וְאַרְבַּע מֵאוֹת שָׁנָה״. [12] אָמַר לָהֶן אֲלֶכְּסַנְדְּרוֹס מוֹקְדוֹן: ״הַחֲזִירוּ לוֹ תְּשׁוּבָה״! [13] אָמְרוּ לוֹ: ״תְּנוּ לָנוּ זְמַן שְׁלֹשָׁה יָמִים״. [14] נָתַן לָהֶם זְמַן. [15] בָּדְקוּ וְלֹא מָצְאוּ תְּשׁוּבָה. [16] מִיָּד הִנִּיחוּ שְׂדוֹתֵיהֶן כְּשֶׁהֵן זְרוּעוֹת, וְכַרְמֵיהֶן כְּשֶׁהֵן נְטוּעוֹת וּבָרְחוּ, [17] וְאוֹתָהּ שָׁנָה שְׁבִיעִית הָיְתָה.

LITERAL TRANSLATION

[1] Once again the people of Egypt came to argue against Israel before Alexander of Macedonia. [2] They said to him: "Surely it says: 'And the Lord gave the people favor in the sight of Egypt, so that they lent them [valuables].' [3] Give us the silver and gold that you took from them." [4] Geviha ben Pesisa said to the Sages: "Give me permission, and I will go, and argue against them before Alexander. [5] If they triumph over me, say to them: 'You have triumphed over an ordinary person among us.' [6] And if I triumph over them, say to them: 'The Torah of Moses our master triumphed over you.'" [7] They gave him permission, and he went and argued with them. [8] He said to them: "From where do you bring a proof?" [9] They said to him: "From the Torah." He said to them: "I too will bring you a proof only from the Torah, [10] for it is stated: 'And the sojourning of the children of Israel, who dwelt in Egypt was four hundred and thirty years.' [11] Give us the wages of six hundred thousand [workers] whom you enslaved in Egypt for four hundred and thirty years." [12] Alexander of Macedonia said to them: "Give him an answer!" [13] They said to him: "Give us three days' time." [14] He gave them time. [15] They checked and did not find an answer. [16] Immediately they abandoned their fields which were sown, and their vineyards which were planted, and fled. [17] And that year was a Sabbatical Year.

TRANSLATION AND COMMENTARY

שׁוּב פַּעַם [1] **On another occasion the people of Egypt came to present a claim against** the people of **Israel before Alexander of Macedonia.** [2] **They said to him: "Surely** the verse **states** (Exodus 12:36): **'And the Lord gave the people favor in the sight of Egypt, so that they** lent **them** valuables.' [3] **Give us** back **the silver and gold that you borrowed from** our ancestors." [4] When **Geviha ben Pesisa** heard the demands put forward by the Egyptians, he **said to the Sages: "Give me permission, and I will go and argue against** the Egyptians **before Alexander of Macedonia.** [5] **If they triumph over me** in the debate, you can still **say to them: 'You have** only **triumphed over an ordinary layman,** and you must now contend with the Sages of Israel.' [6] **And if I triumph over them** in the debate, you can **say to them: 'The Torah of Moses our master has triumphed over you,'** and you need not attribute the victory to me." [7] The Sages **gave** Geviha **permission** to represent the Jewish people, **and he went and argued with** the Egyptians before Alexander the Great. [8] Geviha **said to** the Egyptians: **"From where do you prove** your claim against the people of Israel?" [9] **They said to him:** "We prove it **from** your own **Torah."** Geviha **said to them: "I, too,** then, **will bring you a proof from that** same **Torah** that we do not owe you anything, [10] **for the verse states** (Exodus 12:40): **'And the sojourning of the children of Israel, who dwelt in Egypt, was four hundred and thirty years.'** During that entire period the Egyptians forced the people of Israel to serve them with hard labor. [11] **Give us** now **the wages** owed **to the six hundred thousand workers whom you enslaved in Egypt for four hundred and thirty years."** [12] The Egyptians did not immediately respond to this counterclaim, and **Alexander of Macedonia said to them: "Give** Geviha **an answer."** [13] The Egyptians **said to** Alexander: **"Give us three days' time** to consider the matter." [14] Alexander acquiesced and **gave them time** to think it over. [15] **They checked** the matter, **but they were not able to find a** convincing **answer.** [16] **They immediately abandoned their fields as they had been sown, and their vineyards as they had been planted, and fled.** [17] The Gemara adds that **this** contest took place **during a Sabbatical Year,** so the people of Israel greatly benefited from the produce that the Egyptians left behind.

NOTES

Therefore, though he was a great Sage, he could still refer to himself as "an ordinary person." (*Tzofnat Pa'ane'aḥ.*)

TRANSLATION AND COMMENTARY

וְשׁוּב פַּעַם [1]On yet **another occasion the descendants of Ishmael and the descendants of Keturah came to present a claim against** the people of **Israel before Alexander of Macedonia.** [2]**They said to him: "The land of Canaan belongs to us and to you,** the people of Israel, [3]**for the verse states** (Genesis 25:12): **'And these are the generations of Ishmael the son of Abraham,** who Hagar the Egyptian woman, Sarah's handmaid, bore to Abraham.' [4]**And** another **verse states** (Genesis 25:19): **'And these are the generations of Isaac the son of Abraham.'** The land of Canaan which had been given to Abraham should be divided evenly among all his heirs. We, too, have a share in the land." [5]When **Geviha ben Pesisa** heard this demand, he **said to the Sages: "Give me permission, and I will go and argue against them** (the descendants of Ishmael and Keturah) before **Alexander of Macedonia.** [6]**If they triumph over me** in the debate, you can still **say** to them: **'You have** only **triumphed over an ordinary layman,** and you must now contend with the Sages of Israel.' [7]**And if I triumph over them** in the debate, you can **say to them: 'The Torah of Moses our master has triumphed over you,'** and you need not attribute the victory to me." [8]The Sages **gave** Geviha **permission** to represent the Jewish people, **and he went and argued with** the descendants of Ishmael and Keturah before Alexander of Macedonia. [9]Geviha **said to them: "From where do you prove** your claim to a portion of the Land of Israel? [10]**They said to him:** "We base our claim on what is stated **in** your own **Torah."** Geviha **said to them: "I, too,** then, **will bring you a proof from the Torah** that you are not entitled to any part of the Land of Israel, [11]**for the verse states** (Genesis 25:5-6): **'And Abraham gave all that he had to Isaac.** [12]**But to the sons of the concubines, which Abraham had, Abraham gave gifts,** and sent them away from his son, while he yet lived, eastward, to the east country.' [13]**If a father gave his sons deeds of gift** and divided his property among them **during his lifetime, and** he **sent one** of his sons **away from the other, does** the **one** son **have any** claim **against the other** son?"

מַאי "מַתָּנוֹת" [14]Having cited the verse mentioning the gifts which Abraham gave to his sons, the Gemara asks: **What is** meant here by **"gifts"?** [15]**Rabbi Yirmeyah bar Abba said: This teaches that** Abraham **handed over**

LITERAL TRANSLATION

[1]And once again the descendants of Ishmael and the descendants of Keturah came to argue against Israel before Alexander of Macedonia. [2]They said to him: "The land of Canaan is ours and yours, [3]for it is written. 'And these are the generations of Ishmael the son of Abraham,' [4]and it is written: 'And these are the generations of Isaac the son of Abraham.'" [5]Geviha ben Pesisa said to the Sages: "Give me permission, and I will go, and argue against them before Alexander of Macedonia. [6]If they triumph over me, say: 'You have triumphed over an ordinary person among us.' [7]And if I triumph over them, say to them: 'The Torah of Moses our master triumphed over you.'" [8]They gave him permission, and he went and argued with them. [9]He said to them: "From where do you bring a proof?" [10]They said to him: "From the Torah." [11]He said to them: "I, too, will bring you a proof only from the Torah, [12]for it is stated: 'And Abraham gave all that he had to Isaac. But to the sons of the concubines, which Abraham had, Abraham gave gifts.' [13][If] a father gave his sons deeds of gift during his lifetime, and sent one away from the other, does one have anything against the other?"
[14]What is [meant by] "gifts"? [15]Rabbi Yirmeyah bar Abba said: This teaches that he gave

[1]וְשׁוּב פַּעַם אַחַת בָּאוּ בְּנֵי יִשְׁמָעֵאל וּבְנֵי קְטוּרָה לָדוּן עִם יִשְׂרָאֵל לִפְנֵי אֲלֶכְּסַנְדְּרוֹס מוֹקְדוֹן. [2]אָמְרוּ לוֹ: "אֶרֶץ כְּנַעַן שֶׁלָּנוּ וְשֶׁלָּכֶם, [3]דִּכְתִיב: 'וְאֵלֶּה תֹּלְדֹת יִשְׁמָעֵאל בֶּן אַבְרָהָם', [4]וּכְתִיב: 'וְאֵלֶּה תּוֹלְדֹת יִצְחָק בֶּן אַבְרָהָם'". [5]אָמַר לָהֶן גְּבִיהָא בֶּן פְּסִיסָא לַחֲכָמִים: "תְּנוּ לִי רְשׁוּת וְאֵילֵךְ וְאָדוּן עִמָּהֶם לִפְנֵי אֲלֶכְּסַנְדְּרוֹס מוֹקְדוֹן. [6]אִם יְנַצְּחוּנִי, אִמְרוּ: 'הֶדְיוֹט שֶׁבָּנוּ נִצַּחְתֶּם'. [7]וְאִם אֲנִי אֲנַצֵּחַ אוֹתָם, אִמְרוּ לָהֶם: 'תּוֹרַת מֹשֶׁה רַבֵּינוּ נִצַּחְתְּכֶם.'" [8]נָתְנוּ לוֹ רְשׁוּת, הָלַךְ וְדָן עִמָּהֶן. [9]אָמַר לָהֶם: "מֵהֵיכָן אַתֶּם מְבִיאִין רְאָיָיה"? [10]אָמְרוּ לוֹ: "מִן הַתּוֹרָה". [11]אָמַר לָהֶן: "אַף אֲנִי לֹא אָבִיא רְאָיָיה אֶלָּא מִן הַתּוֹרָה, [12]שֶׁנֶּאֱמַר: 'וַיִּתֵּן אַבְרָהָם אֶת כָּל אֲשֶׁר לוֹ לְיִצְחָק וְלִבְנֵי הַפִּילַגְשִׁים אֲשֶׁר לְאַבְרָהָם נָתַן אַבְרָהָם מַתָּנֹת'. [13]אָב שֶׁנָּתַן אֲגַטִין לְבָנָיו בְּחַיָּיו, וְשִׁיגֵּר זֶה מֵעַל זֶה, כְּלוּם יֵשׁ לָזֶה עַל זֶה כְּלוּם"?
[14]מַאי "מַתָּנוֹת"? [15]אָמַר רַבִּי יִרְמְיָה בַּר אַבָּא: מְלַמֵּד שֶׁמָּסַר

RASHI

אגטין — כתבים, שלא יטול אחד בחלק חבירו, כמו שעשה אברהם לישמעאל, שלא ליטול במה שנתן ליצחק, כלום יש לזה על זה כלום.

NOTES

מַאי "מַתָּנוֹת"? **What is meant by "gifts"?** Since the verse states, "And Abraham gave all that he had to Isaac," what

לָהֶם שֵׁם טוּמְאָה.
[1]אָמַר לֵיהּ אַנְטוֹנִינוּס לְרַבִּי: [2]״גּוּף וּנְשָׁמָה יְכוֹלִין לִפְטוֹר עַצְמָן מִן הַדִּין. [3]כֵּיצַד? [4]גּוּף אוֹמֵר: ׳נְשָׁמָה חָטָאת, שֶׁמִּיּוֹם שֶׁפֵּירְשָׁה מִמֶּנִּי, [5]הֲרֵינִי מוּטָּל כְּאֶבֶן דּוּמָם בַּקֶּבֶר׳. [6]וּנְשָׁמָה אוֹמֶרֶת: ׳גּוּף חָטָא, שֶׁמִּיּוֹם שֶׁפֵּירַשְׁתִּי מִמֶּנּוּ, הֲרֵינִי פּוֹרַחַת בָּאֲוִיר כַּצִּפּוֹר׳״. [7]אָמַר לֵיהּ: ״אֶמְשׁוֹל לְךָ מָשָׁל. [8]לְמָה הַדָּבָר דּוֹמֶה? [9]לְמֶלֶךְ בָּשָׂר וָדָם, שֶׁהָיָה לוֹ פַּרְדֵּס נָאֶה, וְהָיָה בּוֹ [91B] בַּכּוּרוֹת נָאוֹת, [10]וְהוֹשִׁיב בּוֹ שְׁנֵי שׁוֹמְרִים, אֶחָד חִיגֵּר וְאֶחָד סוּמָא. [11]אָמַר לוֹ חִיגֵּר לְסוּמָא: ׳בַּכּוּרוֹת נָאוֹת אֲנִי רוֹאֶה בַּפַּרְדֵּס. [12]בֹּא וְהַרְכִּיבֵנִי וּנְבִיאֵם לְאָכְלָם׳. [13]רָכַב חִיגֵּר עַל גַּבֵּי סוּמָא, וֶהֱבִיאוּם וַאֲכָלוּם. [14]לְיָמִים בָּא בַּעַל פַּרְדֵּס. [15]אָמַר לָהֶן: ׳בַּכּוּרוֹת נָאוֹת הֵיכָן הֵן׳? [16]אָמַר לוֹ חִיגֵּר: ׳כְּלוּם יֵשׁ לִי רַגְלַיִם לְהַלֵּךְ בָּהֶן׳? [17]אָמַר לוֹ סוּמָא: ׳כְּלוּם יֵשׁ לִי עֵינַיִם לִרְאוֹת׳? [18]מֶה עָשָׂה? [19]הִרְכִּיב חִיגֵּר עַל

LITERAL TRANSLATION

them the name of ritual impurity.

[1]Antoninus said to Rabbi: [2]"The body and the soul can exempt themselves from judgment. [3]How so? [4]The body says: 'The soul sinned, for from the day that it departed from me, [5]I am cast like a dumb stone in the grave.' [6]And the soul says: 'The body sinned, for from the day that I departed from it, I fly through the air like a bird.'" [7]He said to him: "I will tell you a parable. [8]What is this like? [9][It is like] a king of flesh and blood who had a fine orchard, and in it were [91B] fine early figs, [10]and he placed two guards in it, one lame and one blind. [11]The lame said to the blind: 'I see fine early figs in the orchard. [12]Come, and carry me, and we will bring them to eat.' [13]The lame rode on the back of the blind, and they brought them, and ate them. [14]After some time, the owner of the orchard came. [15]He said to them: 'Where are the fine early figs?' [16]The lame said to him: 'Do I have legs with which to walk?' [17]The blind said to him: 'Do I have eyes with which to see?' [18]What did he do? [19]He put the lame on

TRANSLATION AND COMMENTARY

to his sons **the name of** the demon that rules over the forces of **ritual impurity** so that they could practice magic.

אָמַר לֵיהּ [1]Having described the encounters between Geviha ben Pesisa and Alexander the Great, the Gemara now describes a series of discussions between another representative of the Jewish people and another world leader. **Antoninus,** the emperor of Rome, once **said to Rabbi** Yehudah HaNasi: [2]"After a person dies, both his **body and** his **soul can exempt themselves from judgment** in the World to Come for sins that were committed during the person's lifetime. [3]**How so?** [4]**The body can say:** 'It was not I, but rather **the soul** that sinned, and I can prove it, **for from the day that** the soul **departed from me** at the time of death, [5]**I am cast like a dumb stone in the grave,** and am unable to sin.' [6]**And the soul can say:** 'It was not I, but rather **the body** that **sinned,** and I can prove it, **for from the day that I departed from** the body at the time of death, **I fly through the air like a bird,** and am unable to sin.'" [7]Rabbi Yehudah HaNasi **said to** Antoninus: "I **will explain** the matter **to you by way of a parable.** [8]**What is this like?** [9]**It is like a mortal king who had a fine orchard, in which there** grew [91B] **fine early figs.** [10]The king **placed two guards in** the orchard; **one** was **lame and** the other was **blind.** [11]**The lame** guard **said to** his **blind** partner: **'I see fine early figs in the orchard.** [12]**Come, carry me** on your back, **and** together **we will bring them** back with us **to eat.'** [13]**The lame** guard **rode on the back of** his **blind** partner, **and** together **they brought** the figs back, **and ate them.** [14]**After some time, the owner of the orchard came,** [15]and **said to them: 'Where are the fine early figs?'** [16]**The lame** guard **said to** the king: **'Do I have legs with which to walk?'** [17]And then **the blind** guard **said to** the king: **'Do I have eyes with which to see?'** [18]**What did** the king **do?** [19]**He**

PEOPLE

אַנְטוֹנִינוּס **Antoninus.** Many scholars have dealt with the problem of identifying the Emperor Antoninus who is mentioned as a close friend of Rabbi Yehudah HaNasi. One serious problem is that several Roman emperors of that time were named Antoninus. In some sources Rabbi Yehudah Nesia, who was Rabbi Yehudah HaNasi's grandson, is also called "Rabbi." According to chronology, the most likely figure for encounters of this kind in Eretz Israel would be Marcus Aurelius, who was famous as a Stoic philosopher and who might have met Rabbi Yehudah HaNasi before he became emperor.

RASHI

שם טומאה — כשוף ומעשה שדים. **בכורות** — תאני הבכורות.

NOTES

did he have left to give to the sons of his concubines? Since Abraham had already given Isaac all of his physical possessions, the Gemara suggests that he imparted knowledge to his other sons, giving them mastery over demons (*Rashbatz*).

שֵׁם טוּמְאָה **The name of ritual impurity.** Many commentators ask how Abraham could have handed over to his sons the name of the demon that rules over the forces of ritual impurity, since the practice of magic is forbidden by Torah law (according to some, even to non-Jews). Some suggest that "the name of ritual impurity" does not refer to forbidden magic, but rather to permissible occult knowledge (*Rashbatz*). Others propose that Abraham taught his sons how to rid themselves of the powers of impurity (*Gur Aryeh*). Or else, he taught them about the forces of ritual impurity, so that they know how to distinguish between the true service of God and idolatry, and that they be able to guard themselves against the powers of impurity (*Ma'asei Hashem, HaKetav ve'HaKabbalah*).

TRANSLATION AND COMMENTARY

put the lame guard **on the back of the blind** one, **and judged** the two **of them as one.** [1]**So, too, the Holy One, blessed be He, will** in the future **bring the soul and cast it** back **into the body, and judge** the two of **them as one,** [2]**as the verse states** (Psalms 50:4): **'He calls to the Heaven above, and to the earth, that He may judge His people.'** [3]**'He calls to the Heaven above' — this is** a reference to **the soul.** [4]**'And to the earth, that He may judge His people' — this is** a reference to **the body."**

אָמַר לֵיהּ [5]It was further related that **Antoninus,** the emperor of Rome, once **said to Rabbi** Yehudah HaNasi: **"Why does the sun rise in the east and set in the west?"** [6]Rabbi Yehudah HaNasi **said to him: "If** the sun traveled in **the opposite** direction, **you would ask me** why does the sun rise in the west and set in the east!" [7]Antoninus **said to** Rabbi Yehudah HaNasi: **"I** meant to **ask you as follows: Why does** the sun **set in the west?** Let it circle the sky and set in the east. It stands to reason that the sun should return to the place where it had risen." [8]Rabbi Yehudah HaNasi **said to** Antoninus: "The sun sets in the west in order **to greet its Maker.** It is bowing down before the Divine Presence, which resides in the west, [9]**as the verse states** (Nehemiah 9:6): **'And the host of Heaven worships you.'"** [10]Antoninus **said to** Rabbi Yehudah HaNasi: **"But let** it rise in the east, **reach the middle of the sky** at noon, continue a bit and **greet** the Divine Presence by bowing towards the west, **and** then **go up** and set in the middle of the sky!" [11]Rabbi Yehudah HaNasi explained: "The sun rises in the east and sets in the west **on account of workers and travelers** who plan their day by the sun."

וְאָמַר לוֹ [12]It was further related that **Antoninus asked Rabbi** Yehudah HaNasi the following question: **"When is a** living **soul placed in man — at the time**

גַּבֵּי סוּמָא וְדָן אוֹתָם כְּאֶחָד. [1]אַף הַקָּדוֹשׁ בָּרוּךְ הוּא מֵבִיא נְשָׁמָה וְזוֹרְקָהּ בַּגּוּף, וְדָן אוֹתָם כְּאֶחָד, [2]שֶׁנֶּאֱמַר: ׳יִקְרָא אֶל הַשָּׁמַיִם מֵעָל וְאֶל הָאָרֶץ לָדִין עַמּוֹ׳. [3]׳יִקְרָא אֶל הַשָּׁמַיִם מֵעָל׳ — זוֹ נְשָׁמָה. [4]׳וְאֶל הָאָרֶץ לָדִין עַמּוֹ׳ — זֶה הַגּוּף״.

[5]אָמַר לֵיהּ אַנְטוֹנִינוּס לְרַבִּי: ״מִפְּנֵי מַה חַמָּה יוֹצְאָה בַּמִּזְרָח וְשׁוֹקַעַת בַּמַּעֲרָב״? [6]אֲמַר לֵיהּ: ״אִי הֲוָה אִיפְּכָא נַמִי הָכִי הֲוָה אָמְרַתְּ לִי״! [7]אֲמַר לֵיהּ: ״הָכִי קָאָמִינָא לָךְ: מִפְּנֵי מַה שׁוֹקַעַת בַּמַּעֲרָב״? [8]אֲמַר לֵיהּ: ״כְּדֵי לִיתֵּן שָׁלוֹם לְקוֹנָהּ, [9]שֶׁנֶּאֱמַר: ׳וּצְבָא הַשָּׁמַיִם לְךָ מִשְׁתַּחֲוִים׳״. [10]אֲמַר לֵיהּ: ״וְתֵיתֵי עַד פַּלְגָּא דְּרָקִיעַ, וְתִתֵּן שְׁלָמָא וְתֵיעוּל״! [11]״מִשּׁוּם פּוֹעֲלִים, וּמִשּׁוּם עוֹבְרֵי דְרָכִים״.

[12]וְאָמַר לוֹ אַנְטוֹנִינוּס לְרַבִּי: ״נְשָׁמָה מֵאֵימָתַי נִיתְּנָה בָּאָדָם

LITERAL TRANSLATION

the back of the blind, and judged them as one. [1]So, too, the Holy One, blessed is He, brings the soul and casts it into the body, and judges them as one, [2]as it is stated: [3]'He calls to the heaven above, and to the earth, that He may judge His people.' 'He calls to the heaven above' — this is the soul. [4]'And to the earth, that He may judge His people' — this is the body."

[5]Antoninus said to Rabbi: "Why does the sun rise in the east and set in the west?" [6]He said to him: "If it were the opposite, you would also ask me that." [7]He said to him: "I say to you as follows: Why does it set in the west?" [8]He said to him: "To give greetings to its Maker, [9]as it is stated: 'And the host of Heaven worships you.'" [10]He said to him: "But let it reach the middle of the sky, give greetings, and go up!" [11]"On account of workers, and on account of travelers."

[12]And Antoninus said to Rabbi: "When is the soul placed in man

RASHI

יקרא אל השמים מעל — כלומר יקרא הקדוש ברוך הוא לנשמה הבאה לו לתוך גופו של אדם מאל השמים מעל ויקרא אף אל הגוף שבא מן הארץ. **מפני מה שוקעת במערב** — תסובב את כל העולם עד שתחזור למקום זריחתה למזרח ותשקע, דאי הוה הכי לא הוה אמינא לך: "מפני מה שוקעת במזרח" — דנוהג העולם כך הוא, ממקום שיצא שם נכנס. **כדי ליתן שלום לקונה** — להקדוש ברוך הוא, שהשכינה במערב, וכיון שמגעת עד מערב הולכת ומשתחוה לפני הקדוש ברוך הוא שבראה, ולכך שוקעת ונכנסת כפופה לפני הקדוש ברוך הוא. **ותיתי עד פלגא דרקיעא** — דאם לכך מתכוונת למה הולכת בתוך המערב — תבא עד אמצעו של רקיע ותשקע לשם ומשם תשתחוה כלפי מערב, שכן דרך בן אדם שמשתחוה ברחוק לפני המלך ואינו מתקרב כל כך. **משום פועלים** — דאילו כן, היה מחשיך פתאום — שכשחמה באמצע הרקיע מאירה ביותר, וסבורים שעדיין יש שהות ביום והיו פועלין שוהין במלאכתן עד שתחשיכה, ועוברי דרכים נמי לא היו יודעין מתי יחשוך לבקש להם בית לינה, ולכך שוקעת במערב, שכשהולכת ומשתפלת והולכת וכלה אורה יודעין שמגיע שעת חשיכה.

NOTES

הַשָּׁמַיִם מֵעָל **The Heaven above.** The very fact that Heaven is being summoned for judgment implies that the verse is not referring to Heaven itself, but to the soul of man which is regarded as Heaven in relation to his body (*Iyyun Ya'akov*). *Ḥida* adds that the numerical value of the word *hashamayim* (הַשָּׁמַיִם — 395), "the Heaven," is equal to the numerical value of the word *neshamah* (נְשָׁמָה — "soul").

BACKGROUND

שְׁעַת פְּקִידָה אוֹ שְׁעַת יְצִירָה At the time of conception, or at the time of formation? This is not merely an abstract question, since it touches upon ethical and practical problems concerning abortion. Antoninus is asking, in effect, whether a foetus should be viewed as a human being even in the first forty days of its life. If so, killing it would be punishable by humans and by divine power.

TRANSLATION AND COMMENTARY

of conception, or at the time of formation, when the embryo begins to assume human form, forty days after conception?" [1]Rabbi Yehudah HaNasi **said to him:** "Man is given his soul **at the time of** his **formation."** [2]Antoninus **asked him:** "But **is it possible for a piece of meat to stand for** even **three days without salt and not spoil?** Surely not. [3]**Rather,** it must be that man is given his soul **at the time of** his **conception."** [4]**Rabbi** Yehudah HaNasi **said: "Antoninus taught me** the truth regarding **this matter, and** there is even **a** verse which **supports him,** [5]**for the verse states** (Job 10:12): **'And Your providence** [וּפְקֻדָּתְךָ] **has preserved my spirit.'** The word וּפְקֻדָּתְךָ, translated here as 'Your providence,' might also be understood as an allusion to the time of פְּקִידָה, the time of conception."

וְאָמַר לוֹ [6]**Antoninus** also **asked Rabbi** Yehudah HaNasi: **"From when does the evil inclination control man — from the time of** his **formation,** forty days after conception, **or from the time of** his **birth?"** [7]Rabbi Yehudah HaNasi **said to him:** "The evil inclination begins to control man **from the time of** his **formation."** [8]Antoninus **said to him: "If** that **is so,** then surely it **should** cause the fetus to **kick its mother's bowels and force its way out** early in her pregnancy! [9]**Rather,** the evil inclination only begins to control man **from the time of** his **birth."** [10]**Rabbi** Yehudah HaNasi **said: "Antoninus taught me** the truth regarding **this matter,** [11]**and** there is even **a verse** which **supports him** (Genesis 4:7): **'Sin crouches at the door.'** When an infant emerges through the door of its mother's womb, the evil inclination is waiting to control him."

רֵישׁ לָקִישׁ [12]**Resh Lakish cast together** two verses, pointing out the contradiction between them: [13]One **verse states** (Jeremiah 31:7): "Behold, I will bring them from the north country, and gather them from the ends of the earth, **and with them the blind and the lame, the woman with child and** the woman giving birth **together,** a great company shall return there," implying that even in the end of days people will continue to suffer from physical defects and deformities. [14]**And** another **verse states** (Isaiah 35:6): **"Then shall the lame man leap as a hart and the tongue of the dumb sing; for in the wilderness shall waters break out, and streams in the desert,"** implying that all physical

— מִשְׁעַת פְּקִידָה, אוֹ מִשְׁעַת יְצִירָה"? [1]אָמַר לוֹ: "מִשְׁעַת יְצִירָה". [2]אָמַר לוֹ: "אֶפְשָׁר חֲתִיכָה שֶׁל בָּשָׂר עוֹמֶדֶת שְׁלֹשָׁה יָמִים בְּלֹא מֶלַח וְאֵינָהּ מַסְרַחַת? [3]אֶלָּא, מִשְׁעַת פְּקִידָה". [4]אָמַר רַבִּי: "דָּבָר זֶה לִמְּדַנִי אַנְטוֹנִינוּס, וּמִקְרָא מְסַיְּיעוֹ, [5]שֶׁנֶּאֱמַר: 'וּפְקֻדָּתְךָ שָׁמְרָה רוּחִי'".

[6]וְאָמַר לוֹ אַנְטוֹנִינוּס לְרַבִּי: "מֵאֵימָתַי יֵצֶר הָרַע שׁוֹלֵט בָּאָדָם — מִשְׁעַת יְצִירָה, אוֹ מִשְׁעַת יְצִיאָה"? [7]אָמַר לוֹ: "מִשְׁעַת יְצִירָה". [8]אָמַר לוֹ: "אִם כֵּן, בּוֹעֵט בִּמְעֵי אִמּוֹ וְיוֹצֵא! [9]אֶלָּא, מִשְׁעַת יְצִיאָה". [10]אָמַר רַבִּי: "דָּבָר זֶה לִמְּדַנִי אַנְטוֹנִינוּס, [11]וּמִקְרָא מְסַיְּיעוֹ, שֶׁנֶּאֱמַר: 'לַפֶּתַח חַטָּאת רֹבֵץ'".

[12]רֵישׁ לָקִישׁ רָמֵי: [13]כְּתִיב: "בָּם עִוֵּר וּפִסֵּחַ הָרָה וְיֹלֶדֶת יַחְדָּיו". [14]וּכְתִיב: "אָז יְדַלֵּג כָּאַיָּל פִּסֵּחַ וְתָרֹן לְשׁוֹן אִלֵּם כִּי נִבְקְעוּ בַמִּדְבָּר מַיִם וּנְחָלִים בָּעֲרָבָה".

LITERAL TRANSLATION

— at the time of conception, or at the time of formation?" [1]He said to him: "At the time of formation." [2]He said to him: "Is it possible for a piece of meat to stand for three days without salt and not spoil? [3]Rather, at the time of conception." [4]Rabbi said: "Antoninus taught me this matter, and the verse supports him, [5]for it is stated: 'And Your providence has preserved my spirit.'"

[6]And Antoninus said to Rabbi: "From when does the evil inclination control man — from the time of formation, or from the time of birth?" [7]He said to him: "From the time of formation." [8]He said to him: "If so, he should kick his mother's bowels and go out! [9]Rather, from the time of birth." [10]Rabbi said: "Antoninus taught me this matter, [11]and the verse supports him, as it is said: 'Sin crouches at the door.'"

[12]Resh Lakish cast together: [13]It is written: "And with them the blind and the lame, the woman with child and the woman giving birth together." [14]And it is written: "Then shall the lame man leap as a hart and the tongue of the dumb sing; for in the wilderness shall waters break out, and streams in the desert."

RASHI

משעת יצירה — שנקרם כולו בבשר וגידין ועצמות. **פקידה** — משעה שהמלאך פוקד הטיפה ומביאה לפני המקום מה תהא עליה, כדאמרינן בפרק "כל היד" במסכת נדה (טז,ב), מיד נזרקה בו נשמה וחיות. **אמר ליה** — רבי: משעת יצירה. **ואמר לו** — אנטונינוס: וכי אפשר לחתיכה שתתקיים אפילו שלשה ימים בלא מלח שאינה מסרחת — והכי נמי אילו לא היתה נשמה נתונה עד שעת יצירה היאך תתקיים הטיפה שלא תסריח במעיה, וכיון שטיפה מסרחת שוב אינה מולדת. **למדני אנטונינוס** — מדבריו למדתי. **ופקודתך שמרה רוחי** — משעת פקידה נשמר רוחי. **משעת יציאה** — כשיוצא ממעי אמו או משעת יצירה. **אמר ליה** — רבי: משעת יצירה. **אמר לו אנטונינוס: אם כן בועט במעי אמו ויוצא** — אלא משעת יציאתה. **בם עור ופסח** — שחיין עם מומן. **וכתיב אז ידלג כאיל פסח** — דמשמע שמתרפאין.

TRANSLATION AND COMMENTARY

handicaps will vanish." [1]**How** can the two verses be reconciled? [2]Resh Lakish explained: People **will rise up** from the dead **with their defects, and** then they will **be healed.**

עוּלָּא רָמֵי [3]**Ulla cast together** the following two verses which appear to contradict each other: [4]One **verse states** (Isaiah 25:8): **"He will destroy death forever; and the Lord God will wipe away tears from all faces,"** implying that in the future people will live forever and not die. [5]**And** another **verse states** (Isaiah 65:20): **"There shall be no more there an infant who lives a few days,** nor an old man that has not filled his days; **for the youngest shall die a hundred years old;** and the sinner being a hundred years old shall be deemed accursed," implying that people will live long lives, but they will eventually die.

לָא קַשְׁיָא [6]The Gemara explains: **There is** really **no difficulty.** [7]**Here** the verse is speaking **about** the people of **Israel,** who will indeed live forever. [8]And **here** the verse is referring to **non-Jews,** who will live long lives but nevertheless die.

וְנָכְרִים [9]The Gemara asks: **Why are non-Jews needed there?**

הָנָךְ [10]The Gemara answers: We are dealing here with **those** non-Jews **about whom the verse states** (Isaiah 61:5): [11]**"And strangers shall stand and feed your flocks, and the sons of the alien shall be your ploughmen and vinedressers."**

רַב חִסְדָּא [12]**Rav Ḥisda cast together** two verses, pointing out the apparent contradiction between them: [13]**The verse states** (Isaiah 24:23): **"Then the moon shall be confounded, and the sun ashamed, when the Lord of hosts shall reign** in Mount Zion, and in Jerusalem, and before His elders will be His glory," implying that in the future the light of the sun and the moon will dim. [14]**And** another **verse states** (Isaiah 30:26): **"Moreover the light of the moon shall be as the light of the sun, and the light of the sun shall be sevenfold, as the light of seven days,** on the day that the Lord binds up the breach of His people, and heals the strike of their wound."

לָא קַשְׁיָא [15]The Gemara explains: **There is** really **no difficulty.** [16]**Here,** where the verse speaks of the sun and the moon becoming brighter, it is referring to **the Messianic** age. [17]And **here,** where the verse speaks of the sun and the moon diminishing in brightness, it is referring to **the World to Come.**

[1]הָא כֵּיצַד? [2]עוֹמְדִין בְּמוּמָן וּמִתְרַפְּאִין.

[3]עוּלָּא רָמֵי: [4]כְּתִיב: ״בִּלַּע הַמָּוֶת לָנֶצַח; וּמָחָה ה׳ דִּמְעָה מֵעַל כָּל פָּנִים״. [5]וּכְתִיב: ״כִּי הַנַּעַר בֶּן מֵאָה שָׁנָה יָמוּת; לֹא יִהְיֶה מִשָּׁם עוֹד עוּל יָמִים״.

[6]לָא קַשְׁיָא. [7]כָּאן, בְּיִשְׂרָאֵל; [8]כָּאן, בְּנָכְרִים.

[9]וְנָכְרִים, מַאי בָּעוּ הָתָם?

[10]הָנָךְ דִּכְתִיב בְּהוּ: [11]״וְעָמְדוּ זָרִים וְרָעוּ צֹאנְכֶם וּבְנֵי נֵכָר אִכָּרֵיכֶם וְכֹרְמֵיכֶם״.

[12]רַב חִסְדָּא רָמֵי: [13]כְּתִיב: ״וְחָפְרָה הַלְּבָנָה וּבוֹשָׁה הַחַמָּה כִּי מָלַךְ ה׳ צְבָאוֹת״, [14]וּכְתִיב: ״וְהָיָה אוֹר הַלְּבָנָה כְּאוֹר הַחַמָּה וְאוֹר הַחַמָּה יִהְיֶה שִׁבְעָתַיִם כְּאוֹר שִׁבְעַת הַיָּמִים״!

[15]לָא קַשְׁיָא. [16]כָּאן, לִימוֹת הַמָּשִׁיחַ. [17]כָּאן, לָעוֹלָם הַבָּא.

LITERAL TRANSLATION

[1]How so? [2]They will rise up with their defect, and be healed.

[3]Ulla cast together: [4]It is written: "He will destroy death forever; and the Lord God will wipe away tears from all faces." [5]And it is written: "For the youngest shall die a hundred years old; there shall be no more there an infant who lives a few days."

[6]It is not difficult. [7]Here, regarding Israel; [8]here, regarding non-Jews.

[9]And non-Jews, why are they needed there?

[10]They are those about whom it is written: [11]"And strangers shall stand and herd your flocks, and the sons of the alien shall be your ploughmen and vinedressers."

[12]Rav Ḥisda cast together: [13]It is written: "Then the moon shall be confounded, and the sun ashamed, when the Lord of hosts shall reign." [14]And it is written: "Moreover, the light of the moon shall be as the light of the sun, and the light of the sun shall be sevenfold, as the light of seven days."

[15]It is not difficult. [16]Here, during the Messianic age. [17]Here, in the World to Come.

RASHI

עומדין במומן – ואחר כך מתרפאין. **בלע המות לנצח** – דלעתיד לבא מאחר שחיין שוב אינן מתין. **כי הנער** – כלומר כשימות אדם לעתיד ומת בן מאה שנה יאמרו ״נער הוא מת״, כי ״הנער בן מאה שנה ימות״ – אלמא מתין. **וחפרה הלבנה ובושה החמה** – משמע שיהא אורם כהה, וכתיב ״והיתה אור הלבנה כאור החמה״. **באן לימות המשיח** – כשיכלה השיעבוד ״והיתה אור הלבנה כאור החמה״, ולעתיד לבא ״וחפרה הלבנה ובושה החמה״ – מרוב נגהם של צדיקים.

HALAKHAH

ימות הַמָּשִׁיחַ The days of the Messiah. "The only difference between the present time and the days of the Messiah is that in the days of the Messiah Israel will regain its sovereignty and no longer be subservient to other powers, but there will be no changes in the natural order." (*Rambam, Sefer Mada, Hilkhot Teshuvah* 9:2.)

TRANSLATION AND COMMENTARY

וְלִשְׁמוּאֵל [1]The Gemara adds: **And according to Shmuel, who said that the only difference between this world and the Messianic** age **is the servitude of the exile communities, how can these** two **verses be reconciled?** According to Shmuel, in the Messianic age the Jewish communities that were subject to other nations will be freed and return to Eretz Israel. But there will be no changes in the natural order.

לָא קַשְׁיָא [2]The Gemara answers: Even according to Shmuel, **there is no difficulty.** Both verses refer to the World to Come. [3]**Here,** where the verse speaks of the sun and the moon becoming brighter, it is referring to **the camp of the righteous.** [4]And **here,** where the verse speaks of the sun and the moon diminishing in brightness, it is referring to **the camp of the Divine Presence,** where the sun and the moon will pale before the light of God.

רָבָא רָמֵי [5]**Rava cast together** the two halves of a verse, pointing out a certain difficulty: The beginning of **the verse states** (Deuteronomy 32:39): [6]**"I kill, and I make alive,"** implying that God will resurrect the dead. [7]**And** that very same **verse continues: "I wound, and I heal."** If God already said that He will resurrect the dead, why does He have to say that He will heal the wounded? [8]Rava explains: **The Holy One, blessed is He, said** as follows: **Those whom I have killed, I will make live.** [9]**And later, those whom I have wounded** with physical defects and blemishes, **I will heal.**

תָּנוּ רַבָּנַן [10]**Our Rabbis taught** the following Baraita: "The verse states (Deuteronomy 32:39): **'I kill, and I make alive.'** Had I only had this part of the verse, [11]**I might have thought that** this means that God will bring **death to one** person, **and** grant **life to another** person, **as is the manner of the world** today. [12]**Therefore, the verse**

[1]וְלִשְׁמוּאֵל דְּאָמַר: אֵין בֵּין הָעוֹלָם הַזֶּה לִימוֹת הַמָּשִׁיחַ אֶלָּא שִׁיעְבּוּד גָּלֻיּוֹת בִּלְבַד? [2]לָא קַשְׁיָא. [3]כָּאן, בְּמַחֲנֵה צַדִּיקִים; [4]כָּאן — בְּמַחֲנֵה שְׁכִינָה.

[5]רָבָא רָמֵי: [6]כְּתִיב: "אֲנִי אָמִית, וַאֲחַיֶּה". [7]וּכְתִיב: "מָחַצְתִּי, וַאֲנִי אֶרְפָּא". [8]אָמַר הַקָּדוֹשׁ בָּרוּךְ הוּא: מַה שֶּׁאֲנִי מֵמִית, אֲנִי מְחַיֶּה. [9]וַהֲדַר, מַה שֶּׁמָּחַצְתִּי, וַאֲנִי אֶרְפָּא.

[10]תָּנוּ רַבָּנַן: "'אֲנִי אָמִית, וַאֲחַיֶּה'. [11]יָכוֹל שֶׁתְּהֵא מִיתָה בְּאֶחָד וְחַיִּים בְּאֶחָד כְּדֶרֶךְ שֶׁהָעוֹלָם נוֹהֵג. [12]תַּלְמוּד לוֹמַר:

LITERAL TRANSLATION

[1]And according to Shmuel, who said: There is no [difference] between this world and the Messianic age except the servitude of the exile communities alone?

[2]It is not difficult. [3]Here, in the camp of the righteous; [4]here, in the camp of the Divine Presence.

[5]Rava cast together: It is written: [6]"I kill, and I make alive." [7]And it is written: "I wound, and I heal." [8]The Holy One, blessed be He, said: Those whom I have killed, I will make live. [9]And then, those whom I have wounded, I will heal.

[10]Our Rabbis taught: "'I kill, and I make alive.' [11]I might have thought that death will be in one, and life in another, the way the world goes. [12][Therefore,] the verse states:

RASHI

ולשמואל דאמר — בדוכתא אחריתי אין בין העולם הזה וכו׳, אידי ואידי לעולם הבא. **אלא כאן במחנה שכינה** — וחפרה מזיו השכינה. **כאן במחנה הצדיקים** — כאן במחנה רשעים לא גרסינן. **כתיב אני אמית ואחיה** — דמשמע כשם שאני אמית את האדם כך אני מחייהו, כשמת בעל מום — עומד וחי בעל מום. **וכתיב מחצתי ואני ארפא** — שכשהוא מחיה מרפא את המחץ ועומד שלם. **והדר מה שמחצתי** — שלאחר כן מתרפא, וכדלעיל: עומדין במומן ומתרפאין. **מיתה באחד וחיים באחד** — והכי קאמר: אני ממית אדם זה — ומחיה אדם אחר. **כדרך שהעולם נוהג** — שזה מת וזה נולד.

NOTES

אֶלָּא שִׁיעְבּוּד גָּלֻיּוֹת Except for the servitude of the exile communities. *Tosafot* and others point out that Shmuel means that the Messianic age will not be accompanied by any changes in the natural order. But surely the Temple will be rebuilt in the days of the Messiah, and the people of Israel will return to the Promised Land from the four corners of the world.

כָּאן — בְּמַחֲנֵה שְׁכִינָה Here, in the camp of the Divine Presence. Even today the camp of the Divine Presence is illuminated solely by the light of God, and not by the sun or the moon. But the verse teaches that only in the World to Come will this become clear and evident to all (*Ramah*).

אֲנִי אָמִית...מָחַצְתִּי, וַאֲנִי אֶרְפָּא I kill...I wound, and I heal. According to *Rashi,* the two halves of the verse contradict each other. The first half of the verse, "I kill, and I make alive," implies that God will revive the dead as they are, so that those with physical deformities will come back to life with those same deformities, whereas the second half of the verse, "I wound, and I heal," implies that the dead will be resurrected with no imperfections. *Maharsha* adds that Rava had a difficulty with the tenses in the verse. "I kill" and "I make alive" are both future forms, whereas "I wound" is a past form, and "I heal" is a future form. He therefore explains the verse as follows: I will kill, and restore to life when I resurrect the dead, and then those whom I wounded during their previous lifetimes, I will heal after the dead are resurrected.

TRANSLATION AND COMMENTARY

continues: 'I wound, and I heal.' [1]**Just as wounding and healing** must **refer to the same** person, **so, too,** do **death and life refer to the same** person. [2]Thus, we have **here an answer to those who say that there** is no allusion to the **resurrection of the dead in the Torah."**

תַּנְיָא [3]**It was taught** in another Baraita: **"Rabbi Meir said:** [4]**From where do we know about the resurrection of the dead from the Torah?** [5]We know about this from **the verse** that **states** (Exodus 15:1): **'Then sang** [*yashir*] **Moses and the children of Israel this song to the Lord.'** [6]The verse **does not use** the past form *shar,* **'sang,' but rather** it uses the future form *yashir,* **'will sing,'** implying that Moses will come back in the future and sing a song to God. [7]Thus, we have **here** an allusion to **the resurrection of the dead in the Torah.** [8]**Similarly, the verse states** (Joshua 8:30): **'Then Joshua built** [*yivneh*] **an altar to the Lord God of Israel in Mount Eval.'** [9]The verse **does not use** the past form *banah,* **'built,'** [10]**but rather** it uses the future from *yivneh,* **'will build,'** implying that Joshua will return and build an altar to God.' [11]Thus, we have **here** another allusion to **the resurrection of the dead in the Torah."**

אֶלָּא מֵעַתָּה [12]The Gemara asks: **But now** that you draw such conclusions from Scripture's use of the future form instead of the past form, what do you say about the verse (I Kings 11:7): [13]**"Then did Solomon build** [*yivneh*] **a high place for Kemosh, the abomination of Moab"?** [14]Do you think that **here, too,** the verse means to say that Solomon **will build** a high place for Kemosh?

אֶלָּא [15]**Rather,** the verse does not use the past form, because Solomon did not actually build the high place himself; he merely allowed the high place for the idol to be built for his wives. [16]The future form teaches us that **Scripture regards** Solomon **as if he had built** the high place for the idol, because he did not prevent his wives from erecting such a place of worship.

אָמַר [17]**Rabbi Yehoshua ben Levi said: From where do we know about the resurrection of the dead from the Torah?** [18]We know about this **from the verse** (Psalms 84:5): [19]**"Happy are they who dwell in Your house; they are ever praising You** [*yehalelukha*]." [20]The verse **does not use** the past form *hilelukha,* **"they praised You,"** [21]**but rather** it uses the future form *yehalelukha,* **"they will praise You,"** implying that those who dwell in God's house will praise Him in the future. [22]Thus, we have **here** an allusion to **the resurrection of the dead in the Torah.**

‘מָחַצְתִּי וַאֲנִי אֶרְפָּא’. [1]מַה מְחִיצָה וּרְפוּאָה בְּאֶחָד, אַף מִיתָה וְחַיִּים בְּאֶחָד. [2]מִיכָּן תְּשׁוּבָה לָאוֹמְרִין אֵין תְּחִיַּית הַמֵּתִים מִן הַתּוֹרָה”.

[3]תַּנְיָא: ”אָמַר רַבִּי מֵאִיר: [4]מִנַּיִין לִתְחִיַּית הַמֵּתִים מִן הַתּוֹרָה? [5]שֶׁנֶּאֱמַר: ‘אָז יָשִׁיר מֹשֶׁה וּבְנֵי יִשְׂרָאֵל אֶת הַשִּׁירָה הַזֹּאת לַה’. [6]‘שָׁר’ לֹא נֶאֱמַר, אֶלָּא ‘יָשִׁיר’. [7]מִכָּאן לִתְחִיַּית הַמֵּתִים מִן הַתּוֹרָה. [8]כַּיּוֹצֵא בְּדָבָר אַתָּה אוֹמֵר: ‘אָז יִבְנֶה יְהוֹשֻׁעַ מִזְבֵּחַ לַה’, [9]‘בָּנָה’ לֹא נֶאֱמַר, [10]אֶלָּא ‘יִבְנֶה’. [11]מִכָּאן לִתְחִיַּית הַמֵּתִים מִן הַתּוֹרָה”.

[12]אֶלָּא מֵעַתָּה, [13]”אָז יִבְנֶה שְׁלֹמֹה בָּמָה לִכְמוֹשׁ שִׁקֻּץ מוֹאָב” — [14]הָכִי נַמִי דְּיִבְנֶה? [15]אֶלָּא, [16]מַעֲלֶה עָלָיו הַכָּתוּב כְּאִילּוּ בָּנָה.

[17]אָמַר רַבִּי יְהוֹשֻׁעַ בֶּן לֵוִי: מִנַּיִין לִתְחִיַּית הַמֵּתִים מִן הַתּוֹרָה? [18]שֶׁנֶּאֱמַר: [19]”אַשְׁרֵי יוֹשְׁבֵי בֵיתֶךָ; עוֹד יְהַלְלוּךָ סֶּלָה”. [20]”הִילְלוּךָ” לֹא נֶאֱמַר, [21]אֶלָּא ”יְהַלְלוּךָ”. [22]מִכָּאן לִתְחִיַּית הַמֵּתִים מִן הַתּוֹרָה.

LITERAL TRANSLATION

'I wound, and I heal.' [1]Just as wounding and healing are in one, so, too, death and life are in one. [2]From here an answer to those who say that there is no resurrection of the dead from the Torah."

[3]It was taught: "Rabbi Meir said: [4]From where [do we know about] the resurrection of the dead from the Torah? [5]For it is stated: 'Then sang Moses and the children of Israel this song to the Lord.' [6]It is not stated 'sang,' but rather 'will sing.' [7]From here [we know about] the resurrection of the dead from the Torah. [8]Similarly you say: 'Then Joshua built an altar to the Lord God of Israel in Mount Eval.' [9]It is not stated 'built,' [10]but rather 'will build.' [11]From here [we know about] the resurrection of the dead from the Torah."

[12]But now, [13]"Then did Solomon build a high place for Kemosh, the abomination of Moab" — [14]so, too, he will build?

[15]Rather, [16]Scripture relates to him as if he had built.

[17]Rabbi Yehoshua ben Levi said: From where [do we know about] the resurrection of the dead from the Torah? [18]For it is stated: [19]"Happy are they who dwell in Your house; they are ever praising You." [20]It is not stated, "they praised You," [21]but rather, "they will praise You." [22]From here [we know about] the resurrection of the dead from the Torah.

RASHI

מה מחץ ורפוי באחד — ואין רפואה אלא במקום מחץ. **ישיר** — משמע לעתיד.

TRANSLATION AND COMMENTARY

וְאָמַר [1]**Rabbi Yehoshua ben Levi said: Whoever sings a song** to God **in this world** will **merit to sing** that song to Him also **in the World to Come,** [2]**as the verse states: "Happy are they who dwell in Your house; they are ever praising You,"** using the future form *yehalelukha*, rather than the past form *hilelukha*.

אָמַר [3]**Rabbi Ḥiyya bar Abba said in the name of Rabbi Yoḥanan: From where do we know about the resurrection of the dead from the Torah?** [4]We know about this **from the verse** that **states** (Isaiah 52:8): **"The voice of your watchmen is heard; they lift up the voice, together shall they sing,** for they shall see eye to eye, the Lord returning to Zion." [5]The verse **does not use** the past form *rinenu,* **"they sang," but rather** it uses the future form *yeranenu*, **"they will sing."** [6]Thus, we have **here** an allusion to **the resurrection of the dead in the Torah.**

וְאָמַר [7]**Rabbi Ḥiyya bar Abba said in the name of Rabbi Yoḥanan: In the future all the Prophets will sing a song** to God **with one voice,** [8]**for the verse states: "The voice of your watchmen is heard; they lift up the voice, together shall they sing."**

אָמַר [9]Seeming to jump to an entirely new topic, the Gemara says: **Rav Yehudah said in the name of Rav: Whoever withholds a law from the mouth of a disciple** who wishes to learn from him **is regarded as if he had robbed him of the inheritance of his fathers,** [10]**for the verse states** (Deuteronomy 33:4): **"Moses commanded us a Torah, the inheritance of the congregation of Jacob."** [11]The Torah **is the inheritance of all of Israel from the six days of creation.** Thus, whoever denies his disciple access to the Torah is viewed as if he had robbed that disciple of his rightful heritage.

[1]וְאָמַר רַבִּי יְהוֹשֻׁעַ בֶּן לֵוִי: כָּל הָאוֹמֵר שִׁירָה בָּעוֹלָם הַזֶּה זוֹכֶה וְאוֹמְרָהּ לָעוֹלָם הַבָּא, [2]שֶׁנֶּאֱמַר: "אַשְׁרֵי יוֹשְׁבֵי בֵיתֶךָ עוֹד יְהַלְלוּךָ סֶּלָה".

[3]אָמַר רַבִּי חִיָּיא בַּר אַבָּא אָמַר רַבִּי יוֹחָנָן: מִנַּיִין לִתְחִיַּית הַמֵּתִים מִן הַתּוֹרָה? [4]שֶׁנֶּאֱמַר: "קוֹל צֹפַיִךְ נָשְׂאוּ קוֹל יַחְדָּו יְרַנְּנוּ וגו׳". [5]"רִינְּנוּ" לֹא נֶאֱמַר, אֶלָּא "יְרַנְּנוּ" [6]מִכָּאן לִתְחִיַּית הַמֵּתִים מִן הַתּוֹרָה.

[7]וְאָמַר רַבִּי חִיָּיא בַּר אַבָּא אָמַר רַבִּי יוֹחָנָן: עֲתִידִין כָּל הַנְּבִיאִים כּוּלָּן אוֹמְרִים שִׁירָה בְּקוֹל אֶחָד, [8]שֶׁנֶּאֱמַר: "קוֹל צֹפַיִךְ נָשְׂאוּ קוֹל יַחְדָּו יְרַנְּנוּ".

[9]אָמַר רַב יְהוּדָה אָמַר רַב: כָּל הַמּוֹנֵעַ הֲלָכָה מִפִּי תַלְמִיד כְּאִילּוּ גּוֹזְלוֹ מִנַּחֲלַת אֲבוֹתָיו, [10]שֶׁנֶּאֱמַר: "תּוֹרָה צִוָּה לָנוּ מֹשֶׁה מוֹרָשָׁה קְהִלַּת יַעֲקֹב". [11]מוֹרָשָׁה הִיא לְכָל יִשְׂרָאֵל מִשֵּׁשֶׁת יְמֵי בְרֵאשִׁית.

LITERAL TRANSLATION

[1]And Rabbi Yehoshua ben Levi said: Whoever recites a song in this world merits to recite it in the World to Come, [2]as it is stated: "Happy are they who dwell in Your house; they are ever praising You."

[3]Rabbi Ḥiyya bar Abba said in the name of Rabbi Yoḥanan: From where [do we know about] the resurrection of the dead from the Torah? [4]For it is stated: "The voice of your watchmen is heard; they lift up the voice, together shall they sing, etc." [5]It is not stated, "they sang," but rather, "they will sing." [6]From here [we know about] the resurrection of the dead from the Torah.

[7]And Rabbi Ḥiyya bar Abba said in the name of Rabbi Yoḥanan: In the future all the Prophets will recite a song with one voice, [8]for it is stated: "The voice of your watchmen is heard; they lift up the voice, together shall they sing."

[9]Rav Yehudah said in the name of Rav: Whoever withholds a law from the mouth of a disciple [is regarded] as if he robbed him of the inheritance of his fathers, [10]for it is stated: "Moses commanded us a Torah, the inheritance of the congregation of Jacob." [11]It is an inheritance for all of Israel from the six days of creation.

RASHI

נשאו קול יחדיו – היינו קול אחד. **המונע הלכה** – מללמדו. **משׁשת ימי בראשית** – דכתיב "בראשית ברא" בשביל התורה שהיא ראשית, וישראל נקראו "ראשית תבואתה" שעתידין להנחילה – "ברא אלהים את השמים וגו׳".

NOTES

כָּל הַמּוֹנֵעַ הֲלָכָה מִפִּי תַּלְמִיד **Whoever withholds a law from the mouth of a disciple.** These statements regarding someone who withholds a law from his disciple are cited here because of the statement at the end of the passage, that whoever teaches Torah in this world merits to teach it in the World to Come, which is similar to saying that whoever recites a song in this world merits to do so in the World to Come (*Noda Biyehudah, Rashash*).

אוֹמְרִים שִׁירָה בְּקוֹל אֶחָד **They will recite a song with one voice.** Even though we learned earlier in the tractate (89a) that no two Prophets prophesy using the very same expressions, all the Prophets will eventually sing God's praises with one voice. It has been suggested that Rabbi Yoḥanan's statement, that in the future all the Prophets will sing with one voice, implies that in the future ordinary members of Israel, and not only Levites, will serve as Temple singers (*Tzofnat Pa'aneaḥ*).

TRANSLATION AND COMMENTARY

אָמַר [1]**Rav Ḥana bar Bizna said in the name of Rabbi Shimon Ḥasida: Whoever withholds a law from a disciple** who wishes to learn from him, **even fetuses in their mothers' wombs curse him,** [2]**as the** verse states (Proverbs 11:26): **"He who holds back corn** [*bar*], [92A] **the people** [*le'om*] **shall curse** [*yikvuhu*] **him."** [3]**And the** word *le'om* in this context **refers to fetuses, as the verse states** (Genesis 25:23): "Two nations are in your womb and two peoples shall be separated from your bowels; [4]**and the one people** [*le'om*] **shall be stronger than the other people** [*le'om*]," teaching that even a fetus in its mother's womb can already be referred to by the term *le'om,* "people." [5]**And the** word ***kavoh*** (*yikvuhu*) in this context **refers to a curse, as it is stated** in the words of Balaam (Numbers 23:8): **"How shall I curse** [*ekov*] **whom the Lord has not cursed** [*kavoh*]?" [6]**And the word *bar*** in this context **refers to the Torah, as the verse states: "Worship in purity** [*bar*], **lest He be angry."** Thus, the verse that we translated above as: "He who holds back corn, the people shall curse him," may be understood as teaching that someone who withholds Torah is even cursed by fetuses.

עוּלָּא בַּר יִשְׁמָעֵאל [7]**Ulla bar Yishmael says:** Whoever withholds a law from a disciple who wishes to learn will **himself become perforated like a sieve.** [8]**Here the verse states** (Proverbs 11:26): "He who holds back corn, **the people shall curse** [*yikvuhu*] **him,"** which as was demonstrated above refers to someone who withholds Torah from a disciple. [9]And **elsewhere the verse** states (II Kings 12:10): **"And he bored** [*vayikov*] **a hole in the lid of it,"** from which we see that the term *kavoh* means "to drill a hole." Thus, the verse in Proverbs may be understood as saying that someone who withholds Torah will become perforated like a sieve. [10]**And Abaye said:** Such a person will become perforated **like a launderer's sprinkler** used during ironing.

וְאִם לִמְּדוֹ [11]The Gemara asks: **If the master taught his** disciple Torah, **what is his reward?**

אָמַר רָבָא [12]**Rava said in the name of Rav Sheshet:** Such a person **merits blessings like** those enjoyed by **Joseph,** [13]**as it is stated** in the continuation of the verse cited above (Proverbs 11:26): "He who holds back

[1]אָמַר רַב חָנָא בַּר בִּיזְנָא אָמַר רַבִּי שִׁמְעוֹן חֲסִידָא: כָּל הַמּוֹנֵעַ הֲלָכָה מִפִּי תַּלְמִיד, אֲפִילּוּ עוּבָּרִין שֶׁבִּמְעֵי אִמּוֹ מְקַלְּלִין אוֹתוֹ, [2]שֶׁנֶּאֱמַר: "מֹנֵעַ בָּר [92A] יִקְּבֻהוּ לְאוֹם". [3]וְאֵין לְאוֹם אֶלָּא עוּבָּרִין, שֶׁנֶּאֱמַר: [4]"וּלְאֹם מִלְאֹם יֶאֱמָץ". [5]וְאֵין קַבֹּה אֶלָּא קְלָלָה, שֶׁנֶּאֱמַר: "מָה אֶקֹּב לֹא קַבֹּה אֵל"? [6]וְאֵין בָּר אֶלָּא תּוֹרָה, שֶׁנֶּאֱמַר: "נַשְּׁקוּ בַר פֶּן יֶאֱנַף".

[7]עוּלָּא בַּר יִשְׁמָעֵאל אוֹמֵר: מְנַקְּבִין אוֹתוֹ כִּכְבָרָה. [8]כְּתִיב הָכָא: "יִקְּבֻהוּ לְאוֹם". [9]וּכְתִיב הָתָם: "וַיִּקֹּב חֹר בְּדַלְתּוֹ". [10]וְאָמַר אַבַּיֵי: כִּי אוּכְלָא דְּקַצְרֵי.

[11]וְאִם לִמְּדוֹ, מַה שְּׂכָרוֹ?

[12]אָמַר רָבָא אָמַר רַב שֵׁשֶׁת: זוֹכֶה לִבְרָכוֹת כְּיוֹסֵף, [13]שֶׁנֶּאֱמַר:

LITERAL TRANSLATION

[1]Rav Ḥana bar Bizna said in the name of Rabbi Shimon Ḥasida: Whoever withholds a law from the mouth of a disciple, even the fetuses in the womb of his mother curse him, [2]for it is stated: "He who holds back corn [*bar*], [92A] the people [*le'om*] shall curse him [*yikvuhu*]." [3]And *le'om* [can] only [mean] fetuses, as it is stated: [4]"And the one people shall be stronger than the other people." [5]And *kavoh* [can] only [mean] a curse, as it is stated: "How shall I curse whom the Lord has not cursed?" [6]And *bar* [can] only [mean] Torah, as it is stated: "Worship in purity, lest He be angry."

[7]Ulla bar Yishmael says: We perforate him like a sieve. [8]It is written here: "The people shall curse him." [9]And it is written there: "And he bored a hole in the lid of it." [10]And Abaye said: Like a launderer's sprinkler.

[11]And if he taught him, what is his reward?

[12]Rava said in the name of Rav Sheshet: He merits blessings like Joseph, [13]as it is stated:

RASHI

בר = תורה. יקבוהו – ינקבים אותו לשון (מלכים ב יב) "ויקוב חור בדלתו". אוכלא דקצרי – כלי של כובסין שהוא מנוקב ומזלפין בו מים על הבגדים.

BACKGROUND

אוּכְלָא דְּקַצְרֵי Launderers sprinkler.

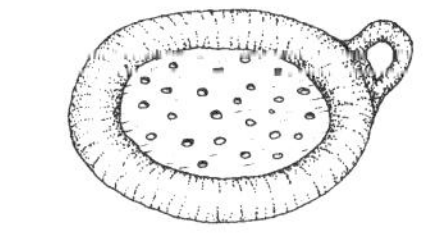

A sprinkler

According to the Geonim, an אוּכְלָא דְּקַצְרֵי was a perforated vessel from which water was sprinkled on clothing during ironing. It was also used to smoke and perfume garments.

NOTES

אֲפִילּוּ עוּבָּרִין Even fetuses. Even though a fetus is not affected by the master who withholds Torah from his disciples, for a fetus is taught the entire Torah by an angel, the fetus nevertheless joins with all the others to curse the master for not sharing his Torah with others (see *Rabbi Yaakov Emden, Torat Ḥayyim*).

מְנַקְּבִין אוֹתוֹ כִּכְבָרָה We perforate him like a sieve. Whoever withholds Torah from a disciple will himself become perforated like a sieve and forget the Torah that he knows. He is punished measure for measure. Since he wants to keep all that he knows for himself, and not share it with others, he is punished by losing all the Torah that he has ever acquired, so that he is left with nothing (*Maharsha*).

"וּבְרָכָה לְרֹאשׁ מַשְׁבִּיר". [1] וְאֵין מַשְׁבִּיר אֶלָּא יוֹסֵף, שֶׁנֶּאֱמַר: [2] "וְיוֹסֵף הוּא [הַשַּׁלִּיט עַל הָאָרֶץ הוּא] הַמַּשְׁבִּיר לְכָל עַם הָאָרֶץ".

[3] אָמַר רַב שֵׁשֶׁת: כָּל הַמְלַמֵּד תּוֹרָה בָּעוֹלָם הַזֶּה — זוֹכֶה וּמְלַמְּדָהּ לָעוֹלָם הַבָּא, [4] שֶׁנֶּאֱמַר "וּמַרְוֶה גַּם הוּא יוֹרֶה".

[5] אָמַר רָבָא: מִנַּיִין לִתְחִיַּית הַמֵּתִים מִן הַתּוֹרָה? [6] שֶׁנֶּאֱמַר: "יְחִי רְאוּבֵן, וְאַל יָמֹת". [7] "יְחִי רְאוּבֵן" — בָּעוֹלָם הַזֶּה; "וְאַל יָמֹת" — לָעוֹלָם הַבָּא.

[8] רָבִינָא אָמַר: מֵהָכָא: [9] "וְרַבִּים מִיְּשֵׁנֵי אַדְמַת עָפָר יָקִיצוּ אֵלֶּה לְחַיֵּי עוֹלָם וְאֵלֶּה לַחֲרָפוֹת לְדִרְאוֹן עוֹלָם".

[10] רַב אַשִׁי אָמַר: מֵהָכָא: [11] "וְאַתָּה לֵךְ [לַקֵּץ] וְתָנוּחַ וְתַעֲמֹד לְגֹרָלְךָ לְקֵץ הַיָּמִין".

LITERAL TRANSLATION

"But blessing shall be upon the head of him who sells freely [*mashbir*]." [1] And *mashbir* [can] only [mean] Joseph, as it is stated: [2] "And Joseph was [the governor of the land, and he] sold [*mashbir*] to all the people of the land."

[3] Rav Sheshet said: Whoever teaches Torah in this world merits to teach it in the World to Come, [4] as it is stated: "And he who waters shall be nourished also himself."

[5] Rava said: From where [do we know about] the resurrection of the dead from the Torah? [6] As it is stated: "Let Reuben live, and not die." [7] "Let Reuben live" — in this world; "and not die" — in the World to Come.

[8] Ravina said: From here: [9] "And many of those who sleep in the dust of the earth shall awake, some to everlasting life, and some to shame and everlasting contempt."

[10] Rav Ashi said: From here: [11] "But go you your way till the end be; for you shall rest, and stand up for your fate at the end of the days."

TRANSLATION AND COMMENTARY

corn, the people shall curse him; **but blessing shall be upon the head of him who sells freely** [*mashbir*]." Just as the first half of that verse may be understood as referring to someone who withholds Torah from his disciple, the second half of the verse may be understood as referring to someone who freely shares his Torah. The verse refers to such a person as a *mashbir*, someone who sells freely, [1] **and *mashbir*** in this context **is** an allusion to **Joseph, as the verse states** (Genesis 42:6): [2] **"And Joseph was the governor of the land, and he it was that sold** [*hamashbir*] **to all the people of the land."** Thus, we learn from the verse that someone who shares his Torah with his disciples is rewarded with the blessings given to Joseph.

אָמַר רַב שֵׁשֶׁת [3] **Rav Sheshet said: Whoever teaches Torah in this world will merit to teach it** also **in the World to Come,** [4] **as the verse states** (Proverbs 11:25): **"And he who waters** [וּמַרְוֶה] **shall be nourished also himself** [יוֹרֶה]." Rav Sheshet transposes the letters of the word וּמַרְוֶה, so that it reads וּמוֹרֶה, "and he who teaches," and he understands the word יוֹרֶה as the future form of that same word. Thus, the verse may be understood as saying that someone who teaches Torah to his disciples in the present will also teach them in the future, in the World to Come.

אָמַר רָבָא [5] **Rava said: Where is** there an allusion to **the resurrection of the dead in the Torah?** [6] This is derived from **the verse** that **states** (Deuteronomy 33:6): **"Let Reuben live, and not die."** This apparent repetition intimates that there is life in two worlds. [7] **"Let Reuben live"** means **in this world; "and not die"** means **in the World to Come.**

רָבִינָא אָמַר [8] **Ravina said:** The resurrection of the dead is alluded to **here** (Daniel 12:2): [9] **"And many of those who sleep in the dust of the earth shall awake, some to everlasting life, and some to shame and everlasting contempt."**

רַב אַשִׁי [10] **Rav Ashi said:** The resurrection of the dead is alluded to **here** (Daniel 12:13): [11] **"But go you your way till the end be; for you shall rest, and stand up for your fate at the end of the days."** "You shall rest" — you shall die; "and stand up" — when you shall be resurrected from the dead.

RASHI

ומרוה גם הוא יורה — מי שמרווה את תלמידו בדבר הלכה, "גם הוא יורה" — לעולם הבא, לישנא אחרינא: ומרוה לשון "מורה". **ואתה לך לקץ ותנוח ותעמוד וגו'** — רמז לו שימות ויעמוד לאחר מכן "לקץ הימין" — לקץ שעתיד הקדוש ברוך הוא להחזיר ימינו לפניו, שהרי "השיב אחור ימינו".

NOTES

קֵץ הַיָּמִין **The end of the days.** Most Biblical commentators understand the word הַיָּמִין as הַיָּמִים, "the days," the letter *mem* having been replaced by the letter *nun* (see *Rashi*). *Ramah* cites the suggestion that the phrase means "the end referred to by the one with the right hand [הַיָּמִין]," about whom the verse states (Daniel 12:7): "And He lifted up His right hand and his left hand to heaven, and swore by that one who lives for ever, that it shall be for a time, times, and a half."

TRANSLATION AND COMMENTARY

אָמַר רַבִּי אֶלְעָזָר [1]**Rabbi Elazar said: Any community leader who leads** his **community with gentleness** — with justice and without anger — **will merit to lead them** also **in the World to Come,** [2]**as the verse states** (Isaiah 49:10): **"For he that has mercy upon them shall lead them, even by the springs of water shall he guide them."**

וְאָמַר רַבִּי אֶלְעָזָר [3]Having cited this statement of Rabbi Elazar, the Gemara now cites a series of statements of Rabbi Elazar on diverse topics. **Rabbi Elazar said:** Know that **knowledge is** of **great** importance, **for** we find that the word "knowledge" **was inserted between two** Divine **Names,** [4]**as the verse states** (I Samuel 2:3): **"For the Lord is an all-knowing God."**

וְאָמַר רַבִּי אֶלְעָזָר [5]**And Rabbi Elazar said:** Know that **the Temple is** also of **great** importance, **for** we find that the word "sanctuary" **was inserted between two** divine **names,** [6]**as the verse states: "In the place which You have made for You to dwell in, O Lord, in the sanctuary, O Lord, which Your hands have established."**

מַתְקִיף לָהּ [7]**Rav Adda Karḥina'ah raised an objection: But now,** according to this reasoning, **vengeance is** also of **great** importance, **for** we also find that the word "vengeance" **was inserted between two** divine **names,** [8]**as the verse states** (Psalms 94:1): **"O Lord God to whom vengeance belongs; O God, to whom vengeance belongs, shine forth"!**

אָמַר לֵיהּ [9]Rabbi Elazar **said to** Rav Adda Karḥina'ah: **When** vengeance **is needed, it is indeed** of great importance, **like** what **Ulla** said, [10]**for Ulla said:** One verse states (Psalms 94:1): "O Lord God to whom vengeance belongs; O God, to whom vengeance belongs, appear," and another verse states (Deuteronomy 33:2): "He appeared from Mount Paran." **These two** instances of **"appearing," why do** I need them? [11]**One for a measure of reward** — the revelation of the Torah at Sinai — **and one for a measure of punishment** — the punishment of the nations that subjugated Israel.

[1]אָמַר רַבִּי אֶלְעָזָר: כָּל פַּרְנָס שֶׁמַּנְהִיג אֶת הַצִּבּוּר בְּנַחַת — זוֹכֶה וּמַנְהִיגָם לָעוֹלָם הַבָּא, [2]שֶׁנֶּאֱמַר: ״כִּי מְרַחֲמָם יְנַהֲגֵם וְעַל מַבּוּעֵי מַיִם יְנַהֲלֵם״.

[3]וְאָמַר רַבִּי אֶלְעָזָר: גְּדוֹלָה דֵּעָה, שֶׁנִּיתְּנָה בֵּין שְׁתֵּי אוֹתִיּוֹת, [4]שֶׁנֶּאֱמַר: ״כִּי אֵל דֵּעוֹת ה׳״.

[5]וְאָמַר רַבִּי אֶלְעָזָר: גָּדוֹל מִקְדָּשׁ שֶׁנִּיתַּן בֵּין שְׁתֵּי אוֹתִיּוֹת, [6]שֶׁנֶּאֱמַר: ״פָּעַלְתָּ ה׳ מִקְּדָשׁ ה׳ כּוֹנְנוּ יָדֶיךָ״.

[7]מַתְקִיף לָהּ רַב אַדָּא קַרְחִינָאָה: אֶלָּא מֵעַתָּה גְּדוֹלָה נְקָמָה שֶׁנִּיתְּנָה בֵּין שְׁתֵּי אוֹתִיּוֹת, [8]דִּכְתִיב: ״אֵל נְקָמוֹת ה׳ אֵל נְקָמוֹת הוֹפִיעַ״!

[9]אָמַר לֵיהּ: לְמִילְּתֵיהּ, הָכִי נַמִי, כִּדְעוּלָּא, [10]דְּאָמַר עוּלָּא: שְׁתֵּי הוֹפָעִיּוֹת הַלָּלוּ, לָמָּה? [11]אַחַת לְמִדַּת טוֹבָה, וְאַחַת לְמִדַּת פּוּרְעָנוּת.

LITERAL TRANSLATION

[1]Rabbi Elazar said: Any community leader who leads the community with gentleness merits to lead them in the World to Come, [2]as it is stated: "For he who has mercy upon them shall lead them, even by the springs of water shall he guide them."

[3]And Rabbi Elazar said: Knowledge is great, for it was placed between two names, [4]as it is stated: "For the Lord is an all-knowing God."

[5]And Rabbi Elazar said: The Temple is great, for it was placed between two names, [6]as it is stated: "[In the place] which You have made [for You to dwell in], O Lord; in the sanctuary, O Lord, which Your hands have established."

[7]Rav Adda Karḥina'ah objected: But now vengeance is great, for it was placed between two names, [8]as it is written: "O Lord God to whom vengeance belongs; O God, to whom vengeance belongs, shine forth"!

[9]He said to him: For it's [an important] matter, it is also so, like Ulla, [10]for Ulla said: These two appearances, why? [11]One for a measure of reward, and one for a measure of punishment.

RASHI

מרחמם — בעולם הזה נהגם לעולם הבא. **שתי אותיות** — של שם, כך שמעתי, לישנא אחרינא: כל שמות על שם דאמרינן בעלמא (חגיגה טז,א) ״צבאות״ — אות הוא בצבא שלו, קרי להו אותיות לשון מופלא. **גדול מקדש** — חשוב הוא. **למילתיה הכי נמי** — דגדולה היא, וכדעולא. **שתי הופעיות** — דכתיב ״אל נקמות ה׳ אל נקמות הופיע״ ואיכא תרי נקמות וחדא הופעה בתרוייהו, ודמי כמאן דאיכא אכל נקמה ונקמה חדא הופעה. **חדא לטובה** — של ישראל שסילק שכינתו מאומות העולם ובא על ישראל וקרי ליה ״נקמות״ משום דתגמול טוב הוא שזכו לשכינה על שאמרו ״נעשה ונשמע״, ״ונקמה״ — היינו תגמול, ואחת לפורענות לנכרים שנפרע מהן ליום הדין, כדאמרינן בפרק קמא דמסכת עבודה זרה (ד,א) ״נוקם ה׳ ובעל חמה״ — לנכרים, שהוא בעצמו ובכבודו נפרע מהן, והיינו הופעה.

NOTES

מִדַּת טוֹבָה וּמִדַּת פּוּרְעָנוּת **A favorable measure, and a measure of punishment.** *Ramah* explains that the measure of reward refers to the compensation that Israel will receive for their servitude to the nations, and the measure of punishment refers to the punishment that the nations will receive for having subjected Israel to them.

[1]וְאָמַר רַבִּי אֶלְעָזָר: כָּל אָדָם שֶׁיֵּשׁ בּוֹ דֵּעָה כְּאִילּוּ נִבְנָה בֵּית הַמִּקְדָּשׁ בְּיָמָיו, [2]שֶׁזֶּה נִיתַּן בֵּין שְׁתֵּי אוֹתִיּוֹת וְזֶה נִיתַּן בֵּין שְׁתֵּי אוֹתִיּוֹת.

[3]וְאָמַר רַבִּי אֶלְעָזָר: כָּל אָדָם שֶׁיֵּשׁ בּוֹ דֵּעָה לַסּוֹף מִתְעַשֵּׁר, [4]שֶׁנֶּאֱמַר: ״וּבְדַעַת חֲדָרִים יִמָּלְאוּ כָּל הוֹן יָקָר וְנָעִים״.

[5]וְאָמַר רַבִּי אֶלְעָזָר: כָּל אָדָם שֶׁאֵין בּוֹ דֵּעָה אָסוּר לְרַחֵם עָלָיו, [6]שֶׁנֶּאֱמַר: ״כִּי לֹא עַם בִּינוֹת הוּא עַל כֵּן לֹא יְרַחֲמֶנּוּ עֹשֵׂהוּ וְיֹצְרוֹ לֹא יְחֻנֶּנּוּ״.

[7]וְאָמַר רַבִּי אֶלְעָזָר: כָּל הַנּוֹתֵן פִּיתּוֹ לְמִי שֶׁאֵין בּוֹ דֵּעָה — יִסּוּרִין בָּאִין עָלָיו, [8]שֶׁנֶּאֱמַר: ״לַחְמְךָ יָשִׂימוּ מָזוֹר תַּחְתֶּיךָ אֵין תְּבוּנָה בּוֹ״. [9]וְאֵין מָזוֹר אֶלָּא יִסּוּרִין, שֶׁנֶּאֱמַר: ״וַיַּרְא אֶפְרַיִם אֶת חָלְיוֹ וִיהוּדָה אֶת מְזֹרוֹ״.

[10]וְאָמַר רַבִּי אֶלְעָזָר: כָּל אָדָם שֶׁאֵין בּוֹ דֵּעָה לַסּוֹף גּוֹלֶה, [11]שֶׁנֶּאֱמַר: ״לָכֵן גָּלָה עַמִּי מִבְּלִי דָעַת״.

LITERAL TRANSLATION

[1]And Rabbi Elazar said: Any person who has knowledge is considered as if the Temple were built in his days, [2]for this was placed between two names, and this was placed between two names.

[3]And Rabbi Elazar said: Any person who has knowledge will in the end become rich, [4]as it is stated: "And by knowledge are the chambers filled with all precious and pleasant riches."

[5]And Rabbi Elazar said: Any person who has no knowledge — it is forbidden to have mercy upon him, [6]as it is stated: "For it is a people of no understanding; therefore its Maker will have no mercy on them, and its Creator will show them no favor."

[7]And Rabbi Elazar said: Whoever gives his bread to someone who has no knowledge — afflictions come upon him, [8]as it is stated: "[They who eat] your bread have laid a snare [*mazor*] under you. There is no discernment in him." [9]And *mazor* [can] only [mean] afflictions, as it is stated: "And Ephraim saw his sickness, and Judah saw his wound [*mezoro*]."

[10]And Rabbi Elazar said: Any person who has no knowledge will ultimately be exiled, [11]as it is stated: "Therefore My people are gone into exile, because they have no knowledge."

TRANSLATION AND COMMENTARY

וְאָמַר רַבִּי אֶלְעָזָר [1]**And Rabbi Elazar** connected together his two previous statements and **said: Any person who has knowledge is considered as if the Temple were** re**built in his days,** [2]**for** we find that the word "knowledge" **was inserted between two** Divine **Names, and** we also find that the word "sanctuary" **was inserted between two** Divine **Names,** as was explained above.

וְאָמַר רַבִּי אֶלְעָזָר [3]**And Rabbi Elazar said: Any person who has knowledge will in the end become rich,** [4]**as the verse states** (Proverbs 24:4): **"And by knowledge are the chambers filled with all precious and pleasant riches."**

וְאָמַר רַבִּי אֶלְעָזָר [5]**And Rabbi Elazar said: Any person who has no knowledge — one is forbidden to have mercy upon him,** [6]**as the verse states** (Isaiah 27:11): **"For it is a people of no understanding; therefore its Maker will not have mercy on them, and its Creator will show them no favor."** If God does not show mercy to people of no understanding, then certainly other people should not show them mercy.

וְאָמַר רַבִּי אֶלְעָזָר [7]**And Rabbi Elazar said: Whoever gives his bread to someone who does not have knowledge — afflictions come upon him,** [8]**as the verse states** (Obadiah 1:7): **"They who eat your bread have laid a snare** [*mazor*] **under you. There is no discernment in him."** This verse may be understood as teaching that someone who gives his bread to someone without discernment or knowledge will be overcome by afflictions, [9]for in this context the word *mazor* **refers to afflictions, as the verse states** (Hosea 5:13): **"And Ephraim saw his sickness, and Judah saw his wound** [מְזֹרוֹ]."

וְאָמַר רַבִּי אֶלְעָזָר [10]**And Rabbi Elazar said: Any person who has no knowledge will ultimately be exiled,** [11]**as the verse states** (Isaiah 5:13): **"Therefore My people are gone into exile, because they have no knowledge."**

RASHI

ובדעת — מפני הדעת מלאו כל החדרים הון. **בשביל לחמך** — שנתת למי שאין בו דעה — ״ישימו מזור תחתיך״.

NOTES

דֵּעָה Knowledge. The term *de'ah*, "knowledge," refers not to factual knowledge, but to understanding and a person's ability to use his knowledge to act properly, both towards himself and towards others. (It was in this sense that *Rambam* referred to the laws relating to ethical conduct as *Hilkhot De'ot*.)

אָסוּר לְרַחֵם עָלָיו One is forbidden to have mercy upon him. It has been suggested that when the Gemara says that one is forbidden to have mercy upon a person who does not have knowledge, it is referring to someone who does not wish to learn and acquire knowledge. Alternatively, the Gemara means to say that someone who does not make use of the essence of his humanity, his knowledge, forfeits his human form, and is no longer deserving of mercy

TRANSLATION AND COMMENTARY

וְאָמַר רַבִּי אֶלְעָזָר [1]And Rabbi Elazar said: Any house in which words of Torah are not heard at night will be consumed by fire, [2]as the verse states (Job 20:26): "Utter darkness is laid up for his treasures; a fire not blown shall consume him; it shall go ill with him who is left in his tent." Rabbi Elazar interprets the verse as referring to someone who does not study Torah at night. "Utter darkness is laid up for his treasures" — during the time of utter darkness, at night, he hides himself from the treasures of the Torah. "A fire not blown shall consume him" — a fire that does not need to be ignited, the fire of Hell, shall consume him. "It shall go ill with him who is left [*sarid*] in his tent." [3]The word *sarid* in this context **refers to a Torah scholar, as it is stated** elsewhere (Joel 3:5): **"And among the remnant** [*seridim*] **those whom the Lord shall call."**

וְאָמַר רַבִּי אֶלְעָזָר [4]**And Rabbi Elazar said: Whoever does not allow Torah scholars to benefit from his property will never see a blessing,** [5]**as the verse states** (Job 20:21): **"None of his food shall be left** [*sarid*]; **therefore shall his goods not prosper."** [6]The word *sarid* in this context **refers to Torah scholars,** [7]**as it is stated** elsewhere: **"And among the remnant** [*seridim*] **those whom the Lord shall call."**

וְאָמַר רַבִּי אֶלְעָזָר [8]**And Rabbi Elazar said: Whoever does not leave over bread on his table,** demonstrating gratitude to God for providing an abundance of food, **will never see a blessing,** [9]**as the verse states** (Job 20:21): **"None of his food shall be left; therefore shall his goods not prosper."**

[1]וְאָמַר רַבִּי אֶלְעָזָר: כָּל בַּיִת שֶׁאֵין דִּבְרֵי תוֹרָה נִשְׁמָעִים בּוֹ בַּלַּיְלָה אֵשׁ אוֹכַלְתּוֹ, [2]שֶׁנֶּאֱמַר: ״כָּל חֹשֶׁךְ טָמוּן לִצְפוּנָיו תְּאַכְלֵהוּ אֵשׁ לֹא נֻפָּח יֵרַע שָׂרִיד בְּאָהֳלוֹ״. [3]אֵין שָׂרִיד אֶלָּא תַּלְמִיד חָכָם, שֶׁנֶּאֱמַר: ״וּבַשְּׂרִידִים אֲשֶׁר ה׳ קֹרֵא״.
[4]וְאָמַר רַבִּי אֶלְעָזָר: כָּל שֶׁאֵינוֹ מְהַנֶּה תַלְמִידֵי חֲכָמִים מִנְּכָסָיו אֵינוֹ רוֹאֶה סִימַן בְּרָכָה לְעוֹלָם, [5]שֶׁנֶּאֱמַר: ״אֵין שָׂרִיד לְאָכְלוֹ; עַל כֵּן לֹא יָחִיל טוּבוֹ״. [6]אֵין שָׂרִיד אֶלָּא תַלְמִידֵי חֲכָמִים, [7]שֶׁנֶּאֱמַר: ״וּבַשְּׂרִידִים אֲשֶׁר ה׳ קֹרֵא״.
[8]וְאָמַר רַבִּי אֶלְעָזָר: כָּל שֶׁאֵינוֹ מְשַׁיֵּיר פַּת עַל שֻׁלְחָנוֹ אֵינוֹ רוֹאֶה סִימַן בְּרָכָה לְעוֹלָם, [9]שֶׁנֶּאֱמַר: ״אֵין שָׂרִיד לְאָכְלוֹ עַל כֵּן לֹא יָחִיל טוּבוֹ״.

LITERAL TRANSLATION

[1]And Rabbi Elazar said: Any house where words of Torah are not heard at night — fire will consume it, [2]as it is stated: "Utter darkness is laid up for his treasures; a fire not blown shall consume him; it shall go ill with him who is left [*sarid*] in his tent." [3]*Sarid* [can] only [mean] a Torah scholar, as it is stated: "And among the remnant those whom the Lord shall call."

[4]And Rabbi Elazar said: Whoever does not allow Torah scholars to benefit from his property will never see a blessing, [5]as it is stated: "None of his food shall be left [*sarid*]; therefore shall his goods not prosper." [6]*Sarid* [can] only [mean] Torah scholars, [7]as it is stated: "And among the remnant those whom the Lord shall call."

[8]And Rabbi Elazar said: Whoever does not leave over bread on his table will never see a blessing, [9]as it is stated: "None of his food shall be left [*sarid*]; therefore shall his goods not prosper."

RASHI

כל חשך טמון לצפוניו – כל לילה צפון ונחבא ממצפוני התורה, שאין דברי תורה נשמעין באותו בית. **תאכלהו אש לא נופח** – זה אשו של גיהנם, שאין צריך נפוח. **ירע שריד באהלו** – מי שרע בעיניו שיש שריד באהלו. **כל שאינו משייר פתיתין** – דצריך לשייר, כדכתיב ״אכול

NOTES

(*Maharsha*). Others explain that the Gemara is referring here to a person who is devoid of knowledge and requests things that will cause him injury. One is forbidden to have mercy upon such a person and accede to his demands (*Margoliyot HaYam*).

כָּל בַּיִת שֶׁאֵין דִּבְרֵי תוֹרָה נִשְׁמָעִים בּוֹ בַּלַּיְלָה Any house in which words of Torah are not heard at night. Some explain this passage in light of what the Rabbis say in praise of studying Torah at night, and the great blessing that such study brings (*Iyyun Yaakov*). *Maharsha* adds that during the day one may not hear words of Torah emanating from a certain house because of all the noise outside. But at night, when the streets are quiet, if words of Torah are not heard from a particular house, it must be that Torah is not being studied there (*Maharsha*).

כָּל חֹשֶׁךְ טָמוּן לִצְפוּנָיו Utter darkness is laid up for his treasures. *Rabbenu Yehonatan* explains that if a house is dark at night, and candles are not lit to illuminate the rooms, that is a sure sign that Torah is not being studied seriously there.

מְשַׁיֵּיר פַּת Leave bread. Some suggest that the ability to leave bread is itself the sign of a blessing (*Ri Almandri*).

HALAKHAH

כָּל בַּיִת שֶׁאֵין דִּבְרֵי תוֹרָה.... Any house in which words of Torah.... "Any house in which words of Torah are not heard at night will be consumed by fire." (*Rambam, Sefer Mada, Hilkhot Talmud Torah* 3:13; *Shulḥan Arukh, Yoreh Deah* 246:24.)

כָּל שֶׁאֵינוֹ מְשַׁיֵּיר פַּת עַל שֻׁלְחָנוֹ Whoever does not leave bread. "Whoever does not leave bread on his table will

TRANSLATION AND COMMENTARY

וְאָמַר רַבִּי אֶלְעָזָר [1]The Gemara raises an objection: **But surely Rabbi Elazar** himself **said: Whoever leaves bread crumbs on his table is considered as if he had served an idol,** for there was a pagan practice to leave the leftover food on the table as an offering to the guardian spirit of the house, an act regarded as idolatry, [2]**as the verse states** (Isaiah 65:11): **"That set out a table for Gad [Fortune], and fill the cup of liquor for Meni** [Destiny]."

לָא קַשְׁיָא [3]The Gemara answers: **This is not difficult.** [4]**Here,** where Rabbi Elazar said that one is forbidden to leave bread crumbs on the table, he was referring to **a whole** loaf placed on the table **with** the crumbs left over from his meal. Such conduct is forbidden, for it resembles an idolatrous practice. [5]And **here,** where Rabbi Elazar said one ought to leave his bread crumbs on the table, he was referring to a person who did **not** bring out **a whole** loaf and place it on the table **with** the crumbs. Such conduct is praiseworthy, for it does not resemble an idolatrous practice. Rather, it looks as if he is leaving the food for the poor.

וְאָמַר רַבִּי אֶלְעָזָר [6]**And Rabbi Elazar said: Whoever changes his word is considered as if he had served an idol.** [7]**Here,** where Jacob was preparing himself to appear before his father Isaac in order to receive the blessing that was intended for his brother Esau, **the verse states** (Genesis 27:12): **"And I shall seem to him a deceiver."** [8]**And elsewhere,** regarding idolatry, **the verse states** (Jeremiah 10:15): **"They are vanity, the work of deception."** Thus, we see that deception is equated with idol worship.

וְאָמַר רַבִּי אֶלְעָזָר [9]**And Rabbi Elazar said: Whoever looks at a woman's nakedness — his bow will be empty** (his virility will be undermined), [10]**as the verse states** (Habakkuk 3:9): **"Your bow is stripped bare."**

[1]וְהָאָמַר רַבִּי אֶלְעָזָר: כָּל הַמְּשַׁיֵּיר פְּתִיתִים עַל שֻׁלְחָנוֹ כְּאִילּוּ עוֹבֵד עֲבוֹדָה זָרָה, [2]שֶׁנֶּאֱמַר: ״הָעֹרְכִים לַגַּד שֻׁלְחָן וְהַמְמַלְאִים לַמְנִי מִמְסָךְ״! [3]לָא קַשְׁיָא. [4]הָא, דְּאִיכָּא שְׁלֵימָה בַּהֲדֵיהּ. [5]הָא, דְּלֵיכָּא שְׁלֵימָה בַּהֲדֵיהּ. [6]וְאָמַר רַבִּי אֶלְעָזָר: כָּל הַמַּחֲלִיף בְּדִיבּוּרוֹ כְּאִילּוּ עוֹבֵד עֲבוֹדָה זָרָה. [7]כְּתִיב הָכָא: ״וְהָיִיתִי בְעֵינָיו כִּמְתַעְתֵּעַ״. [8]וּכְתִיב הָתָם: ״הֶבֶל הֵמָּה, מַעֲשֵׂה תַּעְתֻּעִים״. [9]וְאָמַר רַבִּי אֶלְעָזָר: כָּל הַמִּסְתַּכֵּל בָּעֶרְוָה — קַשְׁתּוֹ נִנְעֶרֶת, [10]שֶׁנֶּאֱמַר: ״עֶרְיָה תֵעוֹר קַשְׁתֶּךָ״.

LITERAL TRANSLATION

[1]But surely Rabbi Elazar said: Whoever leaves bread crumbs on his table is considered as if he served an idol, [2]as it is stated: "That set out a table for Gad [Fortune] and who fill a mixing bowl for Meni [Destiny]."

[3]This is not difficult. [4]This, when there is a whole one with it. [5]This, when there is not a whole one with it.

[6]And Rabbi Elazar said: Whoever changes his word is considered as if he served an idol. [7]It is written here: "And I shall seem to him a deceiver." [8]And it is written there: "They are vanity, the work of deception."

[9]And Rabbi Elazar said: Whoever looks at a woman's nakedness — his bow will be empty, [10]as it is stated: "Your bow is stripped bare."

RASHI

והא אמר רבי אלעזר כל המשייר פתיתין על שולחנו כאילו עובד עבודה זרה, שנאמר "העורכים לגד שולחן" — שכן עושין, שמניחין שלחן ערוך במאכל ומשתה לשם אותה עבודה זרה שקורין גד, וממלאים כוסות של מרקחים נסוכים לעבודה זרה ששמה מני. **הא** — דקאמר אסור. **דאיכא שלימה בהדיה** — שמביא שלימה לאחר שאכל, ונותן על השלחן עם הפתיתין ששייר, דמחזי דלשם עבודה זרה עביד הכי. **והא** — דליכא שלימה בהדייהו, דמזומנין לעני. **הא גדא לביתיה** — לא גרסינן. **המחליף בדבורו** — משנה בדבורו, שלא יהא ניכר. **קשתו נערת** — כח קושי אבר שלו ננער, שאינו מוליד, שנאמר "עריה תעור קשתך" עריה שאתה מסתכל בה ממש בערותה — היא תעיר קשתך, דבר אחר: **המסתכל** — המחשב בעריות דאשת איש, קשתו = גבורת ידו **נערת** — מתהלכת ומתמעטת, כמו (בבא מציעא כט,ב) מלא כסות מנערה אחת לשלשים יום, אי נמי כמו (שמות יד) "וינער ה׳".

NOTES

Others explain that a person must leave bread on his table, so that if a pauper enters at the end of the meal, he will be able to let the pauper eat immediately (*Ramah, Rabbenu Yehonatan*).

הָא, דְּאִיכָּא שְׁלֵימָה בַּהֲדֵיהּ **This, where there is a whole one with it.** There are various readings of this passage. According to the reading of *Ramah*, a person is only forbidden to leave his bread crumbs on the table if he does not also leave a whole loaf with them. But if he leaves a whole loaf with the crumbs, there is no problem, for the idolatrous practice was limited to bread crumbs. Moreover, a person is only forbidden to leave his bread crumbs on the table if he states explicitly that he is leaving them there as an offering to the guardian spirit of the house.

כָּל הַמַּחֲלִיף בְּדִיבּוּרוֹ **Whoever changes his word.** According to *Rashi*, this refers to a person who disguises his voice, to

HALAKHAH

never receive a blessing. But a person should not bring a whole loaf and leave it on the table — that practice resembles idol worship. *Mishnah Berurah* adds that this applies only if bread crumbs were already on the table." (*Shulḥan Arukh, Oraḥ Ḥayyim* 180:2.)

[1]וְאָמַר רַבִּי אֶלְעָזָר: לְעוֹלָם הֱוֵי קָבֵל וְקַיָּים.
[2]אָמַר רַבִּי זֵירָא: אַף אֲנַן נַמִי תְּנֵינָא: [3]״בַּיִת אָפֵל אֵין פּוֹתְחִין לוֹ חַלּוֹנוֹת לִרְאוֹת נִגְעוֹ״.
[4]שְׁמַע מִינָּהּ.
[5]אָמַר רַבִּי טָבִי אָמַר רַבִּי יֹאשִׁיָּה: מַאי דִּכְתִיב: [6]״שְׁאוֹל וְעֹצֶר רָחַם אֶרֶץ לֹא שָׂבְעָה מַּיִם״? [7]וְכִי מָה עִנְיַן שְׁאוֹל אֵצֶל רֶחֶם? [8]אֶלָּא לוֹמַר לְךָ: מָה רֶחֶם מַכְנִיס וּמוֹצִיא, [9]אַף שְׁאוֹל מַכְנִיס וּמוֹצִיא. [10]וַהֲלֹא דְּבָרִים קַל וָחוֹמֶר: וּמָה רֶחֶם שֶׁמַּכְנִיסִין בּוֹ בַּחֲשַׁאי, מוֹצִיאִין מִמֶּנּוּ בְּקוֹלֵי קוֹלוֹת, [11]שְׁאוֹל שֶׁמַּכְנִיסִין בּוֹ בְּקוֹלוֹת, אֵינוֹ דִּין שֶׁמּוֹצִיאִין מִמֶּנּוּ בְּקוֹלֵי קוֹלוֹת? [12]מִיכָּן תְּשׁוּבָה לָאוֹמְרִין אֵין תְּחִיַּית הַמֵּתִים מִן הַתּוֹרָה.

LITERAL TRANSLATION

[1]And Rabbi Elazar said: Forever be in the dark, and live.

[2]Rabbi Zera said: We, too, have learned thus: [3]"We do not open windows in a dark house to see its sickness."

[4]Infer from this.

[5]Rabbi Tavi said in the name of Rabbi Yoshiyah: What is that which is written: [6]"The grave and the barren womb; that earth that is never sated with water"? [7]What is the connection between the grave and a womb? [8]Rather, to teach you: Just as a womb lets in and sends out, [9]so, too, the grave lets in and sends out. [10]And surely these things are a *kal vahomer*: If [regarding] a womb into which we bring in secretly, we take out from it with great noise, [11][regarding] the grave, into which we bring in with great noise, is it not fitting that we should take out from it with great noise? [12]From here an answer to those who say there is no resurrection of the dead from the Torah.

TRANSLATION AND COMMENTARY

וְאָמַר רַבִּי אֶלְעָזָר [1]**And Rabbi Elazar said: Forever be in the dark** — out of the limelight — **and** you will **live** a long life.

אָמַר רַבִּי זֵירָא [2]**Rabbi Zera said: We, too, have learned** a similar idea in a Mishnah (*Nega'im* 2:3): [3]"If a suspicion arose that leprous spots had appeared on the walls of **a dark house** with no windows, **we do not make openings** in the walls in order to allow a priest **to** come and **examine** the house for **leprous spots."**

שְׁמַע מִינָּהּ [4]Indeed, we may **infer from this** that remaining in the dark can be advantageous, for until a priest can properly examine the house and confirm that there is evidence of leprosy, it remains ritually pure.

אָמַר רַבִּי טָבִי [5]The Gemara now resumes its discussion regarding the resurrection of the dead. **Rabbi Tavi said in the name of Rabbi Yoshiyah: What is** meant by the verse **that states** (Proverbs 30:16): [6]**"The grave and the barren womb; that earth that is never sated with water"?** [7]**Why is the grave** compared **to a womb?** [8]**Rather,** this **teaches you** that **just as a** woman's **womb lets in** a man's sperm **and** nine months later **sends out** a baby, [9]**so, too, the grave lets in** the deceased **and** will one day **send** him **out** again when the dead will be resurrected. [10]**And surely this** may be learned by way of **a *kal vahomer*** argument: **If, regarding a womb into which** the sperm **is brought in secretly,** the baby **is taken out amidst great noise,** [11]then **regarding the grave, into which** the deceased **is brought amidst great noise** while the grieving relatives are crying over their loss, **does it not follow that** the dead **will** one day **be taken out amidst great noise,** as the verse states (Isaiah 27:13): "And it shall come to pass on that day, that a great shofar shall be blown"? [12]**Here** we have **an answer to those who say there is no** allusion to the **resurrection of the dead in the Torah.**

RASHI

הוי קבל — הוי עניו ותחיה, קבל — לשון אפל, עשה עצמך אפל ושפל. **בית אפל אין פותחין בו חלונות לראות את נגעו** — "כנגע נראה לי בבית" כתיב, דמשמע נראה מאליו, ועוד דכתיב "לי" — ולא לאורי, נמצא שאפלתו הצלתו, דכל זמן שאין כהן רואהו — אין מטמא בנגעים. **שאול ועוצר רחם ארץ לא שבעה מים** — קבר לא שבע ממתים, ועוצר רחם — בית הרחם שהוא קלור עצור לא ישבע מבעילות, וכן ארץ לא שבעה מים. **וכי מה ענין שאול וכו׳** — למה נסמכו הני אהדדי. **מכניס** — הזרע ומוציא הולד, אף שאול מכניס ומוציא לתחיית המתים. **שמכניסין בה בקולי קולות** — בבכי גדול קוברין את המת. **אינו דין שמוציאין אותו בקולי קולות** — שנאמר "יתקע בשופר גדול".

NOTES

avoid recognition. Even if a person does not mean to deceive anybody at the time, he should avoid such a practice, for it is the way of wicked and deceptive people (*Ri Bacharach*).

HALAKHAH

בַּיִת אָפֵל **A dark house.** "If a suspicion arises that leprous spots have appeared on the walls of a dark house with no windows, we do not make openings in the walls to allow a priest to examine the house for leprous spots, and so the house remains ritually pure." (*Rambam, Sefer Taharah, Hilkhot Tum'at Tzara'at* 14:5.)

[1] תָּנָא דְּבֵי אֵלִיָּהוּ: ״צַדִּיקִים שֶׁעָתִיד הַקָּדוֹשׁ בָּרוּךְ הוּא לְהַחֲיוֹתָן אֵינָן חוֹזְרִין לַעֲפָרָן, [2] שֶׁנֶּאֱמַר: ׳וְהָיָה הַנִּשְׁאָר בְּצִיּוֹן וְהַנּוֹתָר בִּירוּשָׁלַיִם קָדוֹשׁ יֵאָמֶר לוֹ כָּל הַכָּתוּב לַחַיִּים בִּירוּשָׁלָיִם׳. [3] מַה קָּדוֹשׁ לְעוֹלָם קַיָּים, אַף הֵם לְעוֹלָם קַיָּימִין. [92B] [4] וְאִם תֹּאמַר: אוֹתָן שָׁנִים שֶׁעָתִיד הַקָּדוֹשׁ בָּרוּךְ הוּא לְחַדֵּשׁ בָּהֶן אֶת עוֹלָמוֹ, [5] שֶׁנֶּאֱמַר: ׳וְנִשְׂגַּב ה׳ לְבַדּוֹ בַּיּוֹם הַהוּא׳ — צַדִּיקִים מָה הֵן עוֹשִׂין? [6] הַקָּדוֹשׁ בָּרוּךְ הוּא עוֹשֶׂה לָהֶם כְּנָפַיִם כַּנְּשָׁרִים, וְשָׁטִין עַל פְּנֵי הַמַּיִם, [7] שֶׁנֶּאֱמַר: ׳עַל כֵּן לֹא נִירָא בְּהָמִיר אָרֶץ וּבְמוֹט הָרִים בְּלֵב יַמִּים׳. [8] וְשֶׁמָּא תֹּאמַר יֵשׁ לָהֶם צַעַר — [9] תַּלְמוּד לוֹמַר: ׳וְקוֹיֵ ה׳ יַחֲלִיפוּ כֹחַ יַעֲלוּ אֵבֶר כַּנְּשָׁרִים יָרוּצוּ וְלֹא יִיגָעוּ יֵלְכוּ וְלֹא יִיעָפוּ׳״.

[10] וְנֵילַף מִמֵּתִים שֶׁהֶחֱיָה יְחֶזְקֵאל!

LITERAL TRANSLATION

[1] [A Tanna] of the School of Eliyahu taught: "The righteous whom the Holy One, blessed is He, will revive in the future do not return to their dust, [2] as it is stated: 'And it shall come to pass, that he who is left in Zion, and he who remains in Jerusalem, shall be called holy, everyone in Jerusalem who is written to life.' [3] Just as the Holy One exists forever, so, too, [do] they exist forever. [92B] [4] And if you say: [In] the years when the Holy One, blessed be He, is in the future to renew His world, as it is stated: [5] 'And the Lord alone shall be exalted on that day' — what will the righteous do? [6] The Holy One, blessed is He, will make them wings like eagles, and they will fly over the water, [7] as it is stated: 'Therefore, we will not fear, though the earth changes, and though the mountains are moved in the midst of the sea.' [8] And lest you say: They will be in distress — therefore, [9] the verse states: 'But they who wait upon the Lord shall renew their strength; they shall mount up with wings as eagles; they shall run, and not be weary; they shall walk, and not faint.'"

[10] But let us learn from the dead whom Ezekiel resurrected!

TRANSLATION AND COMMENTARY

תָּנָא דְּבֵי אֵלִיָּהוּ [1] **A Tanna of the School of Eliyahu taught** a Baraita: **"The righteous** people **whom the Holy One, blessed be He, will eventually restore to life will not return** once again **to their dust,** [2] **as the verse states** (Isaiah 4:3): **'And it shall come to pass, that he who is left in Zion, and he who remains in Jerusalem, shall be called holy, everyone in Jerusalem who is written to life.'** [3] **Just as the Holy One exists forever, so, too,** those righteous people who will be resurrected shall continue to **exist forever.** [92B] [4] **And** you might **ask:** In the **years when the Holy One, blessed is He, will** destroy this world and **create a new world, as the verse states** (Isaiah 2:11): [5] **'And the Lord alone shall be exalted on that day' — what will the righteous** people **do?** [6] The answer is that **the Holy One, blessed is He, will make them wings like eagles, and they will fly over the water,** [7] **as the verse states** (Psalms 46:3): **'Therefore, we will not fear, though the earth changes, and though the mountains are moved in the midst of the sea.'** [8] **And lest you say** that the righteous **will suffer** great **distress** if they are forced to fly constantly while God refashions His world — **therefore,** [9] **the verse states** (Isaiah 40:31): **'But they that wait upon the Lord shall renew their strength; they shall mount up with wings as eagles; they shall run, and not be weary; they shall walk, and not faint.'"**

וְנֵילַף [10] The Gemara objects: **But let us learn from the dead whom** the Prophet **Ezekiel resurrected** and who are surely no longer alive, that after the dead are restored to life, they will not live forever!

RASHI

שעתיד הקדוש ברוך הוא להחיות — לימות המשיח. לאחר שיחיו שוב **אין חוזרין לעפרם** — בין (לימות המשיח בין לעולם הבא), אלא הבשר מתקיים עליהם עד שישובו ויחיו לעתיד לבא. **ואותן שנים שעתיד הקדוש ברוך הוא לחדש את עולמו** — ויהיה עולם זה חרב אלף שנים אותן לדיקים היכן הם הואיל ואינן נקברין בארץ. **לא נירא בהמיר ארץ** — כשמחליף הקדוש ברוך הוא את הארץ לא נירא לפי שאנו בלב ימים. **וקווי ה׳ יחליפו כח** — שיהא להם כח לשוט ולעופף בלי צער. **ונילף ממתים שהחיה יחזקאל** — שחזרו ומתו כך לדיקים שעתיד להחיות יחזרו לעפרם כך שמעתי, יחזקאל הגלהו נבוכדנצר עם יכניה מלך יהודה והיה יחזקאל מתנבא בבבל וירמיה בארץ ישראל באותן אחת עשרה שנה שמלך צדקיה.

NOTES

וְנֵילַף מִמֵּתִים **But let us learn from the dead.** Our commentary follows *Rashi,* who understands that the Gemara is arguing that we should learn from the dead whom Ezekiel resurrected that, after the dead are restored to life, they will not live forever, but rather will die again. *Maharsha* and others understand the Gemara's question differently: Let us learn from the dead whom Ezekiel resurrected that the resurrection of the dead is indeed possible, against the heretics who denied it. The Gemara answers that we cannot prove anything from the story of Ezekiel and the dry bones, because some commentators maintain that the story is only a parable.

[1]סָבַר לָהּ כְּמַאן דְּאָמַר: בֶּאֱמֶת מָשָׁל הָיָה.

[2]דְּתַנְיָא: [3]״רַבִּי אֱלִיעֶזֶר אוֹמֵר: מֵתִים שֶׁהֶחֱיָה יְחֶזְקֵאל עָמְדוּ עַל רַגְלֵיהֶם, וְאָמְרוּ שִׁירָה וָמֵתוּ. [4]מַה שִּׁירָה אָמְרוּ? [5]׳ה׳ מֵמִית בְּצֶדֶק וּמְחַיֶּה בְּרַחֲמִים׳. [6]רַבִּי יְהוֹשֻׁעַ אוֹמֵר: שִׁירָה זוֹ אָמְרוּ: ׳ה׳ מֵמִית וּמְחַיֶּה מוֹרִיד שְׁאוֹל וַיָּעַל׳. [7]רַבִּי יְהוּדָה אוֹמֵר: אֱמֶת מָשָׁל הָיָה. [8]אָמַר לוֹ רַבִּי נְחֶמְיָה: אִם אֱמֶת — לָמָּה מָשָׁל, וְאִם מָשָׁל — לָמָּה אֱמֶת? [9]אֶלָּא: בֶּאֱמֶת מָשָׁל הָיָה. [10]רַבִּי אֱלִיעֶזֶר בְּנוֹ שֶׁל רַבִּי יוֹסֵי הַגְּלִילִי אוֹמֵר: מֵתִים שֶׁהֶחֱיָה יְחֶזְקֵאל עָלוּ לְאֶרֶץ יִשְׂרָאֵל, וְנָשְׂאוּ נָשִׁים וְהוֹלִידוּ בָּנִים וּבָנוֹת. [11]עָמַד רַבִּי יְהוּדָה בֶּן בְּתֵירָא עַל רַגְלָיו וְאָמַר: ׳אֲנִי מִבְּנֵי בְנֵיהֶם, [12]וְהַלָּלוּ תְּפִילִּין שֶׁהִנִּיחַ לִי אֲבִי אַבָּא מֵהֶם׳״.

[13]וּמַאן נִינְהוּ מֵתִים שֶׁהֶחֱיָה יְחֶזְקֵאל? [14]אָמַר רַב: אֵלּוּ בְּנֵי

LITERAL TRANSLATION

[1]He agrees with the one who said: In truth, it was a parable.

[2]For it was taught: [3]"Rabbi Eliezer said: The dead whom Ezekiel resurrected stood on their feet, sang a song, and died. [4]What song did they sing? [5]'The Lord kills with righteousness, and gives life with mercy.' [6]Rabbi Yehoshua says: They sang this song: 'The Lord kills, and gives life; He brings down to the underworld, and brings up.' [7]Rabbi Yehudah says: It was truly a parable. [8]Rabbi Neḥemyah said: If the truth, why a parable, and if a parable, why the truth? [9]Rather, in truth, it was a parable. [10]Rabbi Eliezer the son of Rabbi Yose the Galilean says: The dead whom Ezekiel resurrected went up to Eretz Israel, and married women, and fathered sons and daughters. [11]Rabbi Yehudah ben Betera stood up on his feet and said: 'I am of the sons of their sons, [12]and these are the tefillin that the father of my father left me from them.'"

[13]And who were those dead whom Ezekiel resurrected? [14]Rav said: They were the sons

TRANSLATION AND COMMENTARY

סָבַר לָהּ [1]The Gemara explains that the Tanna of the School of Eliyahu **agrees with the** Tanna **who said** that, **in truth,** the story of the dry bones that Ezekiel brought back to life did not really happen, but rather **it was a parable,** intimating that just as the dry bones came back to life, so, too, the people of Israel will one day return from their exile to Eretz Israel.

דְּתַנְיָא [2]Not everyone agrees that this was merely a parable. **It was taught** in a Baraita: [3]**"Rabbi Eliezer said: The dead whom Ezekiel resurrected stood on their feet, sang a song** of praise to God, **and** then **died.** [4]**What song did they sing?** [5]**'The Lord kills with righteousness, and gives life with mercy.'** [6]**Rabbi Yehoshua says: They sang this song** taken from the prayer recited by Hannah (I Samuel 2:6): **'The Lord kills, and gives life; He brings down to the grave, and brings up.'** [7]**Rabbi Yehudah says:** The story of Ezekiel and the dry bones **was the truth of a parable.** [8]**Rabbi Neḥemyah said:** If that story was **the truth,** then **why** say that is was **a parable, and if** it was **a parable,** the **why** say that it was **the truth?** [9]**Rather,** we should say as follows: **In truth,** the story of Ezekiel and the dry bones did not really happen, but rather it **was a parable** intimating that the people of Israel would one day return to Eretz Israel. [10]In disagreement, **Rabbi Eliezer the son of Rabbi Yose the Galilean says:** Not only did Ezekiel really restore those dry bones to life, but **the dead whom Ezekiel resurrected** later **went to Eretz Israel, married women, and fathered sons and daughters** whose descendants live to this very day. [11]**Rabbi Yehudah ben Betera stood up on his feet and said: 'I** myself **am** one **of their descendants,** [12]**and these are the tefillin that my grandfather left me from them.'"**

וּמַאן נִינְהוּ [13]The Gemara asks: **Who were the dead** people **whom Ezekiel resurrected?** [14]**Rav said: They were members** of the tribe **of Ephraim who calculated the** promised **end** to Israel's slavery in Egypt **incorrectly,**

RASHI

באמת – בברור. **משל היה** – שהיה מרמז להם על הגלות, כאדם מת שחוזר וחי, כך ישראל ישובו מן הגלות. **מהם** – שאותן תפילין היו שלהם.

NOTES

בֶּאֱמֶת מָשָׁל הָיָה **In truth, it was a parable.** Some explain this expression in light of the rule that every instance of "in truth" is the law, that is to say, Rabbi Yehudah meant to emphasize his position, and so he said: In truth, it is absolutely accepted that the story involving the dry bones was a parable (*Torat Ḥayyim*). Others suggest that Rabbi Yehudah meant to say that in truth Ezekiel restored the dry bones to life, but his main purpose was not to resurrect those dead people, but rather to reassure Israel that they would eventually return to Eretz Israel, and so they should not despair (*Radak*).

בְּנֵי אֶפְרַיִם **The sons of Ephraim.** According to the Midrash (see *Rashi*), members of the tribe of Ephraim calculated the promised end to Israel's slavery in Egypt incorrectly, and as a result left Egypt thirty years too soon. They tried to reach Eretz Israel through the land of the Philistines, but they

TRANSLATION AND COMMENTARY

counting the four hundred years mentioned in Genesis 15:13 from the time that God made His Covenant with Abraham, rather than from the time of Isaac's birth thirty years later. Thus, they left Egypt thirty years too early, only to be killed while on their way to Eretz Israel, [1]**as the verse states** (I Chronicles 7:21-22): **"And the sons of Ephraim; Shutelah, and Bered his son, and Tahat his son, and El'ada his son, and Tahat his son, and Zavad his son, and Shutelah his son, and Ezer, and Elead, whom the men of Gat that were born in that land slew,** because they came down to take away their cattle." [2]**And the next verse states** (I Chronicles 7:23): **"And Ephraim their father mourned many days, and his brothers came to comfort him."**

וּשְׁמוּאֵל אָמַר [3]**Shmuel said:** The people whom Ezekiel restored to life **were people who** during their lifetime had **denied the resurrection of the dead,** [4]**as the verse states** (Ezekiel 37:11): **"Then he said to me, Son of man, these bones are the whole house of Israel; behold they say, Our bones are dried, and our hope is lost; we are cut off."** Just as these people had given up hope of resurrection but were resurrected, so, too, the house of Israel will be rescued, even though they have given up hope.

רַבִּי יִרְמְיָה בַּר אַבָּא [5]**Rabbi Yirmeyah bar Abba said:** The people whom Ezekiel restored to life **were people who lacked the vitality** that comes from keeping the Torah's **commandments,** [6]**as the verse states** (Ezekiel 37:4): **"O dry bones, hear the word of the Lord"** — implying that those people were like dry bones even during their lifetime." If even such dry people can be brought back to life, so, too, can the entire people of Israel.

רַבִּי יִצְחָק נַפָּחָא [7]**Rabbi Yitzhak Napaha said:** The **people** whom Ezekiel brought back to life **had covered** the walls **of the entire Sanctuary with**

אֶפְרַיִם שֶׁמָּנוּ לַקֵּץ וְטָעוּ, [1]שֶׁנֶּאֱמַר: "וּבְנֵי אֶפְרַיִם שׁוּתָלַח וּבֶרֶד בְּנוֹ וְתַחַת בְּנוֹ וְאֶלְעָדָה בְנוֹ וְתַחַת בְּנוֹ וְזָבָד בְּנוֹ וְשׁוּתֶלַח בְּנוֹ וְעֵזֶר וְאֶלְעָד וַהֲרָגוּם אַנְשֵׁי גַת הַנּוֹלָדִים בָּאָרֶץ וגו׳". [2]וּכְתִיב: "וַיִּתְאַבֵּל אֶפְרַיִם אֲבִיהֶם יָמִים רַבִּים וַיָּבֹאוּ אֶחָיו לְנַחֲמוֹ".

[3]וּשְׁמוּאֵל אָמַר: אֵלּוּ בְּנֵי אָדָם שֶׁכָּפְרוּ בִּתְחִיַּית הַמֵּתִים, [4]שֶׁנֶּאֱמַר: "וַיֹּאמֶר אֵלַי בֶּן אָדָם הָעֲצָמוֹת הָאֵלֶּה כָּל בֵּית יִשְׂרָאֵל הֵמָּה הִנֵּה אֹמְרִים יָבְשׁוּ עַצְמוֹתֵינוּ וְאָבְדָה תִקְוָתֵנוּ נִגְזַרְנוּ לָנוּ".

[5]רַבִּי יִרְמְיָה בַּר אַבָּא אָמַר: אֵלּוּ בְּנֵי אָדָם שֶׁאֵין בָּהֶן לַחְלוּחִית שֶׁל מִצְוָה, [6]שֶׁנֶּאֱמַר: "הָעֲצָמוֹת הַיְבֵשׁוֹת שִׁמְעוּ דְּבַר ה׳".

[7]רַבִּי יִצְחָק נַפָּחָא אָמַר: אֵלּוּ בְּנֵי אָדָם שֶׁחִיפּוּ אֶת הַהֵיכָל

LITERAL TRANSLATION

of Ephraim who calculated the end and erred, [1]as it is stated: "And the sons of Ephraim; Shutelah, and Bered his son, and Tahat his son, and El'ada his son, and Tahat his son, and Zavad his son, and Shutelah his son, and Ezer, and Elead, whom the men of Gat who were born in that land slew, etc." [2]And it is written: "And Ephraim their father mourned many days, and his brothers came to comfort him."

[3]And Shmuel said: They were people who denied the resurrection of the dead, [4]as it is stated: "Then he said to me, Son of man, these bones are the whole house of Israel; behold they say, Our bones are dried, and our hope is lost; we are cut off."

[5]Rabbi Yirmeyah bar Abba said: They were people who lacked the vitality of a commandment, [6]as it is stated: "O dry bones, hear the word of the Lord."

[7]Rabbi Yitzhak Napaha said: They were people who covered the entire Sanctuary

RASHI

שמנו לקץ — של יציאת מצרים. **וטעו** — שלא היה להם למנות גזירת ועבדום וענו אותם אלא משנולד יצחק, דהא כתיב (בראשית טו) "כי גר יהיה זרעך" — זה יצחק, דכתיב (שם כא) "כי ביצחק יקרא לך זרע" והם מנו משעת הדיבור לאברהם. ותניא בסדר עולם: אברהם אבינו בשעה שנדבר עמו בין הבתרים בן שבעים שנה היה, ומבין הבתרים עד שנולד יצחק היה שלשים שנה, כדכתיב (בראשית כא) "ואברהם בן מאת שנה בהולד לו את יצחק בנו", נמצאת אומר משדבר עמו בין הבתרים עד שיצאו ממצרים היו ארבע מאות, ואותן שלשים שמן הדבור עד לידת יצחק טעו בני אפרים, ומניין שבני אפרים הן שיצאו קודם זמנן ונהרגו — שנאמר "ובני אפרים שותלח וגו׳ והרגום אנשי גת". **ושמואל אמר** — מתים שהחיה יחזקאל אלו בני אדם שכפרו בתחיית המתים שנאמר (יחזקאל לז) "אבדה תקותנו". **העצמות האלה כל בית ישראל המה** — עצמות הללו סימן לכל ישראל הן שעתידה להם תחיית המתים כמו לאלו שהרי אלו אמרו אבדה תקותנו ועכשו ידעו שאני מחיה את המתים וסימן זה לכל ישראל שגם הם עתידין להחיות ולא מן הדין חיו דהא אמרן הכופר בתחיית המתים אין לו חלק לעולם הבא אלא משום סימן חיו. **שחיפו להיכל** — שהיו מציירין צלמים על קירות ההיכל דכתיב ובא וראה מחוקה על הקיר סביב.

NOTES

were killed by the Philistines. Consequently, when God took Israel out of Egypt, He did not lead them through the land of the Philistines, lest they be overcome by fear of another slaughter. The verse (Psalms 78:9): "The children of Ephraim were as archers, carrying bows, who turned back in the day of battle," has been understood as alluding to the early departure from Egypt of Ephraim's people, and their route to Eretz Israel.

TRANSLATION AND COMMENTARY

pictures of **abominable beasts and creeping things,** [1]for elsewhere in the book of Ezekiel **the verse states** (Ezekiel 8:10): **"So I went in and saw; and behold every form of creeping thing, and abominable beast, and all the idols of the house of Israel, traced upon the wall *all around*."** [2]**And here** in the story of the dry bones **the verse states** (Ezekiel 37:2): **"And He caused me to pass by them *all around*."** Even though these people did not merit resurrection, God restored them to life as a sign of hope to the rest of the people of Israel.

רַבִּי יוֹחָנָן [3]**Rabbi Yoḥanan said:** The people whom Ezekiel resurrected **were the people who had died** at the hand of the wicked Babylonian king, Nebuchadnezzar, **in Bik'at Dura,** as will be explained below. [4]**And Rabbi Yoḥanan said:** Those who were executed by Nebuchadnezzar came **from the Eshel River to Ramat Bik'at Dura.** [5]**When the wicked Nebuchadnezzar exiled Israel, there were among them** certain **young men** who were so handsome that they **put the sun to shame with their beauty.** [6]**The Chaldean women would look at them** and become filled with such lust that they **issued a heavy discharge.** [7]**They told their husbands** about the passions that those young Jewish men were stirring in their hearts, **and their husbands told the king.** [8]**The king issued a decree, and had** the young men **killed.** [9]**But the** Chaldean women **continued to issue a heavy discharge,** because the handsome young men had remained attractive even after their death. [10]**The king issued a** second **decree, and had them trampled,** to mutilate their bodies.

תָּנוּ רַבָּנַן [11]**Our Rabbis taught** the following Baraita: **"When the wicked Nebuchadnezzar cast Hananiah, Mishael and Azariah into the fiery furnace, the Holy One, blessed is He, said to Ezekiel: 'Go, and resurrect the dead in Bik'at Dura.'** [12]**When he resurrected them, the** revived **bones went and slapped that wicked man** Nebuchadnezzar **in the face.** [13]and Nebuchadnezzar **asked: 'What is the nature of these?'** [14]His men **explained to him: 'The friend of these** men whom you had cast into the furnace **is resurrecting the dead**

כּוּלּוֹ שְׁקָצִים וּרְמָשִׂים, [1]שֶׁנֶּאֱמַר: ״וָאָבוֹא וָאֶרְאֶה וְהִנֵּה כָל תַּבְנִית רֶמֶשׂ וּבְהֵמָה שֶׁקֶץ וְכָל גִּלּוּלֵי בֵּית יִשְׂרָאֵל מְחֻקֶּה עַל הַקִּיר סָבִיב וגו׳״. [2]וּכְתִיב הָתָם: ״וְהֶעֱבִירַנִי עֲלֵיהֶם סָבִיב סָבִיב״.

[3]רַבִּי יוֹחָנָן אָמַר: אֵלּוּ מֵתִים שֶׁבְּבִקְעַת דּוּרָא. [4]וְאָמַר רַבִּי יוֹחָנָן: מִנְּהַר אֵשֶׁל עַד רַבַּת בִּקְעַת דּוּרָא. [5]שֶׁבְּשָׁעָה שֶׁהֶגְלָה נְבוּכַדְנֶצַּר הָרָשָׁע אֶת יִשְׂרָאֵל הָיוּ בָּהֶן בַּחוּרִים שֶׁהָיוּ מְגַנִּין אֶת הַחַמָּה בְּיוֹפְיָין. [6]וְהָיוּ כַּשְׂדִּיּוֹת רוֹאוֹת אוֹתָן וְשׁוֹפְעוֹת זָבוֹת. [7]אָמְרוּ לְבַעֲלֵיהֶן, וּבַעֲלֵיהֶן לַמֶּלֶךְ. [8]צִוָּה הַמֶּלֶךְ וַהֲרָגוּם, [9]וַעֲדַיִין הָיוּ שׁוֹפְעוֹת זָבוֹת. [10]צִוָּה הַמֶּלֶךְ וּרְמָסוּם.

[11]תָּנוּ רַבָּנַן: ״בְּשָׁעָה שֶׁהִפִּיל נְבוּכַדְנֶצַּר הָרָשָׁע אֶת חֲנַנְיָה מִישָׁאֵל וַעֲזַרְיָה לְכִבְשַׁן הָאֵשׁ, אָמַר לוֹ הַקָּדוֹשׁ בָּרוּךְ הוּא לִיחֶזְקֵאל: ׳לֵךְ וְהַחֲיֵיה מֵתִים בְּבִקְעַת דּוּרָא׳. [12]כֵּיוָן שֶׁהֶחֱיָיה אוֹתָן, בָּאוּ עֲצָמוֹת וְטָפְחוּ לוֹ לְאוֹתוֹ רָשָׁע עַל פָּנָיו. [13]אָמַר: ׳מַה טִּיבָן שֶׁל אֵלּוּ׳? [14]אָמְרוּ לוֹ: ׳חַבְרֵיהֶן שֶׁל אֵלּוּ מְחַיֶּיה

LITERAL TRANSLATION

with abominable beasts and creeping things, [1]as it is stated: "So I went in and saw; and behold every form of creeping thing, and abominable beast, and all the idols of the house of Israel, traced upon the wall all around." [2]And it is written there: "And He caused me to pass by them all around."

[3]Rabbi Yoḥanan said: They were the dead in Bik'at Dura. [4]And Rabbi Yoḥanan said: From the Eshel River to Ramat Bik'at Dura. [5]For when the wicked Nebuchadnezzar exiled Israel, there were among them young men who put the sun to shame with their beauty. [6]And the Chaldean women would look at them, and issue a heavy discharge. [7]They told their husbands, and their husbands [told] the king. [8]The king decreed, and they killed them. [9]But they would still issue a heavy discharge. [10]The king decreed, and they trampled them.

[11]Our Rabbis taught: "When the wicked Nebuchadnezzar cast Hananiah, Mishael and Azariah into the fiery furnace, the Holy One, blessed is He, said to Ezekiel: 'Go, and resurrect the dead in Bik'at Dura.' [12]After he resurrected them, the bones went and slapped that wicked man in the face. [13]He said: 'What is the nature of these?' [14]They said to him: 'The friend of these is resurrecting

RASHI

וכתיב והעבירני עליהם סביב סביב – כלומר על אותן אנשים שכתוב עליהם סביב עבר עליהם יחזקאל להחיותם. **אלו מתים שבבקעת דורא** – שהמית נבוכדנצר מלך בבל על שהיו יפים כדלקמן. **מנהר אשל עד רבת** – מקומות הן היו בבקעת דורא. **שופעות** – מחמת תאוה. **וצוה המלך והרגן** – **ועדיין היו שופעות** – שהיתה נראית זיו תארם וצוה המלך ורמסום. **ובאו עצמות מן הבקעה וטפחו לו לאותו רשע על פניו** – והלכו להם, ואית דאמרי: שמאותן עצמות היה לו כלים וכשהגיעה שעה שחיו טפחו לו על פיו כשהיה רוצה לשתות בהם. **חבריהם של אלו מחיה מתים** – על יחזקאל היו אומרין שהיה חבירן של חנניה מישאל

BACKGROUND

זָהָב רוֹתֵחַ Molten gold. This description apparently was influenced by the story of the Roman general Croesus, whom the Persians captured. The Persian emperor ordered to have him executed by pouring molten gold down his throat. This method of execution is similar to execution by burning according to Torah law, though it was carried out in a more "splendid" manner.

TRANSLATION AND COMMENTARY

in Bik'at Dura.' But Nebuchadnezzar understood that it was not Ezekiel, but rather God Himself who was resurrecting the dead, [1]and so **he** began with praise **and said: 'How great are His signs! and how mighty are His wonders!** [2]**His kingdom is an everlasting kingdom, and His dominion is from generation to generation.'"**

אָמַר רַבִּי יִצְחָק [3]**Rabbi Yitzḥak said: Let molten gold be poured into the mouth of that wicked man** — let Nebuchadnezzar's mouth be sealed by a cruel mode of execution (out of respect for the king, Rabbi Yitzḥak spoke of "molten gold"). [4]**For had an angel not come and struck him on his mouth,** thus keeping him from further proclaiming God's praises, he **would have attempted to put to shame all the songs and praises that David proclaimed in the Book of Psalms.** God might have preferred Nebuchadnezzar's psalms to those of David.

תָּנוּ רַבָּנַן [5]**Our Rabbis taught** a Baraita: **"Six** other **miracles were performed on that day** that Hananiah, Mishael, and Azariah were saved from death in the fiery furnace, **and they are** as follows: [6]**The furnace** that was sunk into the ground **floated** to the surface, so that everyone could see what was happening there; some of the walls of **the furnace collapsed,** to let people see inside; **the lime** lining of the furnace **melted** from the great heat; **the** golden **idol** that Nebuchadnezzar had fashioned **fell on its face; the** members of **four ranks of governmental power** who had helped Nebuchadnezzar cast Hananiah, Mishael, and Azariah into the furnace **were burned** to death; [7]**and Ezekiel resurrected the dead in Bik'at Dura."**

מֵתִים בְּבִקְעַת דּוּרָא׳. [1]פָּתַח וְאָמַר: ׳אָתוֹהִי כְּמָה רַבְרְבִין! וְתִמְהוֹהִי כְּמָה תַקִּיפִין! [2]מַלְכוּתֵיהּ מַלְכוּת עָלַם וְשָׁלְטָנֵהּ עִם דָּר וְדָר וגו׳ ׳ ״.

[3]אָמַר רַבִּי יִצְחָק: יוּצַק זָהָב רוֹתֵחַ לְתוֹךְ פִּיו שֶׁל אוֹתוֹ רָשָׁע, [4]שֶׁאִילְמָלֵא (לֹא) בָּא מַלְאָךְ וּסְטָרוֹ עַל פִּיו בִּיקֵּשׁ לְגַנּוֹת כָּל שִׁירוֹת וְתִשְׁבָּחוֹת שֶׁאָמַר דָּוִד בְּסֵפֶר תְּהִלִּים.

[5]תָּנוּ רַבָּנַן: ״שִׁשָּׁה נִסִּים נַעֲשׂוּ בְּאוֹתוֹ הַיּוֹם, וְאֵלּוּ הֵן: [6]צָף הַכִּבְשָׁן, וְנִפְרַץ הַכִּבְשָׁן, וְהוּמַק סוּדוֹ וְנֶהְפַּךְ צֶלֶם עַל פָּנָיו, וְנִשְׂרְפוּ אַרְבַּע מַלְכִיּוֹת, [7]וְהֶחְיָה יְחֶזְקֵאל אֶת הַמֵּתִים בְּבִקְעַת דּוּרָא״.

LITERAL TRANSLATION

the dead in Bik'at Dura.' [1]He opened and said: 'How great are His signs! and how mighty are His wonders! [2]His kingdom is an everlasting kingdom, and His dominion is from generation to generation.'"

[3]Rabbi Yitzḥak said: Let molten gold be poured into the mouth of that wicked man, [4]for had an angel not come and struck him on his mouth, he would have attempted to put to shame all the songs and praises that David said in the Book of Psalms.

[5]Our Rabbis taught: "Six miracles were performed on that day, and they are: [6]The furnace floated, and the furnace broke, and its lime melted, and the idol fell on its face, and the four kingdoms were burned, [7]and Ezekiel resurrected the dead in Bik'at Dura."

RASHI

ועזריה ונבוכדנצר היה יודע שהיה הקדוש ברוך הוא מחיה אותם. **פתח ואמר** – להקדוש ברוך הוא אתוהי כמה רברבין פסוק הוא (דניאל ג). **יוצק זהב רותח** – משום דקא איירי בשבחו דנבוכדנצר נקיט נמי לישנא מעליא ולשון קלה. **סטרו** – הכהו מאחורי ידו. **לגנות** – שהיה מסדר שבחות נאות יותר מדוד ואילו אמרן הקדוש ברוך הוא היה נוטה אחריהן יותר מאחרי השירות שעשה דוד. **באותו יום** – שהשליכן לכבשן. **צף הכבשן** – שהכבשן היה משוקע בארץ כעין כבשן של סיד, וצף ועומד על גבי קרקע, כדי שיראוהו כל העולם. **נפרץ הכבשן** – נפלו קצת כותליו, כדי שיוכלו כולם לראות בתוכו. **הומק סורו** – נשפל גאותו, כמו "סורו רע" (קדושין פב,א), לישנא אחרינא: הומק סודו = כמו יסודו נשתלשל, וכן לימדני רבי יעקב בן יקר, אבל מורי גרס: והומק סידו = סיד הכבשן נמסה מרוב חמימות, כך שמעתי, והיתה מושכת למרחוק, ומהבל של אותו הסיד נשרפו אותן שהשליכו חנניה מישאל ועזריה לתוך כבשן האש. **ונהפך** – צלם של זהב על פניו. **ארבע מלכיות** – מלכים ואנשיהם שסייעו לנבוכדנצר להשליך חנניה מישאל ועזריה לתוך האור.

NOTES

בָּא מַלְאָךְ וּסְטָרוֹ The angel came and struck him. The commentators ask why an angel struck Nebuchadnezzar on his mouth, and prevented him from continuing with God's praises. It has been suggested that it would not have been fitting for Nebuchadnezzar, who destroyed the Temple, to have sung more sublime songs of praise to God than did David who built the Temple. Alternatively, the angel struck Nebuchadnezzar on the mouth because he had used the inappropriate expression "son of God [בַּר אֱלָהִין]" (Daniel 3:25). (See *Maharsha, Iyyun Yaakov,* and others.)

וְהוּמַק סוּדוֹ Its lime melted. There are several readings and explanations of this expression. Some had the reading הוּמַק סוּרוֹ. The word סוּרוֹ might denote the flames that go out [סָרוֹת] from the fire (*Geonim*). Or else the word סוּרוֹ denotes power [שְׂרָרָה], the flames that are the power of the fire. Some understand the word סוּרוֹ in the sense of "pride," as in the expression סוּרוֹ רַע. Others had the reading הוּמַק סִידוֹ, "its lime melted," that is to say, the lime that lined the furnace melted from the great heat (*Arukh* and others).

TRANSLATION AND COMMENTARY

וְכוּלְּהוּ גְּמָרָא [1]**All of these** miracles **are known** to us **by** oral **tradition,** except the miracle regarding **the four ranks of governmental power** who were burned to death, for that miracle is known to us from **a verse,** [2]**as it is stated** (Daniel 3:2): **"Then Nebuchadnezzar the king sent to gather together the satraps, the prefects, and the governors, the counselors, the treasurers, the justices, the magistrates, and all the rulers of the provinces,** to come to the dedication of the idol that Nebuchadnezzar had erected." [3]**And** another **verse states** (Daniel 3:12): **"There are certain Jews...**they do not serve your gods, nor worship the golden image which you have erected." [4]**And** after Hananiah, Mishael, and Azariah emerged unscathed from the furnace, **the verse states** (Daniel 3:27): **"And the satraps, the prefects, the governors, and the king's counselors, being gathered together, saw these men."** Four of the ranks of governmental power that were mentioned in the first list are not mentioned here in the second list — "the treasurers, the justices, the magistrates, and all the rulers of the provinces" — teaching us that they had been burned to death by the fire.

תָּנֵי [5]**A Sage of the School of Rabbi Eliezer ben Ya'akov taught** the following Baraita: **"Even in a time of danger a person should not dispense with** the markings of **his dignity,** lest his enemies scoff at him for succumbing to fear, for even when Hananiah, Mishael, and Azariah were cast into the fiery furnace, they were dressed in their finest and most distinguished clothing, [6]**as the verse states** (Daniel 3:21): **'Then these men were bound in their mantles, their tunics, and their hats, and their other garments, and were cast into the midst of the burning fiery furnace.'"**

אָמַר [7]**Rabbi Yoḥanan said:** [93A] [8]**The righteous are greater than the ministering angels, as the verse states** (Daniel 3:25): **"He answered and said, Lo, I see four men unbound, walking in the midst of the fire, and they have no hurt; and the appearance of the fourth is like an angel."** Nebuchadnezzar saw the three righteous men — Hananiah, Mishael, and Azariah — in the fiery furnace, together with an angel, but he mentioned the angel last, indicating that the righteous are more elevated in status than the ministering angels.

[1]וְכוּלְּהוּ גְּמָרָא, וְאַרְבַּע מַלְכִיּוֹת קְרָא, [2]דִּכְתִיב: "וּנְבוּכַדְנֶצַּר מַלְכָּא שְׁלַח לְמִכְנַשׁ לַאֲחַשְׁדַּרְפְּנַיָּא סִגְנַיָּא וּפַחֲוָתָא אֲדַרְגָּזְרַיָּא גְדָבְרַיָּא דְּתָבְרַיָּא תִּפְתָּיֵא וְכֹל שִׁלְטֹנֵי מְדִינָתָא וגו׳". [3]וּכְתִיב: "אִיתַי גֻּבְרִין יְהוּדָאִין". [4]וּכְתִיב "וּמִתְכַּנְּשִׁין אֲחַשְׁדַּרְפְּנַיָּא סִגְנַיָּא וּפַחֲוָתָא וְהַדָּבְרֵי מַלְכָּא חָזַיִן לְגֻבְרַיָּא אִלֵּךְ וגו׳".

[5]תָּנֵי דְּבֵי רַבִּי אֱלִיעֶזֶר בֶּן יַעֲקֹב: "אֲפִילּוּ בִּשְׁעַת הַסַּכָּנָה לֹא יְשַׁנֶּה אָדָם אֶת עַצְמוֹ מִן הָרַבָּנוּת שֶׁלּוֹ, [6]שֶׁנֶּאֱמַר: ׳בֵּאדַיִן גֻּבְרַיָּא אִלֵּךְ כְּפִתוּ בְּסַרְבָּלֵיהוֹן פַּטְשֵׁיהוֹן וְכַרְבְּלָתְהוֹן וגו׳ ׳".

[7]אָמַר רַבִּי יוֹחָנָן: [93A] [8]גְּדוֹלִים צַדִּיקִים יוֹתֵר מִמַּלְאֲכֵי הַשָּׁרֵת, שֶׁנֶּאֱמַר: "עָנֵה וְאָמַר הָא אֲנָא חָזֵי גֻּבְרִין אַרְבְּעָה שְׁרַיִן מַהְלְכִין בְּגוֹ נוּרָא וַחֲבָל לָא אִיתַי בְּהוֹן וְרֵוֵהּ דִּי רְבִיעָאָה דָּמֵה לְבַר אֱלָהִין".

LITERAL TRANSLATION

[1]And all of them are [known] by tradition, and the four kingdoms is a verse, [2]as it is written: "Then Nebuchadnezzar the king sent to gather together the satraps, the prefects, and the governors, the counselors, the treasurers, the justices, the magistrates, and all the rulers of the provinces, etc." [3]And it is written: "There are certain Jews." [4]And it is written: "And the satraps, the prefects, the governors, and the king's counselors, being gathered together, saw these men."

[5][A Sage] of the School of Rabbi Eliezer ben Ya'akov taught: "Even during a time of danger a person should not dispense with his dignity, [6]as it is stated: 'Then these men were bound in their mantles, their tunics, and their hats, and their other garments, etc.'"

[7]Rabbi Yoḥanan said: [93A] [8]The righteous are greater than the ministering angels, as it is stated: "He answered and said, Lo, I see four men unbound, walking in the midst of the fire, and they have no hurt; and the appearance of the fourth is like an angel."

RASHI

מקראי נפקי — דכתיב (דניאל ג) "נבוכדנצר שלח למכנש לאחשדרפניא סגניא" ולבסוף לאחר שבאו מן הכבשן כתיב "ומתכנשין אחשדרפניא סגניא ופחותא" והנך דלא כתיבי — נשרפו. **אל ישנה מן הרבנות שלו** — שהרי חנניה מישאל ועזריה היו לבושין בגדי תפארתן כשהושלכו לכבשן, אל ישנה — שלא יראה מבוהל ומפוחד, ומתביישין שונאיו מפניו. **פטשיהון וכרבלתהון** — עניני מלבושין. **גדולים צדיקים יותר ממלאכי השרת** — דבריישא חשיב לתלתא

NOTES

לֹא יְשַׁנֶּה אָדָם אֶת עַצְמוֹ מִן הָרַבָּנוּת שֶׁלּוֹ **A person should not dispense with his dignity.** *Meiri* explains that this means that a person must stand firm and erect a defense in the face of his troubles as befits his social status, and that he should not display his fears and dejection, or humble himself in any way. *Maharsha* adds that when a person maintains his outward dignity in the face of trouble, he demonstrates that he lovingly accepts the decree of Heaven.

גְּדוֹלִים צַדִּיקִים יוֹתֵר מִמַּלְאֲכֵי הַשָּׁרֵת **The righteous are greater than the ministering angels.** It has been suggested

TRANSLATION AND COMMENTARY

אָמַר [1]**Rabbi Tanhum bar Ḥanilai said: When Hananiah, Mishael, and Azariah came out of the fiery furnace, all the nations of the world came, and slapped** the people of Israel (referred to here euphemistically as **"the enemies of Israel")** on their faces for having bowed down to an idol, [2]**and said to them: "You have a God like this** who performs such wonders, **and** yet **you bow down to an idol?"** [3]**Immediately,** Hananiah, Mishael, and Azariah **began to say** (Daniel 9:7): **"O Lord, righteousness belongs to You, but to us confusion of face, as at this day."**

אָמַר [4]**Rabbi Shmuel bar Naḥmani said in the name of Rabbi Yonatan: What is** the meaning of **the verse that states** (Song of Songs 7:9): **"I said, I will go up into the palm tree, I will grasp its boughs"?** [5]**"I said, I will go up into the palm tree"** — **this is** a reference to the people of **Israel.** I thought that the whole palm tree was mine, that there were many righteous Jews who would suffer death rather than worship a false god. [6]**But now** I see that I **succeeded with only one bough** on which sat **Hananiah, Mishael, and Azariah.**

אָמַר רַבִּי יוֹחָנָן [7]**Rabbi Yoḥanan said: What is** the meaning of **the verse that states** (Zechariah 1:8): [8]**"I saw the night, and behold a man riding upon a red horse, and he stood among the myrtle bushes that were in the glen;** and behind him were there red horses, sorrel, and white"? [9]**What is the** meaning of the words, **"I saw the night"?** [10]When the people of Israel bowed down before the idol, **the Holy One, blessed be He, wanted to** destroy **the entire world** and **turn it into night.** [11]**"And behold a man riding"** — the word **"man"** in this context **refers to the Holy One, blessed be He,** [12]**as the verse states** (Exodus 15:3): **"The Lord is a man of war; the Lord is His**

[1]אָמַר רַבִּי תַּנְחוּם בַּר חֲנִילָאי: בְּשָׁעָה שֶׁיָּצְאוּ חֲנַנְיָה מִישָׁאֵל וַעֲזַרְיָה מִכִּבְשַׁן הָאֵשׁ בָּאוּ כָּל אוּמּוֹת הָעוֹלָם וְטָפְחוּ לְשׂוֹנְאֵיהֶן שֶׁל יִשְׂרָאֵל עַל פְּנֵיהֶם, [2]אָמְרוּ לָהֶם: "יֵשׁ לָכֶם אֱלוֹהַּ כָּזֶה, וְאַתֶּם מִשְׁתַּחֲוִים לַצֶּלֶם"? [3]מִיָּד פָּתְחוּ וְאָמְרוּ: "לְךָ ה׳ הַצְּדָקָה וְלָנוּ בֹּשֶׁת הַפָּנִים כַּיּוֹם הַזֶּה".

[4]אָמַר רַבִּי שְׁמוּאֵל בַּר נַחְמָנִי אָמַר רַבִּי יוֹנָתָן: מַאי דִּכְתִיב: "אָמַרְתִּי אֶעֱלֶה בְתָמָר אֹחֲזָה בְּסַנְסִנָּיו", [5]"אָמַרְתִּי אֶעֱלֶה בְתָמָר", אֵלּוּ יִשְׂרָאֵל, [6]וְעַכְשָׁיו לֹא עָלָה בְּיָדִי אֶלָּא סַנְסַן אֶחָד, שֶׁל חֲנַנְיָה מִישָׁאֵל וַעֲזַרְיָה.

[7]אָמַר רַבִּי יוֹחָנָן: מַאי דִּכְתִיב: [8]"רָאִיתִי הַלַּיְלָה וְהִנֵּה אִישׁ רֹכֵב עַל סוּס אָדֹם וְהוּא עֹמֵד בֵּין הַהֲדַסִּים אֲשֶׁר בַּמְּצֻלָה [וגו׳]"? [9]מַאי "רָאִיתִי הַלַּיְלָה"? [10]בִּיקֵּשׁ הַקָּדוֹשׁ בָּרוּךְ הוּא לַהֲפוֹךְ אֶת כָּל הָעוֹלָם כּוּלּוֹ לְלַיְלָה. [11]"וְהִנֵּה אִישׁ רֹכֵב" — אֵין "אִישׁ" אֶלָּא הַקָּדוֹשׁ בָּרוּךְ הוּא, [12]שֶׁנֶּאֱמַר: "ה׳ אִישׁ

LITERAL TRANSLATION

[1]Rabbi Tanhum bar Ḥanilai said: When Hananiah, Mishael, and Azariah came out of the fiery furnace, all the nations of the world came, and slapped the enemies of Israel on their faces, [2][and] said to them: "You have a God like this, and you bow down to an idol?" [3]Immediately, they opened and said: "O Lord, righteousness belongs to You, but to us confusion of face, as at this day."

[4]Rabbi Shmuel bar Naḥmani said in the name of Rabbi Yonatan: What is that which is written: "I said, I will go up into the palm tree, I will grasp its boughs"? [5]"I said, I will go up into the palm tree" — this is Israel, [6]and now I have only succeeded with the one bough of Hananiah, Mishael, and Azariah.

[7]Rabbi Yoḥanan said: What is that which is written: [8]"I saw the night, and behold a man riding upon a red horse, and he stood among the myrtle bushes that were in the glen, etc."? [9]What is "I saw the night"? [10]The Holy One, blessed be He, wanted to turn the entire world into night. [11]"And behold a man riding" — and "man" [can] only [mean] the Holy One, blessed be He, [12]as it is stated: "The Lord is a man

RASHI

צדיקי, ומלאך לבסוף, דכתיב "ורויה די רביעאה דמי לבר אלהין". **וטפחו לישראל על פניהם** — שהשתחוו לצלם. **אני אמרתי שכל התמר שלי הוא** — שיהיו בהם צדיקים הרבה ולא עלתה בידי וכו׳, ישראל נמשלו לתמר כדאמרינן (סוכה מה,ב): מה תמר זה אין לו אלא לב אחד וכו׳. **והנה איש רוכב על סוס אדום** — בזכריה כתיב. **כל העולם כולו ללילה** — מפני שהשתחוו לצלם.

NOTES

that, since angels can be burned by a heavenly fire, and righteous people were not consumed by a fire raging all around them, it follows that righteous people must be greater than ministering angels (*Binyan Shelomo*).

בִּיקֵּשׁ לַהֲפוֹךְ אֶת כָּל הָעוֹלָם כּוּלּוֹ לְלַיְלָה He wanted to turn the entire world into night. The words "I saw the night" do not tell us the time of the prophecy, for the previous verse states that the prophecy was made during the day. Moreover, the words "I saw the night" follow the word לֵאמֹר, "saying," which marks the beginning of the prophecy itself. Furthermore, the verse state, "I saw the night," and not "I saw in the night." Thus the words "I saw the night" describe Zachariah's vision, that God wished to bring the darkness of night to the world (*Riaf, Ḥayyim Shenayim Yeshalem*).

TRANSLATION AND COMMENTARY

name." "Upon a red horse" — this intimates that **the Holy One, blessed is He, wanted to** destroy **the entire world** and **turn** it **into blood.** [1]**But when He looked upon Hananiah, Mishael, and Azariah,** and saw that they would die rather than serve the idol, **He was pacified,** [2]**as the verse states: "And he stood among the myrtle bushes** [*hadasim*] **that were in the glen** [*metzulah*]. He — the Holy One, blessed is He — stood back from acting in this manner on account of the "myrtle bushes," the *hadasim,* in the "glen," the *metzulah*." [3]**And** the word ***hadasim*** in this context **refers to righteous people,** [4]**as the verse states** (Esther 2:7): **"And he brought up Hadassah,** that is Esther, his uncle's daughter," from which we learn that Hadassah is the name of the righteous woman, Esther. [5]**And** the word ***metzulah*** in this context **refers to Babylonia,** [6]**as the verse** dealing with the downfall of Babylonia **states** (Isaiah 44:27): **"That says to the deep** [*tzulah*], **Be dry, and I will dry up your rivers."** [7]**Immediately, those** agents of destruction (which the Prophet Zechariah envisaged as horses) **that, filled with anger, had become sorrel and red, became white.**

אָמַר רַב פָּפָּא [8]**Rav Pappa said: Infer from this** passage that seeing **a white horse in one's dream is a good** sign.

וְרַבָּנַן [9]The Gemara inquires: **Where did the Sages** — Hananiah, Mishael, and Azariah — **go** after they came out of the fiery furnace, for nothing more is said about them in the Bible?

אָמַר רַב [10]**Rav said:** After having survived the ordeal of the fiery furnace, Hananiah, Mishael, and Azariah **died from the evil eye** that had been placed upon them by their fellow Jews who stared at them with jealousy. [11]**Shmuel said: They drowned in the spittle** of the nations of the world, which said: "You have a God like this who performs such wonders, and yet you bow down to an idol?" [12]**And Rabbi Yoḥanan said: They went to**

מִלְחָמָה ה׳ שְׁמוֹ״. ״עַל סוּס אָדֹם״ — בִּיקֵּשׁ הַקָּדוֹשׁ בָּרוּךְ הוּא לַהֲפוֹךְ אֶת הָעוֹלָם כּוּלּוֹ לְדָם. [1]כֵּיוָן שֶׁנִּסְתַּכֵּל בַּחֲנַנְיָה מִישָׁאֵל וַעֲזַרְיָה — נִתְקָרְרָה דַּעְתּוֹ, [2]שֶׁנֶּאֱמַר: ״וְהוּא עֹמֵד בֵּין הַהֲדַסִּים אֲשֶׁר בַּמְּצֻלָה״. [3]וְאֵין הֲדַסִּים אֶלָּא צַדִּיקִים, [4]שֶׁנֶּאֱמַר: ״וַיְהִי אֹמֵן אֶת הֲדַסָּה״. [5]וְאֵין מְצוּלָה אֶלָּא בָּבֶל, [6]שֶׁנֶּאֱמַר: ״הָאֹמֵר לַצּוּלָה חֳרָבִי וְנַהֲרֹתַיִךְ אוֹבִישׁ״. [7]מִיָּד מְלֵאִים רוֹגֶז נַעֲשִׂים שְׂרוּקִים, וַאֲדוּמִּים נַעֲשׂוּ לְבָנִים.
[8]אָמַר רַב פַּפָּא: שְׁמַע מִינָּהּ סוּסְיָא חִיוָּרָא מְעַלֵּי לְחֶלְמָא.
[9]וְרַבָּנַן, לְהֵיכָא אֲזוּל?
[10]אָמַר רַב: בְּעַיִן [הָרַע] מֵתוּ.
[11]וּשְׁמוּאֵל אָמַר: בָּרוֹק טָבְעוּ.
[12]וְרַבִּי יוֹחָנָן אָמַר: עָלוּ לְאֶרֶץ

LITERAL TRANSLATION

of war; the Lord is His name." "Upon a red horse" — the Holy One, blessed is He, wanted to turn the entire world into blood. [1]When He looked upon Hananiah, Mishael, and Azariah, His mind was cooled, [2]as it is stated: "And he stood among the myrtle bushes that were in the glen." [3]And *hadasim* [can] only [mean] righteous people, [4]as it is stated: "And he brought up Hadassah." [5]And *metzulah* [can] only [mean] Babylonia, [6]as it is stated: "That says to the deep, Be dry, and I will dry up your rivers." [7]Immediately, those that, filled with anger, had become sorrel and red, became white.

[8]Rav Pappa said: Infer from this: A white horse is good in a dream.

[9]And the Sages — where did they go?

[10]Rav said: They died through the evil eye. [11]And Shmuel said: They drowned in the spittle. [12]And Rabbi Yoḥanan said: They went up to Eretz

RASHI

והוא עומד — העמיד הקדוש ברוך הוא עצמו בזכות ההדסים שבמצולה. **האומר לצולה חרבי** — לבבל שיושבת במצולה. **חרבי** — לשון ״חרבו המים״ (בראשית ח). **שרוקים** — צבועים ואחר כך נעשו לבנים, כשנסתכל בצדיקים נח מכעסו. **סוסיא חיורא מעלי לחלמא** — מדקאמר שאדום הוי רמז לקללה. **ורבנן** — חנניה מישאל ועזריה. **להיכן אזלו** — כשיצאו מן הכבשן, דתו לא מדכר להו בכולהו כתובי. **בעין הרע מתו** — שהיו מסתכלים בהן על שהיו תמהין בהן. **ברוק טבעו** — באותו רוק שרקקו אומות העולם בישראל, שאומרין: ״אלוה כזה יש לכם והשתחויתם לצלם״.

NOTES

וְרַבָּנַן, לְהֵיכָא אֲזוּל? And the Sages — where did they go? Our commentary follows *Rashi,* who understands that the words "the Sages" refer to Hananiah, Mishael, and Azariah, who were "the Sages" of their generation. *Ramah* suggests that the words "the Sages" refer to the Sages cited above (92b), who disagreed about what had happened to those whom Ezekiel had resurrected from the dead. The Gemara wishes to know their opinion about what happened to Hananiah, Mishael, and Azariah after they came out of the fiery furnace, for Scripture is silent on the matter.

מֵתוּ They died. *Maharsha* explains that Hananiah, Mishael, and Azariah died, so that they would not be a source of shame for the people of Israel. As explained earlier in the Gemara, whenever the nations of the world saw Hananiah, Mishael, and Azariah, they would chide the rest of Israel for not refusing to bow to the idol.

בָּרוֹק טָבְעוּ They drowned in the spittle. *Ramah* understands this as a metaphor, that Hananiah, Mishael, and Azariah died of shame when the nations of the world reproached the Jews.

יִשְׂרָאֵל, וְנָשְׂאוּ נָשִׁים וְהוֹלִידוּ בָּנִים וּבָנוֹת.

[1]כְּתַנָּאֵי: "רַבִּי אֱלִיעֶזֶר אוֹמֵר: בְּעַיִן [הָרַע] מֵתוּ. [2]רַבִּי יְהוֹשֻׁעַ אוֹמֵר: בָּרוֹק טָבְעוּ. [3]וַחֲכָמִים אוֹמְרִים עָלוּ לְאֶרֶץ יִשְׂרָאֵל וְנָשְׂאוּ נָשִׁים וְהוֹלִידוּ בָּנִים וּבָנוֹת, [4]שֶׁנֶּאֱמַר: "שְׁמַע נָא יְהוֹשֻׁעַ הַכֹּהֵן הַגָּדוֹל אַתָּה וְרֵעֶיךָ הַיֹּשְׁבִים לְפָנֶיךָ כִּי אַנְשֵׁי מוֹפֵת הֵמָּה". [5]אֵיזוֹ הֵם אֲנָשִׁים שֶׁנַּעֲשָׂה לָהֶן מוֹפֵת? הֱוֵי אוֹמֵר זֶה חֲנַנְיָה מִישָׁאֵל וַעֲזַרְיָה.

[6]וְדָנִיֵּאל לְהֵיכָן אֲזַל? [7]אָמַר רַב: לְמִיכְרָא נַהֲרָא רַבָּא בְּטִבֶרְיָא. [8]וּשְׁמוּאֵל אָמַר: לְאַתּוּיֵי בִּיזְרָא דְּאַסְפַּסְתָּא. [9]וְרַבִּי יוֹחָנָן אָמַר: לְאַתּוּיֵי חֲזִירֵי דַּאֲלֶכְּסַנְדְּרִיָּא שֶׁל מִצְרַיִם.

[10]אִינִי? [11]וְהָתַנְיָא: "תּוּדוֹס הָרוֹפֵא אָמַר: אֵין פָּרָה וַחֲזִירָה יוֹצֵא מֵאֲלֶכְּסַנְדְּרִיָּא שֶׁל מִצְרַיִם שֶׁאֵין חוֹתְכִין הָאֵם שֶׁלָּהּ, בִּשְׁבִיל שֶׁלֹּא תֵּלֵד"!

[12]זוּטָרֵי אַיְיתֵי, בְּלָא דְּעַתַיְיהוּ.

[13]תָּנוּ רַבָּנַן: "שְׁלֹשָׁה הָיוּ

LITERAL TRANSLATION

Israel, and married women, and fathered sons and daughters.

[1]Like the Tannaim: "Rabbi Eliezer says: They died through the evil eye. [2]Rabbi Yehoshua said: They drowned in the spittle. [3]And the Sages say: They went up to Eretz Israel, and married women, and fathered sons and daughters, [4]as it is stated: 'Hear now, O Joshua the High Priest, you, and your fellows who sit before you, for they are men of good omen.' [5]Who are the people for whom a sign was performed? Say that it is Hananiah, Mishael, and Azariah."

[6]And where did Daniel go? [7]Rav said: To dig a great river in Tiberias. [8]And Shmuel said: To bring aspasta seed. [9]And Rabbi Yoḥanan said: To bring pigs from Alexandria of Egypt.

[10]Is it so? [11]But surely it was taught: "Todos the doctor said: No cow or sow leaves Alexandria of Egypt unless they removed its uterus, so that it cannot bear young."

[12]He brought small ones without their knowledge.

[13]Our Rabbis taught: "Three were

TRANSLATION AND COMMENTARY

Eretz Israel, married women, and fathered sons and daughters.

כְּתַנָּאֵי [1]This matter which is under discussion between the Amoraim is in fact the subject of a dispute among **the Tannaim,** for it was taught in a Baraita: **"Rabbi Eliezer says:** After having survived the ordeal of the fiery furnace, Hananiah, Mishael, and Azariah **died from the evil eye** of their fellow Jews. [2]**Rabbi Yehoshua said: They drowned in the spittle** of the nations of the world. [3]**And the Sages say: They went to Eretz Israel, married women, and fathered sons and daughters,** [4]**as the verse states** (Zechariah 3:8): **'Hear now, O Joshua the High Priest, you, and your fellows who sit before you, for they are men of good omen** [מוֹפֵת].' [5]**Who are the people** of that generation **for whom a** miraculous **sign** [מוֹפֵת] **had been performed? Say that it is Hananiah, Mishael, and Azariah."** This shows that Hananiah, Mishael, and Azariah returned to Eretz Israel, and were found in the company of Joshua, the high priest.

וְדָנִיֵּאל [6]The Gemara inquires: **Where did Daniel go,** when the others were thrown into the fiery furnace? He, too, did not bow down to the idol, but nevertheless he was not cast into the furnace with them. [7]The Gemara cites several different traditions on the matter: **Rav said:** Daniel went **to dig** out **a great river in Tiberias.** [8]**Shmuel said:** He was sent by Nebuchadnezzar **to bring** choice **aspasta seed** (that would grow into cattle fodder) from a distant land. [9]**And Rabbi Yoḥanan said:** He was sent **to bring pigs** of superior breeds **from Alexandria of Egypt** to Babylonia.

אִינִי [10]The Gemara asks: **Was it** really possible to do **so?** [11]**But surely it was taught** in a Mishnah (*Bekhorot* 28b): **"Todos the doctor said: No cow or sow leaves Alexandria of Egypt unless its uterus has been removed, so that it will not bear** any **young** in its place of destination." The Alexandrians sterilized the animals to prevent them from breeding. How, then, could Daniel import pigs from Alexandria that could still reproduce?

זוּטָרֵי [12]The Gemara answers: Despite the restrictions, Daniel managed to **smuggle out small** pigs that had not yet been sterilized **without** the Alexandrians **knowing.**

תָּנוּ רַבָּנַן [13]**Our Rabbis taught: "Three** parties **took part in that consultation,** which decided that Daniel

RASHI

הוי אומר זה חנניה מישאל עזריה — אלמא חזרו לארץ אצל יהושע כהן גדול. **ודניאל להיכן אזל** — כשהושלכו חביריו לתוך כבשן האש, שלא הושלך עמהם. **למכרא נהרא רבא בטבריא** — לחפור ולהוציא נהר בטבריא, לישנא אחרינא: למכרא נהרא בטורא, בהר. **לאתויי בירי דאספסתא** — להביא זרע של עשב שהוא מאכל בהמה שלחו נבוכדנצר, הכי הוה קים להו. **לאתויי חזירי ממצרים** — שלחו כדי לגדלם לולדות, שחזירי מצרים גדולים הם. **והתניא** — אמר תודוס הרופא לחכמים שהיו אומרים ניטלה האם טרפה, והא אין פרה וחזירה יוצאה ממצרים וכו׳, כדי שלא יהיו מצויין במקומות אחרים, ואף על פי כן חיו. **זוטרי אייתינהו** — ולא העלו על לבם דלפריה ורביה בעי, והניחו להוציאן בלא חתוך האם.

BACKGROUND

לְאַתּוּיֵי בִּיזְרָא דְּאַסְפַּסְתָּא To bring aspasta seed. In antiquity we find material from both the Far East and the West regarding efforts initiated by various rulers to import fine breeds of animals and plants to their countries from distant lands. Similarly, the Bible mentions that Solomon brought horses from Egypt, because that excellent breed was suitable for drawing chariots.

חוֹתְכִין הָאֵם They removed its uterus. In many countries from antiquity to the present severe laws have forbidden the export of various animals or plants, in order to preserve the monopoly on these commodities. Removal of the uterus from the female animals was apparently the method adopted in Alexandria for that purpose.

בְּאוֹתָהּ עֵצָה: הַקָּדוֹשׁ בָּרוּךְ הוּא, וְדָנִיֵּאל, וּנְבוּכַדְנֶצַּר״. [1]הַקָּדוֹשׁ בָּרוּךְ הוּא אָמַר: ״נֵיזֵיל דָּנִיֵּאל מֵהָכָא, דְּלָא לֵימְרוּ בִּזְכוּתֵיהּ אִיתְנַצַּל״. [2]וְדָנִיֵּאל אָמַר: ״אֵיזֵיל מֵהָכָא, דְּלָא לִיקַּיֵּים בִּי: ׳פְּסִילֵי אֱלֹהֵיהֶם תִּשְׂרְפוּן בָּאֵשׁ׳״. [3]וּנְבוּכַדְנֶצַּר אָמַר: ״יֵזִיל דָּנִיֵּאל מֵהָכָא, דְּלָא לֵימְרוּ: ׳קַלְיֵיהּ לֵאלָהֵיהּ בְּנוּרָא׳״. [4]וּמְנַּיִין דְּסָגֵיד לֵיהּ? [5]דִּכְתִיב: ״בֵּאדַיִן מַלְכָּא נְבוּכַדְנֶצַּר נְפַל עַל אַנְפּוֹהִי וּלְדָנִיֵּאל סְגִד וגו׳.

[6]כֹּה אָמַר ה׳ צְבָאוֹת אֱלֹהֵי יִשְׂרָאֵל אֶל אַחְאָב בֶּן קוֹלָיָה וְאֶל צִדְקִיָּהוּ בֶּן מַעֲשֵׂיָה הַנִּבְּאִים לָכֶם בִּשְׁמִי לְשָׁקֶר וגו׳״ [7]וּכְתִיב: ״וְלֻקַּח מֵהֶם קְלָלָה לְכֹל גָּלוּת יְהוּדָה אֲשֶׁר בְּבָבֶל לֵאמֹר יְשִׂמְךָ ה׳ כְּצִדְקִיָּהוּ וּכְאַחְאָב אֲשֶׁר קָלָם מֶלֶךְ בָּבֶל בָּאֵשׁ״. [8]״אֲשֶׁר שְׂרָפָם״ לֹא נֶאֱמַר, אֶלָּא ״אֲשֶׁר קָלָם״. [9]אָמַר רַבִּי יוֹחָנָן מִשּׁוּם רַבִּי שִׁמְעוֹן בֶּן יוֹחַי: מְלַמֵּד שֶׁעֲשָׂאָן כַּקְּלָיוֹת. [10]״יַעַן אֲשֶׁר עָשׂוּ נְבָלָה בְּיִשְׂרָאֵל וַיְנַאֲפוּ אֶת

LITERAL TRANSLATION

in that counsel: The Holy One, blessed be He, and Daniel, and Nebuchadnezzar." [1]The Holy One, blessed be He, said: "Let Daniel go away from here, so that they will not say they were saved for his merit." [2]And Daniel said: "I will go away from here, so that it not be fulfilled in me: 'The carvings of their gods shall you burn in fire.'" [3]And Nebuchadnezzar said: "Let Daniel go away from here, so that they will not say: 'He burned his god in fire.'" [4]And from where [do we know] that he bowed down to him? [5]For it is written: "Then the king Nebuchadnezzar fell upon his face, and bowed down to Daniel, etc."

[6]"Thus says the Lord of hosts, the God of Israel, to Ahab the son of Kolayah, and to Zedekiah the son of Ma'aseyah, who prophesy a lie to you in My name, etc." [7]And it is written: "And of them shall be taken a curse by all the exiles of Judah, who are in Babylonia, saying, May the Lord made you like Zedekiah and like Ahab, whom the king of Babylonia roasted in the fire." [8]It is not stated: "Whom he burned," but rather: "Whom he roasted." [9]Rabbi Yoḥanan said in the name of Rabbi Shimon ben Yoḥai: This teaches that he made them like roasted wheat. [10]"Because they have committed baseness in Israel, and have committed adultery with

TRANSLATION AND COMMENTARY

should not be in Babylonia during the time of persecution: **The Holy One, blessed be He, Daniel, and Nebuchadnezzar."** [1]The Gemara explains: **The Holy One, blessed be He, said: "Let Daniel go away from here, so that** people will **not say that** Hananiah, Mishael, and Azariah **were saved** from death in the fiery furnace **on** account of Daniel's **merit." [2]And Daniel said: "I will go away from here, so that** the verse (Deuteronomy 7:25), **'The carvings of their gods shall you burn with fire,' not be fulfilled in me."** Nebuchadnezzar had bowed down to Daniel, and treated him as a god. Daniel feared that he himself had become the object of the Torah's command to burn idols. Therefore he wanted to leave Babylonia and avoid being cast into the fiery furnace like Hananiah, Mishael, and Azariah. [3]**And Nebuchadnezzar said: "Let Daniel go away from here, so that** people will **not say** about me: **'He burned his god in fire.'"** [4]The Gemara now proves that Nebuchadnezzar had treated Daniel as a god: **From where do we know that** Nebuchadnezzar **bowed down to** Daniel? [5]**For the verse states** (Daniel 2:46): **"Then the king Nebuchadnezzar fell upon his face, and bowed down to Daniel,** and commanded that they should offer an offering and sweet odors to him."

כֹּה אָמַר ה׳ [6]Continuing its discussion of the incident involving Hananiah, Mishael, and Azariah, the Gemara cites the verse that states (Jeremiah 29:21): **"Thus says the Lord of hosts, the God of Israel, of Ahab the son of Kolayah, and of Zedekiah the son of Ma'aseyah, who prophesy a lie to you in My name, etc."** [7]And the next **verse states** (Jeremiah 29:22): **"And of them shall be taken a curse by all the captivity of Judah, who are in Babylonia, saying, May the Lord make you like Zedekiah and like Ahab, whom the king of Babylonia roasted in the fire."** [8]The Gemara notes that **the verse does not state: "Whom** the king of Babylonia **burned** in the fire," **but rather** the verse states: **"Whom** the king **roasted** in the fire." [9]**Rabbi Yoḥanan said in the name of Rabbi Shimon ben Yohai: This** formulation **teaches** us **that** Nebuchadnezzar **treated** Ahab and Zedekiah **like roasted wheat,** roasting them on all sides. [10]The next verse describes the crimes committed by Ahab and Zedekiah (Jeremiah 29:23): **"Because they have committed baseness in Israel, and have committed adultery**

RASHI

באותה עצה – שהלך משם דניאל. **דלא לקיים בי פסילי אלהיהם תרשפון באש** – דנבוכדנצר עשאו אלוה כדכתיב "ולדניאל הוה סגיד", והוה ליה כפסילי אלהיהם שהמקרא הזה היה נוח עליהם לשורפן, לכך היה מתירא. **קליות** – שבלים המהובהבין באש.

NOTES

וַיְנַאֲפוּ אֶת נְשֵׁי רֵעֵיהֶם **And they have committed adultery with their neighbors' wives.** Elsewhere, it is explained that

נְשֵׁי רֵעֵיהֶם״. [1]מַאי עֲבוּד? [2]אֲזוּל לְגַבֵּי בְּרַתֵּיהּ דִּנְבוּכַדְנֶצַּר, [3]אַחְאָב אָמַר לָהּ: ״כֹּה אָמַר ה׳ הַשְׁמִיעִי אֶל צִדְקִיָּה״. [4]וְצִדְקִיָּה אָמַר: ״כֹּה אָמַר ה׳ הַשְׁמִיעִי אֶל אַחְאָב״. [5]אֲזַלָה וַאֲמַרָה לֵיהּ לַאֲבוּהָ. אָמַר לָהּ: ״אֱלֹהֵיהֶם שֶׁל אֵלּוּ שׂוֹנֵא זִמָּה הוּא. [6]כִּי אָתוּ לְגַבָּךְ שַׁדְרִינְהוּ לְגַבַּאי״. [7]כִּי אָתוּ לְגַבָּהּ שַׁדְרַתִּנְהוּ לְגַבֵּי אֲבוּהָ. [8]אֲמַר לְהוּ: ״מַאן אֲמַר לְכוֹן״? [9]אָמְרוּ: ״הַקָּדוֹשׁ בָּרוּךְ הוּא״. [10]וְהָא חֲנַנְיָה מִישָׁאֵל וַעֲזַרְיָה שְׁאַלְתִּינְהוּ, וַאֲמַרוּ לִי: ׳אָסוּר׳״. [11]אֲמַרוּ לֵיהּ: ״אֲנַן נַמִי נְבִיאֵי כְּוָותַיְיהוּ. [12]לְדִידְהוּ לָא אֲמַר לְהוּ; לְדִידָן אֲמַר לָן״. [13]אֲמַר לְהוּ: ״אֲנָא בָּעֵינָא דְּאִיבְדַּקִינְכוּ כִּי הֵיכִי דִּבְדַקְתִּינְהוּ לַחֲנַנְיָה מִישָׁאֵל וַעֲזַרְיָה״. [14]אֲמַרוּ לֵיהּ: ״אִינּוּן תְּלָתָא הָווּ, וַאֲנַן תְּרֵין״. [15]אֲמַר לְהוּ: ״בַּחֲרוּ לְכוֹן מַאן דְּבָעֵיתוּ בַּהֲדַיְיכוּ״. [16]אָמְרוּ ״יְהוֹשֻׁעַ כֹּהֵן גָּדוֹל״. [17]סָבְרִי: לֵיתֵי יְהוֹשֻׁעַ דְּנָפֵישׁ זְכוּתֵיהּ, [18]וּמַגְנָא עֲלַן. אַחְתִּיוּהוּ, שָׁדִינְהוּ. [19]אִינְהוּ אִיקְלוּ, יְהוֹשֻׁעַ כֹּהֵן גָּדוֹל אִיחֲרוּכִי מָאנֵיהּ, [20]שֶׁנֶּאֱמַר: ״וַיַּרְאֵנִי אֶת יְהוֹשֻׁעַ הַכֹּהֵן הַגָּדוֹל עֹמֵד לִפְנֵי מַלְאַךְ ה׳

LITERAL TRANSLATION

their neighbors' wives." [1]What did they do? [2]They went to the daughter of Nebuchadnezzar, [3][and] Ahab said to her: "Thus says the Lord, Surrender yourself to Zedekiah." [4]And Zedekiah said: "Thus says the Lord, Surrender yourself to Ahab." [5]She went and told her father. He said to her: "The God of these people hates licentiousness. [6]When they come to you, send them to me." [7]When they came to her, she sent them to her father. [8]He said to them: "Who spoke to you?" [9]They said: "The Holy One, blessed be He." [10]"But surely I asked Hananiah, Mishael, and Azariah, and they said to me: 'It is forbidden.'" [11]They said to him: "We, too, are Prophets like them. [12]To them He did not speak; to us He spoke." [13]He said to them: "I want to test you just as I tested Hananiah, Mishael, and Azariah." [14]They said to him: "They were three, and we are two." [15]He said to them: "Choose for yourselves whomever you wish to be with you." [16]They said: "Joshua, the High Priest." [17]They thought: Let Joshua whose merits are many, come and protect us. [18]They brought them in, and cast them. [19]They were burned, Joshua the High Priest — his clothes were singed, [20]as it is stated: "And He showed me Joshua the High Priest standing before the angel of the Lord,

TRANSLATION AND COMMENTARY

with their neighbors' wives." [1]The Gemara asks: **What** exactly **did** Ahab and Zedekiah **do?** [2]The Gemara explains: Each of them **went to the daughter of Nebuchadnezzar,** and told her a false prophecy in the name of God. [3]**Ahab said to her: "Thus says the Lord, Surrender yourself to** sexual intercourse with **Zedekiah,"** [4]**and Zedekiah said** to her: **"Thus says the Lord, Surrender yourself to** sexual intercourse with **Ahab."** [5]Nebuchadnezzar's daughter **went and told her father,** who **said to** her: "Surely these prophecies are false, for **the God of these people hates licentiousness.** [6]**When** Ahab and Zedekiah **come to you** again, **send them to me."** [7]**When** the two false Prophets **came** back **to her, she sent them to her father** as instructed. [8]Nebuchadnezzar **said to them: "Who spoke** these words **to you?"** [9]Ahab and Zedekiah **answered: "The Holy One, blessed be He,** Himself." [10]The king said to them: **"But surely I asked Hananiah, Mishael, and Azariah** about the matter, **and they said to me** that sexual activity of that sort **is** strictly **forbidden."** [11]The two false Prophets **answered: "We, too, are Prophets** just **like** Hananiah, Mishael, and Azariah. [12]**To them,** perhaps, God **did not speak** these words, but **to us He spoke** them." [13]Nebuchadnezzar **said to them: "I want to test you just as I tested Hananiah, Mishael, and Azariah."** [14]Ahab and Zedekiah **said to him: "They were three** people, **but we are** only **two."** [15]Nebuchadnezzar **said to them: "Choose for yourselves whomever you wish to be** the third person **with you** in the fiery furnace." [16]**They said** to him: "We choose **Joshua, the High Priest."** [17]The Gemara explains: **They thought** that **Joshua,** the High Priest, **should come** with them, for **his merits were many,** [18]**and** he would **protect them** from the flames. The three — Ahab, Zedekiah, and Joshua — [19]**were brought in, and cast** into the fire. Ahab and Zedekiah **were burned** to death, whereas regarding **Joshua the High Priest,** only **his clothes were singed,** [20]**as the verse states** (Zechariah 3:1): **"And He showed me Joshua the High Priest standing before the angel of the Lord,** and the

RASHI

השמיעי — הסתמכי.

NOTES

Ahab and Zedekiah indeed committed adultery with other people's wives, each one instructing married women to have sexual intercourse with the other. These adulterous relationships continued until they approached the daughter of Nebuchadnezzar, as a result of which they were arrested and put to death.

TRANSLATION AND COMMENTARY

adversary standing at his right hand to thwart him." [1]**And the** next **verse states** (Zechariah 3:2): **"And the Lord said Satan, The Lord rebukes you,** O Satan; even the Lord who has chosen Jerusalem rebukes you; for is not this man a brand plucked out of the fire?" This verse intimates that Joshua, the High Priest, was saved from death in a fire, but his clothing was nevertheless singed like a firebrand. After Joshua was saved from death, [2]Nebuchadnezzar **said to him: I know that you are a righteous man,** and therefore you were saved from the flames. [3]**But why did the fire have** even **a little power over you,** whereas over **Hananiah, Mishael, and Azariah,** the fire **had no power at all?"** [4]Joshua **said to** the king: **"They were three** people, **and I was** only **one,** and my merits did not suffice to save my clothing from the flames." [5]Nebuchadnezzar **said to him: "But surely Abraham was** all **alone** when he was cast into the furnace in Ur, and he survived fully intact!" [6]Joshua answered: **"There were no wicked people with Abraham** in the furnace, **and** so **the fire was not given permission** to harm him. [7]But **here wicked people were with me** in the furnace, i.e., Ahab and Zedekiah, **and the fire was given permission** to burn them. My clothing was also singed in the process." [8]The Gemara notes: **This is** the meaning of **the popular adage:** If there are **two dry firebrands and one moist one, the dry ones set the moist one on fire.**

מַאי טַעְמָא אִיעֲנַשׁ [9]Thep Gemara asks: **What is the reason that** Joshua, the High Priest, **was punished** and cast into the fiery furnace? [10]**Rav Pappa said: Because his sons married women who were not fit for the priesthood, and he did not object to them,** [11]**as the** very next **verse states** (Zechariah 3:3): **"Now Joshua was clothed in filthy garments,** and he stood before the angel." [12]**Now, was it Joshua's way to wear filthy garments?**

וגו׳״. [1]וּכְתִיב: ״וַיֹּאמֶר ה׳ אֶל הַשָּׂטָן יִגְעַר ה׳ בְּךָ וגו׳״. [2]אֲמַר לֵיהּ: ״יָדַעְנָא דְּצַדִּיקָא אַתְּ. [3]אֶלָּא מַאי טַעְמָא אַהֲנְיָא בָּךְ פּוּרְתָּא נוּרָא, חֲנַנְיָה מִישָׁאֵל וַעֲזַרְיָה לָא אַהֲנְיָא בְּהוּ כְּלָל״? [4]אֲמַר לֵיהּ: ״אִינְהוּ תְּלָתָא הָווּ, וַאֲנָא חַד״. [5]אֲמַר לֵיהּ: ״וְהָא אַבְרָהָם יָחִיד הֲוָה! [6]״הָתָם לָא הָווּ רְשָׁעִים בַּהֲדֵיהּ, וְלָא אִתְיְהִיב רְשׁוּתָא לְנוּרָא, [7]הָכָא הָווּ רְשָׁעִים בַּהֲדַי, וְאִתְיְהִיב רְשׁוּתָא לְנוּרָא״. [8]הַיְינוּ דְּאָמְרִי אֱינָשֵׁי: תְּרֵי אוּדֵי יְבֵישֵׁי וְחַד רְטִיבָא — אוֹקְדָן יְבֵישֵׁי לִרְטִיבָא.

[9]מַאי טַעְמָא אִיעֲנַשׁ? [10]אֲמַר רַב פַּפָּא: שֶׁהָיוּ בָּנָיו נוֹשְׂאִין נָשִׁים שֶׁאֵינָן הֲגוּנוֹת לִכְהוּנָּה, וְלֹא מִיחָה בָּהֶן, [11]שֶׁנֶּאֱמַר: ״וִיהוֹשֻׁעַ הָיָה לָבֻשׁ בְּגָדִים צוֹאִים״. [12]וְכִי דַּרְכּוֹ שֶׁל יְהוֹשֻׁעַ

LITERAL TRANSLATION

etc." [1]And it is written: "And the Lord said to the adversary, may the Lord rebuke you, etc." [2]He said to him: "I know that you are a righteous man. [3]But what is the reason that the fire had a little power over you, [but] over Hananiah, Mishael, and Azariah, it had no power at all?" [4]He said to him: "They were three, and I was one." [5]He said to him: "But surely Abraham was alone!" [6]"There were no wicked people with him, and permission was not given to the fire; [7]here, wicked people were with me, and permission was given to the fire." [8]This is what people say: Two dry firebrands and one moist one — the dry ones set the moist one on fire.

[9]What is the reason that he was punished? [10]Rav Pappa said: Because his sons married women who were not fit for the priesthood, and he did not object to them, [11]as it is stated: "Now Joshua was clothed in filthy garments." [12]But was it Joshua's way

RASHI

תלתא — ונפישי זכותייהו. **הלא זה אוד** — מה אוד נחרך — אף הוא נחרך. **אהני** — הועיל. **אקדו** — שרפו. **מאי טעמא איענש** — יהושע, דאהני נורא למאניה, דהאי דאהדר איהו לנבוכדנצר — דחייה בעלמא דחייה.

NOTES

מַאי טַעְמָא אִיעֲנַשׁ? What is the reason that he was punished? *Rashi* understands the Gemara's question differently: What is the real reason that Joshua's clothing was singed? This implies that Joshua's reply to Nebuchadnezzar's question on the matter was merely an evasion. Others explain that the Gemara is asking why Joshua was forced into the company of wicked people like Ahab and Zedekiah, or else, why he was punished with the adversary standing at his right hand to thwart him (see *Maharsha, Iyyun Ya'akov*).

שֶׁהָיוּ בָּנָיו נוֹשְׂאִין נָשִׁים שֶׁאֵינָן הֲגוּנוֹת לִכְהוּנָּה Because his sons married women who were not fit for the priesthood. This offense is recorded in Ezra 10:18: "And among the sons of the priests, there were found such as had taken foreign women, namely: the sons of Jeshua, the son of Jozadak," i.e., Joshua, the High Priest. Similarly, we find in Nehemiah 13:28: "And one of the sons of Joiada, the son of Eliashib, the High Priest, was son-in-law of Sanballat the Horonite."

לָבֻשׁ בְּגָדִים צוֹאִים Clothed in filthy garments. Elsewhere, *Ran* notes that the root לבש, "clothe, wear," sometimes denotes sexual intercourse, as in (Psalms 63:14): "The

לִלְבּוֹשׁ בְּגָדִים צוֹאִים? [1]אֶלָּא, מְלַמֵּד שֶׁהָיוּ בָּנָיו נוֹשְׂאִים נָשִׁים שֶׁאֵינָן הֲגוּנוֹת לִכְהוּנָּה, וְלֹא מִיחָה בָּהֶן.
[2]אָמַר רַבִּי תַּנְחוּם, דָּרַשׁ בַּר קַפָּרָא בְּצִיפּוֹרִי: [3]מַאי דִּכְתִיב: "שֵׁשׁ הַשְּׂעֹרִים הָאֵלֶּה נָתַן לִי". [4]מַאי "שֵׁשׁ הַשְּׂעֹרִים"? [5]אִילֵימָא שֵׁשׁ שְׂעוֹרִים מַמָּשׁ — [6]וְכִי דַּרְכּוֹ שֶׁל בּוֹעַז לִיתֵּן מַתָּנָה שֵׁשׁ שְׂעוֹרִים? [93B] [7]אֶלָּא שֵׁשׁ סְאִין. [8]וְכִי דַּרְכָּהּ שֶׁל אִשָּׁה לִיטּוֹל שֵׁשׁ סְאִין? [9]אֶלָּא, רֶמֶז [רָמַז] לָהּ שֶׁעֲתִידִין שִׁשָּׁה בָּנִים לָצֵאת מִמֶּנָּה שֶׁמִּתְבָּרְכִין בְּשֵׁשׁ [שֵׁשׁ] בְּרָכוֹת, [10]וְאֵלּוּ הֵן: דָּוִד, וּמָשִׁיחַ, דָּנִיֵּאל, חֲנַנְיָה, מִישָׁאֵל וַעֲזַרְיָה.
[11]דָּוִד, דִּכְתִיב: "וַיַּעַן אֶחָד מֵהַנְּעָרִים וַיֹּאמֶר הִנֵּה רָאִיתִי בֵּן לְיִשַׁי בֵּית הַלַּחְמִי יָדֵעַ נַגֵּן וְגִבּוֹר חַיִל וְאִישׁ מִלְחָמָה וּנְבוֹן דָּבָר וְאִישׁ תֹּאַר וַה׳ עִמּוֹ וגו׳". [12]וְאָמַר רַב יְהוּדָה אָמַר רַב: כָּל

LITERAL TRANSLATION

to wear filthy garments? [1]Rather, this teaches that his sons married women who were not fit for the priesthood, and he did not object to them.

[2]Rabbi Tanḥum said [that] Bar Kappara expounded in Sepphoris: [3]What is that which is written: "These six [grains of] barley he gave me." [4]What is "six [grains of] barley"? [5]If you say six [grains of] barley, literally — [6]was it Boaz's way to give a gift of six [six grains of] barley? [93B] [7]Rather, six se'ahs. [8]But is it the way of a woman to take six se'ahs? [9]Rather, he hinted to her that six sons would issue from her in the future, who would be blessed with six blessings, [10]and they are: David, and the Messiah, Daniel, Hananiah, Mishael, and Azariah.

[11]David, as it is written: "Then answered one of the servants, and said, Behold, I have seen a son of Jesse the Bethlehemite, who knows how to play, and is a fine warrior, and a man of war, and prudent in speech, and a comely person, and the Lord is with him, etc."

[12]And Rav Yehudah said in the name of Rav: This entire

TRANSLATION AND COMMENTARY

[1]**Rather, this teaches us that his sons had married women who were not fit for the priesthood, and he did not object to them,** and so he appeared in Zechariah's vision wearing filthy garments.

אָמַר רַבִּי תַּנְחוּם [2]The Gemara continues its discussion of the incident involving Hananiah, Mishael, and Azariah. **Rabbi Tanḥum said that Bar Kappara expounded in Sepphoris** as follows: [3]**What is** the meaning of what Ruth said to Naomi in **the verse** that **states** (Ruth 3:17): **"These six [grains of] barley he gave me"?** [4]**What is** the meaning of the expression **"six [grains of] barley"?** [5]**If you say** that it means **"six [grains of] barley," literally,** there is a difficulty, [6]for **was it Boaz's way to present a gift** to the poor **of** only **six** stalks of **barley?** [93B] [7]**Rather,** it must be that Boaz gave Ruth **six se'ahs** of barley. [8]**But** this, too, is difficult, for **is it the way of a woman to carry** a heavy load of **six se'ahs** of grain? [9]**Rather,** Boaz gave Ruth six seeds of barley, and thus **he intimated to her that six sons would issue from her,** each of **whom would be blessed with six blessings.** [10]Those six descendants **are: David, the Messiah, Daniel, Hananiah, Mishael, and Azariah.**

דָּוִד [11]The Gemara now lists the six blessings given to each of those six descendants of Ruth. **David** was blessed with six admirable traits, **as the verse states** (I Samuel 16:18): **"Then answered one of the servants, and said, Behold, I have seen a son of Jesse the Bethlehemite, who knows how to play, and is a fine warrior, and a man of war, and prudent in speech, and a comely person, and the Lord is with him."**

וְאָמַר רַב יְהוּדָה [12]Regarding this verse, **Rav Yehudah said in the name of Rav: Doeg** the Edomite (it will

LANGUAGE

שֵׁשׁ סְאִין **Six se'ah.** A se'ah is a rather large measure of volume, mainly used for dry measurement. Six se'ahs come to 56-90 liters, a burden which women are unable to carry.

RASHI

שש שעורים — שש גרעינים שעורים ממש. **וכי דרכו של בועז ליתן שש שבלים** — והא תנן (פאה פרק שמיני משנה ה) אין פוחתין לעני בגורן פחות מחצי קב שעורים. **אלא שש סאין** — דשש קבין או שש לוגין ליכא למימר, דלא מייתי בגורן מדה פחותה מסאה. **ליטול שש סאין** — ולישא משוי כזה. **רמז לה** — דשש גרעינין נתן לה לסימן ורמז שעתידין לצאת שש בנים ממנה. **יודע נגן גבור חיל ואיש מלחמה ונבון דבר ואיש תואר וה' עמו** — היינו שש ברכות.

NOTES

meadows are clothed [לָבְשׁוּ] with flocks," and so the metaphor of being clothed in filthy garments is aptly applied to someone who marries a foreign woman. Even though Joshua himself did not take an unfit woman as his wife, Zechariah sees him in his prophetic vision as clothed in filthy garments, because he did not object when his sons married such women.

אֶלָּא שֵׁשׁ סְאִין **Rather, six se'ahs.** It has been suggested that Bar Kappara knew that it was six se'ahs of barley, and not six of some other measure, because the verse uses the feminine form of six, *shesh,* rather than the masculine form, *shisha,* and the only feminine measure is the se'ah (the other possible measures, *kav* and *log,* are both masculine and require the masculine form of the number). (*Margoliyot HaYam.*)

TRANSLATION AND COMMENTARY

be demonstrated below that "one of the servants" is Doeg the Edomite) **said this entire verse with an evil tongue,** praising David before Saul so that Saul would become envious and kill David. [1]This is how the verse should be understood: **"Who knows how to play" — who knows** how **to ask** sharp and relevant questions about the law. [2]**"A fine warrior" —** who also **knows** how **to answer** the questions raised by others. [3]**"A man of war" — who knows** how **to present arguments in the war of Torah.** [4]**"A comely person —** who knows how to **interpret the law** in a convincing manner and prove the validity of his positions. [5]**"Prudent in speech"** — a person **who** knows how to infer by induction and **understand** one **matter from another matter.** [6]**"And the Lord is with him" — the law is in accordance with his** view **in all matters.** [7]The Gemara relates that, **regarding each of** these fine traits for which Doeg praised David, Saul **said to him: "My son Jonathan is** just **like him."** [8]But when Doeg **said to him, "And the Lord is with him,"** [9]**something that was not even** true **about** Saul **himself, he became sick, and jealous of** David, **for regarding Saul,** [10]**the verse states** (I Samuel 14:47): **"And wherever he turned, he did them mischief."** Even though the first part of that verse lists Saul's victories, including his greatness in Torah, his positions were not always accepted as the final law. [11]**But regarding David, the verse states: "And wherever he turns he does prosper"** — the law is always in accordance with his view.

מְנָלַן [12]The Gemara asks: **How do we know that it was Doeg** who praised David before Saul? [13]The Gemara answers: **Here the verse states** (I Samuel 16:18): **"Then answered one of the servants" — the distinguished one among the servants.** The term "one [אֶחָד]" may be understood in the sense of "distinguished [מְיוּחָד]." Who is the most distinguished of Saul's servants? [14]Doeg the Edomite, for **elsewhere the verse states** (I Samuel 21:8): **"Now a certain man of the servants of Saul was there that day, detained before the**

הַפָּסוּק הַזֶּה לֹא אֲמָרוֹ דּוֹאֵג אֶלָּא בְּלָשׁוֹן הָרַע. [1]"יָדַע נַגֵּן" — שֶׁיּוֹדֵעַ לִשְׁאֹל. [2]"גִּבּוֹר" — שֶׁיּוֹדֵעַ לְהָשִׁיב. [3]"אִישׁ מִלְחָמָה" — שֶׁיּוֹדֵעַ לִישָּׂא וְלִיתֵּן בְּמִלְחַמְתָּהּ שֶׁל תּוֹרָה. [4]"אִישׁ תֹּאַר" — שֶׁמַּרְאֶה פָּנִים בַּהֲלָכָה. [5]"וּנְבוֹן דָּבָר" — שֶׁמֵּבִין דָּבָר מִתּוֹךְ דָּבָר. [6]"וַה׳ עִמּוֹ" — שֶׁהֲלָכָה כְּמוֹתוֹ בְּכָל מָקוֹם. [7]בְּכוּלְּהוּ אֲמַר לְהוּ: "יְהוֹנָתָן בְּנִי כָּמוֹהוּ". [8]כֵּיוָן דַּאֲמַר לֵיהּ, "וַה׳ עִמּוֹ", [9]מִילְּתָא דִּבְדִידֵיהּ נַמִי לָא הֲוָה בֵּיהּ — חֲלַשׁ דַּעְתֵּיהּ, וְאִיקַּנְיָא בֵּיהּ. דִּבְשָׁאוּל [10]כְּתִיב, "וּבְכֹל אֲשֶׁר יִפְנֶה יַרְשִׁיעַ", [11]וּבְדָוִד כְּתִיב, "וּבְכֹל אֲשֶׁר יִפְנֶה יַצְלִיחַ". [12]מְנָלַן דְּדוֹאֵג הֲוָה? [13]כְּתִיב הָכָא: "וַיַּעַן אֶחָד מֵהַנְּעָרִים" — מְיוּחָד שֶׁבַּנְּעָרִים. [14]וּכְתִיב הָתָם: "וְשָׁם אִישׁ מֵעַבְדֵי שָׁאוּל

LITERAL TRANSLATION

verse Doeg said only with an evil tongue. [1]"Who knows how to play" — who knows to ask. [2]"A fine warrior" — who knows to answer. [3]"A man of war" — who knows to give and take in the war of Torah. [4]"A comely person — who presents interpretations of the law. [5]"Prudent in speech" — who understands a matter from another matter. [6]"And the Lord is with him" — the law is like him everywhere. [7]Regarding each of them, he said to them: "Jonathan my son is like him." [8]When he said to him, "And the Lord is with him," [9]something that was not even in himself, he became sick, and jealous of him, for of Saul [10]it is written: "And wherever he turned, he did mischief," [11]and regarding David, it is written: "And wherever he turns he prospers." [12]From where do we [know] that it was Doeg? [13]It is written here: "Then answered one of the servants" — the distinguished one among the servants. [14]And it is written there: "Now a certain man of the servants of Saul

RASHI

לא אמרן דואג — לקמן מפרש האחד מן הנערים היינו דואג. **אלא בלשון הרע** — שהיה מספר בשבחו של דוד כדי שיקנא בו שאול ויהרגהו. **לישא וליתן במלחמתה של תורה** — להתוכח בתלמוד. **פנים בהלכה** — שמביא ראיה לדבריו. **דבדידיה נמי לא הוה** — דשאול נמי לא הוה הלכה כמותו, כדאמרינן בעירובין (נג,א) דוד דגלי מסכתא כתיב ביה "יראיך יראוני וישמחו" שאול דלא גלי מסכתא כתיב ביה "בכל אשר יפנה ירשיע".

NOTES

לֹא אֲמָרוֹ אֶלָּא בְּלָשׁוֹן הָרַע He said with an evil tongue. The fact that Saul had asked for a man who knew how to play the lyre, and Doeg proposed David, praising him for traits and qualities that Saul had not mentioned, suggests that Doeg had an ulterior motive to arouse Saul's envy so that he would kill David (*Maharsha*).

הֲלָכָה כְּמוֹתוֹ The law is like him. We find in several places that the Rabbis recognized that a Torah scholar might be brilliant in many ways, while his theoretical analyses do not always correspond to the accepted Halakhah. Conversely, a less brilliant scholar might be endowed with qualities that allow him to arrive at practical conclusions that are accepted as law.

וּבְכֹל אֲשֶׁר יִפְנֶה יַצְלִיחַ And wherever he turns he does prosper. No such verse exists in the Bible (but see Psalms 1:3: "And in whatever he does he shall prosper"). The gist

TRANSLATION AND COMMENTARY

Lord; and his name was Doeg the Edomite, the chief of the herdsmen that belonged to Saul."

מָשִׁיחַ [1]The Gemara continues: **The Messiah** will also be blessed with six admirable traits, **as the verse** that describes the Messiah **states** (Isaiah 11:2): **"And the spirit of the Lord shall rest upon him, the spirit of wisdom and understanding, the spirit of counsel and might, the spirit of knowledge and of the fear of the Lord."**

וּכְתִיב [2]The Gemara adds: Regarding the Messiah, **the verse** also **states** (Isaiah 11:3): **"And his delight** [וַהֲרִיחוֹ] **shall be in the fear of the Lord;** and he shall not judge after the sight of his eyes, neither decide after the hearing of his ears." [3]**Rabbi Alexandri said:** The word וַהֲרִיחוֹ (translated here as "his delight") may be understood in the sense of רֵחַיִים, "millstones." Thus, the verse **teaches that** God **will burden** the Messiah **with commandments and afflictions** as heavy **as millstones.** [4]**Rava said:** The word וַהֲרִיחוֹ may be understood here in the sense of הֵרִיחַ, "smell." Thus, the verse teaches **that** the Messiah will be able to **smell** the parties appearing before him **and judge** between them, [5]**as it is stated** in the continuation of that passage (Isaiah 11:3-4): **"And he shall not judge after the sight of his eyes,** neither decide after the hearing of his ears. **But with righteousness shall he judge the poor, and decide with equity for the meek of the earth."** He will not judge a case on the basis of what he sees or hears, but nevertheless he will judge with righteousness, for he will judge on the basis of a special sense.

בַּר כּוֹזִיבָא [6]It was related that **Bar Koziba** — the pejorative name that the Rabbis gave to Bar Kochva — **ruled** over Israel **for two-and-a-half years** after leading a rebellion against the Roman authorities. After establishing a Jewish state, [7]Bar Koziba **said to the Rabbis: "I am the Messiah."** [8]The Rabbis **said to him: "It is written about the Messiah that he will** be able to **smell** the parties appearing before him **and judge** between

בַּיּוֹם הַהוּא נֶעְצַר לִפְנֵי ה׳ וּשְׁמוֹ דֹּאֵג הָאֲדֹמִי אַבִּיר הָרֹעִים אֲשֶׁר לְשָׁאוּל״.
[1]מָשִׁיחַ, דִּכְתִיב: ״וְנָחָה עָלָיו רוּחַ ה׳ רוּחַ חָכְמָה וּבִינָה רוּחַ עֵצָה וּגְבוּרָה רוּחַ דַּעַת וְיִרְאַת ה׳ וגו׳ ״.
[2]וּכְתִיב: ״וַהֲרִיחוֹ בְּיִרְאַת ה׳ ״.
[3]אָמַר רַבִּי אֲלֶכְּסַנְדְּרִי: מְלַמֵּד שֶׁהִטְעִינוֹ מִצְוֹת וְיִסּוּרִין כָּרֵיחַיִים. [4]רָבָא אָמַר: דְּמוֹרַח וְדָאֵין, [5]דִּכְתִיב: ״וְלֹא לְמַרְאֵה עֵינָיו יִשְׁפּוֹט וְשָׁפַט בְּצֶדֶק דַּלִּים וְהוֹכִיחַ בְּמִישׁוֹר לְעַנְוֵי אָרֶץ״.
[6]בַּר כּוֹזִיבָא מָלַךְ תַּרְתֵּין שְׁנִין וּפַלְגָּא. [7]אֲמַר לְהוּ לְרַבָּנַן: ״אֲנָא מָשִׁיחַ״. [8]אָמְרוּ לֵיהּ: ״בְּמָשִׁיחַ, כְּתִיב דְּמוֹרַח וְדָאֵין.

LITERAL TRANSLATION

was there that day, detained before the Lord; and his name was Doeg the Edomite, the chief of the herdsmen who belonged to Saul."

[1]The Messiah, as it is written: "And the spirit of the Lord shall rest upon him, the spirit of wisdom and understanding, the spirit of counsel and might, the spirit of knowledge and of the fear of the Lord, etc."

[2]And it is written: "And his delight shall be in the fear of the Lord." [3]Rabbi Alexandri said: This teaches that He burdened him with commandments and afflictions like millstones. [4]Rava said: That he smells and judges, [5]as it is written: "And he shall not judge after the sight of his eyes....But with righteousness shall he judge the poor, and decide with equity for the meek of the earth."

[6]Bar Koziba ruled two-and-a-half years. [7]He said to the Rabbis: "I am the Messiah." [8]They said to him: "Regarding the Messiah, it is written that he will smell and judge.

RASHI

נעצר לפני ה׳ — ללמוד תורה הרבה. **אביר הרועים אשר לשאול** — אלמא ההוא מיוחד שבנערים דהיינו דואג, וחזינן הכא דקרי "אביר הרועים". **ונחה עליו רוח ה׳** — איזה רוח — "רוח חכמה ובינה, רוח עצה וגבורה, רוח דעת ויראת ה׳" הרי ששה. הכי גרסינן: **והריחו ביראת ה׳ — אמר רבי אלכסנדריא: שהטעינו במצות ויסורין כריחים,** והיינו והריחו לשון רחים. ולא גרסינן: וכתיב והריחו. **רבא אמר** — מאי והריחו — **דמורח ודאין,** שמריח באדם ושופט ויודע מי החייב, שנאמר "לא למראה עיניו ישפוט ולא למשמע אזניו יוכיח", ואפילו הכי "ושפט בצדק דלים" כגון על ידי הרחה. **בר כוזיבא** — (עס) ממלכי הורדוס היה.

PEOPLE

בַּר כּוֹזִיבָא Bar Koziba. The rebellion of Bar Koziba, his personality, and details regarding the history of the period are not well known to us. From fragmentary accounts in non-Hebrew sources, it appears that the rebellion lasted for three years (135-138), until it was put down by Hadrian. As we know today from original documents found in the Judean Desert, the name of the chief of the rebels was Shimon Bar Koziba, who apparently claimed to be the Messianic king. It also appears that Rabbi Akiba supported that claim, and it was he who called him Bar Kokhba (lit., "the son of a star"), from the verse, "and a star rises from Jacob" (Numbers 24:17). The Sages, who did not accept him as the Messiah, called him (perhaps only later) Bar Koziba (lit., "son of a falsehood"), since he raised false hopes for the Messianic kingdom.

NOTES

of what is stated here is included in the verse (I Samuel 18:14): "And David succeeded [משכיל] in all his ways," the Aramaic translation of משכיל being מצליח ("prosper") (See *Maharsha, Iyyun Ya'akov.*)

הִטְעִינוֹ מִצְוֹת וְיִסּוּרִין He burdened him with commandments and afflictions. The Messiah is burdened with the commandment of redeeming the people of Israel, and he is laden with afflictions, for he bears the iniquities of Israel, as is described in the Book of Isaiah and elsewhere.

דְּמוֹרַח וְדָאֵין That he smells and judges. *Ramah* understands the word מורח in the sense of "detect, sense," as in (Job 39:25): "And he senses [יריח] the battle afar off." He relates the word וְדָאֵין to the word ודאי, and understands it to mean "sure things," the truth. The Messiah will be able to sense the truth in all situations.

TRANSLATION AND COMMENTARY

them. [1]**Let us see whether you can smell** the litigants **and judge** between them." [2]**When the Rabbis saw that** Bar Koziba **could not smell** the litigants **and judge** between them, they understood that he was not the Messiah, and soon thereafter Bar Koziba **was killed.**

דָּנִיֵּאל [3]The Gemara continues: **Daniel, Hananiah, Mishael, and Azariah** were also blessed with six favorable qualities, [4]**as the verse says about them** (Daniel 1:4): **"Youths in whom was no blemish, but well favored, and skillful in all wisdom, and discerning in knowledge, and perceptive in understanding, and such as had strength in them to stand in the king's palace, and whom they might teach the learning and the tongue of the Chaldeans."**

מַאי [5]The Gemara asks: **What is** meant by the words **"in whom was no blemish"?** [6]**Rabbi Ḥama bar Ḥananyah said: They did not even have a scab over a puncture that bled.**

מַאי [7]The Gemara asks: **What is** meant by the words **"and such as had ability in them to stand in the king's palace"?** [8]**Rabbi Ḥama bar Ḥanina said: This teaches that** Daniel, Hananiah, Mishael, and Azariah had unusual powers of self-control, which gave them the strength to stand before the king. **They deprived themselves of laughter, and of idle talk, and of sleep,** [9]**and they controlled themselves when** they felt **they had to relieve themselves,** all **on account of fear of the king.**

וַיְהִי בָהֶם [10]The verse states (Daniel 1:6): **"Now among these were, of the sons of Judah: Daniel,**

[1]נֶחֱזֵי אֲנַן אִי מוֹרַח וְדָאֵין".

[2]כֵּיוָן דַּחֲזְיוּהוּ דְּלָא מוֹרַח וְדָאֵין, קַטְלוּהוּ.

[3]דָּנִיֵּאל חֲנַנְיָה מִישָׁאֵל וַעֲזַרְיָה, [4]דִּכְתִיב בְּהוּ: "אֲשֶׁר אֵין בָּהֶם כָּל מְאוּם וְטוֹבֵי מַרְאֶה וּמַשְׂכִּלִים בְּכָל חָכְמָה וְיֹדְעֵי דַעַת וּמְבִינֵי מַדָּע וַאֲשֶׁר כֹּחַ בָּהֶם לַעֲמֹד בְּהֵיכַל הַמֶּלֶךְ וּלְלַמְּדָם סֵפֶר וּלְשׁוֹן כַּשְׂדִּים".

[5]מַאי "אֲשֶׁר אֵין בָּהֶם כָּל מוּם"? [6]אָמַר רַבִּי חָמָא בַּר חֲנַנְיָא: אֲפִילּוּ כְּרִיבְדָּא דְּכוּסִילְתָּא לָא הֲוָה בְּהוּ.

[7]מַאי "וַאֲשֶׁר כֹּחַ בָּהֶם לַעֲמֹד בְּהֵיכַל הַמֶּלֶךְ"? [8]אָמַר רַבִּי חָמָא בְּרַבִּי חֲנִינָא: מְלַמֵּד שֶׁהָיוּ אוֹנְסִין אֶת עַצְמָן מִן הַשְּׂחוֹק, וּמִן הַשִּׂיחָה, וּמִן הַשֵּׁינָה, [9]וּמַעֲמִידִין עַל עַצְמָן בְּשָׁעָה שֶׁנִּצְרָכִין לִנְקְבֵיהֶם, מִפְּנֵי אֵימַת מַלְכוּת.

[10]"וַיְהִי בָהֶם מִבְּנֵי יְהוּדָה דָּנִיֵּאל חֲנַנְיָה מִישָׁאֵל וַעֲזַרְיָה".

LITERAL TRANSLATION

[1]Let us see whether you can smell and judge."

[2]When they saw that he could not smell and judge, they killed him.

[3]Daniel, Hananiah, Mishael, and Azariah, [4]as it is written regarding them. "[Youths] in whom was no blemish, but well favored, and skillful in all wisdom, and discerning in knowledge, and perceptive in understanding, and such as had strength in them to stand in the king's palace, and whom they might teach the learning and the tongue of the Chaldeans."

[5]What is "in whom was no blemish"? [6]Rabbi Ḥama bar Ḥananyah said: They did not even have a scab over a puncture that bled.

[7]What is "and such as had strength in them to stand in the king's palace"? [8]Rabbi Ḥama bar Ḥanina said: This teaches that they deprived themselves of laughter, and of talk, and of sleep, [9]and they controlled themselves when they had to relieve themselves on account of the fear of the king.

[10]"Now among these were, of the sons of Judah: Daniel, Hananiah, Mishael, and Azariah."

RASHI

"אשר אין בהם כל מום וטובי מראה משכילים בכל חכמה יודעי דעת ומביני מדע ואשר כח בהם" הרי שש, אפילו ריבדא דכוסילתא לא היתה בגופם — שלא היו צריכין להקזה. ריבדא — *פוניור"א בלעז. כוסילתא — שם כלי המקיז — **פלנמא"ל. מן השיחה — שלא היו מספרין בדברים בטלים כדי שלא יתגנו בפני המלך.

NOTES

כֵּיוָן דַּחֲזְיוּהוּ דְּלָא מוֹרַח וְדָאֵין, קַטְלוּהוּ **When they saw that he could not smell and judge, they killed him.** According to the plain sense of the story reported here, it was the Rabbis of Israel who put Bar Koziba to death. But according to other Midrashic sources, Bar Koziba was killed by non-Jews. *Ra'avad* seems to accept what is stated in our passage according to its plain sense, whereas *Rambam* does not relate to our passage at all (*Sefer Shofetim, Hilkhot Melakhim* 11:3). This could be because he relies on the other Midrashic sources (*Kesef Mishneh*) or because he thinks that the Rabbis did not act in accordance with the law (*Leḥem Mishneh*). Alternatively, *Rambam* understands what is stated here, "they killed him," as referring to the non-Jews. In his view, the Gemara means that when the Rabbis saw that Bar Koziba was not the Messiah, they withdrew from him, and as a result he was killed by the non-Jews (*Migdal Oz*). *Ramah,* who understands that the Rabbis themselves put Bar Koziba to death, explains that someone who claims to be the Messiah means that he can judge between litigants on the basis of a prophetic spirit ("he can smell and judge"). Thus, if it is proven that he is not the Messiah, he may be put to death as a false Prophet.

¹אָמַר רַבִּי אֱלִיעֶזֶר: כּוּלָּן מִבְּנֵי יְהוּדָה הֵם. ²וְרַבִּי שְׁמוּאֵל בַּר נַחְמָנִי אָמַר: דָּנִיֵּאל מִבְּנֵי יְהוּדָה, חֲנַנְיָה מִישָׁאֵל וַעֲזַרְיָה מִשְּׁאָר שְׁבָטִים.

³״וּמִבָּנֶיךָ אֲשֶׁר יֵצְאוּ מִמְּךָ אֲשֶׁר תּוֹלִיד יִקָּחוּ וְהָיוּ סָרִיסִים בְּהֵיכַל מֶלֶךְ בָּבֶל. ⁴מַאי ״סָרִיסִים״? ⁵רַב אָמַר: סָרִיסִים מַמָּשׁ. ⁶וְרַבִּי חֲנִינָא אָמַר: שֶׁנִּסְתָּרְסָה עֲבוֹדָה זָרָה בִּימֵיהֶם.

⁷בִּשְׁלָמָא לְמַאן דַּאֲמַר שֶׁנִּסְתָּרְסָה עֲבוֹדָה זָרָה בִּימֵיהֶם — ⁸הַיְינוּ דִּכְתִיב: ״וַחֲבַל לָא אִיתַי בְּהוֹן״. ⁹אֶלָּא לְמַאן דַּאֲמַר: סָרִיסִים מַמָּשׁ, ¹⁰מַאי ״וַחֲבַל לָא אִיתַי בְּהוֹן״? ¹¹חֲבַלָא דְּנוּרָא.

LITERAL TRANSLATION

[1] Rabbi Eliezer said: All of them were of the sons of Judah. [2] And Rabbi Shmuel bar Naḥmani said: Daniel was of the sons of Judah; Hananiah, Mishael, and Azariah were of the other tribes.

[3] "And of your sons who shall issue from you, whom you shall beget, shall they take away; and they shall be *sarisim* in the palace of the king of Babylonia." [4] What is [the meaning of] *sarisim*? [5] Rav said: *Sarisim*, literally. [6] And Rabbi Ḥanina said: That idols were uprooted (lit., "castrated") in their days.

[7] Granted, according to the one who said that idols were uprooted (lit., "castrated") in their days — [8] this is why it is written: "And they have no hurt." [9] But according to the one who said: *Sarisim*, literally, [10] what is "And they have no hurt"? [11] Hurt from the fire.

TRANSLATION AND COMMENTARY

Hananiah, Mishael, and Azariah." [1] **Rabbi Eliezer said: All** four **of them** — Daniel, Hananiah, Mishael, and Azariah — **were of the tribe of Judah.** Rabbi Eliezer follows the homiletical interpretation of "six [grains of] barley" cited above, according to which those words refer to the six descendants of Ruth, including Hananiah, Mishael, and Azariah. [2] **Rabbi Shmuel bar Naḥmani** disagreed and **said:** Only **Daniel was of the tribe of Judah,** but **Hananiah, Mishael, and Azariah were** members **of the other tribes.**

וּמִבָּנֶיךָ [3] King Hezekiah was told as follows (Isaiah 39:7): **"And of your sons that shall issue from you, whom you shall beget, shall they take away; and they shall be *sarisim* in the palace of the king of Babylonia."** [4] **What is the meaning of** the word ***sarisim*** in this context? [5] **Rav said:** The word ***sarisim*** should be understood here **literally** as referring to eunuchs. The Babylonian king castrated Hananiah, Mishael, and Azariah, as was common in despotic monarchies. [6] **Rabbi Ḥanina** disagreed and **said:** The Babylonian king did not castrate Hananiah, Mishael, and Azariah, but they are nevertheless called *sarisim* because **in their day idolatry was uprooted** [*nistarsah*] after it became clear to all that the idols have no substance.

בִּשְׁלָמָא [7] The Gemara now examines the strengths and weaknesses of each interpretation: **Granted, according to** Rabbi Ḥanina, **who said** that the word *sarisim* means **those in whose days idolatry was uprooted,** [8] **this is why the verse** referring to Hananiah, Mishael, and Azariah **states** (Daniel 3:25): **"And they have no hurt,"** which implies that they were whole in their bodies and had not undergone castration. [9] **But according to** Rav, **who said** that the word ***sarisim*** should be understood **literally** as referring to eunuchs, [10] **what is** meant by the words: **"And they have no hurt"?**

חֲבַלָא דְּנוּרָא [11] The Gemara answers: Those words teach that Hananiah, Mishael, and Azariah were not **hurt by the fire** into which they had been cast, but they had indeed been castrated at the king's orders.

RASHI

כלם מבני יהודה — כדכתיב לעיל ששה בנים העתידים לצאת מרות, וחשיב בהדייהו חנניה מישאל ועזריה. דניאל — לחוד קאי אבני יהודה, אבל חנניה מישאל ועזריה לא, ולית ליה הך דרשה דלעיל "שש שעורים". מבניך אשר יצאו ממעיך — בחזקיהו מלך יהודה כתיב. סריסים ממש — שסירסו לחנניה מישאל ועזריה, שכן דרכן של מלכים לסרס את האדם כדי שלא ישא אשה ויהא פנוי לעבודת המלך, ולית ליה הא דחכמים דאמרי לעיל שעלו לארץ ישראל, ונשאו נשים והולידו בנים ובנות. רבי חנניה אומר — לא סרסם, אלא להכי קרו ליה סריסים — שנסתרסה עבודה זרה בימיהם, שבימיהם נודע לכל שאין ממש בעבודה זרה, ופורענות שהיה נביא מתנבא לחזקיהו שיהיו גולים מארצם ויוליכם בהיכל מלך בבל, ורבי שמואל בר נחמני שאמר חנניה מישאל ועזריה משאר שבטים היו — מוקים האי קרא בדניאל לחוד. מאי חבל לא איתי בהון — והלא חבלה היא זו שנסתרסו, ומהאי קרא דלעיל "ילדים אשר אין בהם כל מום" לא מצי פריך, דאיכא למימר בשעה שבאו לנבוכדנצר תמימים הוו וסרסן. חבל די נורא — לא איתא בהון אבל חבלת הגוף מיהא איכא, ופריך לחבלא דנורא לא איצטריך, דהא כתיב קרא "וריח נור לא עדת בהון".

NOTES

מַאי ״סָרִיסִים״? **What is the meaning of *sarisim*?** Even though we find in various Biblical passages that the term *sarisim* refers not to eunuchs, but to high officers (and so the term was understood by the Aramaic translations to those passages), it stands to reason that here the term is not being used in that sense, for Isaiah is prophesying the calamities that will befall Hezekiah's descendants, and becoming officers of high stature is hardly a calamity. Thus, the term must be used here in the sense of "eunuchs," or as Rabbi Ḥanina suggests, "those in whose days idolatry was uprooted [castrated]," for in that sense the word alludes to the calamity that will befall Hananiah, Mishael, and Azariah, that they will be cast into the fiery furnace (*Maharsha*).

[1] וְהָכְתִיב: [2] ״וְרֵיחַ נוּר לָא עֲדָת בְּהוֹן״!
[3] לָא חֲבָלָא, וְלָא רֵיחָא.
[4] בִּשְׁלָמָא לְמַאן דַּאֲמַר: שֶׁנִּסְתָּרְסָה עֲבוֹדָה זָרָה בִּימֵיהֶם, [5] הַיְינוּ דִּכְתִיב: ״כֹּה אָמַר ה׳ לַסָּרִיסִים אֲשֶׁר יִשְׁמְרוּ אֶת שַׁבְּתוֹתַי וגו׳״. [6] אֶלָּא לְמַאן דַּאֲמַר: סָרִיסִים מַמָּשׁ, מִשְׁתָּעֵי קְרָא בִּגְנוּתָא דְצַדִּיקֵי?
[7] הָא וְהָא הֲוָה בְּהוּ.
[8] בִּשְׁלָמָא לְמַאן דַּאֲמַר: סָרִיסִים מַמָּשׁ, [9] הַיְינוּ דִּכְתִיב: ״בְּבֵיתִי וּבְחוֹמֹתַי יָד וָשֵׁם טוֹב מִבָּנִים וּמִבָּנוֹת״. [10] אֶלָּא לְמַאן דַּאֲמַר: שֶׁנִּסְתָּרְסָה עֲבוֹדָה זָרָה בִּימֵיהֶם, מַאי ״טוֹב מִבָּנִים וּמִבָּנוֹת״?
[11] אָמַר רַב נַחְמָן בַּר יִצְחָק: מִבָּנִים שֶׁהָיוּ לָהֶם כְּבָר, וָמֵתוּ. [12] מַאי ״שֵׁם עוֹלָם אֶתֵּן, לוֹ אֲשֶׁר לֹא יִכָּרֵת״? [13] אָמַר רַבִּי תַּנְחוּם, דָּרַשׁ בַּר קַפָּרָא

LITERAL TRANSLATION

[1] But surely it is written: [2] "Nor had the smell of fire passed over them"!

[3] Neither hurt, nor smell.

[4] Granted, according to the one who said: Those in whose days idols were uprooted (lit., "castrated"), [5] this is why it is written: "For thus says the Lord to the *sarisim* who keep My Sabbaths, etc." [6] But according to the one who said: *Sarisim*, literally, does the verse mention the disgrace of the righteous?

[7] They had this and that.

[8] Granted, according to the one who said: *Sarisim*, literally, [9] this is why it is written: "In My house and within My walls a memorial better than sons and daughters." [10] But according to the one who said: That idols were uprooted (lit., "castrated") in their days, what is "better than sons and daughters"?

[11] Rav Naḥman bar Yitzḥak said: [Better] than the sons whom they already had, but died.

[12] What is "I will give him an everlasting name, that shall not be cut off"? [13] Rabbi Tanḥum said [that] Bar Kappara expounded

RASHI

ולא ריחא — עשן האש. **הא והא היו** — סריסים ממש, ושנסתרסה עבודה זרה בימיהם. **טוב מבנים ומבנות** — מכלל דבנים לא הוו להו, דסריסים היו. **מאי טוב מבנים ומבנות** — הכא לא מצי לתרוצי הא והא הוו, דאם כן במאי פליגי. **בנים שהיו להן כבר ומתו** — דלא חיו בניהם, ומיהו לא היו סריסים. **אתן לו** — להם לא נאמר אלא לו, לאחד מהם, והיינו ספר דניאל שנקרא על שמו, והשתא קא פריך פירכא באפי נפשה אגב דאתי בידו ספר דניאל.

TRANSLATION AND COMMENTARY

וְהָכְתִיב [1] The Gemara objects: **But surely** it would not have been necessary to tell us that they were not hurt by the fire, for **it is stated** in another verse (Daniel 3:27): [2] **"Nor had the smell of fire passed over them"!**

לָא חֲבָלָא [3] The Gemara answers: The two verses teach us that not only were Hananiah, Mishael, and Azariah not **hurt** by the fire, but the **smell** of the fire did not even pass over them.

בִּשְׁלָמָא [4] The Gemara comments: **Granted, according to** Rabbi Ḥanina, **who said** that the word *sarisim* means **those in whose days idolatry was uprooted,** [5] **this is why** elsewhere **the verse states** about them (Isaiah 56:4): **"For thus says the Lord to the *sarisim* who keep My Sabbaths,** and choose the things that please me, and take hold of My covenant." The verse calls them *sarisim* ("eunuchs") because idolatry was uprooted ("castrated"). [6] **But according to** Rav, **who said** that the word *sarisim* should be understood **literally** as referring to eunuchs, is it right for **the verse to mention that which disgraces the righteous** — the fact that they have been castrated — rather than refer to them by name?

הָא וְהָא [7] The Gemara answers: In fact, **they** were *sarisim* in **both** senses of the word, for they had been castrated, and in their days idolatry was wiped out.

בִּשְׁלָמָא [8] The Gemara answers: **Granted, according to** Rav, **who said** that the word *sarisim* should be understood **literally** in the sense of eunuchs, [9] **this is why the verse states** about those *sarisim* who will keep God's Sabbaths and His Covenant (Isaiah 56:5): "And to them will I give **in My house and within My walls a memorial better than sons and daughters:** I will give him an everlasting name, that shall not be cut off," for *sarisim,* being eunuchs, have no children. [10] **But according to** Rabbi Ḥanina, **who said** that the word *sarisim* means **those in whose days idolatry was uprooted, what is** the significance of **"better than sons and daughters"?**

אָמַר [11] **Rav Naḥman bar Yitzḥak said:** God consoles the *sarisim* in whose days idolatry was uprooted that He will give them in His house and within His walls a memorial **better than the sons** and daughters **whom they had** formerly fathered, **but** who **died** in the meantime.

מַאי [12] The Gemara asks incidentally: **What is** the meaning of the end of the aforementioned verse (Isaiah 56:5): **"I will give him an everlasting name, that shall not be cut off"?** What is an "an everlasting name," and why does the verse that started in the plural, "And to them will I give," change to the singular, "I will give him"? [13] **Rabbi Tanḥum said that Bar Kappara expounded in Sepphoris** as follows: **This is** a

TRANSLATION AND COMMENTARY

reference to **the Book of Daniel that was called by** Daniel's **name.** "I will give him" — one of them, Daniel, an everlasting name, a book that will forever be called by his name.

מִכְּדִי [1]During the Talmudic period, the Books of Ezra and Nehemiah were regarded as a single entity that was called by the name of Ezra. This brings the Gemara to ask: **Surely most of the matters** found in the Book **of Ezra, Nehemiah ben Hachaliah said them,** [2]**what is the reason,** then, **that the book was not called by Nehemiah ben Hachaliah's name?**

אָמַר [3]**Rabbi Yirmeyah bar Abba said:** Nehemiah did not merit that honor, **because he spoke well of himself** and boasted about his good deeds, [4]**as the verse states** (Nehemiah 13:31): **"Remember me, O God, for good."**

דָּוִד [5]The Gemara asks: Is what Nehemiah said really so bad? Surely **David also** expressed a similar idea (Psalms 106:4): **"Remember me, O Lord, when You show favor to Your people; O visit me with Your salvation"!**

דָּוִד [6]The Gemara answers: There is a difference between the two statements, for **David was asking for mercy,** praying that God would remember him, whereas Nehemiah was stating a fact and demanding that God must remember him.

רַב יוֹסֵף אָמַר [7]**Rav Yosef said:** Nehemiah did not merit having a book in his name, **because he spoke evil of the former** governors, [8]**as the verse states** (Nehemiah 5:15): **"But the former governors who were before me laid burdens upon the people, and took from them for bread and wine, besides forty shekels** of silver; even their servants ruled over the people; but I did not do so, because of the fear of God." [9]**And even about Daniel, who was greater than he was,** Nehemiah **spoke evil,** for Daniel had also been an officer over Israel, and thus an object of Nehemiah's criticism.

וּמְנָלַן [10]The Gemara asks: **From where do we know that** Daniel **was greater than** Nehemiah? [11]The Gemara answers: **For the verse states** (Daniel 10:7): **"And I Daniel alone saw the vision: for the men who were with me did not see the vision; but a great trembling fell upon them, so that they fled to hide themselves."** [12]And regarding what is stated here, **"for the men who were with me did not see the vision,"**

בְּצִפּוֹרִי: זֶה סֵפֶר דָּנִיֵּאל שֶׁנִּקְרָא עַל שְׁמוֹ.

[1]מִכְּדִי, כָּל מִילֵּי דְעֶזְרָא נְחֶמְיָה בֶּן חֲכַלְיָה אֲמָרִינְהוּ, וּנְחֶמְיָה בֶּן חֲכַלְיָה — [2]מַאי טַעְמָא לָא אִיקְּרֵי סִיפְרָא עַל שְׁמֵיהּ?

[3]אָמַר רַבִּי יִרְמְיָה בַּר אַבָּא: מִפְּנֵי שֶׁהֶחֱזִיק טוֹבָה לְעַצְמוֹ, [4]שֶׁנֶּאֱמַר: "זָכְרָה לִּי, אֱלֹהַי לְטוֹבָה".

[5]דָּוִד נַמִּי מֵימַר אֲמַר: "זָכְרֵנִי ה׳ בִּרְצוֹן עַמֶּךָ פָּקְדֵנִי בִּישׁוּעָתֶךָ"!

[6]דָּוִד רַחֲמֵי הוּא דְּקָבָעֵי.

[7]רַב יוֹסֵף אָמַר: מִפְּנֵי שֶׁסִּיפֵּר בִּגְנוּתָן שֶׁל רִאשׁוֹנִים, [8]שֶׁנֶּאֱמַר: "וְהַפַּחוֹת הָרִאשֹׁנִים אֲשֶׁר לְפָנַי הִכְבִּידוּ עַל הָעָם וַיִּקְחוּ מֵהֶם בְּלֶחֶם וָיַיִן אַחַר כֶּסֶף שְׁקָלִים אַרְבָּעִים וגו׳". [9]וְאַף עַל דָּנִיֵּאל שֶׁגָּדוֹל מִמֶּנּוּ סִיפֵּר.

[10]וּמְנָלַן דְּגָדוֹל מִמֶּנּוּ? [11]דִּכְתִיב: "וְרָאִיתִי אֲנִי דָנִיֵּאל לְבַדִּי אֶת הַמַּרְאָה וְהָאֲנָשִׁים אֲשֶׁר הָיוּ עִמִּי לֹא רָאוּ אֶת הַמַּרְאָה אֲבָל חֲרָדָה גְדֹלָה נָפְלָה עֲלֵיהֶם וַיִּבְרְחוּ בְּהֵחָבֵא". [12]"וְהָאֲנָשִׁים אֲשֶׁר הָיוּ עִמִּי לֹא רָאוּ אֶת

LITERAL TRANSLATION

in Sepphoris: This is the Book of Daniel which is called by his name.

[1]Surely all the words of Ezra, Nehemiah ben Hachaliah said them, and Nehemiah ben Hachaliah — [2]what is the reason that the book was not called by his name?

[3]Rabbi Yirmeyah bar Abba said: Because he spoke well of himself, [4]as it is stated: "Remember me, O God, for good."

[5]David also said: "Remember me, O Lord, in favoring Your people; O visit me with Your salvation"!

[6]David was asking for mercy.

[7]Rav Yosef said: Because he spoke evil of the former ones, [8]as it is stated: "But the former governors who were before me laid burdens upon the people, and took from them for bread and wine, besides forty shekels, etc." [9]And even about Daniel who was greater than he [was], he spoke [evil].

[10]And from where do we [know] that he was greater than he? [11]For it is written: "And I Daniel alone saw the vision: for the men who were with me did not see the vision; but a great trembling fell upon them, so that they fled to hide." [12]"For the men who were with me did not see

RASHI

מכדי וכו׳ — רוב דברים שבספר עזרא, ונחמיה אמרם. **דוד נמי מימר אמר** — הכי, כלומר מאי מחזיק טובה איכא. **רב יוסף אמר** — לאו אהכי איענש, דהא דוד נמי אמר כי האי גוונא, אלא לכך נענש — שספר בגנותן של ראשונים.

NOTES

שֶׁסִּיפֵּר בִּגְנוּתָן שֶׁל רִאשׁוֹנִים Because he spoke evil of the former ones. Thus, Nehemiah was punished measure for measure. He wanted to cause the virtues of those who had come before him to be forgotten, and so his own name was forgotten from his book (*Iyyun Ya'akov*).

TRANSLATION AND COMMENTARY

[1]it was asked: **Who are these men?** [2]And **Rabbi Yirmeyah said (and some say that it was Rabbi Ḥiyya bar Abba who said): This is [a reference to] Haggai, Zechariah, and Malachi.** Now if Daniel saw the vision, and Haggai, Zechariah, and Malachi did not see the vision, it follows that Daniel was greater than the others. If Daniel was even greater than Haggai, Zechariah, and Malachi, who were Prophets, then surely he was greater than Nehemiah, who was not a Prophet. [94A] [3]The Gemara adds in passing: Haggai, Zechariah, and Malachi **were greater than** Daniel in one way, **and** Daniel **was greater than** Haggai, Zechariah, and Malachi in another way. [4]The Gemara explains: Haggai, Zechariah, and Malachi **were greater than** Daniel, **for they were Prophets** sent by God, **and he was not a Prophet.** [5]**And** Daniel **was greater than** Haggai, Zechariah, and Malachi, **for he saw** this vision, **and they did not see** it.

וְכִי מֵאַחַר [6]The Gemara asks: **Now, if** Haggai, Zechariah, and Malachi **did not see** the vision, then for **what reason were they frightened?** As the verse states (Daniel 10:7): "But a great trembling fell upon them, so that they fled to hide themselves."

אַף עַל גַּב [7]The Gemara answers: **Even though** Haggai, Zechariah, and Malachi **did not see anything** themselves, **their star** — the spiritual force that guides all their actions — **saw** it.

אָמַר רָבִינָא [8]**Ravina said: Infer from this that** if **someone is** suddenly **taken over by** inexplicable **fright, even though he** himself **did not see** anything, **his star** must have **seen** something frightening. [9]**What is his remedy?** [10]**He should move from his place four cubits.** [11]**Or else, he should recite the *Shema*** ("Hear O Israel, the Lord our God, the Lord is One") which will provide him with the necessary protection. [12]**And if he is standing in a place of filth** or excrement, where the *Shema* may not be recited, [13]**he should recite the following** spell: **"The goat in the slaughterhouse is fatter than I.** Go to the goat, and leave me alone."

הַמַּרְאָה״. [1]וּמַאן נִינְהוּ אֲנָשִׁים? [2]אָמַר רַבִּי יִרְמְיָה וְאִיתֵּימָא רַבִּי חִיָּיא בַּר אַבָּא: זֶה חַגַּי זְכַרְיָה וּמַלְאָכִי. [94A] [3]אִינְהוּ עֲדִיפִי מִינֵּיהּ, וְאִיהוּ עֲדִיף מִנַּיְיהוּ. [4]אִינְהוּ עֲדִיפִי מִינֵּיהּ, דְּאִינְהוּ נְבִיאֵי, וְאִיהוּ לָאו נָבִיא. [5]וְאִיהוּ עֲדִיף מִנַּיְיהוּ, דְּאִיהוּ חֲזָא וְאִינְהוּ לָא חֲזוּ.

[6]וְכִי מֵאַחַר דְּלָא חֲזוּ, מַאי טַעְמָא אִיבְּעוּת?

[7]אַף עַל גַּב דְּאִינְהוּ לָא חָזוּ מִידֵּי, מַזָּלַיְיהוּ חָזֵי.

[8]אֲמַר רָבִינָא: שְׁמַע מִינָּהּ, הַאי מַאן דְּמִבְעִית, אַף עַל גַּב דְּאִיהוּ לָא חָזֵי, מַזָּלֵיהּ חָזֵי. [9]מַאי תַּקַּנְתֵּיהּ? [10]לִינְשׁוֹף מִדּוּכְתֵּיהּ אַרְבָּעָה גַּרְמִידֵי. [11]אִי נַמִי, לִיקְרֵי קְרִיַּת שְׁמַע. [12]וְאִי קָאֵי בִּמְקוֹם הַטִּנּוֹפֶת, [13]לֵימָא הָכִי: ״עִיזָּא דְּבֵי טַבָּחָא שְׁמִינָא מִינַּאי״.

LITERAL TRANSLATION

the vision." [1]Who are these men? [2]Rabbi Yirmeyah said (and some say [it was] Rabbi Ḥiyya bar Abba): This is [a reference to] Haggai, Zechariah, and Malachi. [94A] [3]They are greater than he [is], and he is greater than they [are]. [4]They are greater than he [is], for they are Prophets, and he is not a Prophet. [5]And he is greater than they [are], for he saw, and they did not see.

[6]Now if they did not see, what is the reason they were frightened?

[7]Even though they did not see anything, their star saw.

[8]Ravina said: Infer from this [that] someone who is frightened, even though he did not see, his star saw. [9]What is his remedy? [10]Let him jump from his place four cubits. [11]Or else, let him recite the *Shema* [12]And if he is standing in a place of filth, [13]let him say thus: "The goat in the slaughterhouse is fatter than I [am]."

RASHI

מאי נינהו — שהיו עמו חגי זכריה מלאכי, וכיון שהם לא ראו והוא ראה אלמא גדול מהם הוה, ומדאשכחן דדניאל הוה חשיב טפי מחגי זכריה ומלאכי דהוו נביאי — שמע מינה דגדול הוה מנחמיה בן חכליה דלא הוה נביא, ואפילו הכי ספר עליו, דלא אפקיה מכלל גנות הראשונים, דניאל היה מבאי הגולה עם החרש והמסגר, ונחמיה הוה מעולי הגולה, זמן מרובה לאחר מיכן. **אינהו עדיפי מיניה וכו'** — איידי דגררא בעלמא קתני הכא, ומילתא באפי נפשה היא, וברוב ספרים אינה כתובה. **מאי טעמא איבעות** — דכתיב "אבל חרדה גדולה נפלה עליהם". **לנשוף** — לדלוג. **במקום הטנופת** — דלא מצי קרי. **לימא הכי** — לחש, כלומר לך אצל העזים והניחני.

NOTES

מַאן נִינְהוּ אֲנָשִׁים? **Who are these men?** Haggai, Zechariah, and Malachi must have been the men who were with Daniel, for Daniel was astonished that those men did not see the vision. Thus they must have been Prophets who were fit to see such a vision, and Haggai, Zechariah, and Malachi are the only Prophets known to us from that period (*Maharsha*).

לִינְשׁוֹף מִדּוּכְתֵּיהּ **Let him jump from his place.** This advice is supported by the Prophets who were at Daniel's side when he saw the vision, for they fled when the great trembling fell upon them, implying that when a person is overcome by some inexplicable fright, he should quickly leave the place where he is standing (*Torah Ḥayyim*).

אִי נַמִי, לִיקְרֵי קְרִיַּת שְׁמַע **Or else, let him recite the *Shema*.** If his fear did not abate, even after he moved to a different place, he should recite the *Shema* (*Meiri*).

TRANSLATION AND COMMENTARY

לְםַרְבֵּה הַמִּשְׂרָה [1]Having mentioned Hezekiah in a previous passage, the Gemara now cites a verse referring to the Messiah which the Gemara interprets as relating to Hezekiah. The verse states (Isaiah 9:6): **"For the increase [לְםַרְבֵּה] of the realm and for peace without end,** upon the throne of David, and upon his kingdom, to order it, and to establish it with judgment and with justice, from henceforth for ever; the zeal of the Lord of hosts performs this." [2]**Rabbi Tanḥum said that Bar Kappara expounded** this verse **in Sepphoris** as follows: **Why is** it that everywhere else that the letter *mem* is found **in the middle of a word,** the letter is **open,** an ordinary *mem* having an opening on the side, **but** in **this** case, the letter *mem* in the middle of the word לְםַרְבֵּה **is closed,** for a final *mem* that is closed on all sides is used instead? [3]**The Holy One, blessed be He, wanted to make Hezekiah the Messiah, and** He had wanted to make Sennacherib into **Gog and Magog,** the enemy kings who will wage the final war against Israel that will presage the advent of the Messiah. [4]But **the attribute of justice said before the Holy One, blessed be He: "Master of the universe!** [5]**If David the King of Israel who sang songs and praises before You, him You did not make the Messiah,** [6]**then Hezekiah for whom You performed all these miracles** — for You saved him from Sennacherib, and cured him of his illness — **but** still **he did not sing** any **song** or praise **before You** in gratitude for all that You did for him — **him You will make the Messiah?"** [7]**Therefore** the letter *mem* in the word לְםַרְבֵּה **was closed.** A final *mem* replaced the ordinary *mem*, intimating that the opening to the final redemption had been closed. [8]**Immediately the earth said before Him: "Master of the universe!** [9]**I will sing a song before You in place of that righteous man,** Hezekiah, **and** then **You can make him the Messiah."** [10]The earth then **began to sing a song before Him, as the verse states** (Isaiah 24:16): **"From the uttermost part of the earth have we heard songs: 'Glory to the righteous.'** But I said, My secret is mine, my secret is mine, woe to me! traitors have dealt treacherously; traitors have dealt very treacherously." The entire verse may be understood as arguments put forward by the earth, the angel in charge of the world, and the Prophet, regarding the Messiah. "Glory [צְבִי]

[1]"לְםַרְבֵּה הַמִּשְׂרָה וּלְשָׁלוֹם אֵין קֵץ וגו׳". [2]אָמַר רַבִּי תַּנְחוּם, דָּרַשׁ בַּר קַפָּרָא בְּצִיפּוֹרִי: מִפְּנֵי מַה כָּל מ״ם שֶׁבְּאֶמְצַע תֵּיבָה פָּתוּחַ, וְזֶה סָתוּם? [3]בִּיקֵּשׁ הַקָּדוֹשׁ בָּרוּךְ הוּא לַעֲשׂוֹת חִזְקִיָּהוּ מָשִׁיחַ, וְסַנְחֵרִיב גּוֹג וּמָגוֹג. [4]אָמְרָה מִדַּת הַדִּין לִפְנֵי הַקָּדוֹשׁ בָּרוּךְ הוּא: "רִבּוֹנוֹ שֶׁל עוֹלָם! [5]וּמַה דָּוִד מֶלֶךְ יִשְׂרָאֵל שֶׁאָמַר כַּמָּה שִׁירוֹת וְתִשְׁבָּחוֹת לְפָנֶיךָ — לֹא עֲשִׂיתוֹ מָשִׁיחַ, [6]חִזְקִיָּה שֶׁעָשִׂיתָ לוֹ כָּל הַנִּסִּים הַלָּלוּ וְלֹא אָמַר שִׁירָה לְפָנֶיךָ — תַּעֲשֵׂהוּ מָשִׁיחַ"? [7]לְכָךְ נִסְתַּתֵּם. [8]מִיָּד פָּתְחָה הָאָרֶץ וְאָמְרָה לְפָנָיו: "רִבּוֹנוֹ שֶׁל עוֹלָם! [9]אֲנִי אוֹמֶרֶת לְפָנֶיךָ שִׁירָה תַּחַת צַדִּיק זֶה, וַעֲשֵׂהוּ מָשִׁיחַ". [10]פָּתְחָה וְאָמְרָה שִׁירָה לְפָנָיו, שֶׁנֶּאֱמַר: "מִכְּנַף הָאָרֶץ זְמִרֹת שָׁמַעְנוּ צְבִי לַצַּדִּיק וגו׳".

LITERAL TRANSLATION

[1]"For the increase of the realm and for peace without end." [2]Rabbi Tanḥum said [that] Bar Kappara expounded in Sepphoris: Why is every *mem* in the middle of a word open, and this one is closed? [3]The Holy One, blessed be He, wished to make Hezekiah the Messiah, and Sennacherib Gog and Magog. [4]The attribute of justice said before the Holy One, blessed be He: "Master of the universe! [5]If David the King of Israel who sang before You songs and praises — You did not make him the Messiah, [6]then Hezekiah, for whom You performed all these miracles and he did not sing a song before You — You will make him the Messiah?" [7]Therefore it was closed. [8]Immediately the earth opened and said before Him: "Master of the universe! [9]I will sing a song before You in place of that righteous man, and You will make him the Messiah." [10]It opened and sang a song before Him, as it is stated: "From the uttermost part of the earth have we heard songs: 'Glory to the righteous,' etc."

RASHI

מ״ם – שבתיבת "למרבה המשרה" סתום, לכך נסתם, לומר, נסתמו הדברים שעלו במחשבה ולא נעשה. לישנא אחרינא: שביקש הקדוש ברוך הוא לסתום צרותיהן של ישראל שבקש לעשותו משיח. ומורי רבי פירש: לפי שנסתם פיו של חזקיה ולא אמר שירה. **כל הנסים הללו** – שניצל מסנחריב ונתרפא מחליו. **שר העולם** – מלאך שכל העולם מסור בידו. **שמענו צבי לצדיק** – שר העולם שאמר: עשה צביונו של צדיק.

NOTES

מִפְּנֵי מַה כָּל מ״ם שֶׁבְּאֶמְצַע תֵּיבָה פָּתוּחַ? Why is every *mem* in the middle of a word open? Were the letter *mem* open, it would allude to the *mem* in the word *mashi'aḥ* (Messiah). Thus the word was written with a closed *mem*, in order to show that Hezekiah could no longer fill the role of Messiah (*Ramah*).

חִזְקִיָּה לֹא אָמַר שִׁירָה Hezekiah did not sing a song. It has been suggested that after the ten tribes of Israel were sent into exile, Hezekiah could no longer recite a prayer of praise and thanksgiving for the miracle that was performed on his behalf, for such a prayer is only recited for a miracle performed on behalf of all of Israel, and not for a miracle

[1] אָמַר שַׂר הָעוֹלָם לְפָנָיו: ״רִבּוֹנוֹ שֶׁל עוֹלָם! [2] צִבְיוֹנוֹ עֲשֵׂה לְצַדִּיק זֶה״. [3] יָצְאָה בַּת קוֹל וְאָמְרָה: ״רָזִי לִי, רָזִי לִי״. [4] אָמַר נָבִיא: ״אוֹי לִי! אוֹי לִי! עַד מָתַי״? [5] יָצְאָה בַּת קוֹל וְאָמְרָה: ״בֹּגְדִים בָּגָדוּ וּבֶגֶד בּוֹגְדִים בָּגָדוּ״. [6] וְאָמַר רָבָא וְאִיתֵימָא רַבִּי יִצְחָק: עַד דְּאָתוּ בָּזוֹזִי וּבָזוֹזֵי דְּבָזוֹזֵי.

[7] ״מַשָּׂא דּוּמָה. [8] אֵלַי קֹרֵא מִשֵּׂעִיר, שֹׁמֵר, מַה מִּלַּיְלָה, שֹׁמֵר מַה מִּלֵּיל וגו׳״? [9] אָמַר רַבִּי יוֹחָנָן: אוֹתוֹ מַלְאָךְ הַמְּמוּנֶּה עַל הָרוּחוֹת — דּוּמָה שְׁמוֹ. [10] נִתְקַבְּצוּ כָּל הָרוּחוֹת אֵצֶל דּוּמָה, אָמְרוּ לוֹ: ״שֹׁמֵר, מַה מִּלַּיְלָה, שֹׁמֵר מַה מִּלֵּיל״? [11] אָמַר שֹׁמֵר, אָתָא בֹקֶר, וְגַם לַיְלָה; אִם תִּבְעָיוּן, בְּעָיוּ; שֻׁבוּ אֵתָיוּ״.

[12] תָּנָא מִשּׁוּם רַבִּי פַּפְּיָס: ״גְּנַאי

LITERAL TRANSLATION

[1] The Angel of the world said before Him: "Master of the universe! [2] Do his will for this righteous man." [3] A heavenly voice came out and said: "My secret is mine, my secret is mine." [4] The Prophet said: "Woe to me! Woe to me! Until when?" [5] A heavenly voice came out and said: "Traitors have dealt treacherously; traitors have dealt very treacherously." [6] And Rava said (and some say [it was] Rabbi Yitzḥak): Until the robbers come, and the robbers of the robbers.

[7] "The burden of Duma. [8] One calls to me out of Se'ir, Watchman, what of the night, what of the night? Etc." [9] Rabbi Yoḥanan said: That Angel who is appointed over the spirits — Duma is his name. [10] All the spirits gathered with Duma, [and] said to him: "Watchman, what of the night, what of the night?" [11] "The watchman said, The morning comes, and also the night; if you will inquire, inquire; return, come."

[12] [A Tanna] taught in the name of Rabbi Papyas: "It is a disgrace

TRANSLATION AND COMMENTARY

to the righteous." [1] **The Angel** who is appointed **over the entire world said before Him: "Master of the universe!** [2] **Do the will** [צִבְיוֹנוֹ] **of this righteous man,** and make him the Messiah. Surely Hezekiah is a righteous man, and You must not punish him just because he did not sing a song before You." [3] **A heavenly voice issued forth and said: "My secret is mine, my secret is mine.** Only I know what detains the Messiah." [4] **The Prophet said: "Woe to me! Woe to me!** [5] **How much longer** must we wait until the Messiah finally arrives?" Another **heavenly voice issued forth and said: "Traitors have dealt treacherously; traitors have dealt very treacherously."** [6] **And Rava said (and some say that it was Rabbi Yitzḥak** who said): The Messiah will not arrive **until the robbers** of Eretz Israel **come, and those who shall rob its robbers.**

מַשָּׂא דּוּמָה [7] A similar idea is found in another prophecy (Isaiah 21:11): **"The burden of Duma.** [8] **One calls to me out of Se'ir, Watchman, what of the night, what of the night?"** [9] **Rabbi Yoḥanan said: The Angel who is appointed over the spirits is named Duma.** [10] **All the spirits gathered by Duma, and said to him: "'Watchman, what of the night, what of the night?'** What does the watchman — God, who watches over Israel — say about the night — about the exile which is likened to the night? When will the exile come to an end, and the Messiah arrive, bringing with him the redemption?" [11] The angel answered: **"'The watchman said, The morning comes, and also the night; if you will inquire, inquire; return, come.'** The watchman — God — said that the morning of redemption will indeed come, and it will also be followed by another night — another period of exile. If you really seek redemption, pray for mercy, return unto me with repentance, and come."

תָּנָא [12] **A Tanna taught in the name of Rabbi**

RASHI

רזי לי רזי לי — נסתרות שלי הן, ואני יודע על מה מעכב. **אמר נביא אוי לי עד מתי** — יבא משיח! **עד דאתי בזוזי ובזוזי דבזוזי** — עד שנתבזזו שונאי ישראל כמה פעמים. **שר הרוחות** — שהנשמות נפקדות אצלו, והיינו ״משא דומה״ כך אמר דומה: אלי קורין הרוחות על עסקי שעיר עשו, ואומר לי: ״שומר מה מלילה״ — הקדוש ברוך הוא שהוא שומר, מה אומר מן הגלות שהוא כלילה. **שומר מה מליל** — מה דבר, מתי קץ הגאולה מליל זה. **אתא בקר** — בתמיה, ואית ספרים דלא כתיב בהו וכון, אמר להם השר: כך אמר שומר, הקדוש ברוך הוא: ״אתא בקר״ — גאולה תבא, ״וגם לילה״ — אבל מתחלה תהיה גלות הרבה. לישנא אחרינא: שיגאלו ויבנה מקדש שני ויחזרו ויגלו גלות זה. לישנא אחרינא ״וגם לילה״ — לרשעים, וכן תרגומו מוכיח ״אית אגר לצדיקיא ואית פורענות לרשיעיא״. **אם תבעיון** — אם תבקשו להגאל. **בעיו** — בקשו רחמים. **שובו** — בתשובה ואתיו לגאולה. **גנאי הוא** — דבר מגונה עשו.

NOTES

performed on behalf of a single tribe (*Tzofnat Pa'ane'aḥ*).

בָּזוֹזִי וּבָזוֹזֵי דְּבָזוֹזֵי **Until the robbers come, and the robbers of the robbers.** Robbers will come and rob Israel, and then other robbers will come and rob the robbers and Israel as well (*Arukh*). *Rashi* and *Ramah* explain that robbers will come and rob Israel, and then a second set of robbers will come and rob whatever is left.

TRANSLATION AND COMMENTARY

Papyas: "It is a disgrace that Hezekiah and his company did not sing a song of thanksgiving on their own, **until the earth began to sing a song,** [1]**as the verse states** (Isaiah 24:16): **'From the uttermost part of the earth have we heard songs: "Glory to the righteous."'"**

כַּיּוֹצֵא בַּדָּבָר [2]**Similar to this, you** can **say** regarding the verse (Exodus 18:10): **"And Jethro said, Blessed be the Lord, who has delivered you** out of the hand of Egypt, and out of the hand of Pharaoh." [3]**A Tanna taught in the name of Rabbi Papyas: "It is a disgrace that Moses and the six hundred thousand** men of Israel, despite all the miracles that they had witnessed in Egypt and at the Red Sea, **did not say** on their own, **'Blessed be** the Lord,' [4]**until Jethro came and said, 'Blessed be the Lord.'"**

וַיִּחַדְּ יִתְרוֹ [5]Regarding Jethro, the verse states (Exodus 18:9): **"And Jethro rejoiced** [וַיִּחַדְּ] for all the goodness which the Lord had done to Israel, whom he had delivered out of the hand of Egypt." [6]**Rav and Shmuel disagreed** about the significance of the word וַיִּחַדְּ, translated here as "he rejoiced." [7]**Rav said:** The term teaches us **that** Jethro **passed a sharp** [חַדָּה] **sword over his flesh,** circumcising himself and converting to Judaism. [8]**And Shmuel said:** The term teaches us **that** when Jethro heard about the defeat suffered by the Egyptians, **his entire body felt** as if it had suffered **cuts** [חִדּוּדִים], in sympathy with what had happened to them. [9]**Rav said: This is** what is meant by **the popular adage:** Take care **not to sneer at a non-Jew in the presence of a convert,** or one of his descendants even **to the tenth generation.**

לָכֵן יְשַׁלַּח [10]The verse states (Isaiah 10:16): **"Therefore shall the Master, the Lord of hosts, send among his fat ones leanness."** [11]**What is** the meaning of the words **"among his fat ones** [בְּמִשְׁמַנָּיו] **leanness"?** The Gemara explains: The word בְּמִשְׁמַנָּיו, "among his fat ones," alludes to the number eight [שְׁמוֹנָה]. [12]**The Holy One, blessed be He, said: Let Hezekiah who has eight names come and punish Sennacherib who has eight names.** [13]**Hezekiah**

הוּא לְחִזְקִיָּה וְסִיַּיעְתּוֹ שֶׁלֹּא אָמְרוּ שִׁירָה, עַד שֶׁפָּתְחָה הָאָרֶץ וְאָמְרָה שִׁירָה, [1]שֶׁנֶּאֱמַר: ׳מִכְּנַף הָאָרֶץ זְמִרֹת שָׁמַעְנוּ: ״צְבִי לַצַּדִּיק וגו׳ ״ ׳ ״.

[2]כַּיּוֹצֵא בַּדָּבָר אַתָּה אוֹמֵר: ״וַיֹּאמֶר יִתְרוֹ בָּרוּךְ ה׳ אֲשֶׁר הִצִּיל אֶתְכֶם״. [3]תָּנָא מִשּׁוּם רַבִּי פַּפְּיָיס: ״גְּנַאי הוּא לְמֹשֶׁה וְשִׁשִּׁים רִיבּוֹא שֶׁלֹּא אָמְרוּ ׳בָּרוּךְ׳, [4]עַד שֶׁבָּא יִתְרוֹ וְאָמַר, ׳בָּרוּךְ ה׳ ׳ ״.

[5]״וַיִּחַדְּ יִתְרוֹ״. [6]רַב וּשְׁמוּאֵל. [7]רַב אָמַר: שֶׁהֶעֱבִיר חֶרֶב חַדָּה עַל בְּשָׂרוֹ. [8]וּשְׁמוּאֵל אָמַר: שֶׁנַּעֲשָׂה חִדּוּדִים חִדּוּדִים כָּל בְּשָׂרוֹ. [9]אָמַר רַב, הַיְינוּ דְּאָמְרִי אֱינָשֵׁי: גִּיּוֹרָא, עַד עֲשָׂרָה דָּרֵי לֹא תְּבַזֶּה אֲרַמַּאי קַמֵּיהּ.

[10]״לָכֵן יְשַׁלַּח הָאָדוֹן ה׳ צְבָאוֹת בְּמִשְׁמַנָּיו רָזוֹן״. [11]מַאי ״בְּמִשְׁמַנָּיו רָזוֹן״? [12]אָמַר הַקָּדוֹשׁ בָּרוּךְ הוּא: יָבֹא חִזְקִיָּהוּ שֶׁיֵּשׁ לוֹ שְׁמוֹנָה שֵׁמוֹת, וְיִפָּרַע מִסַּנְחֵרִיב שֶׁיֵּשׁ לוֹ שְׁמוֹנָה שֵׁמוֹת. [13]חִזְקִיָּה, דִּכְתִיב: ״כִּי

LITERAL TRANSLATION

that Hezekiah and his company did not sing a song, until the earth opened and sang a song, [1]as it is stated: 'From the uttermost part of the earth have we heard songs: "Glory to the righteous."'"

[2]Similar to this, you say: "And Jethro said, Blessed be the Lord, who has delivered you." [3][A Tanna] taught in the name of Rabbi Papyas: "It is a disgrace to Moses and the six hundred thousand that they did not say 'Blessed be,' [4]until Jethro came and said, 'Blessed be the Lord.'"

[5]"And Jethro rejoiced." [6]Rav and Shmuel [disagreed]. [7]Rav said: That he passed a sharp sword over his flesh. [8]And Shmuel said: That his entire body felt like cuts. [9]Rav said: This is what people say: A convert, for ten generations, do not sneer at a non-Jew (lit., "an Aramean") in his presence.

[10]"Therefore shall the Master, the Lord of hosts, send among his fat ones leanness." [11]What is "among his fat ones leanness"? [12]The Holy One, blessed be He, said: Let Hezekiah who has eight names come and punish Sennacherib who has eight names. [13]Hezekiah, as it is written: "For

RASHI

חרב חדה – שמל את עצמו ונתגייר. חדודין חדודין – קמטין קמטין, שהיה מיצר מאד על מפלת מצרים. גיורא עד עשרה דרי – הכי הוא משל בני אדם, ומיהו יתרו לאו עשירי הוה.

NOTES

סַנְחֵרִיב שֶׁיֵּשׁ לוֹ שְׁמוֹנָה שֵׁמוֹת **Sennacherib who has eight names.** According to the plain sense of the text, these different names refer to different kings. But since the prophecy deals primarily with the war between Israel and Assyria, all the kings of Assyria are treated as one. The commentators disagree about how to count the eight names. Our commentary follows *Rashi*, who treats Tiglath-Pileser as one name, and Asnapper, Great, and Noble as three names, even though "great and noble" could be read as adjectives. *The Gaon of Vilna* suggests as follows: Tiglath-Pileser, Tiglath-Pleser, Tilgath-Pilneeser, Tilgath-Pilneser (I Chronicles 5:26), Shalmaneser, Pul, Sargon, and Asnapper. *Rabbi A. M. Horowitz* counts the eight as follows: Tilgath, Tiglath, Pul, Pileser, Pilneeser, Shalmaneser, Sargon, and Asnapper.

TRANSLATION AND COMMENTARY

had eight names, as the verse states about him (Isaiah 9:5): **"For to us a child is born, to us a son is given; and the government is upon his shoulder; and his name is called Pele-yoetz-el-gibbor-avi-ad-sar-shalom."**

וְהָאִיכָּא חִזְקִיָּה [1]The Gemara asks: **But** surely he had nine names, for **there is** also the name **Hezekiah!**

שֶׁחִזְּקוֹ יָהּ [2]The Gemara answers: Ḥezekiah [חִזְקִיָּה] was not actually his name, but rather a descriptive term reflecting the fact **that God** [יָהּ] **strengthened him** [חִזְּקוֹ]. [3]**Another explanation** of that designation may be suggested: He was called **Hezekiah,** because **he strengthened** [חִיזֵּק] **Israel**'s faith in God [יָהּ], **their father in Heaven.**

סַנְחֵרִיב [4]The Gemara continues: **Sennacherib** also had eight names, **for the verses** regarding the kings of Ashur **state: "Tiglath-pileser** (II Kings 15:29)," "Tilgath-**Pilneeser** (II Chronicles 28:20)," **"Shalmaneser** (II Kings 17:3)," **"Pul** (II Kings 15:19)," **"Sargon** (Isaiah 20:1)," and **"the great and noble Asnapper** (Ezra 4:10)," the last designation counting as three.

וְהָאִיכָּא סַנְחֵרִיב [5]The Gemara comments: **But** surely he had nine names, for **there is** also the name **Sennacherib!**

שֶׁשִּׂיחָתוֹ רִיב [6]The Gemara explains: Sennacherib [סַנְחֵרִיב] was not actually his name, but rather a descriptive term reflecting the fact that he was a person **whose talk** [שִׂיחַ] **was strife** [רִיב] — whatever he said led to quarreling and contention. [7]**Another explanation** of that designation may be suggested: **He spoke** [סָח] **and snorted forth** [נִיחֵר] **words** [דְּבָרִים] **against Heaven.**

אָמַר רַבִּי יוֹחָנָן [8]**Rabbi Yoḥanan said: Why did that wicked man merit to be called** (Ezra 4:10) **"the great and noble Asnapper"?** [9]**Because** even when he tried to persuade the people of Jerusalem to surrender to him, and voluntarily go into exile, **he did not speak ill of Eretz Israel,** [10]**as the verse states** (II Kings 18:32): **"Until I come and take you away to a land like your own land"** — a land like your own land, but not any better than it.

רַב וּשְׁמוּאֵל [11]**Rav and Shmuel disagreed** about Sennacherib's tactics. **One** of the two Amoraim **said:** He **was a clever king.** [12]**And** the other **one said:** He **was a foolish king.** [13]**According to the** Amora **who said** that he **was a clever king,** Sennacherib reasoned as follows: [14]**If I say to them,** "Until I come and take you away to a land that is **better than your own land,"** [15]**they will say** to me, **"You are a liar,** for no land is better than

יֶלֶד יֻלַּד לָנוּ בֵּן נִתַּן לָנוּ וַתְּהִי הַמִּשְׂרָה עַל שִׁכְמוֹ; וַיִּקְרָא שְׁמוֹ פֶּלֶא יוֹעֵץ אֵל גִּבּוֹר אֲבִי עַד שַׂר שָׁלוֹם".

[1]וְהָאִיכָּא חִזְקִיָּה!

[2]שֶׁחִזְּקוֹ יָהּ. [3]דָּבָר אַחֵר: חִזְקִיָּה שֶׁחִיזֵּק אֶת יִשְׂרָאֵל לַאֲבִיהֶם שֶׁבַּשָּׁמַיִם.

[4]סַנְחֵרִיב — דִּכְתִיב בֵּיהּ: "תִּגְלַת פִּלְאֶסֶר", "פִּלְנְאֶסֶר", "שַׁלְמַנְאֶסֶר", "פּוּל", "סַרְגּוֹן (סרגין)", "אָסְנַפַּר רַבָּא וְיַקִּירָא".

[5]וְהָאִיכָּא סַנְחֵרִיב!

[6]שֶׁשִּׂיחָתוֹ רִיב. [7]דָּבָר אַחֵר: שֶׁסָּח וְנִיחֵר דְּבָרִים כְּלַפֵּי מַעְלָה.

[8]אָמַר רַבִּי יוֹחָנָן: מִפְּנֵי מָה זָכָה אוֹתוֹ רָשָׁע לִקְרוֹתוֹ "אָסְנַפַּר רַבָּא וְיַקִּירָא"? [9]מִפְּנֵי שֶׁלֹּא סִיפֵּר בִּגְנוּתָהּ שֶׁל אֶרֶץ יִשְׂרָאֵל, [10]שֶׁנֶּאֱמַר: "עַד בֹּאִי וְלָקַחְתִּי אֶתְכֶם אֶל אֶרֶץ כְּאַרְצְכֶם".

[11]רַב וּשְׁמוּאֵל, חַד אָמַר: מֶלֶךְ פִּקֵּחַ הָיָה. [12]וְחַד אָמַר: מֶלֶךְ טִיפֵּשׁ הָיָה. [13]לְמַאן דְּאָמַר מֶלֶךְ פִּקֵּחַ הָיָה — [14]אִי אָמִינָא לְהוּ: "עֲדִיפָא מֵאַרְעַיְיכוּ", [15]אָמְרוּ,

LITERAL TRANSLATION

to us a child is born, to us a son is given; and the government is upon his shoulder; and his name is called Pele-yoetz-el-gibbor-avi-ad-sar-shalom (lit., 'Wonder, Counselor, Divine, Mighty, Father, Eternal, Minister, Peace')."

[1]But there is Hezekiah!

[2]That God strengthened him. [3]Another explanation: Hezekiah — that he strengthened Israel regarding their father in Heaven.

[4]Sennacherib — for it is written about him: "Tiglath-pileser," "Pilneeser," "Shalmaneser," "Pul," "Sargon," "Asnapper Rabba Veyakira (lit., 'the great and noble')."

[5]But there is Sennacherib!

[6]Whose talk is strife. [7]Another explanation: Who spoke and snorted words against Heaven.

[8]Rabbi Yoḥanan said: Why did that wicked man merit to be called "the great and noble Asnapper"? [9]Because he did not speak ill of Eretz Israel, [10]as it stated: "Until I come and take you away to a land like your own land."

[11]Rav and Shmuel [disagreed]: One said: He was a clever king. [12]And one said: He was a foolish king. [13]According to the one who said he was a clever king — [14]if I say to them, "Better than your own land," [15]they will say,

RASHI

פלא יועץ אל גבור אבי עד שר שלום — שמחזק ישראל — העוסקין בתורה כדלקמן. **תגלת פלאסר** — שם אחד הוא, דכתיב בימי פקח בן רמליה בא תגלת פלאסר מלך אשור. **אסנפר** — חד, **רבא** — חד, **ויקירא** — חד. **כלפי מעלה** — כדלקמן שחירף על ידי מלאך. **אל ארץ כארצכם** — ולא אמר מוטבת מארצכם.

”קָא מְשַׁקְּרַתְּ“. [1]וּמַאן דַּאֲמַר מֶלֶךְ טִיפֵּשׁ הָיָה — [2]אִם כֵּן, מַאי רְבוּתֵיהּ?
[3]לְהֵיכָא אַגְלֵי לְהוּ? [4]מָר זוּטְרָא אָמַר: לְאַפְרִיקֵי. [5]וְרַבִּי חֲנִינָא אָמַר: לְהָרֵי סְלוּג.
[6]אֲבָל יִשְׂרָאֵל סִפְּרוּ בִּגְנוּתָהּ שֶׁל אֶרֶץ יִשְׂרָאֵל. [7]כִּי מָטוּ שׁוֹשׁ, אָמְרִי: שָׁוְיָא כִּי אַרְעִין. [8]כִּי מָטוּ עָלְמִין, אָמְרוּ: כְּעָלְמִין. [9]כִּי מָטוּ שׁוֹשׁ—תְּרֵי, אָמְרִי: עַל חַד תְּרֵין.
[10]”וְתַחַת כְּבֹדוֹ [יֵקַד] יְקֹד כִּיקוֹד אֵשׁ“. [11]אָמַר רַבִּי יוֹחָנָן: תַּחַת כְּבוֹדוֹ, וְלֹא כְּבוֹדוֹ מַמָּשׁ, כִּי הָא דְּרַבִּי יוֹחָנָן קָרֵי לֵיהּ לְמָאנֵי, ”מְכַבְּדוֹתַי“. [12]רַבִּי אֶלְעָזָר אָמַר: תַּחַת כְּבוֹדוֹ מַמָּשׁ, [13]כִּשְׂרֵיפַת

LITERAL TRANSLATION

"You lie." [1]And the one who said he was a foolish king — [2]if so, what is its advantage?
[3]To where did he exile them? Mar Zutra said: To Afriki. [4]And Rabbi Ḥanina said: To the mountains of Slug.
[5]But Israel spoke ill of Eretz Israel. [6]When they came to Shosh, they said: It is like our land. [7]When they came to Almin, they said: Like our world. [8]When they came to Shosh-tre, they said: For one, two.
[9]"And under his glory shall be kindled a burning like the burning of a fire." [10]Rabbi Yoḥanan said: Under his glory, but not his glory, literally, [11]like the way Rabbi Yoḥanan called his clothing, "that which glorifies me." [12]Rabbi Elazar said: Under his glory, literally, [13]like the burning of

TRANSLATION AND COMMENTARY

Eretz Israel." Thus, I will say to them, "To a land like your own land," and perhaps I will convince them. [1]**And the** Amora **who said** that Sennacherib **was a foolish king** maintains that he should have told them that he would take them to a land that was better than their own land, [2]for **if** it is only as good as their own land, **what is its advantage,** and why should they agree to go into exile?

לְהֵיכָא [3]The Gemara asks: **To where did** Sennacherib **exile** the ten tribes? [4]**Mar Zutra said: To Africa.** [5]**And Rabbi Ḥanina said: To the mountains of Slug.**

אֲבָל יִשְׂרָאֵל [6]The Gemara notes: **But** the people of **Israel** themselves **spoke ill of Eretz Israel,** and praised the land to which they had been exiled. [7]**When they came to** a place which would henceforth be called **Shosh they said:** This place **is** just **like** [*shaveh*] **our land.** [8]**When they came to** a place which would henceforth be called **Almin, they said:** This place is just **like our world** [*almin*], our land. [9]And **when they came to** a place which would henceforth be called **Shosh-tre, they said: One** is like [*shaveh*] **two** [*tre*] — this place is twice as good as our land.

וְתַחַת כְּבֹדוֹ [10]Regarding Sennacherib, the verse states (Isaiah 10:16): **"And under his glory shall be kindled a burning like the burning of a fire."** Rabbi Yoḥanan and Rabbi Elazar agree that the verse implies that the fire burned that which was "under his glory," but not his glory itself. But they disagree about the meaning of "his glory." [11]**Rabbi Yoḥanan said:** The fire burned what was **under his glory, but** the words "his glory" do **not** mean **his glory, literally.** They refer to his clothing, not to his body. Thus, "under his glory" means the body that is under his clothing, and the verse refers to clothing as "glory." This is **like** the opinion of **Rabbi Yoḥanan** himself, who **called his clothing, "that which glorifies me."** Thus, according to him, the fire burned Sennacherib's body under his clothing. [12]**Rabbi Elazar** disagreed and **said:** The fire burned what was **under his glory,** and the words "his glory" mean his glory, **literally,** his body. Thus, "under his glory" means his soul, which is under his body. His soul was burned, but his body remained intact. [13]He was consumed by a divine fire just **like the sons of Aaron,**

RASHI

קא משקרת — שהרי אין ארץ מעולה הימנה, ולכן לא אמר מוטבת מארצכם. **להיכא אגלינהו** — סנחריב לעשרת השבטים דכתיב (מלכים ב׳ יח) ”וינחם בחלח ובחבור נהר גוזן וערי מדי“, הי ניהו אותן מקומות? **אבל ישראל** — כי אגלינהו סנחריב ספרו בגנותה של ארץ ישראל, דכי מטו לאותו מקום ששמו שוש אמרו: ”שויא לארעין“ — זאת הארץ שויא לארצנו, וכשבאו למקום ששמו עלמין אמרו: ”כי עלמין“ — זה המקום שוה לירושלים שנקראת בית עולמים. **כשבאו למקום ששמו שוש תרי אמרו על חד תרין** — כלומר זה יפה פי שנים כמקומנו, ועל שם כך נקראו כל אותן מקומות כך. הכי גרסינן: **תחת כבודו ולא כבודו ממש** — דכבודו ממש משמע בשרו וגופו, תחת כבודו משמע תחת הגוף והבשר, כלומר נשמה שבתוך הגוף, והשתא אמר תחת כבודו ולא כבודו ממש, נשמה שבתוך הגוף, אלא האי כבודו — היינו בגדיו, דתחת בגדיהם נשרפו, וכי הא דר׳ יוחנן וכו׳, דכל הגוף נשרף תחת הבגדים, ולא גרסינן תחת כבודו ולא תחת כבודו ממש, דמשמע דמקרא נפקא לזה, דהאי תחת כבודו לא תחת כבודו ממש, ומהיכא תיפוק ליה האי, — אבל השתא דדרשא בעלמא, דריש ליה. **תחת כבודו ממש** — תחת גופו ממש שהגוף קיים ונשמה נשרפת.

BACKGROUND

אַפְרִיקֵי Afriki. Afriki usually refers to the African continent, especially the Roman province of Africa, which arose in place of Carthage. This region, along the Mediterranean coast, is on the same latitude as Eretz Israel, and its climate is very similar. Here, however, the term might refer to Phrygia in Asia Minor, or to a region in Elam.

הָרֵי סְלוּג Mountains of Slug. It is not clear where this place is, though the term might refer to the Caucasus Mountains.

NOTES

קָרֵי לֵיהּ לְמָאנֵי, ”מְכַבְּדוֹתַי“ He calls his clothing, "that which glorifies me." *She'iltot* cites a reading according to which Rabbi Yoḥanan called his Shabbat garments *mekhabdotai*. By setting aside special garments for Shabbat, he fulfilled the obligation (Isaiah 58:13): "And call the Sabbath a delight, the holy day of the Lord honorable, and honor it [וְכִבַּדְתּוֹ]." Moreover, the Rabbis teach us that in a place where a person is not recognized, his clothing gives him honor.

בְּנֵי אַהֲרֹן. [1]מַה לְּהַלָּן שְׂרֵיפַת נְשָׁמָה וְגוּף קַיָּים, [2]אַף כָּאן, שְׂרֵיפַת נְשָׁמָה וְגוּף קַיָּים.

[3]תָּנָא מִשְּׁמֵיהּ דְּרַבִּי יְהוֹשֻׁעַ בֶּן קָרְחָה: [4]"פַּרְעֹה שֶׁחֵירֵף בְּעַצְמוֹ, נִפְרַע הַקָּדוֹשׁ בָּרוּךְ הוּא מִמֶּנּוּ בְּעַצְמוֹ, סַנְחֵרִיב שֶׁחֵירֵף [94B] עַל יְדֵי שָׁלִיחַ — נִפְרַע הַקָּדוֹשׁ בָּרוּךְ הוּא מִמֶּנּוּ עַל יְדֵי שָׁלִיחַ. [5]פַּרְעֹה דִּכְתִיב בֵּיהּ: "מִי ה' אֲשֶׁר אֶשְׁמַע בְּקֹלוֹ"? [6]נִפְרַע הַקָּדוֹשׁ בָּרוּךְ הוּא מִמֶּנּוּ בְּעַצְמוֹ, [7]דִּכְתִיב: "וַיְנַעֵר ה' אֶת מִצְרַיִם בְּתוֹךְ הַיָּם". [8]וּכְתִיב: "דָּרַכְתָּ בַיָּם סוּסֶיךָ וגו'". [9]סַנְחֵרִיב דִּכְתִיב: "בְּיַד מַלְאָכֶיךָ חֵרַפְתָּ ה'" — נִפְרַע הַקָּדוֹשׁ בָּרוּךְ הוּא מִמֶּנּוּ עַל יְדֵי שָׁלִיחַ, [10]דִּכְתִיב: "וַיֵּצֵא מַלְאַךְ ה' וַיַּךְ בְּמַחֲנֵה אַשּׁוּר מֵאָה שְׁמוֹנִים וַחֲמִשָּׁה אֶלֶף וגו'".

[11]רַבִּי חֲנִינָא בַּר פַּפָּא רָמֵי: [12]כְּתִיב: "מְרוֹם קִצּוֹ". [13]וּכְתִיב: "מְלוֹן קִצּוֹ". [14]אָמַר אוֹתוֹ רָשָׁע: "בַּתְּחִלָּה אַחֲרִיב דִּירָה שֶׁל

LITERAL TRANSLATION

the sons of Aaron. [1]Just as below, the burning of the soul, and the body exists, [2]so, too, here, the burning of the soul, and the body exists.

[3][A Tanna] taught in the name of Rabbi Yehoshua ben Korḥah: [4]"Pharaoh, who blasphemed by himself, the Holy One, blessed is He, punished him by Himself. Sennacherib who blasphemed [94B] through an agent, the Holy One, blessed be He, punished him through an agent. [5]Pharaoh, about whom it is written [that he said to Moses]: 'Who is the Lord that I should obey His voice?' — [6]the Holy One, blessed be He, punished him by Himself, [7]as it is written: 'And the Lord overthrew Egypt in the midst of the sea.' [8]And it is written: 'You have trodden through the sea with Your horses, etc.' [9]Sennacherib, about whom it is written: 'By your messengers you have taunted the Lord' — the Holy One, blessed be He, punished him through an agent, [10]as it is written: 'The Angel of the Lord went out and struck down in the camp of Assyria a hundred and eighty five thousand, etc.'"

[11]Rabbi Ḥanina bar Pappa cast together: [12]It is written: "And I will enter into its farthest height." [13]And it is written: "And I have entered into its farthest lodge." [14]That wicked man said: "First I will destroy the lower habitation,

TRANSLATION AND COMMENTARY

who were consumed by a divine **fire.** [1]**Just as elsewhere,** regarding the death of Aaron's sons, only **their souls were burned, but their bodies remained intact,** [2]**so, too, here,** regarding Sennacherib, only **his soul was burned, but his body remained intact.**

תָּנָא [3]**A Tanna taught in the name of Rabbi Yehoshua ben Korḥah:** "Blaspheming God through an agent is more despicable than blaspheming God directly, and so, too, is punishment meted out by God through an agent a more humiliating form of retribution than punishment meted out by God directly. [4]**Pharaoh, who blasphemed** God **by himself,** and not through an agent — **the Holy One, blessed be He, punished him by Himself,** and not through an agent. **Sennacherib, who blasphemed** God [94B] **through an agent,** adding to the insult — **the Holy One, blessed be He, punished him through an agent,** adding to the humiliation. How so? [5]Regarding **Pharaoh, the verse states** that he himself said to Moses (Exodus 5:2): **'Who is the Lord that I should obey His voice?"** Since he blasphemed God by himself, and not through an agent, [6]**the Holy One, blessed be He, punished him by himself,** and not through an agent, [7]**as the verse states** (Exodus 14:27): **'And the Lord overthrew Egypt in the midst of the sea.'** [8]**And** elsewhere **the verse states** (Habakkuk 3:15): **'You have trodden through the sea with Your horses.'** [9]Regarding **Sennacherib, the verse states** (II Kings 19:23): **'By your messengers you have taunted the Lord.'** Since he blasphemed God through an agent, **the Holy One, blessed be He, punished him through an agent,** [10]**as the verse states** (II Kings 19:35): **'The Angel of the Lord went out and struck down in the camp of Assyria a hundred and eighty five thousand.'"**

רַבִּי חֲנִינָא בַּר פַּפָּא [11]**Rabbi Ḥanina bar Pappa cast together** the two following verses, and pointed out the contradiction between them. [12]**The verse** in the Book of Isaiah that records Sennacherib's blasphemous words **states** (Isaiah 37:24): **"And I will enter into its farthest height,"** implying that Sennacherib threatened to strike at God's heavenly habitation. [13]**But** the parallel **verse** in the Second Book of Kings **states** (II Kings 19:23): **"And I have entered into its farthest lodge,"** implying that Sennacherib threatened to strike at God's habitation in this world, the Temple. How can the two verses be reconciled? [14]**That wicked man,** Sennacherib, **said** as follows: **"First I will destroy** God's **habitation in**

RASHI

בעצמו — הוא עצמו ולא על ידי שליח לא היה ביזוי כל כך, ולכך הקדוש ברוך הוא כמו כן נפרע ממנו בעצמו ולא נתבייש כל כך, דאינו דומה מתבייש מן הגדול למתבייש מן הקטן. **על ידי שליח** — דהיינו בזוי יותר, אף הקדוש ברוך הוא נפרע על ידי שליח ונתבייש יותר. **כתיב מרום קצו** — בישעיה. **וכתיב מלון קיצו** — במלכים, מרום קיצו משמע דירה של מטה, כדכתיב (ירמיהו יז) "מרום מראשון מקום מקדשנו", "מלון קיצו" —

LANGUAGE

לִיטְרָא ***Litra.*** This term derives from the Greek λιτρα, *litra*, which is parallel to the Latin word *litra*.

TRANSLATION AND COMMENTARY

this world, and afterwards I will destroy His **habitation in Heaven.**"

אָמַר רַבִּי יְהוֹשֻׁעַ בֶּן לֵוִי [1]**Rabbi Yehoshua ben Levi said: What is** the meaning **of the verse which states** (II Kings 18:25): [2]**"Am I now come up without the Lord against this place to destroy it?** [3]**It is the Lord who said to me, Go up against this land, and destroy it"?** [4]**What is** meant by **this?** Where did God command Rabshakeh to go destroy the Land of Israel? [5]Rabbi Yehoshua ben Levi explains: Rabshakeh **heard** the words of **the Prophet who said** (Isaiah 8:6-7): **"Since this people rejects the waters of Shiloah that go softly, and rejoices in Retzin and the son of Remaliah.** Now, therefore, behold, the Lord brings up upon them the waters of the river, strong and abundant, namely the King of Assyria, and all his glory."

אָמַר רַב יוֹסֵף [6]**Rav Yosef said: Were it not for the** Aramaic **translation of this verse, I would not have known what it means.** According to the Aramaic translation, the verse means as follows: [7]**Since this people loathed the kingdom of the House of David that led them gently, like the waters of the Shiloah that flow gently, and they wanted Retzin,** King of Assyria, **and** Pekach, **the son of Remaliah,** King of Israel. Therefore, the Lord brings upon them the strong and abundant river, the King of Assyria.

אָמַר רַבִּי יוֹחָנָן [8]The Gemara sets aside the interpretation of the verse in Isaiah momentarily to discuss a reference to Pekach, the son of Remaliah. **Rabbi Yoḥanan said: What is** the meaning of **the verse that states** (Proverbs 3:33): [9]**"The curse of the Lord is in the house of the wicked; but He blesses the habitation of the just"?** [10]**"The curse of the Lord is in the house of the wicked" — this** refers to **Pekach the son of Remaliah,** King of Israel, **who would eat forty *se'ahs* of chicks for dessert** and still not be satiated. [11]**"But He blesses the habitation of the just" — this** refers to **Hezekiah, King of Judah, who would eat a pound of vegetables during a meal** and be satisfied.

וְלָכֵן הִנֵּה [12]Now the Gemara returns to the verse in Isaiah (8:7): **"Now, therefore, behold, the Lord brings up upon them the waters of the river, strong and abundant, namely the King of Assyria."**

מַטָּה, וְאַחַר כָּךְ אַחֲרִיב דִּירָה שֶׁל מַעֲלָה״.

[1]אָמַר רַבִּי יְהוֹשֻׁעַ בֶּן לֵוִי: מַאי דִּכְתִיב: [2]״עַתָּה הֲמִבַּלְעֲדֵי ה׳ עָלִיתִי עַל הַמָּקוֹם הַזֶּה לְהַשְׁחִתוֹ. [3]ה׳ אָמַר אֵלַי עֲלֵה עַל הָאָרֶץ הַזֹּאת וְהַשְׁחִיתָהּ״. [4]מַאי הִיא? [5]דִּשְׁמַע לְנָבִיא דְּקָאָמַר: ״יַעַן כִּי מָאַס הָעָם הַזֶּה אֵת מֵי הַשִּׁלֹחַ הַהֹלְכִים לְאַט וּמְשׂוֹשׂ אֶת רְצִין וּבֶן רְמַלְיָהוּ״.

[6]אָמַר רַב יוֹסֵף: אִלְמָלֵא תַּרְגּוּמָא דְּהַאי קְרָא, לָא הֲוָה יָדַעְנָא מַאי קָאָמַר: [7]חֲלַף דְּקַץ עַמָּא הָדֵין בְּמַלְכוּתָא דְּבֵית דָּוִד דִּמְדַבַּר לְהוֹן בְּנַיַּיח, כְּמֵי שִׁילוֹחָא דִּנְגְדִין בְּנַיַּיח, וְאִתְרְעִיאוּ בִּרְצִין וּבַר רְמַלְיָה״.

[8]אָמַר רַבִּי יוֹחָנָן: מַאי דִּכְתִיב: [9]״מְאֵרַת ה׳ בְּבֵית רָשָׁע וּנְוֵה צַדִּיקִים יְבָרֵךְ״. [10]״מְאֵרַת ה׳ בְּבֵית רָשָׁע״ — זֶה פֶּקַח בֶּן רְמַלְיָהוּ, שֶׁהָיָה אוֹכֵל אַרְבָּעִים סְאָה גּוֹזָלוֹת בְּקִינּוּחַ סְעוּדָה. [11]״וּנְוֵה צַדִּיקִים יְבָרֵךְ״ — זֶה חִזְקִיָּה מֶלֶךְ יְהוּדָה שֶׁהָיָה אוֹכֵל לִיטְרָא יָרָק בַּסְּעוּדָּה.

[12]״וְלָכֵן הִנֵּה ה׳ מַעֲלֶה עֲלֵיהֶם אֶת מֵי הַנָּהָר הָעֲצוּמִים וְהָרַבִּים אֶת מֶלֶךְ אַשּׁוּר״.

LITERAL TRANSLATION

and afterwards I will destroy the upper habitation."

[1]Rabbi Yehoshua ben Levi said: What is that which is written: [2]"Am I now come up without the Lord against this place to destroy it? [3]The Lord said to me, Go up against this land, and destroy it"? [4]What is it? [5]For he heard the prophet who said: "Since this people rejects the water of Shiloah that go softly, and rejoices in Retzin and the son of Remaliah."

[6]Rav Yosef said: Were it not for the translation of this verse, I would not have known what it says: [7]Since this people loathed the kingdom of the House of David that led them gently, like the waters of the Shiloah which flow gently, and they wanted Retzin and the son of Remaliah.

[8]Rabbi Yoḥanan said: What is that which is written: [9]"The curse of the Lord is in the house of the wicked; but He blesses the habitation of the just"? [10]"The curse of the Lord is in the house of the wicked" — this is Pekach the son of Remaliah, who would eat forty se'ahs of chicks for dessert. [11]"But He blesses the habitation of the just" — this is Hezekiah, King of Judah, who would eat a pound of vegetables during a meal.

[12]"Now, therefore, behold, the Lord brings up upon them the waters of the river, strong and abundant, the King of Assyria."

RASHI

משמע דירה של מעלה, בית מלונו. ה׳ אמר אלי עלה אל הארץ וגו׳ מאי היא — היכי אמר לו הקדוש ברוך הוא להשחית? יען כי מאס העם הזה וגו׳ — ומשוש את רצין ובן רמליהו ואתרעו להשחיתה ברצין ובר רמליהו. מארת ה׳ — שלא נשבע מכל מה שהיה אוכל. ליטרא ירק — במדה. ועלה על כל אפיקיו — שאמר לו הקדוש ברוך הוא עלה והשחת.

[1]וּכְתִיב: וְחָלַף בִּיהוּדָה שָׁטַף
וְעָבַר עַד צַוָּאר יַגִּיעַ״. [2]אֶלָּא מַאי
טַעְמָא אִיעַנֵּישׁ? [3]נָבִיא אַעֲשֶׂרֶת
הַשְּׁבָטִים אִיתְנַבֵּי; אִיהוּ יָהֵיב
דַּעְתֵּיהּ עַל כּוּלָּהּ יְרוּשָׁלַיִם.
[4]בָּא נָבִיא וְאָמַר לֵיהּ: ״כִּי לֹא
מוּעָף לַאֲשֶׁר מוּצָק לָהּ״. [5]אָמַר
רַבִּי אֶלְעָזָר בַּר בֶּרֶכְיָה: אֵין
נִמְסָר עַם עָיֵיף בַּתּוֹרָה בְּיַד מִי
הַמֵּצִיק לוֹ.
[6]מַאי ״כָּעֵת הָרִאשׁוֹן הֵקַל
אַרְצָה זְבוּלֻן וְאַרְצָה נַפְתָּלִי
וְהָאַחֲרוֹן הִכְבִּיד דֶּרֶךְ הַיָּם עֵבֶר
הַיַּרְדֵּן גְּלִיל הַגּוֹיִם״? [7]לֹא
כָּרִאשׁוֹנִים שֶׁהֵקֵלּוּ מֵעֲלֵיהֶם
עוֹל תּוֹרָה. אֲבָל אַחֲרוֹנִים
שֶׁהִכְבִּידוּ עֲלֵיהֶן עוֹל תּוֹרָה,
[8]וּרְאוּיִין הַלָּלוּ לַעֲשׂוֹת לָהֶם נֵס
כְּעוֹבְרֵי הַיָּם וּכְדוֹרְכֵי הַיַּרְדֵּן.
[9]אִם חוֹזֵר בּוֹ — מוּטָב. [10]וְאִם
לָאו — אֲנִי אֶעֱשֶׂה לוֹ גָּלִיל
בַּגּוֹיִם.

LITERAL TRANSLATION

[1]And it is written: "And he shall sweep through Judah; he shall overflow and go over, he shall reach even to the neck." [2]So what is the reason that he was punished? [3]The Prophet prophesied about the ten tribes; he set his mind against all of Jerusalem.

[4]The Prophet came and said to him: "For there is no weariness to him that is set against her." [5]Rabbi Elazar bar Berakhyah said: A people that is weary from Torah will not be given over into the hand of him who oppresses it.

[6]What is "At the first he lightly [afflicted] the land of Zebulun, and the land of Naftali and afterward he oppressed her by the way of the sea, beyond the Jordan in the Galil of the nations"? [7]Not like the earlier ones who lightened the yoke of the Torah from themselves. But the later ones who made the yoke of the Torah heavier for themselves, [8]and these are worthy to have a miracle performed for them, like those who passed through the sea and those who stepped across the Jordan. [9]If he retracts — fine. [10]And if not, I will make him contemptible among the nations.

TRANSLATION AND COMMENTARY

[1]**And the** next **verse states** (Isaiah 8:8): **"And he shall sweep through Judah; he shall overflow and go over, he shall reach even to the neck."** As was argued above, after hearing this prophecy Rabshakeh claimed that he and Sennacherib were following God's command. [2]If this is so, for **what reason was he punished?** [3]The Gemara explains: **The Prophet** only **prophesied about the ten tribes** that Sennacherib was to destroy, but **he set his mind** to destroy **all of Jerusalem.**

בָּא נָבִיא [4]When Sennacherib attacked Jerusalem, **the Prophet** Isaiah **went to him and said** (Isaiah 8:23): **"For there is no weariness** [מוּעָף] **to him that is set against her** [מוּצָק]." [5]**Rabbi Elazar bar Berakhyah said:** This verse may be understood as follows: **A people that has become weary** [עָיֵיף] **from Torah** study and observance **will not be given over into the hand of** Sennacherib **who oppresses** [הַמֵּצִיק] **it.**

מַאי כָּעֵת [6]The Gemara asks: **What is** the meaning of the continuation of that verse (Isaiah 8:23): **"At the first** [הָרִאשׁוֹן] **he lightly afflicted** [הֵקַל] **the land of Zebulun, and the land of Naftali and afterward** [וְהָאַחֲרוֹן] **he oppressed her** [הִכְבִּיד] **by the way of the sea, beyond the Jordan in the Galil** [גְּלִיל] **of the nations**"? [7]The verse may be interpreted as follows: Hezekiah's people are **not like the earlier ones** [כָּרִאשׁוֹנִים] — the ten tribes of Israel — **who had relieved** [הֵקֵלּוּ] **themselves of the yoke of the Torah, for the later ones** [אַחֲרוֹנִים] — the people of Hezekiah — **made the yoke of the Torah heavier** [הִכְבִּידוּ] **for themselves.** [8]Therefore, **they are worthy to have a miracle performed for them,** just **like those who passed through the Red Sea** ("way of the sea") after leaving Egypt **and those who stepped across the Jordan** River ("beyond the Jordan") on dry land to enter the Land of Israel. [9]**If** Sennacherib **retracts** his plans **— fine.** [10]**And if not, I will make him contemptible** [גָּלִיל], (used here in the sense of "rolling" in shame), **among the nations.**

RASHI

מאי טעמא — מאחר שברשות הלך, שנביא נתנבא עליו, מאי טעמא איענש. **בא נביא ואמר לו** — כשבא על ירושלים. **כי לא מועף לאשר מוצק לה** — לא נמסר עמו של חזקיה שהוא עיף בתורה ביד סנחריב המציק לו. **בעת הראשון הקל ארצה זבולון וארצה נפתלי וגו׳ לא כראשונים** — עשרת השבטים שהקלו מעליהם עול תורה, אבל אחרונים עמו של חזקיה הכבידו עליהם עול תורה, והיינו דכתיב ״האחרון הכביד דרך הים עבר הירדן גליל הגוים״, ראויין הללו לעשות להם נס כיוצאי מצרים שעברו את הים וכדורכי הירדן. **אם חוזר בו סנחריב מוטב** — ואם לאו אעשה אותו גליל הגוים — שמגלגל בחרפה בכל הגוים, לישנא

NOTES

וְחָלַף בִּיהוּדָה **And he shall sweep through Judah.** The question has been raised: How can the Gemara say that Isaiah prophesied only about the ten tribes that Sennacherib was to destroy, but that Sennacherib himself planned to destroy all of Jerusalem, since the Prophet states explicitly, "And he shall sweep through Judah"? It has been suggested that this prophecy means that Sennacherib was to sweep through Judah and wipe out all those who wished to rebel against Hezekiah, like Shebna and his followers, but Sennacherib himself swept through Judah with the intention of conquering it (see *Maharsha, Iyyun Ya'akov*).

גְּלִיל הַגּוֹיִם **The Galil of the nations.** Our commentary follows *Rashi*, who understands the word *galil* in the sense of "roll." If Sennacherib does not retract his plans, he will

LANGUAGE

רִישְׁנָא Reward. The correct reading for this word is with a *dalet* rather than a *resh*, and it derives from the Persian *dasan*, meaning "a gift." Thus the entire proverb would mean: This reward is for that gift? Is this a fitting return for the gift of King Hezekiah?

פַּרְדַּשְׁנָא Gift. This word is apparently from Middle Persian, possible from the form *pas-dasn*, meaning "a gift in return for a gift, compensation."

TRANSLATION AND COMMENTARY

אַחֲרֵי הַדְּבָרִים [1]The verse states (II Chronicles 32:1): **"After these things and these deeds of integrity, Sennacherib King of Assyria came, and entered Judah, and encamped against the fortified cities, and thought to win them for himself."** The words "after these things and these deeds of integrity," appear to refer to the end of the previous chapter (II Chronicles 31:20), which relates that Hezekiah "did that which was good and right and true before the Lord his God." [2]It may therefore be asked: Is **this gift an** appropriate **reward for this** conduct? Can it be that because Ḥezekiah did what was good and right, Sennacherib came and besieged the cities of Judah? [3]The Gemara explains: The verse states: [4]**"After these things and these deeds of integrity [אֱמֶת]." After what** things? [5]**Ravina said: After the Holy One, blessed be He, swore in excitement** that he would bring Sennacherib against Jerusalem and cause him to fall into Hezekiah's hands. The word אֱמֶת, "truth," does not refer to Hezekiah's fidelity but rather to God's oath, which He seals with truth. [6]For God **said** to Himself: **"If I say to Hezekiah, 'I will bring Sennacherib** against you, **and** then deliver you from him and **hand him over to you,'** [7]**he will say** to Me, **'Neither him do I want, nor his fear.** Rather than bringing Sennacherib against me and delivering me from him, spare me the confrontation.'" [8]**Immediately, the Holy One, blessed be He, swore in excitement: "I will bring Sennacherib** against Hezekiah, and then cause him to fall into Hezekiah's hands," [9]**as the verse states** (Isaiah 14:25): **"The Lord of hosts has sworn, saying, is it not as I pictured it, so has it come to pass; and as I have purposed, so shall it arise; that I will break Assyria in My land, and upon My mountains subdue him; then shall his yoke depart from them, and his burden depart from their shoulders."**

אָמַר רַבִּי יוֹחָנָן [10]**Rabbi Yoḥanan said:** The word אֲבוּסֶנּוּ, translated above as, "I will subdue him," may also be understood in the sense of אֵבוּס, "feeding trough." [11]**The Holy One, blessed be He, said: "Let Sennacherib and his company come and become a feeding trough for Hezekiah and his company."**

[1]"אַחֲרֵי הַדְּבָרִים וְהָאֱמֶת הָאֵלֶּה
בָּא סַנְחֵרִיב מֶלֶךְ אַשּׁוּר וַיָּבֹא
בִיהוּדָה וַיִּחַן עַל הֶעָרִים
הַבְּצֻרוֹת וַיֹּאמֶר לְבִקְעָם אֵלָיו".
[2]הַאי רִישְׁנָא לְהַאי פַּרְדַּשְׁנָא?
[3]"אַחֲרֵי הַדְּבָרִים וְהָאֱמֶת".
[4]אַחַר מַאי? [5]אָמַר רָבִינָא:
לְאַחַר שֶׁקָּפַץ הַקָּדוֹשׁ בָּרוּךְ הוּא
וְנִשְׁבַּע, [6]וְאָמַר: "אִי אָמִינָא
לֵיהּ לְחִזְקִיָּה מַיְיתִינָא לֵיהּ
לְסַנְחֵרִיב וּמָסַרְנָא לֵיהּ בִּידָךְ'
— [7]הָשְׁתָּא אָמַר: "לָא הוּא
בָּעֵינָא וְלָא בִּיעֲתוּתֵיהּ בָּעֵינָא".
[8]מִיָּד קָפַץ הַקָּדוֹשׁ בָּרוּךְ הוּא
וְנִשְׁבַּע: "דְּמַיְיתִינָא לֵיהּ".
[9]שֶׁנֶּאֱמַר: "נִשְׁבַּע ה' צְבָאוֹת
לֵאמֹר אִם לֹא כַּאֲשֶׁר דִּמִּיתִי כֵּן
הָיָתָה וְכַאֲשֶׁר יָעַצְתִּי הִיא
תָקוּם לִשְׁבֹּר אַשּׁוּר בְּאַרְצִי וְעַל
הָרַי אֲבוּסֶנּוּ וְסָר מֵעֲלֵיהֶם עֻלּוֹ
וְסֻבֳּלוֹ מֵעַל שִׁכְמוֹ יָסוּר".
[10]אָמַר רַבִּי יוֹחָנָן: [11]אָמַר
הַקָּדוֹשׁ בָּרוּךְ הוּא: "יָבֹא
סַנְחֵרִיב וְסִיעָתוֹ וְיֵעָשֶׂה אֵבוּס
לְחִזְקִיָּהוּ וּלְסִיעָתוֹ".

LITERAL TRANSLATION

[1]"After these things and these deeds of integrity, Sennacherib King of Assyria came, and entered Judah, and encamped against the fortified cities, and resolved to breach them for himself." [2]This gift for this reward? [3]"After these things and these deeds of integrity." [4]After what? [5]Ravina said: After the Holy One, blessed be He, jumped up and swore, and said: [6]"If I say to Hezekiah, 'I will bring Sennacherib, and give him over into your hand,' [7]now he will say, 'Neither him do I want, nor his fear do I want.'" [8]Immediately, the Holy One, blessed be He, jumped up and swore: "I will bring him." [9]As it is stated: "The Lord of hosts has sworn, saying, is it not as I pictured it, so has it come to pass; and as I have purposed, so shall it arise; that I will break Assyria in My land, and upon My mountains subdue him; then shall his yoke depart from them, and his burden depart from their shoulders."
[10]Rabbi Yoḥanan said: [11]The Holy One, blessed be He, said: "Let Sennacherib and his company come, and let him become a feeding trough for Hezekiah and his company."

RASHI

אחרינא: גליל — לשון גללים, מורי רבי.
אחרי הדברים והאמת האלה — השתא משמע שהיה מדבר בחזקיהו שהיו עסוקין בתורה "בא סנחריב מלך אשור ויבא ביהודה ויחן על הערים ויאמר לבקעם אליו". האי רישנא להאי פרדשנא — וכי מביאין דורון כזה לאדון כזה — וכי מפני שהאמת בחזקיהו בא סנחריב? רבינא אמר מאי אחר הדברים והאמת, אחר שקפץ הקב"ה ונשבע — להביא סנחריב, והיינו אמת, שחותמו וקיומו של הקדוש ברוך הוא אמת. ויעשה אבוס — שיהא כלם פגרים, ויאכלו סוסיהם ובהמתם בתוך עצמות הפגרים כעין אבוס.

NOTES

roll in shame among the nations. Alternatively, the word *galil* is used here in the sense of *gelalim*, "dung." Sennacherib will be treated like dung among the nations. *Arukh* suggests that the word is used here in the sense of *goleh*, "exile." He will be exiled among the nations.

אַחֲרֵי הַדְּבָרִים וְהָאֱמֶת After these things and these deeds of integrity. *Maharsha* argues that the Gemara's interpretation is based in part on the word אֵלֶּה, "these," which is

TRANSLATION AND COMMENTARY

וְהָיָה בַּיּוֹם [1]Regarding the fall of Assyria, the verse states (Isaiah 10:27): **"And it shall come to pass on that day, that his burden shall be taken from your shoulder, and his yoke from your neck, and the yoke shall be destroyed because of the fatness** [שָׁמֶן]." [2]**Rabbi Yitzḥak Nappaḥa said:** The word שָׁמֶן, translated here as "fatness," may also be understood in the sense of "oil." [3]**The yoke of Sennacherib was destroyed because of the oil** provided by **Hezekiah, which burned** all night **in synagogues and study halls** so that the people could engage in Torah study. [4]**What did** Hezekiah **do** to involve the people in the study of Torah? [5]**He stuck a sword across the entrance of the study hall** as a sign and also as a threat, **and said:** [6]**"Whoever does not engage in Torah** study **will be stabbed by this sword."** [7]**They checked from Dan** at the northern tip of Eretz Israel **to Beersheva** on the southern frontier, **and did not find a** single **uneducated person** totally ignorant of Torah law. [8]And they checked **from Gevat to Antipras** on the borders of Judea, **and did not find a boy or a girl, a man or a woman, who were not expert** even **in the** most difficult **laws of ritual impurity and purity.** [9]**Regarding that generation, the verse says** (Isaiah 7:21): **"And it shall come to pass in that day, that a man shall nourish a young cow, and two sheep."** [10]And the verse says (Isaiah 7:23): **"And it shall come to pass in that day, that every place shall be, where there were a thousand vines worth a thousand silver shekels, it shall be for briers and thorns."** [11]**Even though a thousand vines are worth a thousand silver shekels,** so that someone who works the land can become wealthy, people will not work the land, [12]but rather **they will** allow their vineyards to be overgrown by **briers and thorns,** live frugally, and devote themselves entirely to Torah study.

[1]״וְהָיָה בַּיּוֹם הַהוּא יָסוּר סֻבֳּלוֹ מֵעַל שִׁכְמֶךָ וְעֻלּוֹ מֵעַל צַוָּארֶךָ וְחֻבַּל עֹל מִפְּנֵי שָׁמֶן״. [2]אָמַר רַבִּי יִצְחָק נַפָּחָא: [3]חוּבַּל עוֹל שֶׁל סַנְחֵרִיב מִפְּנֵי שַׁמְנוֹ שֶׁל חִזְקִיָּהוּ שֶׁהָיָה דּוֹלֵק בְּבָתֵּי כְנֵסִיּוֹת וּבְבָתֵּי מִדְרָשׁוֹת. [4]מֶה עָשָׂה? [5]נָעַץ חֶרֶב עַל פֶּתַח בֵּית הַמִּדְרָשׁ וְאָמַר: [6]״כָּל מִי שֶׁאֵינוֹ עוֹסֵק בַּתּוֹרָה יִדָּקֵר בְּחֶרֶב זוֹ״. [7]בָּדְקוּ מִדָּן וְעַד בְּאֵר שֶׁבַע וְלֹא מָצְאוּ עַם הָאָרֶץ, [8]מִגְּבַת וְעַד אַנְטִיפְּרַס וְלֹא מָצְאוּ תִּינוֹק וְתִינוֹקֶת, אִישׁ וְאִשָּׁה, שֶׁלֹּא הָיוּ בְּקִיאִין בְּהִלְכוֹת טוּמְאָה וְטָהֳרָה. [9]וְעַל אוֹתוֹ הַדּוֹר, הוּא אוֹמֵר: ״וְהָיָה בַּיּוֹם הַהוּא יְחַיֶּה אִישׁ עֶגְלַת בָּקָר וּשְׁתֵּי צֹאן וגו׳״. [10]וְאוֹמֵר: ״וְהָיָה בַּיּוֹם הַהוּא יִהְיֶה כָל מָקוֹם אֲשֶׁר יִהְיֶה שָּׁם אֶלֶף גֶּפֶן בְּאֶלֶף כָּסֶף לַשָּׁמִיר וְלַשַּׁיִת יִהְיֶה״. [11]אַף עַל פִּי שֶׁאֶלֶף גֶּפֶן בְּאֶלֶף כֶּסֶף, [12]לַשָּׁמִיר וְלַשַּׁיִת יִהְיֶה.

LITERAL TRANSLATION

[1]"And it shall come to pass on that day, that his burden shall be taken from your shoulder, and his yoke from your neck, and the yoke shall be destroyed because of the fatness." [2]Rabbi Yitzḥak Nappaḥa said: [3]The yoke of Sennacherib was destroyed because of the oil of Hezekiah, which burned in synagogues and in study halls. [4]What did he do? [5]He stuck a sword across the entrance of the study hall and said: [6]"Whoever does not engage in the Torah will be stabbed by this sword." [7]They checked from Dan to Beersheva, and did not find an uneducated person; [8]from Gevat to Antipras, and did not find a boy or a girl, a man or a woman, who were not expert in the laws of ritual impurity and purity. [9]Regarding that generation, it says: "And it shall come to pass in that day, that a man shall nourish a young cow, and two sheep." [10]And it says: "And it shall come to pass in that day, that every place, where there were a thousand vines worth a thousand silver shekels, shall be for briers and thorns." [11]Even though a thousand vines are worth a thousand silver [shekels], [12]they shall be for briers and thorns.

RASHI

מגבת ועד אנטיפרס — מקומות שבסוף התחומים. אף על פי שאלף גפן באלף כסף — שהן יקרים, שאין להם רוב כרמים — אפילו הכי "לשמיר ולשית יהיה", שמניחין אותן לאבוד ומבזיין אותן והיו עוסקין בתורה.

BACKGROUND

מִגְּבַת וְעַד אַנְטִיפְּרַס From Gevat to Antipras. Antipras is apparently Antipatras, a city in northern Judea, at the source of the Yarkon, approximately at the site of present day Rosh Ha'ayin. The location of Gevat is not at all clear. Though everyone agrees that it was in southern Judea, some authorities think it was near the Dead Sea while others believe it was slightly north of Beersheba.

NOTES

interpreted in Midrashic manner as if it read אָלָה, "oath," that is to say, God swore that He would indeed bring Sennacherib against Hezekiah, and hand him over to him.

יִדָּקֵר בְּחֶרֶב He will be stabbed by this sword. We find this metaphor of the sword lying across the entrance of the study hall in several places. The sword lies across the entrance, and not inside the study hall, for weapons may not be brought into the study hall. Elsewhere (*Sifrei, Deuteronomy* 40), the Rabbis say that the sword and the book were handed from heaven bound together, meaning that he who does not study the book will be put to death by the sword. It has been suggested that Ḥezekiah chose the sword, in particular, because he made Torah study a royal decree, and someone who rebels against the king's decree is liable to be put to death by the sword (see *Iyyun Ya'akov, Ahavat Eitan*).

TRANSLATION AND COMMENTARY

וְאָסַף שְׁלַלְכֶם [1]The verse states (Isaiah 33:4): **"And your spoil shall be gathered like the gathering of the locusts;** as the running of locusts shall he rove about upon it." [2]**The Prophet** Isaiah **said to** the people of **Israel: "Gather your spoil** from Sennacherib's defeated armies." [3]The people **said to him:** "When you say that we should gather the spoil, do you mean that each individual should **loot** and take whatever he can, **or** that we should **divide up** the spoil evenly among ourselves?" [4]Isaiah **said to them: "'Like the gathering of the locusts.'** [5]**Just like the gathering of the locusts — each and every** locust gathers and eats **for itself, so, too,** concerning **your spoil — each and every one** may gather and take **for himself."** [6]The people **said to** Isaiah: **"But surely mixed into** the spoil of Sennacherib's armies **is property** that once belonged to **the ten tribes** of Israel." Is not that property forbidden to us because of the prohibition against stealing? [7]Isaiah **said to them: "'As the running of locusts** [גֵּבִים] **shall he rove about upon it.'** The word גֵּבִים, translated here as 'locusts,' may also be understood in the sense of 'ponds.' [8]**Just as ponds** of water **raise a person from ritual impurity to ritual purity** when he immerses himself, **so, too, the property of Israel,** [9]**once it falls into the hands of the nations,** and the owners despair of ever recovering it, **becomes immediately permitted** to others." [10]The Gemara notes that this idea is **similar to what Rav Pappa said, for Rav Pappa said:** Even though God forbade Israel to conquer the lands of **Amon and Moab,** those lands **became permitted** to Israel **when** they were conquered by **Sihon,** King of the Emorites.

אָמַר רַב הוּנָא [11]**Rav Huna said: That wicked man** Sennacherib **went on ten journeys on that one day,** [12]**as the verse states** (Isaiah 10:28-32): **"He is come to Ayyat, he is passed to Migron; at Mikhmash he has left his baggage. They passed Ma'abarah: they have taken up their lodging at Geva; Ramah is afraid; Giv'at Sha'ul has fled. Lift up your voice, O Bat-galim; listen Laysha, O poor Anatot. Madmena is removed; the inhabitants of Gevim flee for safety. This very day he will halt at Nob; he will shake his hands against the**

[1]״וְאָסַף שְׁלַלְכֶם אֹסֶף הֶחָסִיל״. [2]אָמַר לָהֶם נָבִיא לְיִשְׂרָאֵל: ״אִסְפוּ שְׁלַלְכֶם״. [3]אָמְרוּ לוֹ: ״לִבְזוֹז אוֹ לַחֲלוֹק״? [4]אָמַר לָהֶם: ״ ׳כְּאֹסֶף הֶחָסִיל׳. [5]מָה אֹסֶף הֶחָסִיל — כָּל אֶחָד וְאֶחָד לְעַצְמוֹ, אַף שְׁלַלְכֶם — כָּל אֶחָד וְאֶחָד לְעַצְמוֹ״. [6]אָמְרוּ לוֹ: ״וַהֲלֹא מָמוֹן עֲשֶׂרֶת הַשְּׁבָטִים מְעוֹרָב בּוֹ״! [7]אָמַר לָהֶם: ״ ׳כְּמַשַּׁק גֵּבִים שֹׁקֵק בּוֹ׳. [8]מַה גֵּבִים הַלָּלוּ מַעֲלִין אֶת הָאָדָם מִטּוּמְאָה לְטָהֳרָה, אַף מָמוֹנָם שֶׁל יִשְׂרָאֵל — [9]כֵּיוָן שֶׁנָּפַל בְּיַד גּוֹיִם מִיָּד טִיהֵר״. [10]כִּדְרַב פַּפָּא, דַּאֲמַר רַב פַּפָּא: עַמּוֹן וּמוֹאָב טָהֲרוּ בְּסִיחוֹן.

[11]אָמַר רַב הוּנָא: עֶשֶׂר מַסָּעוֹת נָסַע אוֹתוֹ רָשָׁע בְּאוֹתוֹ הַיּוֹם, [12]שֶׁנֶּאֱמַר: ״בָּא עַל עַיָּת עָבַר בְּמִגְרוֹן לְמִכְמָשׂ יַפְקִיד כֵּלָיו עָבְרוּ מַעְבָּרָה גֶּבַע מָלוֹן לָנוּ חָרְדָה הָרָמָה גִּבְעַת שָׁאוּל נָסָה צַהֲלִי קוֹלֵךְ בַּת גַּלִּים הַקְשִׁיבָה לַיְשָׁה עֲנִיָּה עֲנָתוֹת נָדְדָה מַדְמֵנָה יֹשְׁבֵי הַגֵּבִים הֵעִיזוּ. עוֹד הַיּוֹם בְּנֹב לַעֲמֹד

LITERAL TRANSLATION

[1]"And your spoil shall be gathered like the gathering of the locusts." [2]The Prophet said to Israel: "Gather your spoil." [3]They said to him: "To loot or to divide?" [4]He said to them: "'Like the gathering of the locusts.' [5]Just like the gathering of the locusts — each and every one for itself, so, too, your spoil — each and every one for himself." [6]They said to him: "But surely the money of the ten tribes is mixed into it!" [7]He said to them: "'As the running of locusts [*gevim*] shall he rove upon it.' [8]Just as these ponds [*gevim*] raise a person from ritual impurity to ritual purity, so, too, the money of Israel — [9]since it fell into the hands of the nations, it immediately became permitted." [10]Like that of Rav Pappa, for Rav Pappa said: Amon and Moab became permitted through Sihon.

[11]Rav Huna said: That wicked man went on ten journeys on that one day, [12]as it is stated: "He is come to Ayyat, he is passed to Migron; at Mikhmash he has left his baggage. They passed Ma'abarah: they have taken up their lodging at Geva; Ramah is afraid; Giv'at Sha'ul has fled. Lift up your voice, O Bat-galim; listen Laysha, O poor Anatot. Madmena is removed; the inhabitants of Gevim flee for safety. This very day he will halt at Nob;

RASHI

לשלל — כל אחד ואחד לעצמו, או לחלוק ביחד אותו ממון שנשאר מחיל סנחריב, לישנא אחרינא: לחלוק לאחרים מה שאנו שוללים, אבל אנו אסורים באותו שלל, שממון שבזזו מעשרת השבטים מעורב בו דאיכא משום גזל. **כמשק גבים שוקק בו** — השקאה של צינורות שמזלפין בהם מים נובעין השקו באותו ממון וטיהרתו, דמה צינורות הללו מעלין את האדם מטומאה לטהרה על ידי טבילה אף ממונם וכו׳, משק = שו״ן בלעז. **בא על עית וגו׳** — ומתרגמינן ״ומני רבני משרייתיה״. **עברו מעברה גבע מלון לנו וגו׳ יושבי הגבים העיזו** — ולא קא חשיב ״עוד היום בנוב לעמוד״, דההוא לאו מסע הוא אלא כדאמרינן לקמן: אותו היום נשתייר מעונה של נוב.

TRANSLATION AND COMMENTARY

mountain of the daughter of Zion, the hill of Jerusalem." On that very day, Sennacherib passed through all the places mentioned in these verses.

הָנֵי טוּבָא הָוְיָין [1] The Gemara asks: But surely **there are more** than ten places listed in these verses!

צַהֲלִי קוֹלֵךְ The Gemara answers: The places mentioned in the verse, "This very day he will halt at Nob," are not counted, as will be explained below. The places mentioned in the verse, [2] **"Lift up your voice, O Bat-galim;** listen Laysha, O poor Anatot," are also not counted, for in this verse **the Prophet** Isaiah means to **say to the congregation of Israel** as follows: [3] **"Lift up your voice, O Bat-galim"** — "the daughter of waves," **the daughter** [*bat*] **of Abraham, Isaac, and Jacob who performed commandments as** numerous as **the waves** [*gallim*] **of the sea.** [4] **"Listen Laysha"** — "listen to the lion [*layish*]." **Him** (Sennacherib), you need **not fear,** for you will be delivered from his hand, **but** you should **fear the wicked Nebuchadnezzar who is compared to a lion,** [5] **as the verse states** (Jeremiah 4:7): **"The lion is come up from his thicket."** [6] **What is** [95A] the meaning of the words, **"O poor Anatot"?** [7] **Jeremiah the son of Hilkiah will in the future prophesy about** Nebuchadnezzar, **from Anatot,** [8] **as the verse states** (Jeremiah 1:1): **"The words of Jeremiah the son of Hilkiah, of the priests who were in Anatot in the land of Benjamin."**

מִי דָּמֵי [9] The Gemara asks: **Are** the two verses really **alike?** [10] **There,** in Jeremiah (4:7), Nebuchadnezzar is referred to as an ***ari***: "The lion [*ari*] is come up from his thicket." And **here,** the verse speaks about a ***layish***!

אָמַר רַבִּי יוֹחָנָן [11] **Rabbi Yoḥanan said:** There is no contradiction, for in Biblical Hebrew **a lion** is called by **six** different **names:** ***Ari, kefir, lavi, layish, shaḥal, shaḥatz.***

אִי הָכִי [12] The Gemara asks: **If** it is **so,** that the places mentioned in the verse, "Lift up your voice, O Bat-galim; listen Laysha, O poor Anatot," are not counted among the places through which Sennacherib passed on that day, then we are left with **too few** stops on his journey. For, according to this, he made only nine stops.

יְנֹפֵף יָדוֹ הַר בַּת צִיּוֹן גִּבְעַת יְרוּשָׁלָם״.
[1] הָנֵי טוּבָא הָוְיָין!
[2] ״צַהֲלִי קוֹלֵךְ בַּת גַּלִּים״ — נָבִיא הוּא דְּקָאָמַר לָהּ לִכְנֶסֶת יִשְׂרָאֵל: [3] ״צַהֲלִי קוֹלֵךְ בַּת גַּלִּים״ — בִּתּוֹ שֶׁל אַבְרָהָם יִצְחָק וְיַעֲקֹב שֶׁעָשׂוּ מִצְוֹת כְּגַלֵּי הַיָּם. [4] ״הַקְשִׁיבָה לַיְשָׁה״ — מֵהַאי לָא תִּסְתְּפִי, אֶלָּא אִיסְתְּפִי מִנְּבוּכַדְנֶצַּר הָרָשָׁע דִּמְתִיל כְּאַרְיֵה, [5] שֶׁנֶּאֱמַר: ״עָלָה אַרְיֵה מִסֻּבְּכוֹ וגו׳ ״. [6] מַאי [95A] ״עֲנִיָּה עֲנָתוֹת״? [7] עָתִיד יִרְמְיָה בֶּן חִלְקִיָּה וּמִתְנַבֵּא עֲלָהּ מֵעֲנָתוֹת, [8] דִּכְתִיב: ״דִּבְרֵי יִרְמְיָהוּ בֶּן חִלְקִיָּהוּ מִן הַכֹּהֲנִים אֲשֶׁר בַּעֲנָתוֹת בְּאֶרֶץ בִּנְיָמִן״. [9] מִי דָּמֵי? [10] הָתָם אֲרִי הָכָא לַיִשׁ!
[11] אָמַר רַבִּי יוֹחָנָן: שִׁשָּׁה שֵׁמוֹת יֵשׁ לָאֲרִי, אֵלּוּ הֵן: אֲרִי, כְּפִיר, לָבִיא, לַיִשׁ, שַׁחַל, שַׁחַץ.
[12] אִי הָכִי בְּצַרוּ לְהוֹן!

LITERAL TRANSLATION

he will shake his hand against the mountain of the daughter of Zion, the hill of Jerusalem."

[1] They are many!

[2] "Lift up your voice, O Bat-galim" — the Prophet said to the congregation of Israel: [3] "Lift up your voice, O Bat-galim" — the daughter of Abraham, Isaac, and Jacob who performed commandments like the waves of the sea. [4] "Listen Laysha" — fear him not, but fear the wicked Nebuchadnezzar who is compared to a lion, [5] as it is stated: "The lion is come up from his thicket, etc." [6] What is [95A] "O poor Anatot"? [7] In the future Jeremiah the son of Hilkiah will prophesy about him from Anatot, [8] as it is written: "The words of Jeremiah the son of Hilkiah, of the priests who were in Anatot in the land of Benjamin."

[9] Are they alike? [10] There *ari*, here *layish*!

[11] Rabbi Yoḥanan said: A lion has six names, and they are: *Ari, kefir, lavi, layish, shaḥal, shaḥatz*.

[12] If so, there are too few!

RASHI

הני טובא הוי — דשתים עשרה הוא דאיכא. **נביא הוא** — קרא ד״צהלי קולך בת גלים הקשיבי לישה״ דחשיבנא ביה תלתא בת גלים, לישה, ענתות, הנהו לאו מן חושבנא נינהו, דנביא הוא דקאמר להו לישראל וכו׳. **מהאי לא תסתפי** — שתנצל מידו, היינו דכתיב ״צהלי קולך״ — אלא אסתפי מנבוכדנצר שנמשל לליש דכתיב ביה ״עלה אריה מסובכו״, והיינו דקאמר ״הקשיבי לישה״. **עניה ענתות** — כמו עניה, כלומר נביאות ירמיה הענתותי היא שעתידה לבא על נבוכד נצר שתמסר ירושלים בידו. **ארי כפיר וכו׳** — ובדוכתא אחריתי מפורש למה נקראו לו כל השמות הללו. **אי הכי** — דכולי קרא צהלי קולך לא מחושבנא הוא, אם כן ליכא אלא תשע מסעות, דהא ״עוד היום״ לאו מחושבנא [נמי הוא], ומתרץ: ״עברו מעברה״ תרתי, אינון, עברו — חד, מעברה — חד, ואיכא עשר מסעות.

NOTES

אִי הָכִי בְּצַרוּ לְהוֹן If so, there are too few. *Ramah* has a different reading of this passage. He sharply rejects the reading according to which the words *Avru Ma'abarah* are counted as two places. He argues that even though the verse, "This very day he will halt at Nob," starts a new idea, "Mount Zion" mentioned in that verse completes the list of ten places through which Sennacherib passed on that day, for Sannacherib surely arrived in Jerusalem.

LANGUAGE

בִּיסְתַּרְקֵי Matresses. This word apparently derives from the Persian *bistar,* cognate with Pahlavi *vistang,* meaning "a carpet."

TRANSLATION AND COMMENTARY

עָבְרוּ מַעְבָּרָה [1]The Gemara answers: **"They passed Ma'abarah** [*Avru Ma'abarah*]" refers to **two** places, *Avru* and *Ma'abarah.*

מַאי [2]The Gemara asks: **What is** the meaning of the words, **"This very day he will halt at Nob"?** [3]**Rav Huna said: That** was the very last **day** that **was left** for punishment to be meted out against Israel **for the crime** perpetrated **at Nob** when that city's priests were slaughtered on account of David (see I Samuel 22). [4]Sennacherib's **astrologers said to him: "If you go** out **now** against Jerusalem, **you will** be able to **defeat it, but if** you do **not** go out now, and wait even another day, **you will no** longer be able to **defeat it."**

אוֹרְחָא [5]It was related that **a journey that would** ordinarily **take ten days took** Sennacherib only **one day,** since he took ten journeys on that one day. [6]**When** Sennacherib and his troops **reached Jerusalem,** his men **cast mattresses for him,** one on top of the other, **so that he** could **go up and sit higher than** the top of **the wall** that surrounded the city, and **see all of Jerusalem.** [7]**When he beheld** the city, **it appeared small in his eyes,** [8]and **he said: "Is this the city of Jerusalem for which I set all my camps in motion, and for which I conquered all the countries?** [9]**Surely it is smaller and weaker than all the cities of the nations that I conquered with my** great **might!"** [10]He then **went up, and stood, and shook his head** in derision, **and waved his hand over the Temple Mount in Zion, and the Courtyard in Jerusalem,** as the verse states (Isaiah 10:32): "He will shake his hands against the mountain of the daughter of Zion, the hill of Jerusalem." [11]His officers **said** to him: **"Let us put out our hand now** against the city and conquer it!" [12]Sennacherib **said to them:** "Now **you are tired.** Rest from the journey, [13]and then **tomorrow, bring me, each of you, a piece**

[1]״עָבְרוּ מַעְבָּרָה״ תַּרְתֵּי נִינְהוּ. [2]מַאי ״עוֹד הַיּוֹם בְּנֹב לַעֲמֹד״? [3]אָמַר רַב הוּנָא: אוֹתוֹ הַיּוֹם נִשְׁתַּיֵּיר מֵעֲוֹנָהּ שֶׁל נוֹב. [4]אָמְרִי לֵיהּ כַּלְדָּאֵי: ״אִי אָזְלַתְּ הָאִידָּנָא, יָכְלַתְּ לָהּ, וְאִי לָא, לָא יָכְלַתְּ לָהּ״.

[5]אוֹרְחָא דִּבְעָא לְסַגּוּיֵי בַּעֲשָׂרָה יוֹמָא סְגָא בְּחַד יוֹמָא. [6]כִּי מָטוּ לִירוּשְׁלֵם שְׁדִי לֵיהּ בִּיסְתַּרְקֵי עַד דִּסְלֵיק וִיתֵיב מֵעִילָּוֵי שׁוּרָה, עַד דַּחֲזְיוּהּ לְכוּלָּהּ יְרוּשְׁלֵם. [7]כִּי חַזְיֵיהּ אִיזּוּטַר בְּעֵינֵיהּ, [8]אֲמַר: ״הֲלָא דָּא הִיא קַרְתָּא דִּירוּשְׁלֵם דַּעֲלָהּ אַרְגִּישִׁית כָּל מַשִּׁירְיָתִי, וַעֲלָהּ כְּבָשִׁית כָּל מְדִינָתָא? [9]הֲלָא הִיא זְעִירָא וַחֲלָשָׁא מִכָּל כְּרַכֵּי עַמְמַיָּא דִּכְבָשִׁית בִּתְקוֹף יְדִי״. [10]עֲלָהּ וְקָם וּמֵנִיד בְּרֵישֵׁיהּ, מוֹבִיל וּמַיְיתִי בִּידֵיהּ עַל טוּר בֵּית מִקְדָּשָׁא דִּבְצִיּוֹן, וְעַל עֲזַרְתָּא דְּבִירוּשְׁלֵם. [11]אָמְרִי: ״נִישְׁדֵי בֵּיהּ יָדָא הָאִידָּנָא״! [12]אֲמַר לְהוּ: ״תְּמַהִיתוּ. [13]לְמַחַר

LITERAL TRANSLATION

[1]"They passed Ma'abarah" are two.

[2]What is: "This very day he will halt at Nob"? [3]Rav Huna said: That day was left from the iniquity at Nob. [4]The astrologers said to him: "If you go now, you will defeat it, and if not, you will not defeat it."

[5]A journey that should take ten days took him one day. [6]When they came to Jerusalem, they cast mattresses for him until he went up and sat above the wall, until they saw all of Jerusalem. [7]When he saw it, it was small in his eyes. [8]He said: "Is this the city of Jerusalem for which I set all my camps in motion, and for which I conquered all the countries? [9]Surely it is smaller and weaker than all the cities of the nations that I conquered with the might of my hand!" [10]He went up and stood and shook his head and waved his hand over the Temple Mount in Zion, and the Courtyard in Jerusalem. [11]They said: "Let us put out our hand now!" [12]He said to them: "You are tired. [13]Tomorrow,

RASHI

אותו היום נשתייר מעונה של נוב – [דמפני עון] שהיה להם לישראל על שנהרגו כהני נוב קבע הקדוש ברוך הוא העונש עד אותו היום, ואותו יום בלבד נשתייר מזמן העונש, ואילו היה נלחם בירושלים באותו היום היה כובשה, והכי משמע קרא: "עוד היום" – אותו יום העמידו לסנחריב על ירושלים בעון נוב. **סגא בחד יומא** – והיינו עשר מסעות שנסע אותו היום. **שדו ליה** – לסנחריב. **בסתרקי** – תחתיו, *טפי"ט בלעז. **עד שראה ירושלים כולה. עלה וקם ומניד ברישיה** – עליה עמד והיה מניד בראשו. **נשדי ביה ידא האידנא** – נלחם בה עתה. **תמהיתו** – תמה הוא להתחיל היום משום חולשא דאורחא, לישנא אחרינא: תמהיתו, נתיגעתם, ודומה ליה (בסנחריב) איתמה למיתב.

NOTES

אוֹתוֹ הַיּוֹם נִשְׁתַּיֵּיר מֵעֲוֹנָהּ שֶׁל נוֹב That day was left from the iniquity of Nob. The question has been raised: How was the crime perpetrated at Nob connected to the inhabitants of Judah and Jerusalem? Moreover, it is stated (below) that even David himself was punished for the crime committed at Nob. It may be suggested that, regarding the incident at Nob, there were two levels of responsibility. The people who were actually involved in the matter — Saul, David, and Doeg — were punished (they or their descendants) for their part in the offense. In addition, the

TRANSLATION AND COMMENTARY

of **stone the size of a seal** from the city wall, and with that alone we will conquer the city." [1] **Immediately: "And it came to pass that night, that the Angel of the Lord went out and struck down in the camp of Assyria a hundred and eighty five thousand: and when they arose early in the morning, behold, they were all dead bodies"** (II Kings 19:35).

אָמַר רַב פַּפָּא [2] **Rav Pappa said: This is** the meaning of **the popular adage: When judgment is delayed, it is** sometimes **canceled** altogether. Sometimes something can be accomplished at a certain time, but any procrastination will lead to total failure. Had Sennacherib attacked Jerusalem on the day of his arrival, he would have been able to conquer the city, but since he chose to wait until the next day, the divine decree was canceled, and Sennacherib's forces were routed.

וְיִשְׁבִּי [3] Having cited the verse, "This very day he will halt at Nob," and having connected it to the crime that had been perpetrated against the priests of that city, the Gemara continues with another story relating to that incident. The verse states (II Samuel 21:16): **"And Ishbi-benob, who was of the sons of the Rafah** [the giant], **the weight of whose spear was three hundred shekels [this was the weight of its brass], he being girded with a new sword, thought to have slain David."** [4] **What is the** meaning of the words **"and Ishbi-benob"**? [5] **Rav Yehudah said in the name of Rav:** This refers to **the man who came** to punish David because **of what happened at Nob.** [6] **The Holy One, blessed be He, said to David: "Until when will this iniquity be hidden in your hand,** and you not be punished for it? [7] **On account of you** the people of **Nob, the city of priests, were killed; and on account of you Doeg the Edomite was banished** from the World to Come; [8] **and on account of you Saul and his three sons were killed.** Your arrival in Nob started the chain of events that brought the death of so many people, and so you must be punished. But it is up to you to decide upon the punishment. [9] **Do you prefer to have your seed destroyed, or that you be handed**

אַיְיתִי לִי כָּל חַד וְחַד מִינַּיְיכוּ גּוּלְמוֹ הֲרַג מִינֵּיהּ״. [1] מִיָּד, ״וַיְהִי בַּלַּיְלָה הַהוּא וַיֵּצֵא מַלְאַךְ ה׳ וַיַּךְ בְּמַחֲנֵה אַשּׁוּר מֵאָה שְׁמוֹנִים וַחֲמִשָּׁה אָלֶף וַיַּשְׁכִּימוּ בַבֹּקֶר וְהִנֵּה כֻלָּם פְּגָרִים מֵתִים״.

[2] אָמַר רַב פַּפָּא: הַיְינוּ דְּאָמְרִי אֱינָשֵׁי: בָּת דִּינָא, בְּטַל דִּינָא.

[3] ״וְיִשְׁבִּי בְּנֹב אֲשֶׁר בִּילִידֵי הָרָפָה וּמִשְׁקַל קֵינוֹ שְׁלֹשׁ מֵאוֹת מִשְׁקַל נְחֹשֶׁת וְהוּא חָגוּר חֲדָשָׁה וַיֹּאמֶר לְהַכּוֹת אֶת דָּוִד״. [4] מַאי ״וְיִשְׁבִּי בְּנוֹב״? [5] אָמַר רַב יְהוּדָה אָמַר רַב: אִישׁ שֶׁבָּא עַל עִסְקֵי נוֹב. [6] אָמַר לֵיהּ הַקָּדוֹשׁ בָּרוּךְ הוּא לְדָוִד: ״עַד מָתַי יְהֵא עָוֹן זֶה טָמוּן בְּיָדְךָ? [7] עַל יָדְךָ נֶהֶרְגָה נוֹב עִיר הַכֹּהֲנִים, וְעַל יָדְךָ נִטְרַד דּוֹאֵג הָאֲדוֹמִי, [8] וְעַל יָדְךָ נֶהֶרְגוּ שָׁאוּל וּשְׁלֹשֶׁת בָּנָיו. [9] רְצוֹנְךָ יִכְלוּ זַרְעֲךָ, אוֹ

LITERAL TRANSLATION

bring me, each of you, a stone the size of a seal from it." [1] Immediately, "And it came to pass that night, that the Angel of the Lord went out and struck down in the camp of Assyria a hundred and eighty five thousand: and when they arose early in the morning, behold, they were all dead bodies."

[2] Rav Pappa said: This is what people say: If a judgment rests, the judgment is gone.

[3] "And Ishbi-benob, who was of the sons of the Rafah, the weight of whose spear was three hundred shekels [this was the weight of its brass] he being girded with a new [sword], thought to have slain David." [4] What is "And Ishbi-benob"? [5] Rav Yehudah said in the name of Rav: A man who came regarding the matters of Nob. [6] The Holy One, blessed be He, said to David: "Until when will this iniquity be hidden in your hand? [7] On account of you Nob, the city of priests, was killed; and on account of you Doeg the Edomite was banished; [8] and on account of you Saul and his three sons were killed. [9] [Is it] your preference that your seed be destroyed, or

LANGUAGE

גוּלְמוֹ הֲרַג A stone the size of a seal. The source of this word is reflected in the alternative reading preserved in the *Arukh,* גולמהרג, which apparenty derives from Persian *gil-mukrak*, meaning "a kind of ball made of lime used for a seal."

RASHI

גולמו הרג — חתיכה של חומה, לשון פרסי אבן רעועה מן החומה ונבקעה. **בת דינא בטל דינא** — כיון שלן דינא בטל הריב, וכן מפני שלא נכבשה בו ביום לא הצליח ממחרת. **וישבי בנוב** — איידי דאיירי לעיל באותו יום שנשתייר מעונה של נוב נקט הכא "וישבי בנוב" — שבא על עסקי נוב. **הרפה** — היינו ערפה. **משקל קינו** — מתרגמינן: מתקל סופיניה. **והוא חגור חדשה** — "והוא אסיר איספניקי חדתא". **נטרד דואג האדומי** — שספר לשון הרע על דוד שנתקנא בו שאול, ולפי שקבל אחימלך את דוד בנוב אמר ליה שאול "סוב ופגע בכהני ה'" נמצא שעל ידך נהרגו ואתה נכשל, ובחטא זה נהרג שאול ושלשת בניו במלחמת פלשתים.

NOTES

neighboring tribes of Israel were also culpable for not objecting when Saul committed the crime. The offending tribes include the tribe of David (Judah) and the tribe of Saul (Benjamin). Since the city of Jerusalem was divided between the tribes of Judah and Benjamin, it, too, bore a certain responsibility for the offense committed in Nob (see *Ri'af* and others).

מַאי ״וְיִשְׁבִּי בְּנוֹב״? What is "and Ishbi-benob"? Were Nob a place-name, the verse should have read: *Ishbi meNob,* meaning, Ishbi from Nob. Since the verse reads, *Ishbi-*

LANGUAGE

לִשְׁכּוֹר בַּזַּאי Hunt with hawks. This appears to be a Persian word, *skar i baz*, meaning "hawking." In this method of hunting, the hunter holds a hawk on his arm, and the hawk chases animals, catches them, and pecks out their eyes. This form of hunting was practiced in Persia and many other countries.

TRANSLATION AND COMMENTARY

over to the enemy?" [1]David **said to** God: **"Master of the universe!** [2]**I prefer to be handed over to the enemy, and that my seed not be destroyed."** [3]**One day** David **went out hunting with hawks,** and **Satan came and appeared to him in the form of a deer.** [4]David **shot an arrow at** the animal, **but it did not reach it,** and David set out in pursuit. [5]Thus Satan **drew** David after him, **until he brought him** all the way **to the land of the Philistines.** [6]**When Ishbi-benob saw him, he said: "This is the one who killed my brother Goliath."** [7]**He tied him** up, **bent him over, lay him down** on the ground, **and placed him under** the beam of **an olive press** in order to crush him. [8]**A miracle was performed for him, and the earth was lowered under him,** so that the olive press did not hurt him. [9]**This is** the meaning of **the verse** that **states** (Psalms 18:37): **"You have enlarged my steps under me, that my feet did not slip."**

הַהוּא יוֹמָא [10]It was further related that the incident described above occurred on **a Friday afternoon toward Shabbat, and Abishai ben Zeruiah was washing his hair with four pitchers of water** in honor of the coming holy day. [11]As he was making his Shabbat preparations, **he** suddenly **saw bloodstains.** [12]**There are** some **who say** that **a dove came, and fluttered** its wings **before him,** as an expression of distress. [13]Taking what happened as a sign, Abishai **said** to himself: **"The congregation of Israel is** compared **to a dove, as the verse states** (Psalms 68:14): **'You shall shine as the wings of a dove covered with silver,** and her pinions with yellow gold.' [14]Surely I may **infer from this that David the King of Israel is in distress."** [15]He quickly **went to** David's **house but** he **did not find him.** [16]**He said** to himself: **"We have learned** in the Mishnah (*Sanhedrin* 22a): 'An ordinary person **may not ride on** the

תִּמָּסֵר בְּיַד אוֹיֵב״? [1]אָמַר לְפָנָיו: ״רִבּוֹנוֹ שֶׁל עוֹלָם! [2]מוּטָּב אֶמָּסֵר בְּיַד אוֹיֵב, וְלֹא יִכְלֶה זַרְעִי״. [3]יוֹמָא חַד נְפַק לְשִׁכּוֹר בַּזַּאי. אֲתָא שָׂטָן וְאִידַּמֵּי לֵיהּ כְּטַבְיָא. [4]פְּתַק בֵּיהּ גִּירָא וְלָא מַטְיֵיהּ. [5]מָשְׁכֵיהּ עַד דְּאַמְטְיֵיהּ לְאֶרֶץ פְּלִשְׁתִּים. [6]כִּדְחַזְיֵיהּ יִשְׁבִּי בְּנוֹב, אֲמַר: ״הַיְינוּ הַאי דִּקְטַלֵיהּ לְגָלְיַת אָחִי״. [7]כְּפַתֵּיהּ, קְמַטֵיהּ, אוֹתְבֵיהּ וְשַׁדְיֵיהּ תּוּתֵי בֵּי בְדַיָּיא. [8]אִתְעֲבֵיד לֵיהּ נִיסָּא, מָכָא לֵיהּ אַרְעָא מִתּוֹתֵיהּ. [9]הַיְינוּ דִּכְתִיב: ״תַּרְחִיב צַעֲדִי תַחְתָּי וְלֹא מָעֲדוּ קַרְסֻלָּי״. [10]הַהוּא יוֹמָא אַפַּנְיָא דְּמַעֲלֵי שַׁבְּתָא הֲוָה, אֲבִישַׁי בֶּן צְרוּיָה הֲוָה קָא חָיֵיף רֵישֵׁיהּ בְּאַרְבְּעָא גַּרְבֵי דְּמַיָּא. [11]חָזֵינְהוּ כִּתְמֵי דָמָא. [12]אִיכָּא דְּאָמְרִי: אֲתָא יוֹנָה אִיטְרִיף קַמֵּיהּ: [13]אָמַר: ״כְּנֶסֶת יִשְׂרָאֵל לְיוֹנָה אִימְתִילָא, שֶׁנֶּאֱמַר: ׳כַּנְפֵי יוֹנָה נֶחְפָּה בַכֶּסֶף׳. [14]שְׁמַע מִינָּהּ דָּוִד מַלְכָּא דְּיִשְׂרָאֵל בְּצַעֲרָא שָׁרֵי״. [15]אֲתָא לְבֵיתֵיהּ וְלָא אַשְׁכְּחֵיהּ. [16]אֲמַר: ״תְּנַן: ׳אֵין רוֹכְבִין עַל

LITERAL TRANSLATION

that you be delivered into the hand of the enemy?" [1]He said before Him: "Master of the universe! [2]It is better that I be delivered into the hand of the enemy, and my seed not be destroyed." [3]One day he went out to hunt with hawks. Satan came and appeared to him like a deer. [4]He shot an arrow at it, but it did not reach it. [5]He drew him on until he brought him to the land of the Philistines. [6]When Ishbi-benob saw him, he said: "This is the one who killed Goliath, my brother." [7]He tied him, bent him over, lay him down, and put him under an olive press. [8]A miracle was performed for him, [and] the earth was lowered under him. [9]This is what is written: "You have enlarged my steps under me, and my feet did not slip."

[10]That day it was a Friday afternoon toward Shabbat, [and] Abishai ben Zeruiah was washing his hair with four pitchers of water. [11]He saw bloodstains. [12]Some say: A dove came and fluttered before him: [13]He said: "The congregation of Israel is compared to a dove, as it is stated: 'You shall shine as the wings of a dove covered with silver.' [14]Infer from this that David the King of Israel is in distress." [15]He went to his house, but did not find him. [16]He said: "We have learned: 'One may not ride on

RASHI

שכר ביזאי – לשון פרסי, קריטא, לישנא אחרינא: כפר היא. **קמטיה** – הכניעו תחת הבד של זיתים ויתיב עלה למעכו. **מכא ליה ארעא מתותיה** – נתרככה הארץ מתחתיו ולא הזיקו, לישנא אחרינא: מכא – נשפלת כעין גומא והיתה מגינה עליו. **בארבע גריבי דמיא** – בארבע סאין של מים, לישנא אחרינא: בארבע כורא דמיא בארבע נודות של מים. **איטריף קמיה** – היתה טורפת ומתחבטת עצמה וממרטת כנפיה והומה ומצערת.

NOTES

benob, Rav interprets the expression as an acrostic for *Ish sheba al iskei Nob*, "A man who came regarding the matter of Nob."

קְמַטֵיהּ **He bent him over.** That is to say, he folded him up inside a garment (*Ramah*).

כְּנֶסֶת יִשְׂרָאֵל לְיוֹנָה אִימְתִילָא **The congregation of Israel is compared to a dove.** Since Abishai knew that the people of Israel were not then in distress, he assumed that something must have happened to David, the King of Israel (*Ramah*).

TRANSLATION AND COMMENTARY

king's **horse, nor** may he **sit on his throne, nor** may he **use his scepter.'** [1]**What is the law in a time of danger?"** [2]Abishai **went and asked** about the matter **in the study hall.** [3]The Sages **said to him: "In a time of danger,** these actions **are permitted."** [4]**He** immediately **rode out on** the king's **mule, and went** on his way, **and the earth shrank for him,** so that he quickly arrived in the land of the Philistines. [5]**As he was going, he saw Ishbi-benob's mother, Orpah, weaving.** [6]**When she saw** Abishai, **she broke** the thread of **her spindle, and threw** it **at him, hoping to kill him** with it, but it did not hit him. [7]**She said to him: "Young man, bring me** my **spindle."** [8]Abishai picked up the spindle, **threw it at** Orpah's **head, and killed her,** and then went to rescue David. [9]**When Yishbi-benob saw him, he said** to himself: **"Now that there are two** of them — David and Abishai — **they will kill me."** [10]**He cast David upward** toward the sky, **and stuck his spear** into the ground beneath him, **and said: "Let him fall upon** the spear, **and die."** [11]**Abishai pronounced a** Divine **Name, and** thus **maintained David** suspended **between Heaven and Earth.**

וְנֵימָא לֵיהּ אִיהוּ [12]The Gemara interrupts the story to comment: David **himself should have pronounced** the Divine Name to save himself!

אֵין חָבוּשׁ [13]The Gemara explains: **A prisoner cannot release himself from prison.**

אֲמַר לֵיהּ [14]The Gemara resumes the story: Abishai **said to** David: **"What are you doing here?"** [15]David **said to him: "The Holy One, blessed be He, said to me** that I must choose whether my seed should be destroyed or I should be handed over to

סוּסוֹ וְאֵין יוֹשְׁבִין עַל כִּסְאוֹ וְאֵין מִשְׁתַּמְּשִׁין בְּשַׁרְבִיטוֹ׳.
[1]בְּשַׁעַת הַסַּכָּנָה מַאי״? [2]אֲתָא שְׁאֵיל בֵּי מִדְרְשָׁא. [3]אֲמַרוּ לֵיהּ: ״בְּשַׁעַת הַסַּכָּנָה שַׁפִּיר דָּמֵי״.
[4]רָכְבֵיהּ לְפִרְדֵּיהּ, וְקָם וַאֲזַל, קָפְצָה לֵיהּ אַרְעָא. [5]בַּהֲדֵי דְּקָא מַסְגֵּי חַזְיֵיהּ לְעָרְפָּה אִמֵּיהּ דַּהֲוָות נָוְולָא. [6]כִּי חֲזִיתֵיהּ פַּסְקָתָהּ לְפִילְכָּהּ שְׁדָתֵיהּ עִילָּוֵיהּ. סְבַרָא לְמִקְטְלֵיהּ.
[7]אֲמַרָה לֵיהּ: ״עֲלַם אַיְיתִי לִי פֶּלֶךְ״! [8]פַּתְקֵיהּ בְּרֵישׁ מוֹחָהּ, וּקְטָלָהּ. [9]כַּד חַזְיֵיהּ יִשְׁבִּי בְּנוֹב, אֲמַר: ״הַשְׁתָּא הָווּ בֵּי תְּרֵין, וְקָטְלִין לִי״. [10]פַּתְקֵיהּ לְדָוִד לְעֵילָּא, וְדָץ לֵיהּ לְרוּמְחֵיהּ, אֲמַר: ״נִיפּוֹל עֲלַהּ וְנִקְטַל״.
[11]אֲמַר אֲבִישַׁי שֵׁם, אוֹקְמֵיהּ לְדָוִד בֵּין שְׁמַיָּא לְאַרְעָא.
[12]וְנֵימָא לֵיהּ אִיהוּ!
[13]אֵין חָבוּשׁ מוֹצִיא עַצְמוֹ מִבֵּית הָאֲסוּרִין.
[14]אֲמַר לֵיהּ: ״מַאי בָּעֵית הָכָא״? [15]אֲמַר לֵיהּ: ״הָכִי אֲמַר לִי קוּדְשָׁא בְּרִיךְ הוּא, וְהָכִי

LITERAL TRANSLATION

his horse, or sit on his throne, or use his scepter.' [1]In a time of danger, what [is the law]?" [2]He went and asked in the study hall. [3]They said to him: "In a time of danger, it is well." [4]He rode on his mule, and stood, and went, and the earth shrank for him. [5]As he was going, he saw Orpah, his [Ishbi-benob's] mother, weaving. [6]When she saw him, she broke her spindle, and threw it at him. She thought to kill him. [7]She said to him: "Young man, bring me the spindle." [8]He threw it at her head, and killed her. [9]When Ishbi-benob saw him, he said: "Now there are two, and they will kill me." [10]He cast David upwards, and stuck his spear, [and] said: "Let him fall on it, and be killed." [11]Abishai pronounced a name, and maintained David between Heaven and Earth.
[12]But let he himself pronounce [it]!
[13]A prisoner cannot release himself from prison.
[14]He said to him: "What do you need here?" [15]He said to him: "Thus the Holy One, blessed be He, said to me, and thus

RASHI

קפצה ליה ארעא – כמו ״לא תקפוץ״ (דברים טו) נתקצרה הארץ והגיע מהרה לארץ פלשתים. לערפה אימיה – דישבי. נוולה – טווה. כד חזיתיה – ערפה לאבישי, סברה למקטליה באותו פלך שהיה בידה ולא נגע בו. אמרה ליה – לאבישי, אייתי לן ההוא פלך דנפל לפניך. הכי גרסינן: פתקיה בריש מוחה וקטלה – השליך אבישי הפלך לראשה ומתה. פתקיה לדוד לעילא – זרקו כלפי מעלה. ודץ ליה – נעץ תחתיו חניתו בקרקע כדי שיפול עליו וימות. ונימא איהו – דוד עצמו לימא שם. אין חבוש – אין דעתו מכוונת לומר השם, והשתא ניצל דוד והשליכו השם ברחוק והלכו אבישי ודוד וחזרו להם. אמר ליה – אבישי לדוד. ומאי בעית הכא – למה באת כאן. אמר ליה – הקדוש ברוך הוא אמר לי רצונך שיכלה זרעך או תמסר

BACKGROUND

פֶּלֶךְ Spindle.

A spindle from the Talmudic period.
This spindle, like many others, has a very sharp point. To be stabbed by such a spindle could be as dangerous as to be stabbed by a dagger.

NOTES

קָפְצָה לֵיהּ אַרְעָא **The earth shrank for him.** Some understand the word קָפְצָה in the sense of "shrank," meaning the distance that had to be traveled got smaller. Others suggest that the word קָפְצָה should be understood in the sense of "jumped, skipped," meaning that a miracle was performed, and he jumped, and immediately arrived at his destination (*Ramah*).

וְדָץ לֵיהּ לְרוּמְחֵיהּ **And he stuck his spear.** Some suggest that Ishbi-benob did not kill David immediately, but rather cast him up toward the sky because he wanted to toy with him and torture him before he died (*Ramah*). Others suggest that Ishbi-benob thought that David had used magic to save himself from being crushed to death by the beam of the olive press, so he tried to kill him in such a way that magic would not be able to save him (*She'elot U'Teshuvot Divrei Rav Meshulam*).

TRANSLATION AND COMMENTARY

my enemy, **and I answered him** that I preferred to be handed over to my enemy." [1]Abishai **said to** David: **"Reverse your prayer,** and say that you prefer to have your seed destroyed, and that you not be handed over to your enemy. This is in keeping with the popular adage: [2]**Let your grandson** be a poor peddler who **sells wax, so that you not suffer privation.** [3]David **said to** Abishai: **"If so, help me.** [4]**This is** the meaning of **the verse** that **states** (II Samuel 21:17): **"But Abishai the son of Zeruiah came to his help,** and smote the Philistine, and killed him." [5]**Rav Yehudah said in the name of Rav:** The verse means that Abishai **helped** David **with prayer.** [6]**Abishai** then **pronounced** another Divine **Name, and brought** David back **down** to the ground. [7]The two of them ran for their lives, and Ishbi-benob **chased them** in order to kill them. [8]**When they reached** a village called **Kubi, they said** to each other: **"Let us stand up against him** [*kum be*]." But they were still afraid, and so they kept running. [9]**When they reached** a village called **Be-tre, they said** to each other: **"Two** [*be tre*] **cubs killed the lion,** and the two of us can overpower him." [10]**They** turned **to** Ishbi-benob and **said: "Go, find your mother Orpah in her grave."** [11]**When they mentioned** Ishbi-benob's **mother's name to him,** telling him that she was dead, **he lost his strength, and** Abishai **killed him.** [12]**This is** the meaning of **the verse** that **states** (II Samuel 21:17): **"Then the men of David swore to him, saying, You shall go no more out with us to battle,** so that you will **not** put out **the lamp of Israel."**

תָּנוּ רַבָּנַן [13]**Our Rabbis taught** a related Baraita: [14]**"The earth shrank for** the following **three** people: **Eliezer the servant of Abraham, our Patriarch Jacob, and Abishai ben Zeruiah."** [15]The earth shrank for **Abishai ben Zeruiah,** as **we said** above. [16]The earth shrank for **Eliezer the servant of Abraham, as the verse states** (Genesis 24:42): **"And I came this day to the well."**

אַהֲדָרֵי לֵיהּ". [1]אֲמַר לֵיהּ: "אַפֵּיךְ צְלוֹתִיךְ. [2]בַּר בְּרָךְ קִירָא לִיזְבּוֹן וְאַתְּ לָא תִּצְטָעֵר". [3]אֲמַר לֵיהּ: "אִי הָכִי, סַיַּיע בַּהֲדַן". [4]הַיְינוּ דִּכְתִיב: "וַיַּעֲזָר לוֹ אֲבִישַׁי בֶּן צְרוּיָה". [5]אָמַר רַב יְהוּדָה אָמַר רַב: שֶׁעֲזָרוֹ בִּתְפִלָּה. [6]אָמַר אֲבִישַׁי שֵׁם וְאַחְתֵּיהּ. [7]הֲוָה קָא רָדֵיף בַּתְרַיְיהוּ. [8]כִּי מְטָא קוּבִי, אָמְרִי: "קוּם בֵּיהּ". [9]כִּי מְטָא בֵּי תְּרֵי, אָמְרִי: "בִּתְרֵי גּוּרְיָין קְטַלוּהּ לְאַרְיֵא". [10]אָמְרִי לֵיהּ: זִיל, אִשְׁתַּכַּח לְעָרְפָּה אִימֵּיךְ בְּקִיבְרָא". [11]כִּי אַדְכַּרוּ לֵיהּ שְׁמָא דְּאִימֵּיהּ, כָּחַשׁ חֵילֵיהּ, וְקַטְלֵיהּ. [12]הַיְינוּ דִּכְתִיב: "אָז נִשְׁבְּעוּ אַנְשֵׁי דָוִד לוֹ, לֵאמֹר לֹא תֵצֵא עוֹד אִתָּנוּ לַמִּלְחָמָה וְלֹא תְכַבֶּה אֶת נֵר יִשְׂרָאֵל".

[13]תָּנוּ רַבָּנַן: [14]"שְׁלֹשָׁה קָפְצָה לָהֶם הָאָרֶץ: אֱלִיעֶזֶר עֶבֶד אַבְרָהָם, וְיַעֲקֹב אָבִינוּ, וַאֲבִישַׁי בֶּן צְרוּיָה". [15]אֲבִישַׁי בֶּן צְרוּיָה, הָא דַּאֲמָרַן. [16]אֱלִיעֶזֶר עֶבֶד אַבְרָהָם, דִּכְתִיב: "וָאָבֹא הַיּוֹם

LITERAL TRANSLATION

I answered him." [1]He said to him: "Reverse your prayer. [2]Let your son's son sell wax, and you not suffer privation." [3]He said to him: "If so, help me." [4]This is what is written: "But Abishai the son of Zeruiah helped him." [5]Rav Yehudah said in the name of Rav: He helped him with prayer. [6]Abishai pronounced a name, and brought him down. [7]He was chasing the two. [8]When they reached Kubi, they said: "Let us stand up against him." [9]When they reached Be-tre, they said: "Two cubs killed the lion." [10]They said to him: "Go, find Orpah, your mother, in the grave." [11]When they mentioned to him the name of his mother, his strength diminished, and he killed him. [12]This is what is written: "Then the men of David swore to him, saying, You shall go no more out with us to battle, so that you will not put out the lamp of Israel." [13]Our Rabbis taught: [14]"For three the earth shrank: Eliezer the servant of Abraham, and Jacob our Patriarch, and Abishai ben Zeruiah." [15]Abishai ben Zeruiah, that which we have said. [16]Eliezer the servant of Abraham, as it is written: "And I came this day

RASHI

ביד אויבך — והכי אהדרי ליה: מוטב שאפול ביד אויב. אמר ליה אפיך צלותיך — הפוך תפלתך ואמור לפניו מוטב יכלה זרעך ולא תמסר ביד אויב, דמה לך בצער בניך. בר ברך קירא לזבון ואת לא תצטער — משל הוא שאומרים בני אדם. סייע בהדן — עזור בתפלתך להפכה. והוה קא רדיף בתרייהו — והם בורחין, שהיה קרוב לארץ פלשתים. וכי מטו קובי — לאותו כפר ששמו קובי שבין ארץ ישראל לארץ פלשתים. אמרי קום ביה — אמרו זה לזה: עמוד כנגדו, ואל תברח, ונכנו, ולכך נקרא קובי, אינהו הוו בקיאי בשמות הכפרים, ועדיין היו מפחדין ובורחין. כי מטא בי תרי — שם מקום. אמרו בין תרי גוריון — בתמיהא. בקברא — שהרגנוה.

NOTES

קִירָא לִיזְבּוֹן **Let him sell wax.** *Ramah* had the reading: קורא נזבון, "let him sell the terminal buds of palm-trees," an item that only poor people deal in. In either case, it is a commodity with a very slight profit margin, which only poor peddlers sell.

אֶל הָעָיִן״ — לְמֵימְרָא דְּהַהוּא יוֹמָא נְפַק. [1] יַעֲקֹב אָבִינוּ, [95B] [2] דִּכְתִיב: ״וַיֵּצֵא יַעֲקֹב מִבְּאֵר שָׁבַע וַיֵּלֶךְ חָרָנָה״. [3] וּכְתִיב: ״וַיִּפְגַּע בַּמָּקוֹם וַיָּלֶן שָׁם כִּי בָא הַשֶּׁמֶשׁ״. [4] כִּי מְטָא לְחָרָן, אָמַר: ״אֶפְשָׁר עָבַרְתִּי עַל מָקוֹם שֶׁהִתְפַּלְּלוּ בּוֹ אֲבוֹתַי וַאֲנִי לֹא הִתְפַּלַּלְתִּי בּוֹ״? [5] בָּעֵי לְמֶיהְדַּר. [6] כֵּיוָן דְּהִרְהֵר בְּדַעְתֵּיהּ לְמֶיהְדַּר, קָפְצָה לֵיהּ אַרְעָא. [7] מִיָּד, ״וַיִּפְגַּע בַּמָּקוֹם״.

[8] דָּבָר אַחֵר: אֵין פְּגִיעָה אֶלָּא תְּפִלָּה, [9] שֶׁנֶּאֱמַר: ״וְאַתָּה אַל תִּתְפַּלֵּל בְּעַד הָעָם הַזֶּה וְאַל תִּשָּׂא בַעֲדָם רִנָּה וּתְפִלָּה וְאַל תִּפְגַּע בִּי״. [10] ״וַיָּלֶן שָׁם כִּי בָא הַשֶּׁמֶשׁ״. [11] בָּתַר דְּצַלֵּי, בָּעֵי לְמֶיהְדַּר. [12] אָמַר הַקָּדוֹשׁ בָּרוּךְ הוּא: ״צַדִּיק זֶה בָּא לְבֵית מְלוֹנִי. יִפָּטֵר בְּלֹא לִינָה״? [13] מִיָּד, בָּא הַשֶּׁמֶשׁ. [14] וְהַיְינוּ דִּכְתִיב: ״וַיִּזְרַח לוֹ הַשֶּׁמֶשׁ״. [15] וְכִי לוֹ בִּלְבַד זָרְחָה? [16] וַהֲלֹא לְכָל הָעוֹלָם כּוּלּוֹ זָרְחָה! [17] אֶלָּא, אָמַר רַבִּי יִצְחָק: שֶׁמֶשׁ שֶׁבָּא בַּעֲבוּרוֹ זָרְחָה בַּעֲבוּרוֹ.

LITERAL TRANSLATION

to the well" — to say that on that day he went out. [1] Jacob our Patriarch, [95B] [2] as it is written: "And Jacob went out from Be'ersheba, and went to Ḥaran." [3] And it is written: "And he struck a certain place, and stayed there all night, because the sun had set." [4] When he came to Haran, he said: "Is it possible that I passed the place where my fathers prayed, and I did not pray there?" [5] He wanted to go back. [6] When he thought in his mind to go back, the earth shrank for him. [7] Immediately, "And he struck a certain place."

[8] Another explanation: *Pegi'ah* [can] only [mean] prayer, [9] as it is stated: "Therefore pray not you for this people, neither lift up cry nor prayer for them, neither make intercession to me." [10] "And he stayed there all the night, because the sun had set." [11] After he prayed, he wanted to return. [12] The Holy One, blessed be He, said: "This righteous man came to My lodging. Shall he leave without spending the night?" [13] Immediately, the sun set. [14] And this is what is written: "The sun shone for him." [15] Did it shine only for him? [16] Surely it shone for the whole world! [17] Rather, Rav Yitzḥak said: The sun that set for him shone for him.

TRANSLATION AND COMMENTARY

Eliezer mentioned this to Rebecca's family in order **to inform** them **that on** the very **day that he left** the land of Canaan, he arrived in Ḥaran. Thus, they would understand that a miracle had been performed on his behalf for the sake of Abraham. [1] The earth shrank for **our Patriarch Jacob,** [95B] [2] **as the verse states** (Genesis 25:10): **"And Jacob went out from Beersheba, and went to Haran,"** implying that he had already reached Haran. [3] **And the** next **verse states** (Genesis 25:11): **"And he struck a certain place, and stayed there all night, because the sun had set,"** implying that he had not yet reached Ḥaran, but was still in Beth-El. How are we to reconcile these two verses? [4] **When** Jacob **came to Ḥaran, he said** to himself: **"Is it possible that I passed the place where my fathers** Abraham and Isaac once **prayed, and** I myself **did not pray there?"** [5] Jacob **wanted to go back** to pray where his fathers had prayed. [6] **As soon as he thought** of going **back** to that place, **the earth shrunk for him,** [7] and he **immediately** arrived at his destination, as the verse states: **"And he struck a certain place."**

דָּבָר אַחֵר [8] The Gemara now cites **another explanation** of that verse: The word *pegi'ah* in this context **refers to prayer,** [9] **as it is stated** elsewhere (Jeremiah 7:16): **"Therefore pray not you for this people, neither lift up cry nor prayer for them, neither make intercession** [*tifga*] **to me."** Thus, the verse means: "And he prayed at the place." [10] It continues: **"And he stayed there all the night, because the sun had set."** [11] **After** Jacob **prayed, he wanted to** resume his journey, for it was still early. [12] But **the Holy One, blessed be He, said** to himself: **"This righteous man came to my lodging. Shall he leave without spending the night** with Me?" [13] **Immediately, the sun set,** and Jacob had to spend the night there. [14] **This is what is** meant by the verse that **states** (Genesis 32:31): "And as he passed over Penu'el, **the sun shone** ***for him.***" [15] The question may be raised: **Was it only for** Jacob **that** the sun **shone?** [16] **Surely it shone for the whole world!** [17] **Rather, Rav Yitzḥak said: The sun that set** early **for** Jacob the night before **shone for him** early now.

RASHI

ויצא יעקב מבאר שבע וילך חרנה — אלמא בא לחרן וכתיב **ויפגע במקום** שעדיין לא הגיע לחרן שהיה עדיין בבית אל. **שהתפללו בו אבותי** — אברהם ויצחק, (אברהם דכתיב ״ויעתק משם״, יצחק — אין מקרא בידי). **הרהר בדעתיה למהדר** — למקום. **קפצה ליה ארעא** — והיה שם מיד, וקרא מוכיח, דכתיב ״ויפגע במקום״ שהמקום פגעו ושקפצה לו הארץ ונתקרב לו המקום. **הכי גרסינן דבר אחר אין פגיעה אלא תפלה** — ונראה למורי דהכא לא מיגרסא הך מילתא. **בית אל** — זה ירושלים, חרן חוץ לארץ. **כי בא השמש** — ויצא השמש לא נאמר אלא ״כי בא השמש״, דמשמע שהיה דעתו לחזור כי עוד היום גדול, כיון שראה כי בא השמש — לן. **ויזרח לו השמש** — משמע השמש שהיה לו כבר שבא בשבילו כבר.

BACKGROUND

שִׁרְיוֹן קְלִיפָּה Coat of mail.

A coat of mail from the Roman period.
Mail is armor made of linked metal plates designed both to protect the wearer and to afford him some flexibility of movement.

TRANSLATION AND COMMENTARY

וּמְנָלַן [1]The Gemara returns to the story of King David: **From where do we know** that after **David** changed his mind and asked not be handed over to his enemy, but rather to have his seed destroyed, his **seed was** indeed **destroyed?** [2]The Gemara explains: We learn this from **the verse** that **states** (II Kings 11:1): **"And when Ataliah the mother of Aḥaziah saw that her son was dead, she arose and destroyed all the royal seed."**

וְהָא אִשְׁתַּיֵּיר [3]The Gemara asks: **But surely** David's seed was not wiped out altogether, for Ahaziah's son, **Joash, survived** Ataliah's massacre!

הָתָם נַמִּי [4]The Gemra answers: **There, too, Abiathar survived, as the verse states** (I Samuel 22:20): **"And one of the sons of Achimelech the son of Achitub, named Abiathar, escaped."** As was explained above, David's seed was destroyed as a punishment for the killing of the priests of Nob. Since one priest survived those killings, one of David's descendants was also spared.

אָמַר רַב יְהוּדָה [5]**Rav Yehudah said in the name of Rav: Were it not that Abiathar was left of Achimelech ben Achituv,** [6]**there would not have been left of the seed of David** even **a** single **remnant or survivor.**

אָמַר רַב יְהוּדָה [7]The Gemara resumes it discussion of Sennacherib's march on Jerusalem. **Rav Yehudah said in the name of Rav: The wicked Sennacherib came against** Jerusalem **with forty-five thousand men, the sons of kings sitting in carriages of gold, and with them mistresses and harlots, and with eighty thousand warriors wearing scaly coats of armor,** [8]**and with sixty thousand sword-bearing men running before him, and the rest** of his soldiers were **horsemen.** [9]**The same** number of soldiers **also came against Abraham** when he fought the four kings of Canaan (Genesis 14). [10]**And the same** number of soldiers **will in the future come with Gog and Magog** in the final battle before the advent of the Messiah.

בְּמַתְנִיתָא תָּנָא [11]**It was taught in a Baraita: "The length of** Sennacherib's **camp was four hundred Persian**

[1]וּמְנָלַן דִּכְלָה זַרְעֵיהּ דְּדָוִד? [2]דִּכְתִיב: ״וַעֲתַלְיָה אֵם אֲחַזְיָהוּ רָאֲתָה כִּי מֵת בְּנָהּ וַתָּקָם וַתְּאַבֵּד אֵת כָּל זֶרַע הַמַּמְלָכָה״. [3]וְהָא אִשְׁתַּיֵּיר לֵיהּ יוֹאָשׁ! [4]הָתָם נַמִּי אִשְׁתַּיֵּיר אֶבְיָתָר, דִּכְתִיב: ״וַיִּמָּלֵט בֵּן אֶחָד לַאֲחִימֶלֶךְ בֶּן אֲחִטוּב וּשְׁמוֹ אֶבְיָתָר״.

[5]אָמַר רַב יְהוּדָה אָמַר רַב: אִלְמָלֵא לֹא נִשְׁתַּיֵּיר אֶבְיָתָר לַאֲחִימֶלֶךְ בֶּן אֲחִיטוּב, [6]לֹא נִשְׁתַּיֵּיר מִזַּרְעוֹ שֶׁל דָּוִד שָׂרִיד וּפָלִיט.

[7]אָמַר רַב יְהוּדָה אָמַר רַב: בָּא עֲלֵיהֶם סַנְחֵרִיב הָרָשָׁע בְּאַרְבָּעִים וַחֲמִשָּׁה אֶלֶף אִישׁ בְּנֵי מְלָכִים יוֹשְׁבִים בִּקְרוֹנוֹת שֶׁל זָהָב, וְעִמָּהֶן שִׁגְלוֹנוֹת וְזוֹנוֹת, וּבִשְׁמוֹנִים אֶלֶף גִּבּוֹרִים לְבוּשֵׁי שִׁרְיוֹן קְלִיפָּה, [8]וּבְשִׁשִּׁים אֶלֶף אֲחוּזֵי חֶרֶב רָצִים לְפָנָיו, וְהַשְּׁאָר פָּרָשִׁים. [9]וְכֵן בָּאוּ עַל אַבְרָהָם. [10]וְכֵן עֲתִידִין לָבוֹא עִם גּוֹג וּמָגוֹג.

[11]בְּמַתְנִיתָא תָּנָא: ״אוֹרֶךְ מַחֲנֵהוּ אַרְבַּע מֵאוֹת פַּרְסֵי,

LITERAL TRANSLATION

[1]And from where do we [know] that the seed of David was destroyed? [2]As it is written: "And when Ataliah the mother of Aḥaziah saw that her son was dead, she arose and destroyed all the royal seed."

[3]But surely Joash was left of him!

[4]There, too, Abiathar was left, as it is written: "And one of the sons of Achimelech the son of Achituv, named Abiathar, escaped."

[5]Rav Yehudah said in the name of Rav: Were it not that Abiathar was left of Achimelech ben Achituv, [6]there would not have been left a remnant or a survivor of the seed of David.

[7]Rav Yehudah said in the name of Rav: The wicked Sennacherib came against them with forty-five thousand men, the sons of kings sitting in carriages of gold, and with them mistresses and harlots, and with eighty thousand warriors wearing scaly coats of armor, [8]and with sixty thousand sword-bearing men running before him, and the rest horsemen. [9]The same also came against Abraham. [10]And the same will come in the future with Gog and Magog.

[11]It was taught in a Baraita: "The length of his camp was four hundred Persian miles,

RASHI

ומנא ליה דכלה זרעיה דדוד – כדאפיך צלותיה. **התם נמי אשתייר אביתר** – מכהני נוב. **שגלונות** – מלכות. **על אברהם** – כשנלחם בארבעה מלכים.

NOTES

וְכֵן עֲתִידִין לָבוֹא The same will come in the future. As was explained above, God originally intended that Ḥezekiah should be the Messiah, and that Sennacherib should fulfill the role of Gog and Magog. Thus, it follows that the number of Sennacherib's troops corresponds to the number of soldiers that will come in the future with Gog and Magog in the final battle before the advent of the Messiah.

רֹחַב צַוַּאר סוּסָיו אַרְבָּעִים פַּרְסֵי, סָךְ מַחֲנֵהוּ מָאתַיִם וְשִׁשִּׁים רִיבּוֹא אֲלָפִים חָסֵר חַד״.
[1] בָּעֵי אַבַּיֵי: חָסֵר חַד רִיבּוֹיָא, אוֹ חָסֵר חַד אַלְפָּא, אוֹ חָסֵר מֵאָה, אוֹ חָסֵר חַד?
[2] תֵּיקוּ.
[3] תָּנָא: ״רִאשׁוֹנִים עָבְרוּ בְּשֶׂחִי, שֶׁנֶּאֱמַר: ׳וְחָלַף בִּיהוּדָה שָׁטַף וְעָבַר׳, [4] אֶמְצָעִיִּים עָבְרוּ בְּקוֹמָה, שֶׁנֶּאֱמַר: ׳עַד צַוַּאר יַגִּיעַ׳. [5] אַחֲרוֹנִים הֶעֱלוּ עָפָר בְּרַגְלֵיהֶם [6] וְלֹא מָצְאוּ מַיִם בַּנָּהָר לִשְׁתּוֹת, עַד שֶׁהֱבִיאוּ מַיִם מִמָּקוֹם אַחֵר וְשָׁתוּ, [7] שֶׁנֶּאֱמַר: ׳אֲנִי קַרְתִּי וְשָׁתִיתִי מָיִם וגו׳ ׳״.
[8] וְהָכְתִיב: [9] ״וַיֵּצֵא מַלְאַךְ ה׳ וַיַּכֶּה בְּמַחֲנֵה אַשּׁוּר מֵאָה וּשְׁמוֹנִים וַחֲמִשָּׁה אָלֶף (וַיָּקוּמוּ) [וַיַּשְׁכִּימוּ] בַבֹּקֶר וְהִנֵּה כֻלָּם פְּגָרִים מֵתִים״!
[10] אָמַר רַבִּי אַבָּהוּ: הַלָּלוּ רָאשֵׁי גְּיָיסוֹת הֵן.

LITERAL TRANSLATION

the width of the necks of his horses was forty Persian miles, the number of his camp was two-hundred-and-sixty ten-thousand thousands minus one."

[1] Abaye asked: Minus one ten-thousand, or minus one thousand, or minus a hundred, or minus one?

[2] Let it stand.

[3] [A Sage] taught: "The first ones passed by swimming, as it is stated: 'And he shall sweep through Judah, he shall overflow and go over.' [4] The middle ones passed standing, as it is stated: 'He shall reach even the neck.' [5] The last ones raised dust with their feet, [6] and did not find water in the river to drink, until they brought water from a different place and drank, [7] as it is stated: 'I have dug, and drunk water, etc.'"

[8] But surely it is written: [9] "Then the Angel of the Lord went forth, and struck down in the camp of Assyria a hundred and eighty five thousand: and when they arose early in the morning, behold, they were all dead bodies."

[10] Rabbi Abbahu said: They were the heads of the troops.

TRANSLATION AND COMMENTARY

miles, the width of the necks of his horses when standing side by side **was forty Persian miles,** and **the number of** soldiers in **his camp was two-hundred-and-sixty ten-thousand thousands minus one."**

בָּעֵי אַבַּיֵי [1] **Abaye asked:** What does the Baraita mean when it states "minus one"? Does it mean **minus one ten-thousand, or minus one thousand, or minus** one **hundred, or minus one?**

תֵּיקוּ [2] The Gemara notes that the question raised by Abaye remains **unresolved.**

תָּנָא [3] **A Sage taught** a related Baraita: **"The first** set of Sennacherib's troops **passed** through the waters of the Jordan River **by swimming, as the verse states** (Isaiah 8:8): **'And he shall sweep through Judah, he shall overflow and go over.'** [4] So much water was displaced by those soldiers that **the middle** set of Sennacherib's troops were able to **pass** through the river **standing** erect, with the water reaching their necks, **as the** continuation of that **verse states: 'He shall reach even the neck.'** [5] When **the last** of Sennacherib's troops passed through the river, **they raised dust with their feet,** for the river- bed was already dry. [6] They **did not find** any **water in the river to drink,** so **they** had to **bring water from a different place, and** only then could **they drink,** [7] **as the verse states** (Isaiah 37:25): **'I have dug, and drunk water.'"**

וְהָכְתִיב [8] **But** concerning the number of Sennacherib's soldiers, **surely the verse states** (Isaiah 37:36): [9] **"Then the Angel of the Lord went forth, and struck down in the camp of Assyria a hundred and eighty-five thousand: and when they arose early in the morning, behold, they were all dead bodies."** The figure mentioned in this verse is considerably less than "two-hundred-and-sixty ten-thousand thousands minus one" mentioned in the Baraita!

אָמַר רַבִּי אַבָּהוּ [10] **Rabbi Abbahu said:** The number found in the verse refers to **the** army's **officers,** each of whom had many soldiers under his command.

RASHI

בעי אביי — האי חסר חד היכי קאמר, אי חסר חד רבוא וכו׳. **ראשונה** — כת ראשונה מחיל של סנחריב. **עברו בשחי** — שטו הסוסים בירדן ונתמעטו המים עד שעברו. **אמצעיים בקומה** — זקופה, ולא היו המים מגיעין אלא עד הצואר יגיע. **שחי** — כמו שחו. **העלו עפר ברגליהם** — שלא היה שם מים כל עיקר. **קרתי** — לשון מקור. **הכי גרסינן: ויצא מלאך ה׳ ויך במחנה אשור אמר רבי וכו׳** — ולא גרסינן והא כתיב ״ויצא מלאך ה׳״ אלמא כל המחנה אשור אינו אלא מאה שמונים וחמשה אלף, ולעיל קתני מאתים וששים רבוא. **הללו** — מאה שמונים וחמשה אלף ראשי גייסות נגידי החיל, שכן עולה לחשבון לכדאמרינן ארבעים וחמשה

NOTES

חָסֵר חַד רִיבּוֹיָא **Minus one ten-thousand.** The question has been raised: What difference does the answer to this question make? The answer to this question does not even help us understand a problematic verse. It has been suggested that the matter does have Halakhic ramifications regarding vows, for if someone vowed to donate a sum of money corresponding to the number of Sennacherib's troops, he can only fulfill his vow after that number has been established (*Melo HaRo'im*). Alternatively, the matter has Halakhic ramifications regarding the meaning of such an expression when it is found in a contract (*Ḥida*).

TRANSLATION AND COMMENTARY

אָמַר רַב אַשִׁי [1]**Rav Ashi said: This** explanation **is also** based on a **precise** examination of the wording of a different verse, **for the verse states** (Isaiah 10:16): "Therefore shall the Master, the Lord of hosts, send **among his fat ones leanness**" — [2]**among the fat or important ones among them.**

אָמַר רָבִינָא [3]**Ravina said: This** explanation **is indeed** based on a **precise** examination of the wording of yet another verse, **for the verse states** (II Chronicles 32:21): **"And the Lord sent an Angel, who cut off all the mighty men at arms, and the leaders and captains in the camp** of the King of Assyria. So he returned shame-facedly to his own land. [4]**And when he came into the house of his god, his own offspring slew him there with a sword."**

שְׁמַע מִינָּהּ [5]The Gemara concludes: We may indeed **infer from these** verses that the number mentioned in the verse refers to Sennacherib's officers, and that the total number of soldiers in his army was far greater.

בַּמָּה הִכָּם [6]The Gemara formulates a question: The verse cited above states that the Angel of the Lord went forth, and smote Sennacherib's troops. **With what** precisely **did he** strike **them?**

רַבִּי אֱלִיעֶזֶר [7]**Rabbi Eliezer said:** The Angel struck Sennacherib's army **with the hand** of God, [8]**as the verse** describing Israel's experience at the Red Sea **states** (Exodus 114:31): **"And Israel saw that great hand."** In the Hebrew, the word "hand" [*yad*] is preceded by the definite article (the letter *heh*), teaching that Israel saw the hand that would be known in another context, [9]**the hand that would in the future punish Sennacherib.**

רַבִּי יְהוֹשֻׁעַ [10]**Rabbi Yehoshua said:** The Angel **smote** Sennacherib's soldiers **with the finger** of God, **as the verse** relating to the plague of lice in Egypt **states** (Exodus 8:15): **"Then the magicians said to Pharaoh, This is the finger of God"** — [11]**this is the finger that will in the future punish Sennacherib.**

רַבִּי אֱלִיעֶזֶר [12]**Rabbi Eliezer the son of Rabbi Yose the Galilean says: The Holy One, blessed be He, said to** the Angel **Gabriel: "Is your scythe sharpened** and ready to kill Sennacherib's soldiers?" [13]**Gabriel said before Him: "Master of the universe,** my scythe **is sharpened and** has been **ready** for this task since **the six days of creation,** [14]**as the verse states** (Isaiah 21:15): **'For they have fled from the swords,** from the drawn sword.'"

[1]אָמַר רַב אַשִׁי: דַּיְקָא נַמִי, דִּכְתִיב: "בְּמִשְׁמַנָּיו רָזוֹן" — [2]בַּשְּׁמֵינִים דְּאִית בְּהוּ.
[3]אָמַר רָבִינָא: דַּיְקָא נַמִי, דִּכְתִיב: "וַיִּשְׁלַח ה׳ מַלְאָךְ וַיַּכְחֵד כָּל גִּבּוֹר חַיִל וְנָגִיד וְשָׂר בְּמַחֲנֵה וגו׳. [4]וַיָּבֹא בֵּית אֱלֹהָיו וּמִיצִיאֵי מֵעָיו שָׁם הִפִּילֻהוּ בֶחָרֶב".
[5]שְׁמַע מִינָּהּ.
[6]בַּמָּה הִכָּם?
[7]רַבִּי אֱלִיעֶזֶר אוֹמֵר: בַּיָּד הִכָּם, [8]שֶׁנֶּאֱמַר: "וַיַּרְא יִשְׂרָאֵל אֶת הַיָּד הַגְּדֹלָה" — [9]הַיָּד שֶׁעֲתִידָה לִיפָּרַע מִסַּנְחֵרִיב.
[10]רַבִּי יְהוֹשֻׁעַ אוֹמֵר: בָּאֶצְבַּע הִכָּם, שֶׁנֶּאֱמַר: [11]"וַיֹּאמְרוּ הַחַרְטֻמִּים אֶל פַּרְעֹה אֶצְבַּע אֱלֹהִים הִיא" — הִיא אֶצְבַּע שֶׁעֲתִידָה לִיפָּרַע מִסַּנְחֵרִיב.
[12]רַבִּי אֱלִיעֶזֶר בְּנוֹ שֶׁל רַבִּי יוֹסֵי הַגְּלִילִי אוֹמֵר: אָמַר לוֹ הַקָּדוֹשׁ בָּרוּךְ הוּא לְגַבְרִיאֵל: "מַגָּלְךָ נְטוּשָׁה"? [13]אָמַר לְפָנָיו: "רִבּוֹנוֹ שֶׁל עוֹלָם, נְטוּשָׁה וְעוֹמֶדֶת מִשֵּׁשֶׁת יְמֵי בְרֵאשִׁית, [14]שֶׁנֶּאֱמַר: 'מִפְּנֵי חֲרָבוֹת נָדְדוּ וגו׳'".

LITERAL TRANSLATION

[1]Rav Ashi said: It is also precise, for it is written: "Among his fat ones leanness" — [2]among the fat ones among them.

[3]Ravina said: It is also precise, for it is written: "And the Lord sent an Angel, who cut off all the mighty men at arms, and the leaders and captains in the camp, etc. [4]And when he came into the house of his god, his own offspring slew him there with a sword."

[5]Infer from this.

[6]With what did he strike them?

[7]Rabbi Eliezer said: He struck them with the hand, [8]as it is stated: "And Israel saw that great hand" — [9]the hand that would in the future punish Sennacherib.

[10]Rabbi Yehoshua said: He struck them with a finger, as it is stated: [11]"Then the magicians said to Pharaoh, This is the finger of God" — this is the finger that will in the future punish Sennacherib.

[12]Rabbi Eliezer the son of Rabbi Yose the Galilean says: The Holy One, blessed be He, said to Gabriel: "Is your scythe sharpened?" [13]He said before Him: "Master of the universe, it is sharpened and ready from the six days of creation, [14]as it is stated: 'For they have fled from the swords, etc.'"

RASHI

אלף בני מלכים, שמנים אלף גבורים, ששים אלף אחוזי חרב, הרי מאה שמונים וחמשה אלף, אבל האחרים שמתו אין מספר, כדאמר: והשאר פרשים אין מספר. במה הכם — המלאך. היד הגדולה — יד הגדולה לא נאמר אלא "היד", דמשמע היד שעתידה וכו׳. מגלך נטושה — שחוזה מגלך להרוג את אלו.

TRANSLATION AND COMMENTARY

רַבִּי שִׁמְעוֹן בֶּן יוֹחַי [1]**Rabbi Shimon ben Yoḥai says: "The time** when the Angel smote Sennacherib's army **was** the season when **fruit ripens.** [2]**The Holy One, blessed be He, said to Gabriel,** the Angel whose responsibility it was to ripen the fruit: **'When you go out** into the world **to ripen fruit, attend to** Sennacherib's soldiers on the way, and destroy them,' [3]**as the verse states** (Isaiah 28:19): 'Whenever it passes **it shall take you — for morning by morning shall it pass over, by day and by night; and the mere understanding of the report shall bring terror'"** — while you are on the way on some other task, destroy them.

אָמַר רַב פַּפָּא [4]**Rav Pappa said: This is** the meaning of **the popular adage:** While you are **on your way, let your enemy hear** from you — appear before him and fill him with fear.

וְיֵשׁ אוֹמְרִים [5]**Some** authorities **say** that the Angel **blew on their noses, and** Sennacherib's soldiers **died,** [6]**as the verse states** (Isaiah 40:24): **"He merely blows upon them, and they wither."**

רַבִּי יִרְמְיָה בַּר אַבָּא [7]**Rabbi Yirmeyah bar Abba said:** The Angel **clapped his hands, and** Sennacherib's men **died,** [8]**as the verse states** (Ezekiel 21:24): **"I will also smite My hands together, and I will relieve My anger."**

רַבִּי יִצְחָק נַפָּחָא [9]**Rabbi Yitzḥak Nappaḥa said:** The Angel **opened their ears, and they heard the song** sung **by** the holy **creatures** in Heaven in praise of God, [10]**as the verse states** (Isaiah 33:3): **"At the lifting up of Yourself the nations were scattered"** — Your loftiness was revealed to them, and they were destroyed.

וְכַמָּה נִשְׁתַּיֵּיר מֵהֶם [11]The Gemara asks: **And how many of** Sennacherib's troops **were left** the next morning after the Angel smote his army?

רַב אָמַר [12]**Rav said: Ten** of Sennacherib's soldiers survived, **as the verse states** (Isaiah 10:19): **"And the rest of the trees of his forest shall be few, that a child may write them down."** [13]**How much can a** young **child**

[1]רַבִּי שִׁמְעוֹן בֶּן יוֹחַי אוֹמֵר: "אוֹתוֹ הַפֶּרֶק זְמַן בִּישּׁוּל פֵּירוֹת הָיָה. [2]אָמַר לוֹ הַקָּדוֹשׁ בָּרוּךְ הוּא לְגַבְרִיאֵל: 'כְּשֶׁאַתָּה יוֹצֵא לְבַשֵּׁל פֵּירוֹת, הִזָּקֵק לָהֶם', [3]שֶׁנֶּאֱמַר: 'מִדֵּי עָבְרוֹ יִקַּח אֶתְכֶם כִּי בַבֹּקֶר בַּבֹּקֶר יַעֲבֹר בַּיּוֹם וּבַלָּיְלָה וְהָיָה רַק זְוָעָה הָבִין שְׁמוּעָה וגו׳ ׳ ".

[4]אָמַר רַב פַּפָּא: הַיְינוּ דְּאָמְרִי אֱינָשֵׁי: אַגַּב אוֹרְחָךְ לְבַעַל דְּבָבָךְ אִישְׁתַּמַּע.

[5]וְיֵשׁ אוֹמְרִים: בְּחוֹטְמָן נָשַׁף בָּהֶן וָמֵתוּ, [6]שֶׁנֶּאֱמַר: "וְגַם נָשַׁף בָּהֶם וַיִּבָשׁוּ".

[7]רַבִּי יִרְמְיָה בַּר אַבָּא אָמַר: כַּפַּיִים סָפַק לָהֶם וָמֵתוּ, [8]שֶׁנֶּאֱמַר: "וְגַם אֲנִי (הִכֵּתִי) [אַכֶּה] כַפִּי אֶל כַּפִּי וַהֲנִחֹתִי חֲמָתִי".

[9]רַבִּי יִצְחָק נַפָּחָא אָמַר: אָזְנַיִם גִּלָּה לָהֶם, וְשָׁמְעוּ שִׁירָה מִפִּי חַיּוֹת, וָמֵתוּ, [10]שֶׁנֶּאֱמַר: "מֵרוֹמְמֻתֶךָ נָפְצוּ גּוֹיִם".

[11]וְכַמָּה נִשְׁתַּיֵּיר מֵהֶם?

[12]רַב אָמַר: עֲשָׂרָה, שֶׁנֶּאֱמַר: "וּשְׁאָר עֵץ יַעְרוֹ מִסְפָּר יִהְיוּ וְנַעַר יִכְתְּבֵם". [13]כַּמָּה נַעַר יָכוֹל

LITERAL TRANSLATION

[1]Rabbi Shimon ben Yoḥai says: "That time was the time of the ripening of fruit. [2]The Holy One, blessed be He, said to Gabriel: 'When you go out to ripen the fruit, attend to them,' [3]as it is stated: 'Whenever it passes it shall take you: for morning by morning shall it pass over, by day and by night; and the mere understanding of the report shall bring terror.' "

[4]Rav Pappa said: This is what people say: On your way let your enemy hear.

[5]And some say: He blew on their noses, and they died, [6]as it is stated: "He merely blows upon them, and they wither."

[7]Rabbi Yirmeyah bar Abba said: He clapped his hands, and they died, [8]as it is stated: "I will also strike My hands together, and I will relieve My anger."

[9]Rabbi Yitzḥak Nappaḥa said: He opened their ears, and they heard song from the mouth of the creatures, and they died, [10]as it is stated: "At the lifting up of Yourself the nations were scattered."

[11]And how many were left of them?

[12]Rav said: Ten, as it is stated: "And the rest of the trees of his forest shall be few, that a child may write them down." [13]How much can a child

RASHI

גבריאל — ממונה על בשול הפירות. הזקק לאלו — לחיל סנחריב להרגן. אגב ארחך — כשתלך לדרכך לפי תומך. לבעל דבבך אשתמע — לשונאך התראה והפחידו. נשף — נפח.

NOTES

כַּמָּה נַעַר יָכוֹל לִכְתּוֹב? **How much can a child write?** Our commentary follows *Rashi*. Similarly, the Geonim say that if a child is given a quill with which to form some kind of symbol, he will form the letter *yod*. *Ramah* explains that the letter *yod* is the letter most easily learned by a young child. We find a view in the Midrash that six of Sennacherib's

לִכְתּוֹב? [1]עֲשָׂרָה.
[2]וּשְׁמוּאֵל אָמַר: תִּשְׁעָה, שֶׁנֶּאֱמַר: [3]״וְנִשְׁאַר בּוֹ עֹלֵלֹת כְּנֹקֶף זַיִת שְׁנַיִם שְׁלשָׁה גַּרְגְּרִים בְּרֹאשׁ אָמִיר אַרְבָּעָה חֲמִשָּׁה בִּסְעִפֶיהָ״.
[4]רַבִּי יְהוֹשֻׁעַ בֶּן לֵוִי אָמַר: אַרְבָּעָה עָשָׂר, שֶׁנֶּאֱמַר: [5]״שְׁנַיִם שְׁלשָׁה [וכו׳] אַרְבָּעָה וַחֲמִשָּׁה״.
[6]רַבִּי יוֹחָנָן אָמַר: חֲמִשָּׁה — סַנְחֵרִיב וּשְׁנֵי בָנָיו, נְבוּכַדְנֶצַּר וּנְבוּזַר אֲדָן. [7]נְבוּזַרְאֲדָן — גְּמָרָא. [8]נְבוּכַדְנֶצַּר, דִּכְתִיב: [9]״וְרֵוֵהּ דִּי רְבִיעָאָה דָּמֵה לְבַר אֱלָהִין״. [10]וְאִי לָאו דַּחֲזְיֵיהּ, מְנָא הֲוָה יָדַע? [11]סַנְחֵרִיב וּשְׁנֵי בָנָיו, דִּכְתִיב: [12]״וַיְהִי הוּא מִשְׁתַּחֲוֶה בֵּית נִסְרֹךְ אֱלֹהָיו וְאַדְרַמֶּלֶךְ וְשַׂרְאֶצֶר בָּנָיו הִכֻּהוּ בַחֶרֶב״.
[13]אָמַר רַבִּי אַבָּהוּ: אִלְמָלֵא מִקְרָא כָּתוּב אִי אֶפְשָׁר לְאָמְרוֹ,

TRANSLATION AND COMMENTARY

write? [1]**Ten,** for if a young child throws ink on a pad, he will form the letter *yod*, the numerical value of which is ten.

וּשְׁמוּאֵל אָמַר [2]**Shmuel said: Nine** of Sennacherib's soldiers survived, **as the verse states** (Isaiah 17:6): [3]**"And gleanings shall be left of him, as in the beating of an olive tree, two or three berries in the top of the uppermost bough, four or five in its fruitful branches."** Just as when an olive tree is beaten, only two or three olives are left on the tree, so too when Sennacherib's army will be smitten, only a few soldiers will survive. How many? "Four or five" — which add up to nine.

רַבִּי יְהוֹשֻׁעַ בֶּן לֵוִי [4]**Rabbi Yehoshua ben Levi said: Fourteen** of Sennacherib's men survived, **as the verse states:** "And gleanings shall be left of him, as in the beating of an olive tree, [5]**two or three** olives in the top of the uppermost bough, **four or five** in its fruitful branches." Two plus three plus four plus five add up to fourteen.

רַבִּי יוֹחָנָן אָמַר [6]**Rabbi Yoḥanan said:** Only **five** people survived — **Sennacherib, and his two sons, Nebuchadnezzar, and Nebuzaradan.** Just as when an olive tree is beaten, not more than four or five olives remain on the tree, so, too, when the Angel smites Sennacherib's camp, not more than five soldiers will survive. [7]As for **Nebuzaradan,** Rabbi Yoḥanan had **a tradition** that he was among the five survivors. [8]As for **Nebuchadnezzar,** we know that he survived the Angel's attack, **for the verse** recording his reaction when he beheld the angel at the side of Ḥananiah, Mishael, and Azariah **states** (Daniel 3:25): [9]**"And the appearance of the fourth is like an Angel."** These words prove that Nebuchadnezzar had encountered the Angel before, [10]since **if he had not** already **seen** an Angel, **how did he know** that the appearance of the fourth was like that of an Angel? [11]**Sennacherib and his two sons** must also have survived the Angel's attack, **for** after Scripture describes how the Angel smote the Assyrian camp, **the verse states** (II Kings 19:37): [12]**"And it came to pass, as he** [= Sennacherib] **was worshiping in the house of Misroch his god, that Adrammelech and Sharezer his sons smote him with the sword."**

אָמַר רַבִּי אַבָּהוּ [13]**Rabbi Abbahu said: Were it not for the explicit verse** regarding this matter, **it would** have

LITERAL TRANSLATION

write? [1]Ten.

[2]And Shmuel said: Nine, as it is stated: [3]"And gleanings shall be left of him, as in the beating of an olive tree, two or three berries in the top of the uppermost bough, four or five in its fruitful branches."

[4]Rabbi Yehoshua ben Levi said: Fourteen, as it is stated: [5]"Two, or three…four or five."

[6]Rabbi Yoḥanan said: Five — Sennacherib, and his two sons, Nebuchadnezzar, and Nebuzaradan. [7]Nebuzaradan — a tradition. [8]Nebuchadnezzar, as it is written: [9]"And the appearance of the fourth is like a son of God." [10]And if he did not see him, from where did he know? [11]Sennacherib and his two sons, as it is written: [12]"And it happened, as he was worshiping in the house of Misroch his god, that Adrammelech and Sharezer his sons struck him with the sword."

[13]Rabbi Abbahu said: Were it not for the written verse, it would be impossible to say,

RASHI

עשרה — שהנער יכול להטיף טיפה של דיו והיינו יו״ד שנשארו עשרה. **ושמואל אמר תשעה** — ונשאר בו עוללות כנוקף זית, שאין נשארין בו אלא דבר מועט שנים או שלשה גרגרים בראש אמיר, כן לא ישתייר במחנהו אלא דבר מועט וכמה — ארבעה וחמשה בסעיפיה פוריה, ארבעה וחמשה — והיינו תשעה. **ארבעה עשר שנים ושלשה ארבעה וחמשה** — ר׳ יוחנן מקרא לא דייק להו, אלא הכי קאמר: הללו חמשה נשתיירו מהן סנחריב ושני בניו, וקרא משמע כנוקף זית — דמשייר מעט בראש ענף, שנים או שלשה גרגרים, כך ישתייר לו מעט ארבעה או חמשה. **נבוכדנצר דכתיב** — גבי [חנניה] מישאל ועזריה תואר ״ורויה די רביעאה דמי לבר אלהין״ — אלמא דחזא גבריאל והכירו בכבשן. **סנחריב ושני בניו** — דכתיב ״ויהי הוא משתחוה בית וגו׳״. **אי אפשר לאמרו** — שהקדוש ברוך הוא בעצמו גלחו לסנחריב.

NOTES

soldiers survived, for when a child makes a scratch on a stone wall, he forms the letter *vav*, the numerical value of which is six.

אִלְמָלֵא מִקְרָא כָּתוּב **Were it not for the written verse.** This passage explains why Sennacherib was not killed with his troops. The Gemara explains that God wanted Sennacherib to return home in shame and die at the hand of his own sons (*Be'er HaGolah*).

TRANSLATION AND COMMENTARY

been impossible for us **to say** this, that God shaved Sennacherib's head with a razor, [1]**as the verse states** (Isaiah 7:20): **"On the same day shall the Lord shave with a hired razor [namely with them beyond the river with the King of Assyria] the head, and the hair of the legs, and it shall also sweep away the beard."** Expressing such an idea without explicit Scriptural support would have been regarded as blasphemy. [2]The Gemara now explains what happened: **The Holy One, blessed be He, came and appeared to** Sennacherib **in the form of an old man.** [3]**He said to him: "When you go to the kings of the east and the west, whose sons you brought** with you to Jerusalem [as it was taught above, Sennacherib brought with him to Jerusalem 'forty-five thousand men, the sons of kings sitting in carriages of gold'] **and led to their death, what will you say to them?"** [4]Sennacherib **said to** the old man: "Indeed **that man** (myself) **dwells in fear,** and does not know what to do." [5]Sennacherib **said to** the old man: **"What should I do?** What advice can you give me?" [6]The old man **said to him: "Go,** [96A] **and disguise yourself,** so that they do not recognize you." [7]Sennacherib asked: **"How should I disguise myself?"** [8]The old man **said to him: "Go bring me a razor, and I** myself **will shave your** head so that nobody will know who you are." [9]Sennacherib asked: **"From where should I bring** you a razor?" [10]The old man **said to him: "Go into that house, and bring** the razor that you find there." [11]He **went** into the house, **and found** the razor. [12]**Ministering Angels came, and appeared to** him **in the form of people, and they were grinding date stones.** [13]Sennacherib **said to them: "Give me the razor."** [14]**They said to him: "Grind** for us **a** ***se'ah*** **of date stones, and we will give you** the razor as your wages." [15]**He** complied with their demand, and **ground a** ***se'ah*** **of date stones, and they gave him the razor** as they had promised. This is the meaning of the verse (Isaiah 7:20): "On the same day shall the Lord shave with a hired razor [namely with them beyond the river with the King of Assyria]— with a razor that the King of Assyria obtained in payment for grinding, work

[1]דִּכְתִיב: ״בַּיּוֹם הַהוּא יְגַלַּח ה׳ בְּתַעַר הַשְּׂכִירָה בְּעֶבְרֵי נָהָר בְּמֶלֶךְ אַשּׁוּר אֶת הָרֹאשׁ וְשַׂעַר הָרַגְלַיִם וְגַם אֶת הַזָּקָן תִּסְפֶּה״. [2]אֲתָא קוּדְשָׁא בְּרִיךְ הוּא וְאִדַּמֵּי לֵיהּ כְּגַבְרָא סָבָא. [3]אֲמַר לֵיהּ: ״כִּי אָזְלַתְּ לְגַבֵּי מַלְכֵי מִזְרָח וּמַעֲרָב דְּאַיְיתִיתִינְהוּ לִבְנַיְיהוּ וְקַטַלְתִּינְהוּ, מַאי אָמְרַתְּ לְהוּ? [4]אֲמַר לֵיהּ: ״הַהוּא גַּבְרָא בְּהַהוּא פַּחֲדָא נַמִי יָתֵיב״. [5]אֲמַר לְהוּ: ״הֵיכִי נַעֲבֵיד״? [6]אֲמַר לֵיהּ: ״זִיל, [96A] וְשַׁנֵּי נַפְשָׁךְ״. [7]״בְּמַאי אֶישַׁנֵּי״? [8]אֲמַר לֵיהּ: ״זִיל אַיְיתֵי לִי מַסְפְּרָא, וְאִיגְזַיֵּיךְ אֲנָא״. [9]״מֵהֵיכָא אַיְיתֵי״? [10]אֲמַר לֵיהּ: ״עוּל לְהַהוּא בַּיְתָא וְאַיְיתֵי״. [11]אֲזַל, אַשְׁכַּחִינְהוּ. [12]אָתוּ מַלְאֲכֵי שָׁרֵת וְאִידַּמּוּ לֵיהּ כְּגַבְרֵי, וְהָווּ קָא טָחֲנִי קַשְׁיָיתָא. [13]אֲמַר לְהוּ: ״הַבוּ לִי מַסְפְּרָא״. [14]אֲמַרוּ לֵיהּ: ״טְחוֹן חַד גְּרִיוָא דְּקַשְׁיָיתָא, וְנִיתֵּן לָךְ״. [15]טְחַן חַד גְּרִיוָא דְּקַשְׁיָיתָא וְיָהֲבוּ לֵיהּ מַסְפַּרְתָּא.

LITERAL TRANSLATION

[1]for it is written: "On the same day shall the Lord shave with a hired razor [namely with them beyond the river with the King of Assyria] the head, and the hair of the legs, and it shall also sweep away the beard." [2]The Holy One, blessed be He, came and appeared to him like an old man. [3]He said to him: "When you go to the kings of the east and the west, whose sons you brought and killed, what will you say to them?" [4]He said to him: "That man dwells in that fear also." [5]He said to Him: "What should I do?" [6]He said to him: "Go, [96A] and disguise yourself." [7]"How should I disguise myself?" [8]He said to him: "Go bring me a razor, and I will shave you." [9]"From where should I bring [it]?" [10]He said to him: "Go into that house, and bring." [11]He went, [and] found it. [12]Ministering Angels came, and appeared to him like people, and they were grinding date stones. [13]He said to them: "Give me the razor." [14]They said to him: "Grind one *se'ah* of date stones, and we will give [it] to you." [15]He ground one *se'ah* of date stones, and they gave him the razor.

RASHI

דאייתיתינהו לבנייהו – כדאמרינן שהביא עמו ארבעים וחמשה אלף בני מלכים. **אשני נפשך** – שנה עצמך כדי שלא יכירוך. **ואגזייך אנא** – אני אגלחך. **קשייתא** – גרעיני תמרים. **טחון** – אלו גרעינין, **וניתן לך** מספרים, והיינו דכתיב **בתער השכירה** – על שם שטרח נתנו לו תער לגלח, ואיזהו שכר נתנו לו – **בעברי נהר**, דברים שדרכן לעשות על ידי נהר, דהיינו טחינת ריחים.

NOTES

אִדַּמֵּי לֵיהּ כְּגַבְרָא סָבָא He appeared to him like an old man. Various explanations have been offered for this strange story, which obviously is not meant to be taken literally. *Ramah* offers five different explanations of the passage on both exoteric and esoteric levels. He suggests that this entire story is Sennacherib's dream. Alternatively,

עַד דַּאֲתָא אִיחֲשַׁךְ. ²אֲמַר לְהוּ: [1]
"זִיל אַיְיתֵי נוּרָא". ³אֲזַל וְאַיְיתֵי
נוּרָא. ⁴בַּהֲדֵי דְּקָא נָפַח לֵיהּ
אִתְלִי בֵּיהּ נוּרָא בִּדְיקְנֵיהּ, אֲזַל
גַּזְיֵיהּ לְרֵישֵׁיהּ וְדִיקְנֵיהּ. ⁵אֲמַרוּ:
הַיְינוּ דִּכְתִיב: "וְגַם אֶת הַזָּקָן
תִּסְפֶּה".

[6] אֲמַר רַב פַּפָּא: הַיְינוּ דְּאָמְרִי
אֱינָשֵׁי: [7] גְּרִירַתֵּיהּ לְאַרַמָּאָה —
שַׁפִּיר לֵיהּ, אִיתְלִי לֵיהּ נוּרָא
בְּדִיקְנֵיהּ וְלָא שָׂבְעַתְּ חוּכָא
מִינֵּיהּ.

[8] אֲזַל, אַשְׁכַּח דַּפָּא מִתֵּיבוּתָא
דְּנֹחַ. [9] אֲמַר: "הַיְינוּ אֱלָהָא רַבָּא
דְּשֵׁיזְבֵיהּ לְנֹחַ מִטּוּפָנָא".
[10] אֲמַר: "אִי אָזֵיל הַהוּא גַּבְרָא
וּמַצְלַח, מַקְרַב לְהוּ לִתְרֵין
בְּנוֹהִי קַמָּךְ". [11] שָׁמְעוּ בְּנוֹהִי,
וְקַטְלוּהוּ. [12] הַיְינוּ דִּכְתִיב: "וַיְהִי
הוּא מִשְׁתַּחֲוֶה בֵּית נִסְרֹךְ
אֱלֹהָיו וְאַדְרַמֶּלֶךְ וְשַׂרְאֶצֶר בָּנָיו
הִכֻּהוּ בַחֶרֶב וגו׳".

[13] "וַיֵּחָלֵק עֲלֵיהֶם לַיְלָה הוּא

LITERAL TRANSLATION

[1] Until he came, it became dark. [2] He said to him: "Go bring fire." [3] He went, and brought fire. [4] While he was fanning it, the fire caught his beard, [and] went and burned his head and his beard. [5] They said: This is what is written: "And it shall also sweep away the beard."

[6] Rav Pappa said: This is what people say: [7] If you scorch a non-Jew (lit., "an Aramean"), and he is pleased, let a fire seize his beard, and you will not be sated with laughter.

[8] He went, [and] found a plank from Noah's ark. [9] He said: "This is the great god who saved Noah from the flood." [10] He said: "If that man goes, and succeeds, he will offer his two sons before you." [11] His sons heard, and killed him. [12] This is what is written: "And it came to pass, as he was worshiping in the house of Nisroch his god, that Adrammelech and Sharezer his sons struck him with the sword, etc."

[13] "And he divided himself against them, he and his servants by night,

TRANSLATION AND COMMENTARY

that is usually performed along the river. [1] **By the time that** Sennacherib **came** back to the old man, **it had** already **become dark.** [2] The old man **said to him: "Go bring** me **fire,** so that I can shave you by its light." [3] He **went** out, **and brought** him **fire.** [4] **While** the old man was shaving Sennacherib's head, and Sennacherib **was fanning the fire**, it **caught his beard, and burned his head and his beard.** [5] **They said: This is** the meaning of **the** end of that **verse,** which **states: "And it shall also sweep away the beard."**

אֲמַר רַב פַּפָּא [6] **Rav Pappa said: This is** the meaning of **the popular adage:** [7] **If you scorch a non-Jew, and he is pleased** by what you have done, **let a fire seize his beard, and you will not be sated with laughter.** If a person does not object when others treat him lightly, those other people will continue to treat him in that belittling manner.

אֲזַל [8] The Gemara continues with its story: Sennacherib then **went and found a plank from Noah's ark.** Attributing Noah's rescue to the ark, rather than to God, [9] Sennacherib **said** to himself: **"This plank is the great god that saved Noah from the flood."** [10] **He said** further: **"If that man,** I myself, **goes** out **and succeeds** in his way, **he will offer his two sons before you."** [11] Sennacherib's **sons heard** their father's vow, **and killed him.** [12] **This is what the verse** means when it **states** (II Kings 19:37): **"And it came to pass, as he was worshiping in the house of Nisroch his god, that Adrammelech and Sharezer his sons smote him with the sword."** Because Sennacherib worshiped in the house of Nisroch (the house of the *neser* — the plank from Noah's ark that Sennacherib turned into a god), his sons, Adrammelech and Sharezer, came and smote him.

וַיֵּחָלֵק [13] Having discussed the defeat of Sennacherib's army, the Gemara now discusses Abraham's battle with the four Kings of Canaan, mentioned in passing above. The verse describing Abraham's battle with those kings states (Genesis 14:15): **"And he divided himself against them, he and his servants by night** [*laylah*],

RASHI

וגם הזקן תספה — דלא כתיב גלוח אלא אראש, אבל אזקן כתיב תספה — לשון כלוי על ידי אור, שכלתה לגמרי. **גרירתיה לארמאה ושפר באפיה** — אם אתה מחרך את הארמאי והוטב בעיניו — הבער לו אש בזקנו, ולא שבעת חוכא מיניה. **בית נסרך אלהיו** — לשון נסר, שהשתחוה לנסר ועשאו אלוה. **היינו דכתיב ויהי הוא משתחוה** — משמע מפני שמשתחוה לשם הכוהו. **ויחלק עליהם** — איידי דאיירי במלאכים, איירי נמי בהאי קרא דכתיב "ויהי בלילה ההוא ויצא מלאך ה׳ וגו׳" נקט "ויחלק עליהם לילה וגו׳".

NOTES

Sennacherib believed that the old man who shaved his head was God Himself. Or else, God brought it about through His providence that Sennacherib met an old man who shaved his head. (See also *Rashba*'s explanation in his *Torah HaOlah*.)

דַּפָּא מִתֵּיבוּתָא דְּנֹחַ **A plank from Noah's ark.** Sennacherib said to himself: This plank from the ark is what saved Noah from dying in the flood like the rest of his generation, and so, too, it saved me from dying with the rest of my troops (*Iyyun Ya'akov*).

TRANSLATION AND COMMENTARY

and struck them." The awkward positioning of the word *laylah*, translated here as "by night," allows the word to be interpreted homiletically. [1]**Rabbi Yoḥanan said: The Angel who joined Abraham** and helped him in his fight against the kings **was named Laylah.** [2]This is supported by **the verse** that **states** (Job 3:3): **"And Laylah said, There is a man child conceived,"** implying that the word *laylah* is the name of an Angel.

וְרַבִּי [3]**Rabbi Yitzḥak Nappaḥa said: An act of the night was performed for him.** Just as the stars helped Barak in his battle against Sisera, [4]**as the verse states** (Judges 5:20): **"They fought from Heaven; the stars in their courses fought against Sisera,"** so, too, the stars helped Abraham in his fight against the four Kings of Canaan.

אָמַר רֵישׁ לָקִישׁ [5]**Resh Lakish said: That** explanation which was offered **by the smith** — Rabbi Yitzḥak Nappaḥa (the word *Nappaḥa* means "smith") — **is better than that** explanation which was offered **by the smith's son** — a designation describing Rabbi Yoḥanan, whose father was a smith.

וַיִּרְדֹּף עַד דָּן [6]The verse describing Abraham's pursuit of the kings states (Genesis 14:14): **"And he pursued them to Dan."** [7]**Rabbi Yoḥanan said:** Abraham pursued the kings only as far as Dan, for **when that righteous man came to Dan, his strength failed him,** because **he saw that his descendants would worship idols in Dan,** [8]**as the verse states** (I Kings 12:28-29): "And he made two calves of gold...**and he set the one in Beth-El, and the other one he put in Dan."** [9]**And similarly that wicked man** Nebuchadnezzar **did not gather courage until he reached Dan,** [10]**as the verse states** (Jeremiah 8:16): **"The snorting of his horses is heard from Dan."**

אָמַר רַבִּי זֵירָא [11]**Rabbi Zera said: Even though Rabbi Yehudah ben Betera sent from Netzivin** the following guidelines: [12]**Be sure** to show honor to **a Sage who forgot his learning through no fault of his own;** [13]**and be sure** to cut **the jugular veins** (in addition to the windpipe or esophagus) when you slaughter fowl, **in accordance with** the position of **Rabbi Yehudah;** [14]**and be sure** to show honor to **the sons of ignorant people**

וַעֲבָדָיו וַיַּכֵּם וגו׳״. [1]אָמַר רַבִּי יוֹחָנָן: אוֹתוֹ מַלְאָךְ שֶׁנִּזְדַּמֵּן לוֹ לְאַבְרָהָם לַיְלָה שְׁמוֹ, [2]שֶׁנֶּאֱמַר: ״וְהַלַּיְלָה אָמַר הֹרָה גָבֶר״.

[3]וְרַבִּי יִצְחָק נַפָּחָא אָמַר: שֶׁעָשָׂה עִמּוֹ מַעֲשֵׂה לַיְלָה, [4]שֶׁנֶּאֱמַר: ״מִן שָׁמַיִם נִלְחָמוּ הַכּוֹכָבִים מִמְּסִלּוֹתָם נִלְחֲמוּ עִם סִיסְרָא״.

[5]אָמַר רֵישׁ לָקִישׁ: טָבָא דְּנַפָּחָא מִדְּבַר נַפָּחָא.

[6]״וַיִּרְדֹּף עַד דָּן״. [7]אָמַר רַבִּי יוֹחָנָן: כֵּיוָן שֶׁבָּא אוֹתוֹ צַדִּיק עַד דָּן, תָּשַׁשׁ כֹּחוֹ. רָאָה בְּנֵי בָנָיו שֶׁעֲתִידִין לַעֲבוֹד עֲבוֹדָה זָרָה בְּדָן, [8]שֶׁנֶּאֱמַר: ״וַיָּשֶׂם אֶת הָאֶחָד בְּבֵית אֵל וְאֶת הָאֶחָד נָתַן בְּדָן״. [9]וְאַף אוֹתוֹ רָשָׁע לֹא נִתְגַּבֵּר עַד שֶׁהִגִּיעַ לְדָן, [10]שֶׁנֶּאֱמַר: ״מִדָּן נִשְׁמַע נַחֲרַת סוּסָיו״.

[11]אָמַר רַבִּי זֵירָא: אַף עַל גַּב דְּשָׁלַח (רַבִּי יְהוּדָה בֶּן בְּתֵירָא מִנְּצִיבִין): [12]הִזָּהֲרוּ בְּזָקֵן שֶׁשָּׁכַח תַּלְמוּדוֹ מֵחֲמַת אוֹנְסוֹ; [13]וְהִזָּהֲרוּ בְּוְורִידִין כְּרַבִּי יְהוּדָה; [14]וְהִזָּהֲרוּ בִּבְנֵי עַמֵּי הָאָרֶץ

LITERAL TRANSLATION

and struck them, etc." [1]Rabbi Yoḥanan said: That Angel who appeared before Abraham was named Laylah, [2]as it is stated: "And Laylah said, There is a man child conceived."

[3]And Rabbi Yitzḥak Nappaḥa said: He performed for him an act of the night, [4]as it is stated: "They fought from Heaven; the stars in their courses fought against Sisera."

[5]Resh Lakish said: Better that of the smith than that of the smith's son.

[6]"And he pursued them to Dan." [7]Rabbi Yoḥanan said: When that righteous man came to Dan, his strength failed him. He saw that the sons of his sons were to worship idols in Dan in the future, [8]as it is stated: "And he set the one in Beth-El, and the other one he put in Dan." [9]And also that wicked man did not take courage until he came to Dan, [10]as it is stated: "The snorting of his horses is heard from Dan."

[11]Rabbi Zera said: Even though Rabbi Yehudah ben Betera sent from Netzivin: [12]Be careful about a Sage who forgot his learning because of compulsion; [13]and be careful about the jugular veins in accordance with Rabbi Yehudah; [14]and be careful about the sons of ignorant people

RASHI

מלאך שנזדמן לאברהם לילה שמו – והוא סייעו. מעשה לילה – שנלחמו בשבילו כוכבי לילה כמו שעשו בשביל ברק. טבא מליה דרבי יצחק נפחא מדבר נפחא – רבי יוחנן דמקרי בר נפחא בכולא התלמוד, כמו (בבא מציעא פה,ב): מאן עייל – בר נפחא, נראה למורי דאביו של רבי יוחנן הוי נפחא ולהכי מיקרי בר נפחא, ואית דמפרשי בר נפחא על שם יופיו. הזהרו בזקן – אף על פי ששכח תלמודו הואיל ומחמת אונסו הוא. הזהרו בורידין כרבי יהודה – דאמר בשחיטת חולין (כז,א): עד שישחוט את הורידין של עוף, הואיל וצולהו כולו כאחד אינו חותכו ומולחו כבשר חיה ובהמה. הזהרו בבני עמי הארץ – שנעשו תלמידי חכמים, לעשות להם כבוד שמהם תצא תורה לישראל, שהרי יצאו שמעיה ואבטליון מבני בניו של סנחריב ומבני בניו של המן למדו תורה בבני ברק, כדלקמן, ואף על גב דאמר רבי יהודה הכי הזהרו בבני עמי הארץ.

שֶׁמֵּהֶן תֵּצֵא תּוֹרָה — [1]כִּי הָא מִילְּתָא מוֹדְעִינַן לְהוּ.
[2]״צַדִּיק אַתָּה ה׳ כִּי אָרִיב אֵלֶיךָ; אַךְ מִשְׁפָּטִים אֲדַבֵּר אוֹתָךְ: מַדּוּעַ דֶּרֶךְ רְשָׁעִים צָלֵחָה? שָׁלוּ כָּל בֹּגְדֵי בָגֶד? נְטַעְתָּם גַּם שֹׁרָשׁוּ; יֵלְכוּ, גַּם עָשׂוּ פֶרִי״. [3]מַאי אַהַדְרוּ לֵיהּ? ״כִּי אֶת רַגְלִים רַצְתָּה, וַיַּלְאוּךָ, וְאֵיךְ תְּתַחֲרֶה אֶת הַסּוּסִים? וּבְאֶרֶץ שָׁלוֹם אַתָּה בוֹטֵחַ? וְאֵיךְ תַּעֲשֶׂה בִּגְאוֹן הַיַּרְדֵּן״? [4]מָשָׁל לְאָדָם אֶחָד שֶׁאָמַר: ״יָכוֹל אֲנִי לָרוּץ שָׁלֹשׁ פַּרְסָאוֹת לִפְנֵי הַסּוּסִים, בֵּין בִּצְעֵי הַמַּיִם״. [5]נִזְדַּמֵּן לוֹ רַגְלִי אֶחָד, רָץ לְפָנָיו שְׁלֹשָׁה מִילִין בַּיַּבָּשָׁה וְנִלְאָה. [6]אָמְרוּ לוֹ: ״וּמָה לִפְנֵי

LITERAL TRANSLATION

from whom the Torah will go forth — [1]something like this we tell them.

[2]"Right would you be, O Lord, if I were to contend with You; yet I will reason these points of justice with You: Why does the way of the wicked prosper? Why are they all happy who deal very treacherously? You have planted them, indeed, they have taken root; they grow, indeed, they bring forth fruit." [3]What did they answer him? "If you have run with the footmen, and they have wearied you, then how can you contend with horses? And do you feel secure in the land of peace? How will you do in the wild country of the Jordan?" [4]This is like a certain person who said: "I can run three Persian miles ahead of the horses, between marshes of water." [5]He met up with a certain footman, [and] ran ahead of him three miles on dry ground and became weary. [6]They said to him: "If ahead of

TRANSLATION AND COMMENTARY

who have become Torah scholars, for it is **from them that the Torah will go forth — we do,** however, **tell them,** the sons of ignorant people who have become Torah scholars, [1]**something like this,** that Abraham's strength failed him when he reached Dan, because he foresaw that his descendants would worship an idol there. If Abraham, who was an absolutely righteous man, became weak when he saw what his descendants would do, these first-generation Torah scholars must recall their ancestry, lest they become too proud.

צַדִּיק [2]The Gemara now discusses a passage in the Book of Jeremiah relating to Nebuchadnezzar, King of Babylonia. The Prophet Jeremiah complained to God about Nebuchadnezzar's successful conquest of Jerusalem (Jeremiah 12:1-2): **"Right would you be, O Lord, if I were to contend with You; yet I will reason these points of justice with You: Why does the way of the wicked prosper? Why are they all happy who deal very treacherously? You have planted them, indeed, they have taken root; they grow, indeed, they bring forth fruit."** [3]The Gemara asks: **How did** God **answer** this argument? The Gemara explains: God's response is found in that very same passage (Jeremiah 12:5): **"If you have run with the footmen, and they have wearied you, then how can you contend with horses? And do you feel secure in the land of peace? How will you do in the wild country of the Jordan?"** [4]**This is like someone who boasted: "I can run** a distance of **three Persian miles, ahead of horses,** even **on marshy land."** [5]**He met up with a certain footman, and ran ahead of him** for a distance of **three miles on dry ground, and** then **became weary.** [6]People **said to him: "If,** while running

RASHI

כי הא מילתא — דלקמן מודעינן להו, כי היכי דחזינן לקמן דלא זכה נבוכדנצר לאותו כבוד אלא מפני זכות ארבע פסיעות כדאמרינן לקמן, הכי נמי אמרינן לבני עמי הארץ דלא זכו לאותו כבוד אלא מחמת זכות מעט שהיה באביהם, מפי רבי, ואית דאמרי דר׳ זירא אדלעיל קאי, אבני סנחריב, אף על גב דשלח רבי יהודה הזהרו בבני עמי הארץ לכבדן שמהם תלא תורה כי היכי דנפקו מסנחריב, כי הא מילתא מודיעים להו לבני עמי הארץ דהא דמוקרין להו — לאו משום אביהם, אלא משום תורה שבהם, שלא תזוח דעתם עליהם ויאמרו אבותיהם לדיקים היו. **מדוע דרך רשעים צלחה** — מפני מה הצליח נבוכדנצר וכבש ירושלים. **אהדרו ליה** — לירמיה. **בצעי מים** — *מרשק״ו בלעז.

NOTES

כִּי הָא מִילְּתָא מוֹדְעִינַן לְהוּ **Something like this we tell them.** It is not at all clear what this line refers to, and what the relationship is between it and what comes before and after. Our commentary follows *Ramah*, who says that this line refers to the statement of Rabbi Yoḥanan, that when Abraham came to Dan, his strength failed him, because he saw that his descendants would practice idolatry there. The sons of ignorant people who have become Torah scholars should recall this story about Abraham to avoid excessive pride. *Maharsha* explains that this line refers to the verse that is cited immediately afterward. Ordinarily it is forbidden to teach an ignorant person a verse such as this, "Right would You be, O Lord," which could lead to skepticism, but we should nevertheless teach it to him, because it is important to know how great is the reward given to someone who honors God and His Torah. The Geonim (and *Arukh* and *Meiri*) had a reading according to which Rabbi Yehudah ben Betera sent out the additional guideline: "Restrain your children from reading the Bible superficially." According to this, "Something like this we tell them" refers to that guideline. Even though the Rabbis warned that young people should not be allowed to study superficially and learn Biblical verses that might give rise to heretical ideas, they may, however, be taught a verse like this, "Right would You be, O Lord," because God responds to Jeremiah's complaint in that very same passage, and there is no danger of misunderstanding.

TRANSLATION AND COMMENTARY

ahead of a footman, you became weary **like this,** then **all the more so** would you become weary were you to run **ahead of horses.** [1]**If,** while running **three miles,** you tired out **like this,** then **all the more so** would you tire out were you to run **three Persian miles,** which is four times the distance. [2]And **if,** while running **on dry land,** you were overcome by fatigue **like this,** then **all the more so** would you be overcome by fatigue were you to run **on marshy land!"** [3]**So, too, you,** Jeremiah, consider the following: **If you are astonished about how I rewarded that wicked man,** Nebuchadnezzar, **for the four steps that he ran in My honor,** [4]then **all the more so** will you be astonished **when** in the future **I reward Abraham, Isaac, and Jacob, who ran ahead of me like horses.** [5]**This is** the meaning of **the verse** that states (Jeremiah 23:9): **"My heart within me is broken because of the Prophets; all my bones shake; I am like a drunken man, and like a man whom wine has overcome, because of the Lord, and because of His holy words."** I am astonished, because of the reward paid to Abraham, Isaac, and Jacob.

הָנֵי אַרְבַּע פְּסִיעוֹת [6]The Gemara asks: **What are these four steps** of Nebuchadnezzar? [7]The Gemara explains: **The verse states** (Isaiah 39:1): **"At that time Merodach-Baladan, the son of Baladan, King of Babylonia, sent letters** and a present to Ḥezekiah; for he had heard that he had been sick and was recovered." [8]It may be asked: **Because** Ḥezekiah **"had been sick and was recovered,"** did Merodach-Baladan **send him letters and a present?** [9]The answer is: **Yes,** he did so in order **"to inquire of the wonder that was done in the land"** (II Chronicles 32:31). [10]The order of events was **as Rabbi Yoḥanan said: The day on which Aḥaz,** the wicked King of Judah, **died lasted** only **two hours.** It was miraculously shortened by ten hours so that he would be buried without the honor of a royal funeral. [11]**When Ḥezekiah was sick and recovered, the Holy One, blessed be He, restored those ten hours to**

רַגְלִי כָּךְ, לִפְנֵי הַסּוּסִים, עַל
אַחַת כַּמָּה וְכַמָּה. [1]וּמָה שְׁלֹשֶׁת
מִילִין כָּךְ, שָׁלֹשׁ פַּרְסָאוֹת, עַל
אַחַת כַּמָּה וְכַמָּה. [2]וּמָה בַּיַּבָּשָׁה
כָּךְ, בֵּין בִּצְעֵי הַמַּיִם, עַל אַחַת
כַּמָּה וְכַמָּה"! [3]אַף אַתָּה, וּמָה
בִּשְׂכַר אַרְבַּע פְּסִיעוֹת שֶׁשִּׁלַּמְתִּי
לְאוֹתוֹ רָשָׁע, שֶׁרָץ אַחַר כְּבוֹדִי,
אַתָּה תָּמֵיהַּ, [4]כְּשֶׁאֲנִי מְשַׁלֵּם
שָׂכָר לְאַבְרָהָם יִצְחָק וְיַעֲקֹב
שֶׁרָצוּ לְפָנַי כְּסוּסִים, עַל אַחַת
כַּמָּה וְכַמָּה. [5]הַיְינוּ דִּכְתִיב:
"לַנְּבִאִים נִשְׁבַּר לִבִּי בְקִרְבִּי;
רָחֲפוּ כָּל עַצְמוֹתַי, הָיִיתִי כְּאִישׁ
שִׁכּוֹר, וּכְגֶבֶר עֲבָרוֹ יָיִן, מִפְּנֵי
ה׳, וּמִפְּנֵי דִּבְרֵי קָדְשׁוֹ".
[6]הָנֵי אַרְבַּע פְּסִיעוֹת, מַאי
הִיא? [7]דִּכְתִיב: "בָּעֵת הַהִיא
שָׁלַח מְרֹאדַךְ בַּלְאֲדָן בֶּן בַּלְאֲדָן
מֶלֶךְ בָּבֶל סְפָרִים וגו׳". [8]מִשּׁוּם
"כִּי חָלָה חִזְקִיָּהוּ וַיֶּחֱזָק", שְׁדַר
לֵיהּ סְפָרִים וּמִנְחָה? [9]אִין,
"לִדְרֹשׁ (אֶת) הַמּוֹפֵת אֲשֶׁר
הָיָה בָּאָרֶץ". [10]דְּאָמַר רַבִּי
יוֹחָנָן: אוֹתוֹ הַיּוֹם שֶׁמֵּת בּוֹ
אָחָז שְׁתֵּי שָׁעוֹת הָיָה, [11]וְכִי
חָלָה חִזְקִיָּהוּ וְאִיתְּפַח,
אַהַדְרִינְהוּ קוּדְשָׁא בְּרִיךְ הוּא

LITERAL TRANSLATION

a footman thus, ahead of the horses, all the more so. [1]If three miles thus, three Persian miles, all the more so. [2]If on dry land thus, between marshes, all the more so!" [3]So, too, you, if regarding the reward I paid that wicked man for the four steps that he ran in my honor, you are astonished, [4]when I pay a reward to Abraham, Isaac, and Jacob, who ran ahead of me like horses, all the more so. [5]This is what is written: "My heart within me is broken because of the Prophets; all my bones shake; I am like a drunken man, and like a man whom wine has overcome, because of the Lord, and because of His holy words."

[6]These four steps, what are they? [7]As it is written: "At that time Merodach-Baladan, the son of Baladan, King of Babylonia, sent letters, etc." [8]Because "Ḥezekiah had been sick and recovered," he sent him letters and a present? [9]Yes, "to inquire of the wonder that was done in the land." [10]For Rabbi Yoḥanan said: That day on which Aḥaz died was two hours, [11]and when Ḥezekiah was sick and recovered, the Holy One, blessed be He,

RASHI

ארבע פסיעות — מפורש לקמן. **על אחת כמה וכמה** — שיהו כל אדם יכולין לתמוה על מתן שכר גדול שישתלם עליהם. **לנביאים** — אברהם יצחק ויעקב. **נשבר לבי בקרבי** — כלומר תמהתי על מתן שכרן. **שתי שעות** — כדי שלא יהא פנאי לספדו ולקברו. **אתפח** — נתרפא. **אהדרינהו הקדוש ברוך הוא** — להנך שעות לחזקיהו, דאותו היום שנתרפא חזקיה היה של עשרים ושתים שעות.

NOTES

אַרְבַּע פְּסִיעוֹת Four steps. According to another reading, Nebuchadnezzar ran three steps in God's honor. According to the Midrash, Nebuchadnezzar was rewarded for this running with three (or four) descendants who ruled the world.

TRANSLATION AND COMMENTARY

him, [1]**as the verse states** (Isaiah 38:8): **"Behold, I will turn the shadow of the dial degrees, which went down in the sun dial of Ahaz, ten degrees backward. So the sun returned ten degrees, by which it had gone down on the dial."** The sun that had set ten hours early on account of Ahaz shone an extra ten hours for his son Hezekiah. When the day was miraculously lengthened, [2]Merodach **said to** his men: **"What is this,** that the day is so long?" [3]They **said to him: "Hezekiah was sick and he recovered."** [4]Merodach **said: "There is a man like this, and I do not have to send him greetings?"** [5]So **they wrote** Hezekiah a letter which read: **"Peace to King Hezekiah, peace to the city of Jerusalem, peace to the great God."** [6]**Nebuchadnezzar,** who **was Baladan's scribe, was not there at the time.** [7]**When he came, he asked** the other scribes: **"What did you write** in the letter?" [8]**They said to him: "We wrote as follows."** [9]Nebuchadnezzar **said to them** in astonishment: **"You referred to Him as a great God, but** nevertheless **you mentioned Him last,** after Hezekiah and the city of Jerusalem? [10]**Rather,** you should **write** the letter **as follows: "Peace to the great God, peace to the city of Jerusalem, peace to King Hezekiah,"** mentioning God first. [11]The other scribes **said to** Nebuchadnezzar: **"Let the one who reads the letter be the messenger."** Let the man who gives such good advice execute the plan. [12]Nebuchadnezzar **ran** out **after** the messenger, but [13]**after running** only **four steps,** he was stopped by the **Angel Gabriel.** [14]**Rabbi Yohanan said: Had Gabriel not come and stopped him, there would have been no remedy for the enemies of Israel** - a euphemism for the people of Israel — for Nebuchadnezzar's reward would have been great, and he would have been granted permission to destroy the remnant of Israel.

מַאי [15]The Gemara raises a question about the verse cited above: **What does** the verse mean by "Merodach-**Baladan the son of Baladan"?** If his name was Merodach, why is he called Baladan here? [16]The Gemara **says: Baladan had been the King** of Babylonia, **but his face changed, so that he looked like a dog,**

לְהָנָךְ עֶשֶׂר שָׁעֵי נִיהֲלֵיהּ, [1]דִּכְתִיב: "הִנְנִי מֵשִׁיב אֶת צֵל הַמַּעֲלוֹת אֲשֶׁר יָרְדָה בְמַעֲלוֹת אָחָז בַּשֶּׁמֶשׁ אֲחֹרַנִּית עֶשֶׂר מַעֲלוֹת. וַתָּשָׁב הַשֶּׁמֶשׁ עֶשֶׂר מַעֲלוֹת בַּמַּעֲלוֹת אֲשֶׁר יָרָדָה". [2]אֲמַר לְהוּ: "מַאי הַאי"? [3]אֲמַרוּ לֵיהּ: "חִזְקִיָּהוּ חֲלַשׁ וְאִיתְפַּח". [4]אֲמַר: "אִיכָּא גַּבְרָא כִּי הַאי, וְלָא בָּעֵינָא לְשַׁדּוּרֵי לֵיהּ שְׁלָמָא"? [5]כְּתָבוּ לֵיהּ: "שְׁלָמָא לְמַלְכָּא חִזְקִיָּה, שְׁלָם לְקַרְתָּא דִּירוּשְׁלֶם, שְׁלָם לֶאֱלָהָא רַבָּא". [6]נְבוּכַדְנֶאצַּר סַפְרֵיהּ דְּבַלְאֲדָן הֲוָה. הַהִיא שַׁעְתָּא לָא הֲוָה הָתָם. [7]כִּי אֲתָא, אֲמַר לְהוּ: "הֵיכִי כְּתַבִיתוּ"? [8]אֲמַרוּ לֵיהּ: "הָכִי כְּתַבִינַן". [9]אֲמַר לְהוּ: "קָרֵיתוּ לֵיהּ אֱלָהָא רַבָּא, וְכָתְבִיתוּ לֵיהּ לְבַסּוֹף"? [10]אֲמַר: "אֶלָּא, הָכִי כְּתוֹבוּ: 'שְׁלָם לֶאֱלָהָא רַבָּא, שְׁלָם לְקַרְתָּא דִּירוּשְׁלֶם, שְׁלָם לְמַלְכָּא חִזְקִיָּה'". [11]אָמְרִי לֵיהּ: "קָרְיָינָא דְּאִיגַּרְתָּא אִיהוּ לֶיהֱוֵי פַּרְוָונְקָא". [12]רְהַט בָּתְרֵיהּ. [13]כִּדְרְהִיט אַרְבַּע פְּסִיעוֹת אֲתָא גַּבְרִיאֵל וְאוֹקְמֵיהּ. [14]אָמַר רַבִּי יוֹחָנָן: אִילְמָלֵא (לֹא) בָּא גַבְרִיאֵל וְהֶעֱמִידוֹ, לֹא הָיָה תַּקָּנָה לְשׂוֹנְאֵיהֶם שֶׁל יִשְׂרָאֵל. [15]מַאי "בַּלְאֲדָן בֶּן בַּלְאֲדָן"? [16]אָמְרִי: בַּלְאֲדָן מַלְכָּא הֲוָה, וְאִישְׁתַּנִּי אַפֵּיהּ וַהֲוָה כִּי דִּכַלְבָּא, הֲוָה יָתֵיב בְּרֵיהּ עַל

LITERAL TRANSLATION

restored those ten hours to him, [1]as it is written: "Behold, I will turn the shadow of the [dial] degrees, which went down in the sun dial of Ahaz, ten degrees backward. So the sun returned ten degrees, by which it had gone down on the dial." [2]He said to them: "What is this?" [3]They said to him: "Hezekiah was sick and he recovered." [4]He said: "There is a man like this, and do I not have to send him greetings?" [5]They wrote to him: "Peace to King Hezekiah, peace to the city of Jerusalem, peace to the great God." [6]Nebuchadnezzar was Baladan's scribe. That time, he was not there. [7]When he came, he said to them: "How did you write?" [8]They said to him: "Thus we wrote." [9]He said to them: "You called Him a great God, and you wrote Him last?" [10]He said: "Rather, write thus: Peace to the great God, peace to the city of Jerusalem, peace to King Hezekiah.'" [11]They said to him: "Let the one who reads the letter be the messenger." [12]He ran after him. [13]When he had run four steps, Gabriel came and stopped him. [14]Rabbi Yohanan said: Had Gabriel not come and stopped him, there would have been no remedy for the enemies of Israel. [15]What is "Baladan the son of Baladan"? [16]They said: Baladan was the king, but his face changed, and he was like a dog, [and] his son sat on

RASHI

רהט בתריה – דשליח. לא היה להם תקנה – שהיה שכרו מרובה והיה לו רשות לאבד שאריתנו.

NOTES

וַהֲוָה כִּי דִּכַלְבָּא **And he was like a dog.** *Rabbi Ya'akov Emden* notes that Baladan's canine appearance is alluded to by

TRANSLATION AND COMMENTARY

and his son Merodach **ascended to the royal throne** in his place. [1] **Whenever** Merodach **wrote** something, **he would write his** own **name and** then **the name of his father, Baladan the King,** as a show of honor to his father. [2] **This is** what **is** meant by the verse that **states** (Malachi 1:6): **"A son honors his father, and a servant his master."** This is an example of a non-Jew honoring his father.

בֵּן יְכַבֵּד אָב [3] The Gemara expands on its explanation of this verse: **"A son honors his father" — that which we have said** regarding Merodach. [4] **"And a servant his master" — as** the verses **state** (Jeremiah 52:12-13): **"Now in the fifth month, on the tenth day of the month, which was the nineteenth year of Nebuchadnezzar King of Babylonia, came Nebuzaradan, captain of the guard, who stood before the King of Babylonia in Jerusalem. And he burned the house of the Lord, and the king's house."** [96B] [5] It may be asked: **Did Nebuchadnezzar** himself ever **go up to Jerusalem,** so that his captain of the guard Nebuzaradan could have stood before him in that city? [6] **But surely a verse** in that very same passage **states** (II Kings 25:6): "So they took the king [Hezekiah], **and brought him up to the King of Babylonia** [Nebuchadnezzar] **to Rivlah."** [7] **And Rabbi Abbahu said:** Rivlah **is Antioch.** And so it would appear that Nebuchadnezzar never came to Jerusalem!

רַב חִסְדָּא [8] **Rav Ḥisda and Rav Yitzḥak bar Avudimi** disagreed on how to understand the verse. [9] **One of** these two Amoraim **said: A figure of** Nebuchadnezzar's **portrait was carved on** Nebuzaradan's **chariot,** and Nebuzaradan treated that image as if it were Nebuchadnezzar himself. [10] **And the other** Amora **said:** Nebuzaradan **stood in** such **great awe of his** King Nebuchadnezzar **that he** always **felt as if he were standing before him.** This is an example of a non-Jewish servant showing honor to his master.

אָמַר רָבָא [11] Having mentioned Nebuzaradan, the Gemara now relates his part in the destruction of the Temple. **Rava said: Nebuchadnezzar sent Nebuzaradan three hundred mules laden with iron hatchets that** were

מַלְכוּתָא. [1] כִּי הֲוָה כְּתִיב, הֲוָה כְּתִיב שְׁמֵיהּ וּשְׁמֵיהּ דַּאֲבוּהּ בַּלְאֲדָן מַלְכָּא. [2] הַיְינוּ דִּכְתִיב: "בֵּן יְכַבֵּד אָב וְעֶבֶד אֲדֹנָיו".

[3] "בֵּן יְכַבֵּד אָב" — הָא דַּאֲמָרַן. [4] "וְעֶבֶד אֲדֹנָיו" — דִּכְתִיב: "וּבַחֹדֶשׁ הַחֲמִישִׁי בֶּעָשׂוֹר לַחֹדֶשׁ הִיא שְׁנַת תְּשַׁע עֶשְׂרֵה שָׁנָה לַמֶּלֶךְ נְבוּכַדְנֶאצַּר מֶלֶךְ בָּבֶל בָּא נְבוּזַרְאֲדָן רַב טַבָּחִים עָמַד לִפְנֵי מֶלֶךְ בָּבֶל בִּירוּשָׁלִָם. וַיִּשְׂרֹף אֶת בֵּית ה׳ וְאֶת בֵּית הַמֶּלֶךְ". [96B] [5] וּמִי סָלֵיק נְבוּכַדְנֶצַּר לִירוּשָׁלַיִם? [6] וְהָכְתִיב: "וַיַּעֲלוּ אֹתוֹ אֶל מֶלֶךְ בָּבֶל רִבְלָתָה". [7] וְאָמַר רַבִּי אַבָּהוּ: זוֹ אַנְטוֹכְיָא!

[8] רַב חִסְדָּא וְרַב יִצְחָק בַּר אֲבוּדִימִי. [9] חַד אָמַר: דְּמוּת דְּיוֹקְנוֹ הָיְתָה חֲקוּקָה לוֹ עַל מֶרְכַּבְתּוֹ. [10] וְחַד אָמַר: אֵימָה יְתֵירָה הָיְתָה לוֹ מִמֶּנּוּ, וְדוֹמֶה כְּמִי שֶׁעוֹמֵד לְפָנָיו.

[11] אָמַר רָבָא: טְעִין תְּלָת מְאָה כּוּדְנְיָיתָא נַרְגָּא דְּפַרְזְלָא דְּשָׁלֵיט

LITERAL TRANSLATION

the royal [throne]. [1] When he wrote, he would write his name and the name of his father, King Baladan. [2] This is what is written: "A son honors his father, and a servant his master."

[3] "A son honors his father" — that which we have said. [4] "And a servant his master" — as it is written: "Now in the fifth month, on the tenth day of the month, which was the nineteenth year of Nebuchadnezzar King of Babylonia, came Nebuzaradan, captain of the guard, who stood before the King of Babylonia in Jerusalem. And he burned the house of the Lord, and the king's house." [96B] [5] Did Nebuchadnezzar go up to Jerusalem? [6] But surely it is written: "And they brought him up to the King of Babylonia to Rivlah." [7] And Rabbi Abbahu said: This is Antioch!

[8] Rav Ḥisda and Rav Yitzḥak bar Avudimi. [9] One said: A figure of his portrait was carved on his chariot. [10] And one said: He was in great awe of him, and he felt as if he were standing before him.

[11] Rava said: Nebuchadnezzar sent Nebuzaradan three hundred mules laden with iron hatchets that can break

RASHI

הוה כתיב שמיה ושמיה דאבוה – כדי שיתכבד אביו, לכך נקרא שם אביו עליו שנקרא מרודך בלאדן, דאי לא כתיב אלא מרודך בן בלאדן לא הוי מיתקרי עליה שמיה דאבוה, דהכי כתבי כולהו אינשי פלוני בן פלוני להכי כתיב מרודך בלאדן. **בחדש החמישי בעשור לחדש בא נבוזר אדן רב טבחים עמד לפני מלך בבל בירושלם** – אלמא: נבוכדנצר סליק לירושלם. **ומי סליק כו׳ והא כתיב** – בההיא פרשתא ויעלו לדקיה אל המלך רבלתה, אלמא ברבלה הוה. **זו אנטוכיא** – ואנטוכיא קיימא לן דאינה מארץ ישראל. **דמות דיוקנו** – של נבוכדנצר. **חקוקה לו על מרכבתו** – של נבוזראדן, ודומה לו כמו שעומד לפניו, ולכך כתיב ״בא נבוכדנצר״ והיינו כבוד. **טעין תלת מאה כודנייתא** – משאוי שלש מאות פרדות. **נרגא דפרזלא** – פטישי ברזל. **דשליט**

NOTES

the numerical value of the word בַּלְאֲדָן, "Baladan," which is equal to the numerical value of the words כִּי דְּכַלְבָּא, "like a dog." Alternatively, the name Baladan might have been interpreted as *Bal adan*, "not a man," but rather some other creature.

בְּפַרְזְלָא שְׁדַר לֵיהּ נְבוּכַדְנֶצַּר לִנְבוּזַרְאֲדָן. [1] כּוּלְּהוּ בְּלַעֲתִינְהוּ חַד דַּשָּׁא דִּירוּשְׁלֵם, שֶׁנֶּאֱמַר: ״פִּתּוּחֶיהָ יָּחַד בְּכַשִּׁיל וְכֵילַפֹּת יַהֲלֹמוּן״. [2] בָּעֵי לְמֶיהְדַּר. [3] אֲמַר: ״מִסְתְּפִינָא דְּלָא לִיעַבְדוּ בִּי כִּי הֵיכִי דַּעֲבַדוּ בְּסַנְחֵרִיב״. [4] נָפְקָא קָלָא, וַאֲמַר: ״שַׁוָּור בַּר שַׁוָּור. נְבוּזַרְאֲדָן, שַׁוָּור, דִּמְטָא זִימְנָא דְּמַקְדְּשָׁא חָרֵיב וְהֵיכָלָא מִיקְלֵי״. [5] פָּשׁ לֵיהּ חַד נַרְגָּא. אֲתָא מַחְיֵיהּ בְּקוּפָא וְאִיפַּתַּח, [6] שֶׁנֶּאֱמַר: ״יִוָּדַע כְּמֵבִיא לְמָעְלָה בִּסְבָךְ עֵץ קַרְדֻּמּוֹת״. [7] הֲוָה קָטֵיל וְאָזַל עַד דִּמְטָא לְהֵיכָלָא. [8] אַדְלִיק בֵּיהּ נוּרָא, גָּבַהּ הֵיכָלָא. [9] דַּרְכּוֹ בֵּיהּ מִן שְׁמַיָּא, שֶׁנֶּאֱמַר: ״גַּת דָּרַךְ ה׳ לִבְתוּלַת בַּת יְהוּדָה״. [10] קָא זַיְחָא דַּעְתֵּיהּ. נָפְקָא בַּת קָלָא, וַאֲמָרָה לֵיהּ: [11] ״עַמָּא קְטִילָא קָטְלַתְּ, הֵיכָלָא קַלְיָא קַלֵית, קִימְחָא טְחִינָא טְחִינַתְּ״,

LITERAL TRANSLATION

iron. [1] One of Jerusalem's gates swallowed all of them, as it is stated: "And now they pound its carved work altogether with hatchet and with hammers." [2] He wanted to go back. [3] He said: "I am afraid lest they do to me as they did to Sennacherib." [4] A [heavenly] voice came out, and said: "Leaper, the son of a leaper, Nebuzaradan, leap, for the time has come for the Temple to be destroyed and the Sanctuary to be burned." [5] One hatchet was left for him. He went and struck [the gate] with the blunt end, and it opened, [6] as it is stated: "He is known as a swinger of axes upward in the thick forest." [7] He continued to kill until he came to the Sanctuary. [8] He lit a fire, [and] the Sanctuary rose up. [9] They tread upon it from Heaven, as it is stated: "The Lord has trodden the virgin, the daughter of Judah, as in a winepress." [10] He became overbearing. A [heavenly] voice came out, and said to him: [11] "You killed a dead people, you burned a burned Sanctuary, you ground ground flour,"

TRANSLATION AND COMMENTARY

sharp enough to **cut through iron,** to attack Jerusalem. [1] But just **one of Jerusalem's gates broke all of** the hatchets, **as the verse states** (Psalms 74:6): **"And now they pound its carved work altogether with hatchet and with hammers,"** which can also be construed to mean: "Its entrance broke the hatchets and hammers." Having failed to gain entry into the city, [2] Nebuzaradan **wanted to return** to Babylonia. [3] **He said** to himself: **"I am afraid lest** the same thing **happen to me that happened to Sennacherib,** whose army was routed while it was camped outside Jerusalem." [4] **A heavenly voice issued forth, and said** to him: **"Leaper, the son of a leaper, Nebuzaradan, leap** forward, and then leap forward once again, and conquer Jerusalem, **for the time has come for the Temple to be destroyed and the Sanctuary to be burned."** [5] Nebuzaradan **had one** unbroken **hatchet left. He went, and struck the gate** of Jerusalem **with the blunt end** of the hatchet, **and** this time the gate **opened,** [6] **as the verse states** (Psalms 74:5): **"He is known as a swinger of axes upward in the thick forest,"** implying that at the right moment, the axe succeeded in breaking the iron gate of Jerusalem. [7] As Nebuzaradan proceeded through the city, **he killed** all those who stood up against him, **until he came to the Sanctuary.** [8] **He lit a fire** to burn down the Temple, **and the Sanctuary rose up** from the ground, trying to escape the flames. [9] But **it was trodden down from Heaven, as the verse states** (Lamentations 1:15): **"The Lord has trodden the virgin, the daughter of Judah, as in a winepress."** [10] Nebuzaradan **became overbearing** and boastful about his success, and so **a heavenly voice came out, and said to him:** [11] **"You killed a people** that was already **dead, you burned a Sanctuary** that was already **burned,** and **you ground**

RASHI

בפרזלא — ברזל חדוד הקוצץ ברזל אחר. **בלעתינהו** — לא בליעה ממש אלא שיברם, שהיו מתפוצצין הפטישים שהכותם בשער לשברה. **פתוחיה יחד** — משמע על פתח אחד הלמו כל הכשילים וכילפות יחד ולא הועיל כלום. **שוור בר שוור** — דולג בר דולג, קום וכבש ירושלים לנבוזראדן קאמר, לישנא אחרינא: שוור בר שוור — מדלג בר מדלג, קפלת פעם אחת עם סנחריב ועכשיו פעם שניה. **בקופא** — מגב הפטיש ולא מחודו, כמו קופא דמחטא (בבא מציעא לח,ב). **יודע כמביא למעלה** — תפלה היא, יודע לפניך אותו סבך עץ קרדומות ששבר בו את ירושלים כאילו הביאו למעלה בכסא הכבוד. **גבה היכלא** — ובקש לעלות לרקיע. **דרכו ביה מן שמיא** — והשפילוהו. **זחה דעתיה** — מתגאה, על שהיה מצליח. **עמא קטילא** — שכבר נגזר עליהם על כך.

NOTES

מַחְיֵיהּ בְּקוּפָא He struck the gate with the blunt end. According to *Rabbi Ya'akov Emden*, the word קוּפָא refers to the wooden handle of the hatchet, as opposed to its iron blade. Nebuzaradan struck the gate of Jerusalem with the wooden handle of the hatchet, and it opened. This fits in well with the words of the verse cited here, עֵץ קַרְדֻּמּוֹת, "the wood of the hatchets."

גָּבַהּ הֵיכָלָא The Sanctuary rose up. *Ramah* explains that the Sanctuary rose up from the ground and then came down, in order to show Nebuzaradan that everything that was happening was taking place by God's will.

TRANSLATION AND COMMENTARY

flour that was already **ground,** [1]**as it is stated** regarding the calamities that will befall Israel (Isaiah 47:2): **'Take the millstones, and grind flour; uncover your locks, tuck up the train, uncover the leg, pass over the rivers.'** [2]**The verse does not state: 'Grind** wheat,' **but rather:** 'Grind **flour'** — you have already been ground into flour, and you will be ground once again." [3]When Nebuzaradan reached the Sanctuary, **he saw the blood of** the Prophet **Zechariah boiling** up from the ground, for Zechariah was murdered in the Temple and was not resting in peace. [4]Nebuzaradan **said to** the priests who were standing there: **"What is that?"** [5]**They said to him:** "That is merely **sacrificial blood that was spilled."** [6]**He said to them: "Bring** me an animal, **and I will test** it and see whether the blood bubbling out of the ground and the blood of the animal that I will slaughter **are similar."** [7]**He slaughtered** an animal, **and** found they **were not similar.** [8]**He** then **said to them: "Reveal** the truth **to me, or else I will comb your flesh with iron combs."** [9]The priests **said to him: "This is** the blood of Zechariah who was both **a priest and a Prophet.** When **he prophesied for Israel the destruction of Jerusalem,** the people **killed him."** [10]Nebuzaradan **said to them: "I will appease** Zechariah, so that his blood will stop bubbling from the ground." [11]**He brought** a group of **Sages, and killed them** right **next to** the blood, **but** the blood **did not cease** bubbling. [12]**He** then **brought** a group of **schoolchildren, and killed them** in that place, **but** the blood still **did not cease** bubbling. [13]**He** then **brought** a group of **young priests, and killed them** there, **but** the blood still **did not cease** bubbling. [14]He kept killing people **until he had put to death nine hundred and forty thousand, but** Zechariah's blood still **did not cease** bubbling. [15]Nebuzaradan then **approached** the blood, **and said: "Zechariah, Zechariah!** [16]I have already **destroyed the best of** your people on your account. [17]**Would it please you that I kill them all?"** [18]**Immediately,**

[1]שֶׁנֶּאֱמַר: ׳קְחִי רֵחַיִם וְטַחֲנִי
קָמַח גַּלִּי צַמָּתֵךְ חֶשְׂפִּי שֹׁבֶל
גַּלִּי שׁוֹק עִבְרִי נְהָרוֹת׳. [2]׳חִטִּים׳
לֹא נֶאֱמַר, אֶלָּא ׳קֶמַח׳ ". [3]חֲזָא
דְּמֵיהּ דִּזְכַרְיָה דַּהֲוָה קָא רָתַח.
[4]אֲמַר לְהוּ: "מַאי הַאי"? [5]אָמְרוּ
לֵיהּ: "דַּם זְבָחִים הוּא
דְּאִישְׁתַּפֵּיךְ". [6]אֲמַר לְהוּ:
"אַיְיתִי וְאִנַּסֵּי אִי מִדַּמּוּ". [7]כָּסֵי,
וְלָא אִידַּמּוּ. [8]אֲמַר לְהוּ: "גַּלּוּ
לִי, וְאִי לָא, סָרֵיקְנָא לְכוּ
לְבִשְׂרַיְיכוּ בְּמַסְרֵיקָא דְּפַרְזְלָא".
[9]אָמְרוּ לֵיהּ: "הַאי כֹּהֵן וְנָבִיא
הוּא, דְּאִינַּבֵּי לְהוּ לְיִשְׂרָאֵל
בְּחוּרְבָּנָא דִּירוּשְׁלֵם, וְקַטְלוּהוּ".
[10]אֲמַר לְהוּ: "אֲנָא מְפַיֵּיסְנָא
לֵיהּ". [11]אַיְיתִי רַבָּנַן, קְטַיל
עִילָּוֵיהּ, וְלָא נָח. [12]אַיְיתִי דַּרְדְּקֵי
דְּבֵי רַב, קְטַיל עִילָּוֵיהּ, וְלָא נָח.
[13]אַיְיתִי פִּרְחֵי כְהוּנָּה, קְטַיל
עִילָּוֵיהּ, וְלָא נָח. [14]עַד דִּי
קְטַל עִילָּוֵיהּ תִּשְׁעִין וְאַרְבָּעָה
רִיבּוֹא, וְלָא נָח. [15]קָרֵיב לְגַבֵּיהּ,
אֲמַר: "זְכַרְיָה, זְכַרְיָה! [16]טוֹבִים
שֶׁבָּהֶן אִיבַּדְתִּים. [17]נִיחָא לָךְ
דְּאִיקְטְלִינְהוּ לְכוּלְּהוּ"? [18]מִיָּד

LITERAL TRANSLATION

[1]as it is stated: 'Take the millstones, and grind flour; uncover your locks, tuck up the train, uncover the leg, pass over the rivers.' [2]It is not stated 'wheat,' but rather 'flour.'" [3]He saw the blood of Zechariah which was boiling. [4]He said to them: "What is that?" [5]They said to him: "Sacrificial blood that spilled." [6]He said to them: "Bring and I will test if they are similar." [7]He slaughtered, and they were not similar. [8]He said to them: "Reveal to me, or else, I will comb your flesh with iron combs." [9]They said to him: "This is a priest and a Prophet, who prophesied for Israel the destruction of Jerusalem, and they killed him." [10]He said to them: "I will appease him." [11]He brought Rabbis, [and] killed them on it, but it did not rest. [12]He brought schoolchildren, [and] killed them on it, but it did not rest. [13]He brought young priests, [and] killed them on it, but it did not rest. [14]Until he killed on it nine hundred and forty thousand, and it did not rest. [15]He approached it, [and] said: "Zechariah, Zechariah! [16]I destroyed the best of them. [17]Would it please you that I kill them all?" [18]Immediately,

RASHI

וטחני קמח — וטחני חטים לא נאמר, אלא קמח, שאין צריך טחינה. **צמתך** — מקום שהקלעים צומתין, בצד הראש. **שובל** — קלע הראש שדומין לשבלים. **גלי שוק עברי נהרות** — פורענות זה היה הקדוש ברוך הוא אומר לישראל: לכו וטחנו קמח, כלומר: טחונים אתם כבר לקמח, ותחזרו ותטחן עדיין, תגלו קלעי ראשיכם ושוקיכם, ותלכו בגלות. **אייתו לי ואינסי** — ואנסה אם דם זבחים הוא. **כסי ולא אידמי** — שחט בהמות ולא אידמי הדם.

BACKGROUND

מַסְרֵיקָא דְּפַרְזְלָא Iron comb.

An iron rake from the Talmudic period.
Rakes or hooks like these were also used as instruments of torture (*harpago*) by the Romans to tear the skin of the victim.

NOTES

דָּמֵיהּ דִּזְכַרְיָה The blood of Zechariah. The story related here regarding Zechariah's blood seems to be based on the words of the prophet Ezekiel (24:7-8): "For her blood is in the midst of her; she set it upon the rock; she poured it not upon the ground, to cover it with dust; that it might cause fury to come, that vengeance might be taken, for I have set her blood upon the bare rock, that it should not be covered." That passage alludes to the murder of the Prophet on the Temple stones, and it intimates that his blood will not be covered until vengeance is taken.

נָח. [1]הִרְהֵר תְּשׁוּבָה בְּדַעְתֵּיהּ. אָמַר: ״מָה הֵם שֶׁלֹּא אִיבְּדוּ אֶלָּא נֶפֶשׁ אַחַת — [2]כָּךְ, הַהוּא גַּבְרָא מַה תֵּיהֱוֵי עֲלֵיהּ״? [3]עֲרַק, שְׁדַר פּוּרְטִיתָא לְבֵיתֵיהּ, וְאִיתְגַּיַּיר.

[4]תָּנוּ רַבָּנַן: ״נַעֲמָן גֵּר תּוֹשָׁב הָיָה. [5]נְבוּזַר אֲדָן גֵּר צֶדֶק הָיָה. [6]מִבְּנֵי בָנָיו שֶׁל סִיסְרָא לָמְדוּ תּוֹרָה בִּירוּשָׁלַיִם. מִבְּנֵי בָנָיו שֶׁל סַנְחֵרִיב לִימְּדוּ תּוֹרָה בָּרַבִּים״. [7]וּמַאן נִינְהוּ? [8]שְׁמַעְיָה וְאַבְטַלְיוֹן. [9]״מִבְּנֵי בָנָיו שֶׁל הָמָן לָמְדוּ תּוֹרָה בִּבְנֵי בְרָק. וְאַף מִבְּנֵי בָנָיו שֶׁל אוֹתוֹ רָשָׁע בִּיקֵּשׁ הַקָּדוֹשׁ בָּרוּךְ הוּא לְהַכְנִיסָן תַּחַת כַּנְפֵי הַשְּׁכִינָה. [10]אָמְרוּ מַלְאֲכֵי הַשָּׁרֵת לִפְנֵי הַקָּדוֹשׁ בָּרוּךְ הוּא: ׳רִבּוֹנוֹ שֶׁל עוֹלָם! [11]מִי שֶׁהֶחֱרִיב אֶת בֵּיתְךָ וְשָׂרַף אֶת הֵיכָלְךָ תַּכְנִיס תַּחַת כַּנְפֵי הַשְּׁכִינָה׳ ״?

[12]הַיְינוּ דִּכְתִיב: ״רִפִּינוּ אֶת בָּבֶל, וְלֹא נִרְפָּתָה״. [13]עוּלָּא אָמַר: זֶה נְבוּכַדְנֶצַּר. [14]רַבִּי שְׁמוּאֵל בַּר נַחְמָנִי אָמַר: אֵלּוּ נַהֲרוֹת בָּבֶל. [15]וְתַרְגְּמָהּ:

LITERAL TRANSLATION

it rested. [1]He entertained the thought of repentance. He said: "If they who killed only one person — [2]thus, this man, what will be with him?" [3]He fled, sent a statement to his house, and became a proselyte.

[4]Our Rabbis taught: "Naaman was a resident alien. [5]Nebuzaradan was a righteous convert. [6]Some of the sons of the sons of Sisera studied Torah in Jerusalem. Some of the sons of the sons of Sennacherib taught Torah publicly." [7]And who are they? [8]Shemayah and Avtalyon. [9]"Some of the sons of the sons of Haman studied Torah in Benei Brak. And even some of the sons of the sons of that wicked man — the Holy One, blessed be He, wished to bring in under the wings of the Divine Presence. [10]The ministering Angels said before the Holy One, blessed be He: 'Master of the universe! [11]He who destroyed Your house and burned Your Sanctuary You will bring in under the wings of the Divine Presence?'"

[12]This is what is written: "We have healed Babylonia, but she was not healed." [13]Ulla said: This is Nebuchadnezzar. [14]Rabbi Shmuel bar Naḥmani said: These are the rivers of Babylonia. [15]And explain it:

TRANSLATION AND COMMENTARY

the blood **ceased** bubbling. [1]Nebuzaradan **entertained the thought of repentance.** He said: **"If they who killed only one person,** the Prophet Zechariah, only achieved atonement after hundreds of thousands of people were put to death — [2]then, **that man** (myself) who has sinned so grievously, **what will be with him?"** [3]**He fled** to a different place, **sent a statement** containing the inventory and disposition of his property **to his house, and became a proselyte.**

תָּנוּ רַבָּנַן [4]**Our Rabbis taught** a Baraita which discusses the conversion of some of the Jewish people's bitterest enemies: **"Naaman was a resident alien** who accepted some of the laws of Judaism — the prohibitions regarding idolatry — but did not undergo complete conversion. [5]**Nebuzaradan was a righteous convert** who underwent complete conversion to Judaism. [6]**Some of Sisera's descendants studied Torah in Jerusalem. Some of Sennacherib's descendants** even **taught Torah to** others in **the community."** [7]The Gemara asks: **And who are** his descendants who became Torah teachers? [8]The Gemara explains: **Shemayah and Avtalyon** were the descendants of converts from Sennacherib's family. [9]The Baraita continues: **"Some of Haman's descendants studied Torah in Benei Brak. And the Holy One, blessed be He, even wished to bring in under the wings of the Divine Presence** for conversion **some of the descendants of that wicked man** Nebuchadnezzar. [10]But **the ministering Angels said to the Holy One, blessed be He: 'Master of the universe!** [11]Is it possible that He **who destroyed Your house and burned Your Sanctuary You** wish to **bring in under the wings of the Divine Presence?'"**

הַיְינוּ דִּכְתִיב [12]The Gemara notes that **this is** the meaning of **the verse** that **states** (Jeremiah 51:9): **"We have healed Babylonia, but she was not healed."** [13]And as **Ulla said: This is** a reference to **Nebuchadnezzar,** whom God wished to heal by bringing his descendants under the wings of the Divine Presence, but none of them converted. [14]**Rabbi Shmuel bar Naḥmani** disagreed and **said:** This verse does not refer to any specific person, but rather to **the rivers of Babylonia** whose waters are not good for drinking. [15]**Explain** the verse

RASHI

פרטתא = שטר צוואה. ואיתגייר — נבוזראדן. גר תושב — שלא קבל עליו שאר מצות, וקבל עליו שלא לעבוד עבודת כוכבים. של אותו רשע — נבוכדנצר. רפינו ולא נרפתה — שהיה הקדוש ברוך הוא מבקש לרפאותו, להכניס מבני בניו תחת כנפי השכינה. אלו נהרות בבל — שהם רעים לשתות.

NOTES

מִבְּנֵי בָנָיו שֶׁל סִיסְרָא **The sons of the sons of Sisera.** There is a tradition according to which Rabbi Akiva was one of Sisera's descendants.

TRANSLATION AND COMMENTARY

as referring to **the bitter rivers of Babylonia.**

אָמַר עוּלָּא [1]The Gemara now relates the sequence of events leading up to the destruction of the Temple at the hand of Nebuchadnezzar. **Ulla said:** The people **of Ammon and Moab were bad neighbors of Jerusalem.** [2]**When they heard the Prophets prophesying** about **the destruction of Jerusalem, they sent** a message **to Nebuchadnezzar,** saying: **"Go out** now, **and come** to Eretz Israel, and conquer it." [3]He sent back, **saying: "I am afraid lest they do to me as they did to the first ones,"** referring to Sennacherib, whose armies were routed outside Jerusalem. [4]**They sent** a message back **to him** in the words of Proverbs 7:19: **"'For my husband** [*ish*] **is not at home, he is gone on a long journey.'** [5]**And** the word ***ish*** [translated here as 'husband'] in this context **refers to the Holy One, blessed be He, as the verse states elsewhere** (Exodus 15:3): **'The Lord is a man** [*ish*] **of war.'"** [6]Nebuchadnezzar **sent** back **to them:** "But perhaps **He is** still **nearby, and He will come** back when he sees that Israel is under attack." [7]The people of Ammon and Moab **sent** a message back **to him,** citing the end of the verse in Proverbs: "God will not return soon, for **'He has gone on a long journey.'"** [8]Nebuchadnezzar **sent** another message **to them:** "But surely **there are righteous people** in Israel **who will pray for mercy and cause Him to come back** and save His people." [9]**They sent** back **to him,** citing the next verse in Proverbs (7:20): **"'He has taken a bag of money** [*kesef*] **with him.'** [10]**And** the word *kesef* [translated here as 'money'] in this context **refers to righteous people, as the verse states** (Hosea 3:2): **'So I bought her to me for fifteen pieces of silver** [*kesef*], **and for a *ḥomer* of barley, and a *letech* of barley'** — which is understood elsewhere as referring to the righteous people whose merits enable the world to exist. God has taken the righteous people with Him, so there is nobody left to pray for His mercy." [11]Nebuchadnezzar

דְּצִינְיָיתָא (צְרִידָתָא) דְּבַבְלָאֵי.
[1]אָמַר עוּלָּא: עַמּוֹן וּמוֹאָב
שִׁיבְבֵי בִּישֵׁי דִּירוּשָׁלַם הֲווּ.
[2]כֵּיוָן דִּשְׁמַעִינְהוּ לִנְבִיאֵי דְּקָא
מִיתְנַבְּאֵי לְחוּרְבָּנָא דִּירוּשָׁלַם,
שְׁלַחוּ לִנְבוּכַדְנֶצַּר: "פּוּק וְתָא".
[3]אֲמַר: "מִסְתְּפֵינָא דְּלָא
לִיעַבְדוּ לִי כִּדְעֲבַדוּ בְּקַמָּאֵי".
[4]שְׁלַחוּ לֵיהּ: "'כִּי אֵין הָאִישׁ
בְּבֵיתוֹ הָלַךְ בְּדֶרֶךְ מֵרָחוֹק'.
[5]וְאֵין אִישׁ אֶלָּא הַקָּדוֹשׁ בָּרוּךְ
הוּא, שֶׁנֶּאֱמַר: 'ה' אִישׁ
מִלְחָמָה'". [6]שְׁלַח לְהוּ:
"בְּקְרִיבָא הוּא, וְאָתֵי". [7]שְׁלַחוּ
לֵיהּ: "'הָלַךְ בְּדֶרֶךְ מֵרָחוֹק'".
[8]שְׁלַח לְהוּ: "אִית לְהוּ צַדִּיקֵי,
דְּבָעוּ רַחֲמֵי וּמַיְיתוּ לֵיהּ".
[9]שְׁלַחוּ לֵיהּ: "'צְרוֹר הַכֶּסֶף
לָקַח בְּיָדוֹ'. [10]וְאֵין כֶּסֶף אֶלָּא
צַדִּיקִים, שֶׁנֶּאֱמַר: 'וָאֶכְּרֶהָ לִּי
בַּחֲמִשָּׁה עָשָׂר כָּסֶף וְחֹמֶר
שְׂעֹרִים וְלֶתֶךְ שְׂעֹרִים'". [11]שְׁלַח

LITERAL TRANSLATION

The bitter rivers of Babylonia.

[1]Ulla said: Ammon and Moab were bad neighbors of Jerusalem. [2]When they heard the Prophets prophesying the destruction of Jerusalem, they sent to Nebuchadnezzar: "Go out, and come." [3]He said: "I am afraid lest they do to me as they did to the first ones." [4]They sent to him: "'For my husband [*ish*] is not at home, he has gone [on] a long journey.' [5]And *ish* can only be the Holy One, blessed be He, as it is stated: 'The Lord is a man [*ish*] of war.'" [6]He sent to them: "He is near, and He will come." [7]They sent to him: "'He is gone [on] a long journey.'" [8]He sent to them: "They have righteous people who will ask for mercy and bring Him." [9]They sent to him: "'He has taken a bag of money [*kesef*] with him.' [10]And *kesef* can only be righteous people, as it is stated: 'So I bought her to me for fifteen pieces of silver [*kesef*], and for a *ḥomer* of barley, and a *letech* of barley.'" [11]He sent

RASHI

צנייתא דבבל — דקלים מרים הם שעומדים בנהרות, לישנא אחרינא:
צינונייתא דבבל — דקלים רעים של נהרות בבל שאין נושאים פירות, לפי שהמים רעים הן לגדל פירות, בסוטה (מו,ב) אמרינן: קושטא הוא דאמריתו הני צנייתא דבבל מששת ימי בראשית איתנהו, ונהר שתחת הני צינונייתא מי מרים נינהו. שיבבי — שכנים. פוק תא — צא ממקומך ובא אל ארץ ישראל ותכבשנה. כי אין האיש — מקרא הוא במשלי. בקריבא הוא — בקרוב הוא, ויבא בעת דוחקם, לפי דרכו של מקרא זה שהם שלחו לו, שומעים אנו שהוא אכל מילתא דהוה אמרי ליה הוה משיב דבר זה. צרור הכסף לקח בידו — צדיקים שבהן מתו. ואכרה לי בחמשה עשר כסף — פדיתי אותה במצרים בחמשה עשר בניסן. כסף וחומר שעורים ולתך שעורים — בזכות צדיקים שנקראו כסף חומר שעורים שלשים סאין, ולתך חמשה עשר סאין, אלו ארבעים וחמשה צדיקים שהעולם מתקיים עליהם בחולין פרק "גיד הנשה" (צב,א), פעמים שלשים כאן וחמשה עשר בארץ ישראל, ופעמים שחמשה עשר כאן ושלשים בארץ ישראל, ובמסכת חולין היכא דקא מפרש האי קרא בצדיקיא, אמרי: אין כסף אלא צדיקים, וכן הוא אומר "צרור הכסף לקח בידו".

NOTES

דְּצִינְיָיתָא (צְרִידָתָא) דְּבַבְלָאֵי The Geonim explain that there is a certain river in Babylonia, near the city of Hizrabah, called Tziriyata [צִירְיָיתָא], whose waters are bitter and not good to drink.

לְהוּ: ״הָדְרִי רַשִׁיעֵי בִּתְשׁוּבָה, וּבָעוּ רַחֲמֵי, וּמַיְיתוּ לֵיהּ״. [1]שְׁלַחוּ לֵיהּ: ״כְּבָר קָבַע לָהֶן זְמַן, [2]שֶׁנֶּאֱמַר: ׳לְיוֹם הַכֶּסֶא יָבֹא בֵיתוֹ׳. [3]אֵין כֶּסֶא אֶלָּא זְמַן, שֶׁנֶּאֱמַר: ׳בַּכֶּסֶה לְיוֹם חַגֵּנוּ׳״. [4]שְׁלַח לְהוּ: ״סִיתְוָוא הוּא, וְלָא מָצֵינָא דְּאָתֵי מִתַּלְגָּא וּמִמִּיטְרָא״. [5]שְׁלַחוּ לֵיהּ: ״תָּא אַשִּׁינָּא דְּטוּרָא, [6]שֶׁנֶּאֱמַר: ׳שִׁלְחוּ כַר מוֹשֵׁל אֶרֶץ מִסֶּלַע מִדְבָּרָה אֶל הַר בַּת צִיּוֹן׳״. [7]שְׁלַח לְהוּ: ״אִי אָתִינָא, לֵית לִי דּוּכְתָּא דְּיָתֵיבְנָא בֵּיהּ״. [8]שְׁלַחוּ לֵיהּ: ״קְבָרוֹת שֶׁלָּהֶם מְעוּלִּין מִפַּלְטֵירִין שֶׁלְּךָ, [9]דִּכְתִיב: ׳בָּעֵת הַהִיא, נְאֻם ה׳, יוֹצִיאוּ אֶת עַצְמוֹת מַלְכֵי יְהוּדָה, וְאֶת עַצְמוֹת שָׂרָיו, וְאֶת עַצְמוֹת הַכֹּהֲנִים, וְאֵת עַצְמוֹת הַנְּבִיאִים, וְאֵת עַצְמוֹת יוֹשְׁבֵי יְרוּשָׁלָיִם מִקִּבְרֵיהֶם; וּשְׁטָחוּם לַשֶּׁמֶשׁ וְלַיָּרֵחַ, וּלְכֹל צְבָא הַשָּׁמַיִם אֲשֶׁר אֲהֵבוּם וַאֲשֶׁר עֲבָדוּם וַאֲשֶׁר הָלְכוּ אַחֲרֵיהֶם׳״.

LITERAL TRANSLATION

to them: "The wicked will repent, and ask for mercy, and bring Him." [1]They sent to him: "He already set a time for them, [2]as it is stated: 'He will come home at the full moon [*kese*].' [3]And *kese* can only be time, as it is stated: 'At the full moon [*kese*] on our feast day.'" [4]He sent to them: "It is winter, and I cannot come because of the snow and rain." [5]They sent to him: "Come on the peaks of the mountains, [6]as it is stated: 'Send the lamb to the ruler of the land from Sela to the wilderness, to the mount of the daughter of Zion.'" [7]He sent to them: "If I come, I do not have a place to sit." [8]They sent to him: "Their graves are superior to your palaces, [9]as it is written: 'At that time, says the Lord, they shall bring out the bones of the kings of Judah, and the bones of his princes, and the bones of the priests, and the bones of the prophets, and the bones of the inhabitants of Jerusalem, out of their graves; and they shall spread them before the sun, and the moon, and all the host of Heaven, whom they have loved, and whom they have served, and after whom they have walked.'"

TRANSLATION AND COMMENTARY

sent back **to them:** "But perhaps **the wicked** in Israel **will repent, and pray for mercy, and cause** God **to come back** and save His people!" [1]The people of Ammon and Moab **sent** back **to him:** "God **has already set a time for their** redemption — seventy years after their exile to Babylonia — but until then you can do as you please, [2]**as the verse** in Proverbs (7:20) **continues: 'He will come home at the full moon** [*kese*].' [3]**And** the word *kese* (translated here as 'full moon') in this context **refers to** a set **time, as the verse states** (Psalm 81:4): '"Blow a shofar at the new moon, **at the full moon** [*kese*] **on our feast day.**'" [4]Nebuchadnezzar **sent** back **to them** another excuse explaining why he cannot come: "**It is winter** now, **and I cannot come because of the snow and rain.**" [5]**They sent** back **to him: "Come** if necessary **by way of the mountain peaks,** where there are no puddles to hinder your advance, [6]**as the verse states** (Isaiah 16:1): **'Send the lamb to the ruler of the land from Sela to the wilderness, to the mount of the daughter of Zion,'** meaning: send a messenger to Nebuchadnezzar who is ruler of the land that he should come to Zion by way of the rocks and mountains." [7]Nebuchadnezzar **sent them** one final excuse: **"If I come, I will not have a place** near Jerusalem where I and my army can **sit** protected from the inclement weather while we besiege Jerusalem." [8]The people of Ammon and Moab **sent** back **to him: "The burial caves** in Eretz Israel **are superior to your palaces.** You can clear them out and live in them. [9]**As the verse states** (Jeremiah 8:1-2): **'At that time, says the Lord, they shall bring out the bones of the kings of Judah, and the bones of his princes, and the bones of the priests, and the bones of the prophets, and the bones of the inhabitants of Jerusalem, out of their graves; and they shall spread them before the sun, and the moon, and all the host of heaven, whom they have loved, and whom they have served, and after whom they have walked.'"**

RASHI

כבר קבע להם זמן — שלא יבא עד שבעים שנה שתשלים גלות בבל. מתלגא וממטרא — מחמת שלגים ומטרים. תא אשינא דטורי — בא דרך תחתית ההרים, וההרים יגינו עליך מן השלגים ומן המטרים. שלחו כר מושל ארץ — שלחו שליח אל נבוכדנצר שהיה מושל ארץ שיבא אל הר בת ציון דרך הסלעים וההרים. לית לי דוכתא — לא יהיה לי מקום סביב לירושלים שנוכל אני וחיילי לישב במקום מכוסה מפני הגשמים. קבריהם של ישראל — מערות שלהן סביב לירושלים, ובהן אתה וחיילותיך יכולין לישב. יוצאו את עצמות מלכי יהודה — שעתידים להשליך מן הקברים העצמות שבקברים שנאמר ״בעת ההיא וגו׳״.

NOTES

אַשִּׁינָּא דְּטוּרָא **On the peaks of the mountains.** *Rashi* and others explain that the people of Ammon and Moab suggested to Nebuchadnezzar that he advance toward Eretz Israel at the foot of the mountains, so that the cliffs and peaks would protect him and his army from the rain and snow.

List of Sources

Aḥaronim, lit., "the last," meaning Rabbinic authorities from the time of the publication of Rabbi Yosef Caro's code of Halakhah, *Shulḥan Arukh* (1555).

Arba'ah Turim, code of Halakhah by Rabbi Ya'akov ben Asher, b. Germany, active in Spain (c. 1270-1343).

Arukh, Talmudic dictionary, by Rabbi Natan of Rome, 11th century.

Arukh LeNer, novellae on the Talmud by Rabbi Ben Tzion Ya'akov Etlinger, Germany (1798-1871).

Baḥ (Bayit Ḥadash), commentary on *Arba'ah Turim*, by Rabbi Yoel Sirkes, Poland (1561-1640).

Be'er HaGolah, commentary on unusual Aggadic passages in the Talmud by Rabbi Yehudah Loew ben Betzalel of Prague (1525-1609).

Bereshit Rabbah, Midrash on the Book of Genesis.

Bertinoro, Ovadyah, 15th century commentator on the Mishnah.

Bet Yosef, Halakhic commentary on *Arba'ah Turim* by Rabbi Yosef Caro (1488-1575), which is the basis of his authoritative Halakhic code, *Shulḥan Arukh.*

Birkei Yosef, novellae on *Shulḥan Arukh* by Rabbi Ḥayyim Yosef David Azulai, Israel and Italy (1724-1807).

Darkhei Moshe, commentary on *Tur* by Rabbi Moshe ben Isserles, Poland (1525-1572).

Ein Ya'akov, collection of Aggadot from the Babylonian Talmud by Rabbi Ya'akov ben Shlomo Ḥabib, Spain and Salonika (c. 1445-1515).

Even HaEzer, section of *Shulḥan Arukh* dealing with marriage, divorce, and related topics.

Geonim, heads of the academies of Sura and Pumbedita in Babylonia from the late 6th century to the mid-11th century.

Hagahot Maimoniyot, commentary on *Mishneh Torah,* by Rabbi Meir HaKohen, Germany, 14th century.

Hagahot Ram Arak, novellae on the Talmud by Rabbi Meir Arak, Poland, early 20th century.

Hagahot Ri Pik Berlin, Rabbi Yeshayahu Pik Berlin, Talmudic scholar, Breslau (1725-1799).

Halakhot Gedolot, a code of Halakhic decisions written in the Geonic period. This work has been ascribed to Sherira Gaon, Rav Hai Gaon, Rav Yehudah Gaon and Rabbi Shimon Kayyara.

Ḥamra Veḥaye, novellae on tractate *Sanhedrin,* by Rabbi Ḥayyim Benevisti, Turkey, 17th century.

Hayyim Shenayim Yeshalem, novellae on *Sanhedrin,* by Rabbi Shmuel Vital.

Ḥokhmat Manoaḥ, commentary on the Talmud by Rabbi Manoaḥ ben Shemaryah, Poland, 16th century.

Ḥoshen Mishpat, section of *Shulḥan Arukh* dealing with civil and criminal law.

Imrei Tzvi, novellae of the Talmud by Rabbi Tzvi Kohen, Vilna, 19th century.

Iyyun Ya'akov, commentary on *Ein Ya'akov*, by Rabbi Ya'akov bar Yosef Riesher, Prague, Poland, and France (d. 1733).

Keli Yakar, commentary on the Torah by Rabbi Shlomo Efrayim of Luntshitz, Poland (d. 1619)

Keneset HaGedolah (see *Shayarei Keneset HaGedolah*).

Kesef Mishneh, commentary on *Mishneh Torah,* by Rabbi Yosef Caro, author of *Shulḥan Arukh.*

Keset HaSofer, laws regarding the writing of Torah scrolls and mezuzahs, by Rabbi Shlomo Ganzfried, Hungary (19th century).

Ketzot HaḤoshen, novellae on *Shulḥan Arukh, Ḥoshen Mishpat,* by Rabbi Aryeh Leib Heller, Galicia (1754?-183).

Kos Yeshuot, novellae on the Talmud by Rabbi Shmuel HaKohen Shatin, Germany (d. 1719).

Leḥem Mishneh, commentary on the *Mishneh Torah,* by Rabbi Avraham di Boton, Salonica (1560-1609).

Lekaḥ Tov, Midrashim and commentary on the Torah by Rabbi Tuvyah the son of Rabbi Eliezer, Bulgaria (11th century).

Levush, abbreviation of *Levush Mordekhai,* Halakhic code by Rabbi Mordekhai Yaffe, Poland (1530-1612).

Magen Avraham, commentary on *Shulḥan Arukh, Oraḥ Hayyim,* by Rabbi Avraham HaLevi Gombiner, Poland (d. 1683).

Maggid Mishneh, commentary on *Mishneh Torah,* by Rabbi Vidal de Tolosa, Spain, 14th century.

Maharal, Rabbi Yehudah Loew ben Betzalel of Prague (1525-1631). Novellae on the Talmud.

Maharam Schiff, novellae on the Talmud by Rabbi Meir ben Ya'akov HaKohen Schiff (1605-1641), Frankfurt, Germany.

Maharik, Rabbi Yosef Kolon, France and Italy (c. 1420-1480). Responsa literature.

Maharsha, Rabbi Shmuel Eliezer ben Yehudah HaLevi Edels, Poland (1555-1631). Novellae on the Talmud.

Maharshal, Rabbi Shlomo ben Yeḥiel Luria, Poland (1510-1573). Novellae on the Talmud.

Maharshashakh, Rabbi Shmuel Shotten, Germany (17th century). Novellae on the Talmud.

Margoliyot HaYam, novellae on tractate *Sanhedrin* by Rabbi Reuben Margoliyot, Poland, 20th century.

Megaleh Amukot, Kabbalistic commentary on the Torah by Rabbi Natan Shapiro, Poland (1585-1633).

Meir Einei Soferim, laws regarding the writing of Torah scrolls, mezuzahs, and bills of divorce, by Rabbi David Krosik.

Meiri, commentary on the Talmud (called *Bet HaBeḥirah*), by Rabbi Menaḥem ben Shlomo, Provence (1249-1316).

Mekhilta, Halakhic Midrash on the Book of Exodus.

Melekhet Shlomo, commentary on the Mishnah by Rabbi Shlomo Adeni, Yemen and Israel (1567-1626).

Melo HaRo'im, commentary on the Talmud by Rabbi Ya'akov Tzvi Yolles, Poland (c. 1778-1825).

Menorat HaMa'or, Anthology of Midrashim, by Rabbi Yitzḥak Abohav (15th century).

Midrash Shir HaShirim Rabbah, Midrash on the Song of Songs.

Midrash Tanḥuma, see *Tanḥuma.*

Mishneh LeMelekh, commentary on *Mishneh Torah* by Rabbi Yehudah ben Shmuel Rosanes, Turkey (1657-1727).

Mishnah Berurah, commentary on *Shulḥan Arukh, Oraḥ Ḥayyim,* by Rabbi Yisrael Meir HaKohen, Poland (1837-1933).

Mitzpeh Eitan, glosses on the Talmud by Rabbi Avraham Maskileison, Byelorussia (1788-1848).

Nimmukei Yosef, commentary on *Hilkhot HaRif,* by Rabbi Yosef Ḥaviva, Spain, early 15th century.

Oraḥ Ḥayyim, section of *Shulḥan Arukh* dealing with daily religious observances, prayers, and the laws of the Sabbath and Festivals.

Pirkei DeRabbi Eliezer, Aggadic Midrash on the Torah.

Pitḥei Teshuvah, compilation of responsa literature on *Shulḥan Arukh* by Rabbi Avraham Tzvi Eisenstadt, Russia (1812-1868).

Ra'avad, Rabbi Avraham ben David, commentator and Halakhic authority. Wrote comments on *Mishneh Torah.* Provence (c. 1125-1198?).

Rabbenu Ḥananel (ben Ḥushiel), commentator on the Talmud, North Africa (990-1055).

Rabbenu Meshulam, French Tosafist, 12th century.

Rabbenu Sa'adya Gaon, scholar and author, Egypt and Sura, Babylonia (882-942).

Rabbenu Shimshon of Sens, Tosafist, France and Eretz Israel (late 12th-early 13th century).

Rabbenu Tam, commentator on the Talmud, Tosafist, France (1100-1171).

Rabbenu Yehonatan of Lunel, Yehonatan ben David HaKohen of Lunel, Provence, Talmudic scholar (c.1135-after 1210).

Rabbenu Yonah, see *Talmidei Rabbenu Yonah.*

Rabbenu Zeraḥyah HaLevi, author of *HaMa'or,* commentary on *Hilkhot HaRif.* Spain, 12th century.

Rabbi David Bonfil (Bonfied), commentary on tractate *Sanhedrin* by Rabbi David Bonfil (Bonfied), France, 11th century.

Rabbi David Pardo, novellae on the Talmud, Italy, 18th century.

Rabbi E. M. Horowitz, Rabbi Elazar Moshe Horowitz, novellae on the Talmud, Pinsk (19th century).

Rabbi Issac Ḥaver, novellae on the Talmud by Rabbi Issac Ḥaver, Poland, 18th century.

Rabbi Tzvi Ḥayyot (Chajes), Galician Rabbi, 19th century.

Rabbi Ya'akov Emden, Talmudist and Halakhic authority, Germany (1697-1776).

Rabbi Yehudah Almandri, author of commentary on *Rif,* tractate *Sanhedrin,* Syria, 13th century.

Rabbi Yeshayahu Pik Berlin, Talmudic scholar, Breslau (1725-1799).

Rabbi Yitzḥak Ibn Giyyat, Halakhist, Bible commentator and liturgical poet, Spain (1038-1089).

Rabbi Yosef of Jerusalem, French Tosafist of the twelfth and thirteenth centuries, France and Eretz Israel.

Rabbi Yoshiyah Pinto, Eretz Israel and Syria (1565-1648). Commentary on *Ein Ya'akov.*

Rabbi Zeraḥyah ben Yitzḥak HaLevi, Spain, 12th century. Author of *HaMa'or,* Halakhic commentary on *Hilkhot HaRif.*

Radak, Rabbi David Kimḥi, grammarian and Bible commentator, Narbonne, Provence (1160?-1235?).

Radbaz, Rabbi David ben Shlomo Avi Zimra, Spain, Egypt, Eretz Israel, and North Africa (1479-1574). Commentary on *Mishneh Torah.*

Raḥ, Rabbenu Ḥananel (ben Ḥushiel), commentator on the Talmud, North Africa (990-1055).

Ramah, novellae on the Talmud by Rabbi Meir ben Todros HaLevi Abulafiya, Spain (c. 1170-1244). See *Yad Ramah.*

Rambam, Rabbi Moshe ben Maimon, Rabbi and philosopher, known also as Maimonides. Author of *Mishneh Torah,* Spain and Egypt (1135-1204).

Ramban, Rabbi Moshe ben Naḥman, commentator on Bible and Talmud, known also as Naḥmanides, Spain and Eretz Israel (1194-1270).

Ran, Rabbi Nissim ben Reuven Gerondi, Spanish Talmudist (1310?-1375?).

Rash, Rabbi Shimshon ben Avraham, Tosafist, commentator on the Mishnah, Sens (late 12th- early 13th century).

Rashash, Rabbi Shmuel ben Yosef Shtrashun, Lithuanian Talmud scholar (1794-1872).

Rashba, Rabbi Shlomo ben Avraham Adret, Spanish Rabbi famous for his commentaries on the Talmud and his responsa (c. 1235-c.1314).

Rashbam, Rabbi Shmuel ben Meir, commentator on the Talmud, France (1085-1158).

Rashi, Rabbi Shlomo ben Yitzḥak, the paramount commentator on the Bible and the Talmud, France (1040-1105).

Rav Aha of Sabha, author of *She'iltot,* Babylonia, 8th century.

Rav Hai Gaon, Babylonian Rabbi, head of Pumbedita Yeshivah, 10th century.

Rav Natronai Gaon, of the Sura Yeshivah, 9th century.

Rav Sherira Gaon, of the Pumbedita Yeshivah, 10th century.

Rav Tzemaḥ Gaon, Tzemaḥ ben Ḥayyim, Gaon of Sura (889-895).

Rema, Rabbi Moshe ben Yisrael Isserles, Halakhic authority, Poland (1525-1572).

Responsa of Ḥatam Sofer, responsa literature by Rabbi Moshe Sofer (Schreiber), Pressburg (1763-1839).

Ri, Rabbi Yitzḥak ben Shmuel of Dampierre, Tosafist, France (died c. 1185).

Ri Almandri, Rabbi Yehudah Almandri. Author of commentary on *Rif,* tractate *Sanhedrin,* Syria, 13th century.

Ri Migash, Rabbi Yosef Ibn Migash, commentator on the Talmud, Spain (1077-1141).

Ri Yolles, Rabbi Ya'akov Tzvi Yolles, Talmudic scholar, Poland (c. 1778-1825).

Rif, Rabbi Yitzḥak Alfasi, Halakhist, author of *Hilkhot HaRif,* North Africa (1013-1103).

Rishonim, lit., "the first," meaning Rabbinic authorities active between the end of the Geonic period (mid-11th century) and the publication of *Shulḥan Arukh* (1555).

Ritva, novellae and commentary on the Talmud by Rabbi Yom Tov ben Avraham Ishbili, Spain (c. 1250-1330).

Riva, Rabbenu Yitzḥak ben Asher, Tosafist, novellae on tractate *Sanhedrin.*

Rosh, Rabbi Asher ben Yeḥiel, also known as Asheri, commentator and Halakhist, German and Spain (c. 1250-1327).

Sanhedrei Ketanah, novellae on tractate *Sanhedrin* by Rabbi Avraham Yehoshua Bornstein, Russia, 19th century.

Sefer Meir Einayim, see *Sma.*

Shakh (Siftei Kohen), commentary on the *Shulḥan Arukh* by Rabbi Shabbetai ben Meir HaKohen, Lithuania (1621-1662).

Shayarei Keneset HaGedolah, a Halakhic work by Rabbi Ḥayyim Benevisti, Turkey, 17th century.

Shelah (Shenei Luḥot HaBrit), an extensive work on Halakhah, ethics and Kabbalah by Rabbi Yeshayahu ben Avraham HaLevi Horowitz. Prague, Poland and Eretz Israel (c. 1565-1630).

She'eilot U'Teshuvot HaMibit, Responsa literature of Rabbi Moshe of Tirani, Sefad (1500-1580).

Shemot Rabbah, Midrash on the Book of Exodus.

Shulḥan Arukh, code of Halakhah by Rabbi Yosef Caro, b. Spain, active in Eretz Israel (1488-1575).

Sifrei, Halakhic Midrash on the Books of Numbers and Deuteronomy.

Sma, (Sefer Meirat Einaim), commentary on *Shulḥan Arukh, Ḥoshen Mishpat,* by Rabbi Yehoshua Falk Katz, Poland (c. 1550-1614).

Smag, (Sefer Mitzvot Gedolot), an extensive work on the positive and negative commandments by Rabbi Moshe ben Ya'akov of Coucy, 13th century.

Talmid Rabbenu Peretz, commentary on the Talmud by the school of Rabbi Peretz of Corbiel, France (13th century)

Talmidei Rabbenu Yonah, commentary on *Hilkhot HaRif* by the school of Rabbi Yonah of Gerondi, Spain (1190-1263).

Tanḥuma, Midrash on the Five Books of Moses.

Tashbatz, Respona literature of Rabbi Shimon ben Tzemaḥ Duran, Spain and Algeria (1361-1444).

Taz, abbreviation for *Turei Zahav.* See *Turei Zahav.*

Tiferet Yisrael, commentary on the Mishnah, by Rabbi Yisrael Lipshitz, Germany (1782-1860).

Torat Ḥayyim, novellae on the Talmud by Rabbi Avraham Ḥayyim Shor, Galicia (d. 1632).

Tosafot, collection of commentaries and novellae on the Talmud, expanding on Rashi's commentary, by the French-German Tosafists (12th and 13th centuries).

Tosafot Ḥadashim, commentary on the Mishnah by Rabbi Shimshon Bloch, Hamburg, Germany (d. 1737).

Tosefot Hokhmei Angli'a, collection of novellae on the Talmud by English Tosafists (13th century).

Tosefot Rabbenu Peretz, Tosefot of the school of Rabbi Peretz ben Eliyahu of Corbeil (d. 1295).

Tosefot Rosh, an edition based on *Tosefot Sens* by the *Rosh,* Rabbi Asher ben Yeḥiel, Germany and Spain (c. 1250-1327).

Tosefot Yom Tov, commentary on the Mishnah by Rabbi Yom Tov Lipman HaLevi Heller, Prague and Poland (1579-1654).

Tur, abbreviation of *Arba'ah Turim,* Halakhic code by Rabbi Ya'akov ben Asher, b. Germany, active in Spain (c. 1270-1343).

Tzofnat Pa'ane'aḥ, novellae and commentaries by Rabbi Yosef Rozin, Lithuania (1858-1936).

Yad Malakhi, a work on Talmudic and Halakhic methodology, by Rabbi Malakhi ben Ya'akov HaKohen, Italy (died c. 1785).

Yafeh Mar'eh, commentary on the Midrash by Rabbi Shmuel Yaffe, Turkey, 16th century.

Yalkut (see *Yalkut Shimoni*).

Yalkut Shimoni, Aggadic Midrash on the Bible.

Yefeh Enayim, cross-references and notes to the Jerusalem Talmud, by Rabbi Yeshayahu Pik Berlin, Breslau (1725-1799).

Yoreh De'ah, section of *Shulḥan Arukh* dealing mainly with dietary laws, interest, ritual purity, and mourning.

About the Type

This book was set in Leawood, a contemporary typeface designed by Leslie Usherwood. His staff completed the design upon Usherwood's death in 1984. It is a friendly, inviting face that goes particularly well with sans serif type.